W9-ANH-410

WITHDRAWN

Gramley Library
Salem College
Winston-Salem, NC 27108

Fassbinder's Germany

FILM CULTURE IN TRANSITION

Thomas Elsaesser: General Editor

Fassbinder's Germany
History Identity Subject

by
THOMAS ELSAESSER

AMSTERDAM UNIVERSITY PRESS

Gramley Library
Salem College
Winston-Salem, NC 2710°

for K.P.E.

Cover illustration (front): R.W. Fassbinder shooting *Lili Marleen*, 1980. Coll. Rainer Werner Fassbinder Foundation / Karl Reiter, Berlin.
(back): *Veronika Voss*, 1981
Cover design: Korpershoek Ontwerpen, Amsterdam
Typesetting: JAPES, Jaap Prummel, Amsterdam

ISBN 90 5356 184 6 (hardbound)
ISBN 90 5356 059 9 (paperback)

© Thomas Elsaesser / Amsterdam University Press, Amsterdam, 1996

All rights reserved. Without limiting the rights under copyright reserved above, no part of this book may be reproduced, stored in or introduced into a retrieval system, or transmitted, in any form or by any means (electronic, mechanical, photocopying, recording, or otherwise), without the written permission of both the copyright owner and the author of this book.

Table of Contents

Introduction: A Work Upstaged by Life?

In the cinema of the post-war period, Rainer Werner Fassbinder is a unique filmmaker. Between 1969 and 1982 – barely more than a decade, which is all he had to make his mark – he transformed the very idea of the German cinema, because by writing himself into German film history, he had to rewrite its history. Yet in the years since, the work he directed has, though not exactly vanished, undergone a strange transformation. A few of the films have entered the canon. FEAR EATS THE SOUL, THE BITTER TEARS OF PETRA VON KANT and THE MARRIAGE OF MARIA BRAUN are among the landmarks of European cinema and have secured him an undisputed place as film artist and *auteur*. But in the process, the work as a whole has become invisible, consumed by Fassbinder's life. What drew the gaze of audiences, but also distracted it, was the enigma of the man who had made these perplexing, provocative but absorbing films: the scandal of openly flaunted homosexuality, the purported self-abuse and the abuse of others seemed to fuel an awe-inspiring productivity, as if a Faustian pact had been sealed with sulphurous thunder. Especially since his death, his lifestyle and the posthumous revelations about it have invariably upstaged the films, it seemed if one wanted to understand the films, one had to look at his life.

He possessed a uniquely creative, but also self-destructive force, yes; but what of his force as a filmmaker for Germany, as a filmmaker about Germany? The biographical literature on Fassbinder has its place, tracking down the anecdotal antecedents of incidents in the films, and often giving the reader a pungent taste of the atmosphere of hate, spite and violence which Fassbinder seemed to inspire and by which he was surrounded.[1] But by concentrating on the pathological and sensationalist aspects of the Fassbinder story, too much space is given to revelations, hearsay and anecdotes about his private behaviour and public posturing. If understandably, perhaps, Fassbinder's former collaborators unburden themselves in their memoirs, airing grievances or long-held grudges with observations that are often sharpened by the keen eye of jealous love, and a language spiced with the baffled memory of hurt, then less directly involved authors ought to take a step back. Some of the English-language studies have tried to put Fassbinder on the Freudian couch, in order to explain his treatment of friends and lovers, his compulsive creativity and his highly manipulative, sometimes generous, often sadistic ways of staying in control. Even where not exactly looking for the key, the single 'Rosebud' clue to Fassbinder, they tended to find a sense of unity of the man and his films in his life, what propelled and compelled it. And since the life was as extravantly spectacular as it was tragically brief, it lends itself especially well to metaphoric or symptomatic interpretations. Among such psychoanalytic approaches, those that focus on Fassbinder's troubled relation with his father and his penchant for humiliating his mother's look-alike are neither the least interesting nor the least plausible, especially since the director himself has often volunteered such explanations himself.[2]

Yet Fassbinder's own candour in this respect is revealing: he finds it amusing to speculate on the connexions between his childhood memories and his films, or to spin some broader cultural reflections from them, but there is little sense of it tapping into his unconscious.[3] For the biographer, on the other hand, the films become source material, raided for clues.[4] They are the record, so to speak, of his acting out, re-enacting and staging the traumas of his childhood: the supposed lack of love from his mother, the feelings of worthlessness and impotence in the face of those who ran his life when he was a child. Fassbinder's adult life and his films, according to this model, are comprehensible as twin tracks whose imaginary meeting point and impossible vanishing point are a return to a childhood blighted by parental discord, political disarray and a manic-depressive personality. Correspondingly, his relations with the people he attracted, used or tolerated in his company became the testing ground and the 'raw material' from which he fashioned the fables of his films or drew the often lurid colours of his characters' feelings. The meaning of both life and work becomes coherent, in such a model, because they are bound together either by an allegorical relationship or a compensatory link. As Ronald Hayman puts it: 'film was a form of therapy in which he could project his identity into the glamorous men and women who spoke his dialogue and obeyed his instructions'.[5]

Reading the work in the light of the life is a strategy which achieves coherence only at a price. If the life explains the films, and the films explain the life, then not only is each the foil for the other, but each makes the other transparent: to the point of tautology. The crucial issue the biographical or psychoanalytic approaches have obscured, if only by taking it for granted, is what makes Fassbinder important in the first place: his films, the resonance they have found, the topics they engage. As Wilhelm Roth remarked, reviewing *Die 13 Jahre des Rainer Werner Fassbinder. Seine Filme, seine Freunde, seine Feinde*

> [Peter] Berling omits nothing, he describes how Fassbinder tyrannized his friends, details the rows and power-struggles with his collaborators, the squabbles over money, the sexual promiscuity, the alcoholic excesses, and finally the suicidal addiction to cocaine. Oddly enough, all these revelations do not seem to damage Berling's (negative) hero Fassbinder. The book becomes a requiem, (maybe an unintentional) mourning work for a wasted and mis-spent life. The paradox remains that out of this life came masterpieces. On this, Berling has nothing to say.[6]

The final sentences have several implications. They can lead one to ponder once more the paradox Roth alludes to: given the self-destructive course of Fassbinder's life and the physical demands of his filmmaking, the enigma is not how did he manage to produce '42 films in 17 years'[7] – a question most commentators elevate to the status of central paradox – but rather, how did he produce 'masterpieces'. This, however, begs a second point. What is a masterpiece in Fassbinder's work, and did Fassbinder set out to make masterpieces: questions demanding precisely the kind of critical study of which the Fassbinder literature is so short.[8]

I would instead rephrase Roth's paradox: the gap left open by the biographical accounts is not only that of a coherent account of Fassbinder's films in sequence,[9] but an account of the films' coherence, which is to say, of the complexity of their underlying design, of the successive transformations of their basic themes. A case could be made for seeing the late films as rewriting the early films in a different idiom, and with a different historical reference: THE THIRD GENERATION (1979) rewriting GODS OF THE PLAGUE (1969), for instance. Put like this, such a project has an old-fashioned, not to say 'retrograde' ring, seemingly wishing to reinstate the 'author' as the locus (and the work as the material manifestation) of an intentional plenitude, whose stages and intricacies it is the task of the critic to reconstruct.

In one sense, this imaginary telos is implicit in any single author study. The temptations such reconstructive fantasies hold for a writer continue to have a powerful attraction for readers. In another sense, the presumed plenitude is far from proven. I do not discuss the work in its totality, or even all the patterns or coherences that might traverse it. I shall be satisfied if this study indicates their direction. My (mis)readings are intended to encourage (re)viewings and (mis)readings, just as they have been prompted by others' (mis)readings. If I were to give a name to the fantasy that has sustained my interest, it would be the possibility that the design underlying Fassbinder's films, and the sense of their rather extraordinary purposiveness (some of the projects pondered for a lifetime like BERLIN ALEXANDERPLATZ, others conceived on the hoof, like LILI MARLEEN[10]), did not mature in modernist isolation or creative solitude. Rather, it must have developed against the pull of an entourage of very demanding friends, lovers and associates; it must have taken shape in the face of the chaos of his personal life; it survived the logistical challenges of 'independent' but nonetheless 'commercial' film production; and it could realize itself in spite of the vagaries of film finance and film distribution in West Germany. In other words, not dividing life from work, but totally intermingling; not 'autobiographical' fusion, but the ability to keep things separate when and where it mattered. I shall come back to this point in my final chapter.

To note the pitfalls of the biographical or auteurist approach does not commit one to the opposite extreme. A purely formal reading, which treats the films as self-sustaining and auto-reflexive artefacts is of course possible, and during the 1970s, Fassbinder was often cited as exponent of an anti-illusionist, modernist or Brechtian counter-cinema.[11] Such interpretations did much to make him popular among student audiences, but they also risked an abstraction: from the context of production, and from contexts of reception other than the 'productive misreadings' Fassbinder at the time shared with other directors of the New German Cinema.[12] The challenge in this study, then, is to keep in view a number of conflicting and shifting contexts: the economic factors that require a filmmaker in a given country to promote himself as artist, star or rebel, irrespective of his own inclination; the fact that a film may attain notoriety because of its subject matter and topical interest and thereby typecast its director; the possibility that the main resistance a filmmaker can oppose to the commodification of his work is to thematize the question of exchange value. Put differently, what is at issue in the chapters that follow are several kinds of reciprocity: between the films and their mode of production, between the historical moment they were made and the conditions under which they were made, between their chronological sequence and their chronological reference. Important, for instance, about the life of Fassbinder is its historicity: how it relates itself to and interprets itself through the history and society of West Germany. Fassbinder's films take this relatively short period of a single decade and build on it a series of concentric circles and reverberating echoes, encompassing the pre-history and the aftermath of modern Germany's greatest catastrophe. Also relevant is the fact that Fassbinder was one of the few directors of the New German Cinema whose films were seen by Germans, and who was able to enter into some form of dialogue with both a public and a public sphere, a dialogue Fassbinder fostered, incidentally, by the astute self-advertising rumour-machine already mentioned. Equally important, Fassbinder seems to have consciously pursued a number of parallels between his personal life and German history, inviting allegorical cross-referencing of biographical and autobiographical elements in his films against the foil of German history, rather than his childhood and its imagined or real deprivations.

The accounts I offer of particular films, such as FEAR EATS THE SOUL, THE MERCHANT OF FOUR SEASONS, DESPAIR, THE MARRIAGE OF MARIA BRAUN, LOLA, VERONIKA VOSS, LILI MARLEEN, IN A YEAR OF THIRTEEN MOONS and BERLIN ALEXANDERPLATZ, hopefully provide the necessary detail for setting out how a film can, at one and the same time, have a degree of internal coherence, form part of an ongoing authorial project, and intervene in a number of public histories. In the course of these chapters, I shall return to the question of whether such an approach makes sense not only of a given film's stylistic strategies but also of its inconsistencies. Implicitly, the chapters will assume that interpretation can illuminate the peculiarly intimate and yet highly mediated relation that obtains between Fassbinder's life and his films. Overtly, however, the main impulse has been to keep the films distinct from the life, if understood as the network of personal ties, erotic dependencies and power-play in which the adult Fassbinder entangled a large number of individuals of either sex, and to see the films across the life, understood as the forces that shape a professional existence and condition the possibilities of working as a film director in Germany in the 1970s. This is a methodological as well as a moral choice. The former I have tried to set out above, notably by redefining the idea of a 'life in history', as it affects both films and filmmaker; the latter is a constant theme throughout the book. Nonetheless, it would be disingenuous not to acknowledge the benefit – and pleasure – I have drawn as reader, critic and historian from the memoirs of the members of Fassbinder's entourage, such as Harry Baer, Kurt Raab, Peter Chatel and others, notably those interviewed by Juliane Lorenz. My debt extends to those scholars who have tried to sift rumour from fact and have begun to document these 'facts', notably Hans Helmut Prinzler, Hans Günther Pflaum, Wilhelm Roth and Michael Töteberg.[13]

As the response to a Fassbinder film has always been a mixture of intrigued amazement, appalled fascination and disarmed frustration, it seems likely that strategies of seduction played a prominent part in his life as well as his work. For reasons which hopefully will become clear in the course of the book, psychoanalysis – rather than being the clue to the life, of which the work is the symptom – may help, thanks to such notions as identification, transference or narcissism, to clarify some dimensions of the film experience and the psychic structures that make it possible. Where Fassbinder mobilizes these structures, he also modifies them, in order to address/ undress/ seduce/ produce a particular kind of spectator. This, at any rate, is part of my argument, after examining the most obvious dynamics that bind together the filmmaker-narrator, the characters and the spectator in Fassbinder's film: that of frame and view, of the different looks and their obstructions, of voyeuristic participation and exhibitionist display. Together, they mark out so many apparently impossible spaces and delineate such distinct fields of the visible that neither the notion of self-reflexivity nor the charge of self-indulgent virtuosity can gain critical purchase. I have attempted a multiple reading of this obvious but finally quite opaque feature of Fassbinder's work, relating it to a topology, a set of tropes as well as to a history. It clearly formulates a 'view' of cinema and of the act of cinematic representation as a fact of private and public existence. It implies a notion of the body in visual and audio space that offers a reflection on the temporalities human perception now inhabits. Most decisively, Fassbinder brings into play such a powerful sense of what it means for men and women to be visible to each other across different kinds of looks, not all of which are attached to an eye, that one comes to understand how human relations – the sole substance of Fassbinder's dramas – can be driven by a startling and even terrifying honesty: a deeply paradoxical situation, given that the cinema so manifestly belongs to the order of appearance, of the simulated and the self-alienated. Evidently, some of my interpretational moves rely on positions debated around questions of subjectivity, the image and the look, but in the course of traversing these by now well-trodden fields of Lacanian film theory, I shall also offer an account of Fassbinder's work that resists this theory, by pointing to other structures which do not so much invalidate as resituate the previously identified issues within a particular history and an ethics of exchange and interaction.

The present book is meant to be used, and therefore a number of 'critical' appendices are added, designed to aid such a possibility, even though they are not intended to replace various reference guides to Fassbinder. I have included an extensively commented filmography, which combines a brief synopsis of each film with its place in several kinds of contexts and preoccupations. A selected bibliography of books and other major publications on the director and his films gives an overview of the growing literature. Besides a brief biographical sketch, there is also a synoptic table of some of the key dates of his life and major political events that seem to have been important points of intervention and reflection.

This volume represents some twenty years of thinking and writing about Fassbinder. Although I never met him personally, and only saw him from afar at the Berlin Film Festival at irregular intervals between 1975 and 1981, I 'followed' Fassbinder's films ever

Gramley Library
Salem College
Winston-Salem, NC 27108

since 1971, when the Goethe Institute London gave me a chance to show THE AMERICAN SOLDIER and WHY DOES HERR R RUN AMOK? at the Gardner Arts Centre of the University of Sussex, well before any of Fassbinder's films had received a public screening in Britain. Some time after his death, the idea of a book took shape, and my subsequent pieces on Fassbinder were written with such a project in mind. In the end, it was not until the tenth anniversary of his death in 1992 that I started to rethink Fassbinder's Germany. Where previously published essays are reprinted (as in the case of DESPAIR, LILI MARLEEN, BERLIN ALEXANDERPLATZ and the final chapter), they have been substantially revised. I have indicated in the bibliography the original places of publication, and I gratefully acknowledge the editors' and publishers' permission to incorporate this material here. My thanks for assistance and many acts of kindness are also due to Mieke Bernink, Desmond Christy, Joan Copjec, Karel Dibbets, Caroline Gauthier, Gerd Gemünden, Milena Gregor, Juliane Lorenz, Andreas Rost, Sally Shafto, Jane Shattuc, as well as the library staff of the Goethe Institute in London, Amsterdam, Paris and Munich.

Amsterdam, August 1996.

1.   Fassbinder Representing Germany

I often ask myself, where do I stand in the history of my country. Why am I a German?[1]

Germany: The 'Nation'

When Fassbinder died in 1982, the obituaries the world over saw in him the chief representative not only of the New German Cinema but of the new Germany. Watchwords were angry, mercilessly critical, honest, incorruptible, the spirit of '68, the beacon of self-righteous anger and aesthetic integrity.[2] It was not always like this, and indeed the notion of Fassbinder representing Germany has something at first sight rather improbable. In order to understand how such obituary assessments could have come about, and how many discontinuous judgements are hidden inside the fulsome tributes, one needs to step back and consider what it means for a filmmaker like Fassbinder, whose life so much overshadowed his work, to 'represent' anything other than himself.

What is a nation, what is national cinema, and how can a filmmaker represent either? In the case of Germany since WW II these are, of course, especially difficult questions. After 1945, few countries were obliged to interrogate their geographical or cultural identity as anxiously as the defeated, devastated and divided German Reich. Not merely because the Yalta and Potsdam Agreements had altered the map irrevocably, handing over the formerly Prussian provinces to Poland and the Soviet Union, and creating the Allied Occupation zones from which emerged the two German states in 1948/49. More decisive was the reason for partition: the fact that the unspeakable crimes visited by Germans on other peoples had been justified in the name of the nation, whose identity, Nazism had asserted, was based both on a common racial origin and a manifest territorial destiny, two constructions of the nation for whose furtherance all means were deemed legitimate.

While the political establishment in West Germany was eager to purge itself of any trace of such aggressive nationalism, and sought to give West Germans a new national identity by defining a new enemy (the Soviet Union and East Germany, its client state), and a new geo-political destiny (the European Community and the North Atlantic Treaty Organization), the intellectual life of the Federal Republic had less clearly defined objectives. Politically, the new enemy was much the same as the old one ('Bolshevism' had already served Hitler), leading to conservative alliances that gave the Germany of Konrad Adenauer and Ludwig Erhard international and domestic objectives reaching back to Bismarck's fight against 'socialists'. Culturally, on the other hand, West Germany did not feel itself to be a nation. Literature, the arts and philosophy were busy catching up on the international movements: abstract painting, the 'new music', Sartrean existentialism, and American authors like Faulkner, Steinbeck and Hemingway became important markers in the 1950s, taking one's mind off the recent past and the burden it presented for the present. Among German authors, it was Thomas Mann in the West and Bert Brecht in the East who set the tone, critically reflecting on what it meant to be a German author, after returning from their Californian exile. Those who had stayed – poets like Gottfried Benn or novelists like Wolfgang Koeppen – became ambiguous figures of what was termed the 'inner exile'. The popular arts, including the cinema, offered an even more disconcerting picture, at least to those commenting on it: the middle classes, the 'Kulturbürgertum' mostly deplored the growing influence of American mass-entertainment in movies and popular music, whereas the left concentrated on what seemed ominous continuities between petty-bourgeois taste of the 1950s and the official entertainment of the Third Reich, as it manifested itself in the unabated hunger for family comedy, 'Schlager' music and heroic melodrama.

Academic writing about nationalism and its responsibility for the Nazi regime often tried to trace its roots to German romanticism and its discovery of the 'Volk'.[3] Here, the popular was identified with the irrational, in turn regarded as the basis for the enthusiasm with which the masses had welcomed the Führer, and was thus deeply distrusted. Such a stance confirmed the sense that nothing short of metaphysical categories could explain the evil that had befallen Germany.[4] At the other extreme, whatever had to do with emotional life was suspect:

> The feeling of German inwardness, as shared beneath the Christmas tree, could be instrumentalized. The famous German Christmas revealed itself as a prepara-
> tion for war.[5]

Yet indicting popular culture for the sentimentality that could be politically exploited was also a kind of counter-move to the explicitly political and economic analyses which Nazism received in the other part of Germany, where proletarian anti-capitalism and anti-fascism became the key elements of the state's self-definition and the cornerstone of East Germany's historical legitimacy as a separate entity.

In a counter-move to this counter-move, a later generation – that of 1968 – consciously sought to distance itself from both these views, blaming instead the education system, authoritarian family values, Germany's lack of democratic institutions, the absence of civic responsibility for the aggressive notions of national identity which led to genocide and territorial expansionism. By drawing attention to some of the historical failures of German society this century, these critics implicated the bourgeoisie as a class and authoritarianism as an ideology in the disasters. Their thinking was indebted to 'Frankfurt School' theories of culture, associated with T.W. Adorno and Max Horkheimer who had, already during their exile in the United States, approached the question of Germany's cultural identity not only as an issue of class, property and ideology, but also psychoanalytically: national identity as a structure of internalization and projection where the bourgeois family is called upon to mediate between the rebellious individual and the authoritarian state. As a consequence, much of the discussion in the 1960s declared the question of cultural or national identity obsolete, preferring to rephrase it either in terms of the new Europe (on the right) or by advocating internationalist political solidarity (on the left). Both sides were, in this respect, caught in something of a dilemma: the right, claiming to speak for the whole of Germany and also its history, had to declare Nazism an aberration, and with it, define culture a-politically and a-historically. The left, when criticising such an idea of national culture as elitist or idealist, risked being denounced as 'communists', mere mouthpieces of East German doctrine and propaganda. What tended to be passed over entirely was a more detailed assessment of German popular culture, both before and after the war, and thus any very differentiated view of what the cinema could contribute as a popular art to the nation's life, beyond being a mere tool for reactionary values or bidding for respectability. One might call it a historical double bind: a commercial cinema that was popular with audiences found itself despised by the critics, even though arguably doing the impossible/impermissible 'mourning work' for that part of the nation's identity and sense of belonging that had been formed as much by mass entertainment as by nationalist propaganda. Genre-bound and with a star-system, its lack of realism could only be perceived as reactionary, by an avantgarde for whom the popular was necessarily nationalist, because during the Nazi period, they seemed two sides of the same coin.

Representing Germany: An Awkward Honour

But in the cinema, what is 'national' and what is 'nationalist' is a complicated issue, and political dates are often an unreliable guide to film-historical developments. It is true that after 1945, it was above all in the cinema that national 'traditions' of entertainment remained apparently most persistent, with the genres of the Nazi period, such as costume dramas, social problem films, musicals, continuing to be produced (often by the same directors and with the stars of the 1940s). But it is also true that many of these entertainment genres dated from the 1910s and early 1920s and therefore were not merely Nazi inventions, however much they may have been abused as propaganda.[6] They retained their popularity even when, in the early 1960s, a new generation of filmmakers challenged the commercial film industry with the Oberhausen Manifesto and their own film productions. The dilemma this poses is either to argue that audiences are still duped by reactionary entertainment, against their better interest, or to accept that even in sentimental melodramas truths are present that speak to people's hopes or fears.

Adopting the slogans of the French nouvelle vague, and inspired by international avantgarde aesthetics, the 'young German cinema' was a self-conscious outsider and minority cinema. It transformed itself into something like a national cinema only much later, mostly with the films of its second-generation directors (Herzog, Fassbinder, Wenders, Syberberg), in the wake of political crises during the 1970s which seemed to threaten the self-definition and social consensus of, precisely, West Germany as a nation. Yet even this notion of a national cinema was double-edged. German audiences abandoned their own commercial cinema in the early 1970s not for the films of Alexander Kluge and Jean Marie Straub (the first generation), nor those of Herzog and Wenders, but for Hollywood block-busters and French comedies. Evidently, one therefore needs to distinguish between a cinema in whose films German audiences wanted to recognize themselves (precisely, the popular German star-and-genre cinema of the 1950s and 1960s and the popular American star-and-genre cinema of the 1970s and 1980s), and – in contrast to both – an auteur cinema whom foreign critics (and audiences) accepted as 'representing' Germany in the kind of parliament of national cinemas which are the big film festivals of Cannes, Venice and Berlin, for instance, or the art-houses of metropolitan film culture in London, Paris and New York.

Among the directors of this second generation, Fassbinder, with his strong regional roots, his love of the Hollywood cinema, and his belief in genre film did not fit any of the categories. In fact, he seemed the least obvious candidate for 'representing Germany', either in the sense that his films gave an image, a descriptive map or an inventory of post-war Germany by treating social and political questions; or in the sense that his films created fictional worlds in which Germans could or did recognize themselves. A filmmaker such as Kluge was much more analytical and focused on the socio-political complex Germany, while Volker Schlöndorff (THE TIN DRUM) and later Edgar Reitz with HEIMAT made more popularly accepted films about aspects of German reality and historical experience.

If representation, then, is given its two meanings, 'speaking on behalf of' and 'constructing a recognizable image of', then Fassbinder can be called a representative of (West) Germany only with qualifications. Even when one equates him with other, perhaps comparable directors abroad, then Fassbinder's Germany is not like Renoir's France, Fellini's Italy, or Bergman's Sweden. Beginning his career as a homosexual avantgarde director, Fassbinder briefly incarnated Europe's answer to the claustrophobic, camp worlds of Andy Warhol's New York. But even as a homosexual filmmaker, he did not represent the post-Stonewall self-confidence of the gay movement. At most, as a conspicuous member of his generation, he 'represented' the counter-culture of the 1970s, being both a figurehead and a scapegoat.

Yet several factors complicate and modify this assessment of non-representation. Throughout the 1960s and 1970s, West German writers and filmmakers often had the status of a representative figure thrust upon them. Novelists like Günther Grass, Heinrich Böll, or Martin Walser were – despite or because of their generally very critical assessment of the Federal Republic – regarded as exemplary Germans: not necessarily because of the breadth of their imaginative vision or their encompassing realism, but by virtue of their moral candour or political commitment. Valued internationally as spokesmen of the new, the better Germany, they were able to credibly represent the new spirit of democracy, born out of the values of Enlightenment rationality. The same was true of academic intellectuals such as Jürgen Habermas, heir of T.W. Adorno and the Frankfurt School, who took upon himself the responsibility of maintaining traditions which would link philosophical and critical thinking in the Federal Republic to the libertarian currents of the Weimar Republic. Their prominent role during these decades was sharply thrown in relief when, with German unification in 1990, this prestige suffered a dramatic decline. Günther Grass and Hans Magnus Enzensberger in West Germany and leading ex-GDR dissidents like Christa Wolf and Heiner Müller not only suffered public attacks on their personal integrity but became symptomatic for a general tendency of toppling cultural icons from their pedestal as national leaders. It was as if, its geographical identity reestablished, Germany began redefining national identity differently, paying less attention to its intellectuals and artists.

A decade or so earlier, between 1974 and 1984, however, it was filmmakers who, perhaps for the first time ever, were regarded as part of the cultural elite, and by that token, they, too, became involved in what Habermas once called 'the legitimation question'. What role, Habermas asked, could artists and intellectuals, the universities and cultural institutions play in a society in which the market of supply and demand was supposed to regulate all services, including those of education and the arts? Could the arts be more than the cultural cachet that commerce liked to give itself, or compensate for ideals that society had long ago struck off its political agenda? The film-directors were often at the sharp end of such questions. Not only were their films invariably funded with subsidies from government institutions, they also benefitted from the official patronage of Goethe Institutes all over the world, which showed their films and presented the directors in person to their foreign audiences. Werner Herzog, Wim Wenders, Hans Jürgen Syberberg, Werner Schroeter, Margarethe von Trotta, Jutta Brückner, Helma Sanders Brahms all at some time found themselves recipients of this ambiguous honour as Germany's ambassadors. The tight relation of the (art) cinema to the state in West Germany, with the many federal commissions, funding bodies, grant authorities and subsidies, meant that there was something 'official' about the German cinema throughout its period of renaissance in the 1970s and 1980s. This was accentuated by the fact that distribution abroad was often co-financed by Inter Nationes, itself the publicity arm of the selfsame Goethe Institutes. Within Germany, the New German Cinema proved hardly ever either popular or fashionable, indicating that those German audiences who had shown their loyalty to the now increasingly moribund commercial cinema, generally did not feel represented in the more 'personal' work of the new directors, and instead, looked to television for their self-representation. Given this absence of a popular German cinema commanding the devotion of German audiences, coupled with a quasi-universal disapproval of popular culture in general, filmmakers, compared to writers, also faced a double dilemma: to be accepted as 'artists' (by the establishment, in order to attract subsidy) and to become popular (in order to be recognized as speaking of and for the people). Those who accepted playing the representatives were furthermore attacked by their less well-known or less pliable colleagues as corrupt or opportunist, or ridiculed as pompous.[7] Few directors were able to balance these demands with ironic distance or a level head, opting instead either for respectability or notoriety.

On the other hand, their official status at home and abroad was due at least in part to the very favourable reception which German films from the late 1970s began to secure internationally. It ranged from an Oscar in 1980 for Schlöndorff's THE TIN DRUM and American mainstream distribution for Wolfgang Petersen's DAS BOOT, to popular acclaim for Fassbinder's THE MARRIAGE OF MARIA BRAUN and Edgar Reitz' HEIMAT, from critical enthusiasm for Hans Jürgen Syberberg's OUR HITLER, to muffled hostility towards Fassbinder's LILI MARLEEN and Herzog's FITZCARRALDO. In each case, however, the directors were treated as more than mere entertainers. They had become elevated to the status of thinkers, apparently taking it upon themselves to speak on behalf of their nation as a whole, and often enough – as in all the titles just mentioned – speaking about German history, itself so often equated with Nazism and its aftermath. Some felt themselves called upon to embody an even more heroic stance, as sages and prophets: in Germany, critics began to talk about 'Our Wagnerians',[8] among whom they listed not only artists like Anselm Kiefer, Joseph Beuys or the composer Karlheinz Stockhausen, but also the writer Heiner Müller and the filmmaker Hans Jürgen Syberberg – embodying ambitions towards the *Gesamtkuntwerk* that may well have been a response to the pressures of being 'representatives'.[9]

But there were also film directors who refused: Herbert Achternbusch, a painter-turned-writer-turned-filmmaker was one of those who vociferously proclaimed his non-availability,[10] but the most prominently uncooperative figure was undoubtedly Fassbinder.[11] One might say that he opted for notoriety, but this would underestimate the complexity of both the situation and Fassbinder's response to it. Wanting to be popular as well as critical, he did not want to manoeuvre himself into either the political avantgarde corner of Straub/Huillet and Harun Farocki, or the clown-as-gadfly antics of Achternbusch, not to mention the persecuted minority stance of a Rosa von Praunheim, the New German Cinema's most militant gay director. And unlike the prominent international names, Fassbinder seemed to feel that being a 'representative' German by being 'critical' of his country and its history was not enough: there had to be another kind of self-presentation and persona.

Fassbinder's move from the programmatic outsider to a more complex and differently provocative stance came at the point in his career when the international fame he began to enjoy made him self-conscious about his work and about being 'German' in a way he may not have been before the mid-1970s. He liked to be famous, sought official endorsements, and was devastated when at the Berlin Film Festival in 1978 he failed to receive the main prize for THE MARRIAGE OF MARIA BRAUN, to him his best film. On the other hand, this kind of slight may have made easier the refusal to be appropriated, even in the face of the inevitable pull in his later years to embody the new Germany. Fassbinder instead tried to make productive the double bind he had himself so clearly recognized, namely that of the *enfant terrible*, the rebel and outsider, whom official Germany needed as one of its 'liberal' alibis as it negotiated a period of economic crisis and near-civil war in the mid-1970s: if he liked to 'bite the hand that fed him', he also could afford on occasion to walk away from the subsidy fleshpots altogether, as with THE THIRD GENERATION.[12]

The Balzac of Germany: Fassbinder's Comédie Humaine

In the aftermath of his sudden death in 1982, however, something like an agreement quickly emerged about Fassbinder's work incarnating peculiarly and even uniquely German traits. Two metaphors established themselves, from Wolfram Schütte's obituary: that with Fassbinder's death the New German Cinema had died, of which he was the driving force, the 'heart', and that Fassbinder had been the Balzac of West Germany, its most perspicacious and passionate chronicler.[13] Is this comparison justified and more than mere hyperbole? In this chapter I want to take a critical look at some of the evidence, and at the same time suggest a more differentiated way of understanding the term representation as it might apply to Fassbinder's films, and to Germany as a country in need of images of itself. According to Schütte, Fassbinder's films reveal a positively nineteenth century voraciousness for documenting a nation:

> Only in retrospect is it possible to see what Comédie humaine Rainer Werner Fassbinder left behind in his oeuvre, how intensely his filmic narratives are saturated with human beings, with the politics, with the history and with everyday life in the context of Germany... Nowhere else is the Federal Republic present in such a broad sweep and with such depth of perspective, except perhaps in the work of Heinrich Böll.... [And] in contrast [to a director like Andrzej Wajda], the paradigmatic character of Fassbinder's oeuvre came about both *against* the establishment consensus and *without* creating a political identity. In his films, no nation recognized itself, though the nation is recognizable in and through the films.[14]

The wealth of characters and situations, of stories, types and people is indeed astounding. One can point to the many classes and social groups Fassbinder's films encompass: aristocracy and landed gentry (FONTANE EFFI BRIEST), haute bourgeoisie (THE BITTER TEARS OF PETRA VON KANT, MARTHA), old money (CHINESISCHE ROULETTE) and nouveaux riches (LOLA), show-business circles (LILI MARLEEN, VERONICA VOSS), petty bourgeoisie (THE MERCHANT OF FOUR SEASONS), working class (MOTHER KÜSTER'S TRIP TO HEAVEN), lumpenproletariat (LOVE IS COLDER THAN DEATH), 'Gastarbeiter' (KATZELMACHER), 'blacks' both foreign and indigenous (FEAR EATS THE SOUL, PIONEERS IN INGOLSTADT). Equally wide is the range of professions: journalists, industrialists, property tycoons, shift-workers, intellectuals, writers, office-workers, trade unionists, farmers, shop-keepers, butchers, bar-tenders, pimps, prostitutes of either sex, petty gangsters, contract killers, dealers, sailors, soldiers, and soldiers of fortune.

Such an urge to document the nation's life on the grand scale is fairly unique in the German cinema – or at least it was, before Fassbinder. Since then, Edgar Reitz might be said to have taken up a project somewhat similar in scale, first with his twelve-part tv series HEIMAT (1979/84) – where the time-span was vast, from 1900-1970, but the setting surprisingly a-typical, with its emphasis on a rural community – and then the 'sequel', DIE ZWEITE HEIMAT (1987/1993), which focuses on a group of young Munich musicians and filmmakers from 1960 to 1970.

That these moves towards panoramic views or national inventories should have assumed tangible shape in the late 1970s in West Germany is no accident. First of all, it came under the impact of the shock, moral and psychological, which the relatively brief period of urban terrorism culminating with the Red Army Fraction, their capture, trial and suicides caused to the Federal Republic's sense of political maturity and historical identity. The crisis' first cinematic reflection was perhaps Volker Schlöndorff's and Margarethe von Trotta's THE LOST HONOUR OF KATHARINA BLUM (1975), but a more broadly based act of 'stock-taking' was the omnibus film GERMANY IN AUTUMN (1977/8), initiated by Alexander Kluge, with contributions, among others, by Schlöndorff, Reitz as well as Fassbinder. It was followed by other films where filmmakers seemed determined to exorcise this critical moment of national self-scrutiny (Margarethe von Trotta's THE GERMAN SISTERS, Reinhardt Hauff's KNIFE IN THE HEAD, Alexander Kluge's THE PATRIOT, Helma Sanders-Brahms' GERMANY PALE MOTHER), using the contemporary situation as also a foil for reflecting on the more subterranean origins of the nation's malaise which led it to a near civil war situation.[15]

Indeed, several of the films just mentioned were the offshoots of a project that again seems to have been originated by Kluge (possibly in conversation with Peter Märtesheimer of WDR) in the wake of the critical success of GERMANY IN AUTUMN, namely to make another omnibus film, to be entitled 'The Marriages of Our Parents'. It was to trace the relation between, as Kluge was to put it in his episode (incorporated in THE PATRIOT), 'a love story and a world war'. While Sanders-Brahms' extended Kluge's formulation into a two-hour, largely autobiographic epic (GERMANY PALE MOTHER), and Reitz conceived his autobiographical HEIMAT around a whole family during and between two wars, Fassbinder's contribution became his best-known and most commercially successful film, THE MARRIAGE OF MARIA BRAUN, scripted by Märthesheimer and his wife Pea Fröhlich, together with Fassbinder himself. This film was not autobiographical.

Fassbinder seemed to have shared the Balzacian ambition to document his society also geographically, providing a kind of inventory of regions: from North Germany (the Prussia of FONTANE EFFI BRIEST, the Berlin of BERLIN ALEXANDERPLATZ, the Bremen of THE BITTER TEARS OF PETRA VON KANT) via the Rhineland (THE MARRIAGE OF MARIA BRAUN), Franconia and Hesse (the Coburg of LOLA, the Frankfurt of IN A YEAR OF THIRTEEN MOONS), to Bavaria in the South, with Munich (THE MERCHANT OF FOUR SEASONS, FEAR EATS THE SOUL), Lake Constance (MARTHA) and the 'hinterland' (THE NIKLASHAUSEN JOURNEY, JAIL BAIT, BOLWIESER). In 1980, Fassbinder stated the reasons and motives quite clearly:

> I'll be making a lot of films until my history of the Federal Republic reaches the present. LOLA and MARIA BRAUN are films about the country as it is today. In order to understand the present, what has and will become of a country, one has to

understand its whole history or at least have worked on it [...]. MARIA BRAUN and LOLA are stories that could only have happened at the moment in time in which they are situated. And they are, I hope, part of a total picture of the Federal Republic, which helps us understand its peculiar democratic contours better – and also the dangers and temptations of this democracy. To that extent, they are both very political films.[16]

The Realities of Representation

Much hinges on the meaning one can give to the word 'political' in this passage. For instance, it does not seem to refer to social realism as a style, the analysis of political institutions, or the sites of industry and business. Furthermore, a director less given to depicting the physical character of a country than Fassbinder is difficult to imagine. One only has to compare his work to that of Antonioni, Tarkovsky or even Godard to realize that Fassbinder's world has no extension in topographical space at all, has no ambitions to open itself to views or vistas, to the feel of the outdoors or convey the qualities of a landscape. If one looks nearer home, to the Herzog of WOYZECK, of KASPAR HAUSER and HEART OF GLASS or the Wenders of WRONG MOVEMENT, KINGS OF THE ROAD and WINGS OF DESIRE (not to mention the two directors' subsequent forays abroad, as in WHERE THE GREEN ANTS DREAM, or TO THE END OF THE WORLD), the difference is, if anything, even more noticeable and absolute. It is not the Germany of Rhine castles (Wenders' WRONG MOVEMENT) and Bavarian mountains (HEART OF GLASS), of romantic Caspar David Friedrich landscapes (KASPAR HAUSER) or the Black Forest (WOYZECK) that we look for in Fassbinder. It is not even to witness bleak border-regions, or villages abandoned by West German prosperity, as in KINGS OF THE ROAD or Niklas Schilling's WILLI-BUSCH REPORT. Karsten Witte once rightly remarked that in Fassbinder 'you find everything of Germany that is not the Lorelei and Neuschwanstein [the fairytale castle of Ludwig of Bavaria miniaturized in Anaheim's Disneyland].'[17]

Similarly, when compared to Schlöndorff, Hauff and Reitz, Fassbinder is still a most unlikely candidate for pioneering a new national cinema: he was completely outside the traditions of cinematic realism. Realism has been important in defining the post-war European national cinemas in at least two respects: firstly, ever since Italian neo-realism came to stand for the idea of a national European cinema, realism as opposed to studio-look and genre cinema – the anti-Hollywood stance – became the defining criteria of national cinema. Secondly, self-consciously national cinemas have often been 'art cinemas' and have drawn quite heavily on indigenous literary traditions, notably the realist novel. This was true of Britain as well as Italy, of Poland as well as East Germany. In due course, it would be true of West Germany as well, so much so that complaints about 'filmed literature' were adduced as proof that the New German cinema had betrayed its radical promises. Fassbinder, by contrast, was in the early 1970s more celebrated for being the director of genre films who imported not literature, but Hollywood melodrama into the European art cinema. And insofar as he might claim a literary pedigree, it was more likely to be the expressionist heritage of Frank

Wedekind, Bert Brecht, Marie-Luise Fleißer, and Odön von Horwath than the realist legacy of either Theodor Fontane or Thomas Mann.

One might object that with his FONTANE EFFI BRIEST, his quotations from Mann's *Tonio Kröger*[18], his adaptations of Vladimir Nabokov's *Despair* and Oskar Maria Graf's *Bolwieser*, the 'mature' Fassbinder did indeed see himself in a classical narrative tradition. But his reading of these texts, as we shall see, is rather different, and when, in 1980 he realized the project that could be said to have been at the heart of his 'Balzacian' enterprise, the massive BERLIN ALEXANDERPLATZ, Fassbinder produced neither a *Bildungsroman* nor a stylistic adaptation of Alfred Döblin's modernist city novel. Instead, it became a highly elliptical and involuted piece of story-telling which, especially in its epilogue, proved to be closer, if anything, to a lugubrious neo-expressionism than to Döblin's experimental-futurist prose.[19]

But interpreted in this way, such stylistic categories do not get to the heart of the matter. We need to remember that Fassbinder's worlds are of resolute and uncompromising artificiality: this was his starting point, and from the intensity of this premise alone do his different stylistic choices become meaningful. A hothouse atmosphere is as much the basic ingedient of the Fassbinder film as the solitary figure in the landscape is for Herzog. Fassbinder not only stayed indoors and hated scouting for locations, he even refused to visit these locations before the shoot, claiming that he needed the element of surprise to fire his imagination.[20] What one gets are 'inner worlds' in which the characters confront each other, but also a materialization of the vicious circles and tightly turned double binds discussed in the following chapter.[21] A space at once permeable to new configurations and closed to the alternative Fassbinder never considered being one: life outside society and without the agonizing company of others.

One could call Fassbinder the chronicler of the inner history of the Federal Republic, provided one does not mean by this a home-movie (blue-movie) 'Deutschland privat'.[22] Rather, it gives one meaning of the label 'political', insofar as it refers to the politics of intersubjectivity, which connects Fassbinder's work to the left-wing politics of the streets in the 1970s and the identity-politics of the 1980s, and also sets it off from both. If the 'Autorenfilm' proved duplicitous when it came to the question of cultural 'representation', Fassbinder might be said to have intervened in the Federal Republic and its society, rather than represented it. But this idea of the political also invites misunderstanding, since the term by now connotes mainly those filmmakers whose politics (because ultra-left or utopian) have remained without practical consequence, while their art has suffered from too explicit an ideological bias, making the films at worst dated propaganda, and at best sociological case-studies. This has been the fate of several directors of Fassbinder's generation, especially those associated with the *Arbeiterfilm*, a genre to which Fassbinder contributed EIGHT HOURS DO NOT MAKE A DAY.

But his films are also political in another sense, one that indicates the limits of the Balzac analogy. Fassbinder's films do not so much create autonomous worlds, as they represent media-worlds, which is to say, they live by the quotations, references, borrowings from newspapers, press photography, popular music, and above all, from other films. One of the characteristics of his work, which furnishes proof of his political acuity and testifies to his sense of history, is precisely this subtle but pervasive awareness of representation always generating a space of media-reality. Two distinct moments are implied: first, Fassbinder never pretends to be giving us people as they 'are', but as they represent themselves, be it as the image they have of themselves or the image they want to give to others. Second, all social reality in Fassbinder already bears the marks of the (mass-) media, so that in each instance the medium has its own material force and does not simply function as a transparent vehicle. This is the case with radio in LOLA and LILI MARLEEN, the press in MOTHER KÜSTER, and the cinema in MARIA BRAUN. But it is also true of literature (as material medium, not as pre-text for fictional material) in FONTANE EFFI BRIEST. Sounds and recorded music, especially in the way Peer Raben scored the films, using popular and classical music, the hits of Rocco Granata in THE MERCHANT OF FOUR SEASONS, the ballads of The Platters (PETRA VON KANT), the voice of Richard Tauber in BERLIN ALEXANDERPLATZ, or Beethoven in JAILBAIT, one finds a quite uncanny sensibility for the historical materiality of the popular. An example of the strong pull which this pre-existing reality created by audio-visual media exerts on the fictional world, to the point of determining its emotional register, is the opening credit sequence of LOLA, where a photo of Chancellor Konrad Adenauer can be seen, bending over to look at a tape-recorder, while on the sound-track and synchronizing with the still image we hear the voice of Freddy Quinn, singing about the longing to return. Two Germanies – of politics and the popular – are here improbably joined, but only together do they make a reperesentable/representative 'reality' of the 1950s.

Political Germany: The Missed Opportunity and The Road Not Taken

Seductive though it is, then, both the idea of Fassbinder's comédie humaine and of Fassbinder the representative German artist may be misleading. Even Fassbinder's political analysis of West Germany has to be approached with caution: as a dissection of Germany's democratic institutions, his films are neither particularly informative nor radical in any documentary sense (with the possible exception of EIGHT HOURS DO NOT MAKE A DAY).[23] Their value as documents lies elsewhere, and it is worth distinguishing different levels: that of a political analysis, and that of a social interpretation, for instance, as well as Fassbinder's complicated relation to the West German left. In the chapter on MARIA BRAUN I shall come back to why his films raise questions of interpretation, but here I merely want to suggest that his allegorical, deadpan-ironic, excessive, melodramatic, or camp modes are not only matters of style but of historical reference.

The political reality Fassbinder could draw on from personal experience was that of essentially four governments: the cold-war Christian-Democrat one, either with or under the shadow of Konrad Adenauer until the mid-1960s, the 'grand coalition', followed by the left-of-centre Social-Democrat government of Willy Brandt, and then after 1974 the right-of-centre Social-Democrat one under Helmut Schmidt. The Chancellorship of Adenauer, which gave West Germany its political identity, lasted from September 1949 to October 1963. It was followed by the cabinet of Ludwig Erhard – under Adenauer often credited with engineering the 'economic miracle' – who in 1966 handed over to a Christian Democrat-Social Democrat 'Grand coalition' with Kurt Georg Kiesinger as chancellor, and Willy Brandt as his deputy and foreign minister. In September 1969 the first majority Social Democrat government came to power under Willy Brandt, coinciding with one of the most turbulent periods of post-war German history, marked by student unrest, ultra-left terrorism, an economic recession and Brandt's determined efforts of *détente* towards West Germany's eastern neighbours, the so-called *Ostpolitik*. But already by the time Brandt was forced to resign in 1974, a conservative turn had begun to make itself felt in the areas of domestic political culture and debate, culminating in the emergency laws which restricted civil liberties (the infamous *Berufsverbot* for political activists among them) and extended the powers of the security services. The chancellorship of Helmut Schmidt, who took over from Brandt, merely underlined the fact that West Germany had become a cautious, essentially conservative consensus democracy. Schmidt's Social Democract-Free Democrat coalition was the last government Fassbinder was to know, for by the time the Free Democrats switched sides and the Christian Democrats under Helmut Kohl returned to power in October 1982, Fassbinder had been dead four months.

It was above all the period from the mid-1950s to the mid-1970s that retained Fassbinder's attention, who treated these two decades as a kind of telescope, whose sections could be pulled out and extended, in order to look backwards towards the history of the German bourgeoisie, the family, the heterosexual couple as it had developed since the foundation of the Bismarckian Reich in the 1870s. In one sense, the films set before 1945 are more concerned with the 'archeology' of post-WW II West Germany than with the actual periods in question, although as we shall see, they do raise a number of properly 'political' questions. The initial cause of Fassbinder's turn to German post-war politics was, as mentioned, the project of GERMANY IN AUTUMN and the plans for a sequel, *The Marriages of Our Parents*. As with other directors who took up the social conflicts of the late 1960s and early 1970s, Fassbinder turned to the topic 'Germany' out of a pressing need to understand the present: in this sense, he was a political animal.[24] It was the crisis of state authority, the legitimation of institutional power and the Law, and the symbolic role of the father as head of the family which set the terms of the conflicts that marked the Federal Republic during the 1970s, as Christian-Democrat values gave way to a Social-Democrat ones, and, within Social Democracy, the leadership passed from Willy Brandt to Helmut Schmidt.[25] By the mid-1970s, the feeling was fairly widespread among intellectuals and even some politicians that something more profound had gone wrong in West Germany: in its relation with German history, its self-definition as a nation, and especially in the rapport between parents and children something had been missed. On the extra-parliamentary left, the notion gained ground that successive governments had squandered opportunities to disentangle Germany from the Cold War, and that after 1945 there might have been a peaceful road to socialism which both

Germanies failed to take or were never allowed to explore. Social historians and literary critics reinvestigated the 'zero-hour' society of 1945, the policies of the Allies, but also the role of the political parties, the trade unions and the secret services in making all but impossible the emergence of a less cowardly selfish or crassly opportunist society. Jean Marie Straub, among the filmmakers, had already in the 1960s, with NOT RECONCILED (based on a novel by Heinrich Böll), made the case for a different reconstruction of the nation than that increasingly identified with the economic miracle. The anti-authoritarian movement in the wake of the student protests of 1968, the opening towards Eastern Europe, and events such as those depicted in GERMANY IN AUTUMN gave the idea of 'Germany' a new topicality, anticipating in some sense but also crucially misreading the terms of the debate that was to follow the fall of the Berlin Wall and German unification in 1989/90, which once more dramatically shifted the very ground of all these dialogues around the nation and its possible histories. Although it might not seem so now, during the time of Fassbinder's most active decade, West Germany was still widely held to be one of the more fragile modern democracies.[26]

By the mid-1970s, a new appraisal of recent German history in feature films could therefore expect to find wide public interest, because it had become increasingly clear to those who had grown up the 1950s and 1960s that the society being built up inside West Germany had not broken with its past, and maybe did not even want to.

> I believe that especially in Germany much is happening right now which indicates that the situation is developing in a backward direction. More precisely, I would say that in 1945, at the end of the war, the chances which did exist for Germany to renew itself were not realized. Instead, the old structures and values, on which our state rests, now as a democracy, have basically remained the same.[27]

Instead of a society engaged in change, uprooted, shaken to its foundations in 1945, Fassbinder, when looking from the 1970s back at the 1950s and the economic miracle, saw a society 'on the make' but not 'on the move'. Avid to acquire the outer trappings of success and respectability, Germans seemed morally stagnating, ultra-conservative, self-deceiving in their certainty, and above all, blind to the insights into their national past. The picture that emerges in films like WHY DOES HERR R RUN AMOK?, THE MERCHANT OF FOUR SEASONS, FEAR EATS THE SOUL, JAILBAIT or FEAR OF FEAR is of a society that is both conformist, immature, 'spießerhaft' while nonetheless supercharged with latent violence, whether directed inward or outward, and therefore at best precarious and at worst dangerously unstable. Fassbinder's interiors in particular connote the petit-bourgeois *Mief*, which breeds the hypocrisy of those who want to appear respectable, a pretense subverted by the resentment and frustration at their failure to convince even themselves.

Yet one tangible result of the nation's moment of self-reflection and family introspection in the wake of the Red Army Fraction's acts of terrorism was the idea for THE MARRIAGE OF MARIA BRAUN, according to some sources suggested to Fassbinder by Peter

Märthesheimer who was keen to give the drama department at the WDR a strong film series with recent history as its focus. The success of MARIA BRAUN led Fassbinder and Märthesheimer to the idea of the so-called BRD trilogy, which also includes LOLA (1981, subtitled 'BRD 3') and VERONIKA VOSS (1981, subtitled 'BRD 2').[28] The importance of these films – especially for Fassbinder's international reputation – is such that they will be discussed in a separate chapter. But the project as a whole, and especially the politics of representation implied, require a look at Fassbinder's relations with the German left during the 1970s, and the versions of the body politic his films develop from these encounters.

Fassbinder and the Left: THE NIKLASHAUSEN JOURNEY

As a political assessment of West Germany, the missed opportunity and the road not taken were hardly original, since they reflected not only the clichés of the left-liberal consensus about the Federal Republic in the 1960s they also rationalized the disappointment of the liberals, and the anger of the left, rueing its own failure to turn the revolts of 1968 into more permanent political structures. Although he sympathized with their causes, Fassbinder's attitude to the political left, whether in the shape of the extra-parliamentary opposition, the international liberation movements or the Red Army Fraction remained distant. He knew Holger Meins and Horst Söhnlein (both members of the RAF), but according to Ingrid Caven, considered direct action stupid and the turn to armed violence self-defeating.[29]

Post-68 militancy, left-wing party politics and urban terrorism were nonetheless the subjects of several of Fassbinder's films, notably THE NIKLASHAUSEN JOURNEY, MOTHER KÜSTER'S TRIP TO HEAVEN, and THE THIRD GENERATION. Even though these films are too variable to either form a 'genre' or to allow one to infer from them their author's voting intentions, a common tenor is the distrust of political activism. But it is less the doubts about the effectivity of direct action than the contradictory motives of the activists that seem to interest Fassbinder: the mixing of the political and the personal, the bids for sexual power or financial gain under the guise of social justice and liberating the masses. On the other hand, to call the salon-communists of MOTHER KÜSTER hypocritical, or the terrorists who suddenly take hostages in THE THIRD GENERATION cynical ego-maniacs assumes a stance the films do not endorse, since it is precisely the duplicity of all motivation and the gaps between intention and its consequences that make up the politics of Fassbinder's films. More likely, at least from a dramatist's point of view, he subscribed to the German enlightenment philosopher Lichtenberg's golden rule: 'do not judge human beings by their opinions, but by what these opinions make of them'.

Looking at Fassbinder's own practice as a filmmaker, it is clear that he did not share the view that the collapse of capitalism was imminent; he thrived on the energy that the circulation of goods, services and money generated, and in this respect was an anarchist who believed in the permanent revolution, of which capitalism was one significant manifestation. Politically, the utopia was for him a conceptual vantage point from which to look at the here-and-now, not as a goal to work towards. More importantly for his work, he was at odds with the post-68 left's disregard of the question of sex and gender, not believing that the struggle for equality could wait until the class-struggle had been won. He also refused to put much trust in political parties, and he never harboured the illusion that the political system of the GDR might provide a more equitable alternative. On the other hand, he was well aware of the peculiar dilemma of the German left, in which even the legal opposition was caught: for much of the 1960s and 1970s, for instance, to criticise the Federal Republic's nuclear policy or to protest against its law-and-order measures meant becoming suspected of sympathizing with the GDR, being a paid agent, or worse still, supporting terrorism: a kind of double bind of political blackmail, applied even to such internationally respected liberal humanists as Nobel Prize winner Heinrich Böll.[30]

While never shy of pronouncing his opinions about those in power, about corruption, cover-ups or the abuses of privilege, Fassbinder did not seem to have had much interest in another form of political interventionism, popular and high-profile in the 1970s: investigative journalism and the documentation of the political elite's own right-wing sympathizing with extremism. The novelist Erich Kuby had made a name for himself during the 1950s, castigating the darker sides of the new democracy and satirizing the scramble for power and wealth in a series of racy books. In the 1960s, Bernt Engelmann was publishing detailed guides to the politically compromised past of West Germany's political class and economic elite, but the star of the 1970s was investigative journalist Günter Wallraff. Putting on ever more audacious disguises and identities, he had reported on the working conditions of miners and Turkish immigrants, had infiltrated businesses and multi-national corporations, right-wing newspapers and Church organizations to expose not only malpractices and criminal conduct, but to demonstrate just how thin the veneer of democracy was on a society still deeply authoritarian, dangerously right-wing and openly discriminating. Fassbinder seems to have had little patience for these heroes of the left, nor much interest in the public scandals revealed each week in the news magazine *Der Spiegel*, owned by the publisher Rudolf Augstein who in the mid-1970s was to rescue the Filmverlag der Autoren, a film production and distribution enterprise that Fassbinder had a major stake in. Relatively few investigative journalists turn up in his films, and where they do, as in MOTHER KÜSTER and VERONIKA VOSS, they are either unscrupulous tabloid hacks out for a scoop, or self-pitying cowards drowning their conscience in booze.

THE NIKLASHAUSEN JOURNEY is Fassbinder's most explicit look at both the rhetoric and the sentiment behind radical activism and ultra-left militancy. Shot in May 1970 for a late-night slot of WDR Television's drama unit, it is clearly inspired by Godard's WEEKEND, using the same basic structure of a picaresque journey through the countryside that ends in violence, a bloodbath and conflagration. Staged as a series of tableaux meant to recall also Glauber Rocha's ANTONIO DAS MORTES, the characters are given to declaiming revolutionary texts, newspaper reports of Black Panther shoot-outs, and passages from Marx' *Das Kapital*. Distinctively German, on the other hand, is the fact that the story is rooted in Bavarian folklore, centred on the contact points between peasant mysticism and agit-prop theatre, the cult of the Virgin Mary and revolutionary messianism. It points to a number of other films made by German directors in the 1970s, from the anti-Heimat films of Schlöndorff (THE POOR FOLK OF KOMBACH), Reinhard Hauff (MATHIAS KNEISSL) and Volker Vogeler (JAIDER-THE LONELY HUNTER), to the anarcho-mystical fables of Achternbusch (SERVUS BAVARIA) and Werner Herzog's HEART OF GLASS. The story of the shepherd boy whose visions of the Virgin Mary are used by very different interests – from a sexually predatory countess to a sinister agent provocateur called the black monk (played by Fassbinder himself) – before he is captured and burnt at the stake, gives rise to several levels of irony and sarcastic humour. Balancing a counter-reformation rococco setting with flower-power hippies, and combining a homosexual bishop addicted to nude boys and the sweaty body odour of young peasants with a law-and-order posse made up of West German policemen and black GI's machine gunning a camping site, Fassbinder lets his most Bunuelian side free range, in what is both a cardboard cut-out satire of the venality and violence of those in power and a rather more touching homage to the Bavarian sense of heartfelt incongruity. Fassbinder also plays on the theatricality of all revolutionary energies, by showing himself 'coaching' Hanna Schygulla in front of a baroque mirror for her big speech to the masses, and preceding the film with a little prologue between himself, Schygulla and an Antonio das Mortes figure with a gun, about the role of the party vanguard in mobilizing the people, and about the legitimacy of masterminding or staging a revolution in order to provoke the people into participation.

It is not difficult to detect behind these cruel Pirandellian games Fassbinder's lack of sympathy for self-appointed demagogues or Jesuit sophistry when it comes to revolution-ary rhetoric about the class-struggle. Yet the care with which some of the set-pieces are put together, notably a speech about Marx' theory of surplus value in an eerily white quarry, a crucifixion staged against a mountain of wrecked automobiles, and a fierce speech from Heinrich von Kleist's *Penthesilea*, delivered by three women in war-paint on a fuming rubbish tip, impart to the film not only a sombre gravity, which is underlined by the church hymns sung acapella or accompanied by drum-rolls. They indicate that Fassbinder is looking for ways to let his characters retain their dignity as human beings, while distancing himself from the foolishness of their acts and intentions, whether official or oppositional, egomaniacal or altruistic.

The Impossible Critique: Neither from Within nor Without

Fassbinder's view on German postwar politics may endorse the notion of 'the return of the repressed' or of fatal continuities, but it was also fundamentally different from both the polemical or activist assaults on the State coming from the left and the superior dismissal of student politics or arguments for even more repression of dissent advocated by the right. The fact that the West German State was internationally the successor of the German Reich gave it the legal right to speak on behalf of both Germanies, but by leaving its judiciary, its scientists, technocrats and business circles (i.e. the educational and expert elite) virtually unpurged, it also forfeited the loyalty and respect of the younger generation, who pointed to the silence on the subject of fascism in the schools' history lessons, and the tainted past of some of its highest officials (Adenauer's political secretary Globke, President Kiesinger, or the so-called 'piggy-back' law in the civil service, for instance, which meant that with each new appointment, a politically compromised, but bureaucratically experienced ex-Nazi could be reinstated). It was also common knowledge that the Americans had preferred the Nazis of yesterday to social democrat dissidents and political emigres, because the former could be trusted as good anti-Communists.

These political scandals, too, rarely served Fassbinder as material for his films. One reason he distrusted such critiques of the system was that they invariably placed themselves 'outside', grounded neither in a viable political alternative nor in a genuine concern for those on whose behalf they claimed to speak. MOTHER KÜSTER'S TRIP TO HEAVEN is in this respect Fassbinder's clearest condemnation of party-politics, trade-unionism and the extra-parliamentary, 'maoist' groupings. By focussing on the sense of moral wrong, the pain of shame experienced by Mother Küster, the need to rescue her own love and loyalty to the husband and father, branded as 'criminal' and 'insane', the film indicates how, in contemporary politics, nobody is able to speak on behalf of or 'represent' the true issues that move people to take action, that 'politicises' the family or the work place.[31]

More generally, what preoccupied Fassbinder was the (im)possibility of a 'critical' position altogether, of what it meant to have a political vantage point at all. Fassbinder's initial solution in his films was the classical strategy of drama: to let the audience see even the villain's point of view. Speaking of the Fascist past of a figure in JAILBAIT, Fassbinder once declared:

> I think I'm one of the few directors in Germany who has a positive relation to his characters ... in some cases, like the girl's father in JAILBAIT when he talks about the war, I'm indulgent almost to the point of irresponsibility.[32]

In other words, while intellectually Fassbinder seemed to support the left's indictment of moral cowardice, he did not use this indictment to caricature the people he portrayed. In this crucial respect, his films were indeed different from those made by the directors of the Oberhausen generation – films like Peter Schamoni's NO HUNTING SEASON FOR FOXES and even Kluge's YESTERDAY GIRL. Where the 'young German film' of the 1960s utilized naturalism as a form of satire, Fassbinder's stylizations, his carefully calculated strategies of identification and distance, discussed more fully in the following chapter, ensured a troubling mix of sympathy and antipathy, beyond clear-cut positions of good and evil. Fassbinder knew that such 'indulgence to the point of irresponsibility' came at a price: the filmmaker's apparently non-judgmental relation to destructive or evil characters did indeed give rise to scandals and controversy. Sympathy for domestic monsters such as Margit Carstensen in PETRA VON KANT, Karlheinz Böhm in MARTHA, Von Instetten, Effi's husband in FONTANE EFFI

BRIEST, or Peter Chatel in FOX AND HIS FRIENDS was interpreted as a sign that Fassbinder was suspiciously fond of depicting emotional cruelty.[33]

In the case of JAILBAIT, Franz Xaver Kroetz, the author of the play on which the film is based, found Fassbinder's reading so 'irresponsible' that he took out a court action. Objecting to what he called Fassbinder's 'pornographic' travesty of his piece, Kroetz managed to enforce an injunction which resulted in cuts and a very limited public release for the film.[34] Fassbinder replied in an open letter:

> Dear Franz Xaver Kroetz, it is a pity that you cannot be altogether honest. Why are you embarrassed to admit that you refused my offer to work with you on a script that would be acceptable to both of us? [...]. Are you embarrassed that you left your play in the lurch? ... Remember those for whom you wanted to write. Think of the ordinary people, ask those who work all day long what they got out of our films. Their replies may come for you as a surprise [...]. To put it with some pathos: it's the first time you have been understood [...]. Everything that is in the film is also in the play. Maybe this now embarrasses you. But it need not, because your play isn't that bad, honestly. Your Rainer Werner Fassbinder.[35]

Disturbingly, there is much love in his films even for those who do evil, as if only morally ambiguous characters can bring the spectator to look at a situation also from 'inside', obliging the viewer to try and understand what has made them the way they are. As a consequence, there is a freedom to Fassbinder's portrayal of evil, in the sense that we can look at the protagonists without the need for the filmmaker to polemicise or the audience to feel superior. This aspect has most consistently caused offence, and not only to Kroetz. Especially when Fassbinder touches on the question of marginal or oppressed groups, he found himself accused of misogyny, of being anti-homosexual and anti-Semitic.[36] But as he pointed out:

> I have always maintained that one can learn most about the majority by looking at the behaviour of the minorities. I can understand more about the oppressors, when I show the actions of the oppressed, or rather, how the oppressed try to survive in the face of oppression. At first I made films where I made the oppressors evil and the victims unfortunate. But in the end, that is not how it is.[37]

What makes the depiction of oppressors and oppressed in his films ultimately so difficult for some audiences is that Fassbinder refuses to assume that there has to be a natural solidarity between victims. Instead, one finds an almost Bunuelian vision of the right of outcasts and underdogs to be as mean, inhuman and evil as anyone else. His portrayal of the victims of society shows what has made them who they are, giving rise to a picture of cruelty among the underclass which reflects but cannot explain the cruelty of the dominant class. The decision of not 'judging' his characters from an external vantage point thus obliges him not to be partisan towards marginal groups solely on the basis of being marginal: his homosexuals are not always nice, his Jews can be exploitative, his communists may be careerists. It is here that Fassbinder's later films rejoin his first success, KATZELMACHER, where Jorgos, the foreign worker from Greece, turns out to be as much a racist and a chauvinist as the others, once he feels his own tenuous position threatened by another foreign worker – this time from Turkey.

Yet if he was 'indulgent to the point of irresponsibility' towards his characters as individuals, such was not the case when it came to political parties, interest groups or organizations. Although, thanks to the anti-theater's rabble-rousing vanguard reputation, he was close to the students' protests of 1968,[38] already by 1970 he had the presence of mind, both in his films and plays, to understand how political action, even in the personal sphere, had a built-in logic of escalation, inexorably feeding on itself. *Bremer Freiheit* (1971), a play written for Margit Carstensen, and based on a historical *fait divers* of a woman who had, in the 1830s, poisoned several men, including her husband, is instructive in this respect. It can be read as a feminist (tr)act of rebellion against a patriarchal order that hydra-like, always sprouts new heads. But as drama, it also puts on show the heroine's need to carry on killing, no longer out of outrage and oppression, just trying to keep under control the momentum started by her grisly deed, until she is finally caught.

Victimisation and isolation are shown to occur not only in a specifically German urban environment, but in settings familiar to a particular audience: the place of work, the family dinner table, the block of apartments with petty neighbours and tyrannical landlords, the supermarket and the launderette, the corner cafe and the local bar. What makes the early films different from the melodramas is not the central preoccupation, which remains the same throughout. Rather, it would be the fact that on the vicious circles that his film so relentlessly trace, Fassbinder's films have a double perspective: one from without, and one from within. The films up to and including BEWARE OF A HOLY WHORE have in common that they are about couple relationships, but seen in the context either of other couples or of the group: the perspective 'from without' is the view of the group on the couple, and thus also reflects the collectivist, anti-family ideologies and aspirations which Fassbinder professed to share with the rest of his generation during the 1960s and early 1970s.

In the films from THE MERCHANT OF FOUR SEASONS onwards, however, the emphasis shifts, and the couple is seen more from within, and from the vantage point of the weaker, if not the losing partner. While the perspective from without maintained an indirect form of address, often perceived as aggressive and even 'sneering,'[39] it also invited the audience to recognize itself in the couple situation *and* to judge it, but judge it from a position that could either be dismissed as cynical and heartless, or praised as politically correct. For instance, when (in THE MERCHANT OF FOUR SEASONS) Irm Hermann, waiting in vain for Hans to come home, and having kept the dinner hot and her daughter starving for hours, finally bursts out in a fit of violence against the child, we sympathize with Irm Hermann's inner rage, with the well-behaved girl playing with her plaits and scraping her spoon, but also with Hans, for skipping his dinner in favour of a schnaps at the bar with his friends. Yet it would be misleading to call such a scene 'distanced'. On the contrary, neither the look at the dynamics of the couple from the vantage-point of the group (in the early films) nor the no-win stalemate in the melodramas gives rise to any kind of supplementary perspective. On the contrary, it merely underlines that the key interpersonal situation around which Fassbinder's work turns is as self-centred as it is self-defeating. This experience Fassbinder himself called emotional exploitation.[40] All of Fassbinder's films, when seen 'from without', are ingeniously drama-tised and occasionally didactic statements about what it means to have power over someone else's capacity for love and thus to live within mutual dependencies structured around generosity and guilt.

Politically Correct or Emotionally Honest: The View from Within

Proving that his heroes' personal predicaments had a wider social significance, Fassbinder's vision became 'political' in the (then commonplace phrase) 'the personal as political', understood, however, as a way of allowing his characters few insights into possible escape routes from the vicious circles that bind them to each other in emotional inequality or exploitation, and instead, asking the audience to imagine a plane of reality or action where such a contradiction might be resolved, which is to say, envisage more fundamental, and thus 'political' changes in the social order. The director's optimism (or what he called his 'romantic anarchism')[41] was focused on the remarkable inventiveness of his stories that demonstrated this very process in action. Graphic portrayals of the predicament across different social worlds and different human situations earned Fassbinder the reputation of a chronicler of German post-war mores, personal vicissitudes and social inequalities; but the very same obstinacy of sticking to this chosen theme is also responsible for the more negative judgement of Fassbinder as a politically naive polemicist with a rather narrow range of social insights.[42]

To get a sense of how persistently he plowed his chosen furrow, one only needs to recall the terms of the conflict in his first half-dozen films: KATZELMACHER uncovers a vicious circle in the sphere of working-class relations to Gastarbeiter, where those kicked by the rest of society find others even more dispossessed than themselves, whom they exploit. A similar downward spiral governs sexual dependencies of whatever form (heterosexual and homosexual in LOVE IS COLDER THAN DEATH, GODS OF THE PLAGUE, THE AMERICAN SOLDIER) where the incompatibility of love *and* money is made explicit by the frequency with which the films feature prostitution, i.e. love *for* money. Inevitably, whereas needing money might appear as a one-way form of dependency, needing love and giving love makes characters equally vulnerable. This more finely spun drama of longing and loss is the subject of films like THE BITTER TEARS OF PETRA VON KANT and I ONLY WANT YOU TO LOVE ME. By contrast, the kinds of exploitation which are shaped by conflicts of race and class (as in WHITY or EIGHT HOURS ARE NOT A DAY) can, in the domestic setting of the family and the couple, also become the point of equilibrium, and even the pivot of a stabilizing mutuality in the relationship (as, briefly, for Emmi and Ali in FEAR EATS THE SOUL, who might be said to find mutual happiness by 'using' each other). It is when examining the subtler but also more devastating dynamics of exploitation within the couple that the vantage point 'from without' will eventually give way to the perspective 'from within'.

The perspective from without, I argued, is that of the group, itself implicitly identified with a 'political' analysis, along the lines inherited by Fassbinder from the anti-authoritarian movements but also the study of Freudo-Marxists like Herbert Marcuse, Wilhelm Reich or Erich Fromm, popularized in the 1960s. The economic and ideological basis of emotional exploitation in Fassbinder's films is never disguised, no more than the class conflicts, directing attention to the demagogical side of the 'class-consensus of afflu-ence' propagated in West Germany during the 1950s and 1960s. How thin this consensus was Fassbinder made apparent in concise scenes of Brechtian logic, such as those binding Elisabeth to Jorgos and vice versa in KATZELMACHER, or similar scenes in the later films, such as JAILBAIT or FOX AND HIS FRIENDS, where the class-barriers close in immediately, once luck or money have run out. But insofar as Fassbinder, privileged as his lifestyle was both in terms of class and money, discovered the same personal problems in all social strata, he gave priority to the depiction of emotional dilemmas. The psycho-dynamics of the characters tends to usurp issues of political economy, and in some cases produces a reversal of roles, where emotional blackmail is seen to cut across classes (e.g. Hanna Schygulla as the proletarian Karin in PETRA VON KANT, blithely compensating her economic dependency on Petra by boasting about heterosexual potency and promiscuity), yet by that very act, affirming the importance of class as a marker of difference.

When a film puts sex and class on a parallel track, as does FOX AND HIS FRIENDS, the story of a proletarian hero who is both sexually exploited and economically ruined by his bourgeois lover, while his lack of education, his peasant manners and naive adulation of middle-class values make him a laughing stock for the snobs he so much admires, the narrative can easily appear didactic, for it seems to lack the dimension of poetic justice or ironic reversal that gives the stages of the Fassbinder plot usually such a grimly satisfying shape. However, FOX AND HIS FRIENDS is the kind of film where the moral point of view is more complex and interesting than the formal pattern, which is why the film marks a certain end-point: the (politically correct) perspective from without sees only an abstract schematicism or a devastatingly total pessimism, which was felt to be 'reactionary' at a time and in a situation – 1974 – when homosexuals were fighting for a fairer and more positive representation in the media.[43] Yet if one applies to FOX AND HIS FRIENDS and other films of Fassbinder's middle period the 'inner perspective', a somewhat different view emerges.[44] It is also worth remembering just how unique Fassbinder's early films were: concerned with exploring the conflicting claims of sexual and class identity, they depict everyday human situations with a casual self-evidence unseen before in post-war German cinema (and even television). At first, subjectivity and social self are represented as parallel spheres, where sexual oppression and the patriarchal family reflect the wider social pressures of capitalism and bourgeois ideology. It is a congruence which preoccupied the German Left and the anti-authoritarian movement more than virtually any other topic.[45] Yet, rather than trying to find a way to free themselves, by showing his protagonists coming to a raised consciousness, breaking out of the family in order to become militants, which was the demand of a certain 'political film practice'[46] and of 'progressive-realist' film theory[47], Fassbinder appears to let his characters rot in their despair.[48] However, the critics who argued that Fassbinder abandoned his heroes to their hopelessness, and accused him of defeatism were perhaps too readily adopting only the 'view from outside', from which the characters' relentless misery does indeed appear as a victim's stance, making every new torture and humiliation appear gratuitously sadistic.

Against such a verdict, it is important to set the possibility that the films cohere in their formal and narrative structure around the tighter and tighter knots of mutual exploitation, because Fassbinder wants to point to a blockage, not so much in his characters' psyche, but in the activist and critical agendas of his audiences. This is particularly evident in the films after 1971, such as MERCHANT OF FOUR SEASONS, FEAR EATS THE SOUL, FOX AND HIS FRIENDS, MOTHER KÜSTER'S TRIP TO HEAVEN, FEAR OF FEAR, and I ONLY WANT YOU TO LOVE ME. They too, have as their dramatic structure the 'vicious circle' in which help proffered invariably aggravates the plight. If there is sadism, it is, however, not directed at the protagonists, but at the audience, perhaps all too easily convinced of their politically enlightened superiority when confronted with simpletons like Franz and Ali, Hans and Fox, Emma and Margot. By grindingly insisting on situations where characters merely dig themselves deeper into their dilemma, Fassbinder draws attention to a subjectivity, where the compulsion to repeat, like other manifestations of the death-drive, have their own place in the psychic economy of his characters – and by extension, his audiences. A quintessentially melodramatic proposition, it lets us see the length to which Fassbinder goes in order to be 'level' with the characters. Yet this liberalism of being 'level' also implies being level with the audience ('what I aim at is an open realism ... that does not provoke people into defensiveness')[49] and gives it a kind of moral horizon which abandons righteous anger in favour of winning the spectators over to a more generous vision of human failings, but also to open them up to a more complex interplay of recognition and identification:

> The viewer should be able to activate things and feelings in himself via the characters, but the structure of the presentation ought to give him the possibility for reflection ... that is, the mise-en-scène ought to be such that it makes distance and reflection possible.[50]

Such might be the 'perspective from within', an indication that Fassbinder refuses the solidarity discourse of the group and the utopian programme of the anti-authoritarian generation: 'Whenever I can imagine a counter-model, I know it must be wrong, [... because] a counter-model always contains within itself that which it opposes.'[51] An interpretation of, for instance, I ONLY WANT YOU TO LOVE ME which sees the father merely as the representative of patriarchy, and thus of capitalism in the home, would make the hero, Peter, a rebel in the image of the oppressor – a position that the social worker in the film tends to take. Sympathetic though she may be, the film questions her (narrative) authority by showing how her advice, even if it does not exactly aggravate Peter's moral and psychic state, nonetheless does not reach him from where he is listening. As in the case of Hitchcock's PSYCHO, medical, ideological or institutional explanations of disturbed behavior in Fassbinder often function as the sign of their own insufficiency. This conviction seemed to define the strategic point at which it became more important for Fassbinder to have access to a mass medium, than to be 'politically correct': at least in this apparently non-partisan attitude Fassbinder was, one might even argue, 'representative' for the audiences with whom he wanted to communicate, while nonetheless taking a stand against 'victim thinking' and thus challenging also a key aspect of contemporary 'identity-politics'.[52]

The Critique from Within and Without: *Soll und Haben*

Throughout Fassbinder's work, one can see this problem of the 'critical' and the 'repre-sentative' stance receiving different answers and formulations. Thus, in the early films, characters represent themselves in their own words, which turn out to be borrowed speech, often borrowed from those who are most responsible for making them marginal. In their struggle for maintaining the illusion of belonging to the 'centre', their personal evil or petty viciousness reveals itself as the deformation that the larger evil imposes on them. In the later films, the commerce of self and other, the dynamics of projection, transference and identifi-cation generate miscognitions of a different order, affecting also the way the master-slave dialectic constantly reworks the antagonisms and power-relations between the characters. That Fassbinder's 'indulgence to the point of irresponsibility' as well as his transferential histories were to become central to his politics is the subject of several chapters, for it affects his representation of all the 'minorities' he names in the passage above: women (in the *BRD Trilogy*), Jews (in IN A YEAR OF THIRTEEN MOONS) and homosexuals (in FOX AND HIS FRIENDS and QUERELLE). The occasion which prompted this statement – as response to one of his television projects being cancelled – also led Fassbinder to mount an especially explicit defence of his concept of a 'critique from within'. The controversy arose because he chose as 'founding text', by which to track the origin and self-definition of the German bourgeoisie, a notoriously anti-Semitic novel from the last century. Gustav Freytag's 1855 bestseller *Soll und Haben* was intended to begin Fassbinder's archeology of the 'representation' of Germany as a process of 'mediated' and necessarily misrecognized self-representation. Freytag's motto is apt: 'The novel should seek out the German people where it is most itself – in its diligence and at its place of work'.[53] Freytag's depiction of the rise of the mercantile bourgeoisie against the feudal land-owning aristocracy relies explicitly and implicitly on a third term, namely German Jewry, which provides the moral and psychological foil for his definition of what is 'German' on the eve of the founding of the (Bismarckian) nation-state. The symptomatic transferential identification on the part of the author/narrator with his (Aryan) hero and (Jewish) anti-hero would have allowed Fassbinder to document the ideology of German nationalism in the making. Conceived as a television 'family' series for the 1977 season, the adaptation was cancelled by the director-general of the WDR, intimidated by a press campaign against Fassbinder on the grounds of the novel's anti-Semitism. Without addressing the personal insinuations, Fassbinder defended the value of the novel for today's audiences:

> Especially the most odious passages in the novel *Soll und Haben* – those demonstrating, as it were, the author's false political consciousness [...] – force us to face perhaps one of the most important issues that tie us today to our history, to the nineteenth century and to our social forebears [...]. *Soll und Haben* tells of how the [German] bourgeoisie in the middle of the last century, after a failed revolution, developed its self-understanding and established its value system, a system that did not progress much beyond the notions of hard work, honesty, righteousness, and that defined the so-called 'German character' by fencing it off in all directions, internally against the proletariat and the aristocracy, and externally against anything alien, and above all against a world view denounced as 'Jewish', but in truth distinguished by its objectivity, humanism and tolerance. It is this bourgeois value system which could, without much trouble, find a home in the ideology of national socialism, but it is also one that extends to today's society – hence the need to confront this novel once more.[54]

What seemed to draw Fassbinder to the novel was also another feature, as telling as the paranoid trait he saw in Freytag's construction of bourgeois German identity. This was the struggle in the text between Freytag the anti-Semitic ideologue and Freytag the journalist: the latter too much interested in a good story – 'exciting, dramatic, sentimental, mysterious' – not to undermine the former's tendentious and racist editorializing. Such tensions, according to Fassbinder, bring out the value of popular fiction, while giving the spectator these very contradictions to think about: 'It is our job, then, to turn a no-holds-barred, sentimental and sensationalist yarn back on its feet, the feet of history, and thus to make Freytag's ideology transparent as potentially fascist.'[55] Fassbinder here remains true to his preference for melodrama as self-revealing yet 'critical', thanks to its own internal inconsistencies.[56] It also defines his attitude to the popular: despising neither the entertainment needs of a prime-time television audience nor reneging on television's remit to educate as well as to entertain.

The fact that *Soll und Haben* was cancelled shows how delicate the balance finally was between the public-service broadcasters' need for artistic figureheads to front the more costly ventures into adapting the nation's literary patrimony for a popular audience, and the cautious approach they took to what they thought these figureheads could be trusted with. After the premature closure of EIGHT HOURS DO NOT MAKE A DAY, and the shunting of the second part of BOLWIESER to a late-night slot on ZDF, it was another proof to Fassbinder why the television series format was the prize to aim for, if one wanted to attract a national audience's attention,[57] and the greatest hurdle to any director who considered that for debates on historical issues to take place at all on television, a film needed to translate complexity also into ambiguity, be it around attraction and repulsion, sexual identity, or as in this case, class insecurity and resentment of the 'other'. The limits of 'public opinion' to tolerating such ambiguity when addressed by a representative public medium were tested by Fassbinder once more in 1980, when his BERLIN ALEXANDERPLATZ was first aired amidst a veritable hate-campaign against the filmmaker, for daring to spend public funds on 'smutty self-indul-gence'.[58] Perhaps speaking through a recognized literary name, be it Freytag, Graf or Döblin, did not, after all, widen the scope for an author to be speaking on behalf of anyone, be it the majority or outsiders, and in this sense, too, Fassbinder was no representative.

'I Don't Throw Bombs, I Make Films'[59]

There are, however, in his work a number of figures or, rather, configurations that seem to have exemplary status, if only because their 'representativeness' is so deeply ambivalent. They manifest themselves in the dialectic of scapegoat and redeemer, or in terms borrowed from Jean Paul Satre's book on Jean Genet, whose *Querelle de Brest* Fassbinder also adapted, they are at once 'saint, actor and martyr'.[60] As in a blueprint, THE NIKLASHAUSEN JOURNEY presented, in the triad of Hans Böhm, the peasant visionary, the Black Monk and Margaretha, a Mary Magdalen figure, the dynamics of leadership and sacrificial lamb, between charisma and imposture, impassioned faith and coolly calculating strategy.

Other Fassbinder films also dissect the logic of conspiratorial groups, foremost among them BEWARE OF THE HOLY WHORE, made the same year (1970). Dealing with the frictions among a film crew at a remote location waiting for the director – and the money – to arrive, it is usually regarded as a wide-open *film-à-clef* about the Fassbinder clique and the shoot of WHITY, the 'Western' with a Southern setting Fassbinder had made in Spain for a production company headed by Ulli Lommel and his wife Katrin Schaake earlier that year.[61] But equally, it is a study of violence generated within close-knit groups, precisely because they are close-knit, mutually and manifold dependent on each other, and therefore in need of a leader, especially one they can join to love to hate. BEWARE OF THE HOLY WHORE has always been seen as one of the turning points in Fassbinder's work,[62] but even stripped of its autobiographical reference, its atmosphere of sullen aggression fuelled by boredom and anticipation conveys much about the milieu of political group work and student communes in the early 1970s, waiting for some kind of thunder and lightning to clear the sultry climate of anti-Vietnam protest or news about Che Guevara's Bolivian campaign, wondering what would finally bring the war home, and reveal the enemy that could be palpably identified and thus frontally attacked.

In this respect, Fassbinder did not have to wait until the events in 1977 that resulted in GERMANY IN AUTUMN to understand the degree to which activist provocation was geared towards making the bourgeois state take the iron fist out of the velvet glove of liberal democracy and dare it to show its own readiness for violence. Intellectually attracted to the ruthless radicalism of the Baader-Meinhof group, but only too aware that the frenzy their action schemes induced in the body politic would isolate them from effectivity and mass-support, Fassbinder had to keep faith with his own political project, which was to make movies that moved people, even if it was in spite of themselves. It was not a matter of making films that 'exposed' the illiberal state or 'condemned' the RAF ('Red Army Fraction', the name the Baader-Meinhof group gave themselves), but to put in the picture the inner workings of anguish, paranoia and the unbearable tension that result.[63]

For a dramatist and story-teller like Fassbinder, then, left-wing politics became a subject at the point at which extremism was caught up in the mirror-maze and political analysis and paranoid projection coincided, while the militants helped create the enemy they had set out to combat. What struck him, especially in the mid-1970s, during the most turbulent years of the Federal Republic, was that in the sphere of the political, the most uncompromisingly critical stance (the view from without) could well turn out to be the most complicit one: playing right into the hands of 'the enemy.' Such is indeed one of the lessons of Fassbinder's bleakest but also funniest settling of accounts with the 'left' that remained by the late 1970s, THE THIRD GENERATION. The title is explained by Fassbinder:

> The first generation was that of '68. Idealists, who thought they could change the world with words and demonstrations in the street. The second generation, the Baader Meinhof group, moved from legality to the armed struggle and total illegality. The third generation is today's, who just indulges in action without thinking, without either ideology or politics, and who, probably without knowing it, are like puppets whose wires are pulled by others.[64]

The film was originally to have been made with television money (by Westdeutsche Rundfunk), but, here, too, the broadcasting company pulled out at the last minute, for fear of touching too sensitive an issue, as did the Berlin Senate which at that time gave subsidies to films that used Berlin locations and facilities. Fassbinder, who allegedly only heard about these decisions days before he was due to start shooting, nonetheless went ahead, partly with his own money, partly by a quickly arranged co-production deal with the Filmverlag der Autoren.[65]

The story is that of a group of urban guerrillas, a mix of drug pushers and political activists, who form a kind of underground cell which, on suspecting that they have been betrayed to the police, decides to strike. They kidnap the director of an American computer company, not realizing that this is part of the trap into which they have been lured. In its sharply etched scenes, its Brechtian intertitles and sometimes satirical, sometimes terrifying intensity, THE THIRD GENERATION is both a ferocious attack and a fond farewell to the spirit of communes, whether political or drug-based: it effectively shows the group as fascistic, but it also makes plausible how individual vulnerability and residual idealism in such a group can be used by the powers that be. In this case, by an international dealer in computer surveillance equipment, in order to increase sales by sowing terror among the business community and politicians. In the end, the militants are shot, though not without creating maximum mayhem, ironically counterpointed to the annual carnival (late February), a dramatic device that Schlöndorff had already used to good effect in the opening scene of another film supposedly sympathetic to the 'terrorist' cause, THE LOST HONOUR OF KATHARINA BLUM (1975).

In Fassbinder, the collusion between terrorists and international capital seems to be the meaning of the film at first viewing, and it is how reviewers saw it when it first came out, endorsed by Fassbinder's own comments in interviews.[66] But two things are striking, upon re-seeing the film, especially in the context of Fassbinder's other films. One is that the power-relations it deals with have been captured within a set of terms that are more widely applicable than to this specific instance, and secondly, that the careful work on both sound and image creates another kind of reality altogether, more inside (every)one's head than in a specific place or period (even though some typical Berlin landmarks are clearly recognizable, such as the revolving Mercedes star on the Europa Centre, and the news on the TV screens together with the carnival costumes allow a precise dating). One could also see it as a companion piece to WORLD ON A WIRE, set in a science fiction realm, and therefore possessing the character of parable or a Brechtian 'model play'.[67]

The wider, 'allegorical' reference of THE THIRD GENERATION concerns the crisis of the idea of individuals as self-motivated and inner-directed, and thus the crisis of historical subjectivity and political agency in the wake of '68. It could be called a double crisis of the subject: what the events of the late 1960s showed was that with the absence of a militant working class, there was no longer even the possibility of a collective revolutionary subject, while at the same time, the bourgeois order could no longer claim, in the face of such massive disaffection, to be the representative subject, who could act on behalf of, in place of society and its members.[68] One of the film's themes seems to be the political double bind in which representative democracies necessarily find themselves: they are there to guarantee equality before the law, yet because this very principle stands in a tension to the articulation of uniqueness, 'roots', particularity, it means that the difference reappears elsewhere in the system, whether in the form of taste and 'distinction', or as the 'identity politics' of invented traditions and genealogies. The question raised by such phenomena as urban guerillas or 'revolutionary cells' was thus how is the singular connected to the collective, to which one answer was the figure of the terrorist, as at once the existential subject (by the mimicry of 'armed struggle'), the embodiment of the singular (the saint), and self-conscious martyr (the ascetic, preparing for fast and sacrifice). The terrorist is a representative, but one with a false mandate, trying to inscribe him/herself 'positively' into history. In the absence of a 'representative' who can credibly figure both the singular and the collective (as does a fascist leader), s/he buys into 'representation' in the form of spectacular action and the highest visibility.[69] Yet to the extent that the terrorist 'responds' to this double bind within the political system of representation, he is a figure not altogether unfamiliar to the Fassbinder hero: he is his alter ego, his 'positive' shadow and diabolical double.

For the only way the Fassbinder hero avoids responding to a false mandate, avoids becoming a terrorist, is by his negativity, his refusal to 'confront' the system or rebel against it. In THE THIRD GENERATION, the terrorists are activists, but they do not have a speaking position, which is where they differ fundamentally from heroes such as Hans, Fox or the many Franz's (of which there is also one in THE THIRD GENERATION who knowingly lets himself be shot).[70] As will be argued in the subsequent chapters, the Fassbinder hero does attain a speaking position by taking the 'system' literally, which is to say, by believing in equality, love, generosity, trust. It is in this sense that Fox in FOX AND HIS FRIENDS triumphs over his cynical exploiters, because he 'answered' the demand of love, and Mother Küster goes to heaven, because she, too, answered the demand to do right by her husband. What they say may be wrong, even what they do is often wrong, but 'where' they stand, *from where they speak* is right, and hence, in this very specific sense, 'representative'.

Macro and Micro: The Networks of Power

The second feature which makes THE THIRD GENERATION not quite the tendentious denunciation of right and left that it appeared to be is the complexity of the film's power-relations, expressed as so often in later Fassbinder in terms of sound-image relations. The questions Fassbinder seems to pose in THE THIRD GENERATION have less to do with what stance to take in the face of such a 'paranoid' state of affairs, where a government might be colluding with its own sworn enemies, each needing the other in escalating acts of confrontation, but rather, what is it that holds such a society together. What, in other words, makes a country like West Germany, then still regarded as rather a fragile democracy, 'successful' socially as well as economically, to the extent that it provides its citizens with high living standards along with a high level of complacency? It was clear what the left's answer was: capitalism and the bourgeoisie keeping at their disposal a thinly disguised police state, and a parliament ready to pronounce a state of emergency to justify the suspension of civil rights (as happened with the extended network of surveillance and computerized identity-checks installed in the wake of terrorist attacks and political kidnapping and assassinations), while the silent majority is willing to pay the political price for their peace of mind. This would be the kind of macro-analysis (including the sort of grand historical parallals one finds in the omnibus film GERMANY IN AUTUMN). But THE THIRD GENERATION concentrates more on the micro-analysis of power and its various networks or *dispositifs*, on the side of those in power, and those 'opposing' them. There, it finds that such direct confrontations and neatly arranged battle-grounds no longer exist. Consequently, the frictions and resistances by which such a society communicates with itself are more difficult to pin down, giving prominence to what one could call the micro-structures of betrayal, of double crossing, of overidentification and disaffection by which the 'system' begets its own 'other' and also, finally, talks to its 'other'. Hence the complicated lines of force that link the characters in THE THIRD GENERATION, where Hanna Schygulla is both the director's secretary and a member of the cell, and Volker Spengler has infiltrated the terrorists' network, betrays them, but when in drag, is himself curiously vulnerable and insecure, as if he had stepped out of the world of IN A YEAR OF THIRTEEN MOONS. All of the characters slide effortlessly from their day-time jobs to their night-time activities, proving how reversible their selves and identities are (they constantly rehearse their aliases and alibis), but also how 'integrated' they are in their disparate and seemingly incompatible lives and lifestyles.

The major resource Fassbinder deploys to give these interpenetrating worlds at once 'body' and a dynamic is his use of sound and overlapping dialogue, the snatches of television image or radio sound contributing to a layered but also 'flat' monitor world, seemingly lacking depth, but intensifying and speeding up interaction. It is as if a new way of regulating proximity and distance was establishing itself, with other rules and new forms of interpersonal relations emerging from an electronic topography of sound space, music, noise and filtered images.[71] It gives the film its double reflexivity, but also resolves the tension between the world of the media – omnipresent in all of Fassbinder – and the human sentiments and passions. These appear to thrive on and energize themselves from being so wholly immersed in the media, underlining how spaces are always interfered with and disrupted in Fassbinder, in contrast, say, to Wim Wenders' contemplative spaces.

Thus, while outwardly (the daytime image) German society in THE THIRD GENERATION appears solid, immobile and (made of) concrete, a slight change of perspective reverses the terms, and a curiously liquid world envelops one, more like an aquarium, constant movement behind glass, transparent but enclosed, claustrophobic and untouchable. THE THIRD GENERATION quite pointedly includes in its plot the German 'Fasching' as a moment of the carnivalesque within the (mis)rule of law, but also showing its necessary obverse, the scapegoating, though random and pointless, which follows such transgressions and mostly seems to include among the victims also the innocent. The very artificiality of the situation, its model character, set against the elliptical tightness of the plot, gives the most caricatural kind of identity to the characters, yet the electronic and audio-visual presence in which they are immersed creates its own invisibility and even opaque substance.

The paradox that arises is that if, at the macro-level, Fassbinder's Germany appears as a conservative and rigid society, at the micro-level, another order of being outlines itself, enveloping bodies irrespective of their social roles, political ideologies or personal status. Possibly under the absolute priority of the economic, whether in the form of personal greed, the profit motive or the expansion of markets, the body politic manifests not the stasis of hierarchical institutions, but radiates movement, releasing through its myriad conspiracies and collusion, its commerce in drugs of whatever kind, a sort of frenzied spiral of energy, regulated if at all around the magnetic poles of sexuality, hightechnology, the mass media and the new kinds of struggles for power they entail even in the private sphere.[72] If, as argued at the outset, Fassbinder's 'political' analysis may have been conventional, his 'social' analysis nonetheless had an eye for a certain dynamic one can recognize as contemporary, where corruption, drugs, crime, terrorism name at once social evils and 'safety mechanisms'. THE THIRD GENERATION shows that society – in order to function at all – has to have built into its fabric the kinds of unconventional, 'illegal' circuits that allow for direct and unmediated confrontation of rich and poor, the interweaving of the powerful with the powerless, of the insiders with the underdogs, of the 'lumpen' with the 'arrivistes': hence Fassbinder's fascination with pimps, dealers and double-crossers and agents provocateurs. These shady figures are, in many Fassbinder films, more credible, more likeable than all the upright citizens, the official representatives, political delegates, or other visible bearers of the social mandate which the director never put in his films. At the limit, any form of dependency and interdependence between individuals – even one that might be called 'exploitation' – is preferable to the autonomous self, the self-assured identity and other ideals of personal development within bourgeois existence. Only the former, it seems, have access to the energies which the 'extra-territorial' relations signified in the films by drugs, money and sex make possible.

Although thereforefore neither his persona nor his characters fit the role of representatives, a number of other configurations in Fassbinder's world appear to reply to the artist-author-film director as 'representative figure' at home and good-will ambassador abroad: besides the 'terrorist' as self-appointed representative, presuming to speak for the (vanished) historical, revolutionary subject, or heading a (fascistic, sado-masochistic) cell, clique or group as charismatic leader, and the sacrificial heroes seemingly going to their predictable, inevitable fate like lambs to slaughter, yet in their way also responding to a symbolic mandate,[73] there is a third possibility, often reserved for the films' strong female characters (the 'Mata Haris of the Economic Miracle') and, as we shall see, sometimes occupied by Fassbinder 'himself': that of the go-between and black marketeer, living in and feeding off the system, needed by the system, but also sacrificed to the system.

Representation, Recognition, Credibility
Such might be the allegorical, retrospective reading of these figurations. At the time, the 'reality' of his situation must have seemed to Fassbinder quite different. The years between 1970 and 1977 were his most prolific ones, a miraculous outpouring of work, and yet, he also found himself quite isolated. After making such a massive intervention in Germany's torpid film culture, after stirring up so many debates, his position was if anything more marginal and precarious than it had been in 1969. Seen as a kind of paria, no part of or party in Germany recognized themselves in Fassbinder, and while he was famous, he cannot be said to have 'represented Germany'. Not even the WDR, the institution he had worked with and brought considerable acclaim to, was prepared to back him. In German public life, he also clearly represented no-one: not the establishment nor the bourgeoisie, not the left nor the right, not the racial minorities nor the sexual minorities. With his major international successes after THE MARRIAGE OF MARIA BRAUN in 1978, his status did change, but only insofar as he was now disavowed at home, rather than isolated: itself a kind of fame. Abroad, on the other hand, he increasingly came to be representative, even credible as a German, paradoxically, because he was so 'excessive', and perhaps because the blend of sentiment and brutality, of sensitivity,

undeniable talent and uncouth directness did in fact convey an 'image': one which further-more may have suited the cautious reserve mixed with outright suspicion that the rest of the world instinctively adopted towards 'representatives' from Germany. It was as if, alongside the caricature of the super-efficient, high-tech German of Audi commercials, the only credible German in the international media was either a Willy Brandt, official representative but also anti-Nazi fighter and returned exile, or a Rainer Werner Fassbinder, disreputable *Wunderkind* and overweight, workaholic self- and substance-abuser.

Perhaps this is another reason why a period in Germany came to an end with his death in 1982. The New German Cinema as *auteur* filmmaking was also 'politically motivated', in the sense that this cinema's economic infrastructure and upgraded cultural prestige were largely due to decisions taken by the social-liberal coalition under Willy Brandt, so that by the early 1980s, German filmmakers such as Volker Schlöndorff or Wolfgang Petersen (whose WWII U-Boat drama DAS BOOT became an international hit) were already on their way to Hollywood.[74] In the year of Fassbinder's death, Helmut Kohl became Chancellor, and with him an official figure began to 'represent' Germany whose very appeal, both at home and abroad, was the fact that he seemed so little traumatized by history:[75] comfortable with being German, *gemütlich* in his physical bulk, provincial in his background, and 'popular' in his tastes, he was able to engineer political reconciliations (as in the various high-profile Mitterand-Kohl, Reagan-Kohl, Gorbachev-Kohl meetings) that eventually even made it plausible for him to take so much of the credit for German unification. With Kohl, the entire issue of 'critical' vs 'representative' figures once more took another turn altogether, for as the chancellor of the *Tendenzwende*, he will be remembered as the politician who helped make Germans seem 'normal' again, both to themselves and to others. While throughout the 1970s, Brandt keenly sensed that German history had to be re-written because of Hitler and the guilt the Holocaust and so many other crimes had left on every German, indeed made every German 'representative', by showing himself at the Warsaw Ghetto as a German willing to seek atonement, on behalf of his country, Kohl's re-writing of Germany history was quite different. True, the Nazi period was also 'written in' (Bitburg and Bergen Belsen, Museums of German History in Bonn and Berlin), but it was no longer the reason why this history had to be re-written.[76] During the 1970s, one is tempted to say, Willy Brandt had in Fassbinder an equally 'representative' fellow-German: a counter-figure but also a complementary figure. Fassbinder, too, was a rewriter of German postwar history, now in the image of its cinema-history, which included Ufa and the Nazi period, and through it a hard look at the historical field itself, as a highly ambiguous arena of contending representations. In Fassbinder's work this field of the visible, of seeing and being seen, of image and body, of spectacle and event, in short, of the politics of 'self' and 'identity' may well define differently what it means to be representative, and, with it, may have helped to redefine the cinema and its representations of history. This is the subject of the subsequent chapters.

2. From Vicious Circles to Double Binds
Impossible Demands in the Field of Vision

Addressing the Audience: No Middle Ground

Fassbinder's ambition may have been to make 'Hollywood films in Germany',[1] but this was to be only partly realized in the years between 1968 and 1975. His furious production schedules set a pace neither his fellow directors of the state-funded New German Cinema nor the (by then) moribund commercial film industry could hope to follow. His energy and charisma put him in command of a working method – the mini-studio with the super-stars, the regular team with the familiar cast of character actors – which could have professionalised filmmaking in Germany, had it not been perceived as an outright critique of the cultural bureaucracies (the 'cinema by committee') almost every other filmmaker depended on.[2] Yet despite the director's notoriety and tabloid fame, his films remained part of an author's rather than a popular cinema, at home and abroad. It was FONTANE EFFI BRIEST, an understated adaptation of a well-loved classic of 19th century German literature that brought him recognition in Germany and mitigated the image of the notorious enfant terrible,[3] while in New York, the retrospective organized by Richard Roud in 1977 had critics proclaim Fassbinder 'the greatest talent in Europe, a new director movie buffs dote on'[4], but it also kept him firmly within the art-house circuit. As Andrew Sarris remarked, Fassbinder's fate was to belong to a country where the cinema knew 'no middle ground between the mandarins and the masses.'[5]

A good example is KATZELMACHER (1969), Fassbinder's second film, which became not only his first claim to fame and author status, but also gave him – via different prizes and subsidies – valuable operating capital for years to come.[6] KATZELMACHER was liked, uniting the avantgarde critics (impressed by the disciplined formal experiments) and those who expected from the cinema a social message, for it commended itself by a prescient analysis of the *Gastarbeiter* problem, in addition to satirizing German petit-bourgeois ambitions and Bavarian complacencies.[7] KATZELMACHER's avantgarde status was also based on the impression that Fassbinder was following Bert Brecht's anti-illusionist precepts. Organized into short tableau scenes, the images are curiously frozen and inert, doubly deprived of depth by Fassbinder's head-on shots and static camera set-ups. When the camera does move, as in the lateral reverse tracking shots of the couples walking past a block of flats, a deliberately shallow space plays off the proscenium-stage against the illusionism of cinema. And yet, there is little evidence that a 'model' of social conflict is intended, in the manner of Brecht's learning plays.[8] Nor is KATZELMACHER a filmed play, despite the fact that it derives from Fassbinder's theatre-piece of the same title.[9]

What KATZELMACHER shares with Fassbinder's other films of the period, less experimental but no less self-conscious, from LOVE IS COLDER THAN DEATH, via GODS OF THE PLAGUE and WHITY to THE AMERICAN SOLDIER, is indeed a certain anxiety about the audience.[10] This chapter is trying to situate this anxiety, as it shifts from confronting one type of spectator to accommodating another, always in pursuit of the goal the director set himself: to make films in which the spectator has a stake. KATZELMACHER is fairly extreme in this respect, but indicative of how some of the 1960s generation of subsidized artists – not only in the cinema – responded to their cultural bondage: in Peter Handke's famous title, they set out to insult the public ('Publikumsbeschimpfung'). Fassbinder rarely returned to aggressing the audience in the way he did in KATZELMACHER, except perhaps in WHY DOES HERR R RUN AMOK,[11] and in retrospect, even KATZELMACHER's sullen terseness can be interpreted differently.[12]

If Fassbinder tried to provoke, it was mostly in order to create a space of unconventional sympathy for his all too conventional characters. KATZELMACHER builds up its powerful portrait of latent violence quite relentlessly, each tableau scene designed to show bigotry and prejudice clashing in non-communication. Yet instead of this pent-up violence releasing itself, for instance, in the repeatedly announced castration of Jorgos, the (Pinter-esque) verbal aggression merely fizzles out. The men gradually tolerate the foreigner in their midst, partly because beneath the macho talk they are all cowards, but also because they recognize that he is already 'castrated': as much a victim of the system as they are. They patronize him, not least because Elisabeth, his landlady, overcharges him for the rent, a fact they seem to approve of, more for its symbolic significance than for the financial benefit that one of them indirectly draws from it. Equally ingratiating is the *Gastarbeiter*'s own social Darwinism: only too ready to complain when a Turk is hired by his firm, Jorgos turns out to be as much a racist as his German tormentors. This final irony neither explains nor excuses anything, and yet it closes the film on a suitably sour note.[13]

For a German filmmaker in the 1970s, to be universally understood the way Hollywood films were was a goal that could only be called 'utopian'. The German commercial cinema, in its dying hour, had settled for the kind of universality best connoted by such lowest-common-denominator indices of a national cinema as pornographic *Heimat* films and high-school comedies. The aspiring directors of the New German Cinema had every interest in distancing themselves from such popularity and tried to appeal instead to international art cinema audiences, whose tastes were formed by festival reports and auteur retrospectives. Fassbinder, who also wanted to have a popular audience, knew only too well that a nation's film culture comprised many kinds of films, and that mainstream cinema always owes a large debt to genre cinema, not just of German provenance: even the Hollywood in people's heads was 'made in Germany,' in the sense that American (as well as other foreign) films shown were all dubbed into German, a practice Fassbinder remembered from his film-going years as a schoolboy, and one that left traces in the dialogues and speech-patterns of his own pastiches of gangster films.[14]

The 'spectator' of German cinema during the 1970s was thus a problematic category not only in the sense of diminishing audiences, but also in their 'other-directedness': what in the 1980s would be called the 'colonization' of the European cinema by Hollywood. Given that most so-called independent filmmaking in West Germany by the mid-1970s was state-subsidized or television-financed, audiences at the box office did not determine what German films were being made, and filmmakers had little direct feedback except via a generally unsympathetic press. They needed to experiment with different ways of addressing the spectator, seeing that they could not rely on a star system, a viable genre tradition, or an indigenous commercial cinema infrastructure.[15]

Once again, Fassbinder was the exception, partly by creating a surrogate star system, partly by pushing further than anyone else the issue of genre. What remained constant in his move from the early gangster film to melodrama, from melodrama to working in television, and from television series to international big budget productions was a concern with the audience's knowledge and expectations of cinema. 'In the theatre, I'm interested in an idea, but I'm not interested in audiences. But how one can work with as technical an instrument as a video camera and ignore the audience is beyond my comprehension.'[16] Even the shift between cinema and television was defined by what underpinned the Hollywood way of making films:

> Right from the start I treated people and filmed them as if they were stars... It's not by putting someone before a camera that he or she becomes a star, but only when they have a certain function, when the image captures them in a particular way, when the camera moves around them in a certain fashion. If the camera isn't Hollywood, then the actor who is in the picture, isn't Hollywood either.[17]

But 'Hollywood' also meant the ability to include the audience in the unfolding of events and character interaction. Fassbinder knew that this required a perversely difficult skill, namely to 'become naive':

> I would not be able to tell a film like MARNIE simply the way Hitchcock does it, because I haven't got the courage of his naivety, simply to tell a story like this and then at the end give the audience this thing, this explanation... I wouldn't have the guts, because it also takes guts.[18]

Instead, Fassbinder at first developed a certain irony as a way of soliciting the spectators' complicity. In GODS OF THE PLAGUE or PIONEERS IN INGOLSTADT, for instance, the viewer is invited to identify with the characters, but also to laugh at them, to recognise their emotional situations and conflicts, and yet to be put off balance by their self-convinced play-acting. None of the customary attitudes of identification (whether the distancing of comedy or the involvement of drama or suspense) sits comfortably on the films. This unsettling, dephasing element could be seen as another debt to Brecht, making a queasy feeling between stifled laughter and embarrassed recognition the filmic equivalent of the famous 'alienation-effect'. But the stylized acting against a starkly simplified, or even seedy decor in Fassbinder draws attention to a different kind of gap: the physical and verbal gestures of the protagonists never match their intentions, and an irrecoverable but spell-binding incongruity surrounds their own role-playing.

Such a mismatch of self-image, between 'being for oneself' and 'seeming to others' may well have come down to Fassbinder via the *nouvelle vague*, where Jean-Luc Godard and François Truffaut advertised admiration for Hollywood, while never pretending to copy the classic simplicity of its story-lines or its story telling. At the same time, Hollywood was never quite the monolith which the myth has made it, and there had been several Hollywoods, even in Fassbinder's lifetime. Often enough, the European adulation for the Hollywood of the 1940s and 1950s became itself a coded rejection of the Hollywood of the 1960s. When Fassbinder came to make films in the late 1960s, the American cinema, itself in a deep crisis, was for the cinephile community already a lost paradise, not only because of the culture gap and the time lag, but because the double displacement of language and historical moment was itself what was most poignant about remembering oneself watching these films: nostalgia and regret became integral parts of what made Hollywood a personal and subjective movie experience as well as *the* formative experience of growing up in post-war Europe.

Already the *nouvelle vague*, however, displayed two distinct attitudes: simplifying a little, the Hollywood of Godard contrasts with that of Jean Pierre Melville. For Godard, the American cinema provided a language for 'making strange' the all too familiar present of Gaullist France, as in ALPHAVILLE or WEEKEND, while for Melville, *film noir* and the hired gunman of the 1940s gave credibility to a nostalgic identification with a macho image, dating from the Resistance and celebrating the existential, but also adolescent virtues of the lone wolf, fiercely loyal above all to ego-ideals of honour and valour. In Germany, with a ten-year delay, both stances vis-à-vis Hollywood resurfaced, with Fassbinder's closer to Godard,[19] while the first films of Klaus Lemke, Rudolf Thome and Roland Klick tried to emulate those of Melville.[20] Yet there is in Fassbinder's early films enough of BOB LE FLAMBEUR and LE SAMURAI once more to blur the distinction, and what strikes one about his gangster trilogy (LOVE IS COLDER THAN DEATH, GODS OF THE PLAGUE, THE AMERICAN SOLDIER) is the discovery of a theme which in both Godard and Melville is much more muted: a vulnerable masculinity behind the macho facade, suffering attacks of sexual anxiety beneath the tough-guy mannerisms. Challenged about this at the time of GODS OF THE PLAGUE, Fassbinder is supposed to have mumbled: 'you're right, it's probably a homosexual film'.[21]

The New Naivety

If Fassbinder found in the egocentricity of the hard-boiled hero and the latent misogyny of *film noir* a useful reference point, it was in order to derive from it some tortuous and ironic comment about a world of false self-images expressing real emotions. Especially in KATZEL-MACHER and GODS OF THE PLAGUE, an underclass aspiring to the stuffy self-righteousness of the German petit-bourgeoisie was held up to a somewhat ridiculous pity as well as inviting pitiful ridicule. What few critics noticed was that the rabid provincial male chauvinists from the Munich suburbs playing at Chicago underworld bosses or hired guns conveyed with their strong need for impersonation one enduring element of all popular entertainment: the pleasure in perverse and reverse identification, the mimetic impulse in masquerade, in short, some of the carnivalesque utopias and transgressions preserved at the heart of much movie lore: 'I don't make films about gangsters, but about people who have seen a lot of gangster films.'[22]

Precisely this cultural camouflage distinguishes Fassbinder's gangster films from those of his other Munich colleagues, also in love with the saturated connotations of Americana: the rock'n'roll played on the American Forces Network, the tastes purveyed by Hamburgers and Hershey bars, the smells alive in chewing gum wrappers and vinyl records, the billboard art available in Hollywood movies and Disney comics. For while FORTY-EIGHT HOURS TO ACAPULCO (Klaus Lemke, 1968), RED SUN (Rudolf Thome, 1969) or DEADLOCK (Roland Klick, 1970) tried to recreate these icons in their films as if colouring by numbers, or in the words of Wim Wenders 'pasting into your school exercise book cut-outs from the funny papers',[23] Fassbinder was aware that his own stance towards Hollywood films – mixing nostalgia, longing, irony and pathos – was a chaos of emotions which had to be up there in all its confusion, because this mix was what spectators could identify with. In other words, the very dilemma of wanting to make films whose prototypes belonged to a culture known only through its images (before the age of jumbo-jets and Florida holidays, none of the characters, no more than the directors or their audiences, had been to the USA) creates a powerful emotional current, one which constitutes a basis for spectator-engagement and character-empathy, and thus an experience which the early films of Fassbinder dignify as 'authentic'.

Yet what ultimately intervenes between the gangster genre and its pastiche in Fassbinder is less the urge of coming out of the closet than an unhappy consciousness about class as much as it is about sex, with a love of cinema alongside a love of men.[24] In addition, going to see Hollywood movies in neighbourhood cinemas – a home away from home, according to Fassbinder – was also where a middle-class boy alienated from his own background became accustomed to projecting his frustrated desires for escape, while feeling a bond with the young men from the otherwise closed-off working-class suburbs. Where families went to the pictures in order to see German comedies and social problem films, Fassbinder probably preferred Montgomery Clift and Liz Taylor, Cyd Charisse and Yvonne de Carlo, Sal Mineo and James Dean. As this cinema was outlawed by parental authority and ignored by the critical establishment until well into the late 1960s, enthusiasm for PARTY GIRL, BAND OF ANGELS, SUDDENLY LAST SUMMER or REBEL WITHOUT A CAUSE was a calculated defiance not only of middle-brow taste, but a gesture of revolt against middle-class morality. Functioning as the small change of universality, it was a shared code between the classes, a bridge for any filmmaker wanting to address both a working-class and a lower-middle-class audience.

By the early 1970s, however, such spontaneously bonding spectators could no longer be assumed, either in the cinema or at the street corner. After twenty-odd years of 'social peace' that had lasted from the Adenauer chancellorship of the early 1950s to the break-up of the grand coalition in 1971, the old class differences and social antagonisms (especially between the working class and the petit-bourgeoisie) seemed once more to threaten the fabric of German consensus politics. Fassbinder thus began his filmmaking career at a moment in time when a battle of sorts came to be waged over the hearts and minds of post-war Germany, with regard to its social conscience and political maturity: admittedly, this was a battle fought more on television than in the cinemas, the latter by then already the protected preserve of art house audiences or children's matinees. Yet working for both film and television, Fassbinder had to address with one and the same kind of film different groups of spectators who did not possess shared self-images or self-interests.[25] Hence a second turn of the screw in the appropriation and transformation of Hollywood naivety:

> The American method of making [films] left the audience with emotions and nothing else. I want to give the spectator the emotions along with the possibility of reflecting on and analyzing what he is feeling.[26]

In the early films, reflecting on the feelings of the characters easily took the form of avoiding even the suspicion of emotion. LOVE IS COLDER THAN DEATH, for example, is a study in detachment and understatement. Reviewers complained that 'the film comes out of an almost unimaginable fear that an emotion might occur which the director wouldn't wish to answer for',[27] and that 'Fassbinder has created a film which tries to avoid any representation of emotion, in order to provoke, by a kind of stylized anti-realism, the thought-processes in the spectator's head'.[28]

But in the later films, especially after THE MERCHANT OF FOUR SEASONS, 'reflecting on feelings' became a way of combining topical subjects – left-wing radicalism (MOTHER KÜSTER), unemployment (EIGHT HOURS DO NOT MAKE A DAY), homosexuality (FOX AND HIS FRIENDS), juvenile delinquency (I ONLY WANT YOU TO LOVE ME), mental breakdown (FEAR OF FEAR) – with a sympathetic, emotionally differentiated portrayal of protagonists who would otherwise be categorized as mere social or statistical case histories. The strength of the Hollywood tradition Fassbinder tried to make his own by adopting Douglas Sirk, whether one thinks of it as the 'women's picture' of the 1940s, or the family melodrama of the 1950s, was the way this successful German director (emigrated to Hollywood in 1938 and rediscovered in the 1970s) had specialized in what could be called negative emotional experiences – love unrequited, hopes dashed, agonized waiting, painful embarrassment, tragic misunderstandings, trust betrayed – in petit-bourgeois or middle-class settings. Moments of deception, manipulation, cruelty, but also equally 'aggressive' manifestations of unconditional love, self-sacrifice, exuberant surrender were the emotions that Fassbinder wanted to convey, across the genre framework of melodrama, in order to allow the spectator to notice the frame, while appreciating the 'new naivety' of authentic inauthenticity.[29]

By the mid-1970s, his films had perfected a style that engaged spectators, striking this chord, irrespective of whether the new naivety was perceived as marrying a post-68 disillusionment about working class militancy to a melancholy social conscience, or as a post-Warhol camp sensibility rediscovering the 1950s German family and their love for sentimental songs by such pop idols as Freddy Quinn, Rocco Granata and Catarina Valente. Here was a director who relished artifice, who forced one's attention constantly to shift between what could have been taken from 'life' and what one recognized from other movies, be they Hollywood spectacles, cheap import soft-core porn, avantgarde low budget productions or television soaps.

This new naivety, however, was far from naive: it deployed conventions, stereotypes and genre formulas in order to capture a truth whose validity may have been emotional but could also be read as political.[30] Especially THE MERCHANT OF FOUR SEASONS was often cited as an example of political cinema, accessible to a mass public, while subtle and formally complex in the way it secured this accessibility.[31] The clash of unmediated and irreconcilable points of view meant that a character's false consciousness became the vehicle for showing up a world of insincerity and bogus values, where the deformation of subjectivity – say, a mother's harsh disappointment in her son or a shrewish wife – merely mirrored the deformations of social reality. This reality, however, was never presumed to be objectively given: Fassbinder's melodramas conveyed at one and the same time the 'point of view from within', while juxtaposing it with a 'point of view from without', which was itself someone else's point of view from within.[32] Alternatively, the new naivety could manifest itself in the adoption of a deliberately restricted vantage point, experienced by the audience as unsettling, wherever it felt exasperated by a protagonist's gullibility, and therefore unable to 'follow' someone like Hans Epp (of THE MERCHANT OF FOUR SEASONS) or Fox (in FOX AND HIS FRIENDS) to his chosen destiny (of suicide). Fassbinder fashioned vicious circles for his characters, as they strove after a happiness that eluded them, precisely because it was the manner of their striving that entrapped them or made them seem willing victims.[33] It was up to the audience to 'distance' themselves, and come either to a higher wisdom or discover a new humility, by appreciating the protagonist's basic humanity.

However, Fassbinder's preference for certain kinds of heroes, such as the small-time criminal, the born loser and those existing on the margins, over more socially 'representative' figures was not merely motivated by ideological critique or for the sake of forcing a particular moral stance. The outsider has always been a useful narrational device for fictional realism, whether in Walter Scott's novels or Stendhal: in Fassbinder, he signals the gap – in terms of verbal articulacy and emotional perspective – that not only makes possible the act of narration itself, based as it is on the knowledge gap of information withheld, but also makes plausible the 'liberal' mise-en-scène discussed in the previous chapter, where each character has his reasons, and however briefly, even the villain's point of view seems justified. Restricted narration is the motor of melodrama as a critical genre, be it in the mode of pathos or that of irony.[34] Its potential to comment on itself derives from the viewer's ability to 'position' him/herself differently vis-à-vis the action: ultimately, on a perch of superior insight or knowledge, but before, on a level with the characters.

In a sense, all classical Hollywood cinema functions in this manner: an uneven distribution of knowledge among the characters, as well as between characters and audience, ensures such emotional or rhetorical effects as pathos and empathy, irony and suspense.[35] To the extent that Fassbinder in his melodramas deployed this system of knowledge gaps he did indeed create 'Hollywood films', and the success of THE MERCHANT OF FOUR SEASONS, EFFI BRIEST, FEAR EATS THE SOUL proved that Fassbinder had learnt well from Douglas Sirk: we often already know the truths the characters are still struggling to discover, and we fear for them as we feel for them. Fassbinder also professed great admiration for Sirk's handling of the obligatory 'happy ending': Sirk allowed the audience to read it against the grain, yet Fassbinder's own manner of reaching narrative closure often differed from both Sirk's and Hollywood practice, not only because, like most European directors, he preferred unhappy endings. Whereas in the classical cinema, the characters' self-awareness (in melodrama) or awareness of the facts of the case (in thrillers or suspense movies) eventually matches that of the spectator, in Fassbinder's films it often remains at variance with the spectator's position of knowledge: witness the bafflingly unresolved or downbeat endings in films like MARTHA, FOX AND HIS FRIENDS, FEAR OF FEAR, which Fassbinder associated with a cinema as universal in appeal as Hollywood but not as hypocritical. These endings, though, can leave an audience with a feeling of frustration, suspecting the director of gratuitous cynicism or heartless irony.[36]

To the extent then that Fassbinder operates within the 'regimes' of knowledge sketched above, his films belong to the classical paradigm, even though he showed no interest in the modes of narration associated with suspense or based on narrative enigmas (thriller, horror, action film). If, on the other hand, one interprets his films as modernist, in the sense that the gaps in the characters' motivation are never filled, one is confronted with a different paradox. The spectator of a Fassbinder film becomes active not so much by wanting to infer the inner state of consciousness of a character, or the transformations that time may bring to a human being overwhelmed by the thereness of the world, as might be the case in an Antonioni film, but by the very impossibility of situating him/herself unambiguously or without self-contradiction: a dilemma which has been increasingly interpreted as sign of a more radical form of cinematic subjectivity, but one still associated with Hollywood rather than Europe: more precisely with the representation of female subjectivity in the woman's film and melodrama.[37]

Broadly speaking, Fassbinder's films complicate the nature of the bond that exists between the screen, the characters and the spectator.[38] But while the director himself made the Hollywood cinema his reference point, to whose intense rapport with the audience he wanted to add 'emotional honesty,' critics tended, as indicated, to see in him the 'modernist' auteur.[39] Yet it is this peculiar quality of the screen-spectator relationship (empathetic to the characters and exasperated in turn, as opposed, perhaps, to the New Hollywood's double address of the 'naive' and 'sophisticated' viewer)[40] that makes it difficult to analyze Fassbinder's narration either in terms of the categories of Aristotelian poetics, or by reference to 'distanciation' and 'deconstruction'. His avowed ambition to make popular films may put him at odds with the goals of anti-illusionism, although arguably, the positions of knowledge in a Fassbinder film do indeed mostly turn out to have a false bottom, constructed as they are 'en-abyme', often sending the viewer down a kind of black hole: not so much of anti-realism as the 'in(com)possibility' of several parallel worlds (one thinks of the role played by coincidence or mere chance in films as different as SATAN'S BREW, CHINESE ROULETTE or LILI MARLEEN).[41]

Chance and ambiguity of another kind characterize MOTHER KÜSTER'S TRIP TO HEAVEN, where, according to Fassbinder, it makes little difference if we imagine Mother Küster shot by the police (which is the German ending) or see her finding autumn happiness in the company of a night watchman in love with her home cooking (the American ending). This apparent indifference to the status of the authorial text has, in the case of MOTHER KÜSTER, been ascribed to commercial opportunism, on the part of a director who by all accounts badly wanted an Oscar nomination. But another interpretation is equally plausible. Not only is the American version a good example of a Sirkean ironic happy ending, testing how naive or credulous an audience is prepared to be after watching the heroine's unrelieved victimization for the best part of ninety minutes; Fassbinder's compliance with the Hollywood norm could also be the sign of a paradoxical artistic integrity. Elsewhere, I argued that at least one kind of inner logic which binds together Fassbinder's work was his ability to accept all manner of constraints, which he almost welcomed, redefining them as vicious circles.[42] Whether they were imposed on him from outside by his working conditions, the state subsidy system or, in this instance, by a foreign distributor, or whether they came from within his own self-tormented creativity and obsessive productivity did not seem to matter: he was quite comfortable with the accusation that he might be 'angepaßt' (meaning 'conformist' or even 'corrupted by the system'), because, as he said, in the end it put him in touch with something he could accept as real and which proved his own existence in history: this, too, an instance of the new naivety.[43]

False Consciousness and Double-Binds

Rethinking the issues of freedom and necessity in the wake of '68, Fassbinder's 'vicious circles' implied also a refusal to accept any value as fixed. But apart from a belief in reversals, the metaphysical core, so to speak, of Fassbinder's new naivety, was his challenge to several kinds of old naiveties, including the belief in 'authenticity,' so prominent in other directors of the New German Cinema.[44] In Fassbinder, there is no safe 'position of knowledge' (whether grounded subjectively in 'personal experience' or objectively, in the dialectic of history), but there is also no 'even exchange' between the 'recognition of desire' (the position from which

I speak) and 'desire for recognition' (the position from which I listen) which became the watchwords of those intent on fusing the political revolution with the psychoanalytic cure.

Earlier than most, Fassbinder began reappraising the ideals, but also the failures of 'May 68', and in particular, the relation between psychoanalysis and radical politics already briefly hinted at in the previous chapter. This rethinking is particularly important in view of another of the old naiveties Fassbinder's films set out to demolish: the idea of false consciousness, at least insofar as it implies as its opposite the possibility of true consciousness. Distrustful of any kind of normative a priori, the films refrain from the political slogans of the day, even the obligatory 'consciousness-raising'. More appropriate than Marxian categories for understanding the dialectic of the vicious circles in Fassbinder's narratives, and how the play of distanciation and fascination worms its way into the viewer's mind, are concepts such as projection, identification, transference and counter-transference. Asked about the direction from which he expected social change to come, Fassbinder once replied that he had always been more interested in Freud than Marx:

> Freud sometimes seems more important than Marx.... The changing of productive relations in society and the exploration of interpersonal communication must be achieved in parallel fashion.... I find that psychoanalysis from childhood on should be the right of every citizen.[45]

This last remark is especially telling, for with the claim of an almost 'civic' right to analysis, Fassbinder placed himself within the mainstream of post-war Hollywood, which had helped to make Freudian notions popular, much more so than in post-war Germany, where seeing an analyst was neither as commonplace nor as socially accepted as in the USA. At the same time, the hope of a convergence of Marx and Freud in the critique of capitalism and bourgeois society was for German student activists, much more than it had been for the radical left in the United States, a cornerstone of the counter-culture, epitomised by Herbert Marcuse, whose teachings tried to reinsert notions of the political economy into the libidinal economy, lest psychoanalysis became a mere hygiene ritual for maladjusted bourgeois egos, and by the critical theory of the Frankfurt School, in the writings of Max Horkheimer, T.W. Adorno, Walter Benjamin, including somewhat apart from this tradition, the essays on popular culture and politics by Ernst Bloch in the early 1930s.

As a vanguard member of the 1960s generation, Fassbinder no doubt shared the outlines of this Freudo-Marxian project. Yet in his films one finds a politically sharper critique than that suggested by either the Frankfurt School's analysis of the 'authoritarian personality' or by Marcuse's belief in the revolutionary potential of alienated students and the social underclass, something altogether less socially marginal and, instead, more ordinarily perverse. Not to yield to the temptation of offering a political solution to the vicissitudes of emotional life was for Fassbinder a double strategy of audience address, manoeuvring between gratifying the demand for a progressive cinema, while appealing to such reactionary emotions as self-pity, nostalgia and romantic yearning: stances not only more prevalent among the student left than it itself admitted at the time,[46] but also typical of the German popular cinema of the 1950s and 1960s, as it manifested itself in *Heimat* films, *Schlager* films, courtroom dramas or *Ärzte* films, all mercilessly deconstructed for their reactionary ideology by critics during the 1960s and early 1970s[47] and all enjoying – then as now – the loyalty of (television) audiences across the generations. It is this 'perversity' which Fassbinder was in tune with, both as the play of identity and identifications which the films oblige the spectator to engage with, and as the index of a particular, historically determined situation a German filmmaker in the 1970s had to work with.[48]

Fassbinder gives a clue to his own thinking on the question of political and libidinal economies when he mentions his interest in Ronald D Laing, the unorthodox British schizo-analyst preoccupied with tracking the origins of psychic disturbance to the nuclear family as 'schizo-genic' institution. Asked in 1977 what he meant when he said that he had read Freud 'cover to cover', the interviewer suggested that his conception of what 'madness' means reminded him of Laing and Lacan: 'I take it you're familiar with them.' – 'Yes, sure. And I saw a film about the experiments Laing does in London.'[49] The fact that Fassbinder watched Laing's filmed docu-drama *Asylum* before making FEAR OF FEAR, his own film about 'schizophrenia and the family', suggests an acquaintance if not sympathy for non-or-thodox psychiatry, and he may even have followed the discussions about madness and the family initiated by Deleuze-Guattari's *Anti-Oedipus*.[50]

Laing's group therapy experiments and his analysis of schizo-genic patterns in close emotional relationships actually cast some light on the typical plot situation of Fassbinder's films, where Ali loves Emmi, but Emmi loves her children, who detest Ali and thus split Emmi's affection, while Ali, rejected by Emmi, returns to Barbara who does not love him but knows how to take care of him. Fassbinder himself has described it in the films of Sirk:

> [In WRITTEN ON THE WIND] Dorothy Malone is the only one who loves the right guy, Rock Hudson, and she stands by her love, which is of course ridiculous. It must be ridiculous, because among people who consider their substitute acts as the real thing, it becomes clear that whatever she does, she does it because she cannot have the real thing. Lauren Bacall is a substitute for Robert Stack, because it must be clear to him that he'll never be able to love her, and vice versa. And because Lauren decides in favour of Robert, Rock falls in love with her even more, because now *he* cannot have her.[51]

The more appropriate term for these vicious circles of substitution and frustrated desire may well be that of the double-bind, as elaborated in Laing's *Knots* and also underpinning Gregory Bateson's grand interactive and communication systems theory, *Steps to an Ecology of Mind*. With *Knots* Laing's 'Jack and Jill' couple tie themselves into double-binds, whose gloomy logic underscores the no-win situation of love relations or family bonds ('I cannot love somebody whom I despise; and since I love you, I cannot believe that you love me, a person whom I despise').[52] Equally apt, but funnier examples are the so-called 'Jewish Mother' jokes[53] or Groucho Marx's immortal 'I wouldn't want to belong to a club that admits me as a member'. Put more generally, a double-bind situation, or 'pathological communication' arises in an interaction between people when the same message functions on two levels, one of which contradicts the other, while the partners in the communication either refuse or are unable to distinguish between these levels, between text and context, communication and meta-communication.[54] Anthony Wilden, among others, has analyzed in detail the 'error' in logical typing which double-binds entail, in the course of a critique of binary, either/or thinking.[55]

The relevance of Groucho Marx for explaining the place of Karl Marx in Fassbinder's films may not at first sight be that obvious. Given that his characters are, on the whole, the exact opposite of verbally duplicitous or dexterous, there would not seem to be much room for laughter. Nevertheless, numerous instances of knotted logic or 'true false consciousness' come to mind from Fassbinder's films, and often it seems as if his characters escape the vicious circles of politically false consciousness only to find themselves in the more interesting, but perhaps also more damaging logic of the double-bind. One striking case is, again, THE MERCHANT OF FOUR SEASONS, where Hans Epp's life is blighted by his mother's rejection when on his return from the Foreign Legion, she scolds him for having come back:

> Mother: The fact that you joined the Foreign Legion is your business. But that you had to drag such a nice, pleasant young man like Manfred Wagner into it as well... The trouble I had with his parents! Making me responsible, me...! Is he also back?
> Hans: Manni is dead.
> Mother: Just as I thought. The best always fall by the wayside, and someone like you comes back.
> Hans: But, Mother, I've changed.
> Mother: What's crooked in the morning doesn't grow straight in the afternoon.[56]

This is no mere lack of recognition by a significant Other, because what Hans' mother tells him is that he would have to be dead before she could love him. It starts a chain of events which culminates in his fatally taking sides against himself and drinking himself to death, but the pattern is established well before, for instance, when Hans explains how he lost his job with the police, after giving in to the advances of a prostitute: 'They had to sack me from the force for what I did. If I couldn't see that, I wouldn't have been a good policeman. And I was a good policeman.'[57]

Similarly, films like MARTHA or BOLWIESER are predicated on the fact that the protagonists' capacity for selfless or self-denying love lands them in deadlocks: when Helmut,

Martha's fiance, hesitates to call the doctor after her mother's second suicide attempt – put on, like the first, in order to punish Martha for marrying – Martha stifles her desire to help. Siding against her mother, she is ready to become an accessory to manslaughter, in order to prove her total devotion to her husband-to-be. But no sooner has Helmut taken in that she has guessed his train of thought, than he telephones for help and turns on her, making a great show of how scandalized he is that she should be capable of such wickedness. Bolwieser, too, finds himself in a corner. Scolded by his wife Hanni for being too bookish and not a 'real man', he forces himself to go out drinking with the village bullies, only to find Hanni revolted when he returns home late, reeking of beer.

Such double-binds, where identity is coextensive with its own denial, flaw most attempts that Fassbinder's heroes – male or female – make in order to integrate themselves into the family, or even their place of work.[58] In the early films the double-binds that lay the grounds for self-alienation can also be class problems. The different episodes of Fassbinder's television series EIGHT HOURS DO NOT MAKE A DAY, for instance, often dovetail around no-win situations at the factory where most of the characters work, in order to show how the logic of capitalism is not only contradictory in the Marxist sense of pitting the forces of production against the relations of production, but divisive and pathogenic, as in the episode where one of the workers is ostracised by his mates and suffers a psychosomatic illness after inventing an improvement which saves the firm from paying the workers the productivity bonus they had been promised.[59] Although Fassbinder, in accordance with the laws of the genre of the family soap, engineered for most complications a happy ending or, as he put it, 'a utopian solution', the series was cancelled prematurely, because, among other things, Fassbinder wanted to show that one of the women committed suicide, despite the fact of having found in her second husband an understanding and devoted partner.[60]

What most often disguises the underlying structure of the double-bind is that the characters' behaviour displays a more obvious pattern: that of an almost provocative masochism. This is again true of MARTHA and BOLWIESER, as in other films with Margit Carstensen (THE BITTER TEARS OF PETRA VON KANT) and Kurt Raab (such as SATAN'S BREW, where the hero's creative talent as a writer only returns to him after he has been whipped by a gang of male prostitutes). So flamboyant is the sadism of Karlheinz Böhm as Helmut in response to Martha's self-humiliations, and so exquisite the torment Kurt Raab as Bolwieser inflicts on himself when he realizes what an ideal foil he is for his male friends' sexual innuendos and misogynist taunts, that one's spectatorial pleasure at the all too perfect 'fit' is probably as strong as one's disquiet over the extent of the cruelty inflicted. The appalled laughter one half-suppresses when watching such scenes suggests that instead of faulty communication, there is after all a circuit that does function, that emotional energy is not blocked but passes and is received, between the characters, as well as between screen and audience. In this respect, MARTHA and BOLWIESER are also Fassbinder's most accomplished comedies, even though the suffering and misery they depict are real enough, and the sense of high-flown feeling grounded and short-circuited lingers on after the laughter has died. It suggests that something inherent in the cinematic situation itself helps to enact a sado-masochistic fit, is impervious to false consciousness, and cuts across the double-binds, while being nonetheless energized by their impossible logic, at least in the films of Fassbinder.[61]

Mirror, Mirror on the Wall...

Instead of making Hollywood films for German audiences, Fassbinder had in fact appropriated the classical system to the point of rethinking not only what it meant to address audiences in what remained of the public space that was cinema, but what it meant to organize the field of vision that is the cinematic apparatus. It suggests that his approach to the three-way interaction between spectator, character and screen space came to differ from that of both classical and modernist cinema, and that via the spaces his films construct, the texture of his sound spaces and sound effects, but above all, via the looks that circulate within these spaces and across them, Fassbinder invited his spectators not only to 'enter' his world, but also managed to pull the ground from under them.

A Hollywood film discreetly or spectacularly puts the viewer at the centre of events. It subordinates camera movement and the characters' looks to our presumed need to know why something has happened and what is about to happen: narration acts as guide, always at our service, rarely asking to be applauded for the unobtrusive skills deployed. Yet almost the first point to make, even on casual acquaintance, about a Fassbinder film is the sense one has of an especially strong investment in vision itself, for its own sake, so to speak. Examples already mentioned are the frontal shots of people sitting behind tables in LOVE IS COLDER THAN DEATH and KATZELMACHER, looking past the camera, though we never know what they are looking at. In other films, a seemingly unmotivated camera movement reveals a space, not while but *before* a character enters it, or it reveals someone else in a space, who seems to be watching us, watching. The typical Fassbinder scene opens without an establishing shot, gives what one imagines is a point of view, maybe because it is angled in a particular way, or taken from behind a beam, as in THE BITTER TEARS OF PETRA VON KANT, from where we see Marlene enter. But there is no reverse shot, and it is in fact Marlene who will be the silent, all-seeing witness throughout. Here, as in so many other instances, one immediately recognizes a Fassbinder film from the obsessive framing of the image, whether by means of doorways (FEAR EATS THE SOUL) or partitions (DESPAIR), or because the shot includes objects that are themselves framed, like pictures on the wall (EFFI BRIEST), a hallway mirror (MOTHER KÜSTER), or huge murals and mounted photos (as in PETRA VON KANT, GODS OF THE PLAGUE and KATZELMACHER).

As a modernist form of deconstruction, this draws attention to the artifice of representation, or critically comments on the claustrophobic, stifling and cluttered world in which these characters are at home.[62] One remembers Sirk's frequent mirror shots in the opulent mansion of WRITTEN ON THE WIND and the final tableau with a picture-window in Rock Hudson's cabin in ALL THAT HEAVEN ALLOWS. But Fassbinder also cites the cinema itself, whether by 'fetishizing' its apparatus and thus barring us from the pleasure of unmediated transparency to which the director himself is nonetheless attached,[63] or by drawing attention to an extra presence, whether originating from the camera, the audience as voyeurs, or some other perceiving instance. While the classical Hollywood cinema disguises such a presence by either motivating it internally or by leaving this extra look unacknowledged (the characters never look at the camera, they do not 'return' our looking at them), Fassbinder often makes us – more or less uncomfortably – aware of our invisible presence, and by extension, of the fact that the 'frame' is not a window on the world outside. Where exteriors are seen, they are often more terrifyingly claustrophobic than indoors, as in the scenes that Margit Carstensen observes from her kitchen window in FEAR OF FEAR, or the cityscape while Brigitte Mira wanders the streets in MOTHER KÜSTER. The outside is the inside also in the opening of BERLIN ALEXANDERPLATZ, where Franz Biberkopf, just released from Tegel prison, is so overwhelmed by the unbounded, unframed world invading him that, overcome by anxiety, he collapses into a nervous heap.[64]

Fassbinder's use of mirror-shots or internal framing is a typical feature of much 'self-reflexive' cinema, in the tradition of European auteurs, from Bergman to Visconti, or Godard to Almodovar.[65] It is also common in the work of Europe's preferred American auteurs, such as Nicholas Ray, Orson Welles, Joseph Losey, as well as emigre directors like Sirk and Fritz Lang. And yet, to explain the frequent mirror shots in Fassbinder's films, neither modernist self-reflexivity nor pastiche finally accounts for the foregrounding of vision and the excess of framing one finds in, say FEAR EATS THE SOUL, EFFI BRIEST, MOTHER KÜSTER or DESPAIR. When, in FEAR EATS THE SOUL, Ali visits Barbara, the owner of the bar, at her home, he is framed in front of the bed by two sets of doors, rather like Elvira in IN A YEAR OF THIRTEEN MOONS, when she pays a visit to Anton Saitz in his office, and where she is seen wandering along a sheer endless corridor of successive door-frames. In both cases, the look which seems to motivate the framing – Barbara's in the first case, that of Saitz's bodyguard in the second – is manifestly insufficient to claim the surplus of seeing thus inscribed in the image.[66] The scenes' excessive symmetry, with their insistence on repetition, doubling and infinite regress, yields a very peculiar kind of geometry, reinforced as it often is by the origins of these frames being themselves represented, in the form of photographs, newspapers, television screens. Two structures – the viewer/film relation and the relation of the characters to the fiction itself – mirror each other infinitely and indefinitely, one putting the other in crisis and pointing to an underlying paranoia, which obliges one to read these perfectly shaped and doubly framed moments as portents of some sort of danger that the characters finds themselves in, or perhaps even the viewer.[67]

By aligning the look of the camera consistently with either the optical or the narrational point of view of the characters in the fiction, the classical cinema provides a certain mastery over this paranoia induced by the apparatus: one feels 'on top of the action' and has a stake in the characters' fate, both of which confirm the spectator as 'subject'. Through shot changes, editing and camera perspectives, and the optically or acoustically organized space, the audience is furthermore given access to the imaginary plenitude of the fictional world.

Where a film or cinematic style blocks or threatens this access, subjectivity manifests itself in negative forms of anxiety, unpleasure, tension. With Fassbinder, such imaginary mastery is often frustrated or, at any rate, reworked in ways that are perplexing, not least by making the spectator aware of how complicit and imaginary this mastery finally is. As Fassbinder put it, describing Chabrol's cinema but implicitly referring also to his own: the director keeps characters and audience like 'insects in a glass case'.[68] If, for instance, neither suspense nor enigma drive the events, then this supplement of 'vision framed' adds an element of fascination, keeping the viewer held under a spell, since there is always someone's look inscribed in what one sees, though one often does not know whose look it is, making it both a threat and a source of uncanny power, holding viewer and protagonist in place.

By foregrounding the look so much, however, Fassbinder also seems to spoil the feast, locking us out, or worse still, catching us out. A good example occurs in FEAR EATS THE SOUL. Emmi and Ali have spent their first night together, they have had breakfast and are about to leave the house. We see them, from across the street, as it were, formally shaking hands, and then each parting in the opposite direction. Before turning the corner, they look back, love in their eyes, managing a brief affectionate wave. But as they disappear, a reverse shot indicates that we were not the only ones witnessing the scene: an upstairs neighbour of Emmi's had been hanging her head out of the window, staring after them.

The scene is in several ways typical of Fassbinder's style of story-telling. As frequently happens in his films, the act of looking is not motivated by a narrative enigma. Voyeurism is both prominently implied and at the same time rendered explicit. Although here it ironically 'places' the neighbour as a mischief-making busybody, such undisguised staring is rarely critiqued: it belongs to his melodramas as much as do the long frontal takes to the early gangster films. In both cases, the awareness of watching marks the entry-point of the spectator into the film, and the manner in which characters interact with each other. One is tempted to say that in Fassbinder's films all human relations, bodily contact, even social hierarchies, and most forms of communication and action manifest themselves (and ultimately regulate themselves) along the axis of seeing and being seen.

Yet to look and be looked at are not neutral activities based on equivalence or reversibility. It implies above all a power-relationship, and one, as feminist theory has persistently pointed out, that is not only gendered but slanted in favour of those who possess the cultural, sexual power of the look: these are invariably men.[69] This axiom has been most consistently demonstrated in classical American cinema;[70] and while it can be applied to Fassbinder, too, what strikes one about his films is that visual relations dominate also at the expense of physical contact or bodily violence, in contrast to the American cinema. Contact that is physical in Fassbinder (especially in the early films) seems less decisive than eye contact, which covers the entire spectrum from extreme hostility and aggression (as in an early bar scene in FEAR EATS THE SOUL) to tenderness and caress, as in GODS OF THE PLAGUE or a number of scenes between Emmi and Ali in FEAR EATS THE SOUL.

In the scene described, as it happens, the bearer of the look, while hostile and aggressive, is not male. One encounters the paradox that the active look can also be a female one: in Fassbinder, women are allowed to look at men (or women) as sexual objects (famously, Emmi and her crones at Ali; Hanni at Franz in JAILBAIT, Petra at Karin in PETRA VON KANT). Of course, it could be argued that this is not surprising in the films of a homosexual director, but Fassbinder has always been quite clear about the sexual orientation of his characters.[71] The question therefore remains: who or what is represented in this look emanating from the neighbour at the upstairs window? Somehow, as a look, it seems second-hand, as if it wanted to be powerful, punitive, censorious, but in the end was really a sham, a kind of imposture. The woman immediately runs to another neighbour, tells her in feigned outrage about Emmi's carryings-on, seeks reassurance from the gossip, and quite clearly, is animated by even murkier motives, mixing envy with spite. The look here is like a mask the neighbour puts in front of her own desire, and Fassbinder's film ridicules this imposture.

The fact remains, however, that this look managed to catch us out. It 'pulled the rug' from underneath our own comfortable and collusive voyeurism, it succeeded in disorienting us, not least by mobilizing in us a good deal of sadism and hostility towards this neighbour, in order to cover our own shame and thus regain our balance. For otherwise, the discovery of having been the watcher watched might ominously leave us without a place from which to look. And yet, Ali and Emmi's farewell handshake at the front door, the crossing of paths, the march in opposite directions, the simultaneous turn of the heads at the corner: is it not like a little ballet, an elaborate domestic pas-de-deux, performed to be seen, already a representation, put on – who knows – for each other, for us, for the neighbour upstairs?

Impossible Viewing Positions

At times, the camera's look cannot be attached to either a person or a narrator: it has a kind of free-floating presence, as the space it traverses becomes itself the space it creates, in an Escher-like involution. This, too, can have unsettling consequences for the spectator, because it produces what could be called 'impossible' viewing positions. One such example is to be found in THE MERCHANT OF FOUR SEASONS where, throughout the film, the action is mostly seen from Hans' point of view, even in the few scenes where he is not present, as in the cheerless and hysterical love-making between Hans' wife and the man she casually lets herself be picked up by one night. By the end of the film, at Hans' funeral, a floating, detached but still somehow subjective point of view suggests a view of the mourners from the vantage point of the deceased. We see metaphorically from beyond the grave, as if his mournful perspective had survived him, or as if he had, already in his lifetime, been somebody who had returned from the dead, which of course is precisely the point Fassbinder is making when the film opens with Hans' mother 'cutting him dead' at his homecoming from the Foreign Legion.

Fassbinder's narratives are at once embodied in and suspended by these relays of looks and poses, gestures and gazes, knitting the characters together in a dynamic that has all the affective density and emotional claustrophobia of lived human relations while preserving the immateriality of a dream or a ghost-story. Metaphorizing once more, one could say that if the vicious circles entrap a character in his fate, they can also ensnare the spectators in an infernal machine into which they are both ambushed and seduced. A number of films have a kind of mirror-maze at their centre, such as the hotel lobby in BEWARE OF A HOLY WHORE. Most graphically and explicitly, it is present in WORLD ON A WIRE (1973), a science fiction epic of parallel worlds, where the windowless room which houses the central computer consists of nothing but walls of mirrors. The illusion of depth and deceptive recesses is made even more confusing by the false eye-contacts between the characters, notably Klaus Löwitsch and Kurt Raab, who in one scene balefully sits in front of a terminal, but in truth closely observes Löwitsch, his boss, walking by behind his back. In CHINESE ROULETTE (1976), glass partitions and trophy showcases divide up the dining room, around which the camera prowls incessantly, mapping out a space at once misleadingly transparent and menacingly blocked at every turn. If in CHINESE ROULETTE the disorientation is in space, indicative of a world of power-play, deception and self-deception, in WORLD ON A WIRE the mirror-maze disorients us in time, as characters 'fall through' or 're-enter' worlds that look the same and are nonetheless a mere 'simulated model' of another, itself a possibly simulated world: reminiscent of the Taoist fable of the butterfly dreaming that he's an man, dreaming that he's a butterfly. Effi Briest, too, gets caught in the mirrors and partitions that surround her in her parents' house, as the world of her husband and daughter recede ever further from her grasp. In DESPAIR, it is again Klaus Löwitsch, loitering near a fairground mirror-maze, who has the misfortune of being 'recognized' by Dirk Bogarde as his double, and in IN A YEAR OF THIRTEEN MOONS, Red Zora takes a dishevelled Erwin/Elvira into the ladies' restroom, where his/her shattered self-image – she had just been dragged in front of a mirror by her lover and told to take a good look at herself, is faithfully reflected in a wall of obliquely placed mirror-panels. In each case, the conventional associations of the mirror as a reflection of the self, of a fragile or fragmented identity are in evidence, but merely serve to hint at their inadequacy as explanations.

Such scenes seem to invoke the famous 'mirror-stage' of Jacques Lacan, explaining the origins of human subjectivity as forever self-alienated, and displaced both in terms of inter-personal relations (it is an 'other' who confers my identity for myself), and deferred in terms of temporality (my mirror-image anticipates the yet to be attained perceptual coherence and sensory-motor control that turns my body into the self that can function as a representation).[72] A mirror in a film is thus a particularly explicit reminder of the situation which obtains in all cinematic representation, as far as film viewing is deemed to simulate and re-stage a much more fundamental experience of subjectivity and bodily identity. In some of the examples from Fassbinder's films, this situation of the screen as mirror (and the mirror in the film as metonymy of this screen) seems indeed appropriate, as characters attempt to situate themselves in their interpersonal relationships, seeking to use the other as the direct or metaphorical mirror which will reflect back onto them an image of themselves. In an interview, Fassbinder made explicit the social symbolic which translates itself into such mutual self-mirroring:

> 'In MARTHA [...] one has the impression that the characters never see each other, but only their own mirror-image, making them strange to themselves. Is this an over-interpretation?' – 'Not at all. In the film we are dealing with two characters, neither of whom really has an identity, because they are such extreme creatures of norms and education.'[73]

Even more frequent, and not signalled by the presence of a mirror, are shots of a character placing himself in front of the camera (he 'returns the look'), except that, as already indicated, the camera is not 'looking', in the sense of not responding to – by motivating, narrativizing or returning – this look. Not the screen, but the invisible fourth wall acts as a mirror, in which the characters seem to be looking at themselves. In KATZELMACHER, for example, the characters are perched on a railing, looking straight ahead, intensely scrutinizing themselves, even though evidently no mirror is either present or can be inferred. Perhaps, then, in Fassbinder's films, what matters is not the act of looking, after all. The look is mainly necessary in order to support someone's desire or need to be looked at, suggesting that much of this cinema is not about voyeurism as it is about exhibitionism.

A Cinema of Exhibitionists?

In the majority of cases where the spectator becomes aware of a prowling, mobile camera, or a frame within a frame, the characters seem to be aware of it, too, as if expecting this look – and being ready for it. Again, this impression might be put down to a certain self-conscious acting style – a hint of inexperience covered up by Brechtian 'role-playing' – if it did not highlight a feature of the characters themselves, and therefore of their narrative dilemmas. Where the presence of the camera draws attention to itself, it is usually because the action revolves around 'being seen.' Some of the most striking instances occur in the early gangster cycle. In GODS OF THE PLAGUE, there is a scene when Carla, the porn-shop owner, is surprised by Günther, returning from the botched bank-robbery to kill the one who betrayed them. As it happens, all three women had been informers, but only Carla is found out. In the midst of applying make-up in front of a mirror, she is shot by him, wailing: 'I needed the money. Because I have to be beautiful for the others'. In other words, she sends her friends to their deaths, in order to be seen by them. A similar logic informs the protagonists' interaction in THE AMERICAN SOLDIER and other films from this period: their desire is not roused by the bank-robbery, the contract-killing or the hold-up, and not even by the acquisition of money or women (though all of these appear as overt goals). A more ambiguously coded desire animates them, not always as explicitly verbalized or enacted as Carla's constantly checking herself in the mirror in GODS OF THE PLAGUE, yet inescapable nonetheless: the desire to play a chosen part 'correctly'. Both men and women have a conception of themselves, determining their behaviour and gestures, of how they wish to appear in the eyes of others: as gangsters, pimps, tough guys, prostitutes, *femmes fatales*. They play these roles with such intense seriousness, maybe because it is the only way they know of imposing an identity on otherwise aimless, impermanent lives. As Günther, the black Bavarian and amateur gangster, puts it (in English!) before he crumples photogenically on the floor: 'life is very precious, even right now'.[74] What authenticates these roles, therefore, is the cinema itself, because it provides a reality more real than the real, sanctioned not only as a world – 'Hollywood' – which everyone wants to inhabit, but as a world that has already been seen by millions. The camera is what the characters look at and look to: to confirm them, to make them real. This, too, is a way of 'making Hollywood films in Germany'. Yet the vanishing point they envision only partially coincides with our position. We are made spectators in a spectacle put on for us, but also exceeding us. The screen becomes the mirror, in the wider sense that both the characters and spectators carry the cinema's 'silver screen' in their heads as well as in front of their eyes.

A given world, it would appear, becomes a reality only because it implies spectators. The characters in KATZELMACHER, for instance, are passive not because they are marginals, and spectators of life. Their waiting is less a waiting for something to happen (as it is with the suburban layabouts in Fellini's I VITELLONI, or Pasolini's ACCATONE) but instead, a waiting for someone who can play the spectator, and thus confirm them, by displaying the sort of behaviour that would conform to the reactions – of shock, outrage, provocation – they expect to elicit. The audience is inscribed as voyeurs, but only because the characters are obliged to be such fervent exhibitionists. Polarised in terms of seeing and being seen, this suspended sense of self subscribes to an idealism as radical as that of Plato's cave, so often invoked to 'explain' the metapsychology of the cinema's apparatus: to be, in Fassbinder's world, is to be perceived, *esse est percipi*.[75]

The gangster and social misfits feel the need to be looked at in order to exist; in the melodramas, by contrast, the aim is to attract the eye that disapproves. Whereas the first resembles a sadistic structure (the spectators are aggressed, until they become exhibitionists-in-waiting, like Jorgos in KATZELMACHER), the second structure is more like a masochistic response: the couple goes out of its way to court rejection and revels in the objectification that disapproval brings. The scene in FEAR EATS THE SOUL analyzed above might confirm this paradoxical pattern, while (in THE BITTER TEARS OF PETRA VON KANT) Marlene, in front of whom Petra and Karin produce themselves, 'materializes' as the necessary complement to the two women's sado-masochistic spectacle. Since what matters is the ability of being looked at, it is not surprising that characters such as Marlene, from whose position the action is shown, do not have a particularly active role to play. They are more like bystanders, or even curiously passive props, whose passivity becomes uncanny, at times malevolent, precisely because they seem to possess the power of the look, without the motivation. If it is most spectacularly the case in THE BITTER TEARS OF PETRA VON KANT, one can also observe it in MARTHA: the lovers are observed by a couple at the fairground; or the camera focuses prominently on the point of view of Olga, the serving maid at the wedding; and later still, it is Inge, Martha's colleague at the library who has a look but no role. In each case, the characters thus privileged by being made the bearer of the camera's point of view are given prominence quite out of proportion to their function as narrative agents. Rather, they are the more or less impersonal support for an 'anonymous' instance of looking. Sometimes, such a look does not even need a human support: rooms are often lit in a way that emphasizes an object by a light source, even though the object picked out does not seem to contribute information to the story. It, too, marks a kind of source of vision, but marks this spot as empty, or at any rate as not yet filled, perhaps much like Van Gogh's famous wicker chair or peasant shoes, inscribing a temporality of either past or future, a mode of expectancy and anticipation, whose sole function it is to signal the principle of inversion (of cause and effect, of source and target), just as the anonymous look inverts the traditional hierarchies of spectatorship and observation: 'I am not interested in showing observation so much as the nature of being observed'.[76]

What could it be that this exhibitionism-which-is-not-one wants to call into existence?[77] Again, the melodramas give a clue. I claimed that they solicit an eye that 'disapproves,' but in fact, it would seem that the gangster films – with their heroes courting provocation by the spectacle they make of themselves, flaunting non-conformism and putting their rebellion on display – are more likely to revel in (bourgeois) reproof. However, their exhibitionism is easily pleased once they are 'recognized' as the gangsters, pimps or mafiosi they style themselves after. As rebels, they need to be seen breaking the rules; or rather, the fact of their behaviour being seen as breaking the rules makes them rebels – first and foremost to themselves, which is to say that their rebellion functions perfectly as the ultimate spectacle of conformism. In the melodramas, on the other hand, the emphasis on being seen is doubled by another structure, which calls attention to a space or place of difference and 'otherness'. Thus, in FEAR EATS THE SOUL, it is true that the neighbour's look of disapproval is already discounted by Ali and Emmi, because it confirms what they already know: that they are 'different', and not ashamed of it. Their sense of identity is supported by a 'negative' look, underlining that in this respect, the young would-be mafiosi, the *Gastarbeiter*, the charwoman with the Polish name, and the Moroccan auto-worker share that they are all outsiders and 'misfits'.

FEAR EATS THE SOUL, THE MERCHANT OF FOUR SEASONS and FOX AND HIS FRIENDS appear to offer a social critique of the pressures to conform and the narrow scope that prejudice tolerates in the way of cultural or racial otherness. But this might be too simple a view, especially if 'conformism' is not judged solely as a negative attribute, the posture of an inward-looking, repressive society, but also as the communal element in any act of 'being seen' in order to 'belong' – the two sides of 'recognition by an other'. The central dilemma of FEAR EATS THE SOUL is a case in point. Ali and Emmi suffer from ostracism because of a liaison that is considered a breach of decorum. But the way it presents itself to the couple is as a contradiction: they cannot be 'seen together', because there is no social space (work, leisure, family) in which they are not objects of aggressive, hostile, disapproving gazes (neighbours, shop-keepers, bartenders, Emmi's sons and daughters-in-law). Yet conversely, they discover that they cannot exist without being seen by others, for when they are alone, their own mutually sustaining gaze proves to be insufficient to confer on them or confirm in them a sense of identity – that delicate balance between their social, their sexual and their ethnic selves, in the interplay between sameness and difference, self and other. Love at home or even a holiday abroad is incapable of providing the pleasure that being looked at by others gives. There is thus, apart from the pressure to conform, also the pleasure to conform in the field of vision, and the tragedy is that the couple are incapable of securely attracting the social eye either in its approving or its disapproving mode.

Only the final scene appears to resolve the contradiction. At the hospital where Ali is recovering from a perforated ulcer, a doctor keeps a benevolent eye on the happily reunited couple. It is a look which no-one but the spectator can see, in a mirror placed on a plane parallel to the camera. The need which is also an impossibility – of being perceived by others and nonetheless remaining a subject (i.e. recognized in one's particular 'difference') – produces both the sickness (Ali's burst ulcer, after he had first slapped himself furiously in the face in front of the washroom mirror) and the cure (presented as a regression to a mother/son, nurse/invalid relationship under the eyes of an institutionally benevolent, sanitised father-figure). Because the mirror inscribes the audience as another – this time 'knowing' – gaze, we as spectators are doubly privileged, but also deprived of the 'happy ending'. Only too aware of the other Alis lying next to Emmis, with the same complaint, we remember the doctor's words: 'he will survive – but he'll be back.'[78] Just as there seems no solution for the *Gastarbeiter*'s choice of evil between Germany, ulcer and work, or Morocco, couscous and poverty, so – in the register of the look – there is no way in which the gaze solicited by Emmi and Ali can both be benevolent and acknowledge difference.

In FOX AND HIS FRIENDS and THE MERCHANT OF FOUR SEASONS the dilemma is similar. Both Fox and Hans seek to attract the eye that will firmly anchor them in the social world to which they wish to belong, having for different reasons fallen out of it, become misfits or outsiders. Initially, Fox ('Fox der tönende Kopf': a pun on the German title of the Twentieth Century Fox Weekly Newsreel) is already, as a public performer, one kind of 'object on view', yet he leaves his fairground job in desperate search of the benevolent eye of his social betters. Hans, as the barrow fruit-vendor, is caught between the surveillance gaze of his suspicious wife and the housewives' gazes he solicits by his mournful courtyard bark: in neither of them does he see himself 'recognized'. Fox ends by making himself the object of the look, even if this means physical death (he dies in the most public place imaginable, the intersection of a Munich subway station). Hans, too, eventually succeeds in having all his friends' attention, even if it means drinking himself to death in front of their eyes. And as we saw earlier, at his funeral, with the family that ignored him standing by his grave and the love of his life tossing a rose on his coffin, he can finally gratify that precious infantile fantasy of watching their tears and their contrition, bitterly regretting their disapproval and neglect. This, too, however, is a fantasy. There is no recognition, no *anagnorisis*: the mourners seem neither sorry nor mourning, but relieved. Nevertheless, however miserable from our point of view the manner of his dying may seem, it secures for the protagonist that second, symbolic death: dying in full view. As Kaja Silverman points out: 'although the subject has no identity without an alienating image, that image may be put in place either by the subject or by the other.'[79] Here it is put in place, literally, by the subject's 'dying to be seen'.

The Look That Shapes a Demand

It might seem that the vicious circles into which the characters enter describe an obvious and well-known 'subject position': that of the victim. Not only do we see Fassbinder's heroes and heroines defeated, rendered homeless, penniless, brutalized, but we also see those who torment, ridicule and exploit them triumph, or at the very least, go unpunished. This is self-evidently true of Hans, Fox, Mother Küster, but it also applies to the eponymous hero of BOLWIESER, whose suffering and disgrace are egregiously in excess of his crime – if being sexually obsessed with one's wife counts as a crime. It also applies to Martha, whose desire to break out of a stifling marriage ends with her becoming a wheelchair-bound invalid, forever at the mercy of her sadistic husband. Given that Fassbinder has always claimed that he only has one theme, namely the exploitation of feeling, and especially the exploitability of love, the conclusion that these are victim's stories would seem unavoidable.[80] And yet, this is, I believe, a misreading not only of Fassbinder's 'politics' but also of the aesthetics of the look I have been describing.

Fassbinder's characters do not see themselves as victims: they never complain, they never hold others responsible for their fate, they never experience self-pity. If we see them as victims, or if we think the director does, it is because of the superior knowledge the narration grants us, without acknowledging it as dramatic irony, which is to say, without providing the frame that would allow us to maintain the 'proper' distance. Fassbinder never tired of stating his disagreement with those who demanded positive 'representations' for minorities and other so-called victims. Not only because this would assume that a 'victim', even if capable of speaking from a position of 'full' subjectivity and self-possession, could represent what it means to be a victim *to another*, and not be caught in an 'impossible' speaking position. It would also put in place precisely those 'frames', those categories of bounded identity (self/other, male/female, belonging/foreign), that Fassbinder's cinema sets out to contest. In either case, to perceive someone as victim is to render a very double-edged service to 'otherness', especially in the field of vision. Making someone a victim 'is the way to maintain the proper distance towards [him... :] our compassion, precisely in so far as it is "sincere", presupposes that in it, we perceive ourselves in the form that we find likeable: the victim is presented so that we like to see ourselves in the position from which we stare at her.'[81] The victim's place is thus also a state of visibility and implies a mode of looking, one which Fassbinder undermines by enveloping the viewer with another gaze that takes away the false security of gazing at the other as victim. As we look at the Fassbinder hero in his abjection and destitution, he actually 'looks' at us, not by meeting our eyes, but behind our backs, so to speak.

Esse est percipi in Fassbinder's films. Yes, but the inverse also applies: if in order to exist one has to be perceived, it is also true that in order to be perceived, one has to be an 'image', a recognizable representation: this, for instance, is the way the classical Hollywood cinema 'sutures' the field of the visible and the field of the look. However, as argued above, the look in Fassbinder is also a kind of imposture, because there is already another look in which the stare, the hostile or desiring look of the characters is enfolded, 'held'. The name for this other look would be 'the look of the camera', which is always already there, having seen then what we see now, and having been seen by the characters before they look at/past us. This abstract, mechanical eye of the cinematic apparatus, with which the spectator is said to identify prior to identifying with either a character or any other (narrational, diegetic) 'point of view',[82] however, is in Fassbinder acknowledged (and not 'repressed' as in classical cinema) by the characters' moves to put themselves 'in front of' this other look, in order to 'claim' from it a certain power. What seems an exhibitionist stance is first and foremost a process of image-making, and there is thus indeed less difference than one might think between Emmi and Ali 'making a picture of themselves' and the neighbour watching them: both parties could be said to be impersonators, or more precisely, image-personators.

Yet in this process of image-into-person, there is, as we have seen, a kind of surplus to their compliance.[83] This extra element is both a surrender to the look, in the intensity of the protagonists' self-abandon, and a challenge, in the 'purity' of their abjection before it. It becomes the source of their strength, albeit negative. What we are likely to interpret, especially in the melodramas, as the characters' gradual loss of self, their self-alienation, at the end of which stand failure, death and suicide, appears as such only when we respond to their look as that of a victim. But from the position of the other look, which is not actually a look because it merely names the gap between the representation and its excess, the same self-alienation can become a form of self-exteriority, a turning outward, as a way of responding to a question we do not hear, answering a call we are not (yet) aware of.

At this point one can return once more to the double-bind: not as the contradiction between the message and that which 'frames' the message, but as such an interpellation, where there are no more 'frames' and instead an impossible 'demand' serves as a kind of question to which the character responds, with utmost literalness and sincerity, and in the process opens up a gap, situating his being in this split between the enunciated and the act of enunciation.[84] For instance, in GODS OF THE PLAGUE, when Joanna, having betrayed Franz to the police inspector, starts crying at Franz's open grave, saying: 'Ich hab' ihn so geliebt' ('And I loved him so much'), she is not voicing remorse at her act of betrayal, nor need it be a sign of her duplicity. Rather, she is affirming both the necessity of her action *and* the sincerity of her feeling. Fully assuming her speaking position, she becomes subject, which is to say, split between the truth of her 'utterance' and the truth of her 'statement'[85], she lives the division that is the Fassbinder protagonist's condition of freedom inside the contradiction, the double-bind. Likewise, Hans in MERCHANT OF FOUR SEASONS takes his mother's injunction, that she preferred him to have died, 'literally'. This is his strength in the final scene (underlined by the flashback to the Foreign Legion): that he knows the 'truth' of her statement better than she does. His 'exhibition' of himself in front of the others as he drinks himself to death becomes the necessary condition for his speaking position, from which he can 'answer' the interpellation, embodied in the double-bind, which we might not even have realized that the film 'took seriously'.

In most cases, however, it is 'love' which Fassbinder's characters seek, and although they seek it out, by 'choosing' the 'other', it is also their peculiar way of positioning themselves in order to respond to a look of which the other is and is not the bearer.[86] Love is that which allows s/he who loves to exteriorize him/herself, and by turning outward (often mistaken for 'objectification'), they open themselves to a demand, one that is by necessity, unfulfillable, impossible. And because love has the structure of a response to a demand that it can never fill, it generates not only stories (as we shall see, Fassbinder's series of 'impossible love stories'), but it can make these stories partake of history, understood as a society's particular, historically determined ways of 'calling' upon its citizens as 'subjects'.

GERMANY IN AUTUMN and Everyday Fascism

This last observation brings into focus the political context in which Fassbinder worked in the late 1970s, when in the wake of escalating acts of terrorism, hostage taking and political kidnappings, the West German government perfected a law-and-order state, suppressing the final vestiges of the politicised student movement and preparing the *Tendenzwende* (a move to the right which resulted in a conservative government in 1982). Events came to a head during the hot summer and autumn of 1977, and a number of filmmakers, coordinated by Alexander Kluge, responded by collaborating on the omnibus production GERMANY IN AUTUMN. The film is centred on a double funeral, that of the industrialist Hans Martin Schleyer, murdered by members of the Red Army Fraction terrorist group, and that of Gudrun Ensslin, who along with Andreas Baader and Ulrike Meinhoff (of the Baader-Meinhoff group) committed suicide inside the maximum security prison Stammheim upon hearing the news that the hijack of a Lufthansa plane in Mogadishu had failed to extract concessions from the German government. Around these very different acts of mourning, both taking place in Stuttgart, a number of self-contained mini-narratives are gathered, broadly illustrating the climate of fear, paranoia, and near civil war which characterized those months of extreme tension, testing West Germany's pluralist democracy to the breaking point. But as Fassbinder's contribution makes clear, neither the story structure provided by a double funeral symmetrically inverted, nor the double father-son axis between the son of Field-Marshall Rommel (then mayor of Stuttgart) and the son of Schleyer, could quite contain the political energies which radiated outwards from the events of Mogadishu and Stammheim.

Set in his own Munich apartment, Fassbinder stages confrontations between himself and his mother, himself and his homosexual lover Armin Meier, himself and his former wife Ingrid Caven via phone-calls to Paris, himself and his alter ego Franz Biberkopf as he dictates shot-breakdowns for his upcoming project BERLIN ALEXANDERPLATZ into a tape-recorder. All these encounters are designed to cast doubts on the fictional-narrative closure on which a founding myth of West German democracy was built, namely that (masculine) ideals of self-discipline, responsibility and citizenship had done away with the authoritarian personality. The core of his episode is the casual but in fact tightly scripted interview in the kitchen with his mother (familiar as Lilo Pempeit from virtually all his films), where he insistently questions her about her politics, until she confesses that the government she feels happiest with would be a dictatorship, adding 'but a gentle, benevolent one'. While his mother, in the face of ever more ubiquitous bureaucratic surveillance systems, would be happy to have Hitler back, and most of the intellectuals portrayed in other episodes of the film cave in to helpless paranoia, Fassbinder opts for another gesture: his exhibitionism (in front of the spectator) not only turns into a quasi-terrorist assault on his interlocutors, it also turns the machinery of surveillance – here represented by all the mounted policemen wielding camcorders filming the mourners at the Ensslin funeral – into an occasion for self-display.[87]

Having established via his mother an analogy between the Federal Republic and its own Fascist past, Fassbinder enacts not so much the general paranoia following the breakdown of authority, but paranoia's narcissistic/exhibitionist obverse. Naked, in frontal view, close to the camera, he (but who is this 'he' that bears the physical features of Rainer Werner Fassbinder?) shows himself mentally falling to pieces under the pressure of police sirens, house searches, and the virtual news blackout in the media. While the obese, heavy yet vulnerable and babyish presence of a body fills the frame, the ambivalence of self-loathing and self-love are projected aggressively on the mother and the lover in turn. The connection between paranoia and narcissistic object choice is made by a montage effect: Fassbinder cuts from his mother advocating the virtues of conformity and submission to himself violently embracing his lover, as they both roll on the floor. Fassbinder and his mother do not exactly 'react' to the events. Rather, they re-situate themselves, they 'answer' the call which emanates – half threat, half invitation – from the frontal viewpoint which is the episode's master-shot. In GERMANY IN AUTUMN, then, one finds two structurally related responses to political crisis, the breakdown of democracy's social symbolic: while one 'solution' is what one might call Fassbinder's mother's 'ordinary authoritarianism' or 'everyday fascism', Fassbinder feels interpellated differently, making (phone-) calls and responding to calls (when the doorbell rings), he tries, in a gesture half-aggressive and half-affectionate, to merge with his lover, assuring himself of himself through his double. Two similar 'solutions' to similarly experienced crises, and located in Germany's past, form the subject of the next chapter.

We can now see why in so many of Fassbinder's films 'exhibitionism' has a double face: one where it calls upon the scene another gaze, in order to conform, in order to be endorsed – and one where we as spectators are not bearers of a look at all, nor voyeurs, but are made to be the witness of what appears to be an act of self-humbling and self-destitution, destined for the self in another 'embodiment'.[88] The field of vision, therefore, in Fassbinder extends to include this 'hold', this demand into which the other look is embedded and embodied. Unlike the 'frame' of recognition which makes a perception an image, a culturally or ideologically replete representation, or the frame of distance and superior knowledge which makes the other a 'victim', this field is not bounded in the terms of the perspectival and the framed at all, even though it includes them.

3.   Murder, Merger, Suicide
The Politics of DESPAIR

'The only emotion I respect is despair' 'DESPAIR *is the most hopeful movie I've made'*[1]

Negative Identity

In Fassbinder, the cinema appears as a magnificent, but also always magnificently failing, efficiently deficient, identity machine. As his characters try to place themselves or arrange others in configurations that promise a heightened experience of self, it is never by means of a self-centred, inward-looking, boundary-drawing insistence on identity, but across as contradictory a field of identifications as Fassbinder's narratives can devise and his camera can capture, providing characters with insinuating others and antagonistic doubles, each with a bewildering array of mirroring possibilities.

Explicitly and implicitly, identity is also the subject of DESPAIR, the film from 1977 that represented Fassbinder's first bid for international recognition, which necessitated a change of genre (the European art film), different financing (including a German tax-shelter company and a French consortium), an international cast, and English language dialogue. These fairly drastic changes outline some of the external conditions of existence of Fassbinder's cinema in the late 1970s, the outer envelope, so to speak, of an authorial identity, at once dispersed across an apparently heterogeneous output of two dozen films, as many theatre productions and several tv series, and concentrated in the cultural capital that being a 'major' European auteur commands.[2] When Fassbinder undertook the filming of Vladimir Nabokov's novel on which DESPAIR is based, the director seemed ready for stardom: New York had discovered him in 1975, glowing profiles had appeared in Paris in 1976, and no film festival seemed complete without the latest Fassbinder. His original mini-studio system had become less incestuous by the addition of trained professionals, including, apart from Michael Ballhaus, Peter Märthesheimer as producer and Rolf Zehetbauer, Bavaria Studio's top art director.[3] With DESPAIR, the sawdust and tinsel glamour of his earlier work became the real glamour of multi-million budgets and solid production values (the film cost six million DM, compared to Fassbinder's previous average of 4-500,000); the script was written by Tom Stoppard, then a celebrity second only to Harold Pinter in the literary script stakes; with Dirk Bogarde he had under contract a star associated with Joseph Losey, Luchino Visconti, Alain Resnais and Liliana Cavani's *The Night Porter*. Together with Andrea Ferréol, Bogarde ensured international distribution for the film, which was shot partly on the sets built for Ingmar Bergman's *The Serpent's Egg* in Munich.

If Fassbinder's films had been about entrapment and imprisonment, vicious circles and double-binds, his change of genres from the gangster film via family melodrama to the European art film reflected, to be sure, his appreciation of the different contexts of reception open to his films, but also a new understanding of the cinema as just such an identity machine, an 'apparatus' poised between thematizing the power of images in the realm of interpersonal relations, and itself embodying a form of symbolic power, affecting ideas of identity and the versions of history by which individuals locate themselves in space and time. In Fassbinder's melodramas, from THE MERCHANT OF FOUR SEASONS (1971) MOTHER KÜSTER'S TRIP TO HEAVEN (1975) and FOX AND HIS FRIENDS (1975) to MARTHA (1973), EFFI BRIEST (1974) and BOLWIESER (1976), the protagonists' motivation centred on how to escape from the family and its substitutes including heterosexual, lesbian, and homosexual double-binds. The films consumed themselves imagining ever new ways of breaking the hold of the exploitative mechanism of the family under capitalism (MERCHANT, FOX) or bourgeois codes of honour (EFFI BRIEST) or mores (MARTHA), and they found their form, their unified perspective by asserting and maybe even celebrating the failure and futility of such an escape. By talking about the family, they also talked about Germany, albeit more by implication and shared assumptions.

With regard to identity in the realm of the intersubjective, the melodramas, even more than the gangster films, problematised identity as a crisis of perception, the self constantly undoing and renewing itself in the struggle between the way the characters perceive themselves and the way that others perceive them. As we saw, the films dramatised the impossibility of an identity either within or without the family as the beginning of a new subjectivity – male subjectivity, but quite often also a specifically female subjectivity – often defined as resistance or refusal to inscribe the self securely into the space of the fictional universe of looks exchanged and looks retained. Anxiety, desire traversed the narratives as an interruption, leaving the traces of excess, in some sense irrecuperable, but none the less finally held and articulated within the conventions of classical narrative, as the pathos of waste, loss and misunderstanding.

The other benefit Fassbinder's melodramas drew from Sirkean classicism was the way questions of identity and subjectivity could be tied to class, money and social status, besides being oedipal dramas of patriarchy. From a political perspective (the 'politics of representation'), melodrama appeared progressive for bringing together and pointing out connections between three different spaces usually isolated from each other: the social space of the middle class, the physical space of the home and the small-town community, and the emotional space of the family. In other words, melodrama implicitly challenges the split and separation between public and private, so fundamental to bourgeois ideology, and thus towards the end of an era it rejoined a problematic dating back to the eighteenth century and the rise of bourgeois tragedy. Nonetheless, radical though it may have been to pinpoint the repressive effects of class, patriarchy and economics on the family in the West German context of the 1970s, recourse to this model of political melodrama also made Fassbinder enemies among the German left when he seemed to be implying in films like FOX AND HIS FRIENDS or MOTHER KÜSTER'S TRIP TO HEAVEN that left-wing convictions and capitalist politics were not that different when it came to measuring the misery inflicted by emotional as compared with economic exploitation. Yet this dissenting view, namely that sexual politics were more likely to be the key to the class struggle, rather than the other way round, proved in the end more politically astute and prescient.

To his admirers as well as his detractors, the move implied by DESPAIR seemed an opportunist one, trading 'relevant' German issues for 'Euro'-decadence, and recognizable working-class characters for aristocrats drawn from literature. From another vantage point, though, the genre Fassbinder turned to with DESPAIR was one where the problem of identity has a long history. The post-war European art cinema, in such classic examples as Alain Resnais' LAST YEAR IN MARIENBAD or PROVIDENCE,[4] Federico Fellini's 8 1/2, Visconti's DEATH IN VENICE, Bergman's PERSONA or Michelangelo Antonioni's L'AVVENTURA or RED DESERT, had always been preoccupied with the (grand-)bourgeois ego divided against itself, the split personality, or the sense of a person suddenly falling out of the symbolic order altogether. DESPAIR aligns itself with this tradition: its setting and social context are unmistakably upper middle class, its hero is a refined, aristocratic dandy, who suffers from a 'dissociated personality' disorder. Identity, for Hermann Hermann, proves to be a negative entity, an unsustainable state, and his journey is one that involves him in gradually shedding all its bourgeois vestiges and trappings of civilized life, exchanging them for identifications, as fragile as they are fraught with danger, towards a self even more stripped and bereft than is usual in the works of the directors Fassbinder was compared with.

The other aspect of the European art film DESPAIR took over was stylistic: its general distrust of depth of field shots.[5] Partly because it suited his own stylistic preferences, and partly because it drew attention to vision and perception, Fassbinder opted for a mise-en-scène notable for the number of rack-focus shots and zooms. This choice returns to the early films' predilection for a flattened picture plane by shooting at right angles to a wall or arranging the figures frontally to face the camera. DESPAIR appears to adapt for the screen one of the literary concerns of Nabokov's novel, namely the modernist interrogation of the status of fictional heroes, the disjuncture between authors, narrators and characters familiar from Proust, Joyce or Faulkner. Yet in a film concerned with dissociation, with false recognition and misperception, such an emphasis on different picture planes and their collapse literalized one of Fassbinder's own themes: the impossible inscription of the protagonist in the fiction considered as the space of perspectival representation. Instead of having a character who acts upon events, the very notion of agency is at stake, as the hero slides off, but is also blocked by surfaces.[6] The lack of depth creates a visual field that defines itself – with one notable exception – not 'within' the picture, but between audience space and screen space, so that the action exists 'in front', 'inside' as well as 'behind' the characters.

A Tale for the 'Viennese Delegation'?

Based on Nabokov's emigre novel, written in Berlin in 1932,[7] which Tom Stoppard's script treats both faithfully and very liberally, the story concerns Hermann Hermann, a chocolate manufacturer of Russian origin, living in Berlin with his empty-headed flirtatious wife Lydia and her cousin Ardalion, a pseudo-bohemian painter with whom she has an affair, while he scrounges off Hermann's rapidly depleting income, as his family business is sliding into bankruptcy. After an unsuccessful attempt at negotiating a business merger, Hermann happens to meet at a fairground mirror-maze a vagrant in whom he detects a perfect resemblance to himself. Over the subsequent weeks he hatches a plan which involves bribing Felix, the vagrant, into putting on his clothes and acting as his double. Felix finally accepts, is then shot by Hermann, who had instructed his wife, after telling her about a mysterious, criminal brother, to collect Hermann's life insurance premium and join him in Switzerland. The scheme fails, mainly because the police have no reason to believe the dead man to be Hermann Hermann. A clue left at the scene gives away the identity of the victim, and it is merely a matter of time until Hermann, now living under Felix's name, is tracked down by the police in his Alpine retreat. The film ends with him making a speech on his arrest, in which he claims to be an actor playing a criminal.

Such might be the plot synopsis. But in the network of symbolic actions that make up the narrative of DESPAIR, the situation is more complex, and two features in particular differ from the novel. The first concerns the fact that Felix, the double, bears little physical resemblance to Hermann,[8] and the second is reflected in the historical setting, which is now fairly precisely located in the Berlin of 1929-1930, with the gradual, perceptible-imperceptible rise of Nazism very much in evidence.[9] For a Fassbinder film, the narration makes quite unusual demands on an audience, with imagined scenes and flash-forwards abruptly interspersed in the narrative flow, the inserts confusingly presented without marking their difference in status.[10] The film had a troubled production history (having been extensively re-edited the night before it was shipped to Cannes), and it generally received a mixed reception when it opened commercially in 1978.[11] If a first viewing, therefore, gives the sense of a lavish but erratic literary adaptation, from which no clear narrative voice or, rather, too many different authorial and stylistic voices emerge,[12] a closer analysis suggests that there is in fact a logic, but dislocated, in order to bring out a structure which, though present in Nabokov's novel, is tighter and organised with a different problem in mind.

Nabokov, reputedly, was no adherent of 'Freudian' models of human motivation, and he may well have intended Hermann Hermann's journey into madness to be a riposte to a psychoanalytic case study (Nabokov's Chocolate Bunny to Freud's Wolf-Man, as it were), spoofing or baiting what at one point in the novel he calls the 'members of the Viennese delegation'. Fassbinder – and Stoppard – on the other hand, give Hermann's chief anxiety ample space to deploy itself, so that his condition can easily be diagnosed as impotence. In the first instance, sexual: his inability to satisfy his wife, or deal with the impudent flaunting of phallic potency on the part of his wife's cousin. At another level, however, sexual impotence is itself a metaphor for other kinds of impotence, notably economic and political, in the light of which Hermann's worry about his sexuality becomes both symptom and repression of the symptom. The film recounts his struggle to cope with this double burden, in a series of confrontations at his office, with his wife, talking to Ardalion, and anxiety attacks that overcome him at a business meeting with his rival, and during a coffee break at an outdoor cafe.

To call 'impotence' the common element that unites these obliquely presented, causally disconnected episodes is to state perhaps too categorically the dilemma that the narrative is designed to explore. For the question the film raises is the following: what exactly is the problem that makes the 'discovery' of his double and the plan to switch identities appear to Hermann Hermann as a way out and a solution? In an obvious sense, he is another Fassbinder hero who feels trapped and who plots escape: and once again, the escape seems to trap him further and more decisively. As in Sophocles' *Oedipus Rex*, or in the famous 'Appointment in Samara', destiny manifests itself in the movement to evade it. What, however, singles Hermann out is his evident reluctance to be drawn into the game that assigns to him the role of the jealous husband, or to act his part in the triangle made up of himself, Lydia, his wife, and Ardalion, her lover. So reluctant is he in fact that he represses all knowledge of her incestuous adultery, and instead imagines himself a masterful and irresistible mate. In one of the scenes where he surprises the two together in Ardalion's studio loft, he is frantically searching for nothing more appropriately inappropriate than one of Ardalion's 'excruciatingly bad' paintings, representing a briar pipe and two apples, but which turns out to show an ashtray and two roses.

Hermann's 'repression' of the signs of his wife's brazen infidelity is not without consequences: he experiences a split, a dissociation, and at night is given to watching himself make love to his wife, as he sits and at the same time sees himself sitting at the other end of the hallway. This 'seeing himself double' is the initial form his condition takes, and follows what, after the credit sequence, is the first scene in the film, in which his wife, naked, moves towards him, her left arm raised, provocatively spraying her shaven armpit with perfume. Her entry can be seen as a metonymic representation of the threat that runs throughout the film: the display of 'nothing there' in the context of sexual desire. Lydia's gaze invites his, but he responds by stepping demonstratively behind a voluminous armchair. To put it like this, however, is to make a correlation between shot and countershot which the film actually interrupts by a marked spatial dislocation. There is no eye-contact, not even negative, between the two characters: both glance directly into the camera, but each shot is held too long to produce a sense of contact, nor is there a cutback to Lydia. It is the spectator who has to make a choice of either bridging the gap that the mise-en-scène opens up or – and this is typical of the film's visual field generally – of constructing the spatial coherence in a different sense, by treating for instance the camera itself as another character.

Elsewhere, Lydia's appetite recalls to Hermann that of his mother 'stuffing chocolates into her silly face'. Again, a 'Freudian' reading offers itself: anxiety produces the image of the voracious, phallic mother as a defence against the incestuous feelings towards her, his own oedipal pathology mirrored in and transferred to Lydia via the incestuous Ardalion: a desire so strongly disavowed as to make Hermann impotent. Shaven armpit or briar pipe, Fassbinder gives the viewer several visual clues towards reconstructing the dynamics of this disavowal: Hermann's search for the briar pipe tries to negate the threat represented by the shaven armpit, hoping to substitute for the lack a fetish object that can represent it metaphorically. This is the structure in which Felix figures as the double: in one sense a substitute for the painted briar pipe never found (an allusion to Magritte's 'ceci n'est pas une pipe'?), and in another sense the schizo- alternative to the paranoid double vision of watching himself watching. At the same time, Felix is an ego-ideal, and everything Hermann is not: young, virile, physically strong, and free of family or social obligations. He also voices a misogyny that Hermann dare not admit to: that women are fickle, deceitful, adulterous. By changing places with Felix, Hermann can put himself in the position of a successful husband without having to fulfil the role in action. Animated by an overpowering desire to liquidate his social persona, and slip out from under a host of impossible demands, Hermann wants to exchange a faltering identity for a fixed one, controlled and circumscribed by the negation of his former self from which it springs. The murder of Felix is a symbolic suicide, but also an execution, in which Hermann can punish himself in the act of shooting Felix, assuming the role of dominance and submission simultaneously. Shooting himself by proxy, he eliminates his own inadequate self, to be reborn, on the 'other side' – here represented by 'neutral' Switzerland – into a life of rugged independence rather than castrated misery. The kind of revenge Hermann has in mind is prefigured in the story he tells Lydia about the allegedly criminal brother: he poisoned his mistress, which makes her the symmetrical equivalent to the chocolate-eating mother/Lydia. Probably regarded by both Tom Stoppard and Dirk Bogarde (as well as Andrea Ferréol) as a grand'guignol fantasy of middle-class mid-life crisis,[13] it does indeed wear its textbook Freudianisms a little too blatantly not to deserve a bit of tongue-in-cheek humour and self-irony which Fassbinder was either unable or unwilling to supply, to the evident bemusement of the critics and deep disappointment of the participants.[14] But this is to put oneself perhaps too firmly on the side of Nabokov and Stoppard, fixated as even a parody would be on the Freudian reading. Fassbinder may have had other ideas – bringing to the fore his radical critique of 'positive' notions of identity, as well as his political agenda, tracing moments of crisis in Germany's national identity. These concerns can perhaps best be studied by looking at a number of particular scenes, starting with the exchange of identity between Hermann Hermann and Felix.

Seeing Double

How crucial the shooting of Felix is can be judged by the fact that is shown twice, to bring out the simultaneity and the contradiction of the two positions, in which the homosexual sub-text becomes a kind of intermediary structure between two impossibilities. The process of transforming Felix into Hermann is shown as the progress of love, expressed in physical gestures, acts of silent exchange. The close-ups of hands, feet, ears, neck, scalp, toes, as Hermann trims, shaves, pedicures and washes Felix before dressing him in his clothes, underscore a heavily eroticised ritual, a love-making which the fatal shot in the back consummates. The murder comes as a point of relief, and Hermann's divided self fuses momentarily in the image of love and death mutually experienced.

As Hermann fires the shot, Fassbinder frames Felix in medium close-up looking into the camera, and almost inaudibly he whispers 'Thank you' as he sinks down. The ringing of the shot is overlaid with the ringing of the doorbell in Lydia's apartment; in rapid succession we see the police investigation, the funeral, Lydia being paid the insurance premium. Finally Lydia, dressed in white, is seen coming towards the camera with open arms, calling Hermann's name, as he stands, also in white, with his back to her on a bridge by Lake Geneva. When he turns round it is Felix, not Hermann, but Lydia seems not to mind, and the two embrace passionately. We realise that the scene has been a flash-forward, a wish-fulfilling fantasy scenario, in which the plot is doubly successful: the police fall for it, and Lydia has accepted the substitution. Felix does indeed replace Hermann at her side, and she authenti-cates the switch by taking him as her lover: female desire has been focused again, and thereby contained. The duplicity of the scene lies not only in the fact that it is 'imagined'; it is a subjective, point of view scene, but one in which the marks of this subjectivity are like the linguists' grammatical shifters ('I', 'you', 'here' 'now') running through and across the characters. Beginning with Hermann's point of view (split between his image in the back-ground and Felix's 'thank you' in the aural foreground), the scene changes to Lydia's point of view via a complex field, made up by a series of glances exchanged between the detective, Ardalion's portrait of Hermann, and the insurance broker, a series of male glances in which Lydia figures as the product, the result, the mediator that brings the spectator to Felix's face looking at the camera and signifying the erasure of Hermann. Thematically, we are given Hermann's vision of his after-life, except that in terms of narrative expectations, Felix appears where Hermann should be. The scene is thus a series of transfers and substitutions, in which Hermann's subjectivity is cut completely loose from any notion of coherent character, investing the whole of the fictional space and assuming an exalted omnipresence.

That it is an impossible escape from his predicament is confirmed by cutting back to the scene of the shooting in the woods. The camera set-up is now different, we no longer have a close-up of Felix's face, there is no beatific expression or any whispered words. The sequence of events stops with the detective glancing at the portrait and disclosing that the man found dead is merely wearing Hermann's clothes and holding his passport: no further resemblance. Does this mean that in order to break out of his bind, Hermann would have to be Felix and Hermann, interchangeably and simultaneously? In one sense, Felix is the 'solution' to the dual constraint of public and private self. To Hermann, unsuccessful businessman and impotent husband, Felix represents the Faustian pact – an idea also found in Nabokov, who clearly let himself be inspired by German Expressionist cinema, replete with doubles, somnambulists, and frustrated bourgeois willing to sell their shadow, or even their immortal soul. Bourgeois individuality, represented by Hermann, would thus emerge as an irresolvable contradiction, and the 'double' stands merely for the figure symbolizing this contradictory inscription of such subjectivity in the social order.

In an obvious sense, of course, Hermann Hermann does not want to inscribe himself in the social order at all: he wants out. But why go to the trouble of devising such an unlikely plot and want to leave behind a double? It seems that Fassbinder, here even more than in his contribution to GERMANY IN AUTUMN, exposes a historically situated subjectivity to the dilemmas and options confronting it in a period of momentous change, the years between the Great Crash and Hitler's coming to power, which for modern Germany condense themselves to something like an 'originary' trauma. What the Freudian plot puts before us is that Hermann's disintegrating personality lays open processes of identity-formation – which, in time travel fashion (or like the psychoanalytic cure), we can inspect in both directions, Hermann un-done and re-done. The crucial fact here is that Hermann has 'chosen' his double, as much as that the chosen double does not look like him.

As often in Fassbinder, the moment of choice is linked to a moment of love, with love in turn both shattering and giving succour to identity, once the lover ventures into the terrain of identification, leaving behind his social roles: here, the bourgeois symbolizations of self. In this respect, Hermann has little else to lose, and by befriending Felix, though apparently the very opposite of a love relationship, based as it is on deception, bribery and broken promises, he nonetheless goes through a number of stages, not all that different from courtship and seduction. As a homosexual romance, it could be fuelled by mimetic desire, with Hermann wanting to discover likeness, except that it should be he who remakes himself in the image of Felix. On the other hand, it is not evident that homosexuality requires desire for the same. Fassbinder himself had always insisted that he did not fall in love with people like himself, even if he made them play aspects of himself in his films.[15] Given the eroticised blend of violence and tenderness surrounding the scene in the woods and the death of Felix, one might think of it as a fantasy of 'incorporation', but ultimately it seems to stand for an act of identification in the more technical sense of regressing to a state where Hermann is no longer aware of separateness and difference from the other.

However, to understand in what sense Hermann's choice has a political side, one has to regard his move as that of a narcissistic object-choice. Just as in GERMANY IN AUTUMN Fassbinder's skill in pointing out the gaps in his mother's position makes her 'cover' the political contradiction (a democracy resorting to violence in order to protect itself from its citizens) by choosing a Führer ('but a kind and benevolent one'), so Hermann Hermann 'covers' his untenable position as husband and head of a failing chocolate business by choosing a double (but one that does not look like him): at issue in these acts of shielding or masking is how violently they draw attention to the process itself, or rather to the gap which the act of covering cannot bridge.

Yet this is what makes the narcissistic element involved so important. For although the narcissist may be in love with his own image, it is not necessarily evident what this image is: is s/he locked into his/her own image as ideal ego, or has s/he invested in others as ego-ideals? In one case, subjectivity will find itself in conflict with the social order and its representations, in the other it will align itself with that order, provided society succeeds in circulating such ego-ideals. Hermann Hermann, it would seem, belongs to the former, which gives his narcissism a politically subversive potential, while 'Fassbinder's mother' represents the latter.

The Break-up of the Bourgeois Subject

The allusions to Nazism in DESPAIR have been criticised, mainly by Nabokov scholars, as a gratuitous vulgarisation and travesty of the original's restraint, given that all these scenes had to be added to the script. But this is to ignore how deeply politics are embedded in the film, and with it, a crucial aspect of Fassbinder's view of modern German history. Nazism appears as both the reverse side and the complementary aspect of Hermann's private hell: to contract out of the sexual and social demands and to split into a paranoid/schizo-self is in the film symmetrically related to contracting into monopoly capitalism, fascism, and Hitler. The narrative pointedly aligns a sexual crisis (Hermann's marriage), an economic crisis (the Great Depression, because of which the 'family firm' can be salvaged only by a merger) and a political crisis (the resignation of the last social-democrat Chancellor Müller, hastening the collapse of the Weimar Republic and the emergence of the National Socialists).

Two figures in whom Hermann mirrors his own options are his production manager – also called Müller – and the director of the rival chocolate firm. In both cases, the conversation revolves round the politics of the day, to which Hermann can only reply with private confessions, in one case about his mother, and to the chocolate manufacturer about living with forged papers. Thus, in the subplot, the personality split is metonymically related to economics, the change from private enterprise manufacture to monopoly capitalism, the proletarianisation of the middle classes, ready to believe in the world-Jewish-Bolshevik conspiracy as a way of venting anxiety and resentment. The white collar supervisor Müller is clearly paranoid about foreigners, Jews, the Versailles Treaty, and in order to allay his fears about the future, he joins the Nazi party. Müller, in other words, chooses the Nazi as his (ego-ideal) double, and when he appears at the office dressed in an SA uniform, the analogy with Hermann (exchanging clothes, switching roles and identities) is made explicit.

However, the connection works more subtly when Müller is first introduced. The morning after Hermann has been watching himself making love to his wife, she drives him to work in their limousine. Hermann, in the car, plays seductively with the hem of her skirt to expose some thigh, and busies himself on her gloved fingers: in the context of the previous night's debacle, the scene functions as a fetishisation and substitution for the potency he failed to muster (the close-ups are inversely matched by the subsequent close-ups of Hermann manicuring Felix). They kiss, and Hermann goes up the steps to his office, not without casting a miserable glance back at Lydia, who immediately checks her face and mouth in the rear view mirror of the car in a gesture which recalls (as does the display of the armpit) Bunuel's heroine in UN CHIEN ANDALOU. We cut to a shot inside the office where Müller, looking out, is actually looking at his own reflection and straightening his tie as he sees his boss arrive. This gesture is symmetrically related to Lydia checking her mouth – both assure themselves of their sexuality in a gender-specific and fetishising manner – and Hermann, who is outside the system of their mirror-glances, acts as the deferment that brings the gestures in relation. He is the mirror in whose reflection they compensate for the lack they perceive in him. The subsequent scenes, where Hermann and Müller talk politics, end with Hermann's face reflected in the glass partition of the inner office, while Müller's face in profile superimposes itself across the glass pane from inside, once more aligning the two, but also keeping them apart. The exhibitionist petty criminal from Fassbinder's early films assumes in Müller a particular historical identity: that of the German petit-bourgeois, over-identifying with the State, and making a public spectacle of his good behaviour and conformism. Compared with Müller, Hermann's paranoia is sanity itself, and to narcissism as repressed paranoia in Hermann corresponds an exhibitionist display of aggression in his supervisor.

Hermann's discussion with the rival chocolate manufacturer, after establishing verbally an analogy between chocolates and German politics (with a number of Stoppardian 'on-colour' puns), is primarily developed visually by the way background and foreground, inside and outside, are systematically juxtaposed. The scene shows the manufacturer directly challenging Hermann's identity ('Is Hermann your first name or your surname?'), and it ends with Hermann caught (and breaking down) in an elaborate play on political colours: 'I was a Blackshirt fighting the Reds in the White Army, then I fought the Brownshirts in the Red Army, and all I am now is a yellowbelly in a brown trade'. Brown evidently being the emblematic colour of a false identity, it condenses politics, repressed homosexuality, the chocolate business, from each of which Hermann tries to escape into madness/exile/neutral territory.

On the visual plane, the conversation is doubled by a view of the factory assembly line, which turns out little brown men in chocolate, all replicas, veritable choc-troops of political doubles, ending like piled-up corpses in a box marked rejects. Fassbinder's image of the fascist state preparing for war and exploiting private paranoia for public conformism considerably deepens a passage in the book where Nabokov's Hermann explains the political significance of the double in terms that recall, more than anything else, a scene from Fritz Lang's METROPOLIS:

> It even seems to me that my basic theme, the resemblance between two persons, has a profound allegorical meaning [...] In fancy, I visualise a new world, where all men will resemble one another as Hermann and Felix did; a world of Helixes and Fermanns; a world where the worker fallen dead at the feet of his machine will be at once replaced by his perfect double smiling the serene smile of perfect socialism.[16]

Nabokov, in these lines, distances himself derisively from his narrator. Fassbinder, who takes his hero more seriously, uses the assembly line as a metaphor for the imbrication of big business, depression economics and the intrusive, para-military state. This connection between private and public life is reiterated in the scene where Hermann, about to seal the letter which will bribe Felix into donning Hermann's clothes, hesitates as he watches just such a line of brownshirts hurling bricks at the window of a Jewish butcher's shop. Their frustration at not being able to smash the window (rhyming as it does with an earlier scene where an irate Müller beats his fists against the wall in the office) acts as a relay in Hermann's mind for the decision he is about to take, Felix now figuring explicitly as the (phantasmatic) supplement to fill the space left by a political impasse as well as the personal one; conversely, Hermann's presence at the scene, his gaze, once more serves to inscribe his dilemma into the specifically historical space of nascent Nazism.

The economic dimension, in so far as it revolves around an analysis of fascism as the extreme political form of state capitalism (an analysis thematized by the decline of Hermann's family firm), enters the narrative in a peculiarly compressed play on words: the pun on 'merger/murder', twice repeated, which involves the merger between two people and the merger of two firms, conflated with a murder that is suicide, and a police state that will murder an entire race, for fear of merging with the hated 'other'. The extreme condensation which Fassbinder here employs to make the private intersect with the economic as well as race may not altogether redeem what is perhaps a laboured pun, but it does point to the paradigm that generates the narrative, determines the logic of the otherwise opaque plot, and is responsible for the elliptical and fragmented storyline. For the pun also suggests that Hermann's dilemma is founded on a double negation, structured symmetrically: to the disavowal of his wife's adultery corresponds the disavowal of any difference between himself and Felix. The two acts of repression (murder and merger, 'threat of castration' and 'denial of difference') confront each other as mirrors, and the paranoia associated with the former is countered with a continually renewed temptation, at once consummated and forever barred with the murder of Felix, to 'regress' to the latter.

The Shattered Mirror and Defective Suture

More exactly, DESPAIR structures both Hermann's disavowal and the double-bind in terms of a defective or partial vision. At one level, the narrative logic is structured along very classical lines, obsessed as the film is with repetition, symmetry, inversion and doubling. In this respect, there is an equivalence between Hermann not recognising what is going on between Lydia and Ardalion, and being over-anxious to discover similarity between Felix and himself. Thus, another structure, about recognition and miscognition, about vision and point of view in general, underpins the narrative as analyzed above, also determined by castration-anxiety and the denial of difference. In other words, the logic that articulates the plot and accounts for the dislocations of DESPAIR's linear narrative is itself shaped by a critique of cinematic representation and its visual metaphors.

I have talked about DESPAIR as if the film ended soon after Hermann shoots Felix in the woods. It does not. Whereas Lydia virtually disappears with the flash-forward that shows her accepting Felix as Hermann, the latter's stay in Switzerland is depicted at length, first as a process of physical deterioration of exterior appearance, but also almost literally as Hermann 'falling to pieces'. Most striking are the scenes at the Swiss hotel where his false position and false identity, his silence, make him an object in other people's speculations, a fragment in their discourse. The process culminates in a sequence that shows a shattered mirror, shards of a broken wash-bowl, and Hermann's hand holding into the frame a passport with Felix's photo. The shots 'rhyme' with the opening credit-scene, where on a reflecting glass table top in Hermann's kitchen, he breaks raw eggs into a bowl in order to mix Lydia her favourite cocktail. This resume of the plot, a visual reminder of the fragility that makes up his identity, is juxtaposed with a particularly graphic 'return of the repressed': the clue left at the scene of the crime, and which points to Felix's identity (and thereby Hermann's), is a solid, carved walking stick; and Hermann's manic laughter when he discovers how the police are being led to his hideout is that of a man who has also read his Freud. The Oedipal trap seems to open only on to a series of interminable and potentially endless substitutions for the initial configuration: briar-pipes, lipsticks, walking-sticks – so many fetish objects circulating within the narrative, 'liberated' as absurd clues and ridiculous traces by the shattering of the self. The film has no closure in terms of the dilemma it poses, and while on the surface it moves towards the false ending of the police thriller (detection and capture), psychologically Hermann is condemned to endless repetition, narrative space itself becoming the mirror-maze where he encountered Felix and now his own shattered image.

This hall of mirrors atmosphere seems to conjure up the ending of Orson Welles' LADY FROM SHANGHAI.[17] But in DESPAIR it is not only indicative of *film noir*'s male paranoia towards femmes fatales, which Fassbinder here parodies. We are also, pace Nabokov, in the world of Jorge Luis Borges' labyrinths, with their Escher-like trompe-l'oeil effects, and Möbius-strip involutions. As in THE BITTER TEARS OF PETRA VON KANT, it is the narrative itself which provides the maze, presenting to the viewer a complicated kind of stereometric shape. Each position taken in the overall design can be inverted or is shown to be reversible, available for occupation by different characters in turn. Whether one thinks of the power-play between Petra and her maid Marlene, the reversal of roles between Karin and Petra, the two couples in CHINESE ROULETTE, or the Hermann-Felix relationship, the more general point is that it underscores the extent to which in a Fassbinder film, identities are nothing but shifting places in a configuration, and as such can be re-placed, if not re-played. The human chessboard situation of CHINESE ROULETTE puts it graphically, as does the end of THE MERCHANT OF FOUR SEASONS, when Hans' employee and ex-friend (again, as in DESPAIR, where he is Felix, a role played by Klaus Löwitsch) at first displaces and then replaces him as father and husband.

The realization of such expendability is almost intolerably poignant, and the misfortunes that befall Hans or Fox (another pawn replaced without being missed) make the films in which they are the heroes end in a moral black hole (literally, in THE MERCHANT OF

FOUR SEASONS, by an open grave). But the relentless negativity especially of FOX AND HIS FRIENDS, where substitution adds the insult of existence disavowed to the injury of humiliation, has itself a reverse side, suggesting that the bleak ending might lend itself to a more enigmatic or ambivalent interpretation, as in DESPAIR, where the hero 'chooses' to be replaced, thereby retrospectively giving also the substitutions in the other films a less negative slant. Turned around, on its axis as it were, every human relationship in Fassbinder appears capable of utterly changing both its meaning and value. Not only the male-female polarity seems to Fassbinder totally reversible,[18] but also the dialectic of the exploiter and the exploited, of the weak and the strong, of the haves and have-nots (as in DESPAIR, where Felix is at the opposite extreme of the socio-economic scale from Hermann). This makes the narratives, despite their relentless negativity, their downbeat or tragic ending much more mysterious, and – as Fassbinder always pointed out – also more hopeful. In DESPAIR, hope and despair seem to hinge on how we read Hermann's desire to find a resemblance between himself and Felix, which in turn, becomes as much a question of our viewing expectations, as of our belief in mimetic love or the reversibility of power-relations.

Puzzling, for instance, is the fact that we are never able to 'get close' to the central character. Throughout, identifying with Hermann is systematically blocked and disrupted, a fact noted by most critics,[19] since one instantly notices that Felix is no physical double of Hermann, but finds that this superior position of knowledge over the hero is never acknowledged by the narrative, it eliminates any suspense and registers more as an exasperation than a willingness to be intrigued by his 'mistake'. Also puzzling is the fact that Hermann's look does not act as a focus or to give direction to our attention, nor does his motivation become clear. His desire is not evident from the movement of the plot itself, for both the sexual and the economic motives are indirectly presented, while the motive we are given in their place, financial gain from an insurance swindle, hardly satisfies. This lack of apparent motivation affects the audience's response also to Lydia, whose occasional nudity is offered to the spectator's gaze, but at no point valorised by male desire. Nor does she exist 'in her own right' as a character. Her role is bracketed by the stereotype of the silly vamp, the exaggerated parody of the alluring female ("Intelligence might take the bloom off your carnality" Hermann says to her at one point). What intervenes between the look and its object is – as in the opening scene already discussed – the camera: an unlocalised immaterial character, a substitute, but covering neither the spectator's point of view nor that of the protagonists. In addition, the few times we see events from Hermann's perspective, this vantage point is undermined by the fact that his vision is so evidently defective regarding crucial elements of the narrative: he sees at once too little and too much.

These two features may, to a spectator expecting a Hollywood-type narrative, merely seem part of the empty formalism so often disliked in European art cinema. But I would argue that DESPAIR reworks quite radically what has undoubtedly been the most original aspects of Fassbinder's style from KATZELMACHER onwards. The split of the spectator's point of view, on the basis of which classical cinema constructs the congruence between 'to see' and 'to know', has always been torn apart rather than sutured in Fassbinder. Instead of motivating the look of the camera via point of view shots and letting these create the visual field, thus building a homogenous fictional space, Fassbinder plays off seeing against knowing or vice versa, mainly by three types of shots. Frontal shots of characters looking (glance-object shots) but without shots of what the character looks at; tableau-like static compositions which by their very symmetry 'cite' an invisible observer (who is outside the fiction, because the shots are never claimed by any of the characters within the film, and because they are organised around an internal frame, accentuating perspectival space); finally, inversely related to the previous type, shots where another spectator perspective is constructed within the action, through a character or characters whose main function it is to observe and who 'anchor' the scene by their presence and gaze.[20]

The point of this defective suture in Fassbinder has always been twofold: to make his characters' dilemma a function of their roles and self-images, as if to say, my protagonists only behave like this because they are being looked at, but if they were not being looked at they would not exist.[21] And secondly, to implicate the spectator in this process as a third term whose invisible presence is no longer that of the voyeur.[22] The paradox of Emmi and Ali in FEAR EATS THE SOUL has already been discussed. Yet the most striking case is no doubt THE BITTER TEARS OF PETRA VON KANT. As the drama of self, double and other unfolds between Petra von Kant and Karin, the spectator becomes ever more aware of Marlene as his/her double within the film. But instead of the narrative taking the spectator's look, via the camera position, and delegating it to, circulating it among and exchanging it with the characters' points-of-view and their off-screen glances, Fassbinder un-couples looking, so to speak, from narration and motivation, and instead, 'embodies' it, and thus doubly locates it, in the fiction and outside, creating a kind of material excess or surplus. In PETRA VON KANT, Marlene's silence is the 'tain' or blind spot in the imaginary mirror that is the screen, her hovering presence seemingly endowing her not only with secret knowledge but an eery power to 'call off the show', to blot out the picture or block out the view, an impression accentuated by the theatrical 'proscenium' space created by filming at right angles to the picture plane.

The one section in the film where Marlene is absent throws into relief her function during the rest: when Petra, on her birthday, has a nervous breakdown, it seems as much due to the removal of Marlene's look as having to confront her mother, representing as it does the absence of control, a moment of totally fragmented and dispersed subjectivity no longer held by the power of Marlene's 'phallic' look, in contrast to the cacophony of female voices associated with Petra's mother and her daughter. At the same time, this section follows most closely the compositional rules of classical narrative, with its point-of-view shots, eye-contact and the spectator sutured into the representational space. Fassbinder seems to be identifying 'Hollywood continuity editing' with the presence of (oedipal) family drama, as if to cite once more Sirk (and the theories of the 'male' look) by designating classical narrative as 'patho-genic'. PETRA VON KANT ends when Marlene, asked to give up her role of silent witness and enter into the sphere of words, walks out rather than speak. Yet this presence virtually outside or at the edge of the fiction is offered to the spectator not as a figure of projection, but merely as an increasingly uncanny awareness of a double. To perceive this manoeuvre also makes the viewer realize that Marlene only appears to be the puppeteer who holds the strings to the mechanism called 'Petra von Kant'. As soon as we recognise our double, we become aware of the 'narrator', and in an attempt to gain control over the film, we need to phantasmatise an author, another instance of control, controlling us. We are plunged into the abyss of the en-abyme construction which the film opens like a trap. If the dedication in PETRA VON KANT reads: 'to him who here became Marlene' (dem, der hier Marlene wurde), in DESPAIR, the dedication could be 'to him who here tried to give up being Hermann'.[23] Who, among the audience, realising that the dedication addresses 'him', would either wish to become Marlene, or have the strength to give up being Hermann?

Another example of a Fassbinder film in which such an absent gaze is both named and erased is THE MARRIAGE OF MARIA BRAUN. As Maria's perennially absent husband, Hermann (once again played by Klaus Löwitsch) has a role similar to that of Marlene in PETRA VON KANT. His disappearance to the front, and his non-return after the defeat of Hitler, become a necessary condition for Maria's story, not only in the sense that there can be no narrative without rupture or absence, but that his absence is the very condition of her love for him. The ideal of true love, on which Maria bases her career, is only disturbed by his periodic return: from the war, from prison, from making his fortune in Canada. What she does she does for Hermann, but only on condition that his place remains empty – but fixed by the temporality and space *where someone once was*. Absence turns her object-choice into an image, which – expelled and phantasmatised into an idée fixe – becomes the guarantee of her identity, self-alienated but secure. Maria represses the return of the source of idealisation, thereby also repressing the knowledge of the source of her economic wealth and sexual power. Her life and identity appear under the sign of a marriage whose consummation is forever postponed and deferred – necessarily so, and in several senses, as the following chapter will show.

Self-Reference as Self-Representation?

Fassbinder has, I would argue, adopted the self-referentiality of the European art-film in DESPAIR, in order to rework also the thematic concern of his own cinema. What in the previous films was largely a matter of presenting the spectator with mirrors of himself as a voyeuristic presence, albeit complexly effaced and staged, becomes in DESPAIR a matter of analyzing more historically determinate relations. The breakdown of identity and its relocation in shifting identifications as described above lead to a filmic mise-en-scène that does more than merely 'distance': it also 'places'.[24] At one stage, Hermann and Ardalion are engaged in a discussion of Lydia in a restaurant. The scene is initially framed as an over-the-shoulder two-shot with Hermann facing in the general direction of Ardalion and the camera. Ardalion's back fills the left-hand side of the frame. The camera then starts a slow travelling shot to the right, which we have to read as a subjective shot from Ardalion's point of view. As Hermann continues to talk, the camera has become stationary, and suddenly Ardalion re-enters the frame, but not, as expected, from the left where we last saw him, to 'claim' the point-of-view shot; instead he enters from behind Hermann, on the right, and Fassbinder cuts at just the moment when Ardalion completely obliterates Hermann in the frame. The point here is not that Hermann has been talking to himself, but that Ardalion has, as it were, delegated his look to the spectator via the camera and thereby marked as a conspicuous absence the point of view of the spectator. Hermann's predicament is that Ardalion has 'set him up' just as Fassbinder has set us up.

Later in the same scene, Hermann is talking about his dissociations to a man he believes to be a psychoanalyst whom Ardalion has introduced him to, against the background of one of Ardalion's paintings depicting a village in the Alps. It turns out that the stranger is in fact an insurance broker, and Hermann has once again been duped into living in a world set up and controlled by Ardalion. In just this way the shots where the camera forces the spectator to claim a point of view not motivated internally by a character are also moments of dissociation for the spectator where his/her identity as invisible observer is called into question. While the scene challenges us by drawing attention to a gap that can neither be repressed nor filled, we nonetheless in the end have to rely on Hermann, doubly duped, to put us right, in his final address to the spectator, which becomes the point at which the spectator is forced to realise that the film as fiction only exists by virtue of that fundamental repression which is the disavowal of the camera as camera, the audience as audience, the actor as actor. But Fassbinder operates this Brechtian reduction only in order to once more invest it with another question which makes the ending of DESPAIR very baffling indeed. After confronting his shattered self in the broken washbowl and cracked mirror, the final scene has Hermann step out of his room to make his speech of surrender to the police who have surrounded the chalet. The fragmented composition gives way to a frontal shot, a direct stare. But the speech itself and the stare are, within the fictional framework, clear signs that Hermann is now insane, himself convinced of the story he had been telling Felix about needing him as an understudy. Hermann's terminal madness, his final identity outside society, outside the law, takes the shape of thinking of himself an actor in a film: which is, of course, what Bogarde/Hermann is at this point, and about to take leave – of his fantasies, his sanity, his role, in fact, of the film itself.

This 'stereometric' tilt, whereby the proof of madness in the story we have witnessed turns out to be the truth of the cinema when considered as a mere illusionist device, both 'places' Hermann's parting words and makes them once more incomplete. On the face of it, the short speech is taken almost directly from Nabokov's novel:

> Hold the policemen, knock them down, sit on them. A famous film actor will come running out of this house. He is an arch criminal but he must escape. I want you to make a free passage for him. I want a clean getaway. That's all. I'm coming out.[25]

The passage of time and the vagaries of English usage have added a meaning to the final sentence that even Nabokov might not have anticipated.[26] Hermann does not just come out of the house, he also comes out of the closet. But Fassbinder added a line to Nabokov's text. Before the frame freezes on the words 'I'm coming out', Hermann says: 'Don't look at the camera', and with this act of naming, Hermann comes out of being a character in a self-contained fiction. The shot frames Hermann/Bogarde's face looking into the camera, and at its edges the barrels of guns are visible, though not those who hold them, obliging us, the audience, to fill their place.

With Hermann's speech, the film attains its closure by substituting one frame of reference for another. The triangular relationships of Lydia/Ardalion/Hermann-Felix are replaced by another triangle made up of actor/camera/spectator, explicitly named and thereby terminating the fiction. If Hermann (whom the murder of Felix has reduced to silence, exile and cunning) attains an identity on the side of madness, this madness also allows him to reappropriate language as the final gesture of a successful transformation. Only now does the play of 'grammatical shifters' which I analyzed in the flash-forward come to rest on that archetypal shifter, the personal pronoun 'I'. Yet the instance of enunciation is nevertheless elsewhere: it must, by the logic of what has been said, be located as and in the metteur-en-scène, the auteur/author.[27]

What can one conclude? Hermann's choice of insanity and his journey into madness equate the enigma in the narrative – who is Hermann, what is his problem? – with the enigma of film narrative: what is the function of a fiction film? 'Lifting' the fundamental repression at the end means abandoning the space of the cinema as the psychological or ideological 'safety-zone' of an identity-machine, for it puts out of action the apparatus that generated the 'fiction-effects' and 'subject-effects' in the first place, by exposing the cinema machine's violent, aggressive, and shattering side. 'Representation' and 'image' are the systems of lack which the cinema both covers up and fetishises for the benefit of the spectator. In other words, in DESPAIR the fictional character, at the point at which he avows himself to be an actor, turns out to be the 'paranoid' construction of the spectator, necessary to make the cinematic apparatus bearable at all. Fassbinder's peculiar mise-en-scène, his use of the false point-of-view shots and of spatial dislocation, takes away the narcissistic supplement of paranoia that makes identification pleasurable in the classical narrative. We can paraphrase the process by allegorizing DESPAIR as a discourse about cinematic identification itself: the film represents the spectator, who 'murders' the fictional character by taking him over, dressing him up in the appearance of his idealised self-image. On the other hand, the spectator commits 'suicide' in order to live (temporarily) in the actor and through him. What Hermann acts out in the murder/merger paradigm are not only 'his' fantasies, but also the spectator's, and Felix is to Hermann what Hermann is to the spectator – the other that is made into the same, at a cost of considerable violence and repression. Fassbinder has literalised the psychic position of the spectator vis-à-vis the screen by indicating its pathological side: the pathology of bourgeois identity-crises that determines – or is it determined by? – the construction of the classical narrative text. The two interlock and mutually predicate each other. In terms of the film, Felix functions as the Fetish, the substitute for the ultimate signifier in this system, the condition for the unification of the subject, and the guarantee for the kind of pleasure that DESPAIR seems destined to frustrate. This is why in this meta-text, Felix and not Lydia is the male hero's object of desire, and why at the same time this desire is camouflaged in a thriller plot with *noirish* genre elements: underlying any cinematic representation, including the oedipal dramas of identity, is a 'dissociation' machine functioning antagonistically vis-à-vis its socially sanctioned, culturally approved uses. The defectiveness of DESPAIR as a classical text is precisely what allows it to deconstruct that text, in the guise of an apparently confusing tale of doubles that do not resemble each other.

The final image achieves closure by its 'zero-ing' of representation and that which is represented: nothing is there except what you see. Dedicated to three artists, among them Antonin Artaud, who wanted to abolish the distance between actor, part and performance, the film has come full circle at the point where the notion of fiction and spectacle is replaced by that of 'performance' as the zero degree of representation. Yet the very logic of the literalisation I have been describing implies, as already indicated, that the author remains in the text and cannot 'come out' either in propria persona or from 'behind' the characters. Fassbinder's film, so dedicated to clarifying the relationship between image, perception, camera and spectator, has as its 'structuring absence' also, it seems, the problem of the self-representation of the author.

My account of the ending is still incomplete. The Alpine scene in which it takes place can be recognised, not without a certain shocked surprise, as the landscape prefigured in the painting of Ardalion that we see, half-finished, on the wall of the restaurant. And as the police surround Hermann's hideout one sees briefly, almost at the edge of the frame, Ardalion, with an easel, 'finishing' his picture. So while in one respect Hermann 'returns the look' and addresses the camera head-on after having sought to appropriate it as a mirror, in another respect DESPAIR, too, is a film in which the closure is achieved by leaving a substitute gaze in the frame. More ironic still, the last scene can be read in terms that make both Hermann and Ardalion delegates of the author's look, even though in the fiction, they functioned as each other's adversaries, in a power-struggle less over the possession of Lydia than over who is 'setting up' whom. Hence a certain ambiguity after all, also about who exactly is whose double in the film. Is Hermann's speech as he 'comes out' a call to arms against illusionism, against representation, or for the ruses of modernism and its modes of deconstructive narration? DESPAIR is an art film, in so far as its self-reflexivity, its use of Ardalion's 'bad painting' as a frame-within-a-frame-within-a-frame, are a comment on 'representation' from within the perspectival-illusionist paradigm; yet it is an anti-art film in so far as the impasse of Hermann's 'coming out' demands a more radical re-thinking of this specular paradigm itself. From one side of the divide, Hermann's fate is one of 'despair', but from another, it is 'eine Reise ins Licht', a journey into light: the light of over-exposure, the kind of 'fading to white' which Fassbinder takes up more fully in VERONICA VOSS. In DESPAIR, the realisation that Hermann may be leaving the space of the narrative is undercut by the knowledge that he is still inside the world of Ardalion, another space of representation: there is no 'outside' to this 'inside'. Or is there?

Beyond the Family: the Benevolent Eye of the State?
Traditionally, the dynamics of the screen as mirror, and cinematic vision as miscognition, of fetishizing the look and suturing the spectator, of self-estrangement and the necessary repression of the look of the camera have been interpreted as determined by, but also effacing the construction of the basic cinematic apparatus. The 'apparatus' figured as the 'final term' both of cinematic modernism's attack on perspectival representation (in the form of art cinema self-reflexivity) and as the model that could explain the 'successful' working of illusionism, its reality-effect and the construction of subjectivity in Hollywood classical narrative.[28]

In Fassbinder, too, as we just saw, there is an acute sense of the cinematic apparatus as having 'basic ideological effects', but there is also, as indicated in the previous chapter, a very particular regime of the look which at once intersects with the various 'modernist', 'Brechtian' and 'deconstructivist' critiques, and largely displaces them in his own practice, by emphasizing the failure of the 'phallic' look, and its reinscription – negatively, through an exhibitionism to which, strictly speaking, no voyeurism corresponds, and in the form of what I have called a response to a 'demand' that emanates from something 'beyond' as well as 'in front of' the image. Although it may ultimately not belong to the register of the 'visual' at all, the solicitation nonetheless is connected to both the problem of the look and to subjectivity. What DESPAIR now suggests, precisely because even more radically than Fassbinder's previous films it deals with a crisis of vision, is that the gap between knowing and seeing figured as an impossible alignment of the look and its object may connect to a historical trauma. For in DESPAIR the problem of vision, of the look intersects with a historical setting, the political and economic crises of the early 1930s in Germany – thematized in the ripple-effects of the pun 'merger/murder' and the tragic-comic encounters of Hermann Hermann with his supervisor Müller and the chocolate baron Mayer.

The ultimate link of these two seemingly so distinct articulations (the crisis of vision/the crisis of politics) must be sought in the family, or rather, in the perennial attempts to escape the bourgeois, patriarchal family as a viable instance of gender-identity, but also as a viable socio-symbolic unit. This, too, relates to the cinema: classical Hollywood has always been about 'family entertainment' and has re-told oedipal dramas, whether 'coming of age' stories of adolescent males or crises of female identity under patriarchy, as in the women's films or family melodrama. In the work of directors such as Sirk, the intensity of the conflicts produced ruptures in the classical mode itself, to become legible as a critique of the institution and its values. In Fassbinder, Sirk's critique finds itself even more exacerbated, so that the cinema comes to stand in a demonstrably antagonistic relation to the family, and this in several respects. First of all, his films invariably figure families, but depicted as sites of emotional exploitation, violent power-struggles and schizo-inducing double-binds. Secondly, the characters' attempted escape from the family focuses on the crisis in symbolic relations outside which find their typical expression in this 'need to be seen', itself the narcissistic 'solution' to the problem of not being able to establish affective bonds around a 'normal' Oedipal development. In the absence of constructing identity within the family, the need to be perceived, to be confirmed, to be looked at takes over the tasks of regulating and at the same time disturbing the articulations of subjectivity. This means that role-playing, spectacle, the street – actions, events and places where the look is symbolically traded – become privileged spaces that actually structure identity outside the family, and in effect replace the family as an identity-generating institution. According to Fassbinder, it was the cinema that became a surrogate family during his adolescence, an alternative space of socialization, affect, identifications, the working out of conflicts.

A film like DESPAIR on one level depicts a de-socialisation process in the way that Hermann Hermann gradually 'loses touch' with his domestic life, his business, the world around him. In his frantic bid to reposition himself 'differently' in the field of vision – substituting someone else to play his roles and switching outward appearances – he responds to a situation which was overdetermined in several respects, being at once a family crisis, a business crisis and a political crisis, all of which Fassbinder, as we saw, translates into the register of sight, vision, perception, deception. That it concerns a crisis of the visual field itself is shown by the parallel re-socialization process of his supervisor Müller, choosing to reinscribe himself into the social symbolic of Nazism, present in the film mainly as a new order of visibility (uniforms, colours, street action). Evidently, Müller's experience of subjectivity, that which allays his crisis of identity is to become an object newly visible, presumably not necessarily for anyone in particular, but under the gaze of an absent Other, fantasized as 'the nation', 'history', 'manifest destiny', the moral imperative: any abstract entity, provided it can be conceived as possessing the power/the reflection of an 'eye'.

In Fassbinder's films, as argued in the previous chapter, both conformism and non-conformism are subject to the rule of wanting to be seen, even though their respective economies differ. The dynamics, as argued in subsequent chapters, gives rise to an acute and complex critique of the representations of the 'other', whose most immediate implication concerns what could be called the fascist public sphere and its 'subject-effects'. Increasingly in the late 1970s, and explicitly when working in the genre of the international art film, the 'need to be seen' is identified by Fassbinder with German Nazism, as a social formation that, especially in its initial 'revolutionary' phase, heavily invested in spectacle, in pageants, the politics of the street, with a simple, cunningly stylized visual iconography prominently displayed on flags, façades and public places. At the same time, because Nazism's claim to power was as a non-conformist rebellion, in fact an oedipal challenge to the symbolic father, in the form of the succession of Chancellors (of the Weimar Republic) perceived as weak, floundering and ineffectual, its social revolution was initially fuelled by a critique of patriarchy, voiced in such all-male groups as the SA. Thus, even Nazism responded to the crisis of the family, although from a para-military, male-bonding, ultra-chauvinistic perspective.

In DESPAIR, the two asymmetrically related 'solutions' to the break-up of the Weimar symbolic order represented by the respective choices of Hermann Hermann and Supervisor Müller formulate a problem, whose relevance goes beyond the film. What, Fassbinder seems to be asking, was Nazism for the German middle class, for the petit-bourgeoisie and the working-class, all of whom supported Hitler? We think we know what it was for those actively persecuted by the regime, for those excluded or forced into exile. But for the 'a-political' Germans, who were addressed and solicited as *included*? Might not the perverse pleasure of fascism, its fascination have been less the sadism and brutality of SS officers, but that of being seen, of placing oneself in view of the all-seeing eye of the State? This eye must not necessarily be imagined as a look: the order of the visible as a whole (uniforms, swastikas, iconography) figures as this eye's mirror. Fascism in its social imaginary encouraged a moral exhibitionism, as it encouraged denunciation and mutual surveillance. Hitler appealed to the *Volk*, but he always pictured the German nation as standing there, observed by 'the eyes of the world'. The massive specularisation of public life, famously diagnosed by Walter Benjamin as the 'aestheticisation of politics', might be said to have helped institutionalise that structure of 'to be is to be perceived' which Fassbinder's cinema never ceases to interrogate.

Evidently, the question of what 'seduced' Germans about Nazism has been asked many times, and the suggestion made here about the importance of specular relations does not presume to be a contribution to this debate. One obvious objection, for instance, would be that the figure of the Führer is such a potent symbol of paternal authority, and the demand for absolute obedience to him so clearly authoritarian, that it is difficult to imagine how this might fit the thesis advanced above for Hermann Hermann and Supervisor Müller, namely of a kind of 'mirror-stage' intervening between the subject and its symbolizations, bypassing the 'oedipal' formation.

However, an author who has studied the psychic make-up of Nazi support, and whose books enjoyed such wide circulation in the 1970s that Fassbinder is bound to have known them, seems to corroborate at least part of the argument of Nazism's appeal having been as a response to the crisis of the bourgeois family. In *Society without the Father* and *The Inability to Mourn*, Alexander Mitscherlich put forward an account of the social psychology of Nazism as well as of Germany during the 1950s post-WW II reconstruction effort – the periods of German history Fassbinder became most interested in – which diagnoses as common traits what Mitscherlich calls 'regression to the pre-Oedipal stage' and the choice of a 'narcissistic love object'. Nazism, according to Mitscherlich, had such wide appeal because it represented a 'regressive' solution to the 'fatherless society' brought about by advanced capitalism's division of labour demoting the male's role as sole provider and weakening parental authority.[29] Instead of (male) egos formed in Oedipal conflict, Nazi bonding encouraged 'manic-depressive' personality structures, alternating between feelings of omnipotence and worthlessness. Into this structure, the leader fits, but not as a father-figure:

> [The mass leader], surprising as it may seem, [...] is much more like the image of a primitive mother goddess. He acts as if he were superior to conscience, and demands a regressive obedience and the begging behaviour that belongs to the behaviour pattern of a child in the pre-Oedipal stage.[30]

Hitler, in other words, projected himself not as the Über-Vater or patriarch, but as the dutiful son of a beloved mother, and thus in the role of the primary love-object, prior to and outside Oedipal division. The original attachment to the mother is revived and rescued in the attachment to abstractions like 'nation' and 'race' (both female nouns in German), in whose loving gaze the male can mirror himself. According to Mitscherlich, this pre-Oedipal bond also helps to explain why the collapse of the Third Reich did not provoke the kinds of reactions of conscience, guilt and remorse that 'the eyes of the world' after 1945 had expected. In *The Inability to Mourn* he writes:

> Thus, the choice of Hitler as the love object took place on a narcissistic basis; that is to say, on a basis of self-love [...].
>
> After this symbiotic state has been dissolved, the millions of subjects released from its spell will remember it all the less clearly because they never assimilated the leader into their ego [...], but instead surrendered their own ego in favour of the object [...]. Thus the inability to mourn was preceded by a way of loving that was less intent on sharing in the feelings of the other person than on confirming one's own self-esteem.[31]

But here we need to remind ourselves of the distinction made earlier between the two types of narcissism, involving the ideal ego and the ego ideal, and the void or gap which narcissism is designed to cover, signifying the presence of that look that does not see, but also formulating a demand that can 'shatter the self', as it shatters Hermann Hermann. The cinematic apparatus, stripped of its mechanisms of identification and the functioning of its reality-effects is thus closer to the look that does not see, that is to say, the 'void' of representation, needing to 'cover' itself by narrative. The classical system of circulating the look, in other words, makes the void 'see', by framing it and investing it with mobile, motivating points of view. In Fassbinder's cinema, at some points, the shield is made to slip, sometimes in an explicitly political context, as in the moment of crisis analyzed in the previous chapter, where in GERMANY IN AUTUMN Fassbinder's mother asks for the return of a benevolent dictator, which is to say, the caring look.

Why did West Germans rebuild such a conservative and conformist society after 1945? If one follows the logic of Mitscherlich's argument, the German economic miracle was sustained psychologically by defence mechanisms against the loss of the ego-ideal and the narcissism of self-hatred and melancholia.[32] In a sense, this is the story told in THE MARRIAGE OF MARIA BRAUN, whose heroine's ambiguous strength lies precisely in her 'inability to mourn', while keeping her ego-ideal intact, via the fiction of the absent husband in whom she has invested (and secured, becaused barred) the gaze, even without him knowing it.[33] As if in a trance, her self-estranged exhibitionism calls upon the scene benevolent eyes, including those of Chancellors Konrad Adenauer and Helmut Schmidt, all of whom gaze in ghostly fashion out of portraits whose frame once contained that of Chancellor Adolf Hitler.

4. The BRD Trilogy, or: History, the Love Story?
THE MARRIAGE OF MARIA BRAUN, LOLA and VERONIKA VOSS

Maria Braun: Irony, Accident and a Slightly Sinister Exchange

Few of the high-points in Fassbinder's career seem as incontrovertible as THE MARRIAGE OF MARIA BRAUN, shot between January and March 1978 and shown for the first time unofficially at Cannes that year[1] (where DESPAIR was in competition), before premiering at the Berlin Film Festival in February 1979. MARIA BRAUN became Fassbinder's most successful film, both critically and commercially. At home it took four million Deutschmarks at the box office, and abroad, it took one million dollars in the United States and played for a whole year at a prestigious Paris cinema. It made Fassbinder an international celebrity, who – to his considerable satisfaction – would be recognized in the streets of New York by passers-by[2] and whose dossier circulated among studio-heads as a promising European director. But MARIA BRAUN also became one of the key films of the New German Cinema, at the centre of a cycle concerned with 'mastering the Nazi past', to which Alexander Kluge and Edgar Reitz, Helma Sanders-Brahms and Hans-Jürgen Syberberg, Volker Schlöndorff and Margarethe von Trotta, Jutta Brückner and Jeanine Meerapfel (among many others) would contribute.

But this is the wisdom of hindsight. When one learns how MARIA BRAUN came to be made, one is struck by the unlikelihood of it existing at all. Or rather, one marvels at the many kinds of irony involved in the process, the role of accident and chance at every turn, seriously suggesting that the argument about the purposiveness of Fassbinder's life and work must be an illusion due to the historian's narrowing retrospective perspectivism. By most accounts, the making of MARIA BRAUN was one of Fassbinder's least happy experiences. Peter Berling even calls it 'one of the decisive self-destructive episodes in Rainer's life'.[3] When the production was ready, Fassbinder no longer wanted to shoot the film, too preoccupied with the preparations for BERLIN ALEXANDERPLATZ to care about much else.[4] Considering how important Hanna Schygulla proved to be for the film's success[5], it is ironic that originally Romy Schneider should have been cast for the part, before her demands, indecisiveness and heavy dependence on alcohol proved too irritating for the impatient director. In the event, the central role is now unthinkable without Schygulla, who carries this film as she had FONTANE EFFI BRIEST. With MARIA BRAUN she became an icon and emblem, bigger than her fictional role and also surpassing her previous screen persona: precisely that which makes a star. This turn of events, too, is not without irony, since Schygulla, who had been replaced after EFFI BRIEST in Fassbinder's fancy first by Margit Carstensen and then Elisabeth Trissenar, was called back into grace and favour at a time when, by all accounts, Fassbinder had definitively tired of her.[6] In another piece of retrospective rewriting, the film's impact consolidated

Schygulla forever after as Fassbinder's leading lady, effectively effacing the gaps and discontinuities in their working relationship.

Rare for Fassbinder, the production on MARIA BRAUN ran over budget, putting his producer, Michael Fengler, under pressure to secure additional funding at short notice, which he raised by 'overselling' the rights. Of the original 50% of the film owned by Fassbinder's Tango Film only some 15% remained, eventually leading to litigations against Fengler, his earliest and most loyal production partner.[7] After this, Fassbinder referred to Fengler, sometimes to his face, as 'gangster', adding 'I'll teach you never to want to make another film with me'.[8] According to Berling, executive producer on the film, and one of the minders Fassbinder tried to interpose in order to keep tabs on Fengler, the main reason why the film was over budget was Fassbinder's cocaine habit, the supply of which had to be assured by Harry Baer and Berling, with the cash coming from Fengler. Some ugly scenes in Coburg, where part of the film was shot, led to Fengler being blackmailed into paying 20,000 DM for compromising photos of Fassbinder's hotel room, and it seems that on some days, Fassbinder never showed up on the set. MARIA BRAUN was also the film after which Michael Ballhaus, Fassbinder's cameraman on eleven previous films, thought it time to quit.[9]

In view of these unhappy circumstances for almost all concerned, its success must have been bitter-sweet, especially when one German newspaper headlined MARIA BRAUN as the film that 'brought people back into the cinemas,'[10] finally almost fulfilling Fassbinder's ambition of making a German Hollywood movie. At the same time, MARIA BRAUN's popularity did not altogether make up for the slight Fassbinder felt had been done when the 1979 Berlin Festival Jury decided not to award him the Golden Bear for best director. Released in the United States the same year as Volker Schlöndorff's THE TIN DRUM (which won the Oscar for best foreign film that Fassbinder had already imagined would be his), the two films together established the New German Cinema as an international brand name, while also assuring that the historical film, especially when critically examining the fascist legacy in the post-war period, became arguably the only genre the New German Cinema is remembered for.

And yet, one cannot help thinking that these ironies and coincidents are no accident: there are good reasons why MARIA BRAUN should have become such an important film, and neither is it an accident that the final result is a Fassbinder film through and through, even when one concedes that the script owes much to the two names that take chief screen credit, Peter Märthesheimer and Pea Fröhlich. Irm Hermann, for instance, remembers Fassbinder telling her the story which would become MARIA BRAUN on one of their walks through Munich's Englische Garten in 1970, eight years before the film was shot.[11] Indeed, in the light of the film's ending, accident is quite an appropriate term for designating not only the particular conflict of unconscious drive and desire that structures the narrative. It describes well the peculiar purposiveness typical of Fassbinder who so often had a sleepwalker's sure-footedness at the edge of the precipice. Fassbinder invariably seemed to know how to turn chance to advantage, and rewrite contingency into design, often developing, extending and making his own an impulse originating elsewhere. His was a quickness of mind that seized opportunities and integrated them in an evolving but nevertheless coherent master-plan. MARIA BRAUN thus became both the cornerstone and the retrospective justification for conceiving of the subsequent two films as belonging to a threesome, the famous 'BRD trilogy', which, as this chapter will try to show, displays a most telling concept of chronology, causality, sequence and consequence – telling above all for Fassbinder's conception of (German) history.

Bankability

Given that MARIA BRAUN came closer than any other film to Fassbinder's ideal of a critical film that is accessible to the general public, it may be worth reflecting briefly on the factors contributing to its success. Some could be regarded as extrinsic, though this need not make them negligible. Domestically, the film received a special kind of publicity when *Stern,* an illustrated weekly mass-circulation journal, agreed to serialize the 'novel of the film', written by Gerhard Zwerenz, a friend of Fassbinder's and occasional collaborator.[12] This Hollywood-style, multi-media marketing concept had never been tried in Germany before, and it ensured that the subject and story of the film were widely known when it went on general release late in March 1979.

As far as its international success goes, it seems evident that what Fassbinder termed Fengler's gangster practices, a co-production and distribution agreement with Trio Film, owned by Hanns Eckelkamp, was highly beneficial for the film, even if it hurt Fassbinder's (and his heirs') bank balance forever after. Eckelkamp, one of the very few German producers with international connexions, began wheeling and dealing on behalf of the film already at Cannes and effectively outmanoeuvred the Filmverlag der Autoren, the domestic distribution partner for both Fassbinder and Fengler's Albatros Film, by selling it to United Artists.

MARIA BRAUN thus became Fassbinder's second attempt at attaining a modicum of long-expected but slow-to-arrive bankability as an important name of European cinema, after his first attempt, DESPAIR, had (at least for this particular purpose) failed, despite its impeccably 'international' literary property (Vladimir Nabokov), cast (Dirk Bogarde and Andrea Ferréol) and writer (Tom Stoppard). Fassbinder had by 1977 hit the ceiling of the German (state-subsidized) national art cinema, without yet reaching the floor of the European (then already mainly French) film industry, and thus becoming a credible partner for an American studio. The success of MARIA BRAUN in both Paris and New York made a Hollywood offer at least a possibility (it certainly resulted in a preliminary financing agreement for a favourite project of Fassbinder's, the adaptation of a novel by Pitigrili called *Cocaine*), but as the experience of his colleague Wim Wenders showed, at that time deeply frustrated with his American friend, Francis Ford Coppola, the prospect of making a film in the United States was probably something a German director ought to desire and dread in equal measure.

Instead of waiting for Hollywood to call, Fassbinder used his now proven international success in a carefully orchestrated, widely publicised quarrel with the German media, possibly in order to bid up his standing at home.[13] He was able to cash some of it in for an increased budget and improved conditions on his next project with Bavaria and the WDR, the 14-part television series BERLIN ALEXANDERPLATZ, nervously announced as the most expensive series ever undertaken by German television. It also led to Germany's most seasoned commercial producer, Luggi Waldleitner, expressing an interest in making an international film with Hanna Schygulla (who insisted on Fassbinder as her director), which resulted in LILI MARLEEN. Horst Wendlandt, another leading German producer, lined up to underwrite LOLA and VERONIKA VOSS (as well as offering Fassbinder the use of one of his Munich penthouse suites after the tragic suicide of Armin Meier in Fassbinder's own apartment). Finally, it also gave Fassbinder the chance to outbid Werner Schroeter by allowing Dieter Schidor, the producer and originator of the project, to conclude a contract with Gaumont for co-financing QUERELLE, and thus ensure world-wide distribution for what would become his last film.[14]

Classical Narrative and European Art Cinema

All these extrinsic reasons suggest that MARIA BRAUN had what it took to be marketed and exploited as a high profile film. Among the more intrinsic sources for its exceptional status in the Fassbinder oeuvre, the simplest but by no means exhaustive explanation for its commercial appeal was that it had both a star and a story: like all popular movies, though unlike many films of the New German Cinema. This story it tells chronologically, coherently and consecutively. The time frame is clearly indicated and the historical context economically conveyed: married in 1943, amid Allied bombing raids and during her soldier-husband's 48 hour furlough, Maria Braun waits in vain for his return after 1945. When his friend, released from a prisoner-of-war camp, reports Hermann Braun dead, she takes up with a black American soldier who becomes her and her family's provider. One night, as they are making love, Hermann suddenly appears, and Maria, coming to his rescue, kills the black soldier. Hermann pleads guilty to the murder and goes to prison. Maria, befriended by the industrialist Oswald, commences a steeply rising career as Oswald's personal assistant and eventual lover, though not without reaffirming her loyalty to Hermann. Released from prison, and seemingly too proud to be 'kept' by Maria, he departs for Canada to make his fortune. Maria, now a partner in Oswald's firm and at the height of her business success, suffers bouts of depression and takes to drink. One day, shortly after the death of Oswald, Hermann returns, this time for good. Maria, confused but overjoyed, gets ready to finally commence a marriage she has been imagining for over a decade, when the couple is interrupted by Oswald's secretary calling on her to read the industrialist's last will. It transpires that, unknown to Maria, the two men had made a pact, with Oswald permitted to enjoy Maria's attentions until his death on condition that Hermann stay away. In return, Hermann and Maria are to be his heirs. As the full import of the news sinks in, Maria goes to light a cigarette in the kitchen, but having previously failed to turn off the gas, an explosion destroys the villa, burying both Maria and Hermann under the rubble, while on the radio one can hear West Germany winning the July 1954 World (Soccer) Cup Final against Hungary.

MARIA BRAUN in this sense is Fassbinder's most 'classically' constructed film: it has a clear dramatic focus, the eponymous heroine, and a recognizably linear pattern of rise-and-fall, as well as a narrative that progresses by a neat series of repetition and symmetries, both direct and inverted. For instance, it satisfyingly reaches closure with the reprise (which is also a kind of mirror-reversal) of the opening image. Like all classical films, its narrative can accommodate a variety of interpretations and responses, being constructed so as to engage different audience interests and to allow German and non-German, male and female, mainstream and highbrow spectators to find a pleasurable emotional and intellectual point of entry. Generically a melodrama, but one whose rise-and-fall structure also gives it the force of a morality tale (both might be said to be secular forms of tragedy), MARIA BRAUN offers an audience enough generic familiarity to encourage direct identification with the heroine's ambitions, goals and disappointments. At the same time, enough mystery hovers over the ambiguous ending. The retrospective doubt it casts on Maria Braun's motivation (whether Maria blew herself up deliberately or by accident, whether she always suspected Hermann to have plotted with Oswald, whether she needed Hermann to absent himself in order to keep her love for him strong and pure) can embolden the audience to speculate about the deeper meaning of the story, without leaving the cinema baffled or confused, proving that structurally motivated ambiguity makes a film especially productive in the spectators' minds. As a piece of story-telling at once linear, transparent and classically realist, while also leaving an ambivalence about what it is that makes the ending ambiguous, MARIA BRAUN might be said to gratify the act of meaning-making itself.

Clearly, the narrative and style of MARIA BRAUN neither inhibit a conventional realist reading, nor demand one. If the cautionary, bitter-sweet tale of a woman's brave attempt to make it in the world of men sufficed for some spectators, to a more intellectual audience it also offered a richly metaphoric texture. Knowing that this was a European auteur's film, MARIA BRAUN's formal symmetries and repetition of motifs invited the sort of reading whereby the referent became the fate of an entire country, rather than of this particular woman. What in a classical film would merely denote its generic form and be part of its deep structure, in Fassbinder become the signs of a different kind of intentionality. Symmetry and repetition are deemed to symbolize the postwar history of Germany, with the apparent changes from one regime to another, from one Chancellor (Hitler) to the Federal Chancellors Adenauer, Erhard, Kiesinger and Schmidt, provoking a shoulder-shrugging 'plus ça change (plus c'est la même chose)'.[15] German history this century, marked by so many ruptures in its political regimes, and so many continuities (among its ruling elites) disguised by new beginnings, appears to the jaundiced eye of the idealist merely cyclical, and even trapped in the endless return of the same. Summing up his review of MARIA BRAUN, Wilhelm Roth writes: 'The German petit-bourgeois of 1930, 1955, or 1975 are identical. Germany a country, in which nothing changes, in which the opportunity of 1945 has been gambled away.'[16] This dialectic of continuity and discontinuity, strongly featuring in the West German Left's view of political and social history, seemed in MARIA BRAUN perfectly mirrored at the level of style and formal organization.

Of course, there are a number of indications to suggest that Germany in the film is more than background and setting. Germany becomes a signifier in its own right from the moment Hitler's portrait comes crashing down, and throughout the narrative similar emblems, such as the American flag, a Hershey chocolate bar or a packet of US cigarettes, direct attention to these objects' symbolic function. When the heroine at one point refers to herself as 'The Mata-Hari of the economic miracle', she not only comments on a moment in the plot, but on the metaphoric nature of her role.

This merely helps to underscore an obvious point of attraction: the strong female character at the film's centre, by 1978 a sign of the Zeitgeist not only in Germany.[17] The mixture of femininity and independence portrayed by Schygulla qualifies her as both an active heroine wanting to be in control, and the emotional focus of suffering, victim of history and the scars of war, while also credibly embodying an indomitable romanticism implied in a story of absent lovers, of yearning with a heavy heart, and hope against hope. Yet while Maria Braun might serve as a role model for young women of the 1970s anywhere in the world and remind an older generation of German women of their lost youth and independence, Schygulla's success, I would venture, has also to do with the degree to which the figure she depicts (and, through her, the film as a whole) lends itself to allegorical or, rather, allegorizing interpretations.

An Allegory of West Germany?

The film was clearly received, especially by foreign critics, as an allegory of West Germany. Insofar as European films and products of a national cinema are invariably 'allegorized' and interrogated as to what they say or give away about their native country, MARIA BRAUN no doubt also helped fill a gap that, at least for American audiences, had been there almost since the 1930s: cinematically speaking, the world knew nothing about Germany, nor how Germans felt about fascism, defeat and reconstruction. Thus, the most commonly accepted reading of Fassbinder's film saw Maria Braun as standing for the pragmatic, post-Hitler Germany. 'This treatment of a woman who picks herself up from the ashes of a war and national disgrace and becomes an efficient, modern business woman is a dramatic metaphor for a nation making a similar transition'.[18] The divided nation's astonishing economic success was, however, bought by a double denial. Predicated on disavowing the fascist legacy and thus periodically visited by a 'return of the repressed', the new Germany seemed seized by nameless bouts of melancholy, indicative of deeper ills, despite material prosperity and outward signs of stability. Having denied itself the fulfilment of emotional needs, sacrificing spiritual values for status and wealth, it wittingly or unwittingly colluded with Cold War rearmament, in which former enemies became allies, and pacts were made, along with fortunes.

But Maria Braun is also 'a modern Mother Courage, with a touch of Polly Peachum and Pirate Jenny' (all Brechtian figures from before 1945) whom Fassbinder makes 'the human metaphor for post-war Germany'.[19] It was even suggested that the film was a protest against the nuclear bomb, with the final blast meant to warn the spectator of impending disaster as Germany permitted Nato nuclear weapons to be stationed on its soil.[20] Other, more specifically feminist interpretations saw Maria Braun's fate symbolize that of many women, not only in Germany, for whom the war and the immediate post-war period had brought the kind of freedom and emancipation which the men, returned from the war and once more reclaiming their patriarchal positions in public life, were busy taking away. In Germany, the film fitted into the debate about the so-called Trümmerfrauen ('women of the rubble'), i.e. the women in the reconstruction period of the late 40s and 50s, and their claims to social benefits as one-time members of the national labour force: 'what also ended in the mid-50s was the participation of women in the reconstruction, and also their entry into the prevailing power structure [...]. Scarcely had the rubble been cleared for their men, then the men came back, and returned to power.'[21] For American audiences, Maria Braun became a German 'Rosie the Riveter', a popular icon in the late 1970s to encourage women to insist on their place in politics, public life and the professions.[22] Taking the film's ending as unequivocally pessimistic, MARIA BRAUN was widely seen in Germany as the negative affirmation of an alternative after 1945 that had not worked: 'as arbitrary as the accident seems that brings an end to [her life and marriage] – this life stands as a symbol that another life is possible... her death is the seal of authenticity of her endeavour to live this different kind of life'.[23] With MARIA BRAUN, then, Fassbinder was taken seriously in Germany, as well as abroad, which meant being taken seriously for the message his work conveyed. Another irony: he finally 'represented Germany' and fitted most closely the role of the artist as prophet and conscience discussed in a previous chapter.

Among so many symbolic readings, it is not surprising that some critics remained unconvinced. They refused to see in Maria's compromises and hangovers, in the subtle corruption that power and wealth bring to her life, a parable of modern Germany. One, for instance, argued that, however much the director had intended it, the figure could not carry the weight of the metaphor, since Fassbinder 'never makes his case', given that he 'expresses complex emotions and an ambiguous political history in broad theatrical gestures'.[24] The fact that female figures in films, propaganda and the visual arts – one thinks of 'Liberty guiding the People', The Statue of Liberty, Germania, Joan of Arc – seem to entertain an oddly close relationship with allegory has often been noted critically, and the question arises as to whether in fact Fassbinder's heroine can and is intended to stand for Germany, itself such an ambiguous historical signifier, in the context of division and defeat. Here the critics' doubts (who nonetheless assumed that a metaphor was intended) may serve to suggest more the limits of such an allegorizing capacity, and to indicate how one might see this limit, or rather, Fassbinder's way of drawing, re-drawing and crossing this limit as one of the purposes of the film, to the point where the powerfully metaphoric constructions which Germany 'under

Hitler' has received in other films of the New German Cinema (such as GERMANY PALE MOTHER, OUR HITLER, or HEIMAT) also come under scrutiny. Thus, in MARIA BRAUN, marriage (highlighted in the full title), the family, and the family under fascism undergo a critique, but also a critique of the critique. As already argued in an earlier chapter, such critical stances in Fassbinder are never delivered entirely 'from without' which is why the question of interpretation is an important one.

Historical Reference or Media Reality?

On the one hand, there is nothing objectionable about such allegorical readings, especially when, as in this case, they could only enhance the success of the film. On the other hand, one still hesitates to remain content with them. Both the precise historical references and the way they play off each other within MARIA BRAUN itself (echoed among the other films of the trilogy, VERONIKA VOSS and LOLA) suggest that the film's stylistic allusiveness and the function of the signifier 'Germany' point also in another direction. The distinction between the classical Hollywood narrative and the European art film was already intended to hint at this. In the art film, the status of history is that of either the absent cause or the allegorical figuration, while Hollywood uses 'history' as a realistically simulated backdrop, often both paralleling and counterpointing the romance (as in DR ZHIVAGO or REDS).

What is most striking about MARIA BRAUN is how full of allusions and references to other works it is, some coming from the cinema, some from literature and the other media. In the first instance, MARIA BRAUN is a woman's picture with all kinds of echoes from Hollywood, notably MILDRED PIERCE by Michael Curtiz, but also THE POSTMAN ALWAYS RINGS TWICE, except that in this case, the femme fatale kills the lover rather than the husband. More central are some German films, from the 1930s, from the so-called 'Durchhalte-Periode' of Nazi cinema (the 'last stand' period from 1943 onwards), and from the immediate post-war era. At the other end of the allusionary spectrum, Fassbinder also evokes such overdetermined icons of the 1950s as chewing gum and American cigarettes. However, rather than put an authentic 1950s pack on the set, Fassbinder coolly has a Camel cigarette packet come into the picture, in close-up, on which one can clearly read the 1970s German government health warning, an ironic meta-commentary on yet another continuity, this time pointing in the direction of the Americans rather than Hitler.

These features oblige us to see the film's historicity first and foremost as a self-conscious artifice and a fabrication, prompting the suggestion that it is a heavily intertextual film.[25] MARIA BRAUN deconstructs/rewrites several different genres, and even several specific films: the newsreel, the post-war Trümmerfilme (such as ZWISCHEN GESTERN UND MORGEN, from which it cites certain visual compositions), the Adenauer-era corruption films (like DAS MÄDCHEN ROSEMARIE), the Hollywood maternal melodrama, and even *film noir*. The most obvious way to comment on this would be to call it a postmodern film, or as already suggested, a 'postmodern parody'.[26] It is thus not just an intertextual film, but a mise-en-abyme of intertextuality: 'the narrative motifs of Hollywood melodrama from the forties and fifties in a film about the fifties,'[27] where one style comments on another.[28]

Fassbinder, by his own admission, was not interested in historical films, but in films about history from the perspective of the present: 'we make a particular film about a particular time, but from our point of view'.[29] This meant that in his films, the past is seen across the traces which it has left in the present, fixed in the representations of that past, across the styles, the gestures, the images that evoke this past in and for the present. In this respect, MARIA BRAUN is a film which functions as a trigger of memories, but at one remove: not so much recalling a reality, as setting up a chain of associations, stories remembered from one's parents, pictures seen in the family album, in short, the standard version of the 1950s as present in the culture at large of the 1970s. Fassbinder seemed happy to work with this material and these associations, as were his set designers and costume makers, thus explicitly repudiating the relevance of authenticity or documentary truth.[30] On the contrary, it was the artefacts turned memorabilia, and the visual records turned coffeetable books, which made them valid as cliches and icons of the postwar period, and thus as the ironically reinstated guarantors of this history.

Nevertheless, or perhaps precisely because of it, for German audiences (and, to some extent, for German television) MARIA BRAUN initiated a cinematic 'history from below', not just a demand for recording the stories and experiences of ordinary people, of the families for whom the problem of getting firewood for their stove or cigarettes to use as 'hard currency' on the black market was more acute than Chancellor Adenauer's assurance on the radio that Germany would never again rearm. Not just the provocative materialism of a Bert Brecht and his 'erst kommt das Fressen, dann kommt die Moral' ('one cannot be virtuous on an empty stomach') is involved, but also the weaving together of fragments of very different lives, a collage of fates rather than one fate ('Geschichten', i.e. individual stories, have an asymptotic relation to 'Geschichte', i.e. history). This is why, in the end, viewers will tend to see Maria Braun's fate as exemplary, even in spite of themselves. Fassbinder understood this, while at the same time, he criticised the notion of history as that which great men say and do, by showing with what indifference or absent-mindedness the Braun family 'consumes' the nightly news or Adenauer first arguing against and then for Germany re-establishing a standing army and joining NATO.

The Sound-Image Intertext

Often, Fassbinder's media reality creates its own historical referents because of something regularly remarked upon in his films, which in MARIA BRAUN plays an especially strategic role: snatches of popular music, sound effects, radio broadcasts, and the resulting sound-image montages or aural counterpoints. They are in many ways both more striking and carry more narrative information than the cinephile quotations and the recreations of famous agency photos. From the monotonously intoned litany of missing persons (even more than the many messages stuck on the boarded fence, it is the radio which convinces the viewer that Maria

Braun is one among many waiting anxiously for news of fathers, husbands, relatives), to the snatches of Louis Armstrong and Glen Miller in the off-limits bar where she presents herself for a job, Maria's state of mind and likely fate are at every point amplified, commented on or ironically undercut by a soundscape even more saturated with historical patina and period flavour than the women's headscarves or the first mention of 'nylons'. Sound in MARIA BRAUN generates a dimension which for the viewer locates the action not so much in a period as in the idea of a period. Here again, it is not simply a matter of using 'authentic' recordings, even though, for a German audience, the voice of Adenauer undoubtedly carries its own particular charge from a time when television did not yet exist.[31] Just as important is the fact that, like all cinema sound, MARIA BRAUN's audio track shifts the boundary between subjective and objective, between character perception and audience perspective. Peter W. Jansen remarked that 'as concretely as these sounds invoke their sources, they are also deployed so subjectively, as part and parcel of the film's subjectivity, so to speak, they intone what lies beyond the perception of the characters who are on the scene [...]. Yet the sounds are part of their consciousness [...] the acoustic assertion of the history of that time'.[32]

These effects are achieved by the principle of sound-image montages, which give the realistic narrative a double background, acting as both interpretative foil and counterpoint. As foil, for instance, the radio broadcasts associate every stage of Maria Braun's rise and fall with a stage in the post-war development of West Germany, documenting the U-turn of the Adenauer government regarding rearmament, the Cold War and NATO. Using radio as a kind of chorus, from announcer to roaring crowd, however, also adds a dimension of counterpoint and sarcastic irony, which is underscored or doubled by yet another structure, namely that of the visual parallels between the opening and the closing. The portrait of Hitler at the beginning ironically or not so ironically is repeated by a framed official portrait of Helmut Schmidt, and the other Chancellors reversed out in negative, suggesting a continuity amid the total change between a dictatorship and a liberal Western democracy. These literal 'framings' of the narrative once more encourage a double, i.e. an allegorical reading, while at the same time never quite disambiguating exactly what the film is finally 'saying' about the relation between the private and the public, the Nazi past and the democratic present. Because of the various counter-movements, Fassbinder continually suspends the spectator between a Hollywood response to his film and an art cinema interpretation.

Sound, then, only adds to the enigma of how Fassbinder's films about Germany are to be read: as realistic, intertextual, allegorical, as parody or pastiche. Each visual source or acoustic channel contributes its own signal, which in turn is so thickly textured as to multiply the referential levels. Superimposed on each other, like so many different sensory memory screens, the references are subtly displaced in relation to one another, none taking precedence in the end, and splitting the spectators' awareness at the very moment of intensifying their attention. In the exchange between Maria, Oswald and his accountant Senkenberg after concluding the deal about manufacturing nylon stockings, for instance, both camera and music become protagonists in their own right, interpreting the realignment of economic, political and erotic power that has taken place. This is perhaps what one reviewer meant when speaking of Fassbinder's 'stereophonic' montage art, obliging the audience to separate the elements before rearranging the parts, to discover the meaning: '[...] throughout the ever present pneumatic drill of prosperity affirms the steady reconstruction of a destroyed country. Fassbinder's directorial skill achieves mastery in this stereophonic art form, where the spectator synthesizes in his head signals sent out on separate channels.'[33]

The same goes for the literary references. If the story of Maria Braun is that of a Hollywood heroine of the 1940s, Hermann's tale evokes (for German audiences: which may be why it need hardly be told) a famous radio-play from the 1950s (*Draußen vor der Tür*, by Wolfgang Borchert), itself inspired by a post-World War I stage play (*Hinkemann*, by Ernst Toller), about a soldier returning from the war, invalid, useless and unwanted. When Maria, trading a piece of family jewellery for a low-cut dress and a bottle of bourbon, replies to the black market dealer who wants to sell her the complete works of the writer Heinrich von Kleist: 'books burn too fast and don't give enough heat', the references and ironies are manifold. Kleist here stands for one of his novellas (*The Earthquake of Chile*), a pessimistic analysis of political tabula rasa thinking (he had in mind the French Revolution), prescient and relevant to Germany's 'zero hour' moral earthquake of 1945.[34] The book-burning refers to the Nazis' infamous action against Jewish and Communist writers in 1933. By opting for the dress with which to please the new powers that be (and herself), Maria not only shows an opportunism that bodes well for her survival (and probably would have stood her in good stead under a different regime, too) but also – allegorically representing the new Germany – turns to America and its culture of jazz, booze and chewing gum. In the debacle that has befallen Germany, then, 'she' does not look to German culture and its humanist traditions to renew herself but, for the sake of success, becomes someone else, assimilating herself – prostituting herself – to the hedonistic, but philistine Other. Such a reading is not that fanciful, since by the 1970s and especially in the 1980s, some German filmmakers felt that Germany had sold its soul with overzealous 'Americanisation' (notably Hans Jürgen Syberberg in OUR HITLER, and Edgar Reitz in HEIMAT). But must one read it this way? There is the fact that Kleist, a writer who was neither banned nor burnt, might be counted among the Prussian patriots whose romantic nationalism Nazi ideology successfully exploited and thus, metaphorically, might be too hot to handle for a Maria who has done her homework. But, taking the scene literally, there is also Fassbinder (who acts the part of the black marketeer) exchanging an in-joke with his star (last seen 'illustrating' the pages of another classic writer in FONTANE EFFI BRIEST), and wishing her good luck with the role as Maria Braun, which will indeed make her famous in America. 'Left-wing melancholy', baroque allegory, cynicism or meta-commentary: Fassbinder multiplies the narrating instances and thus 'frames' the references one inside the other.

A similar principle governs the use of music, invariably composed or compiled by Peer Raben. An attentive disciple of classic Hollywood scoring practice – he introduced Fassbinder to the films of Douglas Sirk – Raben's music pieces often perfectly illustrate the

Fassbinder protagonists' feelings: '[he] could write music as impoverished as were [the] characters.'[35] One is often left wondering whether a character 'hears' the music that expresses his/her state of mind to the viewer or not; in the negotiation scene in MARIA BRAUN already alluded to, an agitated Oswald sits down at the piano, to play (badly) the piece of music audible on the soundtrack throughout, as if he had suddenly entered into a dialogue with his own unconscious or had finally resolved whatever it was that had troubled the relation between him and Maria. The viewer, meanwhile, is startled into becoming aware of the status of film music as commentary. Even without playing so explicitly on the difference between diegetic and extra-diegetic sound, Raben had a knack of 'layering' musical passages, contrasting a subjective emotional point of view with an objective musical commentary, itself in turn resting on another, more 'distancing' musical ambiance.

A particular good example is found in LOLA, where different kinds of music are part of the characters' superego, ego and id. The moral contrast between the new broom in the mayor's office, von Bohm, and the city's corrupt political mafia is illustrated by the contrast between the raucous songs performed by Lola at the local brothel, and von Bohm at home, practising (more or less proficiently) his Vivaldi on the violin. This is both irony at von Bohm's expense and what sets him apart, for Lola, originally out to seduce him and dent his rectitude, discovers her deeper feelings for him when the two are together on a country outing. However, the inner torment of von Bohm to master his sexual obsession with Lola is finally resolved when, instead of Vivaldi, he haltingly intones on his violin the torch song with which Lola drives the men wild. Discussing these shifts of register, and the dialogical dimension, especially in the BRD trilogy and LILI MARLEEN, Norbert Jürgen Schneider remarks:

> Typical for Fassbinder's use of popular hits is that they are not meant ironically, and nonetheless do not function as the illusion of harmony, as they do in other German musicals. The fabricated and self-deceiving emotionality of the pop songs is genuine, because the characters who sing or listen to this music, hang on to its promise for dear life. However, because Fassbinder at the same time shows how gagged, cheated or trapped these characters are in their environment, education and private traumas, he unmasks the pop songs as yet another lie by which they are betrayed.[36]

In VERONIKA VOSS, Schneider distinguishes five levels: diegetic, conveying the atmosphere of the 1950s via the music heard at the time; extra-diegetically, recreating the 1950s mood via Raben's own pastiche composition; extra-diegetic leitmotifs allocated to individual characters; brief musical inserts, connoting shocks of recognition for either the characters or for the viewer about the characters; and finally, a level of commentary, inaccessible to the characters, made up of instrumental passages, mostly percussion.[37] One might add a sixth level, also commentary, when diegetic music dating sometimes anachronistically from the 1960s suggests a thematic connexion or ironically 'places' the conflict, as in the use of Johnny

Cash's 'Sixteen Tons', with its refrain 'I owe my soul to the company store' to underscore Veronika's enslavement to the doctor who supplies her with drugs and obliges her to humiliate herself by begging her former colleagues for film parts she is no longer capable of playing.

In MARIA BRAUN, the snatches of popular songs by such national superstars of the 1950s as Catarina Valente place the film in especially poignant ways, for they render with cloying intensity, as Rocco Granata does in THE MERCHANT OF FOUR SEASONS and Freddy Quinn in LOLA, not so much what it meant to live in the period, as to be put (once more) in touch with the hopes, dreams and pain which that period projected. Projected, one might add, into a future that by now was a present, but one which had in some sense betrayed more than just the lessons of the Nazi defeat that the songs' sentimental longing for the sun and the stars, or for Heimat and home were in any case disavowing. For gone was also the striving for a better future that this past nostalgically evoked.

> [Such] intertwining of musical perspectives, shifting from external to internal without however indicating when the inner core has been reached, conveys a curiously restless kind of longing... Peer Raaben's music, often criticised for being variable in quality, fits Fassbinder's figures like a glove. Like them, there is something simple, naive, sullen and archaic about it (typically, the banal 3/4 beat of many of his themes). But the music lives in a system of dramatic perspectivism, ready at any time to yield to a utopian impulse. And before the listener realizes, the layers converge, and from simple themes there emerge complex collages of avantgarde scoring and bi-tonality, which make of Raben's music the most devastatingly moving film music.'[38]

Telescoping History

If Fassbinder's soundscapes and Peer Raben's music montages give an uncanny illusion of historicity to the representational relays by providing an aural space that extends 'laterally' and in depth, this last passage also hints at a complex temporal dimension, complementing but also disturbing the circularity that might be read from such repetitions as the portraits of West German chancellors rhyming with that of Hitler. To re-invoke the repetitions and symmetries, it is important to note how their function as 'framing devices'[39] has both a specular-perspectival dimension and a structuring role in a temporal displacement that alone makes the parallel, say between Hitler and Helmut Schmidt, something other than a crudely satirical political point. There is, for instance, the equally circular structure of the wailing sirens and hissing bombs at the beginning of the film while Maria and Hermann force the registrar to sign their marriage certificate as the building collapses around them, repeated at the end in the crescendo of the newscaster's voice and the roar of the stadium crowd, as Germany's wins the soccer world cup final, while Maria ignites the escaping gas and her house explodes in flames.

The irony works at several levels, not all of them reinforcing the supposed parallel between Hitler's megalomaniac war bringing ruin to German cities, and West Germany's soccer victory fuelling the same mad chauvinism (such a defamation of soccer would, incidentally, be most uncharacteristic of Fassbinder whose passion for the game is well-documented). The scene creates above all an appreciation for contiguity and coincidence itself, a sense of several temporalities existing side by side, capable of commenting on each other or redefining the notion of causality and counterpoint. If, indeed, Germany becoming world champion in 1954 does bring to an end the rubble years and the post-war matriarchies, then the irony of the new pile of rubble just created by Maria resides in the verbal metaphor, while not excluding a sigh of regret of Fassbinder, the romantic anarchist, for the days immediately after 1945, when the rubble meant that everything was possible and nothing fixed.

In LOLA, too, reference is made to Federal Chancellors Konrad Adenauer and Ludwig Erhard, one by way of a particularly unexpected sound-image montage, the other with a famous speech about the principles of the 'social market economy'. Each refers to a specific political context, but functions also within the circular movements the film enacts, spiralling to a particularly felicitous irony when at the end, one of the male characters is asked whether he is happy: the question is put to him by the daughter of the woman he has just married, at the same place where earlier he first made love to her.

Such loops and spirals within each of the films of the BRD trilogy direct attention to the fact that the three stories are linked to one another by a peculiar temporality. First of all, they show the tension of an inverted chronology (time in which the films are set/time when they were made) typical of Fassbinder's work. Thus, LOLA bears the subtitle 'BRD 3' and was shot in April/May 1981, while VERONIKA VOSS, subtitled 'BRD 2', was completed eight months later, in December 1981. While this inversion may be trivial, and simply reflect the fact that VERONIKA VOSS is set in the early 1950s when LOLA can be dated to the late 1950s, chronologically speaking, the three films do overlap, or rather, they are segued into each other, like the sections of a telescope.

This telescoping of temporalities might be called subjective time or Freudian time, insofar as it enacts the dialectic of forgetting, remembering, repressing and commemorating – the main semantic or tropological field for 'representing Germany' as a nation having trouble 'remembering not to forget'.[40] But these fractured chronologies seem also like attempts to break open the binary oppositions with which this chapter started, between continuity and discontinuity, between the vicious circles of 'plus ça change' and the radical break of the tabula rasa and the zero hour. Given the privileged place the Adenauer years have in Fassbinder's work, the BRD trilogy becomes something of a fulcrum for all his thinking about German history. Yet such treatment of the 1950s as a compressed version of the whole century was also, in the context of modern Germany, something of a polemical device. It prompts the thought of whether the decade was for Fassbinder a metaphor for the different cycles of new beginnings that had marked modern German history, or more a metonymy, where the decade could stand as a part for the whole, or even the speeded up replay of

Germany's entire modern development, after the total destruction, according to the Marxian motto of history always repeating itself, once as tragedy, the second time as farce...

Fassbinder, I noted, always insisted that his films were historical only to the degree that he looked at the past from the vantage point of the present; in other words, how the 1950s look to the 1970s.[41] This might be understood in the sense already discussed, namely what Fassbinder takes from a historical period are the icons, artefacts and representations that the intervening time has selected and authenticated as typical and quintessential, acknowledging the particular kind of a personal, collective media-memory which the proliferation of sound and images in our culture has created. However, it is equally possible that, in light of the frequent 'returns of the repressed' that seemed to dominate the 1970s, Fassbinder did indeed view the 1950s as the locus of traumas requiring a more psychoanalytic time. As we shall see, though, his films were far from endorsing the particular turn towards Freud that became typical for other films of the New German Cinema trying to come to terms with German history and fascism.

If anything, one might compare Fassbinder's handling of temporality to that of Ernst Bloch, and his notion of non-synchronicity or uneven time. There are, in both MARIA BRAUN and VERONIKA VOSS, the spectral presences of ghosts, dead bodies among the living, like the old couple in VERONIKA VOSS or the depressive doctor in MARIA BRAUN, who performs an abortion for her, while shooting drugs in order to do his job at all. His intertextual status refers us to Peter Lorre's underrated masterpiece, DER VERLORENE, a Trümmerfilm depicting a Germany full of displaced Germans, including those who have become guilty but who have no chance to ask or seek forgiveness, before their past catches up with them. The doctor seems just such a figure, displaced and depressed, incapable of either living or dying. In this respect, MARIA BRAUN is in fact full of such walking undead, a veritable time capsule of 'Ungleich-zeitigkeit' [non-synchronicity], where not only different temporalities coexist side by side, but where the dead and the living, ghost, revenant and zombies of the present jostle with those who, like Maria herself, consider themselves 'specialist in [matters of] the future'.

Suffice it at this point to say that one of the most striking consequences of the historical telescoping is the way in which the films decisively interlink with each other, providing a kind of mutually sustaining justification for what it is that gives the trilogy its energy and direction. It suggests that alongside Fassbinder representing Germany by the mise-en-scène of his persona as rebel, outcast and dissident, there is a kind of mise-en-abyme of Germany. Contracted and focussed to a single moment in the trauma of Hitler and Nazism's aftermath, its history now extends back from this fatal point into the 19th century, re-visioned and re-arranged in the light of this terrible teleology, thereby reversing the causal chain. But these twelve years are also extended outward and forward, stretching into a future that knows no statutes of limitation, one that is already predicated upon the burden of responsibility to be carried by subsequent generations who realize that fascism has mortgaged their lives.

The Power of Spectacle: Veronika Voss

The most powerful engine, but also the formal machine for bringing about this mise-en-abyme in Fassbinder's later work, including the BRD trilogy as well as LILI MARLEEN, is no doubt spectacle, and in particular, the cinema.[42] One remarkable instance of such a mise-en-abyme of German history into private history can be found in the narrative of VERONIKA VOSS, which opens with the projection of one of the heroine's own films, as a film-within-the-film. Since VERONIKA VOSS covers the last two years of a former Ufa star turned drug addict, and the film she watches is the story of a woman's heroic struggle to master her need for morphine, the viewing session folds Veronika's past professional role back into her personal present. It thereby frames the current events and interferes with them, as the fiction on the screen anticipates in abbreviated form the fate that is to befall her, while at another level, the screening brings into her life the journalist Krohn, her potential saviour. At yet another level, the visit to the cinema is only one of Veronika's many performances that will divide the action, oscillating between a failed screen comeback and the all too fateful return of a past coming back unbidden.

What makes this opening scene, however, so special is that it refers not so much to a moment in German history, but to a moment in film history, because Veronika Voss' identity – her sole identity as it turns out – is that of a movie star. Based on the real-life actress Sybille Schmitz, once a favourite of Goebbels, but later blacklisted by him, and who committed suicide in 1955, the film introduces another layer of historical referencing when one thinks of some of Schmitz's famous roles, such as the mysterious and elegiac beauty in Carl Dreyer's VAMPYR or the highly strung society lady in Karl Hartl's sci-fi classic FP1 DOES NOT ANSWER (both 1932), about whom the film's scriptwriter Walter Reisch once commented: 'she was a real cuckoo, unhinged and unbalanced'.[43] Fassbinder, who knew her films but was apparently ignorant of her fate, wanted Schmitz to play the mother in PETRA VON KANT when he learned about her suicide twenty years earlier and decided to make her story into a film. His treatment, dating from May 1981, where the heroine is still called Sybille Schmitz, is conceived as a flashback story, in which a reporter, alerted by his girlfriend, a nurse working in a Munich hospital, starts researching the circumstances of her suicide and hits on a number of suspicious characters, including the woman doctor, in whose house Schmitz had been living when she killed herself, and who seemed to be in league with another doctor, an official working for the Munich health department. By issuing and endorsing prescriptions, the two supplied hard drugs to patients for cash, specializing in celebrities from the Nazi period and covering for each other when their charges committed suicide, as appears to have happened on several occasions, when they could no longer pay. The reporter uses his girlfriend as a decoy, but the woman doctor's maid finds out and kills the girlfriend, making it seem an accident. The reporter, suspecting foul play, notifies the police, but he is run over and killed by a car before the matter can be investigated, and the case is dropped for lack of evidence.[44]

VERONIKA VOSS takes over the basic outlines of the treatment, but makes the reporter fall under the spell of the actress when he sees her at one of her own films and then meets her at a tram stop. The film is therefore reminiscent of Billy Wilder's SUNSET BOULEVARD, both telling about a younger man's fascination with a faded movie star, forever expecting and preparing for a come-back. Although still told from the reporter's point of view, VERONIKA VOSS is now the drama of a woman who cannot hold on to her image, and yet is a prisoner of that image. Her addiction to morphine and consequent dependency on Dr Katz is paralleled by a mother-child relationship in what seems a lesbian household, with Dr Katz herself in thrall to the sinister maid. While her physical and psychic disintegration is chronicled as the effect of a threefold withdrawal and loss: of affection, of self-image (or ego-ideal), and of the morphine she takes to compensate for the other two, Veronika's unstoppable descent is punctuated by public performances. After first watching Veronika watch herself on the screen, Krohn, the reporter, also watches her shooting a small scene at a film studio, where she fluffs her lines so many times that the director is obliged to replace her. She gives her most convincing performance, however, when Krohn, accompanied by the police, tries to prize her away from Dr Katz, without success, since Veronika, suddenly panic-stricken at the thought of independence, plays along with Dr Katz' impersonation of a caring friend and host, undermining Krohn's credibility, though not his infatuation. Her most touching, because final, performance comes at a party that Dr Katz gives in her honour, the prelude to her being locked up at home over Easter, while Dr Katz goes on holiday, rightly expecting Veronika not to be alive when she returns.

However, the film is told from Krohn's point of view. What is his interest in Veronika Voss, and in her story, even before she becomes a 'case' with criminal implications? We learn little of Krohn's motivation for an erotic attachment, especially since he seems to be genuinely in love with his girlfriend. But there is enough of a hint of mid-life crisis, of alcohol at work, and the gnawing dissatisfaction with the last-in-line, bottom-of-the-heap existence of a sports reporter, not to make his restlessness plausible. In the film's own terms, though, it is Veronika Voss appearing as if out of blackest night that provides the motivation all by itself for Krohn's life to take a radically different turn. A figure with a past, a figure from the past, she steps on the tram in the Englische Garten like a ghost, which of course is partly what she is. But a ghost of such beauty, such luminosity that she overwhelms Krohn, stepping down from the screen and becoming real, and yet more than real: that primal fantasy of the filmgoer and the daydreamer, always potent, to which Woody Allen in PURPLE ROSE OF CAIRO gave a definitive shape.

But it is also the founding myth and fantasy of a particular genre: that of *film noir*, the obsession with the woman's image on the part of the middle-aged man, whether Dana Andrews in Otto Preminger's LAURA or Edward G Robinson in Fritz Lang's WOMAN IN THE WINDOW. Unlike these mythical *femmes fatales*, Veronika is for Krohn a figure from an overdetermined history – the diabolical past of the Nazi cinema – spreading a very cold but intense light. The fascination of Krohn is also the fascination of Fassbinder, the mise-en-abyme of his life-long ambiguity concerning Ufa, its stars, its directors, its immensely popular and seductive films. In this sense, as Yann Lardeau has noted, Veronika comes to Krohn out of a very particular 'Night and Fog'.[45] But the film can also count on the kind of recognition from the spectator that genre cinema always provides. She is the blonde from Sam Fuller's PICK-UP ON SOUTH STREET and countless other streetcars of desire or subways with brief encounters, yet this particular tram is almost deserted – it takes us back to the trams of the Weimar cinema – Joe May's ASPHALT, for instance, and beyond, to the tram of AFGRØNDEN, where Asta Nielsen first encountered her seducer. So, VERONIKA VOSS eases itself into the thriller format, subgenre film noir without much difficulty. As with MARIA BRAUN, we have a well-established American genre, upon which a typically European art film can graft itself or be segued into. This double reference may explain why VERONIKA VOSS proved rather more successful than LOLA, for we read the new across the familiarity with the old, in an almost imperceptible transfer.

This transfer is historically already anchored in the way the first postwar films dealing with Nazism, whether made in Germany or elsewhere, instinctively seemed to refer themselves to elements of *film noir*.[46] It also explains why Fassbinder has, for this particular story, chosen to shoot in black-and-white. But what kind of black and white! It is a film in which the blacks, the greys promise just a little security and respite, but where the white is deadly. Never before has white seemed so menacing, so evil as in the apartment of Dr Katz, and in the room that will become both prison and grave to Veronika. Not a *film noir*, then, but a *film blanc*, or as Lardeau puts it, not a film in black-and-white, but a film either black or white, in which the white eventually drives out the black, and with it, pushes into oblivion the person that once was Veronika Voss. 'Without shadow a person cannot live, without it a person has no soul because no secrets'[47]: Lardeau sees in Veronika the echo and reinterpretation of an essential motif of expressionist cinema, from the STUDENT OF PRAGUE who sold his shadow, to THE CABINET OF DR CALIGARI, with Veronika the Cesare to Dr Katz' Caligari.[48] Even if one thinks this is a little far-fetched, it emphasizes how pervasively metaphorical the (non-)colour white in VERONIKA VOSS ultimately becomes: from the unnaturally white decor in Dr Katz' apartment, which evokes the clinical abstractions and the presence of death emanating from hospitals and medical installations, here transferred into the domestic sphere, turning the home into its worst perversion, a test laboratory for unspeakably cruel human experiments.[49] White is in this context inevitably also associated with the drugs to which Veronika is addicted, and via drugs, the whiteness of forgetting, oblivion, self-annihilation, but also a blotting, a rubbing out of the stain from whatever the guilt is about that so stubbornly refuses to go away. At the extreme, it is the cinema itself become the medium of forgetting, with Veronika hiding in the light from the life she can no longer control.[50] VERONIKA VOSS: not just a *film blanc*, but a film blank.

Blank, too, in that the mise-en-scène creates around the whites of decor, lighting and overexposed sets a kind of vortex, absorbing love and fascination, inexorably moving towards madness and self-annihilation all that energy which manifests itself in Veronika's struggle, in which so much light but so little warmth is generated from the intensity of her person and her plight. It is, to borrow the German title of another Fassbinder film, DESPAIR, with which it may after all have more in common than seems at first, 'a journey into light': here the film-within-the-film that opens VERONIKA VOSS functions rather like the early scene of Hermann Hermann watching himself make love to his wife, initiating in both films a descending spiral and yet another figuration of the vicious circles on which all of Fassbinder's films are built.

The Star, Show Business, Woman

VERONIKA VOSS can be regarded either as a film about drugs (and in this respect offers some autobiographical speculations, if only insofar as Veronika is unable to maintain the creative force that the drugs so magically seemed to bestow on Fassbinder the director), or it can be seen as a film about the cinema, in particular, the difficult transfer from the old Ufa cinema to the post-war West German movie business, and from Papa's Kino to the New German Cinema.[51] Such might be the allegorical import of the story Fassbinder chose to tell, in which he has more than a casual interest, given his rather less hostile attitude to these traditions than was shown by many other filmmakers of the 1970s, and given his special interest in the stars of the 1950s, such as Karlheinz Böhm or Brigitta Mira, whom he cast in some of the most interesting roles in their careers. Thus, VERONIKA VOSS can indeed be seen as the casting of Sybille Schmitz for a role he was, alas, too late in offering to her in person.

Its relevance and place in the BRD Trilogy is at best oblique and indirect, for although the 1950s are evoked, they cannot be said to feature as strongly as they do in MARIA BRAUN, for instance, and (contrary to the original treatment) the finished film hardly, if at all, refers to Veronika's embroilment with either Goebbels or the regime. At any event, while it may make sense to tell the story of the United States of Eisenhauer across the cinema which was Hollywood, the Germany of Adenauer is generally not known for its cinema (though perhaps undeservedly, Fassbinder might argue), which would make Veronika – even in her 'failure' to become a movie star of the 1950s – rather less an icon across which to figure national history, than say, Marilyn Monroe or James Dean for the same period in the United States.

That the situation is different when it comes to Nazism is an argument I hope to make more fully in the following chapter. In VERONIKA VOSS, the topic of fascism is present only in a displaced form, where it surfaces – the more strongly, one could argue, but also quite controversially – in a subplot not found in the film treatment, namely the story of the old Jewish couple. Survivors of the camps and also in the thrall of Dr Katz, they decide at a certain point to take their own lives rather than be forced to do so by the doctor's implacable greed. If a Dr Katz and her accomplice are ominous figures from the 1950s, whom one might hope to see simply fade away – in more settled or enlightened decades – or be duly punished, the place of Krohn as a 1950s figure is less certain. As the journalist-detective, he does belong to the period (though of another country), as does his obsession with the *femme fatale*, but whether this makes him a representative of either Germany or the Bavarian demi-monde of the 1950s is difficult to decide. In one sense, he too is an outsider, a stranger to the corrupt and affluent world of Katz, but also to the world of the movies, as his ignorance about Veronika's career indicates. He even seems an outsider, not unlike Hermann Braun, to the drama he witnesses and possibly unwittingly helps to precipitate. Like so many Fassbinder heroes, from the American Soldier to the Merchant of Four Seasons, from Bolwieser to Franz Biberkopf, from Hermann Hermann to Hermann Braun, Krohn is a loner, a passer-by and passer-through of life. It is therefore quite difficult to know what value to ascribe to his final gesture when, his girlfriend killed because of him and her death as unavenged and unatoned for as that of Veronika, he goes back to the office to cover yet another football match. This is unmistakeably reminiscent of the game which concludes MARIA BRAUN, and thus signals the kind of silent explosion that in the milieux of the Katzes of Germany will never take place. It may also be the response which the genre of the hard-boiled *film noir* leads us to expect: the mystery unravelled, the detective, misogynist and cynical, resigned and wise to the ways of the world, consoles himself for the loss of both women, probably calculating that one was a bad girl anyway and the other too pure and good to survive except in his memory. However, this genre convention in an art film might just be the kind of gesture by which Fassbinder directs our attention elsewhere, as if to say, Krohn is not who and what this story has been about...

Krohn's ultimate insignificance only underscores the most obvious feature that the three films of the BRD Trilogy have in common: they are centred on a female heroine, each of whom, perhaps even more crucially, lives her life through the realities and values of show business, which constitutes them, makes them into what they are, and gives them a field of action, a terrain for being that exceeds the scope their lives might otherwise have had. All three films have the cinema as historical point of reference: MARIA BRAUN is replete with allusions to other films, VERONIKA VOSS a *film noir* which cites the Nazi cinema as its internal vantage point, and LOLA, finally, was conceived as a remake of THE BLUE ANGEL. Although little has survived of this last concept, Lola's most devastating number is a torch-song called 'Am Tag als der Regen kam'. This just happens to be the title of the film (and, of course, the theme tune) in which Mario Adorf, who in LOLA plays Schuckert, the all-powerful entrepreneur and Lola's sugar daddy, had one of the early triumphs of his acting career. As to show business in the wider sense, Maria Braun would not have made it in the world of business, labour relations and high finance, domains dominated by men, without having first been a bar-hostess and professional entertainer of men. Veronika may no longer have her name in big letters on the silver screen, but she can still put on convincingly the spectacle of suffering that so attracts the sports reporter (and repels Krohn's girlfriend), or inversely, the spectacle of vulnerability and gratitude to Dr Katz which forever puts the police off the scent. And Lola is above all a performer, both in and out of the brothel in which she sings, services Schuckert, and which eventually she owns.

Focussed on performers, the films are also built around a dramaturgical principle of counterpoint: an independent woman making her way, surrounded by men who are both omnipresent and somehow marginal, with the counterpoint revolving around supposedly 'male preserves' such as sports, particularly football, as if to signal ways of talking about politics across the personal and the social. In two of the films, German political events are explicitly invoked: Konrad Adenauer's U-turn regarding German rearmament and Nato (MARIA BRAUN), the economic miracle of the construction boom (MARIA BRAUN, LOLA), Ludwig Ehrhard's 'social market economy' and anti-nuclear protest (LOLA), corruption scandals in local government and the ban of the communist party (LOLA). And yet, invariably, these function in the narrative as amplifications and foils of themes that are centred elsewhere.

The question this raises is why Fassbinder thought that the history of Germany (his grand project in the middle years of his career) was best told through the fate of women.[52] I have already discussed the answer most critics implicitly assumed, namely the allegorizing power of the female when the notions of nation or country are at issue, but I have also hesitated to take this reading for granted. On the other hand, feminist film theory has for some time alerted us to the problematic status of the woman involved in and offered as spectacle. It is not difficult to understand the fate of both Maria Braun and Veronika Voss as that of victims – and above all as victims of the world of men, with their victimization greatly aggravated by being the object of the look, by being implicated in the dehumanizing, commodifying power of spectacle, and thus thwarted in their selfhood, by having no other choice than constituting themselves as objects to be looked at, in order to become subjects. Veronika's exhibitionism of suffering is staged around performances that involve imaging and the gaze; in the scene where she refuses to be 'rescued' by Krohn, all the suspense and drama are in the looks that circulate between Krohn and Dr Katz, Dr Katz and her maid, the policemen, Krohn and Dr Katz.

Similarly in the other two films, crucial scenes are staged as the woman gives herself as spectacle to men. In LOLA, for instance, one scene has Lola wanting to be noticed by von Bohm, even betting on getting from him a formal acknowledgement. She achieves her goal with a true campaign, planned in stages to ensure a double effect of mystery and surprise, the first of which involves being seen, and the second one, being seen to be seen. Early on in MARIA BRAUN, Maria and her friend Vevi sit in the bar, with Vevi pointing out a black soldier at another table. V: 'Don't tell me you haven't noticed him' – MB: 'No. Which one is he' – V: 'The one over there. He was perfectly normal until you came in, now he sits there like he's paralyzed... Look at him: just like Willy Fritsch' [the most popular matinee idol in the 1930s and 1940s). MB: 'How do I look?' – V: 'Great. Why?' – MB: 'Because I want to look great right now.' (Maria walks across:) 'Will you dance with me, Mr Bill?' A complex architecture of shot-countershot between the women and the silently staring Bill orchestrate this exchange.

Yet these examples also indicate that the women in Fassbinder's films are all too aware of both a power and a presence that they draw from being looked at, and are usually prepared to deploy, knowing full well that it is a weapon that can cut both ways. The most ambiguous figure in this respect is undoubtedly Veronika, in love with her own image, needing that image to return to her, but realizing more and more that it is an image which only Dr

Katz can give to her, under specified conditions, and on loan so to speak. One might go further and say that Veronika Voss is a Maria Braun who dared to look into the mirror, when Maria avoided doing so, or that other, self-centred and self-directed side of Maria who, at the very moment she makes herself 'image' for her husband, realizes that she is about to lose all power over that image, and thus over herself, preferring to 'blow it all' rather than commute it into the small change of marital attrition.

If specular power relations are central in each of the films that make up the BRD trilogy, they are ones in which the woman as image is alert to the power of that image, which may well explain the meaning of the signifier 'show-business' in the films, and also define what might be at stake when calling Fassbinder's heroines 'strong women'. But what exactly does this mean? Fassbinder has often talked about why he preferred female lead characters to figure as the film's central consciousness. He has hinted that for him, a woman is more 'medial' (in the sense of being in touch with the *Zeitgeist*, 'sensitive' to both its superficial driving forces and deeper libidinal currents) and unlike a man, can 'lend herself to others but give herself only to herself', in the words of Jean Luc Godard's Nana in VIVRE SA VIE.[53] Maria's own description of herself comes to mind, as 'a specialist in matters of the future' and 'the Mata Hari of the Economic Miracle', which emphasizes her self-understanding as a woman who can adapt herself quickly, who is as mercurial and medial as she needs to be, an opportunist in the best and most literal sense, supple and capable of intervening on both sides at once, where men are blinkered and awkward.[54] Twice Maria's skills as a negotiator are highlighted in the film: once when she knows what women want (nylon stockings), and once when she knows what men want (when dealing with union bosses). At the same time, she is a woman who 'stops at nothing' (in German, the metaphoric phrase is 'geht über Leichen' which would apply to her almost literally, when one thinks of the fate of Bill).

Thus, what holds the films together in the final instance is the mise-en-scène of the woman as image. While this notion has become something of a cliché in feminist film studies, it is in these films of Fassbinder open to a number of different readings: the power of self-display, of female exhibitionism, the reification of the image, the society of the spectacle, the woman trapped in her image or using her image to make it in the world of men, and thus using the energy contained in the image as the power of self-alienation. More precisely, the question arises of how in films about women, and about women as image, the women are nonetheless perceived as strong, rather than as victims, exploited and objectified? A test case is LOLA, and it may be useful to look more closely at the structures that put into play the energies Fassbinder regards as inherent in the notion of woman as spectacle.

Politics, Melodrama and Intelligence: Lola

LOLA is the story of an independent woman who, left with a child, has to balance her options very carefully and pick her way through a treacherous world by being ruthless and resolute, yielding and ultra-feminine at one and the same time. In the story of her long-drawn out and carefully staged seduction of Bohm, she acts as both the means of corruption and that corruption's most potent vaccine: in her relation with Schuckert, the local construction boss, on whose payroll all people that matter have landed in one way or another, Lola displays the kind of emancipation which for the 1970s looking back at the 1950s appears as heroism and courage of a special kind. The brothel in which much of the film is set becomes not only a microcosm of small town society, its patriarchal attitudes and Tamanny hall politics (itself reminiscent of an even earlier period, that of Wilhelmine society with its 'Stammtisch' and Victorian double standards), but also a microcosm of the world of women, in their struggle to be economically independent, run their own businesses and still be part of the male world.

It is here that Fassbinder's particular dramatic skill in deploying the resources of melodrama for a historical chronicle becomes most evident. In LOLA, the uses of melodrama far exceed its function as an instrument of style or mise-en-scène. What is at issue is not so much to give a certain reality the colours of emotion in order to bring it closer to a general public or to make it apparent as artifice by heightening the narrative action and the clash of sentiment and temperament; as so often in the later films, Fassbinder adds through melodrama another, distinct level of experience. The stylistic signs of melodrama, be they in the narrative line (in the case of LOLA: the irresistible rise and fall of municipal planning director von Bohm), in the dialogue (for instance, when Lola says to von Bohm: "I only cry because I'm so happy") or in the music (the sensual pitch that rises to a climax when Lola sings 'Am Tag als der Regen kam') – are all, as is the intertextual and musical 'perspectivism' discussed earlier, in the service of differentiating between an inner and an outer reality, in order to make subjective and objective states or experiences simultaneously accessible to the audience. This 'subjectivity', on the other hand, is not that of the author, of course, but of his protagonists, who are often not the coherently motivated, psychologically unified characters of Hollywood, driven by a single desire, obsessed by an idée fixe, dominated by an unambiguous goal, but divided in themselves, torn and tormented, often acting in ignorance of or in contradiction to their own innermost being, what I called the double-bind as source of energy.

In other words, what makes Fassbinder's characters so fascinating is ultimately their intelligence. Not in any scholarly or professional sense (say, von Bohm's competence as planning chief, or Schuckert's financial wizardry, though in the confrontation between the men, this mutual recognition of talent plays an important role); rather, it is the sort of intelligence which enables the characters to stand by their own contradictions and inconsistencies, in a manner that energizes their capacity for action rather than blocking it. Melodrama and its reversals of fortune are here not the expression of a world of emotions for those who cannot think, or victims of circumstance, and instead, the very signs of self-knowledge, honesty and lack of cant. In the case of the main protagonists of LOLA, this may seem a particularly extravagant or perverse claim, given that the film is so often read as the exact opposite: a document of the moral hypocrisy, mealy mouthed opportunism and corrupt influence-peddling that was supposed to have typified the West Germany of the economic miracle. But looked at from a little closer, Lola, von Bohm, Schuckert and even Esslin, the Bakunin-reader, disappointed idealist and left-wing melancholic, along with von Bohm's secretary and Schuckert's stuck-up wife all manifest to varying degrees and on varying occasions a particular brand of insight and acuity which makes LOLA one of the wittiest, sharpest but also most sardonic post-war German films altogether. One can speak of different kinds of intelligence: sensual, moral, and political. For instance, Schuckert's wife shows political intelligence when, instead of scratching out her rival's eyes on learning that Lola will marry von Bohm and therefore have access to the highest social circles of town, she says to her: 'you're a woman to reckon with'. Von Bohm's landlady shows sensual intelligence when she lets him know that his new seersucker suit is a mistake, a judgement confirmed by Lola's moral intelligence when she qualifies the suit as 'hypocritical'. Sensual intelligence is not only Schuckert's preserve (whom Lola calls, not without respect the 'spirited pig'), but also von Bohm's, when he practises the hit of the Capri-fisher on his violin as ardently as he does Schubert.

Put more generally, the kinds of intelligence on display might help resituate what is at stake in LOLA. Not, I would argue, the story of THE BLUE ANGEL, in which a sexually frustrated bureaucrat is made a fool of by the night-club singer Lola-Lola who coolly recognizes the masochist in Rath beneath his authoritarian bluster. Nor is it the story of a good and morally upright person, seduced into success by money, sex and the promise of power, nor even the tale of someone who thinks himself morally superior, but whose arrogance meets its just deserts. On the contrary, it would seem that such interpretations lack intelligence, in the sense I have just been attributing to Fassbinder's characters, precisely by implicitly assuming moral superiority and better political judgement, of the kind sometimes found among the anti-capitalist left of the 1970s (the 'third generation') that so irritated and depressed Fassbinder. Phrased the other way round, one could say that a film like LOLA asks itself, how is it possible that a society like the Federal Republic of Germany actually works? One might be tempted to think that LOLA gives the answer: because the ruling class is corrupt, immoral and mercenary. But this only proves that the critics of capitalism have learnt nothing, or at any rate, that even the sympathetic critics of Fassbinder's films seriously underrate his characters. Of course, the question is: why was this society so successful in becoming both a leading capitalist power and a consensus democracy, when by rights it should not have been either, given the provincialism, the venality and hypocrisy, the lack of public spirit when it came to confronting the past, and finally, the hypochondria and self-pity usually ascribed to West Germans? This problem is so central to the films of Fassbinder's BRD trilogy precisely because it is so much harder to answer than might appear at first.

Thus, the issue of corruption in LOLA is really quite complicated, as can be seen from one key scene, for instance, when the prostitutes waiting for customers in the brothel start a long discussion about the difference between one who counts for something and one who pays (revolving around the pun of 'zählen' and 'zahlen'). Or again, in the manner in which the new breed of entrepreneurialism and the social market economy are thematized, the film takes a fairly differentiated stance. With the kind of contemporary perspective that Fassbinder was interested in, the film recognizes the double role of what is now called the 'medium-size' businesses ('Mittelständische Betriebe', the backbone of Germany's industrial strength as a supplier of specialized tools and high surplus value niche products) as the buccaneers of 'primitive accumulation' who had to operate on the margins of a bureaucracy still tainted by fascist state dirigism and a legality as yet untested. Schuckert, for instance, leaving Church on Sunday morning, gives money to striking workers outside and makes a donation to the 'Friends of Bakunin', to the great consternation of both his wife and the anarchist Esslin: 'if I give my money over there (pointing to the Church), I don't see why I shouldn't give it over here'. The film is exceedingly sympathetic towards Schuckert, not only because he makes an excellent – and sexy – villain, but because the kind of risks he takes function within the world the film portrays as catalysts, while his sort of speculator's nimbleness always energizes those around him. Even without spelling out the parallels between Schuckert and Fassbinder himself, or between rebuilding a market economy in the Germany of the 1950s and rebuilding a film industry in the 1970s – both negotiating a modus vivendi between state support and private capital – it seems evident that Fassbinder saw a figure such as Schuckert in several dimensions, much in the way he saw the commercial producers he increasingly did business with: Wendlandt, Waldleitner, Eckelkamp, Gaumont, Hollywood...

The logic of LOLA implies that it becomes a matter of political intelligence – even from the point of view of democracy, and not only out of expediency or cynicism – for von Bohm eventually to comprehend that the purpose of his job as the city's chief planning officer cannot be, as he threatens at one point, 'to go all out and ruin' property tycoon Schuckert and his local power cartel. It is therefore not only weakness and sexual infatuation that makes von Bohm give in, but also the insight, never directly named but implied by the very emphasis Fassbinder puts on the intelligence of his characters and the dramatic structure of the intrigue, which proceeds in a suitably dialectical fashion.

One of the most striking stylistic features of LOLA points in a similar direction. I am referring to the many short scenes, often only briefly sketched, before a direct cut moves the viewer to another, rarely causally or chronologically consecutive scene. Barely has the audience gained a foothold in the action, when Fassbinder jerks them away, boldly racking the focus or covering the lens in order to redirect our attention. It is not only the director's way of letting the viewer know who is 'in charge' among these power-hungry sharks in the provincial pond called Coburg, but his way of obliging us to understand that the action also contains another level of abstraction and reference, from whence the connexions among the fragments and the logic that binds them into a narrative become comprehensible.

Love Story vs The Family

This logic needs to be analyzed further, and it seems to imply a redefinition of how one sees the films linked to the topic of Germany. When I started with the question of what makes the main protagonists of these films 'strong women', the answer which emerged was that neither their allegorical figurations emblematically representing the nation nor their victim status quite accounted for their narrative and emotional functions. A strong woman turned out to be a woman in show business, at the centre of a nexus of power and spectacle, in which the traditional 'woman-as-image', 'woman-to-be-looked-at' merely indicated that there had to be another structure beneath that of voyeurism. Given that their intelligence is much in evidence, as is their ability to deploy it to their own advantage, these female heroines at once instantiate and subvert the basic configurations in Fassbinder, which is that all politics, all action in the world of men becomes spectacle, becomes show business. Yet the way they subvert it may at first glance look like being the very means that victimizes them: their capacity to love.

All of Fassbinder's films have in common that they are love stories. What the films of the BRD trilogy have in common is that despite being 'about' Germany, they are still love stories, a point worth insisting on for two reasons: one, it directs our attention to the kinds of love story he tells, and two, this feature makes them different from other films of the New German Cinema, dealing with fascism and its aftermath. First of all, Fassbinder's films are unconventional love stories on their own terms: MARIA BRAUN is predicated on the central relationship remaining unconsummated (but in the minor key there is Oswald's love for Maria), VERONIKA VOSS is a love story between two times two women (with in the minor key, Krohn's love for Veronika), and LOLA is a love story between sex and power (with the minor key provided by von Bohm's love for Lola).

The real perversity, however, is elsewhere. By opting for love stories as the moral if not the dramatic core, Fassbinder's BRD trilogy runs in a counter-current to other films concentrating on the German family and on family history, such as THE GERMAN SISTERS, GERMANY PALE MOTHER, and HEIMAT, which are, respectively, a sister-sister story, a mother-daughter story, and a family saga, faintly echoing Hollywood genres of the 1970s and 1980s having to do with history and oppression, like THE COLOR PURPLE or ROOTS. Ever since DW Griffith, there is no mystery about the importance of the family in mainstream cinema either as representation or as addressee.[55] The rise to prominence of the family in the New German cinema, on the other hand, was a gradual process, tied to the rediscovery of history, or rather its absence when history is conceived as change. For the clearer it became to the generation of the 1960s that the society built up in West Germany since 1945 had not broken with the essentially patriarchal-authoritarian structures associated with Wilhelmine, Weimar and Nazi Germany, the more the family became a key point of attack. For the new Left, the historical references were rarely the opposing ideological and economic systems of the two Germanys, and much more Germany's Fascist past with its impact on the present, while the psychological reference point was the family, the conflict between the generations, the guilt-laden and traumatic contacts between fathers and sons, mothers and daughters.[56] As a consequence, national identity, personal identity, the German question were diffusely filtered through or symbolized by oedipal scenarios and their affective ambivalences. This was true not only of the cinema. It could also be seen in the wave of autobiographical and confessional novels which began to appear in the 1970s, often written in order to finally settle accounts with parental authority figures and their representatives, and where the almost forgotten childhood of a whole generation was being exorcised by showing its long shadow still falling over the present.[57]

In one sense, the focus on the family in the New German Cinema is only a more localized variant, textured with historical references, of a phenomenon common to most Western societies, suffering from the so-called 'fatherless society' and the 'crisis of patriarchy'. While social psychologists like Alexander Mitscherlich or Christopher Lash saw in it the conflicting pressures that capitalism and paternity exert on male role models, and sociologists point to the increase of single-(female) parent families, Hollywood's concentration on young boys and adolescents with oedipal crises as heroes (from STAR WARS to ET, from BACK TO THE FUTURE to THE TERMINATOR) might just be an astute calculation of their primary audiences – young males between fourteen and twenty-four. Significantly, some of the films of the New German Cinema that did best internationally such as Werner Herzog's AGUIRRE and KASPAR HAUSER, Wim Wenders' PARIS TEXAS, and even Edgar Reitz' HEIMAT feature the return of prodigal sons or the revolt of self-exiled orphans.[58] But whereas most of the Hollywood films revolve around a doubly displaced father image (as, for instance, in the INDIANA JONES trilogy, returning as superfather and then going away), in most German films it is the absence of fathers which gives rise to sentimental Kaspar Hauser stories.

This would set up a paradigm: two symmetrically related models of what happens when the bourgeois family falls apart: one is New Hollywood, the other the New German Cinema, one reaching the big public, the other withering on the vine, even before anyone properly understood what it was all about. Against these, Fassbinder's cinema appears as the third possibility. I argued earlier that his films mount not only a critique of the bourgeois German family, but a critique of the critique one finds in the films of the New German Cinema (the mother/daughter films no less than the family round the dinner table, or father/son stories). It is not as if Fassbinder did not show family life. We have seen, in previous chapters, that there are plenty of families, and his films are not short of portraits of appallingly destructive marriages. THE MERCHANT OF FOUR SEASONS, MOTHER KÜSTER'S TRIP TO HEAVEN, FEAR OF FEAR, MARTHA, FEAR EATS THE SOUL are so full of non-functioning couples that evidently Fassbinder had as little need to believe in marriage as he had every need to believe in love. The family for Fassbinder is not only the Laingian schizo-factory discussed earlier, damaging the individual for life because it does not give him/her the resources to create out of the double-binds the new deal of (Deleuze-Guattari's) rhizomatic energies, circuits and productivities. More important in the representation of the past and of Germany than the choice of socio-political topic was the shift from family sagas to love stories in view of a different kind of economy.

Taking out a Contract

If conventionally love leads to marriage, especially in the cinema, then Fassbinder's films go against the grain, since here, a woman's love leads to a pact, with the consequence that all these love stories are centred on a contract. In MARIA BRAUN, it is between Oswald and Hermann, but also between Maria and Hermann. In VERONIKA VOSS, the deal is between Veronika and Dr Katz,[59] and in LOLA between von Bohm and Schuckert, between Lola and von Bohm, between Schuckert and Lola, and indirectly, between Schuckert and Marie, Lola's daughter. A contract identifies in the first instance separate parties and recognizes separate interests, and thus a minimum of acceptance of otherness. This ability to make such distinctions is often thematized in Fassbinder, sometimes as the (ambiguous) ability to disengage personal emotions from business: in this form it recurs in both MARIA BRAUN and LOLA. It is usually interpreted negatively, as in MARIA BRAUN, for instance, where Hermann says to Maria: 'Is this how it is among people outside? so cold?' when she tells him about her business career. But the film does not encourage us to side with Hermann: this may be the way Fassbinder signals intelligence, for Maria's behaviour highlights not coldness but the capacity to differentiate, not in order to keep separate, but as the necessary prerequisite for union. The pronouncements are thus not mere cynicism on Maria's part, as can be seen by a similar and similarly strict differentiation she insists on with Oswald ('let's say that I wanted you'). It may have, as we shall see, also a forward-looking, utopian dimension, indeed it is a prelude to a love which, in a reversal of early Fassbinder, is still a love that is colder than death (see below). For what seems to operate is that, paradoxically, in these films, women withdraw themselves from established circuits of exchange in order to participate in others, even though these other conduits are not outside the dialectic of the gendered systems of exchange, where women are objects of exchange between men. The emphasis on these acts of exchange, I shall argue, becomes also the promise of a radical reversal, the possibility of absolute equality.

In this sense, MARIA BRAUN is a much more radical challenge to what one means by value. And not only of the values of marriage, loyalty, honesty, business ethics, but of the category of value itself. In the margins of the widely held view of Maria Braun as the symbol of German capitalism,[60] there is something else, more properly a dialectic between the strong women, on the one hand, and a new kind of economics on the other, superficially perhaps to be labelled 'capitalism' but potentially pointing in a different direction. For although at the end of MARIA BRAUN the pact between Oswald and Hermann merely seems to confirm the old paradigm, of a woman traded between two men, it is done so openly, so triumphantly, and yet at the same time, also so much in keeping with Maria's own values (the wheels within wheels structure of her desire) that one wonders whether it is not also overtaken by yet another structure which goes beyond the rise of capitalism in West Germany and the left-wing pessimism of the road not taken (supposedly the themes of MARIA BRAUN). For in the end, everyone has become so wealthy as to allow them to suspend all exchange values in the gesture of the gift, itself the mark of a quite different economy.[61]

If the (marriage-)contract is thus a double act of defiance, against the 'family' as either schizo-factory or theatre of traumatized patriarchy, the function of love in this constellation is first of all to provide a focus for 'coldness', in the sense of the ability to differentiate, and secondly, to legitimate an ethics of intransigence, itself the 'cold' side of romantic yearning and of idealized self-denial. For this intransigence cuts both ways: it differentiates between Maria Braun or Lola lending themselves to others but giving themselves only to themselves, while preserving the possibility that such a self necessarily constitutes itself through an 'other,' this 'other' being in some sense the product and object of a – strictly speaking – impossible love.

One can now see why the strong Fassbinder woman is both involved in showbusiness and intransigent in her demand for love, knowing full well that at stake is an impossible love. It is her way of initiating a different form of exchange, in the course of which a structure other than that of being-looked-at, a way for power to circulate other than via the woman-as-sign is established, which in its turn deconstructs and resituates the power potential of the look, while reaffirming the principles of exchange and the economies of desire.

The example of LOLA may help to clarify this point. What, one is led to ask, is it that the characters want in the end? A cynical view is that Lola wants sex, power and money, deftly exploiting the infatuation of Bohm and the class-and-status anxiety of Schuckert. A more charitable view, derived from Sirkean melodrama, is that all characters have been chasing unattainable objects, thus demonstrating the law of desire as formulated by Oscar Wilde: 'the only thing worse than not getting what you want is getting what you want'. Yet it might be worth entertaining the hypothesis that the film aims at a new definition of what an individual might consider to be of value, and thus what might be desire, both in relation to oneself, and in one's dealings with others, notably in terms of what one learns from others about one's own value.

In this context, the figure of Esslin, go-between, outsider and jaundiced chorus, has a role at once structurally crucial and ideologically implausible (because caricatural). Adjusting his self between von Bohm, the 'Friends of Bakunin' circle, the Mayor and Schuckert, he is able to calculate his value fairly precisely and to set his price accordingly. His trajectory in the film is that of the ultimate opportunist, changing his masters more often than his shirts, but by that very token he is also the demonstration of the functional relativity of value per se. On the other hand, the manner in which von Bohm becomes for Lola and Lola for von Bohm an object of value and eventually of love is one of the film's moral centres, not least because their mutual accumulation of value for each other proceeds in a highly asymmetrical manner, considering for instance that Lola's initial interest in von Bohm derives from the tremor of uncertainty his appearance in town causes the local big-wigs. Given her own ambivalent power-relation to these local dignitaries, it is easy to sympathize with Lola as she hopes by attracting von Bohm's attention and erotic interest to participate in his political power potential by proxy (she calls it "indirect"). However, as we saw, when she finally falls in love with him, it is for none of these premeditated reasons, but because the two of them make music together, singing folk songs in an empty church on a Sunday date.

The Stock Exchange of Impossible Equivalences

This stock-exchange of values, constantly redefining and in-differentiating its claims across the film's various erotic and erotetic encounters, gives LOLA both its inner dynamics of suspense and its external, political provocativeness. But the play of tolerances can only deploy itself so promiscuously because Fassbinder is dealing with a society in the process of transformation and reconstruction, of boom-and-bust, as was indeed the case with the Federal Republic of the 1950s. The salt in this soup, however, is once more the protagonists' all-round intelligence, which – because of its sovereign ability to live with contradictory positions, with twists on the political stage and turns in the moral stakes – seems uniquely equipped to enter into very different and for the spectator often unexpected alliances with others, in which emotional, power-political or economic factors polymorphously-perversely combine and mingle. One already mentioned instance is the way the women in the film circulate according to the most archaic patriarchal law as objects of exchange between the men (Lola between Schuckert and von Bohm, Schuckert's wife, the housekeeper and even Lola's daughter Marie between different male authority figures), which nonetheless frequently allows them to initiate new modes of exchange by suddenly upending value systems most vulnerable in the micro-power politics of a small-town society still reverberating from historical shock but also from the shock energies of risk capital and rapacious entrepreneurism.

It is worth noting the elaborate contractual arrangements by which the brothel changes ownership and passes into the possession of Lola's daughter. The terms of the deed and the working out of its implications make up the final part of the film, leaving on one level the bridegroom von Bohm as the cuckolded dupe and Lola triumphant, but on another level allowing Schuckert to give something away in order the better to keep it, while also effectively putting von Bohm as legitimate pater familias in charge of an enterprise in which everyone is everyone else's symbolic stand-in, guardian and thus 'representative'. What seems a cold-hearted move by an inveterate gold-digger turns out to be a most elaborately 'democratic' system of checks and balances between Lola, von Bohm and Schuckert, presided over by Cupid or Eros in the form of an ex-prostitute's illegitimate daughter. In its multi-layered reciprocity the deeds in LOLA resemble nothing so much as the pacts in MARIA BRAUN between Oswald and Hermann, between Maria Braun and Oswald, between Hermann and Maria Braun which, although non-equivalent, nevertheless, when superimposed, contrive to make every-one rich – in death.

Thus the circles close upon themselves which in truth are neither circles nor closed. They allow Fassbinder to manifest himself in a double guise: as the author who succeeds in giving his work the inner logic and coherence, the amplitude and reverberation of a 'work' (the potentially pompous but strategically highly marketable concept of the trilogy), and as the artist whose political intelligence manages to keep faith with the idea of the group as a viable community, with the ideal of a permanent revolution of values, and with anarchism as a political vision – as if in the early 1970s he had put aside his Bakunin only in order to reclaim him the more insistently at last, no longer to combat inequality in a world based on scarcity, but to maintain non-equivalence in a world coming to terms with superfluity and abundance. Equality and irreducible singularity are still the twin poles of a dignified human existence. But instead of being the vanishing point of a political programme which cannot but be utopian, these values have become the variables in a staging of human agency and desire that is designed to keep open the processes which assign value and singularity that determine their constellations and regulate their exchanges. Among these processes, or so at least it would seem in MARIA BRAUN and LOLA, capitalism as an economic system has its role to play and even proves itself the liberator of energies, for only when human beings no longer need to struggle for their naked survival, only when they possess, besides an intelligence of the head, the body and the heart, also a bank account and a business card, can they enter into and entertain an economy of the gift, as the protagonists of these two films try to create. This of course also indicates their limits, or rather their status as figures of a design, a pattern, and thus creatures of an artist's vision. Far from merely presenting to a moribund society the distorting mirror of satire, or the sarcasm of the disgruntled revolutionary, LOLA is finally a surprisingly optimistic film, tender to its characters and to that extent directed towards their future, without sacrificing its sharply targeted project of being an image of a past period and its mores.

Conclusion

This chapter has been trying to look at three of Fassbinder's most celebrated films within a set of interlocking concerns, which on the one hand had to do with the act of reading or interpretation – seeing them as at once complexly allegorical texts in relation to a doubly mediated history – that of representations of Germany and of film history, between Hollywood and the European cinema.

But an effort was also made to give some definition to what it means that at the centre of each film stands a woman – at once a sign and a centre of energy, at once a 'representative' figure and one that slips from under any form of official representation. Instead, the figure claims attention by virtue of a peculiarly paradoxical mixture of opportunism and intransigence, of manipulated image and self-directed egotism – a paradox I have tried to define across the notion that these films embody particular kinds of love stories – love stories coming after marriage, coming outside marriage, coming separated from 'family'. What makes these love stories, or rather this love of which they are the stories, notable is how they open up within the political and social field a certain kind of space, the space of uneven exchange and incommensurability. With it, they become political not because they are set *against* world historical or political events, but because the nature of the relations they provoke and necessitate are inherently political. I have called them 'contracts' or 'pacts', in which these love stories find their stability and logic, as well as proposing a more utopian and (permanently) revolutionary dimension to the conduits of intercourse and desire.

Whereas, as we have seen in a previous chapter, Fassbinder's directly political analysis tended to be at once pessimistic and neo-liberal, satirizing the revolutionary left in films like THE NIKLASHAUSEN JOURNEY and condemning the ultra-left and its unholy alliance with the right in THE THIRD GENERATION, the BRD Trilogy takes a hard look at the dominant Christian Democrat status quo. Recognizing it to be deeply entangled in fascism, Fassbinder nonetheless makes a distinction between the class-nature of West German politics (the German bourgeoisie) and the economic system (American capitalism). While there are few signs of sympathy with the German bourgeoisie (whose history Fassinder tried to outline in his aborted adaptation of Gustav Freytag's *Soll und Haben*), his estimation of capitalism is both nuanced and contradictory. Liberal in their politics, the films of the trilogy allow us to recognize the nature of Fassbinder's radicalism: capitalism and show-business are, on the one hand, best embodied in women, in individuals capable of striking a bargain and sealing a deal – which may also be a pact with the devil, as VERONIKA VOSS might suggest, but as the chapter on LILI MARLEEN will indicate in more detail, show-business deals can also take one straight back to German history.

In the BRD trilogy the contracts are not at the margins, but at the very centres of German society's power structures, mostly dominated by men (VERONIKA VOSS may be regarded as the exception), but 'open' to women thanks to the ambivalent, reversible, soft-and-hard circuits between power and show-business, the 'politics of spectacle' which women seem to enter, often at great risk to themselves. This radicalism gives the films a certain paradoxical other-worldy serenity, and suggests an almost Nietzschean 'gay science' with regards to capitalism, criticised from within, by hinting at utopian dimensions in its different economies. In this specific and limited sense, the BRD trilogy is after all the celebration of a certain energy and of a certain optimism about the capacity of Fassbinder's characters not only to establish 'working' circuits of desire and exchange, but to be able to sustain them under the law of the spectacle, and thus by extension, the (media worlds of) cinema.

However, it is also clear that the optimism the films may exude comes from Fassbinder's assessment of his favourite period, the 1950s, as one of rapid change and transformation, where an anarchic vitality permeates even the sinister dealings of black marketeers, corrupt politicians, venal bureaucrats and drug-peddling doctors. Although this picture may itself be *noir*-tinted by a romantic-nostalgic vision, it is not the least of Fassbinder's achievements to have wrested from this generally drab period an image at once vibrant, intelligent and differentiated, while making sure to locate this potential not in the period as such, but in his characters – larger than life and yet the very essence of life.

5. Fassbinder, Reflections of Fascism and the European Cinema

> '... even the dead will not be safe from the enemy, if he wins. And this enemy has not ceased to be victorious.'[1]

Mastering the Past?

In the previous chapter I argued that the BRD trilogy is best seen as Fassbinder's perversely optimistic invitation addressed at the Germans of the 1970s to take a look at the Germans of the 1950s: their marriages, their dependencies and depressions, the origins of their wealth and 'Wohlstand'. A far more difficult and fraught undertaking was to extend a similar invitation to that same Germany of the 1970s to try and deal differently with the 1940s, a time when those who would be parents in the 1950s were still singing 'today we own Germany, and tomorrow the world', or were falling in love, despite – or maybe because – of falling bombs and fallen brothers or fathers. Viewed from the 1970s, the Nazi years were invariably regarded under the sign of the 'return of the repressed', provoking the sometimes unspoken but always unanswerable question of whether the country had 'mastered its fascist past'.[2] While it was generally agreed that the correct reply must be in the negative, it would be hard to conceive of a country that dwelt as intensely on a recent period of its history as the Federal Republic.[3] Yet already in the 1960s a gap was noticeable between the way most Germans thought about the Nazi period and how the world at large expected them to think about it. Some historical circumstances need to be recalled. Unlike Spain after 1936, Germany in 1945 did not come out of a fratricidal civil war, and thus one could not speak of a divided people having to grow together once more. It remained a divided people, which gave one part the chance to unite (also against the other) by becoming militants on a new battleground, that of the Cold War. 'Liberation' had happened from the outside, and thus for much of the existence of West Germany, the question 'May 1945 – liberation or defeat' hung like a cloud over public life.[4]

Public events, such as the anniversaries commemorating the end of World War II or the state visit by Willy Brandt to Poland and his genuflection at the Warsaw ghetto memorial in 1970, sparked off public controversy and drew worldwide attention, indicating that what continued to generate heat did not always shed new light. At times these occasions displayed such a peculiar logic where accident and bad timing, coincidence and misjudgments of tact played a prominent part that one could almost call them the Freudian slips in the nation's inner speech about history,[5] as in the 'tension between remembering and forgetting',[6] many a public parapraxis came to pass. When in THE MARRIAGE OF MARIA BRAUN the heroine lights a cigarette in the kitchen where she forgot to turn off the gas, Fassbinder found in her fatal lapse of attention an appropriate, though uncharacteristically apocalyptic image for this return of the repressed that often enough staged itself around dates like May 8th (the end of the war in Europe). The subterranean reverberations of this final scene potently add to the reasons why the heroine has, as we have seen, persistently been taken to stand for 'forgetful' Germany. Yet by the same token, such scenes could hardly hope to reassure those who had suffered under Nazi rule that Germans were prepared to face up to their historic responsibilities. The contradictions were all too plain to see: in the decade after the Nürnberg trials, the Allies were remarkably lenient and forgiving, allowing many high-ranking ex-Nazi to return to respectability and thus most of Germany to conveniently forget.[7] The question of how Hitler could have won such widespread support for his racist policies and all-out war of aggression was an issue mainly confined to academic history, and the 1950s and 1960s were periods where there seemed little inclination to debate individual guilt or openly express shame or remorse.

Those who did or tried to confront these questions faced the double problem of how to begin to account for fascism without appearing to 'explain' it, and thus explaining it away. Among historians, this dilemma gave rise to the 'fascism-debate' of the 1970s, between 'intentionalists' (who saw German fascism as the systematic implementation of Hitler's racist and imperialist goals) and 'functionalists' (who regarded Nazism as the ad-hoc alliance of divergent socio-economic interests, held together only after Hitler had declared war, and bonded to the Führer by criminal complicity in the 'Final Solution'). The controversy deepened into the so-called 'historians debate' during the 1980s, when Jürgen Habermas detected in the writings of German academic historians, foremost among them Ernst Nolte and Andreas Hillgruber, an unacceptably revisionist project, designed to historicise the Nazi period in order to 'normalize' it, by comparing the extermination of the Jews, as Nolte seemed to do, to earlier genocides (the Boer war, the destruction of the Hereros, the Ottoman massacre of the Armenians, Stalin's Gulags) and later ones (Idi Amin's Uganda, the killing fields of Pol Pot).[8] The most controversial revisionist argument, however, was Hillgruber's who implicitly juxtaposed the victims of the concentration camps with the hundreds of thousands of women and children killed in the Allied bombing raids that resulted in the firestorms of Dresden and Hamburg, or the several million civilians who perished during the mass-expulsions from the Eastern provinces of the Reich after capitulation.[9]

The Limits of Representation

Among writers and artists, the task of how to represent in the medium of fiction or drama the extermination camps or the collusion of individuals and institutions like the Church proved a daunting dilemma. On one side stands the belief that to preserve the respect and honour due to the dead, and record the 'permanent scar on the face of humanity',[10] all forms of fictional narrative, dramatization and figurative speech must be qualified as *mis*representations, not least because they put a presence where there can only be absence. On the other side, there is the concern that such literalness and reticence might itself be merely a mode of representation, a rhetoric, which – more worrying still – will appear to confine the events to a fast receding point in time, making us powerless to invoke their actuality when similar barbarities once more defy understanding and defeat the will to action.

While agreed that conventional narratives were inappropriate to an event of such extremity as the Holocaust, writers like Peter Weiss (in *Die Ermittlung*) and Rolf Hochhuth (in *Der Stellvertreter*) were confronted with the question of whether their particular aesthetic choices and artistic solutions had not betrayed realities and experiences whose very nature made them unrepresentable. If these lives and deaths could only be commemorated in silence or documented by an uncompromising literalness, with only the survivors' testimony and the victims' names allowed to speak, then – it could be argued – Germans, however well-meaning, had no place in this work of either remembrance or representation.

For filmmakers, the dilemma was if anything even more acutely testing. How to represent fascism, without appearing to re-enact its horrors or yield once more to its fascination? It is easy to see why the cinema has, in this debate, been very much in the firing line. Images have traditionally been regarded as that which most readily elicits effects of 'melodrama, sentimentality, prurience', regardless of whether fictional or documentary.[11] Here the limits of representation have acted as a particularly effective taboo, ensuring that virtually no film was made in West Germany during the 1950s or 1960s that featured Jews or concentration camps.[12] While Alain Resnais made NIGHT AND FOG and Andrzj Munk made THE PASSENGER (a film about a women's camp in Poland), only some of Wolfgang Staudte's films (SCHWARZER KIES and HERRENPARTIE) obliquely alluded to the fate of German Jews or Nazi war crimes in formerly occupied countries.

It is in this context that one must see Fassbinder's forays into the subject, and the moral-historical perspectivism which in his films joins the 1970s to the 1940s. I have, in the previous chapter, argued that Fassbinder, throughout his career, deployed filmic means to create a very specific form of 'historical' memory, among which his use of melodrama and violent juxtaposition of contrasts, sentimental pop songs and improbable coincidences have a strategically important place. Thus, the 'effects of melodrama, sentimentality and prurience' form part of Fassbinder's aesthetic and moral universe, prompting the question of whether they do not in his work constitute 'limits' which any discussion of representation may have to confront, including one that wants to approach German Fascism, Auschwitz, and the relationship between Germans and Jews. For what terms such as melodrama signify, however much they may be coloured by negative judgements of taste and decorum, is an affectivity, and therefore an aspect of subjectivity crucial not just to the cinema. These emotions, one could argue, ought to legitimately belong to any engagement with matters of life and death, on the part of those to whom history has given the role of readers or spectators, but also for those who are charged with passing on compassion and preserving memory. The film experience is, par excellence, a site of mimetic emotions, caught in an ambiguous play of affect and identification, and therefore demands a 'melodramatic' interpretation more obviously than a 'modernist' hermeneutic one.[13] Cinema, in this respect, is on the side of excessive, perverse, psychotic or clichéd representations rather than ruled by an aesthetics of detachment and distance. The possibilities and limits this assumption offers for an understanding of several of Fassbinder's works, including a play, is the subject of the following chapters, in which a distinction will be made between the representation of the 'Third Reich', the representation of the Holocaust, and the representation of Jewish-German relations *after* the Holocaust. Precisely because these realities are mutually interdependent and inextricably bound together *in history*, we need to understand how and why they have been played off against each other, or are regarded separately in historical, narrative or fictional representations.

One of the tell-tale signs, for instance, of an apologetic discourse has always been to separate the 'internal' history of the 'Third Reich' from its 'external' policies (the war, the extermination of the Jews), by pointing out that Hitler achieved the unification and modernization of Germany (where Bismarck and the Weimar Republic had failed), before the war undid it all, or to argue that since out of a population of 700,000 German Jews 'only' about 250,000 perished in the camps (and most of them in the years 1942-45), the majority of Holocaust victims died as a direct or indirect consequence of the war, and therefore must be seen in the context of the exceptional situation created by war.[14] On the other hand, an argument that sees the 'Final Solution' not only as the implicit 'telos' of Nazism, but as the single reality that informed every aspect of Nazi Germany from 1933 onwards risks separating Hitler's racial policy from the regime's other principal aims: the 'overcoming' of democracy, the subversion and destruction of communism and organized labour, the domination of Europe by the German Reich and the attainment of world-power status. That it all but 'succeeded' in one of its aims, the near-destruction of European Jewry, does not mean the objectives it 'failed' to attain are no longer part of the representational reality of the 'Third Reich'. But then, so are other representational realities, which may have to be looked at separately from any of the overt political and ideological aims of Nazism, in order to grasp their meaning, and connection with Nazism. Hans Dieter Schäfer, for instance, has analyzed some of the contradictory 'life worlds' existing side by side in Germany during the 1930s and 1940s, which include such popular culture phenomena as a lively trade in jazz and swing records, even though they were officially banned, or the thriving tourism by sea and road to countries (including the USA) on which Germany was to declare war. What Schäfer calls 'everyday schizophrenia' becomes a little less inexplicable when seen against Nazism's (successful) promotion of a consumer culture which reconciled many Germans to the regime's curtailment of civil liberties.[15]

Since representations are the consequence of acts of selection, part of the task of analysis is to understand the rhetorical tropes by which presence and absence, inclusion and exclusion signify each other. One such 'representational reality' that Fassbinder looked at closely was, as we saw in the chapter on DESPAIR, the Nazi regime's specular and spectacular self-representation. In the chapter devoted to LILI MARLEEN, I shall take up the more specific case of how spectacle and power collude with each other in creating such a reality, while at the same time posing more clearly than before the question not only of what can be represented, but what can be said to whom and by whom, in this case by a German to Germans about this period of their history, and thus about the very status of history when represented by the cinema. This is especially delicate, since Fassbinder's films provide many of the examples that seem to cause great concern to the author of an incisive and critical study of what he calls the 'new discourse' on fascism, Saul Friedländer.[16]

The New German Cinema's Turn to History

> [LILI MARLEEN] is my first attempt to make a film about the Third Reich. And I will certainly be making other films about the Third Reich. But that's another subject, just as the Weimar Republic is another subject. This cycle will also be continued. Maybe at the end, a total picture will emerge of the German bourgeoisie since 1848... I think, there is a logic in all this. Just as I think that the Third Reich wasn't just an accident, a regrettable lapse of history, as it is so often portrayed. The Third Reich does have a sort of logic, as well as what carried over from the Third Reich to the Federal Republic and the GDR.[17]

In order to understand some of the reasons why Fassbinder became committed to a project such as LILI MARLEEN and what kind of 'logic' his 'history of the bourgeosie' might bring to the fore, one needs to first recall the special circumstances which led German filmmakers to take up historical topics in the mid-1970s, when for the previous decade, neither the commercial nor the art and avantgarde cinema seemed particularly interested in any aspect of the past, least of all the fascist past. Werner Herzog's work rarely featured Germany even as geography. Fassbinder, too, preferred to explore in his first films the one-dimensional, unreflecting state of mind of his heroes, rather than the possibility that they might have a history beyond the moment. But when Wim Wenders was asked why American music, comics and movies had been, during his adolescence, what he called his 'life savers' he replied: 'Twenty years of political amnesia had left a hole: we covered it with chewing gum and Polaroids.'[18] Fassbinder, who filled the void with movie-going, might have replied in a similar vein.

Barely a decade after the beginnings of the so-called New German Cinema, and following the international success of films as diverse as Syberberg's OUR HITLER (1977), Fassbinder's THE MARRIAGE OF MARIA BRAUN (1978), Volker Schlöndorff's THE TIN DRUM (1980) and Wolfgang Petersen's DAS BOOT (1981), this cinema, insofar as it was recognized as a 'national' cinema, appeared set to have its identity firmly located in a brooding obsession with Germany's recent past as a nation. What, then, was it that prepared the ground for directors to cut a passage through this 'amnesia' to Nazism and German history as a film subject? One answer, when looking at the films, is that the New German Cinema discovered the past when filmmakers turned to the home and found fascism around the family dinner table (as in Helma Sanders-Brahms' GERMANY PALE MOTHER). The anti-authoritarian movement, certain contemporary events (those depicted in GERMANY IN AUTUMN, for instance), but also the more conservative and revisionist turn of academic historians already mentioned gave 'German history' a new topicality at the end of the 1970s,[19] well before the fall of the Berlin Wall and unification dramatically shifted the ground of all the debates at the very end of the 1980s.

But these factors in themselves might not have swung German filmmaking so dramatically in the direction of historical topics in general and fascism in particular. The taboos mentioned above were too strong, especially since they were exacerbated by two complexes which were at one and the same time the traces of historical traumas and instances of conceptual impasses. One appears specific to Germany and German history, namely the question of continuity and discontinuity, of new beginnings and recurring cycles, of 'the return of the repressed', and the desire for radical breaks. The defeat of Nazism by the Allies in 1945 is one such radical break. It has served politicians as the founding myth of the Federal Republic, the 'Stunde Null'.[20] Filmmakers, however, have treated the very idea of a 'zero hour' of German history as problematic, and many found in a novella by Heinrich von Kleist, *The Earthquake of Chile*, an appropriate fictional precedent: Kleist took a natural disaster as the foil for criticising the *tabula rasa* thinking of the French Revolution. As a rhetorical trope, the 'Chile complex'[21] can best be understood as a condensation of the question of historical change (or lack of it, continuity: 'what carried over from the Third Reich to the Federal Republic and the GDR') with historical agency (who does what where and to whom: an obvious problem with a historical period marked by extraordinary crimes against humanity, for which the victors demanded 'collective responsibility' from the German nation, while virtually all of its citizens in advance pleaded 'not guilty').

The other complex is the 'limits of representation' debate already alluded to, now centered on the question of how faithfully the audio-visual media, and narrative films in particular, can represent the forces at work in the historical process. Does the cinema not have a tendency to liquidate history altogether, in the sense of a reality and a truth established independently of a narrative, favouring instead the representation of a subjective experience that alone makes history coherent and intelligible? But, then, what place do personal life-stories have in representing historical cataclysms, and finally, what kind of evidence are images, and especially moving images, for understanding history?[22]

In West Germany the question of how to represent and narrate German history thus not only affected professional historians and writers, but troubled filmmakers, too. One need only recall Wim Wenders' polemical essay on Joachim Fest's HITLER-EINE KARRIERE (1977)[23] or Syberberg's and Reitz's interventions in the HOLOCAUST debate.[24] Conscious that there was no easy way out of this problem, discussions in West Germany tended to revolve around a term that has a special resonance not only in the debates about representation, but in the philosophy of the bourgeois self and its sense of identity: 'authenticity'. There was talk of authentic 'Filmbilder' (Wenders), authentic 'Filmstoffe' (Kluge), or Reitz's demand that 'films, literature, images (must) come into being which bring us to our senses and restore our reflexes.'[25] So pervasive was the reaction to the presumed threat of the 'vanishing of the real'[26] brought upon by the media's 'historical obsession' that one can almost speak of an authenticity complex possessing the New German Cinema.

The Hitler-Welle, or Show Time for Hitler

Fetishizing the value of authenticity was itself a reactive move, as it tried to respond to what had become another kind of return of the repressed, a shamefaced nostalgia for the 'good old times', expressing itself in a desire to remember the 'Third Reich' as it was lived by Germans, rather than as it was represented by others. On the conservative side, during what came to be known as the 'Hitler-Welle', the new right, often made up of overt Nazi sympathizers, tried to reclaim what it thought was its due: the prerogative to remember childhood pleasures and sentimentalize its lost illusions. On the left, under the slogan 'Let's work on our memories', a liberal intelligentsia wanted to confront the parent generation by way of incontrovertible evidence and documents, while a fashion-driven memorabilia boom blurred these distinctions, bringing the period back into consciousness in fiction and non-fiction books, biographies and memoirs, films, television documentaries, comic-strips and collectibles.

When representing Nazism, the cinema has an especially ambivalent task, because 'never before and in no other country have images and language been abused so unscrupulously [...], never before and nowhere else have they been debased so deeply as vehicles to transmit lies.'[27] Added to the fact that German fascism has left a more complete account, in sight and sound, in visual records and staged celebrations, of itself and its version of history than any previous regime, this amounts to a particularly heavy moral and aesthetic legacy on the history of cinema. Moreover, German fascism was the first political ideology which borrowed the materials, the techniques and the mise-en-scène of its self-image from the cinema and from show-business: fabric and drapery, flood lights and recorded sound, scaffolding and plaster became the preferred props and elements: cinema, theatre, music drama, pageantry and what has been called 'Stimmungsarchitectur' (mood-architecture) found their way from stage and screen into public life. As a result, cinematic representations of 'Nazism' after Nazism are of necessity involved in a dimension of self-reference or mise-en-abyme. They are confronted with a choice of evils: either adhere to a stringent form of understatement and visual asceticism, in order to counter the visual pleasure and seduction emanating from the regime's spectacular stagings of itself,[28] or expose the viewer once more to the fascination, making the emotional charge residing in these images and stagings part of the subject matter itself. While the rhetoric of sobriety and understatement (usually accompanied by a monotone, sombre voice-over) became itself a cliché way of dealing with fascism in post-war documentaries, the presentation of the fascination 'from within' is precisely the mark of the 'new discourse' detected by Friedländer in Italian, French and German films of the 1970s. In either case, the regime's self-representation as show, its erotisation of power and charisma is not only a 'reality' that films have to engage with, it is also a 'signifier' of Nazism they cannot escape from. In this sense, visual fascination is as present in the German films made about Nazism in the late 1940s and 1950s, where a *film noir* atmosphere wanted to signify the 'demonic' quality of Hitler and his henchmen, as it is when a filmmaker practices an 'aesthetics of resistance' against specular seduction, such as Jean Marie Straub in NOT RECONCILED.

The watershed which signalled a renewed interest in fascism as a film subject came around 1970, when Luchino Visconti's THE DAMNED (1969) and Bernardo Bertolucci's THE CONFORMIST (1970) chose to do battle on the enemy's terms, so to speak, the territory of fascination, sex, death, violence, melodrama: not least because the enemy was also the enemy within, the cinematic self in another guise. Its representational reality rather than its historical meaning was what made fascism a material reality for a certain (idea of) cinema in the first place, which in turn signalled the crisis of another (idea of) cinema: that of (neo-)realism. The choice of topic for these directors, we have to assume, was neither naive nor speculative, but one that recognized the legacy of Nazi aesthetics (even where its politics had lost its appeal) in present-day commodity culture, also given to conspicuous waste and spectacular destruction. In the age of the block-buster, who does not recognize the seductive appeal of creating a substitute world, of treating power as a work-of-art, in short, the eros and thanatos of objectification? Visconti and Bertolucci spoke to these thoughts, unequivocally.

Yet what of popular or commercial films, like Mel Brooks' THE PRODUCERS (1968) or Bob Fosse's CABARET (1972), which also made much of the affinity between fascism and showbusiness, underlining this 'aesthetisation' of politics, already crucial to Walter Benjamin, and also analyzed by Susan Sontag?[29] Do they not confirm Friedländer's worry that the lure of 'kitsch and death' in Nazi self-representation carries over into films that use fascism as a backdrop for a love intrigue? Does the spectacle of putting-on-a-show, the song and dance routines and parodies of goose-stepping Nazi in Brooks' production number called 'Spring-time for Hitler' not make light of the obscenity of a regime that put on the mask of entertainment and glamour, so as to hide the energy it put into destruction, terror and contempt for human life?

Such questions are unanswerable, because the answer is already contained in the question. Whatever one might infer about the 'intentions' of the makers, such as claiming that CABARET asserts a vitality which defies the life-denying exercise of totalitarian power, or that THE PRODUCERS uses the resources of humour, stereotypes and parody to challenge unmitigated evil, there will be the counter-argument that rhetorical strategies such as irony or inversion can be misunderstood, ignored or not even noticed by the audience. This, however, is the nub of the problem: the dilemma of a hypothetical reception invalidating a hypothetical intentionality, so often invoked when one is dealing with 'popular' or mass audiences. The convenient solution is to posit the open or deconstructive 'text', as if the term 'postmodernism' had to be invented specifically in order to acknowledge the inroads the popular has made into the institutional context of high culture.

Perhaps CABARET can serve as an example for the complexities of text and reception with a popular film. In the story of the night-club performer's friendship and entanglement with a homosexual Englishman and his lovers, several themes are central which do and do not have anything to do with the nascent fascism that forms the backdrop, of which one is precisely that of the fascination with the 'other', the oscillation between alien and familiar. But more remarkable than the film's portrayal of Germans of all classes and convictions in a sympathetic, or at any rate, non-judgemental light motivated by a foreigner's perspective (though it did mark a significant enough shift in Hollywood representations of Germans) was the fact that it dared to use its Nazi setting for a musical. The association of such a sinister chapter of history with jazzy music seemed to be designed to court the charge of trivialization, yet the radical shift in genre from sombre Wagnerian music drama (for instance, in THE DAMNED) to light entertainment was defiant in several respects: it made a claim for popular music and the musical as genre to be taken 'seriously' (a complex cultural process that had taken place during the 1960s on a very wide front), and it also argued for sexuality to be granted a 'political' dimension. CABARET's discourse on 'perverse sexuality' and dandyism as a form of political resistance cut across the stereotypical identification of fascism with sexual perversion. It opened the way for representing homosexuals as themselves a persecuted group, and for understanding sexuality (in this case, the 'polymorphous' sexuality and androgyny of the Sally Bowles figure) as a subject position that responds to this specific historical reality, to the point of embodying a form of heroism.

CABARET's generic identity as a backstage musical about show people in Berlin on the eve of Nazism made it a hybrid text. This hybridity is not quite the same as postmodern openness, precisely because it is a necessary condition for any international commercial film, and thus, rather than being suspended between critical intentions and misinterpreted reception, CABARET (and its huge international success) can be most usefully regarded as a historical fact about 1972. As such, the film records a number of (transgressive) cultural shifts (about popular music, gender and sexuality) which have become commonplace, but which at the time needed to articulate themselves in the context of a particular referential world – Germany in the 1930s – which itself connoted transgression, danger, transition. It could do so successfully, because it rewrote a popular intertext, THE BLUE ANGEL, already famous for (heterosexual) decadence. CABARET represented its diegetic universe as a blend of youth, the politics of the street, impending apocalypse and sexual adventure, suggesting a number of *Zeitgeist* parallels between the 1930s and the 1970s, which however shallow they may seem to a social historian, allowed the film to have a multivocal speaking position, made coherent by its star, who successfully 'addressed' these new and shifting audiences.

Taking Back Neo-Realism

This speaking position could be called typical of the new discourse of fascism: for some a diffuse amalgam of kitsch and sentimentality, violence and nostalgia, for others a rather more productive, open and even 'honest' engagement with history, sexuality and the body. To those who find the blend suspect, one might reply that such are the emotions and sensations the cinema has been accused of since its beginnings, which leads to the interesting suggestion –

half argued by a director like Hans Jürgen Syberberg – that the cinema is inherently fascist. But such a perspective, while worth arguing, is somewhat foreshortened. A missing link in the debate is perhaps the fact that through 'discovering' the topic of fascism, the European art cinema of the 1970s and 1980s (particularly the Italian cinema) decisively broke with the dominant post-war representational mode, namely realism, whether one thinks of the neo-realism of Rossellini and De Sica, or the realist ideology of virtually all the 'new' cinemas of the 1950s and 1960s in France, Britain, Poland or West Germany. Visconti's THE DAMNED, Bertolucci's THE CONFORMIST, or Fellini's ROMA (1972) had, in a sense, 'taken back' neo-realism (which of course, in such textbook examples as Rossellini's ROME OPEN CITY [1945] or Visconti's OSSESSIONE [1943] was itself essentially melodramatic).[30] Moreover, these directors had made a subjectively slanted, melodramatically or operatically spectacular representation of history the dominant model of historical representation in cinema.[31] This probing of the new image worlds of electronic reproduction and the breakdown of the divide between 'inner' and 'outer' reality which they entail still form the major preoccupation of the cinema, and it has brought an as yet unabated turn to melodramatic, erotico-pornographic, horror and fantasy subjects, as typical of the post-1970s Hollywood as it is of contemporary European cinema.[32]

One can, therefore, with some justification, identify within these major shifts and reorientations of both popular cinema and art/auteur cinema a tendency in the 1970s that, especially for European filmmakers, made fascism a preferred reference point: Visconti and Bertolucci were followed, in quick succession, by Louis Malle's LACOMBE LUCIEN (1973), Liliana Cavani's THE NIGHT PORTER (1974), Lina Wertmuller's SEVEN BEAUTIES (1976), Joseph Losey's M KLEIN (1976), Ingmar Bergman's THE SERPENT'S EGG (1978) and François Truffaut's THE LAST METRO (1980). Although these films hardly form a genre or even a coherent group, there are enough areas of contact to merit a more systematic analysis of their preoccupation with Nazi emblems, Nazi iconography and the building up of a kind of stock repertoire of architectural props, clothes, haircuts and accessories that began to function as instant signifiers of fascism.[33]

Such an analysis can proceed from different perspectives and, consequently, construct different vantage points on its subject. Looking at the afterlife which Nazism appeared to lead in the popular media generally, Friedländer saw the films, with their ambiguous celebration of style detached from a clear moral and historical stance, confirm a dangerous confusion between critical distance in historical understanding, and a form of exorcism that seemed to end up playing the devil's advocate.[34] Other analyses sprang from nationally specific points, such as the realization that a rather radical change in attitude had occurred in France with respect to the Occupation period and the Resistance. Michel Foucault, for instance, attributed it to the demise of Gaullism in 1968-69 which dissolved the strategic post-war alliance de Gaulle had forged between the nationalist right (government-in-exile) and the collaborationist right (Pétain and Vichy). What he feared from the sympathetic portrayal of collaboration (in LACOMBE LUCIEN) and the revelations of just how widespread and highly placed collaboration had been in occupied France (in Marcel Ophuls' LE CHAGRIN ET LA PITIÉ [1970]) was not the false glamorization of Nazism. Rather, it supported a negation of the Resistance, together with the denial of popular (socialist) struggles, and thus a subversion and erosion of what he called 'popular memory'.[35]

Jean Baudrillard, taking a characteristically wide sweep, analyzed the phenomenon in the context of a general nostalgia and detected in the cinema's 'retro-fashion' a distinct 'retro-scenario': Western Europe, locked into the political stasis of the Cold War, and with its intelligentsia demoralized by the post-1968 defeat of its revolutionary dreams, nostalgically imagines through the cinema a time when a country's history still meant individual victims, still signified causes that mattered, and decisions of life and death. The attraction of a return to history as story and image was the illusion it could give of a personal or national destiny: a need fascism had tried to gratify on a collective scale. For Baudrillard, too, retro-cinema was therefore less a move towards coming to terms with the past than the fetishization if not of fascinating fascism, then of another trauma located in the present: the absence of history altogether.[36]

Historicising vs Relativizing: Different Theories of Fascism
What the debate about retro-fashion, nostalgia and historicism highlights with respect to Nazism is a certain deficit in the traditional, or even scholarly accounts of Fascism, a historical experience which, precisely, has lost none of its topicality at the end of the twentieth century. To the extent, however, that it is a historical experience, which in Europe alone has profoundly affected millions of people, it matters whether it is analyzed by historians, by ethnographers and psychoanalysts, or indeed by filmmakers and film-scholars. This does not mean that a work of history, a novel or a film cannot be judged in the light of the many disciplines that have studied fascism, but it stands to reason that each will do so differently: a novel, for instance, may legitimately be more concerned with the perspective of a single individual than an economic treatise. With regard to film, then, I would argue, the discovery that fascism is a mirror of the cinema's own concerns with the ethics of spectacle must be a crucial historical fact of the 1970s 'revival': so much so that in most cases without such a shock of recognition of cinema's 'fascist' potential there would have been no Bertolucci's THE CONFORMIST, or Pasolini's SALO. Quite differently articulated, though equally central is the shock of complicity in Fassbinder's LILI MARLEEN.

Such historical 'revisionism' has itself to be seen in the broader context of 'historicizing fascism'. Initially, this had been the goal of Marxist analysis. One remembers Max Horkheimer's dictum from the 1930s: 'those who do not wish to speak of capitalism should also be silent about fascism',[37] taken up after the war in order to counter the personalization of fascism in the figure of Hitler. What the notion of Hitler as a uniquely aberrant individual and the Nazi elite as a gang of common criminals sanctioned was the screening out of the political and economic factors that had made fascism part of the modernizing forces of industrialization and the crisis cycles of finance capitalism. Furthermore, it exculpated those sections of German society that had helped Nazism to power and had maintained it there, notably the banking establishment and heavy industry, the judiciary, the army and the civil service. Declaring tabula rasa in 1945 allowed the Adenauer government to make its peace with most of them, a fact to which several of Jean Marie Straub's protagonists are, precisely, NOT RECONCILED.

However, by the early 1970s, the 'historicizing' argument had moved on, to focus on the inadequacies of the structural or conjunctural models that Marxists had been putting forward. Instead of calling fascism the 'crisis management' of capitalism, the 'new' debates either stressed the European or international dimension of the phenomenon (for instance, by taking up the earlier theses of Ernst Nolte[38]) or gave the psychic-libidinal dimension a greater weight (Alexander Mitscherlich's attempt to explain, for instance, the allegiance of the masses to the Führer[39]). While the first has surfaced again in the historians' debate, the second, psychoanalytic approach did not find favour with historians, but was hugely influential among writers and filmmakers, especially in West Germany. Hence the paradox that a 'theory of fascism' regarded as almost irrelevant by professional historians came to assume a major cultural and explanatory power for filmmakers and film historians, leading to the posited affinity of modern cinema and fascism.

In the European art cinema, the analogy was elaborated, but also limited along at least three quite distinct lines: as the theme of specular seduction, show-business and the technology of sight and sound (THE LAST METRO, LILI MARLEEN); as sexuality, in its vitalist, gendered and perverse dimensions (THE CONFORMIST, SEVEN BEAUTIES, THE NIGHT PORTER); and finally, as the loss of self, melancholy and 'mourning work' (THE SERPENT'S EGG, DESPAIR, M KLEIN).[40] However, one needs to be cautious about the label 'European'. France, Italy, Germany: each country's cinema recorded these affinities and mirror-images in distinctive ways. While in Italian films class decadence and deviant sexuality became major issues (THE DAMNED, SALO), in German films, it was often the family and patriarchy that found themselves scrutinized via the Nazi setting (GERMANY PALE MOTHER, LILI MARLEEN). As the divergent explanations offered by Baudrillard or Foucault show, even within one country, the specificity of historical reference must be addressed, or conversely, the films' several entry-points need to be seen within generic or institutional frameworks.

The preoccupation with fascism in the cinema of the 1980s was thus a complex European phenomenon, not satisfactorily explained either by references to the appeal of political pornography or to the Germans' failure to 'master their past'. Furthermore, for countries without a strong and continuous tradition of filmmaking, international success may depend on an ability to 'market' the national history as international spectacle. Common currency, such as the iconography and shorthand symbolism of Nazism, establishes a signifying system no less complete, or replete with antinomies and binarism, i.e. possible narratives, than say, the American West or the Civil War. It might be argued that fascism was Europe's last genuinely shared historical experience (as sign-world), the negative image of unification, against which the troubled transformation of the nation state within the European

Community could be assessed. Or, conversely, fascism could be seen as the most violent, spectacular face/phase of capitalist production and of (symbolic) consumption prior to the age of the supermarket and the mass media.

Among German historians, the ambiguity was a different one. A problematic symmetry opened up between those whose moral conscience insisted on the uniqueness and singularity of the Holocaust, and those who in an ideological move wanted to claim the same uniqueness for Hitler and his regime, absolving the generations before and after from responsibility. Yet since any argument that would isolate the period of Nazism from the rest of German history was unsustainable on both historical and moral grounds, the conservative right put forward its own demand for historicizing fascism. This time, however, not in order to point to the continuities of fascism with Germany's social structure throughout most of its modern history, but in an attempt to relativize Hitler's policies, to compare the regime's crimes to those of other totalitarianisms, and as already indicated, thereby to 'contextualize' the Final Solution.

This skewed symmetry was to become one of the focal points of the historians' debate in the 1980s, just as it had haunted West German politics throughout the 1970s. It was in some direct sense the background to West German filmmakers' own return to fascism as a film subject. Compared to what may or may not have been the causes in France and Italy, theirs was an even more complex story of reaction, regrouping and response. The New German cinema came to films about history late, almost a decade after Visconti's THE DAMNED, at least as far as its fictionalization was concerned. For most of the 1960s and 1970s documentary approaches predominated.[41] Only when a series of political events replete with uncanny historical parallels led Alexander Kluge early in 1978 to gather together a number of his colleagues to make the film GERMANY IN AUTUMN can one detect a different kind of self-reflexion in the New German cinema's relation to the fascist legacy, and also to its possible and impossible historicisations: as discussed in the previous chapter, two highly publicised funerals provided the framework for an oblique meditation on some of the asymmetrical repetitions in recent German history.[42]

As an 'omnibus film', GERMANY IN AUTUMN attempted to combine discursive and argumentative sections with dramatizations, which may explain why it had relatively little response among the general public. Yet barely a year later, another fictional treatment of the topic fascism was to have a public impact of unexpected proportions, the screening on German television of the US-produced four-part series HOLOCAUST.[43] Thus, the trigger for German directors to rethink the representation of history on film came, like the defeat of fascism itself, from outside. It stood under the shock of the enormous public response, and in particular, the overwhelmingly emotional outpourings the story of the Weiss and Dorf families had elicited from German television viewers.

> An American television series [...] accomplished what hundreds of books, plays, films, and television programmes, thousands of documents, and all the concen-

tration camp trials have failed to do in the more than three decades since the end of the war: to inform Germans about crimes against Jews committed in their name, so that millions were emotionally touched and moved.[44]

The emotions touched were themselves of a complex kind; while the metaphor of 'floodgates opening up' recurred almost stereotypically, and expressions of guilt, shame and remorse were made public with sometimes hysterical and sometimes exhibitionist fervor, there was also much outrage and condemnation about the screening.[45] Among those who charged the series with trivialization and embarrassing sentimentality, because it represented the unrepresentable and imaged the unimaginable – the concentration camps and gas chambers – were also filmmakers. While some felt perturbed that a Hollywood soap opera on *the* German subject should have moved millions to tears where their own films had been ignored, others felt roused to respond to the challenge. Not only did it seem that, in the words of Günter Rohrbach, then head of drama at WDR who had bought the series, 'after HOLOCAUST television can no longer be what it was before',[46] the New German cinema could also no longer be what it was before. When, in quick succession, Syberberg's OUR HITLER (1977), Fassbinder's DESPAIR (1978) and MARIA BRAUN (1978), Helma Sanders Brahms' GERMANY PALE MOTHER (1979) and Alexander Kluge's THE PATRIOT (1979) appeared on the screens, along with Schlöndorff's THE TIN DRUM (1979), Fassbinder's LILI MARLEEN (1980), and finally, in 1984, Edgar Reitz' 11-part HEIMAT (begun in 1979), it was clear that some sort of dam had burst among the filmmakers, too, to release maybe not the floodgates of tears opened up by HOLOCAUST, but nonetheless a more profound 'reflection of fascism' than Friedländer was perhaps willing to grant.

For these directors, HOLOCAUST and its German reception posed a double problem. First of all, the series had 'successfully' combined the representation of the Third Reich with the representation of the Holocaust: it had made of it one story. Secondly, it had been able to arouse strong feelings by 'personalizing' history, concentrating on two individual cases, juxtaposed and counterpointed, and utilizing the strategies of Hollywood dramaturgy most discredited by film theory in order to direct spectator empathy and identification. Put differently, it had neither 'historicised' fascism in the left-wing sense, nor 'relativised' it in the right-wing sense. But then, it had not treated the Holocaust sui generis either, because by preferring the genre of the family melodrama, it was offering identification to each and every viewer. One could say that HOLOCAUST had provided a coherent subject position, but at the price of de-historicising fascism altogether, and universalizing it, in the form of a soap opera.

Clearly, these options were not open to a German film. Few directors of the 1980s represented Auschwitz or the Holocaust (although a screening of Resnais' NIGHT AND FOG plays an important role in Margarethe von Trotta's THE GERMAN SISTERS),[47] and instead of 'historicising' fascism along the left-right divide, many of the films, especially those made for television, found a primary orientation in what among historians is known as 'Alltagsgeschichte' ('the history of everyday life'). It connotes a kind of micro-analysis of history, from the perspective of 'ordinary people' and their ways of living through the years between 1933 and 1945: Nazism as a daily reality, as a 'normality' putting to the test individual attitudes and human behaviour. Such a study of Nazism as everyday history had been a point of discussion among historians since the late-1970s. Martin Broszat, for instance, had argued that in order to be able to talk about the 'Third Reich' as 'the German people's own history' and thus for individuals to take responsibility for what had occurred, Germans had to cease viewing it as external and separate and to mobilize private or family memories. Rather than regard Hitler as the nation's pied-piper and themselves as having acted in a trance ('der Nazi-Spuk', 'the Nazi-spell' was a common term of post-war disavowal), personal stories and reminiscenses had to be evoked and told, in order to get out of what one historian called 'the quasi-hypnotic paralysis of most of the German people with regards to the Nazi past'.[48]

Several successful television series (for instance, Eberhardt Fechner's TADELLÖSER & WOLF) and countless documentaries were to be based on this concept, yet the international apotheosis of filmed everyday life was Reitz' HEIMAT, which followed the destiny of the Simon family from 1918 to 1982. If HEIMAT suggested that the German cinema, too, had recourse to melodrama for its view of history, then this was both its strength and weakness: strength, in that it reached a large number of individuals, in Germany and elsewhere, giving unusually detailed and engrossing insights into rural life before 1945; weakness, in that 'Alltagsgeschichte' can indeed be apologetic in tendency if not intent, and has, among historians of the Holocaust often been regarded as a revisionist ploy for 'normalization' and 'routinization', especially where it blanks out the death camps, on the grounds that few 'ordinary' Germans would have experienced the deportations and exterminations first-hand. HEIMAT also confirms Baudrillard's thesis, when one considers that the insistence on the family has something of a fetish-function, because it clings to a notion of the authentic in 'everyday experience' as if it was a quality that could somehow be recovered, and represented on film.[49]

The charge levelled against HEIMAT of being apologetic – Jim Hoberman spoke of 'blatant tokenism' and 'born again Germany'[50] – is one horn of the dilemma faced by German directors, of which the fascinated gaze at kitsch glamour was the other. Yet in fairness to Reitz, HEIMAT could also be seen as 'deconstructing' some of the conservative values it appeared to extol, notably the 'blood and soil' rootedness of its main characters and the authenticity that their close-knit family life represents. For what appears to be the motor and motive of historical change is ultimately technology and consumer culture. Reitz shows no rural, pre-industrial idyll, and instead, his characters' lives and histories are transformed by modern communication technologies: the women go to the movies (to see a film called HEIMAT), and the men either spend their time with ham radio sets, are busy with precision optics or have a passion for still photography, when not on active duty as newsreel cinematographers on the Eastern front.[51] A deconstructive turn is also present in the other, even more controversial response to HOLOCAUST, Syberberg's OUR HITLER. One of its central arguments, as we shall see, is that the Nazi deployment of radio made the State into a 'live' media experience, thanks to a permanent public address system. Together with Fassbinder's LILI MARLEEN the most obvious example of a film to take the historical imagination associated with Nazism (spectacular in the public sphere, and a family soap opera in the home) and turn it into a representational mode of excess, melodrama and contradiction, Syberberg's mega-film could qualify for the epithet 'postmodern', in the specific sense of three areas of intervention: pastiche and rewriting; show-business and power; the media public sphere of radio and cinema.[52] If Reitz's contribution to breaking down the divide between high culture and popular culture is a tour de force of 'Alltagsgeschichte', Fassbinder's attitude to popular culture implicitly replies to Syberberg's OUR HITLER, where an uncompromisingly high-culture proposition (that modern show-business is in some sense more fascist than Nazism) underpins the rather shrill identification of Hollywood cinema with Hitler.[53]

A Death in the Family: Mourning Work and The Oedipal Trap

Films such as HOLOCAUST, OUR HITLER, HEIMAT and LILI MARLEEN were, beyond their existence as films, also media events, discursive realities cascading through the representational reality of television, phone-ins, newspapers, leader columns, learned journals. The question of the subject positions they created and the speaking positions they assumed were vital aspects of their reality in culture. While in HOLOCAUST, the subject positions offered led to a facile identification with the victims of the Holocaust, OUR HITLER and HEIMAT were anti-HOLOCAUST in that they tried to open a more tortuous and underground path to subject positions of the divided German self (the monologue of the schizophrenic child-murderer from Fritz Lang's M [1931], or passages from Himmler's Posen speech at crucial points in OUR HITLER) and a retreat to the domestic self (Reitz in HEIMAT creating a Mother Courage who doesn't lose her children to the war). If HOLOCAUST's assumption that to show people going to the gas chambers in a film could give an idea of 'what it was like' was a deeply offensive presumption, how is one to take the analogy between the child-murderer in M and Adolf Hitler (in OUR HITLER), and how does one 'become naive' in Reitz' HEIMAT about the persecution and deportations of Jews, barely mentioned throughout 16 hours of film?[54] For Reitz, it was Hollywood's speaking position that offended about HOLOCAUST, while for some viewers of HEIMAT, it was the speaking position of a barely disguised anti-Americanism that offended.[55] By dividing Germans into those who stayed and those who went away (to the United States, as emigrants or exiles), and by speaking from a German New Left position (for which the United States was the enemy), while trying to identify with the old German Left (wiped out by Hitler and Stalin), Reitz' film appeared to be speaking from the 'green-red' position of the German ecology movement, itself a politically ambivalent stance.

Both Syberberg and Reitz may argue that their films are in a 'double frame', so to speak. HEIMAT, for instance, is for Reitz a story within a story ('thousands of stories based on irritatingly detailed experiences which do not contribute to judging or explaining history, but whose sum total would actually fill this gap'[56]), and thus a (single) story of the Simons family 'framed' by the many stories (too well known, according to Reitz, to need retelling) of the Holocaust. Similarly, the multiple ironies and incongruities constructed in OUR HITLER could be seen as the mise-en-abyme of all possible speaking positions, and thus proof of the impossibility of speaking 'as a German' about the Holocaust and the 'Third Reich', while needing to testify that the unspeakable happened. However, in light of the directors' public interventions (Syberberg's having become increasingly political[57]), it is important both to protect the films' mise-en-abyme or framing ironies from their makers' personal statements and to acknowledge the difficulties the cinema has as a mass medium to institutionalize preferred readings other than by creating ambiguous subject positions.[58] There had been, after all, those 'hundreds of documentaries' about fascism and the Holocaust, none of whose unambiguous subject positions provoked either the emotional outbursts following the screening of HOLOCAUST or the debates occasioned by HEIMAT, OUR HITLER and LILI MARLEEN. The question is thus one of the 'political unconscious' of a popular text, which by definition exceeds the control of the maker, and which becomes a cultural or historical fact precisely because of this excess.

In their public utterances, directors like Reitz and Syberberg tended to claim for their work a particular form of authenticity, a term which, as already indicated, had to bear quite a heavy rhetorical burden in the New German Cinema's sense of history. It stood for such traditional categories of history as agency (which in the films became a negative and subjective category: a matter of guilt and responsibility), change (which emerged as the psychic 'return of the repressed'), and truth (which became an almost religious need to bear witness). These transformations of key historical terms into values of the subjective, the psychic and the spiritual could almost serve as another definition of *Trauerarbeit* (work of mourning) in which memory and commemoration wanted to establish a continuity across the very awareness of separation and loss, in a mode that converts the mirroring effects of nostalgia into the 'sorrow and pity' of the self recognizing and tolerating otherness. *Trauerarbeit* in this sense is 'oedipal time', the coming to terms with the absent father, or the father's absent authority, the problem of how to relate to the loss or narcissistic internalization of love objects.[59]

By contrast, in Fassbinder, neither 'authenticity' nor *Trauerarbeit* are operative terms. As argued in the previous chapters, his structures of self and identity are not introspective, but are part of a particular geometry of representation, a scenario of differently enfolded looks, exchanged between or received by the characters but not confined to them, and embracing/exceeding the spectator. Both visually and in his narratives, Fassbinder in effect distances himself from the oedipal time of the family romance and the primal scene of 'the marriages of our parents', giving the spectator no illusion of depth, of entering or penetrating the recesses of the fiction: his flat, evenly or underlit images invite no 'inwardness', but merely complicate infinitely a visual surface, put 'en abyme' by the multiple frames and overlaid action spaces of sound and image.

Fassbinder's refusal of illusionistic depth and his rare, highly stylized use of flashbacks, as in THE MERCHANT OF FOUR SEASONS or in BERLIN ALEXANDERPLATZ,[60] can also be seen as part of a more fundamental stance opposed to the Oberhausen generation of German filmmakers and their film-politics. The Oberhausen Manifesto of 1962, the founding moment of the Young/New German Cinema, was supported by the slogan 'Papa's Kino is dead': an oppositional and parricidal gesture of confrontation typical of avantgarde aspirations, but which in the event was promptly denounced by a more radical male avantgarde (Jean Marie Straub, Vlado Kristl, Hellmuth Costard, for instance) and also by women filmmakers such as Ula Stöckl, who saw in the slogan an underlying oedipal sentimentality and patriarchal presumptions. While Fassbinder did not belong to any of these factions, it became clear from his preference for actors tested in 'Papa's Kino' (Karlheinz Böhm, Adrian Hoven, Mario Adorf, Brigitte Mira, Barbara Valentin, Conny Froboess) that he never seemed to have felt the need to draw a sharp line between himself and the cinema of the 1940s and 1950s in order to become either productive or a 'self'.

The political and polemical rifts after Oberhausen can be retraced also in the modes used to represent history, leading to distinct strategies and attitudes, which, as it happens, can be mapped around the issue of *Trauerarbeit* and oedipal time. In retrospect, it seems that the New German Cinema was polarized between endorsing a commemorative return to the past (in the films of Kluge, Reitz and Syberberg, all committed to 'work of mourning'), and those who insisted on a radical break (Kristl's self-destructing political fables like DER BRIEF, Straub's idea of 'resistance' in NOT RECONCILED, Harun Farocki's essayistic 'learning play' approach to history in BETWEEN TWO WARS). Fassbinder, on the other hand, took a third option (though it may not have appeared as an option at all), for which agency and authenticity were not attributes of the unitary (or oedipal) self but emerge negatively, from the constantly shifting and fractured relation between subjectivity and otherness. If the royal road in the 1970s of West German cinema to German history was family history, and if one can speak of a veritable oedipalization of this history, Fassbinder's own strategy appears in a quite different light: either more excessive and parodic where he subscribes to the oedipal paradigm (in MARIA BRAUN and LOLA) or overturning the paradigm altogether (as in BERLIN ALEXANDERPLATZ).

Given that Fassbinder thus had a quite different concept of representation and reference in his films, seeking another kind of truth in the way in which one style, one image, one representation commented on another in a universe of media-saturated reality, it is safe to assume that his reconstruction of the last 100 years of the German bourgeoisie – had he been permitted or lived to complete it – would have differed fundamentally from, say that of Reitz in HEIMAT. On the evidence of the films we have (and as indicated in the quotation by Fassbinder cited above, they do focus on significant periods of the 20th century in Germany), the difference lies in the heterogeneous literary sources Fassbinder used (writers such as Gustav Freytag, Theodor Fontane, Oskar Maria Graf, Alfred Döblin) and in the fact that not the epic time of duration typical of a dynasty and its sequence of generations mattered to him, but the brief moments of collapse and crisis, the spasms and sudden explosions (as in the opening of MARIA BRAUN), the apparently gratuitous accidents in history (as we shall see in

LILI MARLEEN), or the traumatic single domestic event (the beating to death of Ida by Franz Biberkopf in BERLIN ALEXANDERPLATZ). Also, instead of meaning gradually emerging out of the chronicle of small incidents and minute changes, Fassbinder prefers (even in BERLIN ALEXANDERPLATZ) the moral point of pathos (as in VERONIKA VOSS) or the sharp irony of the fable (as in LOLA). Finally, Fassbinder's essentially melodramatic concept of continuity and discontinuity, in which the specular dynamics of space and vision play a much greater role than do dream-time and character-specific subjective recollection,[61] also implies that his idea of temporality in history differs from that of the chronicle, the family saga or even soap opera. In the chapter on IN A YEAR OF THIRTEEN MOONS, I shall argue that if anything, temporality in Fassbinder has more in common with time travel and science fiction than with nostalgia, authentic moments and mourning work.

6.   ...wie einst? LILI MARLEEN

Fascism: Seduction by the Rapist; Consumerism: Seduction by the Pimp?[1]

Brass Values

With these contradictory ideological intertexts in mind, the background to LILI MARLEEN, the history of its reception, and its place in Fassbinder's work become themselves more oblique, but by the same token, also more interesting. The project originated in the base proprietary rights of Luggi Waldleitner, one of West Germany's oldest established and most industry-oriented producers, who owned the song and its title. Manfred Purzer, also a member of Papa's Kino, though of Fassbinder's generation, and active in commercial filmmaking as writer, director and producer, had acquired the film rights to singer Lale Andersen's autobiography (*Der Himmel hat viele Farben*) and turned it into a script. This script he sold to Waldleitner who had not failed to notice that with Hanna Schygulla after MARIA BRAUN, Germany had a female star of international appeal, perfect for playing yesterday's divas. She, on the other hand, refused to have Purzer direct her: Purzer was known in the world of German film funding as an astute operator but also as a right-winger close to the Munich political establishment. Insisting on Fassbinder, who by then had vowed never to work with her, Schygulla put the director in a dilemma, for he in turn, while not at all averse to working for a professional producer with the kind of money and connexions that Waldleitner could bring to such a project, was rather less keen to team up again with the actress he had become bored with.

The irony of this state of affairs is worth underscoring. Given on the one hand the Svengali myth of Fassbinder and Schygulla, and on the other, the Waldleitner-Purzer team's image as the incarnation of everything that the 'New German Cinema' had revolted against, Fassbinder, by agreeing to make LILI MARLEEN, seemed to conclude not one, but two devil's pacts: with Papa's Kino and with the kitsch-and-glamour Hitler-nostalgia wave. Not surprisingly, the quality papers reverberated with howls of protest, there was talk of ominous parallels with the Nazi years, of the revenge of the fathers on the sons, while a barely disguised Schadenfreude accused the enfant terrible of having sold out.[2]

What could have been the attraction for Fassbinder? In one sense, the perversity of the proposal must have been irresistible, given the quite vertiginous circuits of exchange it opened up, and how it turned set ideas and expectations upside down even at the project stage. It is as if the very improbability of the elements coming together here and their mutual friction allowed Fassbinder to participate in a process by which capitalism itself stripped history to the skeleton of its own truth, in this case to that which survives from a dangerously sentimental past and a louche bourgeois lifestyle as bankable assets. The director's position was, it would appear, not unlike that of his heroine, complicit in the exploitation of a personality as the figurehead of a particular regime. The singer, her story and the song attracted Fassbinder because he could see in it the image of himself. The popularity – the transgressive *frisson* – of Nazi nostalgia was part of the price (or the prize?) for having access to operating capital in the only valid currency apparently available to directors of the (German International) film industry in the 1970s: marketing and mirroring the world's fascination with fascism.

Seen in this light, LILI MARLEEN permitted Fassbinder to demonstrate that fascism, some forty years on, could not be regarded as exclusively German – a position only apparently close to the apologetic normalisation thesis discussed above – as well as showing that it was not merely historical. Rather, it seemed to be the constant shadow cast by the crisis cycle of capitalism and of globalized markets, commodifying but also charging with desire the material and immaterial fetish objects of the past. The crystallisation points of this process were the constantly displaced 'theaters of event,' those concentrations of spectacle power realised through the mass media and the new technologies, themselves in turn promoted and naturalised by the ubiquity and collusive unity of war, spectacle and show. In the unmediated, pure presence of the song "Lili Marleen" on the airwaves during World War II, 'hard' military rule and consolidated corporate interests became 'soft', through the relay of the product, the personality, the image and the sound. Power had channelled, dispersed, and liquified itself, until it had become almost as insubstantial and dematerialised as the airwaves on which the radio signals travelled that transmitted it.

Lale Andersen's Story

But this may be anticipating too much. LILI MARLEEN is in the first instance a film about fascism which constructs its narrative around a paradoxical but historically authenticated montage effect: the fortuitous encounter of a love song and a world war. Purzer's screenplay was based on what was the central event in Lale Andersen's life, the series of coincidences that made a song, originally called 'Der Wachposten' written by Hans Leip, with music by Norbert Schulze, the hit of 1943, when it was played every night by Radio Belgrade, the German Army broadcast station in occupied Serbia. Adopted also by other Wehrmacht radio stations, and even heard on Allied and Russian radio, it became a kind of signature tune for the men in the trenches all over Europe. The song was briefly banned by propaganda minister Goebbels for being defeatist, but this ban was lifted again in the face of massive protests. In itself, the case is interesting because it demonstrates that Nazi policy vis-à-vis popular culture and especially popular music was not as monolithic as the notion of the perfect propaganda machine might lead one to expect, for it would seem that in several areas of public life, pressure from the base could and did lead to changes in policy.[3]

On the other hand, the story of Lale Andersen herself is not without interest. An avantgarde cabaretist in the late 1920s in Berlin, she met on a tour in Switzerland in the early 1930s a young Jewish composer, Robert Liebmann, living in Zurich with whom she fell in love. Their frequent meetings in Munich and Zurich in subsequent years aroused the suspicions of the Gestapo, and they both came under surveillance. Whether she actually participated in any political activity, either in connexion with the Jewish rescue organisations in Switzerland that Robert was active for, or with an underground resistance group which included the writer Günther Weissenborn is not entirely clear, though this is what Andersen claimed in her memoirs, in which – as so often with prominent Nazi entertainers' memoirs – the attempt to exculpate herself veers between an almost culpable naivety, claims of opposition to the regime, and a palpable fascination with the men of evil she was once close to. In Andersen's case, there is, however, as documented evidence, the love affair with a Jewish man, the temporary ban of the song, an attempted suicide, and the international protests which rumours of her internment and/or death at the hands of the Nazis provoked.

These, then, are some of the elements of fact and fiction that could be woven into female melodrama and a performer's bio-pic, which is what Purzer had done. The story starts in Munich in 1938, where the couple – called Willie and Robert in the film – have installed their love nest, about to be interrupted by Robert's Jewish backers, angry at the risks he is running, and also by the Gestapo, ready to pounce. Willie is at that time working in a Munich nightclub, where she premieres her new song, with mixed results, but is befriended by a high-ranking Nazi who in due course becomes something like her manager and persuades her to record the "Lili Marleen", which she does on the very day that Hitler invades Poland. On a subsequent trip, Robert is arrested by the police and interrogated, while Willie is contacted by Robert's family who persuade her to assist in undercover operations. Not an experienced spy and closely watched by her Nazi protectors, with whose help she soon rises to wealth and fame, she breaks under the strain of so many conflicting pressures and attempts suicide during one of her much-publicised tours. In order to stop rumours of her having been killed, the doctors are instructed to patch her up for a final appearance, which she manages to resounding applause, as Allied bombs are pounding German cities. Robert, who was exchanged at the Swiss-German border, has disappeared from her life, and when after the war Willie attends one of his concerts in Zurich, she is snubbed by his family and ignored by Robert, now married to a Jewish woman.

For Fassbinder, it is the song's legendary popularity that he wanted to take from history, recognizing like Waldleitner that the song's lasting aura had swallowed both the life and the love affair of Lale Andersen.[4] If this transfer of self to image is typical of the function of mass culture and the nature of an entertainment industry, it is because they require their products to be both objects (commodities) and signs (elements of a discourse). Could Bert Brecht have envisaged that his materialist aesthetics of the 'Messingkauf' (buying a trumpet for its brass value) which he had advocated as the proper way of dealing with the works of his classic predecessors would become sound capitalist practice for men such as Luggi Waldleitner, who bought a piece of history for a song (-title)? To talk of commercialisation or exploitation is perhaps to miss the point. A consumer culture congested by overproduction of both commodities and discourses must consider it progress when it can produce commodities directly as discourses, and can code repetition as a mode that combines waste-disposal with recycling. Consumption is managed, regulated, and assured by periodic de- and revaluations, which is to say, by either adjustment or redefinition of the material support of the signifiers: that Lale Andersen is remembered thanks to a song she neither wrote nor owned rather than the reverse is in some sense an important cultural truth, one which forms the subject of Fassbinder's film, since it records the struggle of the heroine to redefine her subjectivity and identity at once through and against this materiality of the signifiers to which she finds herself attached.

The historical montage of Fassbinder's film in the form of a bio-pic or a love story is thus a trompe l'oeil effect, achieved by suppression and foreshortening the specific material instances mediating between "Lili Marleen," Lale Andersen, Fascism and a world war. But even where these instances appear as discontinuities, cuts, abrupt transitions (as they do in the film), this, too, is deceptive because the logic that articulates the story as a series of incoherences, accidents, strokes of good or bad luck and devastating non-sequiturs is itself the reflex of different aggregate states of power: energising, re-forming and reinforcing itself constantly across the gaps of the many media forms, institutions, representations, coercive instances, channels of communication, which in their ensemble make up the circuits of production and consumption in a totalitarian, but also 'modern' capitalist society. The modalities and manifestations of the invisible substance of power also produce subject-effects: emotions, intensities, in short drama, horror, tragedy, melodrama. This may be the secret of power's hold on desire, ruled by the same disjunctive logic of exchange and transformation that concentrates economic or political power on one side, while splitting and dividing the subject on the other.

Fascism as Media World

Fassbinder takes the reversal operating between person and song, public history and private story into his analysis of fascism: from the vantage point of Lale Anderson/Lili Marleen's commodity status, the war and show-business change places, production and consumption change places. Because of this emphasis on a topsy-turvy, looking-glass world of upside down values and identities, Fassbinder's films about the 1930s and 1940s are at one level anxious allegories of what in the last chapter I called the cinema's historical self-reference: foregrounding those aspects of German history (Nazism) which make them a subject for filmmaking. The connection between fascism and show business, for instance, appears to be the implicit perspective not only in LILI MARLEEN but also VERONIKA VOSS and even DESPAIR: films focussing on the nexus of power and subject effects. What emerges is the notion that cinema has a claim on history, where this history is spectacle and make-believe, deception and self-deception. Fassbinder's characters are caught up in show-making and entertainment worlds, these being addictions on a par with being hooked on drugs. His perspective therefore contrasts sharply with that of other directors' films dealing with everday life and ordinary folk (or with 'the personal as political') under fascism (HEIMAT, GERMANY PALE MOTHER), but it also differs from the *film noir* atmosphere from the immediate post-war period when films evoked fascism in the visual idiom of Expressionist cinema (e.g. Wolfgang Staudte's THE MURDERERS ARE AMONG US, 1946).

Of all the films that in the 1970s and early 1980s had fascism as their subject – and not only in Germany – it was LILI MARLEEN that took furthest the alignment of fascism and show-business, seeing (the German experience of) Nazism as a thoroughly 'modern', purposively political programme that set out to organize its followers' desire, libido and leisure.[5] By splicing together in one narrative the Second World War and the buoyant entertainment industry of radio and the phonograph, via a female star performer and a patriarchal oedipal melodrama, Fassbinder tries to pinpoint the transformation of totalitarian power into a spectacle redolent of cinematic fascination, where military and logistical power is commuted into erotic glamour, by way of three related themes: mobilization of the masses, the productivity of a war machine, and the consumption of spectacle. Not coercion and fear, but the war machinery side by side with the technology of sound and image reproduction emerges as the drug that keeps the population vital and productive. What seems central to this big budget movie wanting to break into the international film business is the extent to which Fassbinder can acknowledge that in the relation between the mass media and warfare, and thus in the significance of any historical parallel between them, the common element is consumption. Prior to the age of consumer society, war was the traditional way of managing the overproduction attendant on production for profit. In the struggle for new markets, war has in common with cinema (or for that matter any service industry) the logistics of supply, manpower, transport and distribution. In the fight with overproduction, the rapid obsolescence of weapon systems during peace time and their rapid material destruction during war have their parallel in cinema's (or in the media of mass entertainment's) creation and rapid exploitation of blockbusters.

If one approaches LILI MARLEEN with this dimension of self-reference in mind, some interesting parallels suggest themselves between Fassbinder's film and Syberberg's OUR HITLER, in other ways its antithesis, since Syberberg's is a self-consciously art and avantgarde film while Fassbinder's is just as self-consciously commercial. Both directors seem to agree that the cinema can deal with history only when and where history itself has acquired an imaginary dimension, where the disjunction between sign and referent is so radical that history turns on a problem of representation, and fascism emerges as a question of subjectivity within image and discourse (of power, of desire, of fetish objects and commodities) rather than one of causality and determinants for a period, a subject, a nation.

One of the central arguments of OUR HITLER is that the Nazi deployment of radio broadcasts, live transmissions, mass rallies and civilian mobilisation campaigns turned the State into a twelve year state-of-emergency, experienced by many Germans as communality, participation and direct address. The argument seems at first glance built on a relatively straightforward antithesis, in which the film industry, fascism and Hollywood are aligned on one side, from the vantage point of an art cinema which engages in a heroic struggle with the commercial cinema over the right to inherit nineteenth century popular culture, with its romantic myths, its kitsch objects, its sentimentality and peasant piety, as well as its wit, sarcasm and peasant slyness.[6] But even if one recognizes here the director's special pleading from the embattled position of a minority cinema struggling with Hollywood over Germany's domestic audiences, the case against Hitler as a "failed" Cecil B. DeMille, mistaking Europe for a movie set, is perhaps not just a polemical frivolity.

Just as Albert Speer conceived his buildings in view of their "ruin-value," and Ufa under Goebbels put more manpower and resources into completing KOLBERG in 1945 than the Wehrmacht into defending La Rochelle, so the marketing of movies the Hollywood way is to Syberberg the verso of war, itself the most spectacular production of industrial waste, production for waste as spectacle. The mass media in OUR HITLER emerge as a power apparatus of specular seduction, because they gave Nazi ideology its semblance of self-evidence. The appeal of *Lebensraum* and *Volksgemeinschaft* was finally not an appeal to history, national identity or a promise of manifest destiny. Rather, its meaning was the experience of immediacy and presence itself, conjured up by night-time radio broadcasts to the nation, creating the German Volk as the synthetic product of a media conglomerate which combined press, radio and cinema. The logistic capacities of this new apparatus were such that, at the height of the war, live transmissions could join battle fronts with the home front, in order for soldiers to intone "Silent Night" simultaneously in Murmansk and Tobruk, in Kiev and St Malo. What satellite technology routinely achieves today, half a century ago still required the resources necessary for a world war. It is at this point that OUR HITLER equates film production and cinema with the logic of militarization and warfare. The argument is similar to Fassbinder's when he makes LILI MARLEEN and its capacity to gather audiences central to his view of fascist ideology as a marketing strategy in the sphere of politics. Except that Fassbinder's view is more dialectical, since what makes LILI MARLEEN special is that its popular appeal outstripped both the Nazis' attempts to co-opt and contain it, and the frontiers neatly separating friend from foe, Axis soldiers from Allied soldiers.

Syberberg's polemical point is that Hollywood cinema and now television, in the name of democracy and the right to consume, have made the Riefenstahl aesthetic of TRIUMPH OF THE WILL the international norm: politics has become a photo-opportunity, public life a perpetual festival of presence, action, live-ness, where spectacles of destruction or feats of prowess and the body beautiful are feeding national or individual fantasies of omnipotence. Fassbinder's point is that popular culture taps into sources – needs, desires, yearnings – which are not simply manipulated by the powers that be, and therefore retain a degree of ambivalence and autonomy vis-à-vis ideology and politics. The continuity Syberberg draws between fascism and the modern entertainment business in OUR HITLER is still indebted to the Frankfurt School (an influence he has, more recently, repudiated in the most virulent terms),[7] according to which one kind of capitalism was trying to solve its crises by building up a war economy, while another kind of capitalism is solving its crises by enticing people to buy, spend and consume. What in fascism was the will towards self-representation (perversely, the anticipated promise of democracy, but also, according to Benjamin's famous formulation, the attempt to give the masses not the 'right to change property-relations' but 'the chance to express themselves')[8] has in post-war societies become the narcissism of the consumer. By naturalizing the mirroring structures of spectacle, cinema has played a crucial role towards bringing about such a transformation. The aesthetics of the show, according to Syberberg, is democracy's tribute to totalitarianism, not only because the past can always be rewritten as a movie, but because individual or collective experience is no longer passed on, other than as an object of consumption, in the visual system of identification, projection and doubling that is the cinema and television. Fassbinder's assessment of popular culture implicitly replies to Syberberg's (where the proposition that modern show business is more fascist than Nazism underpins the at first sight gratuitous and cranky bracketing together of Hollywood cinema and Hitler), because of his acute awareness of the heterogeneity, excessiveness and indeed surreality of the subject-effects and solidarities brought into play by movies or popular music.

Both directors represent fascism and the cinema at the level of the referent by way of citation and cliché (sidestepping issues of how 'accurately' a film can 'deal with' fascism, or 'convey' its horror or seduction). Instead, they concentrate on the (technological, emotional, rhetorical and psychic) *dispositifs* fascism seems to have in common with the mass media. Thus, they usefully draw attention to one particular history of the cinema's (and television's) power-potential: for creating a public sphere ('mobilisation') and for affective/emotional engagement. But where Fassbinder parts company with Syberberg is in not subscribing to the latter's barely disguised anti-Americanism, which gives him critical leverage against fascism while not obliging him to engage with the Holocaust. OUR HITLER, in particular, is recognizable as the high-water mark of a certain post-1968 anti-Americanism, whose critique of Hollywood can also be found in Godard's demand for 'two or three Vietnams, in the heart of the Hollywood-Mosfilm-Cinecitta-Pinewood Empire'.[9]

By contrast, Fassbinder's emplotment of the Third Reich via melodrama and genre is integral to his approach to historical representation. His films make emotion their subject not only because he wanted to address a mass audience; Nazism paradoxically was one of the few periods in modern German history when the division between high culture and mass culture had become less absolute, and a certain popular culture, as manifested in Ufa films, popular music and the radio-broadcasts of classic concerts, assumed a new historical significance, precisely because of the massive investments in the technology of sound and vision.[10] This process, where regional and folk cultures were selectively taken in charge by a centralized state and the modern technologies of representation, is the material basis against which the Nazi entertainment cinema assumed the political significance often too readily subsumed under the blanket term propaganda.[11] This popular culture – like most popular culture – was political not in the first instance because of what it showed, but because of what it also hid from view: for instance, the fanatic ruthlessness with which the regime destroyed and eradicated other cultures, crafts, skills and artefacts on an incalculable scale. Fassbinder's black market melodramas, from DESPAIR and LILI MARLEEN to MARIA BRAUN and BERLIN

ALEXANDERPLATZ, convey some of the obverse sides of this 'modernisation' process, however much the films focus on the nuclear family and the couple: the very excess of the emotional turmoil racking the characters points to the dislocations caused by this first society of the spectacle, while the thematics of devaluation and the apparently arbitrary reinscription of value are in each case central.

Love Is Colder Than Death?

The motive of this reinscription is, however, not to be sought in the domain of politics or warfare. It appears in its domestic, intimate form as a love story. What undoubtedly also attracted Fassbinder to the Waldleitner-Purzer proposal was that LILI MARLEEN is a love story, and even more so, that it is an impossible love story. Clearly, a mainstream film such as both producer and director had in mind had to contain a romance plotline to complement its quest-adventure (in this case an espionage-counter-intelligence story), but LILI MARLEEN extracts its heroine from this narrated his-and-her-story, and implicates her in ways that challenge directly the metaphorical construction of classical narrative. As already indicated, the jumps and disjuncture in the story-line are here inseparable from the flux and current of sexuality and desire, where among the accidents, ruptures, border crossings and coincidences 'love' for Fassbinder (and his heroine) always inhabits the spaces in between.

In this respect, a line of development can be traced from Fassbinder's early films to his melodramas, and from his domestic melodramas to his historical melodramas. The trajectory initially presented love stories where the desire of the central character displaced itself ceaselessly in relation to an unattainable object and where the quest terminated in literal or symbolic death (THE MERCHANT OF FOUR SEASONS, THE BITTER TEARS OF PETRA VON KANT, FEAR EATS THE SOUL, FOX AND HIS FRIENDS). In each case, the object seemed, more or less explicitly, to be the maternal body – a reading which the films, however, attempted, as it were, to foreclose by a rather didactic use of coincidences, underscoring their non-psychological structure. When, for instance, in THE MERCHANT OF FOUR SEASONS, Hans hires as his assistant the very man whom his wife has taken as her (casual) lover, the fact that Hans remains ignorant of the irony is less important than the narrative economy that results from the construction of a dramatic hinge between sexual and economic exchange. Ironic coincidences, in films like FOX AND HIS FRIENDS or FEAR EATS THE SOUL, appeared as part of Fassbinder's strategy of redefining melodrama as social parable, but in the later films, the structural use of coincidence – although if anything even more striking – nevertheless functions differently, namely to remove even the suggestion of an unattainable (but imaginable-phantasmatic) object as the driving force.

If one looks at DESPAIR, MARIA BRAUN, and LILI MARLEEN, one notices that all three films begin with a moment of break, in which an apparently 'successful' heterosexual object choice is disturbed by the more or less violent entry of a completely different referent. In DESPAIR, it is the Wall Street Crash that seems bound up with the hero's mental dissociation, and in MARIA BRAUN an explosion at the Registrar's office anticipates both the violent collapse of the Third Reich and the couple's separation. These political or economic signifieds are casually embedded in the narrative, but the relations of equivalence established between psychological motivation and political issues and events become increasingly precarious. Whereas in DESPAIR it is still possible to believe in an essentially metaphorical discourse which holds the film in place until it deconstructs itself before the spectator's eyes as a fiction of filmmaking ('I am a film actor. Don't look at the camera. I am coming out'), the relation between love and war in MARIA BRAUN or LILI MARLEEN becomes the very occasion for putting forward a non-congruent, non-metaphorical universe. The collisions, divisions, and separations that structure these films when read metaphorically appear preposterous, which has led some critics to dismiss LILI MARLEEN as just that: a preposterous exercise in bad taste. This judgement is founded on the assumption (possibly provoked by the manner in which juxtaposition teases the spectator with the promise of a hidden analogy) that the film constructs its story coherence on the offensively naive metaphorical relationship between fascism and the song, between a doomed love affair and a world war ending in defeat. Yet in LILI MARLEEN both the love story and the references to fascism are depicted in ways that effectively dismantle the metaphoric armature of popular romance and historical melodrama when set against 'real events'.

Similarly, in the case of MARIA BRAUN, where Fassbinder appears to establish a link between emotional privation (a wife pining for her husband) and economic investment (a gold-digger turning successful businesswoman), leaving open the question of whether economic activity is a substitute for sexual gratification or whether sex functions in any case merely as the consolation prize compared to the erotics of (economic, political) power. In this respect, Maria Braun inverts the conventions of melodrama, where the economic is often excluded as a possible sphere of action for the heroine, in order to give her romance/marital situation the force of emotional excess. In MARIA BRAUN, renunciation and emotional coldness explicitly underpin a certain puritan work ethic, which provides the meta-psychological, allegorical level, where Maria embodies the energy and melancholy that 'Germany' invested in the reconstruction of the national economy.

Such a New Left reading of (Sirkian) melodrama by critics, however, does not convincingly account for the perversity of the film, since Maria Braun seems to mourn her missing husband even after his release, and she engineers situations that send him first to prison and then to Canada where he, too, can make a fortune. The marriage survives, so one senses, because it remains based on separation and is practically unconsummated, except in death, and under circumstances that return to and repeat, in the form of parody and 'farce,' the historical explosion which opens the film. As argued in the previous chapter, there is considerable figurative ambiguity about this ending: whether it is an intratextual deferral of the initial violence, thereby constructing the terms of a difference that gives the narrative the circularity of its closure, or the representation of an orgasmic moment that subsumes a psychic and a political referent in a common metaphor: winning the world (cup)/losing the world (she had built up). Another way of construing the film from its ending is to say that MARIA BRAUN revolves around the heroine's attempt to retain absolute control over the terms of her own libidinal economy when the 'real' economy is at its most anarchic, and by that very fact, the recto is the economic miracle of which the verso is Maria Braun's apparently self-denying but therefore the more absolutely self-fulfilling love.

By contrast, LILI MARLEEN resembles less MILDRED PIERCE or Lana Turner in MAGNIFICENT OBSESSION, and is more like Sirk's A TIME TO LOVE AND A TIME TO DIE in the way it sets a love story against the background of historical events.[12] But it repeats the move of MARIA BRAUN in that Willie's love, too, is depicted as forceful and significant only insofar as it is based on separation, rupture, non-fulfillment. The story about love is doubled (or multiplied perhaps) by a story, not, as in MARIA BRAUN, about necessary erasure of the love object, but about an objectification of this love in a form that both contains it and betrays it, namely the song 'Lili Marleen'. In order to appreciate the significance of this shift, from the cancellation of the love object to its substitution by mechanical reproduction in the form of a phonograph record, one needs to recall how LILI MARLEEN both refers itself to the codes of melodrama and systematically turns them in upon themselves. Fassbinder points up the limits of melodrama as social parable and narrative form at precisely the moment when one of the major ideological premises of his earlier work appeared to change, namely that 'love' – whether given or withheld, whether betrayed or upheld against all odds – 'is the most insidious and efficient instrument of oppression,'[13] i.e. the supreme source of value and the supreme instrument of inequality and exploitation. In all his early films, emotional, sexual, and economic exploitation are metaphors for each other, substitutable fields that make love 'colder than death.'[14]

Exploitation: Another Form of Circulation of Value

The central paradox around which, as we have seen, Fassbinder's early work turns is that in a fallen world, love remains the only valid currency, but it lends itself to any form of speculation and calculation of gain and loss. Like Jean Luc Godard, who had linked economic and emotional relations under capitalism through the metaphor of prostitution (the ubiquity of exchange-value criticised from a romantic perspective of use-value), so that in his films only the active pursuit of prostitution (MY LIFE TO LIVE, TWO OR THREE THINGS I KNOW ABOUT HER, EVERYMAN FOR HIMSELF) promises freedom, Fassbinder saw in the way that love was traded within the family the condition for perpetuating exploitation at all levels of society. However, in his later films, he was to shed any residual romanticism about alienated use-value as the basic source of value in Western societies, and instead began to analyze the unexamined value judgements in the very notions of exploitation and prostitution.[15]

In an obvious, though perhaps superficial sense, LILI MARLEEN exemplifies the two (traditional) sides of sexual 'exploitation': on the one hand, Willie prostitutes herself to the Nazi regime in exchange for fame and wealth; on the other, she is in control, exploiting the men who think they exploit her for the regime, in order to launch herself on a career which, as it turns out, exceeds the powers of the regime to control her. This, it seems, poses a dilemma:

how can she be on the right side (morally) and on the wrong side (physically); how can she work for the Resistance and at the same time be a figurehead and showcase for the Nazis; how can she love Robert, the persecuted pariah, and accept the luxury and glamour with which the Führer himself surrounds her? But to think of her as either exploited or prostituting herself is to hold her to the same binary alternative as her lover does. One sees here a constellation of factors which could structure a much simpler film, a classical melodrama or even a classical *film noir*, where male desire, generated and simultaneously divided by the jealousy that results from the oedipal triangulation (the visible Henkel standing for the invisible Hitler standing for the symbolic *Übervater*), but salvages itself from its own contradictions through the phantasmatic production of the woman as both victim and villain (*femme fatale*).[16] The film and the figure of Willie are, however, more complex, and insofar as the heroine's position in the psycho-political constellation is that of a 'double-agent', she is closer to Maria Braun, the self-declared 'Mata Hari of the economic miracle'.

It is indeed through the constant return to periods of economic crisis and collapse, combined with the dramatisation of an unfulfilled and unfulfillable desire, that Fassbinder represents 'exploitation' as itself a problematic term, insofar as it is merely the partial and particular form of another predicament. Recognising that her desire is unfulfillable – that any desire is unfulfillable – Willie withdraws herself from the sphere of authority and control, from the calculations of gain and loss. The question becomes no longer one of degrees or kinds of exploitation from the vantage point of non-exploitation and authenticity, but of understanding that which underpins and gives currency to exploitation in the first place, namely the system(s) of exchange: whether 'fair' or 'unfair', equivalent or uneven, material or symbolic. In short, what Fassbinder exposed to examination is the realm of substitution, of metaphor and desire, where narrative form and the social production of meaning and value converge.

Willie is even-handed; she consents to lend her voice and body, her image and her performance to the Nazi regime, but she also lets herself be used by the other side. Her attempted suicide, for instance, is seized upon by the Jewish resistance as an occasion for publicising to the world press certain facts about the concentration camps. In a countermove, the Nazis revive her in order to bring her back on stage, parading her before the same international press as evidence that the Jewish claims – not about Willie/Lili Marleen, but about the concentration camps – are slanderous propaganda. The facts of her attempted suicide and of the concentration camps, different realities and incommensurate in themselves, are subsumed under her star image as pure sign, available for manipulation and transfer from one discourse (show biz performance) to another (genocide and politics). Yet instead of the film, and its heroine, judging this a perversion of true value or a violation of her identity, both accept it as the law by which she lives. Her final appearance in public even enacts a blissful version of death and transfiguration, as under the glare of the spots she bleaches into pure light, a transparent body, dematerialised, the human substance which has supported it all but used up. For it is as if only by fully participating in becoming a site of sign-production that

Willie escapes being constructed as an object – of desire and exchange, a commodity. Freedom, defined as the right to difference, comes on the side of the sign and its circulation, not by trying to resist it.

Political Resistance and the Pact of Non-fulfilment

LILI MARLEEN opens with the lovers in each other's arms. The stereotypical goal of the melodrama is here its point of departure. The subsequent narrative develops out of the interruption of this embrace which ensues when Robert's brother enters the room to remind him of his duty toward his father and the Jewish resistance group operating from Switzerland against the Nazis. The scene sets out all the antinomies – Jew/Aryan, Nazi/underground, Germany/Switzerland, father/lover – that simultaneously structure the conflicts that keep the lovers apart and that make their love possible in the first place. But since non-fulfillment is not only the driving force but also the goal of the narrative, the conflicting terms are never mediated in a 'classical' narrative resolution.[17] Robert's insistent demand to know which side Willie is on never receives an unambiguous answer. Rather, the condition of their love is that it remains fully exposed to the territorial and moral divisions that the film sets up. As in MARIA BRAUN, desire creates, along with the object, the separation and divide that bar fulfilment, which both films represent as, among other things, a geographical border.

At one level, the narrative movement of LILI MARLEEN simply illustrates the pressures that force the lovers to identify themselves with groups opposed to their love – the Jewish resistance on the one side, the Nazi and show business on the other. Both remake themselves in the image and the terms of the worlds they reluctantly inhabit, at the same time as they try to use these terms to intensify their love. The world of moral and political obligations which Robert chooses turns out to be dominated in every respect by his father, so that he is defined completely by the oedipal limits of patriarchy. The world of spectacle, show, performance, and self-display which Willie chooses is synonymous with Nazism. The difference between Robert's and Willie's 'inscription' into the social symbolic reproduces the sexual difference which society traditionally sanctions. The Law of the Father allots duty, work, renunciation to him and specularity, image, objectification to her. For, true to one trope of melodrama, Willie's love for Robert is of course her true act of (political) resistance. It is she who has the will to tolerate uncertainty, and the strength to put up with the in-between, the mixed, the Jewish-Aryan amalgam, the jagged lines demanded by survival strategies and frequent border crossings. By contrast, both the Nazis and the Jews are depicted as funda- mentalists, concerned with purity and clear lines of demarcation, making Willie defy not only the Nazi's racial laws, but also the Jewish family's patriarchal law.

This 'intransigence' and the misunderstandings it gives rise to are most clearly in evidence in the all-night recording session during which the song is cut. The scene as a whole is crucial in that it sets up many of the film's most revealing ironies. After several takes, Willie's Nazi protector agrees to a short break; it is 6.00 a.m. They turn on the radio for the news just in time to hear Hitler announce, "Since 5.45 a.m. this morning, the German Army is returning fire." Not only has war been declared, but outside in the park, Willie's lover is waiting, having crossed the border illegally and against his father's orders. As Willie steps into the cold dawn, horrified that Robert has put himself at serious risk by entering the grounds of the Gruppenführer's villa, Robert, not unreasonably, wants to know whether she still loves him. Dissatisfied with her protestations, he asks which side she is on, to which she replies 'on your side, as long as I live. But I'm not free to choose how to live in order to survive.' The outbreak of the war coinciding with the recording of the song and both interrupted by the unexpectedness of his visit perfectly illustrate what she means. The improbabilities and coincidences which here introduce the referents 'world war' and 'love story' clearly exceed all fictional verisimilitude, especially since the narrational device of the radio-broadcast providing vital plot information is a self-consciously cited cliché from B-picture productions. These three moments of drastically unequal weight and significance are made to coexist within the same narrative space, in breach even of the logic of excess of melodrama, and give rise to one of the most meticuluously staged scenes in the whole film. A geometry of glances linking characters and spaces builds up a complex architecture of fictionality, challenging the viewer to regard these coincidences as a conceptual montage in which the film's major themes and their interdependence are given a three-dimensional representation, so to speak. Otherwise the incongruity between the private, the anecdotal, and the historical remains so radical and unbridgeable as to offend the sophisticated viewer's sense of proportion and even propriety. For to read the coincidence between the end of a recording session and the start of a world war as significant on the diegetic level – as a moment of symmetry, as an explanation of why the song was so meaningful during the war – amounts to having to dismiss the film as 'a slap in the face'.[18] The scene must appear grotesque, unless one sees the film as pressing narrative coincidence to the point where it deconstructs itself as a Brechtian 'distancing device'.

Yet such a modernist reading goes, it seems to me, against the grain of a film which, after all, is a product of the commercial film industry for the mass-market. Another way of construing the incongruity of this scene is to assume that Fassbinder here resorted to the logic of the gag,[19] precisely because of his awareness of the limits of melodrama in the face of representing fascism. Melodrama's particular modes of disjuncture and discontinuity are always in the service of either irony or pathos. Yet both depend on the spectator assuming a secure position of knowledge, which is to say, they presume a narrative which establishes a strong sense of closure. The 'success' of HOLOCAUST, I argued, was due to its depictions of fascism and the 'Final Solution' in the mode of tragic irony and intense pathos, made possible by a pre-construction of the spectator as one who is in the know: about the terrible end in store for the protagonists, but also about fascism's historical and geographical boundary, in short, about the fact that the Americans put an end to it, and that, however terrible it was, it has entered into the past tense. A series like HOLOCAUST furthermore tries to contain fascism by confining its effects on domestic life, making the (bourgeois) family the norm, threatened and disrupted by the blandishments (in one case) and the persecutions (in the other) associated with the regime's racism.[20] Fassbinder's challenge was – as in all his films – how not to make the bourgeois family the norm against which danger, threat, and disruption of equilibrium are measured, and how not to put the spectator 'in the know', whether this was the security of hindsight or the expectations of a narrative that cast fascism in the rise and fall of pattern of a Hollywood gangster film.[21] In LILI MARLEEN, May 1945 is not the endpoint of the narrative; at some unspecified point, Willie goes to Zurich, and after her non-encounter with Robert, disappears into the night. Here, too, coincidence and dramatic irony are presented as terrible anticlimaxes. With its asymmetries and non-equivalences, the film disturbs the formal closure of popular narrative, while still retaining all the elements of popular story-telling.

Six Million: Fascism and Consumer Society

This, then, is why the narrative of LILI MARLEEN appears so episodic, haphazard even, and liable to the sudden and surreal reversals which the film chronicles in the several episodes that turn on puns in bad taste and other gruesome gags. For instance, to illustrate the popularity of the song, Fassbinder confronts its success with the Nazi's success in liquidating and destroying surplus material (human and technological): 'Six million' – Willie's face beams as she is told by her Nazi friend how many listeners are tuning in to "Lili Marleen" every night. 'Fantastic,' she says, trying to hug herself with both arms to confirm that this means her. Turned to the camera in medium close-up, Schygulla's face basks in the new identity that her status as superstar, confirmed by record sales and audience ratings, reflects back on her.[22] Six million: the figure connects her fans – mainly soldiers dying in the trenches – and the Jews dying in concentration camps, as it equates mass consumption of entertainment with the organized deaths of warfare, slave labour and genocide. The convergence of soldier and fan is turned by Fassbinder into a terrible gag when Willie's pianist-turned-soldier takes his platoon over the top and straight into the machine gun fire of the Russians whom he confuses with German troops because they, too, are playing "Lili Marleen".

This tragic mistake exemplifies the more general principle of one sign serving several referents. But the image of the song floating on the airwaves can also stand for the principle of the 'floating signifier' which structures the film as a whole, linking the different episodes and leapfrogging from sign to referent and back, as mistakes and misunderstandings 'productively' circulate. The principle strongly emerges in the sequence where Willie attempts to prove to her lover that she is on 'his' side, even though she works for the Nazis and seems intimate with Henkel, the Obergruppenführer. But nothing is as it seems: The Jewish resistance needs someone to smuggle out of Poland the clandestine footage documenting the existence of concentration camps; Willie can be the carrier pigeon under cover of her Eastern Front entertainment tour; but she needs an alibi for a meeting with her lover, so a car ride is arranged, during which the film reel is slipped to her; Henkel, guessing what has happened, attempts to recover the film hidden in her bra; Willie deliberately misinterprets his gesture as a sexual advance, which she rebuffs with the help of her pianist friend, whose sudden assertion of (feigned) manhood costs him his life, because it starts off another chain reaction leading to his being called up to active duty, and the fatal mistake already mentioned. During a body search ordered by the Nazi command, Henkel offers to transmit the film to the Jewish resistance as a sign of his love for her, even though he knows that for Willie the film is merely a sign of her love for Robert. The film reaches Switzerland at the same time as Robert's father is negotiating the release of his son captured by the Nazi who demand (and get) the film in exchange for Robert's return. Thus the footage, important in its referentiality, is never actually shown, but exists productively as sign, circulating as token and value in a number of discourses about love, loyalty and sacrifice, while also materially changing hands in a number of conflicting deals which in the end cancel its referentiality when the Nazi take possession of it. Both sides seem prepared to operate according to the object's semiotic 'code', except for Robert's brother, a fundamentalist and materialist who, as he says 'hate(s) these dirty deals' and, refusing to submit to the logic of exchange between sex and politics, prefers to be a 'terrorist'. He blows up the bridge between Germany and Switzerland, severing the connexions in the vain hope that clear lines of division, between good and bad, right and wrong can be redrawn.

Submission to the Patriarchal Law

What is scandalous to many viewers of LILI MARLEEN is that the relation family/fascism is presented as a structural symmetry onto which the antagonism Jew/Aryan is mapped as an additional confirmation that the heroine must find her subject position outside either set of value systems and the narrative constraints they connote, at the same time as she represents an object – of value, of exchange – to both sides. Her lover's anti-fascism is thus entirely recuperated within patriarchy, while his Jewish identity is equally inscribed in the law of the father, and therefore does not appear as heroically 'other' (neither victim to be pitied nor brave resistance fighter), with all the shocking provocation that this juxtaposition of Nazi terror and Jewish patriarchal terror was bound to elicit.[23]

The logic which directs Robert's father first to pay for all of Willie's 'debts' in order to accumulate enough evidence to obtain an expulsion warrant from the Swiss government, and then to allow Willie to accompany Robert to Munich so that the lovers can be served the warrant and legally separated at the German-Swiss border, is the mirror equivalent of the logic which directs the Nazis to use Willie and Robert as bait for each other and as pawns in the circuit of exchange that results in the release of Robert and the transfer of Jews to Switzerland. The same chiasmic path defines the journeys of the reel of film as it makes its way from Poland via Germany to Switzerland and back and "Lili Marleen" as it circulates between contending forces both within and outside Germany. Robert and Willie's love affair is thus always masterminded, by 'both sides', but does this mean the parallels that emerge between the actions of the Jewish resistance and the Nazis have to be regarded as part of a conspiracy which locates the lovers as victims? Surely, the point is not to suggest that the Nazis and the Jews were equally to blame, but rather, that for Willie, the politics of fascism and race, and the politics of gender and subjectivity cannot be conflated. By resisting all constructions of herself in the terms of (the narrative's) binary oppostions, she achieves a particular kind of freedom. She becomes a sign without submitting to a referent, or rather, because several referents – notably her star image and the phonographic record – are simultaneously attached to her, her desire and subjectivity can exist outside either possession or fulfillment. Neither her show business 'personality' nor the song she records express her, except in the way they permit her to constitute herself outside fascism and outside the family.

The film therefore makes a distinction between the vicissitudes of Robert's and Willie's displaced desires. As these are so carefully delineated, LILI MARLEEN is in actual fact two films, depending on whose destiny one is most concerned with: a melodrama and an anti-melodrama. Robert's story follows the lines of the typical German melodrama of the mid-30s, exemplified, say, by Sirk's SCHLUSSAKKORD (1936), where a woman separated from her husband is able to 'be' with him by listening to him conduct Beethoven on the radio. As in so many of the composer bio-pics from Ufa and Hollywood during the 1930s and 1940s, an unrequited love and the lashings of sexual frustration give rise to virtuoso performances and masterpieces. This identification of art and an unhappy lovelife is deconstructed by Fassbinder, because in LILI MARLEEN it is explicitly attributed, in a complexly edited scene near the film's end, to the castration anxiety which empowers the Law of the Father. The face-to-face meeting of Willie and Robert at the Zurich opera house is mediated by the glances of two women – Robert's mother and his (new) wife. These glances are themselves intercut at several points, however, by an image that cannot be located within the diegetic space of the narrative, but acts as a kind of master shot for the sequence as a whole: it is a frontal mirror shot of Robert's father as a benevolent but threatening spectator of both the triumphant performance onstage and the embarrassing scene backstage. Robert's escape into the world of performance has not liberated him from anxiety, unlike Willie's spectacular resurrection after her attempted suicide has released her into the realm of myth and legend – that of 'Lili Marleen' giving her, as she says, 'a passport to being no longer afraid.'

Willie's story thus invites a reading that turns the melodrama on its head, for she, too, sublimates and displaces her unfulfilled desire in music and performance, but in contrast to Robert, oedipal sublimation-repression does not work, and on the contrary, is spectacularly betrayed by the very technology that is about to determine her subsequent fate. The metaphoric status of 'Lili Marleen', as an expression of her longing for Robert is explicitly established by a phone call she places backstage to Robert in Zurich, as she is about to sing the song for the first time in a Munich nightclub, and where she speaks of her love and longing for him. Due to a fault in the amplification system, her frank and reiterated declaration of love can be heard throughout the bar, to the great hilarity of the guests and to the detriment of her performance. The attempt to fix her subjectivity in this way is a disaster, quite literally, insofar as her cabaret number gives rise to a brawl, started between a group of young Germans in SA uniforms and some English visitors. The ensuing demolition and devastation of the premises foreshadow a future point in the narrative, for it is staged and edited so as to rhyme with the depiction of air raids and bombs exploding in German trenches. These shots are themselves intercut with those of bouquets of flowers being tossed on stage in tribute to her smash hit. Fassbinder both links these distinct moments and undercuts their metaphorical status by relying on a pun: 'Lili Marleen' is a 'Bombenerfolg', a devastating smash hit, while the bombs are falling and human bodies are erupting from the ground like the flowers showering the stage on opening night.

Twice more, Fassbinder makes the point that no psychological, causal, or intentional relationship exists between the singer and the phonograph record. If Willie's longing for Robert does not improve her singing and the first performance is a flop, the fact that her Nazi protector nonetheless insists on recording the song serves to emphasise that it is not her desire that speaks, but someone else's desire for her. Even this might have remained an act without consequence, had it not been for the coincidence of the war breaking out. But it takes the additional fortuity of the Belgrade radio operator finding a stray copy of it among looted spoils for the song to air and become the phenomenal hit, symbolizing for others what it does not symbolize for her. At the climax of her career, Willie dances about in the luxury apartment given to her by the Führer; holding a mirror in front of her, she exclaims, 'we've made it, we're above the clouds.' Taschner, her pianist and companion, responds as if to complete her sentence, 'and the irony is, you have no voice and I'm a lousy pianist.' This is the most Sirkian moment in the film: sharply undercutting subjective euphoria with a sobering objectivity. Irony is piled upon irony: Taschner's comment severs, in the most direct and brutal way, any organic or necessary connection that might be thought to exist between singer and song, self-expression and success, talent and recognition, authenticity and exhibition value. It advises us, as spectators, against construing the relationship between love and war as metaphorical – but also as merely coincidental. Whereas the Hollywood bio-pic is committed to the opposite logic, namely to inflect the hero or heroine's accidents of life and circumstances with the deeper meaning which destiny and hindsight confer on them, Fassbinder appears to revel in demonstrating the non-sequiturs and accidents. But these accidents are in some sense merely the corrosive agent that strips away the coating of verisimilitude and the glue of choice and agency that usually holds together a biography. What needs to be exposed is that other structure, that other logic – the one by which history can become a song, and a life can become the effect of an image and a commodity.

Fassbinder became increasingly concerned with the historical moments of rupture (the inflation period, World War II, and the early postwar years), and he redefined melodrama as his way of deconstructing the hidden discursiveness in the realm of history, social reality, and the psyche, on the basis of a rigorous and everywhere enforced celebration of the arbitrary. Hence the textuality of his later films which parody the social text that is monopoly capitalism. LILI MARLEEN develops in a series of gags and jokes in order to point to the logic, this time by no means arbitrary, governing the economic and symbolic systems by which our society reproduces its power relations and thus lives its history.

It is almost entirely within this perspective – which is obviously also the perspective of Fassbinder's own construction as a filmmaker, as a performer in the cultural contexts of sign and commodity production – that fascism becomes specific, and that one can find in LILI MARLEEN a representation of Nazi Germany. For although the (by 1980) already cliched iconography of the 'mode-retro' pervades the film, along the Nazi insignia and colour schemes, Fassbinder is even less intent on recreating period accuracy than Visconti in THE DAMNED or Bergman in THE SERPENT'S EGG (two films that Fassbinder had carefully studied). The emphasis on spectacle and show lends glamour to Nazism; but without invoking its conventionalized sign-language Fassbinder could not establish the important metonymic link he needs to draw between Nazism and representation, on the basis of which the story elements function as so many metaphors of warfare: the wars on the military fronts, the propaganda and media wars, the 'secret wars' between the Nazis and the Jewish resistance organisation.[24] It is this multiplication of wars and of theatres of war which forms the historical but also the argumentative basis for portraying the period as one of crisis, of rigorous and businesslike administration of chaos, during which established systems of value and traditional forms of cohesion are at the very least suspensed if not altogether destroyed. And as always in Fassbinder, such a state of affairs is ambivalent – a melting pot and a test laboratory, destructive and disruptive, but releasing energies of an unexpected kind.

First of all, there are the material energies inherent in a modern industrialized society. Fassbinder presents war from the point of view of production: it is seen as an acceleration and a unifying force which, by speeding up the productive and reproductive cycles of the economy, gets rid of material surplus, and to that extent, Hitler's arms build-up could be seen as the conventional way of resolving capitalist crises of over-production. By linking rearmament with show-business, LILI MARLEEN depicts warfare and mass culture as almost alternative ways of achieving a similar aim: intensify consumption. The Fascist war economy and its show business operations appear as a kind of immense and universalised black market where, in the manner of all military dictatorships, the Nazis impose their own rate of exchange – fixed from moment to moment – which determine ethical values (what counts as morality) and referential values (what counts as reality).

Material energies are doubled by semiotic energies: Fassbinder's view of show business as an instrument that splits sign from referent is mirrored in the picture of fascism as a form of crisis management in the economic sphere, called upon to regulate – by brute force – the acceleration of production. Eliminating surplus by simple destruction, while at the same time developing radio and the record industry, using war to organise an elaborate system of mass transportation and communication, Nazism becomes a particularly flamboyant figuration of capitalism in the sphere of representation – not merely because of its gigantic aspirations or the brutality of its public life, but more because of its power to reorganise a society's moral, material and erotic relations in the direction of spectacle or rituals of communal consumption of sounds and images.

Material Girl and Immaterial Song

The identification in LILI MARLEEN of mass coercion (the Nazi regime and the army) with mass consumption (show business and the electronic 'global village' of radio and later, television) is interesting in another respect. For one of the questions which Nazism raises for Fassbinder, as it did for Syberberg, apart from its relation to material production and capitalism, and the monstrous scale and consequences of its demographic planning, was its ability to create a public sphere, a mass audience. The song of "Lili Marleen", endlessly repeated as a nightly ritual above and between the sights and sounds of war, is such a fascinating phenomenon, partly because of the discrepancy between the pure presence of the song, hermetically sealed by its technological immediacy from any contact and context, and the ceaselessly destructive and intensely busy machinery of war which it serves. Media technology, in this case, binds together a whole array of social and communicative activities (performance, recording, broadcasting, listening, phoning and letter-writing) around something which, while still in need of some sort of material support (a phonograph record, a receiver, a broadcasting station), nonetheless has no essence in itself other than to act as a kind of mirror surface for the projection or reflection of desire.

What exactly is this desire? "Lili Marleen", like Willie, voices a protest, a refusal, a critique even: it says no to war, and yes to memory, loss and love ("For you and I again to meet/Under the lantern on the street/Like times gone by, Lili/Gone by, Lili Marleen"). One can see why the Nazi leadership felt ambiguous about it, because it gives expression to a death wish at the same time as it disguises and disavows it ("Out of the earthly soil, out of the silent realm/Your loving lips could lift me, as if in a dream/And late, when the fog is rolling in/I'll stand beneath the lamp again/Like times gone by...").

This double impulse may well explain the song's popularity during the war; it certainly explains the symptomatic significance which it is granted in the film. As a protest and a refusal, its message would seem to be at odds with its social and political function as a nightly theme song: to boost morale and unite the *Volksgemeinschaft* behind the *Führer*. The stark opposition of love and military discipline in the song, its 'politics of subjectivity', is, however, recuperated by the ritual and turned to the advantage of the regime. But the situation is even more complex. Not only is the song repeated nightly (and throughout the film), it is itself entirely built on repetition and refrain ("wie einst" – like times gone by). Conjuring up a lost object and a lost moment, both of which the song re-presents and re-possesses through the refrain and the overall melodic structure, the song is clearly obsessional and fetishistic.

How is it that mass subjectivity becomes so intricately bound up with this obsessional song? As Robert is tortured by the Nazis, who play him broken snatches of the song, we are given a vivid representation of the hounding persistence of the compulsion to repeat and of the frustration, violence or aggression it entails. The utterly subjective death-wish expressed in the song stands in symmetrical relation to the historical death towards which its listeners are headed. For, by the film's terms, popular music, always complicit with voicing and representing subjectivity and desire, works in tandem with an entertainment industry that extends its dominion and economic control more and more firmly into the same area – that of the subject. Here the split, unreconciled in most contemporary theory of culture, between the economic structure of the mass media and the political meaning of subjectivity, is made obvious.[25] As the products of culture reveal their commodity/sign status, which destines them for consumption or the devaluation/revalorisation processes of the market, so the subjectivity that articulates itself across these products can speak mostly of loss and destruction, nostalgia and death. In this respect, the particular sensibility, the powerfully melancholic, Saturnalian turn of LILI MARLEEN is perhaps the precisely perceived demonstration of its political function, the negative truth about its objective condition: to represent radical subjectivity trapped in commodity form.[26]

The more often the song "Lili Marleen" is repeated, the more it becomes a pure signifier, shifting between any number of conflicting discourses. Caught in a cycle of repetition, it no longer denotes anything, but merely connotes a wholly abstract, generalised structure of absence or loss and reinforces the primary impulse to yield. Yet the song colludes with fascism only insofar as its repetitive form installs within the subject that same synthesizing force which unites the social system to Fascist politics, unites it, that is, under a single figure, a single image, a single insignium.[27]

Empires of Signs

The disjunctive though metonymic relations between performer and song on the one hand, and between song and material object/commodity on the other, are fundamental to Fassbinder's idea of the cinema since they implicate, by way of a series of displaced analogies and en abyme constructions, the film object and its author/performer. The song, insofar as it exists prior to and apart from its material shape as record or infinitely repeatable performance, may function as a mode of self-expression, a declaration of love, of morbid protest, of a desire for nostalgic return. Its value as a token of subjectivity, however, contrasts with its exhibition or circulation value, since any traces of an authorial self become literally immaterial as soon as the work signifies other 'subjectivities' in the iterative acts of consumption. Rather like a linguistic shifter, the song says 'I' and 'you', 'here' and 'now' for everyone and at all times, thus establishing the commodity as sign, with every act of appropriation becoming an act of subjectification.

This sign form is, above all, the trace of the technical and economic power inherent in the mass media, reorganising, from the point of view of consumption, both the production of materials and of meaning. As these abstract processes of power emerge in concrete contexts (here, as a song that serves to console friend or foe as each faces annihilation; that becomes an instrument of torture, a political weapon in a propaganda war, a means of turning an individual into a star), they require for their material support not a work that is original or profound, but one that can be bland, banal, devoid of any but the power to circulate.[28] The mass media artefact is thus not the product of a field of combative forces – between the author struggling for self-expression, for example, and the industry which exploits him or her – but of the site where, through immense technical and logistic effort, all forces are neutralised. The conjunction of Nazism and "Lili Marleen" illustrates the way the logistic-military machinery stages the perfect spectacle as the one from which all external referents are emptied.

Yet there is at work here another, countervailing force. "Lili Marleen" also obliquely, stubbornly opposes itself to all the forces that attempt to appropriate it. When Willie says, "I only sing", she is not as politically naive or powerless as she may appear. Just as her love survives because she withdraws it from all possible objects and objectifications, so her song, through its very circularity, becomes impervious to the powers and structures in which it is implicated. Love and song are both, by the end of the film, empty signs. This is their strength, their saving grace, their redemptive innocence, allowing Fassbinder to acknowledge the degree to which his own film is inscribed within a system (of production, distribution and reception) already in place, waiting to be filled by an individual, who lends the enterprise the appearance of intentionality, design and desire for self-expression. It is this system, after all, that transforms him from partner in a deal (proposed by Luggi Waldleitner? Manfred Purzer? Hanna Schygulla?) into an auteur, a star, the name above the title. Whereas Jean Marie Straub and Daniele Huillet construct their films around the notion of the resistance of their materials to the filmic process,[29] one might say that Fassbinder constructed his films around the notion of the inability of materials to resist. It is not through resistance, but through self-cancellation that materials achieve purity and transcendence in his films. The spectacle becomes a form of escape, which is why her attempted suicide is such an ambiguous gesture: she dies twice, in effect – once by cutting her wrists, and a second time by stepping into the white light of her final stage appearance.[30] Whereas her lover unifies himself in the performance of classical music, she undoes herself in the performance of a pop song, consenting to becoming the depersonalized fetish object which is "Lili Marleen", the song endlessly playing, the record endlessly turning.

It would therefore be inaccurate to say that the song "Lili Marleen" is a metaphor, or even a representation en abyme of Fassbinder's film of that title. And yet, LILI MARLEEN – the fictional narrative and the historical pre-text, the song and its reiterated performance in sound and image – does create a symbolic field of receding and nested references that places the film both as material object and, in the act of consumption, within the mirror-image of its own subject. To point to an obvious trace of this process: Hanna Schygulla plays a woman called Willie, singing a song in which a first-person narrator (a man) addresses an unnamed woman by invoking another woman, named Lili Marleen. Once this song has become popular, because it provides a subject position and a temporality for lonely men in the trenches, Willie autographs pictures of Hanna Schygulla with the name Lili Marleen. Hanna Schygulla is not Willie (in the tautology elaborated over decades by the star system which allows actor or actress to "use up" the fictional character they portray by inhabiting his/her persona), she is Lili Marleen, because both are identical imaginary objects (or discursive effects) for two historically distinct audiences (soldiers of World War II and cinema spectators now) constructed in relation to one another as the other's mise-en-abyme. Fassbinder, in LILI MARLEEN, demonstrates the permanent slippage of actress, character, name and addressee, organized around something as ephemeral and banal as a popular song, albeit one that, like the cinema, commands its own imaginary and mythological space within history. This space can neither be metonymically collapsed with history (in the sense that one might be tempted to say that the song "Lili Marleen" stands for the use of the mass media under fascism), nor metaphorically separated from it (by treating the song as a symbolic representation of the cinema, for instance). What is at issue is precisely the complex status of the song as object, irreducible and recalcitrant to the uses it served, and at the same time, product, expression, and signifier of a historical period. A spiral movement joins not only author to actress, and actress to part, and part to song, and song to film, and film to commodity, but also moves laterally, where the commodity film becomes the experience cinema, for an audience that identifies with star, and across the star with the fiction, repeating the infinite regress which the film both enacts and deconstructs, and deconstructs in order to enact.

A Clearing in the Forest: Temporality and Melodrama, Sequels and Prequels

We seem to have come back to what we started from: the peculiar processes by which history can become a song title and a person merges with a commodity. Yet these processes, so apparently destructive of self and happiness, paradoxically now appear almost as moments of freedom and resistance. With this, Fassbinder makes a plea on behalf of his female heroine and her conception of selfhood, but he also mounts a most optimistic argument on behalf of popular culture, in the midst of fascism, resisting fascism. This is worth bearing in mind for two reasons: firstly, it marks him off, as we saw, from quite a number of fellow-filmmakers whose antipathy to what they perceive as the 'Americanisation of Europe' (where American invariably stands for little else but popular culture) makes them at times equate Hollywood with Hitler. And secondly, it suggests, on the part of Fassbinder, a position vis-à-vis capitalism and commodity culture that goes well beyond the ideological critique and even the utopian horizons of his generation, the post-68 politicised intellectuals of Germany and Western Europe.

Hopefully, the chapter has also offered some arguments why Fassbinder's decision to work on this most sensitive topic with the formulas of melodrama, the mise-en-scène of spectacle, and the visual tropes of fascination, aesthetisation or glamourisation can be seen as not only inherent in the very nature of the project, but as elements of a self-referentiality and a discourse in which these very signifiers of 'Nazism' could be made productive – for a reflection on the nature of cinema as a historically overdetermined dispositif, and also on the cinema's own textuality: between realism and metaphoric speech, postmodern pastiche and socio-historical allegory.

In this last respect, the films of Fassbinder offer the greatest challenges, since they belong to a cinema which, while addressing a mass public (and thus committed to genre cinema and fictional realism), nevertheless works at deconstructing this generically coded realism for another audience and for another discourse. Three traits characterise the latter: the use of the female actress as fictional character and star; the peculiar temporality within which the narrative is embedded, and finally the 'supertext' that unfolds not just within one film, but establishes itself across several films and ultimately, the director's whole oeuvre.

As for the first point, the female star around which LILI MARLEEN turns is of course Hanna Schygulla. I already mentioned how fraught Fassbinder's relation with her had by that time become. Made world-famous with MARIA BRAUN, Schygulla should have played the lead in LOLA, but lost the part to Barbara Sukowa, because she was foolhardy enough to be seen deciding this casting herself, and thus invite Fassbinder's disfavour, who seemed already piqued that Schygulla stole the thunder on LILI MARLEEN. And yet, this battle of wills between actress and director is preserved in the film, making her even more uniquely qualified to embody the fictional person the film constructs out of Lale Andersen's life, the only one who could credibly and movingly represent the two sides of Willie: an absolute demand for love, and an equally absolute withholding, in the sense of connoting a stance less sacrificial than renunication and more purposively determined than refusal. That the refusal was as much Fassbinder's and that her walking away from Robert at the end of the film marks the zenith of her career adds a further twist.[31]

Schygulla in MARIA BRAUN and LILI MARLEEN, but not in LOLA or VERONIKA VOSS, introduces my second point. For insofar as the idiosyncratic relationship that Fassbinder at this point entertained with Schygulla unites and yet also fractures the BRD trilogy, we need to think LILI MARLEEN into the equation, in order for the outlines of the overall design to become visible. As already hinted in one of the preceding chapters, the three films of the BRD trilogy – shot out of sequence – are held together by the possibility that they form sequels. If we add the film that was made between MARIA BRAUN and LOLA, namely LILI MARLEEN, which clearly has key themes in common with the trilogy, then LILI MARLEEN's status in the series might be that of a 'prequel' chronologically: 1938-1946 Lili Marleen, 1945-1954 Maria Braun, 1956 Veronika Voss, 1957 Lola. Four women, four love stories, four ambiguous gestures of complicity and resistance.

But in Fassbinder's historiographic telescoping of space and time, where he conjugates the 1970s across the 1940s and 1950s, LILI MARLEEN might also offer something like a causal explanation of the origins of the themes dealt with in the others, with each film not only like the anticipation but also the memory of the other. Looked at from another perspective – a narrative one – each film is also an interpretation, or an alternative version, a revision. MARIA BRAUN, VERONIKA VOSS and LOLA fit as a group, not only because of the way the three films are chronologically segued into each other, but because the two others are in a sense other versions of the 'ending' of MARIA BRAUN (whose ending as we have it is already an alternative ending to the one written in the script, which is again different from the one Hanna Schygulla would have liked to have seen). VERONIKA VOSS is the story of a Maria Braun who more and more gives in to her depressions, who becomes addicted first to alcohol and then to drugs, a woman who, after becoming thoroughly disenchanted with men, enters into a fatal bond with another woman. By contrast, LOLA tells the story of a Maria Braun who, though sobered by her returning Hermann, decides to run Oswald's firm with the help of loyal Senkenberg, playing the various interests off against each other. Become the cynical, razor-sharp survivor-type, Lola, even if the men have taken over the show again, nonetheless knows not only how to run her life, but how to run that of the men as well. Or perhaps, given the similarity in the endings of the two films, LOLA is best seen as a parodic version of MARIA BRAUN, where everyone gets what they want in the end, while in LILI MARLEEN, as in Sirk's melodramas, nobody gets what they want.

Such a formulation, however, does not plumb some of the depths at which these different films cohere by forming a network of more or less subterranean cross-references. In particular, the figure of Lola, so apparently similar to Maria Braun is also her opposite, seeing that Barbara Sukowa is the ying to Hanna Schygulla's yang. One cannot but remember that Sukowa's other major role for Fassbinder was that of Mieze, the much-suffering, dedicated girlfriend of Franz Bieberkopf, the hero of BERLIN ALEXANDERPLATZ, 'given' to Franz by Eva, played by none other than Hanna Schygulla. When one then compares Lola's calculated self-control with Mieze's intensely selfless and unreflected abandonment to the man she loves, one wonders, again, how Lola might once have been a Mieze, or what could have happened in Mieze's life – had she survived – for her to become a Lola?

If this seems idle speculation, it is in fact prompted by one of the more mysterious scenes of LILI MARLEEN, where Willie, escaping from the advancing Red Army and hiding in the woods near Berlin, is told by Henkel, now camouflaged in civilian clothes, about a gruesome sex crime committed at this very spot in the late 1920s. This murder in a forest clearing refers to the violent death of Mieze in BERLIN ALEXANDERPLATZ, obliging the viewer to reflect, across the association of Willie and Mieze, about the meaning of a love and a loyalty that has to prove itself in a seemingly pointless death. That this should take place in a forest clearing, on the other hand, attains its ominous resonance not primarily in BERLIN ALEXAN-DERPLATZ, but in LILI MARLEEN, because a film about Nazism and the World War inescapably associates at the sight of false forest idylls the massacres and random executions that took place at Katyn or in Galicia, committed by German SS or Soviet commandos, whose victims were Jews and partisans, Polish officers and retreating German soldiers, linking individual fates and collective moments of horror across places that at first seem to have nothing to do with each other, like Willie and Mieze, like LILI MARLEEN and BERLIN ALEXANDERPLATZ, like BERLIN ALEXANDERPLATZ and LOLA.

The effect is that LILI MARLEEN and MARIA BRAUN are not the only ones of the four women's films with an ambiguous ending: taken together with LOLA and VERONIKA VOSS, they all but oblige the viewer to imagine the jigsaw puzzles into which these so differently shaped pieces might fit.[32] Anticipation, explanation or alternative resolution: it seems that the chronological intersplicing of the Fassbinder films dealing with German history is doubled by an even more mysterious causality, and the complexly retroactive relationship the works have on each other. It suggests that Fassbinder's notion of history includes time and events being in some ways open to revision, almost 'reversible', or at any rate, open precisely to these other readings, which are even more than readings: they are re-writings. In the following chapter, this particular motif and its many ramifications will be looked at more closely, to suggest why it is part of Fassbinder representing Germany, but also why it leaves the viewer with such a strong sense that these women's stories are haunted by their 'others': 'others' that the films looked at so far hardly name at all.

7. Frankfurt, Germans and Jews
The City, Garbage and Death

A Nation without Dreams: Memory and Identity in Germany[1]

What the 'Hitler Wave' of the early 1970s and its focus on the 'home front' barely brought into public discussion was one central fact of Nazi ideology: anti-Semitism.[2] Its presence in Germany preceded Nazism, but its significance changed utterly when Hitler came to power, for with the planned genocide of the 'Final Solution' it became the turning point of modern German history. Yet neither the Eichmann trial in Jerusalem in 1964, nor the Auschwitz and Majdanek concentration camp trials of Frankfurt in 1963 and Hamburg in 1967 provoked a fundamental soul-searching.[3] The history of European Jews and the unimaginable destruction of their centuries-old culture remained, like the origins of fascism generally, a subject for academic historians, while the attitude of Germans to Jews after Auschwitz barely featured even there. Over many years and against often shamefully bureaucratic manoeuvres, the representatives of what remained of the Jewish community in West Germany had to fight case by case to persuade federal and municipal authorities to erect monuments to the victims of the Holocaust, to preserve the internment and concentration camps as commemorative sites, and to have streets named after eminent German Jews.[4]

Yet if Nazism was to be 'mastered', one needed to come to an understanding of anti-Semitism, and if anti-Semitism was to be understood, actions were called for that went beyond paying disability pensions to survivors and concluding compensation agreements with the state of Israel. Primo Levi, liberated by the Russians in Auschwitz and passing through Munich in October 1945 on his way back to Italy, scrutinized the faces of the people for some sign of acknowledgement or apology:

> But nobody looked us in the eyes, nobody took up the challenge: they were deaf, blind and mute, locked into the ruins of their houses like fortresses of wilful ignorance, still strong, still capable of hatred and contempt, still prisoners of the old cage of arrogance and guilt.[5]

According to Hermann Glaser, a cultural historian, Levi might have said the same about the majority of Germans thirty or forty years later.[6] It seemed that no amount of public pronouncements against racism could oblige Germans to take upon themselves some of the burden of responsibility which the Nazi terror against Jews had passed on as their country's unavoidable legacy. Although officially West Germany, and especially the conservative right, had been demonstratively philo-semite ever since Konrad Adenauer's first pro-Israel statements, the taboo around anti-Semitism, whose historic roots and particular logic demanded to be exposed and explained, remained in place.[7] Fassbinder recalls how as a child, people used to silence him in the corridor, and say in a hushed voice: 'that's a Jew over there, you better behave, and be nice to him'.[8]

West Germany's deficit, as far as anti-Semitism is concerned, has had two central aspects: a lack of knowledge about the history of German-Jewish culture, so essential for an understanding of German intellectual life at least since the Enlightenment, and secondly, the absence of a sense of personal guilt or public shame about the fact that so many German civilians tolerated or colluded with the injustices committed by the authorities against the Jewish citizen in their midst. The latter has been summed up in the by now somewhat formulaic phrase as 'the inability to mourn', the lack of 'Trauerarbeit'. There is another dimension, though: the hypocrisy of public life, where known former Nazis, war criminals and high-ranking officials of the regime were rehabilitated and allowed to return to their old jobs in the judiciary, the medical profession, or the economically decisive banking sector. As one side of official Germany got on with what a commentator has called the 'biggest resocialization and reintegration programme ever,'[9] another side was busy paying lip-service to the principles of universal justice, insisted on the clean break, and exhorted the public to be vigilant against 'totalitarianism'. But after such a 'cold amnesty' and in the face of 'the terrible peace made with the murderers'[10], it is perhaps not surprising that these double standards should produce the Freudian slips of public figures, or the various forms of tactlessness by politicians already referred to.[11]

The cynicism this bred among the wider public probably did little to help foster contriteness in private. Double standards and bitter resignation were the symptoms of a 'repression' which ensured that the Federal Republic did not succeed in agreeing with its citizens the terms, the narratives or gestures that could allow them to remember the shocking realities of the Nazi regime, to mourn its victims, or begin to 'normalize' the German-Jewish relationship. For West Germany also failed to master – perhaps no more or less than other countries, but under more pressing circumstances – the personal and interpersonal dimensions of the Jewish tragedy, of which mourning-work was only one aspect. It might also have included an accountability to subsequent generations, not least to prepare them for another fact, namely that to the rest of the world, Auschwitz was to stand for a reality so dark, stark and ungraspable, that the very word 'German' seemed to become forever, and sometimes exclusively, associated with it. This education into accountability scarcely happened, no more than an analysis of the psychological mechanisms that underpin racial hatred. Badly in need of elucidation, for instance, were also the historical circumstances that already in the 1920s gave credibility to notions such as those which made the Jews responsible for capitalism, but also for its opposite, Bolshevism, thus justifying the Nazi war-within-a-war: the irrational genocidal war against the Jews within the war for territory and geo-political power against the whole of Europe. Unprepared for the hostility towards Germans wherever they went abroad, this younger generation in the affluent and newly mobile 1960s began to turn on their parents and the West German state with a virulence and intensity unparalleled elsewhere, escalating political protest to armed terrorism, and keeping this dissent alive longer than elsewhere. The acts of violence during the 1970s, complexly motivated, but challenging the very moral basis of the West German reconstruction effort, seemed to have further hardened the resistance of the parental generation to cease disavowing or to admit to remorse. This, certainly, is the version Fassbinder gives the viewer in the dialogue with his mother in GERMANY IN AUTUMN. But even among the protest generation of 1968, few were ready to identify their own lives with the Holocaust or Jewish existence in any tangible way.

After decades of persistent denials of having known about Jewish persecution or the camps, and a public policy once described as the 'instrumentalization' of anti-Semitism,[12] the 1970s also saw the beginnings of a change. Partly in the aftermath of the Six-Day War of 1967 and the escalation of the Arab-Israeli conflict in the 1970s, which sharply polarized political opinion in Germany, often blurring the old distinctions, with supporters of the Palestinian cause finding themselves automatically accused of anti-Semitism,[13] while racist slurs against Arabs could count as expressions of solidarity with Israel, public awareness of German-Jewish history and German anti-Semitism took on a different dimension. For instance, the Arab-Israeli conflict gave visibility in the media to the presence of Jews in West Germany, thanks to their representatives commenting on current events in the Near East,[14] while in the face of the rise of the new Right in West Germany, the Left re-examined its views of racism, previously too often 'explained' as a mere by-product of class antagonism and economic exploitation.[15]

Prostration after Provocation?

But what finally changed the nature of attention most dramatically, as already discussed, was the impact of the US television series HOLOCAUST, first screened in Germany late in January 1979, and telling the story of two German families – one 'Aryan', one Jewish – from Hitler's rise to power to the Jewish family's annihilation at Auschwitz. The reaction has been exhaustively described and analyzed: the shock of recognition, the tears, the confessions, the helpless and hysterical outbursts on talk shows and phone-ins, but also the outrage and controversy over the fact that it should be an American mini-series (often denounced as 'soap opera') which had awakened the conscience of ordinary Germans.[16] Problematic to the critics was the melodramatic and manichean construction of the series, as well as the question of means and ends, which is to say, the consequences. Were the effects ultimately no more than titillation, or had HOLOCAUST produced a profound and lasting catharsis? The conclusion was that for a time at least, it put in the minds of more Germans than ever before that there was indeed a past which belonged to them, for which they had to be accountable, whether they chose to or not. Grief-stricken Germans complained that they could never again feel pride in who they were, or live their lives without offering a permanent apology for existing at all. While some were prepared to ask what actions might possibly redeem them in the eyes of the world, others wondered when 'a line should finally be drawn under this past', since Germans, too, in order to play their part in a future Europe, must be entitled to patriotism.[17] Identity and self threatened to become a twisted architecture of prostration after provocation, with subliminal aggression anticipating the imputation of a wrong.[18] Neil Ascherson, a foreign correspondent in Germany in the 1970s, once remarked that 'some Germans when they greet you in the street sound as if they want to say: "come over here, so I can prove my superiority to you".'[19]

Ascherson's barb, like Levi's 'cage of guilt and arrogance' contains an insight that Fassbinder, too, made his own when pinpointing the place of anti-Semitism in the formation of West German identity: the need to construct an 'other', against whom to define the self – often by attributing to this other truths unpalatable or hateful to the self. Even before the reactions to the HOLOCAUST screenings, Fassbinder seemed well aware of these mechanisms, and was keenly alert to the dramas of an identity sustained by emotions springing from disavowal and the need for negative definitions. One of his projects in 1977 – an adaptation of Gustav Freytag's novel *Soll und Haben* – set out to examine precisely this: why, in the struggles for assertion against the landed aristocracy, and in order to draw a sharp boundary against the emergent proletariat, the Jew became the self-defining 'other' for the German bourgeoisie. Meant to inaugurate his history of modern Germany, the TV series was to underline the value system and self-images of this class, and the manner in which they depended on an anti-Semitism that did not register as such since it was taken for granted.[20]

But it was the year before, in March 1976, that Fassbinder provided, in the form of a theatre play, the catalyst for an evidently long-overdue debate between Germans and Germans, Germans and Jews, in which anti-Semitism and Jews after Auschwitz were suddenly centre stage.

Open Season for Revisionists?

Apparently written during two flights back from New York early in 1975, and intended as a farewell note addressed to the Frankfurt cultural bureaucracy,[21] *Der Müll, die Stadt und der Tod (The Garbage, the City and Death)* had, during the last month of Fassbinder's contract at the Theater am Turm, caused an uproar of the kind rarely seen in West Germany before. Ostensibly about the links between property speculators, prostitution and corrupt municipal authorities – and thus containing roughly the same cast of BRD protagonists as LOLA – the play is set in the once fashionable but by then seedy West End area of Frankfurt and features a Jewish slum landlord and property developer. The unexpectedly heated and widely publicised controversy that the play sparked off even before it was published or performed hardly touched on the target of Fassbinder's satirical scorn, the city administration. Nor did critics comment on the fact that the play spoke rather more in sorrow and sadness than in anger. But an inflammatory review by Joachim Fest, whose biography *Hitler – A Career* had turned the groundswell of nostalgia and incipient revisionism into the 'Hitler-Wave', put something else in the spotlight: Fassbinder's play as symptomatic for the West German Left.[22] Although Fest's review bears all the signs of defining an 'other' in order to deflect from the self and to saddle the hated Left with the ingrained racism of the Right, his accusations of 'Left-wing anti-Semitism' and 'red fascism masterminded from Moscow' stuck, and assured that Fassbinder's subsequent attempts to deal more specifically with the topic were also doomed. Apart from the *Soll und Haben* project which was cancelled, a Fassbinder screenplay, based on a novel by Gerhard Zwerenz from 1973, was refused federal funding and was never produced. Since Zwerenz' *Die Erde ist unbewohnbar wie der Mond (The Earth is as uninhabitable as the Moon)* had already furnished Fassbinder with some of the characters, as well as the Frankfurt setting for *Der Müll, die Stadt und der Tod* (henceforth *MST*), it is fair to assume that the funding authorities fought shy of getting embroiled in such an explosive issue (citing their statutes, which prohibited the public purse from subsidizing works that 'incited racial hatred and contempt for human dignity'). On Fassbinder's side, the film would have allowed him to put his case in the medium for which the subject was in any case intended, especially since the play remained unproduced, and in the aftermath of the Frankfurt debacle was banned for performances during his lifetime by Fassbinder himself.[23]

The general consensus, therefore, is that all of Fassbinder's attempts to come to terms with anti-Semitism must be considered 'failures'.[24] Robert Katz, for instance, calls *The Garbage, the City and Death* 'the most costly act of frivolousness Fassbinder ever committed'.[25] However, even though there is no film 'authored' by Fassbinder on which to base oneself, the overall structure, as well as some of the specifics of the play are too much in line with the moral and emotional concerns of Fassbinder's other work for there to be good reason to dismiss it. Furthermore, the commotion that *MST* (and to a lesser extent, the film that was made of *MST*, Daniel Schmid's SHADOWS OF ANGELS) touched off seems at the heart of the intervention which 'Fassbinder' (as author, media-figure and absent centre of a body of work) represented for the 1970s and the struggle for West Germany's cultural identity in the shadow of Nazism.

For the public controversy around *MST* did nothing less than make of the play a 'social text', at once an index of the kinds of miscognition that arise when a work of art manages to create a scandal and thus a public sphere, and proof that Fassbinder was indeed an artist in touch with the subterranean currents of his time. Dismissively treated as 'media events', such controversies and misunderstandings – 'parapraxes of the public sphere' is what one might call them – can be exemplary, as was the case here, for the way participants in the debate argued past one another in an emotionally loaded situation, and still gave away truths fundamental to an historically overdetermined moment.

Two such 'moments' need to be distinguished. One was the controversy sparked off by Fest's article in March 1976, and carried on in the pages of *Die Zeit* and elsewhere during April. Based on a book that never made it past the review copies, it involved mainly prominent journalists and writers, along with an interview response and a press statement by Fassbinder himself. The second 'moment' came nine years later, in October 1985, when after lengthy debates about censorship and a public row which cost a Frankfurt theatre director his job, another theatre director, Günther Rühle, formerly a colleague of Fest's, finally decided to stage the play. This time, however, it was the Jewish community in Frankfurt who took to the streets and, staging a sit-in in the theatre, forced the production to take place behind closed doors, for an invited audience of critics only.

As a media event, the second occasion was the more widely reported and commented upon. Six years after the HOLOCAUST screenings, a general public interest could be assumed, and Fest, also back in the fray, could even claim that 'the books, films, plays, television programmes dealing with anti-Semitism can now only be counted in the hundreds', while conceding that Germany might well be witnessing a backlash, given the 'surfeit of appeals to remember'.[26] The protests against the play in 1985 must therefore be seen in another political and cultural context, where not only the deep malaise within West Germany regarding historical anti-Semitism generally and Nazi policy in particular played a part, but also the growing will of the conservative government to finally find a politically acceptable formula for 'integrating' this period of German history into the overall history of the nation. These issues were known in academic circles as the 'Historikerstreit' (the historians' debate) where, as already mentioned, Jürgen Habermas prominently polemicised against historians Ernst Nolte and Andreas Hillgruber.[27] In the political arena they signified the Kohl administration's attempts to 'normalize' German history by affirming its loyalties to the Western Alliance, itself defined via that old 'other', 'communist totalitarianism'. Symbolized by the 1984 Kohl-Mitterand meeting at Verdun to commemorate the First World War, and in 1985 by the Kohl-Reagan visit to the Bitburg military cemetery, this desire to present West Germany as a mature democracy having definitively stepped out of the shadow of the Hitler years and become the cornerstone of a United Europe and the Nato Alliance survived even the Bitburg occasion which became, thanks to worldwide protests, a setback and a public relations disaster for the German Chancellor.[28]

The ongoing political realignment of German foreign and domestic policy towards creating the image of a country at peace with itself and its neighbours also entered into the Frankfurt Fassbinder controversy. To many, it seems that here was a theatre director, who for no better reason than to make his mark in a new job, was rocking the boat by dragging out of oblivion a play that the author, now dead, had himself disowned, causing offence to the Jewish community and embarrassing all kinds of diplomatic initiatives. The latter sentiment, for instance, was voiced by Manfred Rommel, Mayor of Stuttgart and son of Field Marshall Rommel, when awarding the Peace Prize of the Frankfurt Book Fair to the Mayor of Jerusalem.[29] But the planned production also marked a watershed for the Jewish community in Germany. Offical representatives, such as Heinz Galinski and other members of the Central Council of Jews in Germany had always been diplomatic and mindful of German sensibilities.[30] Wary guests and model citizens, they tried to blend into West German public life as much as possible, presumably also in order to be able to negotiate reparation payments away from the limelight, and to ensure for the members of the German Jewish community fair and speedy settlement of claims and grievances. In the 1980s these Jewish community leaders were beginning to be viewed with suspicion by a younger generation, opposed to what they regarded as an 'appeasement policy' when it came to speaking out against, for instance, former

Nazi judges attaining high office in West Germany, as in the case of the President of Baden-Württemberg whose brutal sentencing right up to the last weeks of the war was apparently rated less severely by official Jewish spokespersons than by many politicians, not only on the far left.[31]

Among the leaders of the squatters' movement and housing battles of the 1970s in Frankfurt (integral part of the West End real estate scene to which Zwerenz' novel directly, and Fassbinder's play indirectly, refer) was also one of the representatives of this younger generation of self-confident German Jews. His name was Daniel Cohn-Bendit, better known internationally as the legendary Danny-the-Red or 'juif allemand' figurehead of the May '68 revolt in Paris, who in the 1980s became a prominent politician in the Frankfurt environmental party, for a time the Social Democrat's coalition partner in the State of Hesse. During the 1985 controversy, Cohn-Bendit advocated that the Fassbinder play should be performed, while at the same time welcoming the militancy of the Frankfurt Jews who protested against the play. The important point for Cohn-Bendit was that in the protests, German Jews manifested themselves in public as an identifiable collective and pressure group, finally taking up their rightful place as Germans in a society that had, not least because of the 'Gastarbeiter' and their children, de facto become multi-cultural and multi-ethnic. For him, this was the only alternative to the revival of anti-Semitism, racism and other forms of social and political discrimination.[32]

Fassbinder: an Anti-Semite?

With these general, historical shifts inside West Germany in mind, it may be easier to understand why Fassbinder's play could act as a catalyst, and why Frankfurt, one of the traditional centres of Jewish intellectual life in Germany before the war, had to be the setting, not only of the play, but also of the controversies it provoked. What also needs to be looked at, however, is exactly how it was that Fassbinder – in his play – had managed to give offence, when under the general circumstances outlined, other occasions or cultural events might equally well have served to bring these tensions to the surface.

The play uses strong language, both sexually explicit and racist, as is appropriate, Fassbinder argued, to the mind-set of the characters he puts on show. What is absent is a central consciousness that reflects and thus deflects, mediates and thus mitigates the naked impact of Fassbinder's purposive verbal assault. The prostitute Roma B at one point ruminates about the habits of her pimp:

> and then he asks me, how was his dick, Roma, big or small? Did he have staying power, or did he come straight away? Did he groan, he wants to know. Names and all – I tell him, I can't remember, it's not important to me. And then [his fist] comes crashing down, I see stars sparkle in the sky. So I learn to let myself be fucked with open eyes and ears. What's it to him, I wonder? Does he go to the toilet, to masturbate and be a different person?[33]

And Hans von Gluck, a competitor in the real estate business, complains:

> He sucks us dry, the Jew. Drinks our blood and puts us in the wrong, because he's a Jew and we are guilty. [...] If only he'd stayed where he came from, or if they had gassed him, I'd sleep better tonight. They forgot to gas him. That's no joke, that's how it thinks in me.'[34]

Those who read the review copies of the play were repelled by its crudity and 'pornography', which could not but compound the unease over the unsavoury anti-Semitic sentiments expressed in such lines. In *Die Zeit* of April 9th, 1976, Jean Améry called it: 'Genet sans génie. A pseudo-Paris come down in the world to Frankfurt. Ill-digested George Bataille. Transgression at a discount. A bit of cleverly-inserted Threepenny Opera Berlin. And the lot, God forgive him, delivered in the diction of Büchner, but completely off-key.'[35] Those who thought it had some merit artistically either saw it as a literary exercise, in the manner of Fassbinder's anti-theater stunts, a collage of quotations from the Expressionist drama of Bert Brecht and Ferdinand Bruckner, the plays of Ödon von Horwath, with a helping from Christopher Marlowe's *Jew of Malta*,[36] or they conceded that is was 'politically naive, maladroit, unfinished.'[37]

Critics who claimed to be morally offended focused on the characters, and among the characters on one in particular, and in this one character on the fact that Fassbinder does not give him a proper name, but calls him 'The Rich Jew', thus imputing the generic identity of the stereotype. Coupled with the anti-Semitic tirades by two self-avowed anti-Semitic characters and a monologue in which 'The Rich Jew' explains his strategic function for the city council, because as a Jew in West Germany he is both an untouchable and cannot be touched, this seemed sufficient evidence to prove that the play was, although probably not intended to be, anti-Semitic, dangerously close to giving welcome ammunition to Germany's latent anti-Semites.[38] It was also pointed out that, among Frankfurt's 5000-strong Jewish community, most lived on modest pensions and quite a few on social security benefits.[39]

If anything seemed proven by these diverse reactions, it was that the Fassbinder play laid itself wide-open to misreadings. To chide the author for taking risks, for acting irresponsibly, and to wag a finger at him for not having taken care to forestall the responses seems disingenuous, given that Fassbinder's work, especially that for the theatre, was always meant to stir up a response.[40] Asked, by Benjamin Henrichs, a leading theatre critic, whether he had made an error of judgement by not anticipating the misunderstandings the play would give rise to, Fassbinder replied:

> Absolutely not. Theatre-work is always a spontaneous reaction to a given reality. [...] True, the play dispenses with certain precautions, and I think this is completely defensible. I have to be able to react to my reality without making compromises. [...] I think, the public reactions, such as they were, have if anything confirmed

that it was right [to raise the issue in this way]. I think it is better when these things are discussed openly, that way they are less dangerous, instead of whispering about them with one's hand cusped.[41]

As a social text, it was probably this capacity to give rise to 'misunderstandings' that makes *MST* important for the history of West Germany and distinguishes it from literary classics (say, a play by Samuel Beckett or Harold Pinter). Modernist works, by attenuating the referential dimension and by using a style carefully honed and crafted, limit potential misreadings, supported as they are by a specialist literary criticism which outlaws some interpretations as interferences while canonically sanctioning others. Fassbinder's play, on the other hand, is in this sense neither literature nor a modernist work. As late as 1991, Reinhold Grimm, eminent Germanist scholar and Brecht specialist, recommended that on the evidence of the play, Fassbinder the dramatist should be consigned to oblivion, 'the more thoroughly [...] the better'.[42] Full of literary borrowings, foul language, political slogans and emotional excesses, the play is wilfully impure and is as much a pastiche of expressionist pathos as of the genre of the (1960s) happening. What *MST* successfully provoked was a manifestation of the moment's political unconscious, with all the contradictory identifications and position taking this entailed. Alas, the debate also demonstrated the truth of a sentence from the play: 'we're getting lost in discussions, when we've made up our minds long ago.'[43]

For in this respect, the controversy exposed the vulnerability of West German culture as a municipal-regional subsidy culture and thus inherently heavily politicised, in the sense of demanding from the artist to be a moral guide, not only speaking through his work, but having to represent a constituency.[44] In such a culture, art is expected to create a very traditional public sphere, in which consensus and balance must perforce prevail. Fassbinder saw the contradiction clearly:

> I fear that [our cultural committees] have now found their aesthetic criteria. Finally. Unfortunately. For years they had none, and that was lucky for us. [...] The committees and television bodies were truly shocked about what happened, at a certain point in the German cinema. Suddenly, there were so many kinds of film, they couldn't understand them anymore, couldn't get a grip on them [...]. It would contradict all my expectations if the state that financed these films were to say, let's pay for plurality and freedom, and let these people really reflect their reality. This sort of thing is more likely to happen in a purely commercial system such as Hollywood.[45]

Perhaps here lies the reason why, in the end, the (subsidized) theatre never did engage Fassbinder's best energies, and why he chafed at the bit of the German subsidy cinema, preferring the risks of working with a commercial producer like Waldleitner.[46] As playwright he remained an experimentalist, whose open texts, written 'without precautions' aimed at a confrontation in the spirit of Artaud, therapeutic or cathartic only insofar as they envisaged the possibility of an audience capable of being disturbed and even offended. Yet at the end of the Fassbinder controversy there was neither enlightenment nor recognition, neither a purging of affect nor a new kind of insight: frustration and exhaustion reigned, not least because the contending parties, made up of journalists and politicians, were speaking not in their own names but on behalf of others whom they, more or less legitimately, could claim to represent, but whom they also disenfranchised by presuming to know. Fassbinder – and even his play – remained, in both historical moments, truly the absent one.

Garbage, City and Death

In this respect, *MST* was a failure, because it never reached a public. An added problem, when trying to assess the importance of Fassbinder's aborted film projects though is the fact that a stage play and a film for either the cinema or television are such different aesthetic objects, both from the point of view of their perceptual texture and as acts of critical reception and the circulation of cultural capital. The challenge is to imagine what *MST* as printed on the page might have in common with the film Fassbinder had hoped to make (and the one Daniel Schmid did make).[47] Written in the expressionist or Brechtian manner, with short scenes and sketches, *MST* consists often of no more than a series of monologues, like the ones already quoted. It builds up a logic of argumentative juxtaposition rather than a narrative sequence, and its causality is that of jagged transitions and internal frictions instead of the smooth and fluid continuity that is typical of Fassbinder's films even when they take place in the most boxed-in and claustrophobic interiors.[48] In SHADOWS OF ANGELS, for instance, the notorious monologue of Hans von Gluck becomes a lugubrious bedside oratorio, and the mercy-killing of Lily/Roma B at the hands of The Rich Jew a slow-motion dance for a tender farewell.

Once imagined in filmic terms, *MST* has a coherence in its choice of motifs, characters and story-complexes. In fact, they seem remarkably familiar from Fassbinder's films. As so often in his middle period, the core relationship is that between two characters whose intelligence and insight set them apart from the rest. In this case, these are Roma B and The Rich Jew, both of whom have seen and suffered too much to entertain any illusions or ambitions, but whose peculiar look at life is as if from beyond the grave. It gives them a special dignity, impersonality and humility, with which they carry their respective burden. Roma B because she is the daughter of an ex-Nazi, whom she merely reminds of the son he never had.[49] Her pimp beats her as token of his love and sends her out on the streets even though she is ill, because his pride as a man demands that when gambling it is her money he loses, rather than money he could borrow from his friends. The Rich Jew, too, knows what is being expected of him, from his enemies and his so-called friends, since for each he is a mere cipher, a fixed value in an equation which ultimately does not concern him:

> The plan isn't mine, it was in place before I came. It is none of my business if children cry, if the old and the sick suffer. And when some howl with anger, I just

shut my ears. What else could I do? [...] Should my soul stand up and be counted for decisions taken by others, and which I only execute with the profit I need, in order to afford what I need? Need, need – what a funny word [....] The city needs the unscrupulous businessman who enables it to change and move with the times.[50]

What does become his business is his relation with Roma B, whose services he buys, initially in order to use her as a weapon against her father Müller One, an unrepentant, vile Nazi with a wheelchair-bound wife. By profession a transvestite, he performs Zara Leander torch-songs in a bar where The Rich Jew seeks him out, suspecting him of having murdered his parents. Convinced that fascism will triumph in the end, Müller One remains unfazed when Roma B confronts him with this allegation:

> I didn't bother about each and everyone I killed. I wasn't an individualist, I am a technocrat. But it's possible that I am the murderer of his parents, and in any case, I would have liked to have been, and therefore I am.[51]

But as The Rich Jew gets to know Roma B, he begins to care about her, while she, come up in the world because of associating with him, finds herself ever more isolated. Franz B in the meantime has fallen in love with a man, whose friends whip, drown, sodomize and beat him with chains to his heart's content. Tired of living in cities where life is more like death than death itself, Roma B begs to be killed, but everyone is too busy to attend to her request, until The Rich Jew takes mercy on her and strangles her with his tie. When the police need to produce her killer, they arrest Franz B, the perfect fall-guy, just 'asking' for it.

Strikingly consistent as the themes are with other Fassbinder work, *MST* shows them in more schematic configurations, when compared with films like FOX AND HIS FRIENDS, BOLWIESER, SATAN'S BREW, LILI MARLEEN or LOLA. Furthermore, with its Jacobean feel, the play contains elements of the baroque 'Trauerspiel'[52] which it combines with the difficult didactic form Brecht called the 'Lehrstück', or model-play, in which impossible moral dilemmas – Fassbinder's double-binds – are played through and played out.[53] The important power-relations in *MST* function on the sado-masochistic model: that between Roma B and Franz B, but by implication also that between The Rich Jew and the City, except that both are complicated by the fact that The Rich Jew as well as Roma B are both inside their respective power-structures and outside them. In one case, the non-congruence of need and desire between the characters is crucial: it is 'resolved' for the masochist Franz B by the blasphemous, grotesque punishment he receives, and 'resolved' for Roma B by a sacrificial death, meaningless, because discounted and disowned by the City, which treats as a mere bureaucratic inconvenience a protest message addressed to its conscience. In the case of The Rich Jew, it is the apparently perfect fit between his 'need' and what the city 'needs' which is tragic and makes all his activities – whether objectively good or evil – meaningless in advance.

The play is thus a morality play, but also a hall of mirrors, like so many of Fassbinder's films, except more so. Structurally, it has a great deal of affinity with the director's other paranoia films, WORLD ON A WIRE and THE THIRD GENERATION, in that the power-triangles are at one and the same time topsy turvy, inside-out and mutually sustaining, interdependent. The small-time pimp Franz B who always loses is superficially opposed to the big-time speculator The Rich Jew who cannot lose, but what ties them together is not only that they love the same woman, but also that they are both tools and ciphers in the games of a male gang with whom they collude: that Franz B should become the 'stand-in' for The Rich Jew as (non-) murderer of Roma B is therefore doubly appropriate, reminiscent of the narrative logic underlying both LOLA and LILI MARLEEN. While the function of most of the secondary characters in *MST* is to invert or double the central relationships between Franz B, Roma B and The Rich Jew, these in their turn trace a determinate pattern, or rather, enact a muted but intricate pas-de-deux. It underlines the fact that like a prism, whichever way one turns the action, a new perspective will emerge.

To begin with, two kinds of anti-Semitism are at issue: Müller One's anti-Semitism is that of pathological antagonism, but without hatred or resentment. A technocrat of extermination, he represents the coldly rational side: the Eichmanns or Mengeles, minds who could plan and organize genocide on an industrial scale and with the dispassionate dedication of the laboratory specialist. Now two-faced and a creature changing identity between night and day, he is nonetheless of one mind, impenitent and convinced. Against Müller One conceding the likelihood of his having killed The Rich Jew's parents, one can set The Rich Jew's not even ironic remark, after meeting him, 'what a charming man, one could almost forget that his name is Müller'[54], which underlines the asymmetrical mirroring between the two, which is in fact one of The Rich Jew's mysterious sources of power. Hans von Gluck represents the second, hysterical side of anti-Semitism, full of hatred and enjoyment, gloating at the Jew's imagined power and punishment ('And I rub my hands with glee, at the thought of how he gets short of breath, there in the gas chamber'). In SHADOWS OF ANGELS von Gluck makes this speech lying in bed, as if in a fever dream, but to him applies what Henryk Broder calls 'anti-Semitism not in spite of Auschwitz, but because of Auschwitz.'[55]

When viewed from the point of view of the underdog, Franz B's figure goes back to KATZELMACHER, encompasses Fox in FOX AND HIS FRIENDS, and is also present in the way Kurt Raab plays Bolwieser in the film of that title. But most of all, Franz B anticipates Franz Biberkopf, especially as presented in the epilogue, 'The dream of the dream of Franz Biberkopf'. One of the astute touches is that Franz B is not an anti-Semite (he does not care about Jews one way or another); instead, he is a rabid anti-Tennisite, hating tennis players with an irrational but irresistible passion.[56]

Roma B as Müller One's daughter refuses to be drawn into the generational chain of either seeking retribution or atonement: she goes with the Jew for entirely different motives (at first simply because she loves Franz B and wants to make sure that he feels like a 'man' in front of his mates). When she learns that she is a pawn in The Rich Jew's revenge on her father, she reacts with indifference, although she fully understands that here might lie her salvation (since she could so easily give a meaning to her life by sacrificing herself for her father's crimes).[57] Instead, we have to infer that the more Roma B gets drawn into the configuration Nazi-Jew, the more she lives the West German-Jew relationship under the shadow of the Nazi-Jew relationship, and one also sees the logic of why the more she loves the Jew, the less she wants to live. If one reads the play as centred on Roma B, one finds the constellation of a woman who, faced with a kind of contract (agreeing to disagree totally) between two men (her father and The Rich Jew), loses the will to live, which, of course, is also one way of reading the heroine's ambiguous decision at the end of MARIA BRAUN.

On the other hand, her strength is being sapped by the other triangle, which is that of Franz B's contract with Oscar von Leiden, a sado-masochistic love-pact. The various triangles balance each other, but are articulated at different levels: the sexual one is contrasted with the racial one, and one is about painful pleasure, while the other about painful unpleasure. Again, as with MARIA BRAUN and LOLA, one can see the play trying to 'conjugate' different possibilities of how characters can relate to each other, and in this sense, the play uses The Rich Jew and anti-Semitism as clichés of a totally debased and degraded form of human intercourse. These, however, are necessary, for the central relationship between Roma B and The Rich Jew to develop and define itself, which is to say, to define a love story, the more moving and tragic in that it has to shed all this earthly ballast in order to transfigure itself: it has to descend into the filthiest filth, in order to shine – as so much else in the play, a profoundly religious conception of body, love and salvation. In the end, however, her motivation remains unclear, and if the play does have a structural problem, it seems to lie in not clarifying or deepening the character of Roma B to the point where one might understand her better. As it stands, her suicidal drift is somewhere between the relentlessly downward spiral of FOX AND HIS FRIENDS and the fever-pitch panic of VERONIKA VOSS. In SHADOWS OF ANGELS, even the tenderness in the final deadly embrace motivates her despair poetically rather than in properly dramatical terms, as we see her and The Rich Jew dancing a kind of tango of self-immolation.

When the play is viewed from the point of view of The Rich Jew, we recognize in him right away certain other figures in the Fassbinder universe. He is a relative of Oswald in MARIA BRAUN, and in the same business as Schuckert, the building speculator in LOLA. He sits on top of a corrupt power structure like Lenz in THE THIRD GENERATION, and at the centre of a spider's web like the mysterious boss Vollmer in WORLD ON A WIRE. For The Rich Jew, two contracts are in play: one with the city that makes him untouchable, and one with Roma B. The fact that the latter contract is one of revenge (though again with a woman as the object being traded) does not seem to affect the dynamics of their relationship. Along the axis of 'Germany (not) mastering its past', The Rich Jew is the 'return of the repressed'. But he is also the figure who has come back from the dead, and paradoxically, because different from Schuckert's 'pig with a zest for life', he is the only one who has energy and method in a city of the dead. If he is a vampire as Hans von Gluck complains, The Rich Jew does not suck blood, but represents the avenging angel who simply by his presence renders the others sick with their own guilt, hatred and resentment.

This is also the reason why The Rich Jew, quite logically, cannot have a name. As the focus of all the ills in the city, he is the composite picture/figure which German anti-Semitism has been projecting on the Jews ever since the crises of modernity early this century made them the conspiratorial force that was supposed to lurk behind both capitalism and bolshevism. The Rich Jew, as Fassbinder points out, knows that he speaks in the borrowed clichés of his enemies, or in more psychoanalytic terms, that he is spoken to by their language, in the way that 'it thinks in me' for Hans von Gluck: 'The Jew is the only one in the play [...] who is capable of understanding that the language he speaks is a deal that [these] people have concluded with each other'.[58] To show a poor Jew, or a 'good' Jew as some critics have argued, in order to 'correct' the generic cliché of The Rich Jew is therefore an absurd proposition. In fact, it would amount to another form of discrimination, since it says either 'it's alright to be anti-Semitic when it is directed against rich Jews' (a trap into which some of the pro-Arab Left in Germany were ready to fall), or it says, 'I don't mind being a philosemite but for that I can expect the Jews to behave themselves.'[59] Hence, it is precisely the cliché of The Rich Jew which has to be put on display, in order to tackle the phantasmatic figure which nourishes anti-Semitism. 'The Jew' in Fassbinder is de-individualized as a matter of principle, since in order to discuss anti-Semitism, the play has to refer to the Jews as imagined by a German, be s/he an overt anti-Semite or 'merely' someone who lives or has grown up in a society and a culture 'contaminated' (Broder) by anti-Semitism (as so many of the participants in the 1985 debate demonstrably were).

One might ask whether there is not also another point of view, around which the play becomes perfectly 'coherent' and legible: not the position of one of the characters, but of West German society and its repression of the 'pleasures' (once) inherent in Nazism and anti-Semitism. From this perspective, the play's centre is constituted by the *Müller* Gang. For them, City officials by day, homosexual homophobes by night, both The Rich Jew and Franz B are outsiders, especially in relation to what holds them together as insiders, namely repression and disavowal themselves, which becomes the strongest bond between the members of such a society. The collusions between the knowledge of crime, the knowledge of its cover-up, and the 'normalization' that the successful cover-up of the crime represents act like the internal cement, while the shared resentment about a guilt imposed from outside becomes the wall that makes it conscience-proof. Together, the memory of crime and the anticipation of guilt represent the deepest symbolic code shared by all. Fassbinder is therefore not in the first instance concerned with (primary) anti-Semitism, but with a kind of secondary (post-Auschwitz) anti-Semitism, what Henryk Broder has called the 'German-Jewish Gemeinschaftswerk' (cooperation work) and Eike Geisel (even more sarcastically than Broder) 'Familienzusammenführung' (reuniting families).[60]

The accusation that Fassbinder's play is anti-Semitic seems to me therefore as untenable as the assertion that Fassbinder was an anti-Semite. If it is the case that his play did stir up latent West German anti-Semitism, the 'hatred of the perpetrators for the victims' (Broder), and confusingly compounded it by what in Robert Neumann's definition – quoted by Fassbinder – constitutes philosemitism ('philosemites are anti-Semites who love Jews'), then one can, as Broder, Cohn Bendit and others have argued, only welcome the opportunity, not granted to Fassbinder in his lifetime, to bring this crucial aspect of German self-understanding into the discussion. What Fassbinder has done would then have been nothing more reprehensible than to use a highly charged idiom and some drastic but legitimate dramatic techniques of world theatre in order to hold a mirror up to the German audience he was hoping to reach.

The Otherness of the Other, or 'The Importance of Being Jewish'

Nevertheless, when all is said, there is still a problem about 'the figure of the Jew' in *SMT*, especially if one wants to see him as only one of the 'Jewish figures' in Fassbinder's work: their role and function turn out to be quite complex and apparently conflicting. One could summarize them under three headings: firstly, Jews in Fassbinder are privileged figures of projection, serving as the archetypal 'other' in a whole range of contexts and discourses. Secondly, Jews are outsiders, but more in terms of being figures imperturbably, unassailably outside: waiting patiently, sometimes as if biding their time, sometimes merely watching from the outside. Finally, Jews are figures in whose presence a German must 'choose', who enjoin upon Germans a decision, a moment of self-reflection and even a break, a rupture.

It is possible to recognize in this composite image not only a figure imbued with moral or magic power, but a kind of mythological being, outside society and history, and thus in some respects it might be argued as phantasmatic or phantasmagoric as the century-old image of the Jew of anti-Semitic literature and thought. Put slightly differently, Fassbinder's Jew, before he is a person of Jewish faith or race, is first of all the figure of the Other, or more precisely, he occupies the place of the Other. On the one hand, this place is necessary, in order for Fassbinder to set in motion the mechanism of how the self defines itself across an other, how identity is a function of identifying an other, who in the case of Fassbinder's films is invariably defined as antagonist. Thus, the Jew becomes the antagonistic other, mirroring the repressed, unacknowledged part of the self to which identity is tied, irrevocably. Fassbinder even speaks of a second 'original sin':

> Because of the time between 1933 and 1945, but not solely because of what happened then, the history of the Germans and the Jews is now linked forever, something like a second original sin will be fixed in those who were born and will live in Germany, an original sin which does not lose its importance because the sons of the murderers are today washing their hands in innocence.[61]

The problem with this notion is that such a conception of Jews, while it may not de-humanize them in the way that anti-Semitic clichés do, nonetheless depersonalizes their specific histories and fates, including those now generally subsumed under another generic term, namely 'Auschwitz'. There is thus a conflict pre-programmed into the figure of The Rich Jew, when so much circumstantial political and historical material is also present (though not in the play). For as argued, The Rich Jew is a figure of projection, intended to expose the mechanism of creating an other, one who does not remain passive but who defends himself by using the projected power – the paranoid power of a phantasm, at one and the same time mythical, economic, sexual – as 'capital' in the extended sense of the term: as his physical means of survival ('the profit I need in order to afford what I need') and as his symbolic currency in his interaction with society. But what if individual Jews refuse to recognize themselves, or rather, refuse to accept 'otherness' as a category they either can or want to be identified with? This clearly happened in the case of *MST*, since neither the purported 'real-life' model of The Rich Jew, nor the German (or French or Dutch)[62] Jewish communities were prepared to accept 'otherness' as their defining feature. Seyla Benhabib has put the dilemma succinctly:

> Whereas a Daniel Cohn-Bendit can immediately identify with and exercise solidarity with the Jews – precisely because they *are* the outsiders in this case – the Jews who live in post-war Germany find the company into which Fassbinder has thrown them abhorrent. Once again, they see themselves identified as the other, and in this otherness [...] as threatening. In other words, a Cohn-Bendit can accept a political message and the political community into which Fassbinder has put him, because he sees the moment of redemption in that otherness, whereas the Jewish community in Germany, which in the post-war period gained or has tried to gain respectability, seeks to rid itself of that otherness.[63]

With such a position, however, the debate also shifts ground, placing anti-Semitism in a wider context, one that we now generally refer to when speaking of 'identity-politics', the question of the relation of minorities to the majority, or the dynamics of oppression, where the outsider, or the victim compete for cultural as well as political representation. This, too, however, might be unsatisfactory, given that the Jewish community rightly insists on the uniqueness of the Holocaust, and by implication, on the historical fact that it happened in Germany and at the hands of Germans, while simultaneously wanting to promote a state of normalcy as the basis of their existence as Germans in Germany.

As far as Fassbinder is concerned, it is probably true that he saw the Jewish question as similar to that affecting all minorities, and thus his Jewish characters do indeed inscribe themselves in the wider concerns of his work of how to represent minorities. Fassbinder had always insisted that he refused, as a matter of principle, to give positive images of minorities or society's victims, arguing that such positive images are merely another form of discrimination.[64] He was perfectly aware, in other words, of the possibility of allegorical or mythological representations – themselves 'positive' images, in the sense of being charged with energy – lending themselves to discriminations:

> To accuse me of anti-Semitism is just an excuse, because [in the projected series *Soll und Haben*] I explicitly tried to set out how anti-Semitism has come about. [...] I do not think it is anti-Semitic to tell about the mistakes a Jew has to make, in order to survive at all. The best way to describe the oppression of a minority is to show which mistakes and even crimes members of a minority are forced to commit, as a consequence of being oppressed.[65]

Fassbinder thus abstained from giving a favourable image of minorities because it seemed a more insidious form of oppression. Yet even when he did show 'victims' as they see themselves, he 'deconstructed' their identity as a fiction: one that emerges from the non-congruence between self-image and the image others have of the self.[66]

The Unrepresentability of the Jew

In a similar vein as Seyla Benhabib – though from a more hostile position – Gertrud Koch has argued that Fassbinder falls into the anti-Semitic trap because his Jew, even with this stance, is not only 'other' but his otherness is invariably constructed allegorically. Thus, the Jew is a figure who is as necessarily unassimilable, in an allegorical discourse in which he is associated with death, with the mortification of the flesh, an association that in Fassbinder's moral and representational universe has a very specific meaning. In her illuminating essay Koch pinpoints the problem these chapters have constantly returned to, namely the status of the Fassbinder film as a 'realist text', as an allegory or as a mode oscillating between different referentialities. By analyzing Fassbinder's allegorical strategies, Koch argued that the Jewish figures do not form part of the galleries of victims and outsiders Fassbinder depicts, and therefore that the case Fassbinder makes about his 'identity-politics' does not apply. For Koch, Fassbinder's allegorization of the Jew in such films as IN A YEAR OF THIRTEEN MOONS, BERLIN ALEXANDERPLATZ and VERONIKA VOSS shows first a clichéd conception of the Jew as sacrificial figure. But Fassbinder also operates 'a displacement of the sacrificial fantasies away from the Jews onto those figures who are predestined [...] to experience suffering of the body and the torments of the flesh'.[67] As such, they become figures of desire, foremost the Jew Anton Saitz, a concentration camp survivor, for whom Elvira in IN A YEAR OF THIRTEEN MOONS willingly changes more than her life.

In other words, what is characteristic for Koch of the fantasy structure of Fassbinder's films about the representation of Jews is that they give rise to self-sacrificial desires (Koch includes LILI MARLEEN, arguing that Willie is ready to die for her Jewish composer-lover), but that Jews have to pay a price for being cast in this role, not the least of which is that they are relegated to a kind of mythical universe, and thus are expelled from history, while in another, complementary move, they become stern patriarchal figures of cold intellect, shut out from the writhing and tormented flesh which signifies juissance, life and death in Fassbinder's sado-masochistic universe.

Koch's very sophisticated argument is indebted to the case made by Saul Friedländer against what he has called the new discourse of fascism, of which Fassbinder, according to Friedländer, is a prime example. This discourse, as already mentioned, turns Nazism, its iconography, its fantasies of power into a 'mythology', and thus removes it not only from history, but makes it available for all kinds of libidinal investments, from the pornographic to the political, via kitsch, nostalgia and a nihilistic cult of death. The vanishing point of Friedländer as well as of Koch, but perhaps expressed most clearly by Eric Santner[68], is the demand that Jews be represented as subjects, whereas artists like Fassbinder, even if ideologically on the left, cannot but objectify, allegorize or mythologize their representations.

In the end it is thus not the problem of casting the Jew as other, it is a fundamental non-representability that is at issue. This non-representability in fact rehearses much of the same ground that another debate has already covered, namely that about the non-representability of Auschwitz.[69] Indeed, the whole Frankfurt episode could be rewritten in terms of the ethics and aesthetics of representation, as part of the discussion that has in this context pitted realists against allegorists, documentarists against fictionalists. What we have come across earlier as the demand for positive role models, which in this case would mean 'balancing' the The Rich Jew against the 'good Jew', now returns as the debate about the signifier 'Jew' as at once unique and universal. The latter, in turn, threatens to open the way towards 'historicising', normalizing, or even relativizing the Holocaust, or making the individual case, whether that of (the real) Anne Frank or (the fictional) Weiss family from the TV series HOLOCAUST 'stand for' the fate of six million Jews, taking in the attempt at identification the fatal risk of trivialization. In all such cases, it is clear that there cannot be a 'normal' Jew, because then the fact that s/he is a Jew is no longer a fact of discourse, but simply an anecdotal fact of birth. The argument seems to have come full circle, because it leaves us with the dilemma – the vicious circle – how can it be possible in relation to the signifier 'Jewish' within a discourse about Germany not to have recourse to the figure of the Other? To this dilemma, Fassbinder sought to give his own answer also in the play, notably in a line recognized by the more astute commentators[70] as a crucial passage: Hans von Gluck's shocking and shockingly revealing 'that's no joke; that's how it thinks in me' – a sentence that focuses on the process of the subject-effect produced by racisme *and* language.

Gluck's sentence makes explicit what was implicit in the split speaking positions of characters who had 'exteriorized' their double-binds, such as Joanna in GODS OF THE PLAGUE, or had 'lived' them by literalizing them, like Hans in MERCHANT OF FOUR SEASONS.[71] More clearly than any other character, he voices the difference between subject of utterance and subject of statement, between what he says and what is said. The sentence is also revealing in that it can be read as a comment on all those occasions, especially in public life, where this split, and its peculiar significance when the saying and the said concern German-Jewish relations are repressed. It almost seems as if the 'identity-politics' of West Germany consisted of this double movement, where a publicly expressed anti-Nazism and philosemitism had to do battle not with its own unconscious, but with its own speaking position. Public occasions, especially when dates were commemorated or historical events celebrated, proved particularly treacherous. There was, as already discussed, May 8th, the date in 1945 of the German Reich's unconditional surrender. The many mishaps and misunderstandings which this day has given rise to in the last forty years could fill an entire book,[72] documenting how the Federal Republic was never able to decide whether the nation was celebrating its liberation or mourning its greatest defeat, or both, or neither, until Chancellor Kohl, by inviting President Ronald Reagan to Bitburg, hoped in vain to cut the Gordian knot, and tried to make it an event where Germany and the USA could simply assume that they had always been Allies in a common war against Communism.

May 8th, however, was not the only instance in (West) German public life where history as the return of the repressed suddenly intervened to draw unwanted attention to the speaking positions of prominent Germans. On November 9th, 1988, a ceremony took place in Bonn to commemorate the 50th anniversary of the *Kristallnacht*, the beginning of the open persecution and deportation of German Jews. Philipp Jenninger, the President of the Upper House of the Federal Parliament, gave a keynote speech, which caused so much consternation that he was obliged to resign. Reading the speech in print, one is struck by the writer's intense and emotional identification with the victims, especially in the passages where he quotes at length and in horrifying detail an eyewitness report of mass-executions. But, speaking as a German rather than a Jew, he also tried to think himself into the minds of the ordinary German of 1938. Jenninger's speech might be called a post-HOLOCAUST and post-HEIMAT attempt to address two constituencies simultaneously: Germans and Jews, the memory of those who lived in places like Schabbach (Reitz' fictional village in HEIMAT), and the memory of those who were transported to camps like Auschwitz. The attempt singularly failed, not only because there is no historical discourse in which these two realities can coexist as compatible subject positions, but also because Jenninger had entirely misunderstood his own speaking position. What might conceivably have passed if spoken as an individual deeply troubled by a sense of responsibility and the need for atonement apparently could not be said by the representative of the highest elected body of the nation. Representation here taking on its full meaning of representing an event while also speaking on behalf of someone, those on whose behalf Jenninger spoke clearly did not feel the event was represented as they wished to hear it.[73] By trying to remove the frame that separated these two incompatible discursive registers, Jenninger was left without a place from which to say anything at all. Since then, the *Kristallnacht* has become, in another historical turn, once more an overdetermined date, allowing two quite dissimilar events and their reverberations to superimpose themselves on each other, one 'muting' the other.[74]

On such occasions history has a way of overtaking the most carefully scripted speaking positions, so that mastering the past also implies an 'un-mastering' of history, accepting the 'parapraxes' which can insert themselves into one's speaking positions. The historical semiotics at work here can be studied all over Eastern Europe, and they extend beyond individuals and texts: they comprise, for instance, the way a nation speaks to itself about its history in the form of public holidays and public memorials, or when naming streets and designating sites as part of national history. It was surely no accident that Jürgen Habermas, for instance, when starting the polemic which subsequently became the historians' debate, made a connection between the writings of scholars like Nolte and the German Federal Government's plans to fund two new historical museums, one in Bonn for the history of the Federal Republic, one in Berlin for the history of the German nation, even though Nolte had taken no part in these decisions. The government's attempt to distribute history strategically, so to speak, and create an asymmetrical duality, was, however, proven premature thanks to the irruption of an another historical event: the fall of the wall and German unification.

By what is therefore also no coincidence, the publication which Habermas singled out for comment shows the same dual structure of dissimilar events obliged to share one and the same representational or discursive space that so often typifies divided and now united Germany's dealing with representations of its recent history. Andreas Hillgruber's *Zweierlei Untergang* ('Two Kinds of Ruin') combines in one volume an essay on the 'Shattering of the German Reich', with one on the 'End of European Jewry'.[75] This brought into a deceptive, and as it would turn out, provocative symmetry the story of the collapse of Hitler's Eastern front in the last year of the war and an assessment of the 'Final Solution', its planning and ruthlessly methodical implementation. The provocation resided not in the texts themselves, nor the case they put forward.[76] More problematic was the parallel that the juxtaposition seemed to draw between the evacuation and expulsion of the German population from the provinces east of the Oder and the extermination of Jews, herded from all over Europe into the death camps of the East. Yet what caused major offense was Hillgruber's candid admission that, as a German historian, he could not but empathize with the injustice, suffering and death inflicted on the German population during the cold winter months of 1944/45. Had Hillgruber, who was himself part of the exodus, made these statements in the context of a biographical account, 'few would have quarrelled', as Perry Anderson put it. But by claiming empathy and identification while speaking as a German historian, Hillgruber had 'slipped with one step from the understandable to the indefensible.'[77] In one sense, the reason for the indefensible is obvious: the position of empathy assumed by Hillgruber creates in the same space of narration two kinds of victim, each competing with the other: those of the Holocaust, whose singular and exemplary fate is as though invalidated by dramatizing, back to back, the possible or actual Soviet retribution meted out to the civilian population of Germany's former Eastern provinces.

Surely, one could object, even the Germans must be allowed to mourn their dead? Might Hillgruber not be understood as following the advice of Alexander Mitscherlich who had suggested that West Germans suffered from a particular kind of self-alienation, the 'inability to mourn', which meant that they were also unable to love, either themselves or others.[78] But such 'mourning work' is also politics, and as the example of Syberberg or

Hillgruber shows, it carries a high risk. Too often, it has seemed that 'mourning work' stops short at the stage of self-pity and sentimentality ('what is terrible about Germans is not their brutality, but their sentimentality' the Jewish novelist Amos Oz once remarked), thus acknowledging compassion only at the price of playing victims off against each other. As already alluded to in the chapter on MARIA BRAUN, much of the New German Cinema presented a view of history in which Germany appears as a nation of victims, either by choosing women as protagonists, or by allegorizing the country as a female body, vulnerable and maltreated: in both cases as if vying for victim status.[79] But if 'mourning work' cannot open up that space of otherness, what can? What kinds of affect might possibly 'unlock' numbness and apathy, reconcile memory and hope, commemoration and forgetting, or mediate between pity, sentiment and shame? Fassbinder, it seems to me, had begun to think about this problem in his offending theatre play in such an unusual, unorthodox way, that the moral and emotional place from which his characters spoke clearly exceeded in their dividedness and self-contradiction the space available for them in the German public sphere or the Frankfurt stage. It was perhaps, after all, only in the cinema and on film that he could be sure to be in full command of his own, as well as his characters' speaking positions.

8.   Beyond 'Schuld' and 'Schulden'
IN A YEAR OF THIRTEEN MOONS

Sequels and Revision

The opportunity to take up central aspects of *Der Müll, die Stadt und der Tod* presented itself to Fassbinder two years later, under what at first glance appear to be wholly different circumstances. In May 1978, on a trip to New York, Fassbinder split up with Armin Meier, his lover of four years' standing. Armin Meier returned to Munich on his own, while Fassbinder went directly to the Cannes Film Festival. On what was probably Fassbinder's birthday (May 31st: the body was found almost a week later), Meier committed suicide in their joint apartment, having taken an overdose of sleeping pills. The death caused a minor public scandal and was exploited in the tabloid press. There were calls for a criminal investigation, and Fassbinder received anonymous death threats: that Armin Meier had not been able to cope with the separation proved once again how dangerous it was for him to love and, even more so, for others to love him.

Fassbinder's response to the tragedy was to take on more work. Whether he could call on his 'usual knack of turning occasions from his private life into material for his films'[1] in order to master his distress, or whether a monument to his friend was Fassbinder's very personal form of mourning is a point that biographers have often debated since.[2] The film which resulted three months later, though 'dedicated to the memory of Armin Meier', is at all events only intermittently based on the latter's life: neither a biography nor autobiographical, it is not even the fictionalisation of a homosexual relationship.[3]

Yet IN A YEAR OF THIRTEEN MOONS has always been recognised as one of Fassbinder's most 'personal' films: the sensationalist pre-text made sure of that, but it was also personal in the more banal sense that Fassbinder, apart from producing, writing and directing the film, also did the camera-work and the editing.[4] Yet this hardly explains why IN A YEAR OF THIRTEEN MOONS has such an exceptional place in the overall oeuvre. Wolfgang Roth called it Fassbinder's

> most radical [film]. It goes under the skin because of the concentration of the means. There is no trace of self-pity: any possible mawkishness is banished by a merciless despair that is unique in the whole of German cinema. Volker Spengler as Elvira makes himself vulnerable to a degree only possible because of total identification with the figure he plays, whom he pushes to such an extreme that he reaches a degree of artifice which transcends the apparent naturalism of his acting.[5]

From the opening scene, where Elvira is beaten up and kicked to the ground by three homosexuals, evidently scandalised when discovering that she is a 'woman', to the final shot of him/her dead in her apartment, with most of the protagonists in her life eventually gathering round, the film does not let go, piling up humiliation upon humiliation, dead-ends upon dead-ends, sparing the viewer none of the ghastly revelations about Elvira's past, the injustices done to her, the embarrassments inflicted on her.

Insofar as IN A YEAR OF THIRTEEN MOONS takes hints from Armin Meier's life, it tells the story of 'a person's last five days on earth' before he commits suicide when abandoned by his long-time lover and rejected for a second time by the love of his life. In its claims for wider significance, it seems closer to the underlying project of *Der Müll, die Stadt und der Tod* than to Meier's fate either before or with Fassbinder. This assertion must be a contentious one, since it is by no means evident how such a singular situation as that of Armin's death, with its share of futility and pathos, might lend itself to a political interpretation, be it focused on Germany or not.

The story is relentlessly linear. The transsexual Erwin/Elvira Weishaupt is woken one morning by the unexpected but evidently long awaited return of her partner, Christoph, who, it turns out, has only come back to pack his bags and leave for good. Erwin/Elvira's pleas and remonstrations lead to a violent quarrel which ends with her lying, half-dressed, in the street outside, where she is picked up by Red Zora, the 'tart with a heart' who buys her a brandy. They spend the day together, touring also the abattoir where Erwin once worked as a butcher, and visiting the convent where the orphan Erwin was brought up by Sister Gudrun. Reprimanded by his estranged wife for having given an interview about her life, Erwin/Elvira pays a call on Anton Saitz, an influential property speculator for whose sake she became a woman, asking him to forgive the indiscretion. He barely recognises her, but promises to have coffee at her apartment. There, he makes love to Red Zora, while Elvira, ever more distraught, cuts off her hair, puts on men's clothes and walks out, to ask her wife and daughter to take her back. But it is too late to return to family life, and the next morning, Erwin/Elvira is found dead in her apartment.

Even from such a simple plot summary, a number of themes suggest themselves. Is it a meditation on unhappy love? An examination of sexual deviancy and subsequent social discrimination? Is it a plea for tolerance of the 'other' in his/her otherness? Or is it a study of extreme pain and terminal despair in the face of rejection? The critics at the time were not unanimous. 'A wild bellow of a shriek that Fassbinder had to let out to stay sane' one reviewer called it,[6] while David Robinson found it unappealing and stark, and much too singular a case history.[7] By contrast, Richard Roud, Fassbinder's staunchest American advocate, was deeply touched, and saw it as the 'parable of the weak being exploited by the strong,' showing how 'those who live by the emotions [are] exploited by those who don't.'[8] Other critics agreed that the film had little to do with Armin Meier. They saw it as a statement about Frankfurt, and by extension, about the psychic immiseration of life in the soulless cities of modern corporate capitalism.[9]

The raw anguish and disturbing power of this achingly naked film are as inescapable as they are hard to define, and there is a temptation to stay with the biographical, if only in order to come to terms with its unsettling impact. Arguing that IN A YEAR OF THIRTEEN MOONS, whose ostensible occasion appears to speak against any further subtext whatsoever, is responding to the pressures of a particular German, historical trauma is therefore not without risks.[10] Formally an 'experimental' art film – one critic called it 'rough', in contrast to the 'polish' of the more commercial MARRIAGE OF MARIA BRAUN – the film nevertheless constructs a narrative which, like all narratives, can be seen as an imaginary 'solution' to a real problem, which raises the moot point of what might have been the problem to which Elvira's suicide is the solution? If Fassbinder himself has given a clue when he remarked how important it was for him to turn this death into 'a decision for life',[11] we might note that Erwin's decision to become Elvira is in this respect also a solution, albeit one that, in not winning Anton Saitz's love, appears to have failed.

It therefore makes sense to regard the narrative as that of an impossible love story, which, as noted in previous chapters, is so often both the emotional matrix and the narrative motor that Fassbinder's films need for generating their socio-historical allegories. Once more, the genre would be that of melodrama, with its vicious circles, and a plot that carefully traces how tightly bolted all the exits are by which the characters attempt to escape their fate. But in the case of Erwin/Elvira, the dilemma at the heart of all the different impossibilities is not the vicious circle of A loving B, but B loving C, and C only loving/hating himself (cf. Fassbinder's description of Sirk's WRITTEN ON THE WIND, or the narrative crux of his own FEAR EATS THE SOUL, where Ali loves Emmi, but Emmi loves her children and depends on her neighbours, who are revolted by Ali, so that Emmi has to choose between either becoming an outcast like Ali or casting out Ali by betraying him). In IN A YEAR OF THIRTEEN MOONS, Erwin once loved Anton, who did not love him, but suggested he might love him, if only Erwin were a woman, whereupon Erwin 'becomes' a woman, merely to find that Anton, instead of acknowledging in Erwin 'Elvira' (the sameness and otherness of the person before him) bursts into laughter. Denying his responsibility and refusing the gift, he pays him off instead and sends him away. However, as if this was not enough, Fassbinder complicates matters by assigning to the impossible couple a historically particular, uniquely German 'impossibility': Saitz is Jewish and 'grew up' in Bergen-Belsen.[12]

The fact of Saitz being Jewish and a survivor from a Nazi concentration camp is not the only link between IN A YEAR OF THIRTEEN MOONS and *Der Müll, die Stadt und der Tod*. There is the common setting (the city of Frankfurt), a key scene (the meeting with a Jewish property developer), and a central character who ends by committing suicide, an act at once noticed and ignored by those around. The most explicit parallel is the monologue addressed by one of the property developer's bodyguards to Erwin/Elvira as she waits for admission outside Saitz's office:

In the old days, all hell was loose here [...] we bought up old buildings and cleared them. Sometimes it got really tough, but we always managed to pull it off. God knows! Then we tore the old shacks down and built new, mostly high-rise office blocks, and then sold them at a good profit. Pretty slick, eh? [...] The city was helping us. The police chief is a friend of his [i.e. Saitz] and so was the mayor, then. Quite a few on the council were in on it, too. Anyhow, the original scheme wasn't his. It was already in place, the eviction orders were there, the building regulations were there. He just did the dirty work for the ones who made the real decisions. Outwardly, though, they kept their distance, since they wanted to get re-elected. They'd rather have the power than the profit, which they preferred to make a present of, to us, for instance.[13]

For those in the know, these explanations transform IN A YEAR OF THIRTEEN MOONS into a sequel to the Frankfurt play, covering, as it were, the period after 'The Rich Jew' has been paid off by the city fathers, with his real estate business fallen on harder times, as the new office blocks are standing empty.[14] Without this intertext, Erwin/Elvira's story is perhaps more reminiscent of that archetypal Fassbinder victim tale told in FOX AND HIS FRIENDS, whose male hero is exploited and abused by his lovers, and ends up rejected and driven to suicide. The semi-public nature of Erwin/Elvira's suicide also recalls that of Hans in THE MERCHANT OF FOUR SEASONS, who drinks himself to death in front of his assembled friends. Yet IN A YEAR OF THIRTEEN MOONS is ultimately not about victimhood, since this implies a subjectivity and a negative identity that Erwin/Elvira, despite her manifest torment and unhappiness, emphatically rejects. For insofar as it is a sequel, the film is also a 'revision', with the central relationship between Erwin/Elvira and Saitz, as we shall see, fuelled by a different emotional energy than that between Roma B and The Rich Jew, while the roles of Christoph, Red Zora, and Erwin/Elvira's wife and daughter are worked out with greater emotional subtlety than are comparable characters in FOX AND HIS FRIENDS or THE MERCHANT OF FOUR SEASONS. This shift away from victimhood, and the frankness that results, has to do with the nature of the relationships Erwin/Elvira is open to with those she encounters, all of which are marked by great mutual understanding and even greater tenderness.[15]

More plausible than a story of victimisation would be the suggestion that it is about outsiders: marginals, deviants, foreigners, outcasts and social failures. In the circumstances, even Anton Saitz is a figure placed far from the seat of power, relegated to watching re-runs of old Jerry Lewis movies on television and playing childish games with his bodyguards. Each outsider, furthermore, lives in a world of his/her own, establishing no more than tenuous contact with others.[16] There is solidarity between Erwin/Elvira and Red Zora (up to a point: she readily sleeps with Saitz, even in the presence of Elvira), but little between Erwin/Elvira and other kinds of 'others': the Croats who beat him up; Christoph, her exasperated 'husband'; the macho world of Saitz; Saitz's black bodyguard Smolik with the Bavarian accent, or the North African with the American accent hanging himself in an empty office, not to mention the Turks in the video arcade. It is this combination of emotional honesty in their dealings with each other, and their ultimate isolation from each other, as outsiders in a society that seems to have no centre, which gives the film's characters their bleak finality and confirms all the false solutions and blocked exits as nobody's fault and nonetheless inevitable. Running against this tight grid of hopelessness, however, is another dynamic, at once more paradoxical, because even more desperate, and more utopian, because following the laws of a different genre from that of melodrama. For this to become apparent, one has to consult the extensive notes Fassbinder wrote while preparing the film.

Fassbinder's 'Impossible' Fantasy

The 40-page treatment for IN A YEAR OF THIRTEEN MOONS seems to have been written almost immediately after Fassbinder's return from Cannes, for the film was shot over 25 days in July and August 1978. As published, the treatment is divided into three parts: 'The Year of Thirteen Moons' ('in which emotionally sensitive humans are especially vulnerable and in mortal danger'),[17] 'A Biography' (of the orphan Erwin Weishaupt, disowned by his mother, brought up in a convent, denied an adoption and apprenticed to a butcher), and 'A Film' (the story of the five final days in the life of the transsexual Erwin/Elvira who, abandoned by his lover, refused a home by his wife and daughter, betrayed by the man for whose sake he changed his sex, is finally left to die in the cellar of the writer who had exploited his story in the tabloids).

Just as Erwin/Elvira Weishaupt's story is not that of Armin Meier, so the story Fassbinder wrote as a treatment is not the film he made, or rather, as he points out, there is a year, there is a biography, and there is a film. Despite the harrowing immediacy which gives such a powerful illusion of the autobiographical and of raw, unscripted referentiality, the film is in fact very carefully constructed, and shaped to serve ends that have little to do with what the treatment calls 'A Biography'. The film, in this respect, lets each part of the treatment comment on the others, so that information, left out of the film, can serve as vantage points from which the events take on new meanings. Thus, Erwin/Elvira's love story is conceived, from the very start, as one that only exists because in some crucial respects, it cannot be. But the reasons for this impossibility are located in gaps that the film deliberately seems to create. For while in other impossible love stories, such as that of MARIA BRAUN or Willie in LILI MARLEEN the ostensible impediment is that of circumstance (the war, or the incompatibility for a woman to combine love and career), here the impossibility is of a different nature: an asymmetry so radical and extreme that it casts doubt on the very notion of a lover, of a being who can love and still be a person, a subject, an identity. Yet, this radicalism is, as it were, only gradually revealed underneath other impossibilities, most evidently that of gender, and the impossible sexual identity that marks the body and person of Erwin/Elvira. IN A YEAR OF THIRTEEN MOONS figures transsexuality and Erwin/Elvira's body as both cause and effect of the impossible love that ties her to Anton Saitz. Hers is an impossible love story not only because this love is unrequited, or because the lovers' families are feuding with each other, or even because a man loves another man. As Saitz tells it: 'He always used to look at me so strangely, so I asked him what he was really thinking. And he told me he loved me. Then I said that would really be nice, if he was a girl. And he thought so too. And then it just happened – he was a girl.'[18] What seems to be at stake is that a man becomes a lover by inverting the biological and morphological signifiers of sexual identity, though not because he 'feels' a woman, or identifies with women, but because he tries to be his beloved's love object.[19] Her love becomes an act of making the other master of one's desire, yet by putting the other in charge of her desire, Elvira finds herself without either socially accepted or bodily secured signifiers of the self, and thus at maximum risk.

This dilemma the film thematizes in two ways. It consistently disarticulates gender in terms of different aspects of maleness and femininity in body and dress, in public appearance and gender address, proliferating the sites of distress and the signs of undress. Christoph pulls a half-naked Elvira in front of a mirror to show her how shapeless and sexless her face and body have become; Red Zora takes a dishevelled Elvira to a ladies' toilet in a night-club; Elvira visits Saitz in a black costume, wide hat and high-heel shoes, but is pushed, stumbles and falls, crumbling into an unsightly pile of uncovered flesh and ill-fitting clothes.[20]

IN A YEAR OF THIRTEEN MOONS also disarticulates film image and voice in such key scenes as the one at the slaughterhouse, where we hear Elvira's voice but do not see his/her image, or at Sister Gudrun's inside the convent walls, where we see her (having fainted) while others 'speak' him (on his behalf, by presuming to know his feelings when his adoption was cancelled). From another vantage point, the stations of Erwin's life all disarticulate several social roles: those of lover, husband, father, orphan, but also Elvira/Erwin's professions: as master-butcher, as Christoph's business adviser and as female 'hustler'/prostitute. Especially in respect of the latter, the impossibility of this identity is drastically demonstrated in the very first scene: a man who out of love for a man has a sex change into a woman, dresses as a man, in order to attract men who are attracted to men, because ashamed to pay for sex 'as a woman' whereupon s/he is beaten up because the men s/he attracts cannot find the sign of manhood they desire, despising her instead for being a woman dressed as a man. Sexual identity is at once staged and cancelled, in successive moves of double-binding impossibility. However, it seems as if the impossibility of a stable sexual identity is introduced in such stark terms not least in order to provide the metaphoric terms for another impossibility. This other impossibility the film approaches through the genre of the science fiction film, and in particular, the time travel film. It may at first glance seem strange to call such a persistently linear tale of a human being's one-way street to self-anni-hilation a time travel film, but there are several reasons why this seems the apposite genre to identify the current that runs counter to the melodramatic one.

Already the title alludes to an unusual temporal dimension, a time out of time, so to speak. For as the pre-credits put it: 'when a moon year is also a year with thirteen new moons, it often results in inevitable personal catastrophes'. Secondly, what Elvira does in these final days is to revisit the sites and persons, the places and stations that have determined her/his life, but now retraced in reverse order: the abattoir where he worked as a butcher, his former wife and daughter, the convent where he was brought up as an orphan, and most important of all, Anton Saitz's headquarters, as the person for whose sake he underwent his sex change operation. It is as if the film of Erwin/Elvira's life was once more unreeling backward, as it is said to do at the moment of death, so that her actual death is not so much an undoing of a life as it is this undone life's re-living, in the time-traveller's future-anterior mode of anticipating its inevitability, now undertaken in the knowledge of a repetition that experiences 'difference' without being terrified by alterity.

Finally, there is another reference to science fiction, not mentioned in the film, but prominent in the published treatment.[21] We learn that Elvira, on the day she finds herself abandoned by Christoph, eventually falls asleep reading a science fiction novel called *World on a Wire*, based on an idea which strikes her as eminently sensible and profoundly true, namely that the world she lives in is nothing but an experimental model for another, possibly 'higher' world, which has set up hers, mainly in order to try out and test, using real human beings, certain situations and responses.[22]

This inner framing of the fiction, whether explicitly present in the film or not, confirms the impression that this is a world of immanence without transcendence, where hierarchies are inverted and identities reversible because lives are lived in the mise-en-abyme of their own impossibilities. Anton Saitz, too, is in a time loop, not only because he is caught in the ups and downs of the cycles of the so-called 'real economy'. Playing the Jerry Lewis figure in the Jerry Lewis-Dean Martin film which is itself a time loop (YOU'RE NEVER TOO YOUNG, where Jerry Lewis disguises himself as a teenage girl in order to join a high-school parade as one of the cheerleaders), Anton enacts a temporality as well as a compulsion to repeat whose infinite regress of 'Jerry Lewis' mirrors Elvira's situation vis-à-vis Anton, one wanting to be the other being another, the other wanting to have the other and becoming another. Although their parallel lives are fated to meet only in infinity, Elvira's body has to be seen as a kind of 'time machine' where the shifts of gender, or rather, the shifting articulations of gender – male, female, homosexual, asexual, transsexual – succeed each other, not consecutively, but interchangeably. The indescribably agonising experiences Elvira narrates about her/his life take on the status of terrible 'experiments' of what it means to be human. Erwin/Elvira's body in its very indeterminacy becomes a kind of 'theatre of cruelty', in which a series of contests of identity and reciprocity are being staged.

'Negative Symbiosis' and the 'Auschwitz Bonus'

In this tale of suspended identities, the Jewish theme and Bergen-Belsen as the password to Saitz's inner sanctum may seem a tactless and embarrassing irrelevance. Worse still, here is a 'good' German, rebuffed, scorned and derided by a 'bad' Jew, as if to turn the tables on the historical facts. Such a view might be justified, if this was indeed a fictional account of a factual case. But the basic modality of the film, its tense and time structures speak against it, and the logic of the episodes, as well as the deeper logic of the problem Fassbinder sets himself to 'solve', has to do with two kinds of hypotheticals. One is the 'if-only' of melodrama, the tense of regret, so to speak, and the other the 'what-if' of science fiction, the tense of 'thinking the impossible'. As always in his films, the action encircles a cluster of emotional and moral blockages, double-binds, dead-ends. An impossible love story that is both tragic and ridiculous; a confession of love which is met with a rebuff, but so is the confession of having confessed this love to a tabloid journalist, for Saitz greets Elvira's indiscretion with indifference. No forgiveness mitigates her anxiety of having given offence, as Elvira and Saitz are caught in the moral dilemma of how to acknowledge a debt, how to reply to a demand, and how to 'return' a gift. At another level still, the encounter brings together two people, neither of whom should be alive, at least if one attends to their tragically complementary fates: Erwin, it transpires from the 'Biography' (though not the film), is an orphan because offspring of the infamous Nazi 'Lebensborn' project, the attempt to force nature to collaborate in the creation of an Aryan 'Über-Mensch', the super-(Ger)man. Anton Saitz, for his part, was a child at Bergen-Belsen, and stigmatised as 'Unter-Mensch', he should have perished like his parents. Two Germans, two orphans, two extremes around the signifier 'race', two lives that have, in a sense, already suffered one death.

By the time of the film, however, the intended super-German has become a non-being (a no-'body') in contemporary Germany, while Anton, once feared – faithful to the old anti-Semitic cliché – as a super-Jew, has also become a non-person in the Frankfurt of 1978.[23] From such a perspective, Erwin/Elvira and Anton are each other's mirror images of impossibility, making this love story embody the intolerably poignant confrontation of two human beings who are each other's 'other', across a time shift and a history which is a personal disaster for both: the Holocaust for Anton Saitz, and the master-racial fantasies of National Socialism for Erwin Weishaupt. In response to this disaster, the conjuncture of the melodrama of unrequited love and the 'world-on-a-wire' science fiction story represent a genre context that both frames a historical dilemma and formulates a hypothetical proposition, each of which has to be looked at separately.

The historical dilemma is, of course, the relationship of Germany to its 'others' par excellence, the Jews. But as we have seen in the previous chapter, this is a relationship that in some profound sense is 'unrepresentable',[24] since it has to encompass their mutual response *after* Auschwitz, but also *because of* Auschwitz, and thus involves a way of thinking a past as well as a present within a single continuum which cannot contain both. Germans and Jews are henceforth tied together by such monstrous guilt and almost equally monstrous innocence, which together form a kind of inescapable 'symbiosis':

> Since Auschwitz – what a sad ruse – one can in fact speak of a 'German-Jewish symbiosis,' albeit of a negative one. For both Germans and Jews, the result of the Holocaust is now the starting point of their self-understanding; a sort of diametrically opposed communality, whether they like it or not. Germans and Jews are, thanks to this event, newly implicated with each other. Such a negative symbiosis, engineered by the Nazis, is likely to determine for generations to come the relation

each group has to itself and above all, to the other [...]. It is almost as if the phenomenon Auschwitz, seemingly belonging to the past, has its future as a factor forming consciousness still ahead of it.[25]

At the heart of this symbiosis, then, are once more the parapraxes of an unresolved double identification, lived as the uneasy truce that ranges from studied avoidance to cautious collusion, as German-Jewish coexistence within West Germany has remained bounded by anti-Semitism, in both its unreconstructed, historical form, and in its modern, contemporary version.[26]

The Federal Republic, as already indicated, had a fairly consistent record of disavowing anti-Semitism, mainly compensated by an official philo-Semitism, which as many commentators have pointed out, always risks being anti-Semitism's obverse and equivalent.[27] Its many public manifestations in the 1950s and 1960s have been exhaustively catalogued, as the Federal Republic sought international recognition, for which it needed to show to the world its *entente cordiale* with the State of Israel.[28] Nevertheless, even this 'formal' philo-Semitism found itself at times under strain in subsequent decades, notably after the Six-Day War, when a philo-Semitism, available at little cost on the German right, tried to score domestic points off an almost equally risk-free anti-Zionism on the German left. As far as dealings with the Jewish community living in Germany were concerned, the unresolved ambivalence covered over by demonstrative philo-Semitism was the symptom of a deeper, but real impasse: how to find a language and a social space for the larger questions of guilt, whether collective or individual, which this legacy of anti-Semitism entailed. However much official Germany subscribed to some version of its formal responsibility and juridical accountability for the crimes of Nazism,[29] the matter mostly figured in post-war West Germany as the debt of a guilt that had better *not* be called in, the 'negative symbiosis' here naming the mutual, silent agreement to defer terms and suspend this particular exchange. In the words of one sharp observer: when a Jew, faced with another German's profession of innocence, said: "'I believe you,'" he actually meant: "I take your disavowal as your good faith'"[30], which, using a more Sartrean vocabulary, could also be translated into the Jew's obligation to reassure his German friend that the latter's bad faith is taken as his authenticity. From this dynamic of a guilt that anticipates its own discovery, while at the same time finding its 'sincerity' already discounted in advance, a constellation arose, which left at once profound and nonetheless largely uncommented marks on German post-war culture.[31] Given that it remained over long decades an impasse which neither words nor gestures seemed to bridge, many actual deeds and much commerce and communication on the part of Germans were in turn fated to fall under the clumsy calculus of how this 'Schuld' (guilt) might be turned into the manageable change of 'Schulden' (debts),[32] how 'Wiedergutmachung'/compensation might somehow even out the irredeemable imbalance between suffering inflicted and suffering acknowledged, and repayments might be handed out generously, where regret was slow in forthcoming, and such as it was, mainly undertaken in a largely futile hope to 'square' accounts.[33]

An illustration of just how hopeless this attempt at squaring accounts was destined to remain is an anecdote told by Viennese Jews who 'envied' their German cousins the benefits of what they called the 'Auschwitz bonus':

> When my father and I visited our relatives in Frankfurt in 1964, we found a parking ticket on our host's car as we exited from a movie theatre. Irate about this, my father's cousin drove to the police station and demanded to speak to the officer who had penalised him for parking in a clearly prohibited area. Without attempting to justify his actions [...,] he asked the officer in a hostile tone whether he had taken showers during the war. When the startled policeman, who was probably in his mid-fifties, answered affirmatively, my father's cousin shot back: 'Well, I just wanted you to know that you washed with soap which you Nazi made out of my family.' Shocked and speechless, the policeman tore up the parking ticket.[34]

What makes the incident, whether real or invented, so telling is that one can read it as the tragic-comic demonstration not only that two wrongs do not make a right, but also of the reverse conversion of *Schulden* into *Schuld*, where 'the German's' hypothetical guilt is played off – angrily, but also sadistically – against 'the Jew's' actual debt (the parking fine): the two cancelling each other out, and yet not cancelling each other out, in an act of exchange that is both grotesquely asymmetrical and yet appropriate precisely because it underlines the fundamental asymmetry which the exchange cannot obliterate and simply serves to highlight.[35] Displaying the structure of a (Freudian) joke, the story of the 'Auschwitz bonus' also thematizes the power of the victim, which is, of course, an illusory, because borrowed power. More accurately, it is the power of 'having-been-the-victim,' and as such it exerts itself, by its very nature, rarely towards the guilty one, but often towards the 'innocently guilty,' those 'blessed with the grace of late birth'[36] – who in turn will eventually demand that 'enough is enough', that the 'closed season' must come to an end, that 'a line must be drawn'[37] – a situation which leaves both parties to the exchange at once frustrated and cheated.

Loving the Other: The Temporalities of Anger and Regret

Reversal of terms as a response to the monstrous asymmetry is thus a key feature of the social discourse as well as the psychic economy under which Jews and Germans have so often come into contact with each other after Auschwitz. Fassbinder's choice of the couple Erwin/Elvira and Anton Saitz may not seem quite so gratuitous or arbitrary, once it is granted that in the light of the 'negative symbiosis' (as example of the impossibly enmeshed states of identification) and the 'Auschwitz bonus' (as the illusory power of the past victim), the central relationship of IN A YEAR OF THIRTEEN MOONS does indeed take on an allegorical significance. By figuring such a constellation – not as it 'objectively' presents itself to an outside observer, but in its necessarily slanted, even twisted subjective reality – the film doubly motivates this apparently most insidious form of reversal, where an 'innocent' Erwin/Elvira is 'victimised' by Anton Saitz. A primary mechanism of projection is here exposed – Peter Gay once spoke of the German-Jewish relationship as a 'history of largely unexamined counter-transference'[38] – addressed especially at the (West German) spectator. The new constellation also makes clear in what sense the film amounts to a 'revision' of *Der Müll, die Stadt und der Tod*. Rewriting or reworking the Roma B/The Rich Jew relationship in the (non-) encounter of Elvira and Anton, Fassbinder throws into sharp relief the universally human, but also historical, conditions under which such a love story might be conceived as the (impossible) solution. More radical, more open, more specific in the motivation that drives the central character, IN A YEAR OF THIRTEEN MOONS is less schematic than the Frankfurt play and therefore also more concise, more economical in the constellation of its characters. Franz B and Roma B are now clearly one figure: that of Erwin/Elvira.[39] Even Roma B's father, the Nazi who earns his living by dressing up as a woman, could be seen as present in Erwin/Elvira's unresolved gender and overdetermined biography.

Yet how can such a composite, 'constructed' figure emerge, or more to the point, what is her function? The 'background' of this affair, as told by Elvira to the journalist, draws attention to certain power-relations: While working as a butcher, Erwin is befriended by Anton Saitz, who uses him to run some dangerous and illegal operations which make Saitz a wealthy man, but land Erwin in jail. Rejoicing in the opportunity to prove his love, Erwin takes the blame, though when he meets Anton after his release, he is spurned, which only makes Erwin more fervent in his love. A post-Genet staple of homosexual romance fiction, this story-within-the film only helps to underscore the 'experimental' nature of the central issue in IN A YEAR OF THIRTEEN MOONS. Erwin's act of sacrifice has to be extreme, even unreasonable: the moral force of the story derives from the fact that someone is prepared to change himself for love, irrespective of the cost to himself and his own identity. And while most of us are capable of sacrifice for a loved one, and in fact find happiness in making such sacrifices, they are rarely such radical, such irreversible ones. Similarly, Anton's character has to be extreme, because the nature of this sacrifice demands, both in its psychological as well as its historical truth, that Anton be as he has become: brutal, inconsiderate, letting Erwin go to prison, and yet not wanting anything to do with Elvira. For is it not a tribute to the truth of one's love when one loves someone who is not loveable? This line of thought and feeling is represented in the film indirectly, via Elvira's story in the slaughterhouse scene of how she gave a new sense of purpose and self-respect to Christoph.[40] Both Christoph and Saitz – even more than The Rich Jew in *Der Müll, die Stadt und der Tod* – are monsters of ingratitude, and they have to be in order for there to be the possibility of true love, the proof of love.[41] For it would, after all, be too easy for a German to love a Jew, on condition that he is a nice, upright one.[42] Such is the 'answer' Erwin/Elvira gives to the question of how to 'represent' German-Jewish relations after Auschwitz. Yet this dynamic, this uneven power-relation, also indicates the utopian, impossible, 'failed' nature of the response embodied in the figure of Elvira's love/sacrifice, and thus marks a kind of vanishing point for any lived intersubjectivity. To represent a German Jew as a 'just another German' would either be to 'deny' Auschwitz (and ignore the implications of the 'negative symbiosis'), or it would presume having access to the subjectivity of the 'other' : precisely what German society as a whole, caught in the dialectic of a philo-Semitism at once overcompensating and repressing anti-Semitism, has singularly failed to find the terms for. This dilemma goes some way towards explaining why there have been so few representations of Jews in post-war German cinema, given that most directors are non-Jewish.

At the level at which 'Schuld' becomes the loose change of 'Schulden', or the Auschwitz bonus is reluctantly being redeemed, there can evidently be no solution to the tragi-comedy of German-Jewish relations. The two terms indicate, as it were, both a tantalising proximity and an unbridgeable distance, both the wished-for instrumentalization (on the part of the Germans) and the insisted-on impossibility (on the part of the Jews) implied in this exchange, for it is irrevocably marked (and at the same time marred) by the lack (or lack of agreed definition) of what might serve as currency in this hopelessly uneven exchange. Thus, confronted with the German-Jewish 'historical dilemma', the Elvira-Saitz affair merely reproduces the moral deadlocks and emotional double-binds, from which so many other Fassbinder films draw some of their strongest subject-effects.[43] IN A YEAR OF THIRTEEN MOONS seems to go beyond these customary double-binds as its time schemes break up both the binarisms and the asymmetries so far described. Other modalities and temporalities open up a different space and another dimension, notably towards the 'hypothetical proposition' already mentioned. For the reverse identification holding Elvira in thrall also extends itself to the time schemes of the 'if-only' of melodrama and the 'what-if' of science fiction, where IN A YEAR OF THIRTEEN MOONS tries to formulate another kind of question and speculates on another kind of answer: by loving Saitz, Erwin seems to be asking 'what would a German (after Hitler) have to be like, who would s/he have to become, in order to be loved by a Jew (after Bergen Belsen)'? Such a 'what-if', however, implies as its own mirror inverse a complementary question: 'what must/what might a Jew have felt like (before Hitler) if s/he thought of him/herself as German?' Taken together, the 'what-ifs' imply a supplement in the logic of melodrama and unrequited love, while the modality of the 'if-only', expressing in the first instance the force of desire and longing, proves itself also open to the affect of regret and even remorse. In other words, these 'questions' produce as their 'answer' the body of Erwin/Elvira, and with it, her indescribable psychic pain, but also a body capable of signifying a more radical kind of empathy.

Here the logic of the sex change, the 'conversion' of Erwin into Elvira exceeds any sexual pathology (whether seen as case history or fictional biography), in order to find its place in the larger allegorical scheme. Choosing the most extreme form that human society and culture know of suspending identity, irrespective of faith, nationality and ethnicity, namely the one attached to gender and sexual difference, Fassbinder shows a man who decides to open up to the play of intensity and contradiction, of passion and hurt, not his memories, nor his prospects, but something altogether more fundamentally involved in the tragedies of the history he is investigating, namely masculinity, as the bedrock of patriarchy, but also of the fascist body.[44] Erwin becomes Elvira not in order to 'come out' as a homosexual, nor as a 'woman' but as a being floating between these forms of gendered identity, and thus a person open for all forms of inscription of the love of the other, including the other's rejection or derision of this love. The indeterminate gender identity of Elvira is especially open to accommodating the intensities of anger others project on her, which require a different temporality in order to give shape to a relationship whose very meaning is based on a sense of time that knows no past, because it lives in the perpetual present of hatred, of grievance so intense as to be beyond justice or forgiveness. To this extent, Erwin/Elvira is an idealised, utopian figure, capable of expressing in her very being this temporality of regret, a time experience dominated by the wish to undo something that cannot be undone, to turn back the clock, and re-turn to the moment in time prior to the moment that now makes both anger and regret such voiceless elements of historical reality.

Fassbinder's chosen route to the 'what-if' of Erwin/Elvira's 'conversion' as an implicit answer to the 'if-only' of regret can be useful contrasted with another 'if-only', which also wants to be an expression of regret: that of the filmmaker Hans Jürgen Syberberg, whose own revisionism might be called a 'failed' 'what-if' temporality applied to the German-Jewish question. In *Vom Unglück und Glück der Kunst*, a book of reflections and ruminations published in the wake of German unification, Syberberg speculates about what has gone wrong with Germany: not only in 1871 (the foundation of the German Reich) or 1914 (the outbreak of WWI), 1919 (the failed 'Socialist' Revolution), or 1933 (the Nazi take-over), but also in 1945. Why had West Germany not seized the chance to cleanse itself to become once more the 'Kulturnation' of Goethe and Schiller, of Kleist and Richard Wagner? After first acknowledging the damage done by the post-war rehabilitation of a compromised civil service and judiciary, Syberberg gives himself space for a kind of fantasy, in the mode that also joins the regret of 'if-only' to the speculative 'what-if'. He dreams of what might have become of German (popular) culture, had it not been for Hitler, but even more so, had it not been for Germany's liberators. Without the Americans and their mass culture, whose dominance he regards as a direct result of Hitler's defeat by Hollywood, a truly German art might have rebuilt itself without 'foreign' influences.[45]

However, Syberberg joins to these speculations a further thought: namely, what might post-war German cultural life have become if only its younger generation had not embraced so fervently the melancholy pessimism of Germany's pre-war Jewish intellectuals, in a misguided effort at atonement. Making Walter Benjamin and TW Adorno the good conscience by which to assuage their own (parents') guilt, and taking over from them the negative perspective on German romanticism, nationalism and popular culture, the generation of the Sixties, according to Syberberg, missed dealing with the German question in an indigenous way, and therefore had self-exiled and alienated themselves from what it meant to be German as fatally as had the masses who embraced Hollywood, Disneyland and American popular music.[46]

That these reveries have something deeply offensive needs little comment. As Eric Santner argues, Syberberg's thoughts on contemporary Germany are stained by a dangerous, because largely unconscious anti-Semitism.[47] What can also be observed are the peculiar temporal shifts in this fantasy, as the sentiment of regret, the grieving over all that has gone amiss with modern German history, not so much 'scapegoats' German-Jewish cultural philosophy and thought but places it in a reverse order, where the lucid diagnostics of Frankfurt School critical theory from the 1930s and 1940s is treated as if it was a 1960s 'seduction' of German youth.

In contrast to Syberberg's 'what-if' logic, Fassbinder's way of conceiving a modality of regret wants to have no truck with either official statements of regret (whose hypocrisies are also hateful to Syberberg), or with conjugations of history such as Syberberg's. Unsentimental, without 'self-pity' or 'mawkishness', IN A YEAR OF THIRTEEN MOONS allegorises German-Jewish relations in a form already familiar from Fassbinder's other films: as a matter of love, which is to say, as an inherently impossible and yet necessary exchange.[48] By presenting the relation as such, we come to recognise it as impossible twice over: impossible because what has been done in history even 'love' cannot undo, and impossible because those like Elvira willing to take the risks have no position from which to speak, no identity to draw on, no self from which to be the other's 'other'. Insofar as its impossibility is couched in the terms of 'love', Fassbinder presents also a challenge that says: a German might at the very least have to go this far, in order for the post-Auschwitz Jew to be able to respond at all.

Otherness after Over-identification and Assimilation

Treated as a matter of the 'Euclidean space' of equations, equivalencies and even exchanges, the German-Jewish 'negative symbiosis' is thus as unrepresentable as it is irresolvable. It remains an asymmetry that always threatens to capsize whatever fragile equilibrium the parties might attempt to negotiate. Anton Saitz must always laugh and cry, whether an Erwin wants to establish the currency conversion of *Schuld* into *Schulden*, or an Elvira tries to square accounts by offering a common solidarity of victims. In neither case is there a basis (neutral or otherwise) on which the currencies could be fixed, and thus an exchange sustained. Where Fassbinder's film breaks new ground is that his central character is not, as most fictional characters are, engaged in establishing a stable identity across a quest for love, for recognition, or by making the other the mirror of the self. On the contrary, IN A YEAR OF THIRTEEN MOONS is, if anything, about an inverse quest: the dissolution of the self, the un-making of identity. While quite a number of films of the New German Cinema from the 1970s and 1980s touching on (German) history are oedipal quests, whether centred on men (KASPAR HAUSER, HEIMAT, THE JOURNEY) or women (GERMANY PALE MOTHER, THE GERMAN SISTERS, THE HUNGER YEARS), the 'terminal' subject in IN A YEAR OF THIRTEEN MOONS is no longer rebelling against a father, nor in search of figurations of the maternal.[49] An altogether different process seems to be at work, though one that by now strikes a familiar note.

Fassbinder's heroes and heroines, one might say, attain through their impossible loves very different states of selfhood: some, by a kind of radical exhibitionism, catch in the gaze of the other a fleeting, unstable mirror-image of their selves. Such is the case of Emmi and Ali, in FEAR EATS THE SOUL, the morning after their first night together.[50] Alternatively, a character's desire might be to inhabit the other, as with Hermann Hermann in DESPAIR, whose over-identification with Felix leads to killing 'himself' in order to become the other. At the limit, love may signal the desire for incorporation by the other, a desire for self-annihilation in and through the other, as if this self-annihilation might prepare incorporation by the other: such is the story of QUERELLE. What one finds in IN A YEAR OF THIRTEEN MOONS, however, seems different from any of these. Early on, Christoph drags Elvira in front of a mirror, screaming: 'Look at yourself [...] Look! Now, do you see why I don't come home anymore?' to which Elvira replies: 'I see myself loving you,'[51] as if to underscore that her quest only begins after such a self-confirming love is no longer possible, and with it, the exchange of looks and the specular relations that these entail can no longer secure the self.

Circulating in the film after the break-up with Christoph is a new element, crucial for understanding not only the trajectory of this particular narrative about German-Jewish identities after Auschwitz, but also for Fassbinder's wider project of re-drawing the boundaries of selfhood and otherness. This element is Erwin/Elvira's body, or rather, the way his/her body gradually reveals itself as a site of impossibilities, at once 'embodying' irresolvable antinomies and transcending them, becoming the vehicle for temporal shifts and virtualities of existence capable of putting a past in touch with a future. For what does the introduction of such a 'self-divided' but also 'double' body mean? First of all, it affirms the material immanence of the basic categories one normally thinks about self and other: the shift to the body confounds categories of otherness based on presence/absence, inner/outer, exclusion and inclusion, requiring a different modality by which 'love' manifests itself. Erwin/Elvira's love is literally written on her body, in such a way as to mark this body with the signs of its 'Germanness'.

What specifically might this marking of the body mean for that blend of covert rejection and over-identification that allegedly typifies the German situation of modern philo-Semitism covering old anti-Semitism? How can it mitigate the alternatives of failed assimilation and integration on one side, and expulsion or annihilation on the other, and perhaps put an end to the 'negative symbiosis'? Here, the most striking aspect of Erwin/Elvira is his/her suffering: raw, piercing and seemingly without relief or respite. But this is to see it under its negative signs. One could equally well regard it as the bliss of suffering. When visiting the abattoir s/he once worked in, Erwin/Elvira replies to Zora's question of how she can bear a place where animals are being killed, for 'that's against life':

It's not against life at all. It is life itself. The way the blood steams, and death, that's what gives an animal's life meaning in the first place. And the smell, when they die and they know that death is coming and that it's beautiful and they wait for it. [...] Come with me, I'll show you. It'll smell, and we'll see them die and hear their cries, cries for deliverance.[52]

Elvira's affirmation of suffering has been interpreted within the complex psychic economy of masochistic ecstasy,[53] but it also has been examined as a sign of Fassbinder's covert anti-Semitism, in that he consistently reserves the (spiritually higher) 'torments of the flesh' for his German characters, in contrast to whom his Jewish figures are cold and remote.[54] The association made here by Elvira of suffering with deliverance is amplified with a materiality – of steaming blood, of smells and cries – which in some sense precedes both the negative theology of the mortified flesh discussed by Koch, and the 'heteropathy' of exteriorized identification analysed by Silverman.

The Historical Body Transfigured as the Open Wound

The argument up to now has been that the reinscription of a body so clearly but also so contradictorily marked as that of Erwin/Elvira into German post-war history necessarily changes the terms by which this history can be understood, but also carried further towards a future. And if this history – at whatever level we look at it, is traversed by oppositions, double-binds and stalemated confrontations, then one would expect such a body to expose a terrain where this situation can be reconfigured. The only way to picture this is to regard Elvira's suffering as a kind of 'open wound', transcending not only the fatal asymmetries of *Schuld* and *Schulden*, but also positing as a 'radical' alternative the body without skin: 'tender' in both senses of the word. Seen as a shedding of all skins, as a self-flaying, the narrative of Elvira's five last days, the stations on her path to 'deliverance,' reorganises itself around different intensities. One can distinguish a threefold movement 'beyond': the past beyond longing and regret, the body beyond gender, and love beyond identification and incorporation. Thus, for instance, Erwin/Elvira's visit to Soul Frieda's apartment and to Sister Gudrun's convent can be seen as the attempts to appropriate her own past without trying to re-incorporate this past's memories: Soul Frieda's dream of the cemetery in which are buried not the dead, but the brief times 'a person [...] was truly happy' or 'his' remarks about 'that outward manifestation which I call my body' become more comprehensible when set next to Sister Gudrun's narrative of the intense longing Erwin felt as a boy when waiting for the visits from his step-parents-to-be, to which Elvira responds by fainting, a form of ex-corporation of anticipated happiness too precious to forget, and too painful in its non-fulfilment to retain. Elvira could also apply to herself the words Soul Frieda has pinned to his wall: 'what I fear the most is if one day I'm able to put my feelings into words...'.

Insofar as IN A YEAR OF THIRTEEN MOONS is a melodrama, it is a film of suffering, muteness and repression. Integral to the genre is that the suffering self be incapable of giving voice to his or her feelings. Yet whereas in its 'classical' form film melodrama finds a conduit of 'expression' by way of symptoms, either visited on the physical body of the protagonist (as in Fassbinder's MARTHA) or more often on the metaphoric body of the film (represented by its mise-en-scène, its colour scheme, its decor),[55] IN A YEAR OF THIRTEEN MOONS must be called a post-classical melodrama, in that it no longer functions along the lines of the repression/expression model, but by a more radical displacement and reversal of values. The 'I' that in this film suffers so excruciatingly and flamboyantly is an 'I' that does not repress suffering, nor does it voice it directly, but 'ex-corporates' it: suffusing the film in ways the filmic discourse fails to contain, except by modulating sound effects, light, music, ambient noise into an almost abstract figuration, as in the scene of Elvira weeping in the video arcade.

Crucial in the process of ex-corporation, however, is the slaughterhouse scene: while the beasts are butchered, stripped and flayed, Elvira can be heard telling Zora about her life with Christian, how she made a 'man' of him, quoting a famous passage from Goethe's play *Torquato Tasso*, which directly alludes to the relation of pain to expression, of incorporation and excorporation, of containment and silence: 'und wenn der Mensch in seiner Qual verstummt, gab mir ein Gott zu sagen was ich leide' ('And if as a man, I am silenced in my agony, a god taught me to speak of how I suffer'). Yet the ironic point in this scene is a double one: first of all, Elvira does not 'identify' with Tasso, the poet touched by God, more with the humans falling silent in their pain. But given the passage already quoted about the animals, it is clear that Elvira actually 'identifies' most directly with the animals, who also do not fall silent like humans but 'speak' – yet what speaks in them is not the poetry of words, but the poetry of the flesh, flayed and skinned, the beautiful wound opening up – the most literal form of excorporation that the film provides as the key to its preferred mode of 'bodily' being.

'Working through' or 'Putting on'?

Finally, we can return to our initial question, by reversing it: what has any of this German-Jewish history to do with (the life and death of) Armin Meier? The starting point, it could be argued, was the dilemma facing Fassbinder with the fact of Meier's death. The moral question he was confronted with was that of guilt, both as he may have felt it about this suicide, but perhaps even more so, as others projected on to him and expected of him to take upon himself. It therefore joins, in a very direct way, the larger issue of what could be the modalities of 'mourning work' in a situation not of one's making and yet part of one's personal accountability. Being so publicly blamed and made responsible for Armin Meier's death as Fassbinder was at the time, he seems to have been determined to explore what it meant to be made to feel guilty, and yet not feeling guilty, although prepared to take some form of responsibility.

The question I have only touched upon in passing, however, is whether a film like IN A YEAR OF THIRTEEN MOONS signifies in film history and the wider media world by virtue of 'intervening' or 'working through', of 'documenting' or 'disavowing', of 'putting-on' or 'putting forth' the symbolisations of masculinity, as in their narratives of the quest or the journey they encounter traumatic formations of race, gender or ethnicity. Each mode may well require a reading, a hermeneutics appropriate to its textuality, and to the institution which mediates its reception and thus helps determine its meanings. With it, another set of boundaries is being crossed, namely those that have traditionally divided mainstream cinema from art cinema or the avant-garde according to their referential status: seen against the 'untranscendable horizon' of the modern cinema as also a range of commodities, all films become texts are necessarily allegories.

It suggests that some of the films subsequent to IN A YEAR OF THIRTEEN MOONS, among them especially BERLIN ALEXANDERPLATZ and QUERELLE, might also be given such a double reading. As the cinema at the end of its first century comes out of the great figures of the imaginary into another kind of relation with the real, attending more closely to the non-symbolizable in both the socius and the self, one can see Fassbinder's films standing at a very crucial crossroad. No longer does desire in IN A YEAR OF THIRTEEN MOONS make its pact with the law, in order to recognise itself, in order to structure itself as 'desire' and recover itself from the death drive. Where once desire needed the law (or crime) in order to assume a shape at all, even if the shape it assumed was also that which prevented it from fulfilling itself, an ultimately unrepresentable entity, namely the body as sole support of the self seems to have taken over as the materiality, as well as the currency of exchange. Even the author of *Querelle*, Jean Genet, imagined this relation as oppositional, and therefore lived his contestation in the protective environment of the law of bourgeois society, but it seems that Fassbinder at the end of his life could not or would not enter the security zone in which law and crime are mutually implicating each other as two sides of the symbolic that makes subjectivity possible. In this respect, THE THIRD GENERATION is an almost nostalgic film, representing a certain kind of symbolic order, already vanishing at that point. The situation in which Fassbinder found himself for his last films – and indeed for VERONIKA VOSS – was no longer that of a homologous relation between a benevolent/criminal father and a benevolent/criminal state, but a society in which even this balance no longer operated (nobody guards the guardians at the end of VERONIKA VOSS...), which makes VERONIKA VOSS more the story of Roma B and Elvira than the story of Maria Braun or Lola: figures of an anticipatory bodily transfiguration, beyond masochism.

In the following chapter, BERLIN ALEXANDERPLATZ will be read as the story in which a German must choose 'his other' and does so, also in the hope of finding 'deliverance'. What we can say, finally, about IN A YEAR OF THIRTEEN MOONS is that Fassbinder tried to 'normalise' German history in exactly the opposite sense of the present generation of politicians. Fassbinder, too, it seems wanted to know how and why he was German, but not without pointing out the price to be paid for once more being German. Not by metaphorizing 'the other',[56] not by 'symptomatizing' the Jew,[57] but in his films, and with certain of his characters, going down a road, at the beginning of which for every German, according to Fassbinder, stands anti-Semitism and its relation to German identity. Living in Germany after Auschwitz meant learning to 'become German', which is to say to also 'become a German Jew' and conversely, to be able to conceive of 'becoming Elvira'.

To end the present chapter on this thought is to speculate how Fassbinder, who died too early to have imagined the fall of the wall, might have been formulating in IN A YEAR OF THIRTEEN MOONS some pertinent and yet perhaps too poignantly utopian advice also for a post-unification Germany, where the task of 'becoming German' appears doubly urgent, not only as East and West Germans have to renegotiate each other's otherness, but as the legacy of Germany's twentieth century once more seems to determine the future of Europe in the twenty-first century. Fassbinder's way of doing his mourning work for Armin Meier, I am suggesting, can help reflect upon the question of a European cinema, after auteurs and new waves, after national cinemas and oppositional avant-gardes: a cinema beyond identification and distanciation, as it moves from 'representing' reality to 'inhabiting' both past and future, in and through the media.

9. Franz Biberkopf's/ex-changes
BERLIN ALEXANDERPLATZ

> *Berlin Alexanderplatz helped me develop a theoretical point without*
> *becoming theoretical, forced me to take a moral stand*
> *without being moralizing, to accept the commonplace as*
> *the essential and the holy, without being either common or*
> *sanctimonious.*[1]

The Life-Plan

Encouraged by Fassbinder's more than usually candid essay 'The Cities of Man and His Soul' which he published towards the end of the series' first public broadcasting in Germany,[2] the general view of BERLIN ALEXANDERPLATZ is that this 14-part television production was the culmination of Fassbinder's ongoing cinematic autobiography, best read as something like the blueprint, the ground-plan of the house he so often wanted his films to become.[3] A paradoxical situation, when one considers that Fassbinder was filming a major work of modern German literature, a 'classic' many times covered in commentaries and interpretations, which had already been made into a successful film in 1931.[4] As not only an intensely personal project, but as a kind of 'spiritual autobiography', this adaptation of a novel written some thirty years before Fassbinder came across it seems to have cast a very particular light – or shadow – on his life.[5] Fittingly for Fassbinder, one might even say that his life was imitating a work of art,[6] and this was indeed a possibility Fassbinder seriously entertained, because in the essay he tells of the shock reading, first as a fourteen-year-old and then again, five years later, a book in which he recognized himself so completely that he saw in it a vision of his existence, as if his life had already been lived.[7] Conversely, one might say that across Alfred Döblin's 1929 novel *Berlin Alexanderplatz – Das Leben des Franz Biberkopfs* a voice not only spoke to him, but passed on to him, like the witches to Macbeth, a riddle, a message, which for the rest of his life he would be trying to decipher, encouraging Fassbinder '[...] to work on something which finally [...] relatively completely was to become what one calls an identity'.[8]

But Fassbinder also speaks of the film as a kind of 'experiment', which in turn suggests a certain degree of detachment, also present in the quotation heading this chapter. As such, it may imply a relation of film author to literary text quite different from the ways one normally thinks of either adaptation or self-expression of and through someone else's text or body.[9] Was it a dialogue with Döblin, an act of mimicry and masquerade, or a necessary gesture of liberation? After the many allusions to it in his previous films, did Fassbinder shy away from tackling the film project earlier, because he realized that its hold on him probably remained more 'useful' to his work the less he tried to exorcise it? In one sense, chronologically and thematically, it fits into the mosaic Fassbinder pieced together for his epic of modern Germany – BERLIN ALEXANDERPLATZ joins other films (EFFI BRIEST, BOLWIESER, DESPAIR, LILI MARLEEN, THE MARRIAGE OF MARIA BRAUN, LOLA, VERONIKA VOSS, THE MERCHANT OF FOUR SEASONS, IN A YEAR OF THIRTEEN MOONS, THE THIRD GENERATION) in which self-destruction, self-sacrifice and death become the peculiar entry-points of embattled subjectivity into (German) history.[10] In another sense, it gives a male – and one who by his name Franz was in the early films so often associated with the losers at the bottom of the social heap – a fate of suffering and emotional destitution more culturally familiar from the representation of female characters. As with the other central figures in the melodramas, an impossible love – between two men – opens up bodies and private beings to the more or less violent inscriptions of Germany's political and social history. Yet unlike the stark, historically overdetermined impossibilities of Erwin's love for Anton Saitz in IN A YEAR OF THIRTEEN MOONS, the love between Franz and Reinhold at the centre of BERLIN ALEXANDERPLATZ is, according to Fassbinder, in its very nature outside the social realm:

> It by no means concerns a sexual relation between two people of the same sex. [...] No, what goes on between Franz and Reinhold is no more no less than pure love, unendangered by anything social. That is, this is how it ought to be. But since, of course, both of them are social creatures, they are incapable of understanding this love, accepting it. They cannot simply submit to, be enriched and made happy by a kind of love that is in any event extremely rare among human beings, [for it is a love] which does not lead to visible results, which cannot be paraded, cannot be exploited and therefore cannot be made useful.[11]

The question this chapter tries to raise, then, is what might be implied by positing such a love's utopian vantage point, whose disinterestedness stands in such contrast to the idea of an 'experiment', and why does it have to be at once outside society and yet actually determined by society. The answer seems to point to the self-divesting, de-individualizing energy inherent in such a love, and the disarticulating, de-humanizing forces at work in the processes of social modernity, so apparently similar in their attack on individuality and the bodily self, and yet so different in their experience of identity. Both love and society, in other words, thoroughly take Franz Biberkopf apart – before they reassemble him. In order for this movement around a perilous identity between two deaths to become manifest, one needs to look at the logic of the story as told by Fassbinder, and also at the gaze with which his film accompanies its hero in the course of this unbearably cruel but ostensibly necessary experiment.

Narrative, Interminable...

As Fassbinder freely admitted, he had always found the first third of Döblin's novel, before the appearance of Reinhold, a 'turn-off'.[12] Out of the modernist prose jungle that is *Berlin*

Alexanderplatz, Fassbinder cut a relatively simple story, making sure that Biberkopf does not, as often happens in Döblin's collage novel, disappear from narrative view in the undergrowth of statistical, documentary and archival information about Berlin as a metropolis and home to several million souls.[13] Yet, in Fassbinder's BERLIN ALEXANDERPLATZ, too, it is not until episode five (entitled 'A Reaper with the Power of the Good Lord') that Franz encounters Reinhold, and even thereafter, their story, taking up some ten hours of screen time, makes anything but a cogent narrative, at least by the standards of television series or feature film production. Critics were apt to point to the liberties Fassbinder had taken with the original, or blamed the lighting levels, judged too low for television.[14] Yet the widely voiced difficulties of comprehension have their roots elsewhere: to begin with, the role of the camera, agent of Fassbinder's narration, makes exceptional demands on the concentration of the viewer. A complex and cluttered visual space even by Fassbinder's standards allows the camera to inscribe a peculiarly unsettling look, obtrusive in that it is often attributable only to secondary figures, and sometimes to no on-screen character at all. While the presence of narrators (including Fassbinder's own voice-over commentary) and other narrational in-stances are thus overstated, the logic of the actions, their sequence and causal connexions are massively understated, giving the characters' interchanges a tantalizingly elliptical quality, leaving the viewer baffled as to their motives or goals. For instance, had BERLIN ALEXAN-DERPLATZ been a more conventional adaptation (of an admittedly highly unconventional novel), or more commercially calculating, the enigmas on which the plot turns would probably have been: what exactly brought about the original act of violence which cost Ida her life? Why does Franz, at a crucial point and without any apparent reason, let Reinhold back into his life? What exactly goes on in Franz at the time of Mieze's death, given that he must have had more than a hint of what Reinhold was up to? In Fassbinder's film, these and similar questions are neither what drives the narrative forward nor are they finally resolved. There is a striking and repeated shift of emphasis from narrative action to tableau composi-tions with static takes, lingered over longer than is needed to absorb the information contained. In a film that mostly takes place indoors, this further dilates the already labyrinthine causality linking the individual scenes across the episodes. That the scenes interlock is evident, but how they do so is determined by an unstated logic which gives the narrative a powerful inner compulsion (startlingly manifest by the repetition of a location or a set-up), but also blocks the more overt motivation of the character's actions.

However provocative such elliptical storytelling may be in a big budget television production designed for a mass market, it finds its justification in the tenacity with which Fassbinder pursues his simple but fundamental concerns across a vast number of characters, situations and incidents: there is an enigma in this story, a mystery which has to work the body of the text, rather than the words and actions of the characters. The wealth of material amassed by Döblin is selected and subordinated in Fassbinder to a different organizing principle, so that the film's convoluted and seemingly meandering storyline must be seen against the single-mindedness with which Franz carries his baffled good intentions – to be a decent human being – into the trials and defeats life puts in his way. In this sense, the central question animating BERLIN ALEXANDERPLATZ is not in the first instance, as Fassbinder claims, a love story between two men, but the central protagonist's undeterred quest for an existence where his very particular 'economy' of feelings – an unbroken continuum from the gentlest tenderness to extreme violence – can manifest itself in and through the encounters of social life rather than against or outside it. Biberkopf's story is therefore not a private fate parallelling, mirroring or mimetically repeating the public life of Germany during the latter part of the 1920s, but an integral, complete particle of that public life.

Put differently, Fassbinder's film is constructed in the classical manner, in that here, too, a male's quest for identity across an 'other' stands at the centre, but it is a non-classical film in that his identity is put to the test not according to the narrative transformations that confirm the hero in his full self-possession. Instead, the narrative 'empties' him, readies him for his complete merger with the social body.[15] This process of emptying, furthermore, follows a triple logic: of alternation, of repetition, and of attrition, suspended between two traumatic acts of violence against women: the battering to death of Ida, and the killing of Mieze. Although formally, the narrative movement of repetition and alternation is not that different from the structure and ideological purpose of classical cinema's oedipal journeys, Biberkopf's quest is one not of affirming identity across the conflicting demands of law and desire, but to negate such identities. The film signals everywhere the destructive and pathological nature of identity when posited as the macho values of (self-) possession, pursued in the phallic mode, and across a series of fetish objects. Over and over Fassbinder repeats the scene of Franz beating Ida, killing her, one presumes, rather than permitting himself the thought that she might be leaving him. Also in contrast to the classical symbolic structure, the single most frequent constellation that does *not* stabilize Biberkopf's identity is the formation of the heterosexual couple (with Ida, Lina, Minna, Cilly, Fränze, Mieze all victims of this failure).

The second feature characteristic of the inner logic of the narrative in BERLIN ALEXANDERPLATZ is the way its crisis points punctuate the flow at regular intervals not in order to give the action a different direction or provide a reversal. Instead, they mark moments of dispersal, of energy dissipating itself in all directions, a kind of bleeding away of narrative drive, so that one only becomes aware of such critical moments in retrospect – where they reveal themselves to have invariably involved peculiarly skewed acts of substitution and exchange. At first sight, however, this principle, to which I shall return, remains buried in the motivational gaps, the unexplained transitions, the sense of a story stuck in its groove. While overtly, the narrative has a relentless downward drift, in which the incremental principle of escalating loss holds sway, with Biberkopf at first losing his job, then his arm and finally his loved one (a logic underscored by repeated acts of betrayal), another dramatic line in the film is much more ambiguously poised, making it difficult to decide whether Franz, at these moments of loss, is experiencing extremes of suffering or jubilation.[16] This ambivalence in the emotional life, of course, permits of no resolution, least of all one achieved through narrative division and closure. The extent to which it is irrecoverable is indicated by the epilogue – 'my dream of the dream of Franz Biberkopf' – which responds to the fact that the quest Franz is embarked on is neither a 'pilgrim's progress' nor a cathartic purging, but finally forms a sort of loop, a permanent 'action replay', where the compulsion to repeat eventually signals the death, if not of the protagonist, then of his narrative. Strictly speaking, therefore, the story of Biberkopf in BERLIN ALEXANDERPLATZ does not terminate, but exhausts and disperses itself: in a constant vacillation between violence inflicted and violence received, between an atmosphere heavy with love undeclared and one thrilling with sensual-sexual abandon. A movement of attrition 'renders' all of this affectivity ever more physical and bodily based, for as Eric Rentschler has observed:

> BERLIN ALEXANDERPLATZ lingers in the mind, indeed haunts the viewer as a markedly corporeal experience [.... It] is nothing less than an encyclopedia of bodies responding to modernity: street violence and domestic beatings; individuals in crowded spaces shrieking, moaning, rejoicing; an arm run over and a hand burned; people in transit, meeting and coupling in public places, having serious conversations while urinating or [engaging in] sexual intercourse in a toilet stall. One escapes the city into small cubby holes, smoke-filled bars or rented rooms cluttered by a printing press and reddened by incessantly blinking neon lights. Fateful walks through the woods, the inescapable procession through the slaughter house.[17]

'The Punishment Commences'

Generically, BERLIN ALEXANDERPLATZ could be called a passion play, in the way it is divided into fourteen stations, leading to the hero's eventual 'crucifixion' and even ironic resurrection. This is how Döblin conceived his novel, where two Biblical mythologies of suffering – that of the Old Testament Job and of Christ the Redeemer – are braided into a seemingly single journey to the end of night. Fassbinder was especially impressed by this ecumenical blending of Jewish and Christian mythologies, underscoring Döblin's courage in 'treating every scrap of action, however banal, as significant and momentous in and for itself, as part of [...] a mysterious mythology', and pointing out how he had embedded into the story 'another, more impenetrable and secret narrative, part of a novel within the novel'.[18] It is this mysterious, allegorical but also contrapuntal layering of the fate of the proletarian 'former transport worker, pimp, murderer, thief and finally once more pimp' Franz Biberkopf which seems to have given Fassbinder the conviction that his adaptation could re-focus the novel around a new centre – the increasingly more ecstatic and more murderous love of Franz for Reinhold – without betraying either Döblin or his own youthful self reading Döblin for the first time. But Fassbinder's detachment from both these acts of empathetic identification and prophetic decipherment are also evident in his narration, where the impenetrable crystallizes into a single constellation, endlessly repeated, subtly varied, but permitting of no solution in the terms in which it confronts the protagonist: once more a vicious circle, though here depicted as the shuttlecock movement of the hero between unacceptable binary choices.

The first three episodes of BERLIN ALEXANDERPLATZ almost didactically demonstrate the terms of a possible stability for the contending selves in Franz Biberkopf – a socialized existence – but also the price to be paid and the reasons for his violent oscillations. The world he is released into, after his stint in Tegel prison, is divided into fixed either/or choices. For instance, one is either inside prison or outside; one is either heterosexual or homosexual;[19] either a Communist or a Nazi;[20] one either has work or is unemployed, and one's business is either legitimate or illegal. In fact, the film chronicles Biberkopf's fight against these powerful binarism and symmetries, instinctively unable to live by the divisions they impose, which also explains why his attempts to settle for an identity within the situation of the heterosexual couple must be doomed, given the set of rigidly policed differences it entails.

From the opening scene of Franz's release, Fassbinder's focus is on liminal states, on boundaries crossed and thresholds traversed, with the prison gates opening up the first of such thresholds, on which he hesitates, before he collapses with an agonized scream: the irony is underlined by the fact that this first episode is called 'the punishment commences', as if to signal not only that the law is ineffectual in providing an individual with the ability to decide the meaning of good and evil, right and wrong, but that in this case it has failed to put crime and punishment into a correlation to each other. For Biberkopf, 'justice' may have been done, but it is not felt to have been done: time in prison has merely delayed the reckoning, or even more ominously, it is obliging him to 'discover' the crime of which the life we are about to witness is so evidently the punishment.

Picked up by a Talmud scholar who offers him shelter, Biberkopf is saved from a nervous breakdown by being told stories, bonding both teller and listener into a community of sorts, but one that cannot bridge division, for as Nachum says, 'they may not feed you, but they make you forget'. A more violent oscillation between either/or accompanies the quest for sexual identity. Exposed to rejection by a prostitute who taunts and laughs at his impotence, Franz seduces – or rapes – Minna, the sister of Ida: 'Blow the trumpet, hallelujah! Franz Biberkopf is back. Franz is free!' Identity is here asserted in the mode of phallic masculinity. But making love to the double of the woman he has killed, reveals a possibly even more crippling 'inadequacy', circumscribing and prescribing the precarious terms of his new-found identity. It points down one path along which his quest will often lead him, but equally often will leave him defeated and humiliated. For Minna is only the first in a long line of doubles, all of whom establish Biberkopf's dependence on finding substitutes, in a psychic economy built on repetition. Minna is soon replaced by Lina, herself – one presumes – another Ida: generous, lively and a loving provider for his bodily needs, she is introduced to him by his old friend Meck. The Meck-Lina-Biberkopf triad serves as a normative, albeit quickly superseded reference point for what one might call the possibility of Franz's 'useful' (that is, oedipal) identity, even if in the socially 'negative' mode of parasite and pimp. Its very stability (as the post-war, proletarian norm) proves its undoing, for it pales into irrelevance in the face of a possibility which is as utopian as it is traumatic, which shatters Biberkopf in precisely the way ideal love in BERLIN ALEXANDERPLATZ is at once free of all social utility and permeated by society and history. This crucial turn of events occurs after Lina introduces Biberkopf to her uncle Lüders, an unemployed door-to-door salesman of shoelaces and small household goods with whom Franz teams up to eke out an existence on the margins of economic destitution and social uselessness, a parasite and nuisance who in the hierarchy of respectability is only just above the common street beggar.

Utopia and Trauma

One day, working with Lüders one of the tenement buildings they specialize in, Biberkopf is asked inside by a young woman in black, evidently a war widow. Noticing a portrait of her deceased husband, he is struck by the man's uncanny resemblance to himself, and the widow, overcome with emotion, dissolves in his arms. The scene mirrors the one of Franz making love to Minna substituting for Ida. To his own surprise, Biberkopf acquiesces, taking pleasure in being (mistaken for) someone else, his double, as it were, with whom he 'shares' a woman. Elated and moved by the experience, he divides with Lüders the money given to him by the widow.

The moment is central to both the narrative economy of the series (in its understatedness and elliptical treatment) and to the psychic economy of Franz Biberkopf. Hence the trauma of its violation, betrayal and profanation. What can be glimpsed, but only as an instant flash in the form of a 'positive' image, are the outlines of a kind of utopia, the vision of a way of being *in* the world without being *of* the world, where *eros* and *agape*, but also an ethical imperative and a bodily transfiguration miraculously come together as a new experience of identity, in the strange circuit of erotic, economic and family ties that briefly binds Biberkopf to Lüders and to Lina, Lina to the widow, the widow to her dead husband, and the husband to Biberkopf. They are all each others' doubles and stand-ins, making up a relay of giving and receiving, a de-territorialized and exteriorized manner of being for each other, in a time-shifting and space-shifting continuum, where the dead can come back to life, and even murder can be undone.

Yet Lüders, envious and bigoted, perceives in the widow's emotion towards Biberkopf, and Biberkopf's quasi-religious epiphany only a despicable sexual act, which makes Franz a lucky punter and the widow the goose ripe for plucking. He takes terrible revenge on her, blackmailing and all but raping her. In Lüders we meet the film's first repressed homosexual, whose heterosexuality is 'pathological', similar to Biberkopf's when killing Ida or fleeing in horror and humiliation from the prostitute, in contrast to the 'new' Franz, whose sexuality is precisely located in that area of indeterminacy where he henceforth tries to discover who he is and what it means to be 'decent'. Meeting the widow, Biberkopf lends himself to another's grief and longing, in a moment that liberates him from the nexus of property, jealousy and possessive sexuality. Lüders, however, feels threatened because his best friend fills the role usually assigned for women, to be an object of exchange. He only sees prostitution and sordid sex, where for Biberkopf there is substitution, even transsubstantiation and sharing. That the scene is central to the narrative logic is paradoxically confirmed by the way Fassbinder treats it as a mere peripheral incident, deliberately veiling the causal chain that leads Biberkopf back to zero and to his break with both Lüders and Lina, in long drawn-out confrontations that manage to avoid naming exactly what it was that prompted the widow to shut the door in Biberkopf's face: the gap of knowledge between the viewer (who has seen what Lüders did) and Biberkopf (who does not) is never fully bridged, but the consequences take up an entire episode ('A Handful of Humans in the Depth of Silence') whose almost wordless, but in fact densely 'argued' descent into hell – a depraved but strangely democratic community of alcoholics, outsiders, marginals, opportunists and survivors – marks another major point of self-divesting dispersal, where Biberkopf is 'taken apart', in order for the pieces to be once more shuffled before they are put together again.

Franz's extended dark night of the soul hiding out in a concrete hovel, too drunk to care, and not drunk enough to be indifferent to the world's pain, repeats the breakdown after his release from prison and an earlier crisis which follows the violent rejection by his former (wartime) comrades, when in the polarized/politicised post-war Berlin he refuses to sing the Communist International, preferring the (nationalist, but to him above all patriotic) 'Watch on the Rhine'. Once again, a mode of being 'decent', a manner of charting identity beyond the either/or is shattered, misunderstood, instrumentalized.

Fassbinder here defines the only law by which Biberkopf seems capable of desiring: not the emotional security of the heterosexual couple, nor the financial security of a job, but the more insecure and dangerous logic of symbolic exchange, where identity is a balance between, simultaneously, a narcissistic double,[21] sexual role reversals, and an economy based on charity, on money given or shared, rather than of money earned or accumulated. This (erotic-economic) utopia, in which desire functions not according to the oedipal law of fetishizing or repressing lack, collapses with Lüders' betrayal. A pattern begins to establish itself, where – perhaps in line with Fassbinder's 'romantic anarchism'[22] – sexual 'promiscuity' or bisexuality is to psychic life what the black market is to economics: a (temporary?) suspension of the (fixed) currency, in favour of a more unpredictable, perverse or reversible circuit of the signifiers of value, plenitude and ecstasy.

Eternal Triangle or Unholy Trinity? Prostitute, Client, Pimp

I have stressed the scene with the war widow, because it provides the necessary counterfoil for understanding some of the more 'mysterious' aspects of the relationship which, according to Fassbinder's own remarks,[23] structures BERLIN ALEXANDERPLATZ: the relation of Franz and Reinhold, which is often seen as the only emotional circuit that the series charges with live energy. But when Reinhold finally appears – a member of Pums' gang of thieves, fences and pimps, and also introduced to Franz by Meck – the encounter is not only the foundation of that fatal attraction which Franz will never be explain to himself,[24] but it configures for us, the viewers, also another system of exchange, reconfiguring the terms that have already been put in play. The Franz who meets Reinhold may have been pieced together differently (Meck playing the re-assembler to Lüders', and later Reinhold's dis-assembler), but he tries to re-establish another circuit of equivalences and exchanges, based on recognition and miscognition, for Reinhold is immediately and mistakenly recognized by Franz as his double.[25] In a scene parallelling the first meeting with Lüders, where the symmetry was based on both men being long-term unemployed, Franz assumes that Reinhold has done time at Tegel. Even though Reinhold denies ever having been to prison, the friendship develops around this shared experience and its simultaneous disavowal: a situation of miscognition is set up which continues throughout and proves the most durable of all the asymmetrical symmetries the film establishes between its central characters.

Here another aspect of BERLIN ALEXANDERPLATZ's circular design becomes apparent: twice more Franz is betrayed by a friend, and twice more he will start from zero. With Reinhold's entry into Franz's life, the exchange of women between the men becomes an explicit and open part of the relationship. For Reinhold the passing of discarded mistresses to Franz is the friendship's founding and sustaining moment, but for Franz, as I have tried to indicate, being a sexual surrogate (active or passive) neither starts with Reinhold's, nor is it a sufficient condition for his sense of self. What is crucial to Biberkopf's own quest are the different channels and opportunities which working for Pums, the friendship with Reinhold, taking over Fränze from or sharing Cilly with Reinhold, have opened up to him by way of trading services and gifts, bodies and glances, gestures and acts. In a sense, Biberkopf becomes intoxicated with the possibilities of these forms of exchange, seemingly free of a single denominator, open-ended and reciprocal. Amid a society disintegrating, ravaged by political extremism and embittered polarisations, he lives by a different psychic and moral reality: sexual barter, narcissistic doubling and stolen goods are his answers to the political and social crises of the Weimar Republic, constantly alluded to but never 'represented'. One might in fact compare this part of the film with Hermann Hermann's and Supervisor Müller's respective 'answers' to the aggravated stage of the same crisis of institutions and values in DESPAIR, discussed in an earlier chapter, although in BERLIN ALEXANDERPLATZ Fassbinder seems more optimisitic and also more radical as to the prospects of his protagonist. Out of what looks like grossest exploitation, crime and sordid degradation, Biberkopf draws his own spiritual integrity, underlined in a scene where in the company of Reinhold he visits the Salvation Army, to do penance among the poorest of the poor.

The fact that women are still the main objects of this multi-level exchange might point to the male-centred utopia here invoked.[26] But the possibility that something else is also at stake can, I think, be seen in Eva, Franz' ex-mistress and the most 'active' (though not necessarily masculine) among the female characters, who gives Franz money, introduces him to pimping, and occasionally uses him sexually. The relations of power she enacts and represents make sure that the economy practised by Biberkopf does not solely function along the traditional gender divide. This requires a return to one of the key circuits of exchange in all of Fassbinder's work, that of 'prostitution'. Fassbinder's films have often explored the relationship between pimp, prostitute and client, not least because it is the most graphic and flagrant example of the tight imbrication of an economic and an emotional system of dependence and exploitation.[27]

Paradoxically, however, it also has for Fassbinder the fascination of an ideal form of exchange in which three terms are related in a system of non-symmetrical equivalence: as an agent of a symbolic exchange, the prostitute is merely the go-between between client and pimp (the male-defined system, and typical of Reinhold), but the emotional contract works as a double circuit: the pimp protects the prostitute and gives her the security which allows her to lend herself to the client whose need for security and identity she gratifies (the female-centred system, embodied by Mieze). In reality, of course, the system is distorted and degraded several times over: the economic aspect overlays the emotional one, in a sort of grotesque parody of a capitalist service industry. In actual fact, the triadic relationship is more a set of dual relationships hierarchically positioned to each other (pimp-client, with woman/money as exchange; pimp-prostitute, with security/money as exchange; and prostitute/client, with money/sex as exchange). Fassbinder's early gangster films are invariably playing through these different permutations, free of moralizing or didacticism. In BERLIN ALEXANDERPLATZ he consciously returns to these motifs, now vastly complicated by the added twist that 'strong' female characters (mostly incarnated by Hanna Schygulla, who here plays Eva, or Barbara Sukowa who played the title part in LOLA, and here has the part of Mieze) introduce into these scenarios.

The Ethics of Loss and the Economics of Abundance

Biberkopf is an archetypal Fassbinder hero not least because he appreciates perverse couplings, not only of a sexual kind. Through Reinhold and Pums, for instance, Franz tries to redraw binary divisions apart from those of gender, such as employed/unemployed, legal/illegal, rich/poor. A hallmark of the 'other' economy is that it operates with the traditional figures of the in-between and the go-between, outlawed by respectable society: the thief, the fence and the black marketeer.[28] Franz is initially taken on by Pums as the substitute for a gang-member suddenly arrested by the police, and he invests this 'place-holding' for someone else with a moral urgency incomprehensible to all, except perhaps Eva. This state of bliss is shattered, when under pressure from Cilly, he interferes in Reinhold's passing on of women and breaks the circuit of exchange by refusing to take Trude. It leads to his second betrayal: Reinhold pushes Franz out of a speeding car, causing him to lose an arm. But instead of blaming Reinhold for the incident, Franz seems to welcome it.

This is the narrative's major provocation, because at first sight it is so undermotivated: we never quite understand why Reinhold did push Franz from the speeding car, and secondly, we never learn from Franz why he is so ready to forget, and so anxious to forgive. The least satisfactory explanation is Franz's infatuation with Reinhold, masochistically seeking humiliation and punishment. For from the perspective I have tried to indicate, Franz's response is quite logical, in that it exactly follows the pattern established earlier: is not his arm merely another sacrifice, another 'gift', entitling him to a (non-equivalent) reciprocity by creating an asymmetry (now inscribed on his body) which allows him to renegotiate the terms of the contracts that bind him to the one(s) he loves? Without an arm, he is useless on the labour market, and available to being supported by women: he accepts Eva's 'gift' of Mieze, who in turn adopts him as her pimp and is proud to be earning his living. For the women, his loss signifies that he is a man willing to renegotiate the 'phallic' mode of masculinity, comparable to Erwin/Elvira's gift of love for Anton Saitz (also played by Gottfried John, the actor who is Reinhold). As for Reinhold, the amputated arm is only in one sense an icon of Franz's 'sex-change' (though in a crucial scene the wound does figure as just that).[29] Rather, it redefines the kind of complicity (sinner and sacrifice) that joins them together in mutual identification, a fact that only emerges fully in the Epilogue.

Key to Biberkopf's character, and the point where the symbolic orders of gender and economics intersect, is his mutilation. The missing arm signifies Franz's acceptance of a fundamental lack (part of his spiritual quest of common humanity), it communicates his 'incompleteness' as a man (which Mieze is called upon to compensate), but most powerfully and disturbingly, it is a token of a desire to actively seek out a different masculinity, encompassing sexual relations and those of exchange. None of those around him can quite understand the feeling close to jubiliation that so often seems to overcome Biberkopf when the loss of his arm is at issue. That it involves a transgressive notion of gender (the fear of dismemberment and the social/sexual stigma of the handicapped)[30] is evident, but just how transgressive it also is in the economic relations of work, wage and property comes out only in the scene where Pums sends him money for his part in the robbery of the clothing store. Biberkopf first needs to clear up a double misunderstanding: suspecting his motive to be revenge, Pums thinks in terms of a squaring of accounts, that Biberkopf merely wants to come back in order to get even. But Franz does not want to work in order to earn money. Instead, it is work for the sake of work that he seeks, and money is merely a means for making gifts: the missing arm is thus yet another – extremely brave, extremely bold – attempt on the part of Biberkopf to realize his own utopian system of uneven exchange. Pleased by the money as the confirmation that he is once more accepted into one kind of exchange ('a fair day's wage for a fair day's work') and released from the position outside as a 'useless cripple', he nonetheless fails to understand why Mieze gets angry, pleading to be allowed to stay. Since she draws her identity at this point from her position as his provider, she refuses to accept the money even as a gift, and makes him promise to pass it to the poor (which he does). Significantly, the work for which he is paid involves a deft use of his disability, lying flat on the ground and passing bales of cloth from Meck through a hole in the floor to Reinhold: happy to serve as the link in a chain formed by his two best friends.[31]

Lack Liquidated or Equal Exchange?

So far I have analyzed the logic of the plot mainly from the vantage point of Franz, but in actual fact, the relations between all the characters are handled in complex and subtly contradictory ways. Episodes and encounters are rarely one-off: each event usually has its parallel, its equivalent elsewhere in the series, and thus serves mirroring functions of contrast, balance or (false) closure, like the pair Mieze and Franz in the woods/ Mieze and Reinhold in the woods. Displaying an almost classical economy of repetition and symmetry at the formal level, and burying the links between the episodes deep within the narrative semantics of his film, Fassbinder's work on a moral economy different from Hollywood's oedipal tales is the more striking, especially since even here, he is able to remain true to the Sirkean system that gives every character his or her point of view.

Almost all social intercourse takes the form of surrogate action, some intersecting comically, but more often with tragic results. Herbert, Eva's suitor, who is fighting a kind of underworld war with Pums, uses Eva as a go-between to Franz, and Franz as an involuntary informant. Reinhold interrogates Mieze to find out what Franz has told her about him. Mieze, unable to conceive a child, tries to persuade Eva to become pregnant by Franz in her stead. Each character has reasons/desires/schemes that allocate to the others specific roles, functions, symbolic positions. Thus, although the film constantly shows couples, they are all open towards or implicated with a third term, forming constellations which overlap but never wholly converge. Each dual relationship is in fact determined by its place in a semi-disguised triadic one, of which the social bracket or label is prostitution, but the inner paradigm aims at re-establishing the complex free-trade zone I have described around the traumatic event with Lüders and the widow. Here is the basic antinomy of the film, which indicates Franz's special status: while the fantasies which have Franz as their object are paranoid (such as Reinhold's idea of friendship), fetishistic (Mieze's wish for a Franz-child) and phallic (Eva's pleasure in playing the symbolic male), Franz's own relationship with each of them is tragic precisely because he tries to be openly 'polymorph', non-exclusive and go beyond the binary binds, but mostly comes to grief as it comes up against the others' differently organized psychic economies.

Reinhold, for instance, is a caricature of paranoid masculinity. He needs women as fetishes, but dreads their fetishizing power over him. The structure of repressed homosexuality requires that he can only be with a man if a woman is being traded, and he can only be with a woman if a man is there to take her off his hands. What precipitates Mieze's death (and thus brings us back to the initial and initiating tragedy, the death of Ida, to which Mieze's death symmetrically corresponds) is the fact that from Reinhold's point of view, Mieze interrupts this circuit by trying to establish a counter-circuit. In the Mieze-Eva deal (persuading Eva to have a child by Franz) Franz occupies the place which is allocated to the women in the Reinhold-Franz deal, but symmetrically inverting it. On one level, the seduction of Mieze by Reinhold represents an exacerbated repetition of Lüders' attempted rape of the widow, and on another, it is a second attempt to maim Franz's symbolic body. By taking away

Mieze, Reinhold once more 'amputates' Franz, depriving him of the substitute phallus she had become, and at the same time 'devaluing' her as phallic stand-in, which is what Mieze senses when she worries about Franz sending her away or selling her to Reinhold. Mieze dies, because in Reinhold's world the gift is merely the other side of possession. He wants women, in order to give them away, and although he does not want Mieze for himself, he wants her in order to be able to give her (back) to Franz. Since she refuses, he eliminates her: not being able to give her away, he throws her away.[32] Possession and the gift: two ways of wielding (the signifiers of) power. But Reinhold misconstrues Franz' economy of desire, and just as Franz accepts the loss of his arm, he accepts the loss of Mieze: by putting himself outside the phallic order, he cannot be 'castrated'. Franz, for instance, tells Reinhold about Mieze's idea of him having a child with Eva in, of all places, the men's room, immediately after asking Reinhold, without embarrassment or lewdness, to wash and button him up: no conflict in his imaginary between the assertion of sexual prowess and childlike dependence.

Eva, on the other hand, is structurally related to Reinhold: she, too, supplies Franz with women. But she is also a more phallic version of Mieze: having been rejected as Franz' mistress, Eva has taken herself out of the position of the female that can be traded (we never see her with a client), to become Franz' benefactress, effectively paying him to have sex with her. This does not stop her from being to Franz the equivalent of a male friend and moral authority. Mieze, for her part, would like Eva as her surrogate, in order to realize her love for Franz, symbolized by a child, within the 'normal' oedipal triad. Via Eva, she wants to 'have' the phallus (the child as fetish), while 'being' the phallus and maintaining her role as the breadwinner. Her relationship to Franz is in fact the relationship of Elvira to Christoph, as told to Zora in the slaughterhouse scene of IN A YEAR OF THIRTEEN MOONS.[33]

In these, essentially 'family' dramas, through which Fassbinder can invoke the narrative logic (and symmetries) of Hollywood without obeying the manner of implementing the mechanisms of narrative resolution, the characters are symmetrically placed in relation to each other. One could even construct a Greimasian semantic square with at its respective corners: impotent/barren/potent/fertile. The couple Mieze/Franz (barren/potent), the couple Eva/Herbert (fertile/impotent) intersect with the couple Reinhold/Franz (repressed homosexual/ bisexual). Reinhold and Mieze are not direct sexual rivals for Franz (Reinhold: 'I don't want to steal Franz from you, but there were some funny things between us') and instead rivals for phallic power over him, while Mieze and Eva are more like doubles, even though Eva was once the rival for the place of Ida (to whom she lost Franz): a place now occupied by Mieze, if only by virtue of nearly being killed by Franz when confiding in him about being in love with someone else.

BERLIN ALEXANDERPLATZ, viewed under the aspect of its (oedipal or pre-oedipal) triangles, tries to work out configurations of exchange in a generalized economy of scarcity and want (leading to the crash and the collapse of the Weimar Republic). By contrast, a film like THE MARRIAGE OF MARIA BRAUN enacts its systems of exchange under inverse conditions, out of a historical moment emerging from or moving away from the zero degree of generalized destitution (the collapse of the 'Third Reich'), after the reform of the currency. By the end of the film, the central characters attempt to put themselves in a situation of equal exchange, by making economic signifiers of value (the wealth of the German economic miracle) stand for the non-equivalence of oedipal desire. The narrative – concluding, as one will recall, with the death of Maria and her husband in a gas explosion – has its own alternative ending ironically inscribed, for the three main protagonists (Maria, her husband Hermann, and her lover Oswald) bequeath their respective fortunes to each other: Maria to her husband, Oswald to Maria, and Maria's husband to Oswald. Since by the end, all three are rich beyond their needs, these gifts cancel each other out. The irresolvable triangulation of desire – Oswald loving Maria, Maria loving her husband (a love unconsummated by his absence), but desiring Oswald as she had desired the black soldier – is 'transcended' by the symbolic exchange of wills, a mutually sustaining ritual, which turns (sexual) desire into the indifference of material wealth. What obstinately remained asunder in life is sutured beyond the grave, so that, as one would expect, lack liquidated puts an end to desire. Contrary to the capitalist logic of unlimited accumulation, it is the Freudian law which finally represents the 'economic miracle': plenitude and in-difference are the limit states and thresholds that consummate the 'marriage' of Maria Braun.

A Wanted Man

In BERLIN ALEXANDERPLATZ, by contrast, one is far from such consummation, or indeed, the end of difference in death. Reinhold's blackmailing/prostituting/annihilating (repeating Lüders' reaction) seems as much a defense against castration anxiety as Mieze's sudden falling in love seems designed to counter her fear of abandonment (repeating the situation of Ida). Both are strategies 'from within' the patriarchal law against which Biberkopf's economy of giving/sharing/circulating tries so strenuously to set itself up as a hopeful alternative. But the risks are high, psychic as well as bodily. Beyond the law of castration anxiety, and seeking a non-phallic identity leaves the Fassbinder hero with two impossible choices. He can be a total outcast, neither needing human society nor being 'wanted' by it, and therefore staying outside the circuit of desire. Such is the state of Biberkopf, when in his total abjection (in episode four) he lives like an animal in a fox hole of a room, surrounded by empty beer-bottles. This exclusion is like a return to the situation in Fassbinder early gangster films: LOVE IS COLDER THAN DEATH or THE AMERICAN SOLDIER render explicit the implicit structure of desire in Hollywood *film noir*.[34] For the ultimate goal of the *noir* hero, and the reason why even his death represents the fulfilment of a wish seems to be that he is 'wanted': if not by the femme fatale, then at least by the police, which is to say, he is finally receiving a 'demand' from the symbolic order through which the love or power of the Other manifests itself to him.[35]

The inverse side of the non-phallic alternative is to regress to a pre-oedipal state of fusion or dependence.[36] If Biberkopf's bouts of drunken stupor fairly typify one extreme, the kind of dependence which develops between Franz and Mieze can be seen as the other extreme. Reconciled, after the terrible beating Franz had given her, by a day outing in the country, Mieze insists on washing Franz like a baby, who offers her food with his mouth like a bird and crouches on the floor, barking like a puppy. What for Mieze is in a sense the enactment of a wish-fulfilling fantasy – having (of) Franz (as) a child – by doubling economic with physical dependence and thus mastering the impossible oedipal dilemma of having/being the phallus, signals to Franz the end of the relationship. He now takes Mieze along to one of the gang's regular meetings, a gesture which in fact releases her into general circulation.[37] While Franz is playing pinball with Reinhold, she is passed on to Meck, who is blackmailed by Reinhold into acting as go-between for the rendezvous which will result in her death. It is as if to let go of sexual difference and the phallic definition of identity is to be exposed to infantilization or death. The tragedy is that of sexual difference: Mieze enacting the oedipal logic of her situation (both Eva and Mieze are given reasons for 'choosing' to live under the phallic law themselves) collides with that same logic as it applies to Franz: in the struggle over oedipal identity, her victory spells his defeat, but also vice versa. The drama between Franz and Mieze is already played out before Reinhold enters, which explains – at the deeper, 'mysterious' level of the narrative – why Franz can forgive Reinhold even Mieze's murder: he knows that he himself killed this love, had to kill this love.

To understand this paradox, one has to move once more from the libidinal economy to the general economy, for Franz' attempts to situate his life (and that of Mieze) within 'uneven' circuits of exchange – the 'economic dimension' – are his defense against identifying the non-phallic with the pre-oedipal. But the conditions which make such symbolic exchanges possible are themselves strictly circumscribed. They presuppose a (social) situation of political insecurity and rapid change, of sudden discrediting or overturning of traditional value systems, that is to say, conditions that throw into relief a society's markers of difference, be they of class, wealth, or gender. For Fassbinder these moments are 'revolutionary breaks', and in his pick of period as well as social milieu, he consistently chose historical instances when the basis of value was being redefined, when an apparently stable moral currency suddenly began to collapse. As we saw in previous chapters, many of his films pursue an economic or political crisis into its sexual or familial reverberations, seizing on the fact that German history during the past hundred years has been riven by such crisis moments.[38]

These critical moments, however, expose a double-edged phenomenon: politically, the most 'revolutionary breaks' this century have been those of fascism and of multinational capitalism, destroying traditional value systems by fundamentally altering the productive relations. Historically, there is a substantial difference whether an economic system determines the 'rate of exchange' of social intercourse and moral value by totalitarian means, subjecting heterogeneity to the single principle, as in fascism, or whether a system is able to enforce a kind of universal and unlimited equivalence, by a ceaseless exploitation on a global scale of the differentials in time and space, of labour supply and raw materials, discovering ever new aggregate states of profitability and speculation, as in contemporary capitalism. But in terms of sexual politics, Fassbinder's position is more ambiguous: the romantic anarchist in him seems to be dreaming a historico-economic fantasy, in which any dominant currency needs to collapse, in order for there to be the right conditions of symbolic exchange. Hence, an indulgent sympathy in Fassbinder also for economic freebooters: black marketeers, petty gangsters, pimps, entrepreneurs and other kinds of 'Mata Haris' of the free market economy who make their living within the interstices of the system. What under one aspect may appear as exploitation and the power to dictate the terms of a transaction is in another respect a form of enterprise, where acts of exchange require the materialist poetry of savage thinking, of wheeling and dealing, of the opportunist's quick response and the speculator's risk-taking.

Fassbinder was nothing if not aware of the perversity of such a position, making him politically so left-wing that one could mistake it for a right-wing stance. Yet it informed his faith in the cinema, as it informed his practice as a filmmaker. Well-known, for instance, is the fact that he preferred financing his films from the most unlikely sources (at any rate, for an 'independent' auteur), to the extent that he fully participated in the deals, the write-offs, the tax shelters, the distribution guarantees of the international film industry, while at the same time utilizing the opportunities of the German film subsidy system, by exploiting its provisions and rejecting its ideology of public service and cultural cachet. 'In the end,' he used to say, 'you can make films only the capitalist way, backing your hunches and taking risks.'[39] In this respect, BERLIN ALEXANDERPLATZ was one of his greatest gambles, consuming the highest budget that until then television had invested in a series, but also making fifteen-and-a-half hours' worth of film which were greeted with howls of protest: the scenes were so 'badly' lit that you could not see what was going on![40] What could possibly have motivated the director to such a desperate act of perversity? Perhaps a first answer would be that it allowed Fassbinder to direct our attention to what we don't see, or don't want to see, in order to encourage the viewer to do more than seeing, or to see without 'seeing'! A second answer must be to consider once more the 'impossible demands in the field of vision'.

The Limits of Specular Space

Fassbinder's films, I argued in that chapter, are in a certain sense exhibitionist rather than voyeurist, because an 'other' is always inscribed in the representation, whether this other is a look locatable in a character, drawing attention to the 'presence' of the audience, or situating itself more puzzlingly and problematically 'outside' or 'behind' the representational frame altogether.[41] In BERLIN ALEXANDERPLATZ this kind of 'visual field' is congruent both with Biberkopf's vow to be a good person (i.e. not to construct his identity around the struggle for phallic power) and with the more general issue of reversibility or asymmetry in the sites of symbolic exchange that the series so frequently opens up. In this respect, the drama of Biberkopf's impossible choices, of the threats to his selfhood and his attempts to live identity differently can also be charted along the different 'specular regimes' that Fassbinder associates with certain characters and situations.

To take as an example the opening of BERLIN ALEXANDERPLATZ: any plot summary of the first episode would be quite misleading without some idea of the 'geometry of representation' that underpins the events: the visit to the prostitute is preceded by Biberkopf looking at a cinema poster, his humiliation turns into flight when, in order to arouse him, but also to ridicule him, she reads a passage from a pseudo-scientific pornographic magazine; finally reaching home, Ida's framed photograph stares at him as he enters his room (paid for by Eva). So petrified is he of Ida's gaze that it sends him off to seek the eyes of Minna, Ida's sister. On a second visit to Minna, he is secretly followed by Meck; when Biberkopf challenges him in the courtyard, the two men are watched by Minna from behind her bedroom curtains. Benevolently surveyed or suspiciously eyed, provided for by one woman and haunted by another, accusingly scrutinized or merely watched out of curiosity: Fassbinder makes it clear that Biberkopf's newly won freedom is, from the start, a function of a certain ceaseless specular machinery that throughout the film sustains his identity, at the same time as it unravels it.[42]

In the configuration of the characters, showing and being seen are also important indices of their relations, allowing for different gazes, different pairs of eyes to be inscribed in the unfolding action. One of the most explicit examples is the scene where Reinhold brings back Cilly in order to get rid of Trude. The violent quarrel is, as it were, staged for Cilly's benefit, it requires her presence as both a woman and a spectator: across her terrified face, rather than the screams of Trude, Reinhold assures himself of his 'male' identity. This structural configuration is repeated several times more; an analogous one, for instance, is the scene where Biberkopf gets rid of Fränze, in front of the newsvendor, in order to make room for Cilly. An even more explicit repetition occurs (an attempt on the part of Franz to invert its symbolic significance) when Franz hides Reinhold under the bed, before Mieze returns, in order to 'show' Reinhold what a really good woman is like. For Franz, the set up does not seem 'perverse' since Mieze's supreme value to him can only be demonstrated if it happens within an affective circuit that includes Reinhold. There is evidently no question of sharing Mieze with Reinhold sexually: in asking Reinhold to stay and by hiding him, Franz wants in one sense to 'show off' Mieze, but in another, neither the voyeuristic look nor the exhibitionist being-looked-at look defines his mode of existence in the world for him. This is why an explicitly voyeuristic moment such as Reinhold hiding and looking as Mieze returns inevitably misfires, as if the structure of the looks Franz has set up and put in place was itself the 'cause' for Mieze's confession, for the oedipal violence and jealous rage that ensues, when she tells Franz that she is in love with someone else, wanting him to console her, and instead of which he nearly kills her. Reinhold's eyes seem to reawaken in Franz the same anxiety that had led to the violence lashed out on Ida, where it was his landlady, Frau Bast, who lent the scene her horrified look. Thus, the 'classical' system of looks in BERLIN ALEXANDERPLATZ is invariably the sign of an ambiguous reversibility of cause and effect and associates the possibility of extreme violence, as if to point to a deeper dialectic of violence and the look, but also bringing out the imbalance and instability which any 'inscription' of vision means for the visible.

For as in other Fassbinder films, the emphasis given to the looks lingering in the frames, the exchange of glances, the restless camera and the many close-ups of characters intently looking straight ahead out of the frame are clearly marked as excess, if only because so often, no narrative knowledge passes along the lines of sight thus traversing the space. Excess also, because of all the images with mirrors, windows, partitions, or the frequent compositions dominated by obstructions to vision, and because there is a virtual absence of any direct view of any of the characters. The frame appears always cluttered, divided and usually open only towards the spectator inscribing him/herself as a presence, though often 'across' an object partially blocking the view: the hand printing press or the gramophone are so prominently stationed in Biberkopf's room that they almost become silent witnesses, even more mysterious than Marlene, in PETRA VON KANT. For how do we look at objects, when these are themselves endowed with a look, even though they have no eyes? At all events, there is no illusion of immediacy, no sense of an action simply 'taking place': to the aural gesture of voice-over narration corresponds the visual gesture of 'showing', drawing attention to the events as always already having been seen.

Similarly, something always seems to intervene in the characters' interaction with each other (on the principle that during every encounter, be it aggressive or amorous, an 'image' intersects with another 'image'). In the case of the various couples, their relationship is never directly dual, partners rarely 'face' each other except across a picture, a representation, a projection or a fantasy: it is as if simply by looking at one another, Fassbinder's characters make each other 'unreal'. Likewise, there are very few moments where the camera assists that convergence of seeing and knowing one is used to from Hollywood, nor do the characters by looking at each other trade the sort of intimacy and knowledge which exchanging looks usually signifies. Because for Fassbinder, every dual relationship is by necessity a triadic relationship (with in most cases, the third term implied, hidden, known to neither party, or at best to one party), the unevenness in the balance of power on-screen transmits itself to the spectator-screen relation. Fassbinder's boldness in opting for a mise-en-scène so radically different from conventional television aesthetics must therefore be seen as more than an act of wilful provocation aimed at the habitual viewer.[43]

This brings me back to the question of violence in BERLIN ALEXANDERPLATZ. Brute force, especially when directed against women, stands for a non-symbolized phallic power placed outside all possible circuits of exchange, being the ever-present original trauma from which Franz fails to recover. In another sense, it is the non-symbolized power of visual representation, of cinema. It was Eric Rentschler's argument, referred to above, that Fassbinder engages the viewer in a politics of the body, 'a visceral practice that privileges direct impact over rhetoric, that places the tangible over the discursive.'[44] This acutely conveys one level of the film, explaining why many television viewers found the film unacceptably disturbing, although possibly not because of the violence or physicality per se, but because of its seemingly non-discursive, and also non-narrative function (an objection Fassbinder had in a sense already anticipated when he spoke about a love that has no visible results or consequences, cannot be exploited and is therefore not useful).[45] At another level, however, the violence and physicality is far from non-discursive. As I have tried to show, its mode of discursivity may not be language, but the general economy of capitalist exchange, and the symbolic economy of (oedipal) identity, into which Fassbinder inserts the special economies practised by his hero: that of an uneven exchange of the gift, and the 'black' or utopian economy of the 'polymorphously perverse' who in the realm of the senses tries to transgress the binary divides of active and passive, giving and receiving, male and female, hetero and homo, while all the while putting his body on the line. For it is this body, and the margins of its unsymbolizability – in other words its excess and its violence – that make it both capable of what Fassbinder called 'pure love' and enmeshes it in society and history. But just as the 'body' of Biberkopf is strategically placed at the cusp of the different economies, marking the border to pure matter and pure force, as well as being the flesh through which the alternative economies can be embodied, so Fassbinder's peculiar mise-en-scène enacts a double register in the field of vision – opposing to the perfectly discursive look of the classical system the 'embodied', obstructed, excessively physical look of his camera – excessive because rarely bound by the narrative motivating camera movement or the characters' motivating point of view editing into a system of even exchange.

'Wir wissen was wir wissen, wir haben es teuer bezahlen müssen'[46]

What I've been trying to describe have been some of Fassbinder's strategies for articulating the emotional, sexual and gendered – in short, oedipal – energies of his protagonist(s) and then 'feeding' them into the circuits of economic and class relations, especially as these revolve around two indicators of value and exchange crucial for the period, the unstable labour market with high unemployment, and the unstable currency with its cycles of hyper-inflation. These 'negative' factors of instability, however, develop their own dialectic, because they allow Biberkopf – without his ever being aware of it – to explore new ground in the way human beings conduct their 'business' with each other: they paradoxically liberate and exhilarate him at the same time as they maim him physically and destroy him mentally. This doubleness the epilogue once more puts in phantasmagoric images and sounds, where, according to some commentators, Fassbinder may have overreached himself, compared to the work of Fellini and Pasolini, after whom he possibly modelled himself.[47] Yet the function of the epilogue, its place in the overall 'allegorical' scheme is not in doubt: it is to show this drama once more, now 'out of time' and out of history and narrative, in a different space of non-symbolization and non-discursivity: that of the 'holy', the transfigured. History and the subject confront each other here in another symbolic for which the cinematic may not have a language other than that of violence. Hence the groteque forms it takes, hence the unbearable stripping, once narrative is taken away, once the disembodied look no longer circulates.

In 'choosing' Reinhold, Franz opens himself up to ambivalence and possibility, he refuses the politics, sexual and racial divides on offer, while being nonetheless the opposite of apolitical, in the best and the worst sense.[48] Precisely because he is ordinary, the ordinary German, the figure through whom 'Fassbinder' can not only love Germany but love himself, Franz Biberkopf becomes someone through whom the viewer can begin to understand what it means to have been a German, and maybe what it means once more to become German. Hence the irony of the motto 'we know what we know, the price we paid was not low' which works in both directions: 'we' (the West Germans) have paid a heavy price – maybe heavier than most people know, for we know what we know – but 'we' have also not benefitted from this knowledge, because the price 'we' paid has not translated itself into the kinds of economies of loving which the Erwin/Elviras and the Franz Biberkopfs are prepared to enter into, or expose their bodies to: the motto – which is taken from Döblin's text – brings one back, projects one forward once more to the apparently untranscendably asymmetrical economies of 'Schuld' and 'Schulden' discussed in the previous chapter. That Biberkopf in the epilogue should be nailed to the cross and then taken down again is a melancholy blasphemy. Suffering no longer brings transfiguration and no transsubstantiation: on the contrary, what the epilogue leaves the viewer with is an eternity without transcendence, and thus, at the very end, we are confronted with the question of the mortal body: not only Franz Biberkopf's, or those bodies 'mortified' in such devastating detail belonging to Ida and Mieze, but also Fassbinder's – his body, his body-image, his 'body of work'.

10. Historicising the Subject
A Body of Work

> *In the final analysis, all that matters is the body of work that you leave*
> *behind when you've disappeared. It's the entirety of the*
> *oeuvre that must say something special about the time in*
> *which it was made...otherwise it's worthless.*[1]

Too late, too soon

Writing about Fassbinder more than a decade after his death is both too late and too soon.
Too late to have much to add to the already voluminous literature, too soon to presume to
have a perspective on the phenomenon Fassbinder. As the 1992 celebrations around the tenth
anniversary of his death amply proved, in Germany itself, Fassbinder's films still split the
critical establishment and baffle audiences.[2] During his lifetime, the director had passionate
detractors, but also a number of loyal followers, who watched his progress from sub-Holly-
wood B-pictures to middle-class melodramas to international super-productions with a
steadfast belief in his genius. His fellow-filmmakers respected him more than they admired
him, and while he was alive, statements from Wenders, Schlöndorff or Herzog rarely went
beyond conventional acknowledgement or grudging praise. Jean Marie Straub had, soon after
their collaboration on THE BRIDEGROOM, THE COMEDIENNE AND THE PIMP (1968), added
Fassbinder to his own list of international pornographers, and no-one seemed to detest him
more heartily than the gay filmmaker Rosa von Praunheim.[3] Politically, the Left denounced
his self-advertised anarchism as crypto-fascist, while the Right saw in him an irresponsible
Maoist demagogue.

In the absence of a 'place' for Fassbinder in the history of his native cinema,
contrasting so strongly with his overwhelming presence as one thinks back on pre-unification
German filmmaking, it is tempting to resort to auteurism, that time-honored but treacherous
classification of the unclassifiable under the sign of unity. And true enough, as an auteur,
staking a claim to a number of themes and variations, Fassbinder easily imposes a stamp and
an identity. As a fact of cinema, however, he has something of the Dracula figure about him,
'undead' and unburied, haunting and vampirizing those who came after, having left neither
legitimate heirs nor outright usurpers, and instead, passing on his bite in unsuspected ways.[4]
So much so that German critics were talking about 'the Fassbinder myth': oddly enough, as
something which had to be dismantled, demystified and destroyed.[5] Indeed, one cannot help
feeling that he has become a figure more monstrous, more phantasmagoric than when he was
alive and public outcry or fresh scandals followed him everywhere. During his lifetime, it
was at least his restless productivity, his role as impresario and figure-head of the New German

Cinema that made up the myth and brought his astonishing talent to the attention of an international public.

With the demise of the New German Cinema (coinciding as some have argued, with Fassbinder's death in 1982),[6] the shadow on the German cultural scene is not cast by his films, but by his life. More precisely, his lifestyle, as recalled, recorded and fantasized by his friends and lovers: it caught the limelight and came in for mostly devastating scrutiny. Fassbinder's fate has been to attract biographers – Kurt Raab, Peter Chatel, Harry Baer, Gerhard Zwerenz, Ronald Hayman, Robert Katz, Peter Berling – who have chronicled (often not without relish) the ever more astonishing revelations which his entourage made public piece-by-piece about their carryings-on in his company: it seemed to confirm the most macabre view the general public could have had of the gay community and sub-culture. After these accounts of perversity, psycho-terror and dependency (which made him the bogey for people who probably had never seen a film of his), it came almost as a relief when in 1987, with the posthumous premiere of *Die Stadt, der Müll und der Tod*, controversy focused once more on his work, rather than his person. The protests around the play served as a reminder that Fassbinder might also have been concerned with political and moral issues.[7] Yet in 1988, in part due to Kurt Raab, one of his closest collaborators, staging his own slow dying of AIDS as a kind of televisual horror-show, the name of Fassbinder was once again associated with the darkest, most taboo-ridden, most distressing, but also most prophetic-apocalyptic aspects of the 1980s.

Fassbinder's life *or* his films, his life *and* his films: can one separate them, indeed should one separate them? Do they not make up the communicating vessels that are responsible for the very fascination and exasperation still emanating from the word 'Fassbinder'? Here, surely, is a director who practised an unparalleled symbiosis between living and filming, loving and hating, working and dying. Ronald Hayman hit on an engagingly domestic image, when he compares Fassbinder feeding his art from his life and his life with his art, calling him a 'cook with two stockpots on the go', who 'robs one to enrich the other'.[8] The metaphor can be extended, for there is another sense in which Fassbinder had different pots on the fire: he worked in several media simultaneously (theatre, film, television, and it seems, even radio), as well as in different genres (gangster films, melodramas, black comedies, historical spectaculars, literary adaptations, filmed plays, queer cinema), a fact which in itself marked him off from other European auteurs, and brought him closer to the Hollywood figure he always wanted to be, that is, a 'commercial' director. Paradoxically, it also confirmed that he never quite abandoned his origins in the sub-cultural avantgarde.

Living and working in the 1970s – the decade that like no other was dedicated to closing the gap between reality and utopia, between life and art – Fassbinder, as we saw, touched in his films on a great number of broad cultural and political debates: around class (as in his early films, dealing with the Munich sub-proletariat and petit-bourgeois shopkeepers, or the workers' films set in the Ruhr industrial region, made for television – EIGHT HOURS DO NOT MAKE A DAY), ethnicity (the Greek origins of the eponymous KATZELMACHER), race and colour (especially but not exclusively in FEAR EATS THE SOUL), radical politics (communists and ultra-leftists in MOTHER KÜSTER'S TRIP TO HEAVEN, urban terrorists in THE THIRD GENERATION) and sexual identity (the gay scene in FOX AND HIS FRIENDS and QUERELLE; the lesbian relation in THE BITTER TEARS OF PETRA VON KANT, pubescent sex in JAILBAIT, the post-menopausal sexuality of the heroine in FEAR EATS THE SOUL). Enough sociology and cultural studies, in short, to fill an entire curriculum of Modern German Studies.

Forgetting Fassbinder?

So why this difficulty with Fassbinder's *film* legacy? As contradictory and multi-faceted a talent as his is likely at once to energize and paralyze a country's cinema culture, and filmmaking in Germany in the 1980s and 1990s has taken quite different directions from his, whether one regards his agenda to have been German history, German film history or even 'gender'. Perhaps because history in the 1990s has everywhere returned with such immediate urgency and force, it may take more than another decade for there to be a 'return' to Fassbinder the filmmaker in Germany itself. There are also other, more mundane reasons for the impression that Fassbinder may have become a forgotten filmmaker: the legal situation of his estate was for many years the subject of litigation,[9] the rights on some of his films have either expired or were never properly cleared,[10] and several other obstacles have made access to his scripts, his drafts, and personal papers – and therefore sound research – difficult.[11]

But the sense in which Fassbinder's films have been 'forgotten' even internationally becomes apparent when comparing him with one of his fellow-directors: as Fassbinder's notoriety declined, so Wim Wenders' critical reputation rose. During the 1980s Wenders became the director par excellence of postmodernism, endlessly problematizing and celebrating Europe's relationship with the United States, deftly tying and untying a precarious authorial identity around the shuttle-cock motion between PARIS, TEXAS and Paris-Tokyo (NOTEBOOK OF CITIES AND CLOTHES), between Berlin (WINGS OF DESIRE) and Ayres Rock, Australia (TO THE END OF THE WORLD).[12] Against this geopolitical map and time-traveller's mindscape (FARAWAY, SO CLOSE, indeed), Fassbinder's world looks extremely parochial. He may have had apartments in Paris, visited brothels in North Africa, and gone to the leather-bars of New York, but his home was obstinately and unambiguously West Germany: Munich, Frankfurt, Bremen, Coburg in his films, but in the end only Munich seemed to matter. Even the Berlin of DESPAIR and BERLIN ALEXANDERPLATZ was ultimately 'made in Bavaria (Atelier)'.

Two critical vantage points therefore offered themselves on why Fassbinder's work has entered into a period of eclipse, or suffered premature burial in pious retrospectives. One was that his life finally devoured his work (when previously, it had been the other way round). The lifestyle and the anarcho-communitarian ideal it wanted to signify (extended families, elective affinities, non-heterosexual bonding beyond the couple) could not and did not survive the catastrophe of AIDS. The second inference was that because his topographical and emotional home, West Germany, formally ceased to exist in 1990, the changing balance of forces in Europe brought Germany not only out of its political quarantine, but also put an end to the morose, yet often enough self-laceratingly direct introspection which perhaps was Fassbinder's chief contribution to world cinema, and – at the time – one of the main reasons for his reputation as a creative force. More concretely, from KATZELMACHER and GODS OF THE PLAGUE to IN A YEAR OF THIRTEEN MOONS and THE THIRD GENERATION Fassbinder had also given spectators a quite physical, not to say tactile sensation of bodies agonizingly and violently in contact with each other.[13] Taken together, the films deepened into a visually sumptuous, emotionally claustrophobic, and often enough magnificently mundane image of West Germany, which afforded – according to one's point of view – an intimate, unvarnished, or an obscene, pornographic gaze on this particular, generally underexposed body politic.

Whether he set out to make skin-flicks of the German soul is a moot point. Yet the reasons so far advanced for explaining Fassbinder's eclipse as a filmmaker are not wholly convincing. He was neither quite the post-'68 romantic anarchist whose vision of love and communal living became irrecoverable after AIDS, nor Bavaria's native son swept aside by Germany's new strategic self-importance since unification and the end of the cold war. There must be other ways of approaching the 'resistance to/of Fassbinder', but also without cutting the Gordian knot by either sifting out the masterpieces and discarding the rest, or by making of him an *auteur*, who 'expresses' himself, which is to say, half explains himself in his films and half gives himself away in them. Once past the handful of themes, such as 'emotional exploitation' or 'sado-masochistic power-games', the auteur-critic can either make Fassbinder's homosexuality the key to his films, or chart the rise-and-fall of an overreacher. Another option, as we saw in the previous chapter, was to read Fassbinder across his relations to BERLIN ALEXANDERPLATZ as at once his life plan and his testament, following Fassbinder's own gesture of 'allegorizing' his existence through Döblin's novel, but then proceed to metaphorically translate this allegory of a life (back) into the films.[14] Both approaches would be, as Douglas Crimp put it, 'continuing to move in the wrong direction',[15] not to mention the fact that along none of these lines is it easy to like Fassbinder or even to see in him an artist worth attending to. Lugubrious, oppressive, humorless, his films seem so steeped in misanthropic cynicism and petit-bourgeois sentimentality that the odd moments of authenticity are merely symptomatic of a director who mistakes his own 'fucked-up', alienated relationships as a metaphor of post-war Germany.[16] This, surely, indicates one has not even begun to do justice to the devious subtlety of his work, its political and historical scope, or to appreciate its astonishing 'honesty', even if it is of a quite different kind from what is normally understood by the term.[17]

Probing this risky kind of honesty about Fassbinder's Germany was, of course, the central purpose of the preceding chapters, which wanted to both restate and resituate the paradox at the heart of his work: given the chaos of his personal life and the physical demands of filmmaking, drugs and alcohol may account for the manic nature of his productivity, but they do not explain a body of work of such perseverance or indeed, coherence. Re-viewing his films, across their generic diversity and even their stylistic unevenness, one cannot but be struck by the persistence of an overall conception, which is to say, the rather extraordinary purposiveness of the oeuvre. This I attempted to document, for instance, by emphasizing the 'serial', 'sequel', 'prequel' connexions between the films, either made with the same actors and slightly varying the same story-line, or looking at the same constellation from different vantage points and across different historical configurations.[18] But the inner drive, so to speak, must also be located elsewhere: a fractious energy battering against this work's overall unity, even as it struggles to assert it. This energy, I argued, could feed upon the vicious circles and the double-binds, make constraints productive and take off from formidable obstacles, including the passionate hatred or personal attacks he provoked among those close to him, amplified by the hostilities and *Schadenfreude* shown so often towards him in the German press.

To explain this resilience, one could point to an existential contradiction. The recurring motifs, the familiar configurations and metaphors in his films spell out an obsession, a trauma he quite consciously refused to shake off. If it had its origin in childhood, it was already as an adolescent that Fassbinder perceived the full value of an anxiety that could make him at once productive and clear-sighted about the society in which he lived. Nurtured, so that it could become a renewable resource, this contradiction centres on giving and receiving, on taking and exchanging, on the obligation and the gift. These are always uneven relations of exchange, whose 'balance' requires a shift of registers, whether this register is the symbolic exchange of art and make-believe, or the emotional currency of sex and violence, love and psycho-terror, or the ecomonic currency of a glamorous lifestyle that could at any moment disappear with a tax debt or a cancelled television contract.[19]

This uneven exchange, and the various circuits established to energize its trans-actions provide the sparks that bridged the gap opening between two of his film titles 'Love is Colder than Death' and 'I Only Want You to Love Me' which do indeed seem to span the two polarities within his life as well as in his filmmaking. An inner drive to surround himself with people he could have a hold on constantly came into friction with but also recharged itself across an outer constraint: the parlous state of postwar German cinema, where 'inde-pendence' meant serving at least two masters. In a sense, nothing more mysterious was Fassbinder's 'theoretical' vantage point on Germany than the fact that May 1945 could be thought of as a *tabula rasa*, an 'originary' moment (May 1945 being the year, as well as the month of his birth) when all the values could be reorganized. Ultimately, the two things that 'move' in Fassbinder's world are values and value systems (defined by a Marxist-capitalist vocabulary of use-value, exchange-value, circulation-value), and secondly (sexed, sexual-ized, and sexually available) bodies which can be stared at or look back, can be subjected to ocular micro-dismemberment, but also can be 'put together' again. These movements of bodies and values make up Germany, whose history is traversed by such moments of possible 'freedom', the seismic shifts becoming vantage points for charting the fate of different kinds of free-floating libidinal energy, but also for moments of extreme individual danger and self-shattering intensity, as identities are dislocated and bodies wrenched apart. The same 'explosions' also serve as (ethical) vanishing points, from which Fassbinder can critique a West Germany stuck in a sterile tit-for-tat, rigid in its anxious search for an always ungraspable, but fortified 'identity', devoid of humour or self-irony, but also incapable of sustaining either the schizo-doubleness (of so many of Fassbinder's minor characters) or the field of contradictory identifications into which Fassbinder's historical melodramas lead his strong, cunning and perverse women and weak, simple and gullible men.

From Vision to Mission

It is likely that Fassbinder was aware of what compelled him; at a certain point in his career, his vision metamorphosed into a mission, one he took upon himself quite dutifully, and even at times mechanically: to be the chronicler of West Germany.[20] It was no mean achievement, even if the rancid complacency overlaid by self-hatred he so often castigates in his Germans may well have been too partial and selective a moral outlook. Yet before he arrived, there was nothing in the German cinema even remotely close to the social panorama he chose to deploy. One only needs to remind oneself of what was discussed in an earlier chapter: the different classes and social groups Fassbinder's films encompassed, the range of professions, as well as the regions. I also alluded to the way in which, taken as a whole, Fassbinder's films organize themselves around a different chronology, not that of their year of production, but of the time in which they are set. Such a typically bourgeois, typically 19th century 'romanesque' ambition to document a society from top to bottom, inside out, from North (Prussia) to South (Bavaria), is an ambition especially paradoxical in a director who in other respects is totally removed from the Forsythe Saga tradition of the realist novel, and who has so often been celebrated as the avantgarde filmmaker who rediscovered popular Hollywood melodrama for the European art cinema. Several other projects in German cinema and television have a comparable scope (starting with Eberhard Fechner's TADELLÖSER & WOLF [1974/75], and including Edgar Reitz's HEIMAT [1984] as well as Berhard Sinkel's TV series VÄTER UND SÖHNE [1987] about an industrialist's family), testifying to a strong urge to re-appropriate a past which, for so many Germans, the legacy of Hitler had 'taken away', blighting and blocking the very belief in a 'future'. Yet comparing Fassbinder to Reitz, two directors who in their values, convictions and style are diametrically opposed, only underlines the singularity, even in his native country, of Fassbinder's films taken as a whole, and of BERLIN ALEXANDERPLATZ as these films' and modern Germany's mise-en-abyme.

By commuting his emotional life into the means of production and vice versa, he extracted from both his life and his filmmaking a perspective and a project. It made him one of the last 'modernists' (in Fredric Jameson's sense), leaving his unmistakable signature on all his films. But unlike the European cinema's other modernists who cultivate impersonality and screen out the biographical (in the manner of Bresson, Rivette, or even Godard), Fassbinder's project emerged from a constant crossing of the boundary between the personal and the professional. It might have provoked reflection on him as someone trying to give his life the truth of art (in the manner of an Oscar Wilde), or of a life lived for 'art' (to appropriate

Mallarmé's famous dictum that 'all life is destined to end in a book'). Instead, it (mis-?)led commentators into ferreting out assiduously the parallels between life and work, especially where it concerned calculated cruelties towards his friends serving as material for his films.[21] A fascinatingly lurid, but in the end futile endeavour when it does not bring one closer to understanding what might be significant about this oeuvre of so many films in so short a period: a decade, moreover, during which Germany, as we saw, according to many commentators had missed another historic chance.

Was Fassbinder a romantic, a realist, or a modernist? And what of the suggestion that he was already a post-modernist? This claim, too, would not be difficult to sustain. For a start, several Fassbinder films belong to what one might call the stock of Ur-stories common to the New German Cinema: motifs from MARIA BRAUN turn up in Alexander Kluge's THE PATRIOT, Helma Sanders-Brahms' GERMANY PALE MOTHER and Janine Meerapfel's MALOU; THE MERCHANT OF FOUR SEASONS returns in Herzog's STROSZEK, the world of KATZELMACHER can be found in scenes out of Hans Jürgen Syberberg's REQUIEM FOR A VIRGIN KING. Such borrowings and reworkings, on the other hand, are typical of Fassbinder himself who is not only a consummate literary adaptor in the white irony mode, but a gifted pasticheur. Having been so often compared to Balzac, it is worth reminding oneself how Fassbinder's films, despite the many internal echoes, do not create an autonomous, fictional universe, but media-worlds, which is to say, visual and aural spaces of references from newspapers, press photographs, popular music, and above all, from other films. In previous chapters, I discussed some of the allusions across the different media in THE MARRIAGE OF MARIA BRAUN, LOLA and VERONIKA VOSS, but the same holds for virtually all his films. Besides the 'horizontal axis', there is the 'vertical' one, what I have called Fassbinder's intertextual telescoping, in which different temporalities, plot situations and character developments from the various films are lined up and realigned with each other.[22]

But if at first, Fassbinder made films about films, he had, by 1977 decided that the cinema 'inhabited' a world of its own,[23] if necessary, a parallel 'world-on-a-wire', an electronic, virtual but for all this no less real a world, and furthermore, one that was as likely to 'betray' as it might 'redeem' the physical world of bodies, encounters, memories and sensations. This could suggest that Fassbinder had a postmodern view of the media and representation. Yet the reason why the analogy between his films and the C19th realist tradition ultimately breaks down is not a postmodern view of the vanishing historical referent. Rather, his ambition to cover all social strata and classes was founded on a distrust of the documentary character of literature (or, for that matter, film) and instead, was driven by the conviction that filmmaking is a form of 'experiment', and this in a double sense. As regards Germany, writing its social history meant entering the test-lab of its social imaginary, recording the materiality of its image making and the traces of its sounds and voices. But it was also an experiment, insofar as his films laid bare the mechanisms of miscognition within recognition, of speaking past each other when speaking with another, and of transference, overidentification or objectification 'failing' any effort at identity-formation in the face of excluded otherness. Such a national history, conceived as the echo-chamber of its sounds and images, as the self-deception of its self-definitions has a special place in Germany, given the determination of Nazism, the nodal point of Germany's ambivalent modernity, to implement a 'society of the spectacle' in order to black out the society of forced industrial expansion, slave labour and the death-camps, and to proclaim a national identity based on expulsion and extermination of all 'others'.

As we saw, Fassbinder's cycle of films about the 1930s and 1940s tended to foreground those aspects of Nazism which underline the specular, paranoid or narcissistic features of its public and private spheres. The connection between political power and show business is one of the most prominent perspectives in LILI MARLEEN, LOLA and VERONIKA VOSS. Fassbinder found in the Nazi regime's use of radio as a new technology and as a machine of social control a pertinent way of locating both the present situation of the commercial film industry and state-sponsored German culture as well as a metaphor for the medium that would in time displace radio and cinema, namely television. Yet as we saw, Fassbinder was in fact going against the current of his Italian predecessors Visconti and Bertolucci, or his German contemporaries Syberberg, Reitz and Kluge, all of whom had in one form of another focussed in their films about fascism on the operatic, self-mirroring, media-obsessed aspects of totalitarian regimes. LILI MARLEEN wanted to push furthest the deconstruction of cinema itself as a concentrated power potential (and therefore not unlike fascism), while also showing fascism as the first 'modern', self-consciously political organization of mass-entertainment. By forcing together into one narrative the Second World War and the blossoming entertainment industry of radio and the phonograph, Fassbinder dramatized the transformation of this power potential into 'over the top' spectacle. The film works out how military and logistical power gets commuted into spectacle power, by way of the related themes of mobilization, productivity and 'presence' (or aura), the latter figured as the effacement of the boundary between the roles of 'witness' and 'consumer' in the age of tele-technical reproduction, and all of them together preparing a version of modernity as a society driven by media events.[24]

The fact that Nazism becomes historically specific in LILI MARLEEN from such a (post-modern? neo-marxist?) vantage point, as a regime active in the cultural arena of sign and commodity production, has been heavily criticized.[25] But what Fassbinder's focus makes visible is not trivial and certainly not apologetic. The war economy and its showbusiness operations appear as a kind of stock exchange of values where those who have 'cornered' the currency of representation – in this case the Nazi regime – may try to impose their own rates of exchange, but, as the film also shows, these are liable to sudden, terrifying or surreal reversals, such as the song's (unwelcome) popularity and its consequences.

If (as Hollywood has always known) cinema intersects with history only insofar as a given past has itself acquired a pseudo-mythical dimension, then fascism emerges in Fassbinder's films, consistently and critically, as a question of subjectivity within image and discourse (of power, of desire, of fetish objects and commodities). Is it then the law of desire and thus the rule of ceaseless displacement as the 'semiotic' principle holding Fassbinder's historico-fictional universe together? It would be one of the strongest arguments in favor of Fassbinder as a postmodern director, but it would, I think, be a misunderstanding. Firstly, by presenting fascism as the subject's relation to libidinally fraught and therefore pleasurable representations, rather than as the subject's exposure to the repressive power of a specific political system, Fassbinder questions historical subjectivity from the vantage point of a new kind of ethics (of sex and death). Rather than conceding the point of postmodern relativism, he seems to suggest that a media reality such as manifested itself during fascism is in fact the pre-condition for both a (repressive, paranoid) attempt at identity and for a different kind of subjectivity, one that can embrace contradictory identifications and still assume responsibility and make choices.

This can perhaps be clarified by briefly looking at a number of parallels with other directors, also concerned with the politics of the subject. Identified with the 1970s, Fassbinder's work prompts – around the twin themes of eros and thanathos – comparisons with Pier Paolo Pasolini and Nagisha Oshima. All three directors came from countries which espoused fascism as their way of 'modernizing' a feudal society, and all three directors took fascism as the historical key to understanding the formation not only of their country's post-war present, but also for an exploration of social marginality, and by extension, the material conditions of subjectivity.[26]

Although Fassbinder never made a film as explicitly about sex, death and political power as Pasolini's SALO or Oshima' EMPIRE OF THE SENSES (though QUERELLE comes close), he shares with them the conviction not only that history can give a hold and a perspective on contemporary society, but that the historical referent, vanishing though it may be as a determining force, can nonetheless be seized in the form of resentment, anger, refusal and desire, in short, at the level of a psychic and possibly 'perverse' investment which may overturn the existing order: such a promise of revolution – existential, sexual, ethical – was a long way from the post-'68 slogan of the personal as political, but also from the postmodern political cynicisms of, say, Pedro Almodóvar. Nearer to Pasolini and Fassbinder in spirit was Derek Jarman, who in some of his films, most poignantly in EDWARD II, deconstructed class-war and history (understood by Jarman as the remembering and passing down of certain versions of power and masculinity, and not others) and set against them the investment of single-sex love, jealousy and finally, death.

Fassbinder and Brecht: Know Thyself and Be Thine Own Enemy

Without further elaborating the parallels, or indeed, the differences between these directors, there are a number of moments in such a constellation unique to Fassbinder, most usefully examined by recalling how he utilized melodrama as an 'if only' temporality and the modality of impossible love, including impossible self-love. Fassbinder was unusually intelligent, which manifested itself not least in his ability to take sides also against himself. Volker Spengler put it succinctly: 'In whatever métier, if you want to achieve something or be productive, you have to generate the aggression, the defiance, the resistance within yourself, in order to even begin to have a partner in dialogue. And in this, Rainer was unsurpassed.'[27]

In knowing how to take sides against himself Fassbinder resembled the young Brecht, who in one of his early short stories, *Bargan läßt es sein*, created a figure who invented his own enemy, or rather, who fell in love with another man, Croze, who used, abused and betrayed him. Not a masochist, Bargan cunningly makes his own a dictum Brecht took from R.L. Stevenson: 'he who finds an enemy, finds a treasure, and who knows, maybe even himself.'[28] Similarly, instead of an either-or world, Fassbinder's was a both-and world, but one where his 'sentimentality' became a most powerful strategy for putting himself in the place of both lover and loved, both sadist and masochist. He not only saw two sides at once, he was in two sides at once. This was his intelligence, and this was his honesty (even when he 'lied'), perhaps his humanity (even when it seemed sheer perversity to put oneself 'inside' an anti-Semite). The doubleness of the perspectives as they emerge from the films' speaking positions thus become the very hallmark of a certain conception of truth, rather than proof of what many around him interpreted as his inveterate duplicity or hypocrisy.[29]

The contradiction can be resolved if one can entertain the notion that Fassbinder may have had no inner life, or rather, that he needed no inner life, in the way one usually imagines this to be one's most precious possession or the lack of which one most carefully shields from others. But the impression not only from the interviews is that Fassbinder probably found his interior life quite uninteresting, which in turn allowed him to project the egocentric selflessness one finds so startling in his protagonists – their nakedness, their disarming candour, in their dealings with others, however shabby their motives and devious their objectives.

This radical exteriorization was not only the goal of his characters and the dynamic of his narratives, both 'exhausting' themselves in the process, but also the secret of Fassbinder's productivity. Hence one's unease with psychoanalytic interpretations of his personality, and the interest instead in understanding how he made others give their inner life in order to make it enter his films, how – again like Brecht – he was able to think in other people's heads and hearts. In this sense, he was a catalyst who attracted so many kinds of contradiction that his gift as 'medium of antagonism' made him a 'merchant of four seasons', someone who could utilize the subtle gaps always opening up between supply and demand, sitting inside and outside, creating himself the gradients he then used for new circuits of exchange. Yet this kind of existence needed crises, thrived on them, and when there were none, he made them happen, which is why Kurt Raab could epitomize Fassbinder as *der sanfte Kaputtmacher* (the gentle wrecker).[30] This, too, not unlike Brecht, who used up his collaborators, tested human relationships for the degree of their *Verwertbarkeit* ('utilitizable value'), and who found himself constantly challenged as the appropriator of other people's labour. Fassbinder's and Brecht's 'systems' of authorship were in many ways similar also with respect to 'intervening' in so many different media, exploiting them, in order to gain access to or stay in the market. Like Brecht's plays, Fassbinder's films testify to his presence even when he was not there.

No wonder that some of his collaborators, who gave their love, their emotions, their lives, had the feeling that his filmmaking was a kind of moloch devouring everyone, including himself.

Fassbinder and Kafka: The Anti-Patriarchal Production Machine

Thus, other ways of situating an author, without invoking the force-field of self-expression or the redundancy of self-identity, now seem to become possible. Among these, one that suggests itself is Gilles Deleuze and Felix Guattari's model of the writer in a minor literature which they develop in their study of Kafka.[31] There, they set out to rescue Kafka from two kinds of readings – the psychoanalytic-biographical and the metaphysical-transcendental one – and instead, they stress the political-historical-interventionist dimension of his work. Two characteristics are highlighted in Deleuze and Guattari's definition: that for Kafka, his letters, diaries, and novels were three modes of writing, each equally important, each serving a distinct function in what they term his 'writing machine'. Secondly, that in Kafka's case writing meant finding between the Czech of his peasant ancestors (remote because he had to learn it), the Yiddish of his ethnic group (too bodily, too unformed for him to feel anything but nausea and shame), and the German of his job, his literary world ('this paper language'), a language that was his own, or rather, one which became his own once he had drawn the consequences of the fact that his writing happened within several impossible languages.

According to Deleuze and Guattari, the Kafka writing machine developed along three lines of force: the segmental line (of institutional constraints, social and civil existence, the family), which in his case, was the Germano-Austro-Hungarian Empire with its bureau-cratic-military-legal caste- and class-system, in which Kafka and his father were completely caught up, and across which they fought their apparently overdetermined oedipal-biographi-cal relations. By 'wiring' the domestic oedipal rivalry into the legal and administrative circuits of the Prague political machinery, Kafka discovered a second line traversing his existence, the line of break, in which women had the key role which was also a most ambiguous role: they are, in his stories, the guardians of the law, but at once 'below' the law and above it, in ways that both break and reassert the segmental line. It was along the break-line of this 'casting' of women that Kafka could deploy his writerly energies – as opposed to the permant 'power-cuts' that ruled his emotional and sexual life – towards a third path, the 'line of flight' which Deleuze and Guattari call, in view of a theme in so many of the short stories, the movement towards 'becoming animal': most explicitly demonstrated in *The Metamorphosis*, *The Burrow*, *The Singer Josephine*.[32]

The minor literature model is thus firstly a way of reading a body of work as anti-oedipal and, to this extent, anti-autobiographical in the traditional sense. Secondly, it is a way of opening it up towards its own politics, that of seeking consistency and substance not in identity, but in traversing boundaries, tolerating tensions, positioning itself in the territory of language and power, which is to say: domination, colonization, minoritization, hegemonies – without depriving itself of the energies thus put in circulation. In this sense, a minor literature is to be read as a problem-solving machine, as a way of deblocking, re-energizing and re-motivating an existential project when it looks like having no exit.

What is the significance of this model for an understanding of Fassbinder? Literally, of course, it does not apply, since Fassbinder 'wrote' in his native German. But in other respects, it suggests a number of analogies, especially in the way the elements of Fassinder's life seemed constantly to re-arrange themselves to become meaningful in his work. There are the productively impossible 'languages' for a German director: of Hollywood, Ufa and the European art cinema; the break-line of bisexuality in his life, and masculinity and the feminine in his work; finally, 'exploitation', Fassbinder's code-word for the ambivalent and reversible interactions between minorities, power and domination. What matters, though, is how these complexes externalize themselves in Fassbinder. The close symbiosis of his film-making and his bodily existence in all its aspects, for instance, only makes sense when seen as the setting up and maintenance of a number of networks and 'machines': the strategically seductive use of his homosexuality; his alcohol and drug abuse (both pharmaceutical drugs and cocaine); his nomadic existence, even when not on the set, between aeroplane trips and car-rides (where he usually conducted love affairs, business deals and wrote film scenarios or plays). Above all perhaps by the way he shrewdly 'energized' the segmental lines of the (German) film business (television, public funded theatre, the auteur cinema, and money from the state), in order to achieve his 'German Hollywood' films. Looked at coldly from the outside, it was a sex, money, drugs machine; looked at from the inside (by his friends) it was a sadistic, manipulative power-game machine; but at one remove, from an empathetic distance, and granting it the seriousness of a project, it was a most extraordinarily productive machine that generated the over forty films, not counting theatre plays, TV series, published essays, acting parts we now associate with the name 'Fassbinder'.

As evident from the previous chapters, I see the networks of Fassbinder's productivity organizing themselves principally around two kinds of ensembles: the production apparatus of his 'family' and 'mini-studio', and the cinematic apparatus of frames, mirrors and looks, of sound spaces, time shifts and aural topographies. Into these enter and from these emerge the impossible love stories, the 'strong women' moving between different instances of the law, and living identities that are 'non-oedipal' and therefore grounded also in a different concept of gender and family, which is to say, who invent – mainly around melodrama's modalities of 'if-only' – different temporalities and performances of the self.

Surrogate Families

At first, Fassbinder's 'mini-studio', building on the *anti-teater* experience, kept these systems in balance: a small galaxy of actresses, ranging from Hanna Schygulla, Ingrid Caven and Margit Carstensen to Barbara Sukowa, Elisabeth Trissenaar and Rosel Zech was complemented by a permanent team consisting of the ubiquitous Peer Raben, Renate Leiffer, and (as production manager) Christian Hohoff, with a number of actors doubling as assistant directors (Kurt Raab, Harry Baer). The women were made by him into 'stars' (i.e., they fully partook in the exteriorizing metamorphoses of self enacted by the cinematic apparatus). Given the importance of female roles, this treatment of actresses has come in for much comment, both by himself and others.[33] Ingrid Caven put it very sharply, 'this man had the courage of thinking in terms of structure and form; as far as content goes, he mostly dealt with this by himself outside the normal working days. He required a certain distance, had to imagine an outside, in order to project onto it what the [women] with their voices and bodies could bring to a film.'[34] Rosel Zech was even more tongue-in-cheek when she reported Fassbinder once quipping to her: 'what can you do with women, except make films with them?'[35]

In contrast, the men were mostly bound to him by emotional, financial or sexual dependencies he was reputed to have exploited, either by manipulating their loyalty (playing them off against each other), or by bribing them with a calculated mixture of bullying and magnanimity.[36] Such biographical speculations would once again be improper if the double-binds implied were not also signs of a 'machine' powerful enough to shape both the human and the story material, giving the films at once a broad sweep and their narrow focus.[37]

The surrogate family and the vantage points both inside and outside the family were archaic, atavistic, pre- and post-oedipal: they constantly created but also destroyed identities, venturing outside the family, outside the usual mechanisms of socialization. Whether one takes the *ménage à trois* with Peer Raaben and Irm Hermann in the late 1960s, the extended family of the *anti-teater* period, the Theater am Turm team, the love and money nexus, the luxurious recreation of the working class or peasant family, or his participation in the hip international gay subculture: in each phase of his life, Fassbinder was able to use his deprivation of the nuclear family to his advantage, namely in order to create other kinds of families, and with them, other ways of regulating how in his vicinity emotional and material goods were bought and sold, traded and kept.[38] A fairly consistent line runs from one kind of extended family to another, while the 'cultural meaning' of these families is forever changing: from the first extended family with his grandmother, to the prostitutes across the hall in his mother's Munich apartment, from the time he and Raben were briefly Irm Hermann's and Ursula Strätz's pimps, to the grace-and-favours games of the *anti-teater* period, Fassbinder adeptly seemed to impersonate un-bourgeois and all-too bourgeois family lives, immersing himself in all its different variants, including the final years of relative domesticity with Juliane Lorenz.

The Sexual Politics of Victimhood

Where did this double circuit of the 'family firm' immanent in Fassbinder's life and exteriorized as the working conditions of an 'independent' filmmaker come together to produce new knowledge? Where did it generate *across the films* the 'line of break' that could open up a deadlock, re-energize a stalemate? My contention has been that one can see it happen around the shifting spaces the 'outsider' inhabits in the field of 'representations' called Germany, reworking fantasms of identity into embodied subjectivities as they form, deform and unform themselves in gestures of love and sacrifice, exploitation and victimization.

Central to views of Fassbinder have always been the notion of victimhood, as both an analytical category and a form of spectatorship.[39] Especially in the early films, victims were often seen as the living, suffering proof of capitalism and authoritarian patriarchy. Mostly female, they were the voiceless and silent accusers of the system, and thus became the bad conscience of a male society they did not understand (or understood too well). In the later films, victims were often homosexuals, brutally or cynically exploited by other gays, as in FOX AND HIS FRIENDS and IN A YEAR OF THIRTEEN MOONS, or lesbians, victims of power-games and infatuation (THE BITTER TEARS OF PETRA VON KANT). It is this conception which most bothered gay critics. Richard Dyer, for instance, found Fassbinder's view of victims problematic in a several respects. Firstly, the depiction of suffering seems to become a kind of end in itself, for even if it was not 'gloating', it endorsed the dominant representational code of female suffering as beautiful (in FONTANE EFFI BRIEST or MARTHA). Secondly, Fassbinder not only reduplicated patriarchal image values, he also made sexual oppression merely a metaphor of class oppression, showing a gay character such as Fox victimized as a proletarian without indicating that gays are also oppressed as gays. With his proles presented as brutalized and sexist (as in JAILBAIT), and gays like Fox relentlessly and stupidly duped, Fassbinder's sexual politics embodied what Walter Benjamin had diagnosed as 'left-wing melancholy', a kind of self-pitying defeatism about the liberating potential or solidarity that can come out of being an underdog or outsider, leaving the spectator in a disempowered state, where resistance and struggle seemed pointless and futile.[40]

A different reading of the figure of the victim would have to start from the assumption that victimhood in Fassbinder may not necessarily be the negative state the protagonists try (and fail) to escape from, but already a 'solution', a way of repositioning the dialectic of oppressor/oppressed, refusing the complicity of the power struggles over sexual or class identity. Some of Fassbinder's protagonists seek salvation and integrity not outside the barriers of sex and class, but by living exploitation 'from within'. Only when stripping themselves of the self's symbolic or fetish supports (most harrowingly and graphically in IN A YEAR OF THIRTEEN MOONS and VERONIKA VOSS) do they arrive at self-acceptance. What appears to be defeatism or mere self-abandonment, in fact founds another truth of selfhood and thus corresponds to a different – differently gendered, and in the present society unliveable – morality. Death, unbearably pointless as it may seem, is not a defeat for them, but the memorial to a victory as yet deferred. Against a belief in the transcendence of struggle, or the assumption of a subject speaking from 'full knowledge', Fassbinder's harsher view of subjectivity and death admits only of immanence, an immanence bereft, furthermore, of the tragic hero's anagnorisis or recognition.[41]

The question, however, remains whether one can conclude from this that Fassbinder's films embody, even if negatively, the utopia of non-phallic sexuality, as I, for instance, tried to argue for MARIA BRAUN and BERLIN ALEXANDERPLATZ. The film's epilogue, but also QUERELLE affirm Fassbinder's world as one of intense brutality, violence, aggression and torment – torment inflicted so often from thoroughly gendered, not to say 'sexist' motives.

QUERELLE in particular makes it difficult to read the explicit thematization of homosexual desire in the perspective of a post-68 but already post-modern Foucault: 'Another thing to distrust is the tendency to relate the question of homosexuality to the problem of "Who am I?" and "What is the secret of my desire?" Perhaps it would be better to ask oneself, "What relations, through homosexuality, can be established, invented, multiplied and modulated?"'[42]

Given the divergence of views on this issue, Fassbinder's sexual politics will continue to provoke further readings. Thus, Kaja Silverman has interpreted the epilogue of BERLIN ALEXANDERPLATZ as the 'ruination of masculinity', arguing for masochistic ecstasy as the subjectivity that forms the limit-point of the ambiguous and lethal desire which binds Franz Biberkopf to his tormentor-executioner Reinhold. For Silverman, however, it would be a mistake to see in the epilogue merely a truth which the preceding film represses; rather, she locates in the fantasy that animates the film an entirely different scenario, which counters the more obvious 'sadistic' reading of the film's (and the epilogue's) violence with a 'masochistic' reading, where what she calls 'heteropathic' identification (identification with the aggressor), and the spectacle of 'psychic detumescence' determine the text's movement towards self-annihilation, sought in order to anticipate the self's humiliation, rejection and extinction by the love that cannot but express itself in violence: 'I hope that this analysis of BERLIN ALEXANDERPLATZ has once again conjured forth the image of the squirrel throwing itself down the throat of the snake'.[43] Relating Fassbinder's theatricalization of homosexual desire to Freud's fantasy scenario of 'a child is being beaten', Silverman sees in BERLIN ALEXANDERPLATZ one of the rare attempts by a filmmaker to get 'inside' male subjectivity, driven by the wish to love another man, and to accept in the other man all the violence and aggression that constitute idealized masculinity in our culture. The mode of this acceptance, however, can only be by living out the destruction that it brings to the loving subject. In a particularly bold move, Silverman is able to rescue this reading as 'utopian'.[44]

Stripped of this utopia, and locked into the physical immanence of mortal bodies, masochism is also the key to Fassbinder in Steven Shaviro's interpretation of QUERELLE.[45] In his reading, no politically progressive, liberating significance is given to homosexual desire, seen as necessarily liminal, even if a deeply gratifying dimension of wish-fulfilling fantasy attaches itself to the self's destruction. Although rejecting Silverman's psychoanalytic model of masochism, Shaviro confirms the self-shattering aspect, but insists on the essentially phallic imaginary of Fassbinder's explicitly homosexual films. Both Silverman and Shaviro refer to Leo Bersani, who in a famous essay has trenchantly argued against a 'liberal' or non-phallic view of homosexuality in queer cinema and gay sub-cultures, providing a theoretical framework for what might be called post-AIDS versions of late Fassbinder.[46] Even without attributing prophetic foresight to his films, it is therefore possible to maintain that Fassbinder was perfectly capable of thinking 'beyond AIDS'. His distrust of doxa and ideology would have stopped him from seeing homosexuality 'out of the closet' as the new religion of sweetness and light.

Thus, in order to locate Fassbinder's sexual politics, both Silverman's concept of masochism and queer theory do furnish convincing arguments for why AIDS has not made Fassbinder's films obsolete. At the same time, the complexity of the question of gender in Fassbinder should also guard one against reading all of Fassbinder as 'really' about homosexuality, a point made by the director himself, when asked whether FEAR EATS THE SOUL and PETRA VON KANT were not what his interviewer calls camouflage films.[47]

So perhaps what is needed is a critique of the critique of victimhood in Fassbinder's cinema: not only around the false symmetry of sex and class, or the difference between a sadistic gaze and masochistic ecstasy, but situated also in a historical perspective. The question is whether the difficulty with Fassbinder's work, and the resistance it provokes, does not have something to do with the fact that any debate about victimhood has to include a consideration of its significance in recent German history, itself complexly refracted in the German cinema. There is in Fassbinder a dimension which, understandably, has not been of major concern to the largely Anglo-American debate about his sexual politics. Throughout Fassbinder's films about Germany, an oblique, if persistent critique is mounted of what has been one of the most typical features of the New German Cinema's 'coming to terms' with the fascist past, usually summed up by the term 'mourning work', and covering such diverse modes as 'history from below' (*Alltagsgeschichte*), as in HEIMAT, the critique of Nazism from the woman's point of view as a critique of patriarchy (e.g. GERMANY PALE MOTHER, or THE GERMAN SISTERS), the staging of a baroque 'teatrum mundi' (Syberberg's OUR HITLER) or more literally, the documentation of two funerals, resonant with historical echoes, as in GERMANY IN AUTUMN.[48] Initially conceived as a way of recovering buried memories, and reconciling Germans to their lost ego-ideals, by admitting the divisions and discontinuities within their historical selves, thus making space for the acknowledgement of 'the other', *Trauerabeit* also carried its risk, as the 'Historikerstreit' showed, when, as discussed earlier, Andreas Hillgruber empathized with the injustices and the death toll suffered by the German population evacuated or evicted from East Prussia, Sudetenland and Bohemia after the collapse of the Eastern front. 'Mourning work', in other words, risked stopping short at the stage of self-pity, granting compassion only at the price of playing victims off against each other. Often no doubt unconsciously, but in Hillgruber quite explicitly, two kinds of victims, 'theirs' and 'ours' were being compared, in an attempt to correlate what is incommensurate. The New German Cinema often presented a view of history in which Germany appeared as a nation of victims, either by choosing women as the central protagonists, or by allegorizing the country as a female body, vulnerable and maltreated: in both cases without leaving room for other victims.[49]

It is in the way he avoids the temptation of such false book-keeping and fatal kinds of balancing of accounts, in short, such equivalence thinking, that Fassbinder differs from some of his fellow German directors, pursuing an agenda perhaps not even shared by Pasolini or Oshima. Fassbinder's 'strong' female characters (Maria Braun, Willie in LILI MARLEEN, Lola, Veronika Voss) refuse victim thinking, not least because it presumes to create empathy at the price of exonerating them from a responsibility which no solidarity among victims can efface. But the status of victim also locks the subject into binary reciprocity, which, as we have seen in the discussion of his sexual politics, Fassbinder's cinema constantly tries to break open, radicalize or displace. As a consequence, it may be possible to see the utopian dimension in Fassbinder's films about Germany not primarily, as Silverman argues for BERLIN ALEXAN-DERPLATZ, in the ideal of masochistic ecstasy, but in the insistence – here true to the tradition of the anarcho-libertarian credo Fassbinder always professed – that the couple as a love relationship can only exist when it recognizes its place in other circuits of exchange. Thus, the second (historical) dimension not considered in the debate about Fassbinder's notions of victimhood is what I have called the motif of the black markets in Fassbinder, and which is a constitutive part not only of his sexual politics, but of his view of German history. In other words, Fassbinder's films draw part of their energy from their engagement with two discursive fields, that of 'mourning work' and *tabula rasa* thinking, both of which are anchored in the specific circumstances of German history and its representations.

In Fassbinder's world one often notices that the victims are not powerless, but have their own weapons, not least because they have nothing to lose. So, there is always an inverse side, just as Fassbinder plays Fox, but in 'real life' is Eugen, or Maria Braun may be Mata Hari or Mildred Pierce, but she is also duped by her husband and by Oswald, who make a pact behind her back. There is always exchange, uneven exchange, and the tables can be turned. In fact, a story does not seem worth telling to Fassbinder, until and unless he can locate the pivot, the point of its reversibility. This 'rage' for reversibility has to be seen against the background of the rigidly patriarchal society which was West Germany, and the double retreat from the traumas behind its founding identity: anti-Semitism (the fear of the other) and Nazism (the craven and pleasurable submission to a power without morality) had both been made to 'disappear'. Fassbinder's 'answer' was to open his films up to the ambiguous play of both displacements: the love of the other (without castrating the other's power to avenge himself), and the masochistic pleasure of self-abandonment, abjection. If Fassbinder is thus such a potent commentator on West Germany, it is because he takes the repressed logic of its social relations and human intercourse to its ultimate stage, where the ground on which this rigid identity is built gives way on all sides. Hence his stories are told from a vantage point of self-sacrifice, of the one who has nothing to lose because s/he looks forward to losing this self. The play of uneven exchange, of exteriorisation and death is part of a politics of the wager, of taking risks, crucial to the emotional economy and even of the spiritual aspirations of the Fassbinder character.

The Black Marketeer

Hence also the ambiguity of the black-marketeer, who is both a sinister figure and a saviour, a devaluer and a revaluer, without needing the brute force of imposing the value of exchange (as did Nazism). The black-marketeer is both a historical figure in the context of post-war Germany, and the 'explanation' of West-Germany's moral impotence, its inability to impose itself culturally or ethically in the post-war world. The connexion would be that after the death of the Führer – ambiguously gendred according to Mitscherlich – it is a maternal image that takes over, one we find in Fassbinder almost over-represented in all its ambivalence, but this image enters into an alliance with, gets blurred by, and finally succumbs to the new image of a male, of a patriarchal figure, but castrated: that of the pimp, the black marketeer. But while the woman becomes more phallic in the process of this transformation, the man necessarily becomes a transvestite. In one sense, therefore, the pimp and the go-between only emerge because of the fatherless generation, where he constantly 'tests' the mother. Yet as a transsexual, he enacts a mode of exchange that 'tests' the whole affective economy, doing without father and mother, without dependencies of this kind. The homosexual made a female would be at the vanguard because able to engage in symbolic relations, beyond nature and biology, fully in the realm of culture and society.

Thus, the importance of uneven exchange has, to my mind, been underestimated when discussing the kind of utopian economy of the subject which makes self-annihilation and self-sacrifice such crucial vantage-points in Fassbinder's moral universe. For it is against the background of an ideal of non-equivalence and symbolic exchange that the figure of the victim attains its rightful place. From Jorgos in KATZELMACHER to Fox in FOX AND HIS FRIENDS, from Ali in FEAR EATS THE SOUL to Erwin of IN A YEAR OF THIRTEEN MOONS : they all play out, like Franz Biberkopf in BERLIN ALEXANDERPLATZ, the drama of a very peculiar radicalism, that of divesting themselves of the means of exchange – power, money, phallic identity – in order to attain an almost mystic transfiguration: not by dying as sacrificial animals, but in and through their deaths daring those that survive to reflect on what it means to give and to take, which is to say, what it means to 'love'. Nowhere has Fassbinder staged the possibilities and hazards of such open circuits of exchange more starkly, once the heterosexual-reproductive and patriarchal-oedipal lineage of the family and the couple are bracketed, than in his contribution to GERMANY IN AUTUMN, his IN A YEAR OF THIRTEEN MOONS and THE THIRD GENERATION, while for other, more overtly economic, moral and political acts of exchange, Fassbinder in his later films (e.g. VERONIKA VOSS, QUERELLE, and the planned *Cocaine*) chose drugs and drug-trafficking as the suitably ambiguous and provocative metaphor.[50]

What I am suggesting is the possibility of seeing Fassbinder's sexual politics of male subjectivity in a wider semantic field. Together with his representation of German history as a series of crises in a society's exchange values – with fascism, the post-war period and the 1970s all emerging as 'black markets' – his sexual politics form a configuration which could be called the tragedy of 'ir/reversibility'. Contrasting the temporality of loss and nostalgia with that of forgetting and remembering, and the causality of guilt and retribution with that of debt and restitution, it also includes the reversibility of sexual violence (the sado-masochistic bind) and the reversiblity of State violence and terrorism (the structure of THE THIRD GENERATION), all of which, however, are bounded by the irreversibility of the body and death. Fassbinder's (seemingly postmodern) depiction of fascism as a media reality is thus less apologetic than aimed at keeping alive issues of accountability, which is to say of both politics and ethics. The anachronisms of Fassbinder the chronicler, the doubled time shifts of his films about Germany already alluded to, with their asymmetric relationship of fascism to the 1970s (in GERMANY IN AUTUMN and IN A YEAR OF THIRTEEN MOONS), or their use of drugs as the metaphor of forgetting/remembering (in THE THIRD GENERATION and VERONICA VOSS) make the reversibility of roles (of oppressor/oppressed) and gender (transsexuality) the very condition not for revisionism, but for unexpected shocks of recognition. Distrustful of explanations of how it could have come to Hitler,[51] his films turn on how to (re-)present the present, in order for the past to make sense. While this might well support the case that German unification has made Fassbinder's films once more relevant, because another (false) squaring of accounts seems to be the order of the day, it also draws attention to the other necessary reversal which both confirms the principle of uneven exchange and points to its ultimate limit.

This 'limit' takes two characteristic forms: both have to do with Germany, and both have to do with the body. One centres on the relationship between 'crime' and 'punishment' and the temporalities of melodrama and science fiction, the other on the way a 'body of work' may involve 'work on the body'. Earlier I referred to an energy battling against coherence in the films as a whole, which suggests another way of reading Fassbinder: backwards, from the end as it were, in a kind of unravelling of the 'house that Rainer built'. The move towards undoing, the shattering aspect, the anarchic impulse to tear the self down seems equally pressing in his work, pointing to different values and intensities, to different circuits of communication and exchange, which include the body's presence as perceptual surface, receptive to emotions such as hate, to suffering directly represented and violence valorized, but also to tenderness as suspended hurt and the tenderness of the intended touch: the body offered as gift and symbol, but also as that which cannot be symbolized. In Fassbinder's world, the mind-body divide can find itself turned inside out, where the body is that which thinks, has the 'presence of body' to take risks, be analytical and alert also in the hypothetical mode, while the mind is that which is inert, merely there, neither logical nor critical...

Such a reversibility of the 'exchange rate' within and between human beings, sometimes figured as a sado-masochistic double bind, sometimes as selves living entirely in the other, obtains in Fassbinder in the economic sphere and in the sexual sphere, it traverses bodies and genders, but it has its ground in the cinema's relation to time. What I have called Fassbinder's media reality is thus the precondition for temporal reversibility – the cinema as time-machine – which presents itself here as the only hope for a historical reversal, not with the intent of disavowal or the need for a tabula rasa, but in the paradoxical mode of melodrama: the only 'answer' possible to the impossible 'squaring of accounts', because it inhabits the time of the 'if only' and the 'negative' spaces of subjectivity, because it feeds on excess and can tolerate contradiction. In this sense, Fassbinder's fractious energy comes from his characters forever asserting 'this is not it', while trying to respond to a symbolic mandate, at least to the extent that they are always more concerned with the place from where they speak than what they speak. The effort of placing themselves so that they can be seen – as argued, the source and goal of their mobility in cinematic space – can now be re-interpreted as the effort to occupy a speaking position that is 'right', and thus to answer the 'ultimate' question put to a German, when the look behind the look needs to be confronted. By the same token, this speaking position has to be that of the outsider, the figure par excellence to provoke that other look into revealing itself – behind all the looks of desire, disapproval and projection.

Outsiders, then, but not victims. Likewise, less figurations of absolute or even social evil, but figures of an often powerful negativity. Only after depriving his villains of psychology or sociology did Fassbinder take the crucial step towards a 'historical' dimension. Granted the immanence of Fassbinder's ethical universe, it is the absence of either malice or desire in someone like Reinhold which attracts to him the energy that stirs one's interest in Franz Biberkopf's strange passion. To understand what Fassbinder understood about Biber-kopf is to share a very peculiar quest, namely to want to know why the punishment begins when the prisoner is released... In Fassbinder's world, one has to 'find' not only one's enemy in order to know oneself, but one has to choose one's double, not so much to lose oneself (which may or may not be the case), but to learn from him about the nature of one's crime. This crime, in the case of the Germans of Fassbinder's generation, must be connected with Nazism. But it cannot be the Holocaust as such, a fact that, in spite of everything one knew, was in the 1970s at once too impersonal in its imcomprehensible enormity, and already too remote as a living memory. Nazism could most conveniently be projected, in the form of assigning guilt, upon one's parents. But when, like Fassbinder, one worked outside the patriarchal paradigm the task was different. One had to discover for oneself – if not within oneself – less the sense of guilt or shame, so often demanded from Germans, but the 'innocent' side of the crime: one 'became' German, by starting on a long journey in both directions: into worlds before the crime, and yet already after the crime, suffering the punishment, but still in ignorance of the crime. 'We know what we know, the price we paid was not low': after such knowledge, what (price) forgiveness, Fassbinder might have said, although – if one looks at his contempt for the self-satisfaction of his countrymen – he might also have said: after so much self-forgiveness, what (use is) knowledge? At the same time, the journey undertaken by his films is one away from identity, towards the more arduous, perilous and perverse strategies of identification: from KATZELMACHER (identifying with the victim) to QUERELLE (being the victim identifying with the many figures of the executioner), Fassbin-der's whole work revolved around the drama of 'identifying': as the very precondition of recognizing the self in the other and the other in the self, but also as a threat: where the self might abandon itself before it is ready to give itself away. With this as the central theme of his work, Fassbinder possessed one of the very few genuinely new visions of how the Germans he sought to reach might make contact again with their past, their desire for identity, without shunning the price needed to be paid for assuming a history from which in 1945 they had decided to cut themselves off, after seeing how far it had cut them off.

Body-Politics: Bad Guys and Gay Bodies

The logic of what I have been arguing here implies that if the past is as monstrous as that for which Fassbinder's generation felt obliged to account, then the representation in the light of which it has to 'make sense' will necessarily bear features of this monstrosity. Usually in the cinema, this becomes a question of verisimilitude, where the represented is supposed to approximate the depicted. But what might pass as costume drama for some national cinemas clearly will not do in the case of German history. Not to be a 'realist' filmmaker is thus as much a question of integrity, as it is, paradoxically, a matter of credibility. Put perhaps too bluntly, one might venture that, at a certain point, German post-war filmmakers confronted the fact that throughout most of its history (at least since the end of the First World War), the German cinema had achieved international fame mainly through its villains: Dr Caligari, The Golem, Dr Mabuse, Nosferatu, Rotwang, Jack the Ripper, 'M'. With Werner Herzog's films (AGUIRRE, FITZCARRALDO, NOSFERATU, COBRA VERDE), and Hans Jürgen Syberberg's OUR HITLER, the New German Cinema renewed a tradition where deep-seated Gothic self-representations meet equally deep-seated anti-German preconceptions. Less calculatingly, it is of course a matter of respect for the 'other' and of, precisely, assuming historical responsibility, when German films acknowledge the need to show not 'realistic' but 'credible' Germans, which must include credible villains. Without conforming to the stereotypes of the 'Hun' in popular culture, but without denying or disavowing the reality they parody either, German filmmakers have on occasion tried to create 'representative' figures whose relation to Germany takes a form that brings others close to that history, in terms that must include the incomprehensibility which is Nazism, Auschwitz, and the war, without presuming to 'represent' it. In other words, what would it mean to show yourself as 'bad' as the other says you are, and thereby at least recognize the speaking position of this other?

Insofar as the discussion of Fassbinder's sexual politics and the German cinema's 'mourning work' have both focussed on the construction of the victim, the necessary reversal of perspective here proposed requires one to ask what kind of investment his films have in the figuration of the villain. But while with Mario Adorf, Karlheinz Böhm and especially with the roles he gave to Gottfried John (e.g. Saitz IN A YEAR OF THIRTEEN MOONS and Reinhold in BERLIN ALEXANDERPLATZ), Fassbinder did create a number of suitably ambiguous and troubling villains,[52] he took the question of representation far more literally than his fellow-filmmakers, who – when we think of Herzog, Wenders, Syberberg – were always willing to become the cultural ambassadors of a better Germany, a role Fassbinder resolutely refused.

In its place, there was his own persona: arrogant and sentimental, driven and masochistic, lucid and inarticulate, poetic and brutal, hypersensitive and coarsely vulgar. His appearance, in the meantime, carefully fashioned to accommodate, but also to transcend 'the ugly German', gave him the mask, the shield through which he could regulate distance and proximity, nakedness and disguise. Perhaps it is after all not surprising that few Germans wanted to recognize themselves in him: he was not a 'good' German nor a dutiful son, prepared to apologize politely to the world about his parents possibly having been wrong. An unshaven, dishevelled, beer-bellied monster, he seemed visibly pleased to stick out in the smooth *Wirtschafts*-wonderland. On the other hand, so calculated was this appearance that it is safe to assume that it was more than an affront, more than an obscene gesture to give himself the space to breathe. What is so visibly there is first of all a body, vulnerable and mortal, unavailable for the usual inscriptions of identity and coherence in the world of show business or the media. It therefore pays to give attention to the way the director's body and voice enter so many of his films – from the voice-over commentary in EFFI BRIEST and BERLIN ALEXAN-DERPLATZ, to his acting parts in THE AMERICAN SOLDIER, WHITY, BEWARE OF THE HOLY WHORE, FOX AND HIS FRIENDS, GERMANY IN AUTUMN, MARIA BRAUN, and LILI MARLEEN, including a cameo-appearance as movie spectator in VERONIKA VOSS. That a more classical director comes to mind at this point – Alfred Hitchcock – may not be altogether an accident, and as with Hitchcock it would be seriously underestimating Fassbinder's 'body-politics' if one saw these personal appearances merely as a play of cinephile citations and self-references. In this, he is also close to the Orson Welles of LADY FROM SHANGHAI in the use he makes of the 'persona' he constructed for himself and the 'body' he put on show, in films such as FOX AND HIS FRIENDS, or GERMANY IN AUTUMN.

Even placing him in the line of director-actor-showmen (with all the variations of ego-ideals and alter-egos this allows) does not, however, account for the roles he allocates himself in such films as MARIA BRAUN, LILI MARLEEN or BERLIN ALEXANDERPLATZ, where he plays a black marketeer, an underground resister, a pimp and go-between, each more unsavory than the other.[53] Taking up a moral space and function which, as I tried to indicate, is central to his universe, his physical presence intimates that what is at stake is not only a figure of economic reversal and sexual barter, but a stand-in for the ultimate mediator, 'saint and martyr', awaiting the Redeemer. The black marketeer, in other words, becomes a redemptive figure in a world of pure immanence, one obliged to negotiate mere debts where a more original guilt is at stake, but also unable to do so: this seems to me the ultimate significance of the Franz figure in his work, and the fact that Fassbinder so often embodies him, rather than merely identifying with him.[54]

More prosaically, the fat body also becomes the locus of resistance to so much that has to do with cinema, with image and self-image, with the mirror and the ego-ideal. Here, it lays itself across Germany's debt-and-guilt history, refusing the oedipal fate of sons becoming (like) fathers (in GERMANY IN AUTUMN): unassimilable to the body politic, it nonetheless claims its place within it. The paradox is that Fassbinder's films preached a body that evacuates itself of need, desire, of all means and manner of exchange, in order that it become an icon, an empty sign, because in the media world, in the history that is the media, only this kind of body, the self-identical body of the star remains, which is to say, has the power to signify – an epoch, a history, a life. Looked at closer, the very secret of Fassbinder's cinema, insofar as it speaks a truth about movie making, becomes apparent: the cinema has to destroy in order to create, it works with the same material as life and therefore can only substitute itself for life, which in turn requires a very particular form of sacrificial self-exposure.

This may explain the irony that as a movie icon, Fassbinder's body is in its own way as powerful as any the German cinema has bequeathed to the century, as memorable as that of Emil Jannings and Marlene Dietrich, Conrad Veidt and Peter Lorre. In this double, and doubly paradoxical sense, his body has become the untranscendable limit of exchange, as if Fassbinder had 'resolved' in his own way the question I started with ('his life *or* his films, his life *and* his films?) by creating a body of work in the literal sense, in that, accepting its ungainly shape and what it seemed to connote, he reinvented his body in the image of his work, gave to it an essential part of the meaning of his work, and thus made himself and it enter history.[55]

And yet, Fassbinder risks having lived and died in vain, if this work remains mere movie lore. Germany, no longer disavowing Fascism, Auschwitz, or its role in the disasters of the 20th century, is simply adding their representations to its national heritage, in order to move on. The turn to the body and its identifications has not happened: no Franz Biberkopf has recognized his Reinhold, no Erwin has turned into Elvira to make an Anton Saitz love him. In this sense, Fassbinder's films do have something to say about Germany after unification, if anyone cared to look and listen.

These remarks may remind one why Fassbinder has been an unfashionable filmmaker to commemorate, and why he remains a difficult German to celebrate. The inscription of awkwardly human, all too imperfect bodies into the social symbolic, or of non-equivalence into the different personal and public economies hardly seems a promising project, at a time when the ideal of perfect exchange rules unchallenged and unchecked. Yet it is fair to say that when one is prepared to reflect about the world this leaves, Fassbinder's parables of non-innocent victims, unsavory saviors and scapegoat villains may yet come to seem uncannily apt. They may in fact already be timely, given that the 'new Europe' whose in turn brutally bloody and murkily bureaucratic emergence we are witnessing has created another of those historical moments of crisis so prized by Fassbinder, where not only the formerly command economies of Central and Eastern Europe, but 'developing' along with 'developed' societies have become as much 'black markets' as 'common markets', on which the very currencies of exchange – whether economic, ethical or interpersonal – are seriously in doubt.

Appendix One

A Commented Filmography

...wer jetzt kein Haus hat baut sich keines mehr.[1]

The House That Rainer Built

In the course of several interviews, Fassbinder returned to a remark he had made early in his career, to the effect that his films are like a house. In 1982, he put it like this: 'I want to build a house with my films. Some are the cellar, some the walls, and others still, are the windows. But I hope that in the end, it is a house.'[2] It is a suggestive, if also somewhat facile metaphor.[3] It gives a glimpse of Fassbinder's 'houselessness' which is not the same as homelessness, and of course, it is a metaphor that suggests Germany, a house bombed to the ground, in ruins, rebuilt, divided, and to many in the 1970s, a mere façade.[4]

This commented filmography picks up the metaphor of the house indirectly, in order to complement the more obvious structuring principle, that of the chronology, and as a counter-weight to the authorial unity of the self-expressive, self-sufficient 'work'. While Fassbinder's spatial image is therefore a telling one also in its wider cultural resonances, a chronological division of his work is in fact no less suggestive, and no less misleading. At first glance, Fassbinder's films fall conveniently into distinct genres, which in turn can be divided into periods: the years 1969 to 1970 (the gangster films), 1971 to 1976 (the melodramas), and 1976 to 1981 (the German history films). But such a classification, even if it does not altogether violate either the films' chronology or Fassbinder's stylistic develop-ment, leaves unexamined some of the pressures that provoked these changes, such as the desire to reach different audiences (from 'underground' to art house to mainstream national and international spectators), the different budgets and financing conditions, and also the undoubtedly genuine change of outlook following the encounter with the cinema of Douglas Sirk.

As to conveying the sense of coherence without giving the illusion of a 'rounded' work, one can point to externally and internally unifying markers. There is, for instance, the basic structural configuration: the triangles of relationships, usually open-ended (in Fassbin-der's life) but forming vicious circles in the films, where they are at first male-centred, and later centred on women. Among the male characters, one can speak of the seven lives of Franz B (eight, if one includes *Der Müll, die Stadt und der Tod*) and ask what does he stand for? Is he a 'holy fool' or 'merely' a masochist, is he stupid and naive or does he have second sight? The men Franz loves, the Brunos, Eugens, Reinholds seem unworthy of such love, but they possess a mysterious power that translates itself into a hold almost beyond death: 'you in me, more than myself'. The women start out as prostitutes, devoted to their pimp. They accept this uneven relationship, money from many, in exchange for loving one as (God)given. But they also betray their men to the police, to other men, and then weep at their grave (the fear of the women's infidelity, of their power to deceive and dissimulate, of betrayal as their natural weapon makes the early heroines sharply drawn caricatures of a recognizable male phantasm). This figure is invariably associated with Hanna Schygulla, who is allowed, via expiring as Effi Briest, to metamorphose into the archetypal strong woman of the later films, her instinct for survival still intact, her infidelity become intelligence, her prostitution a showbiz career and her love the very signifier of impossibility.

Matters become more complicated where Hanna Schygulla is replaced by Margit Carstensen, Fassbinder's other incarnation/projection of the feminine: in MARTHA, PETRA VON KANT, FEAR OF FEAR, SATAN'S BREW, the plays *Blut am Halsband der Katze* and *Bremer Freiheit*, MOTHER KÜSTER, THE THIRD GENERATION she is the demanding woman with a strong urge to test the other's power to subdue her, ice-cold and masochistic at the same time. In the history films, it is the women who love, and the men who cheat on them, but in complicated ways, because of central importance is a pact, to mediate between (impossible) love and (intolerable) marriage. BERLIN ALEXANDERPLATZ brings both the men and the women together once more, in a massive panorama of all the possible combinations of male and female binding and bonding, violence and tenderness, suffering and bliss...

What also unifies the work is the team, which consisted of a remarkably stable infrastructure: Peer Raben for the music, Kurt Raab for the sets, later Harry Baer (as 'artistic assistant' and production manager); the women in charge of the editing (first Thea Eymez, then Juliane Lorenz), the woman in charge of costumes (Barbara Baum), the continuity assistant Renate Leiffer; the three cameramen, Dietrich Lohmann and Xaver Schwarzenberger, but above all Michael Ballhaus who shot twelve films with Fassbinder after which he thought it best to move on. Lesser known figures behind the scenes were his producers (Michael Fengler with twelve films, and Peter Berling, apart from his most important television producer, Peter Märthesheimer) and accountants (after Raben's disastrous stint, Fassbinder's mother).

The second unifying factor were, of course, the actors. The extended family (mostly playing supporting parts, like Irm Hermann and Ingrid Caven, or occasionally starring, like Kurt Raab in BOLWIESER and SATAN'S BREW and Harry Baer in GODS OF THE PLEAGUE and JAILBAIT) and some ex-members of the theatre troup (Ursula Strätz, Rudolf Waldemar Brehm); the 'stars' Hanna Schygulla, Margit Carstensen, Elisabeth Trissenaar, Barbara Sukowa who generally did not belong to the inner circle; regulars like Ulli Lommel, Peter Chatel, Gottfried John, Volker Spengler who were professional actors, as were those familiar from television series like Klaus Löwitsch or Walter Sedlmayr; then, Günther Kaufmann, El Hedi ben Salem, Armin Meier: Fassbinder's lovers who had small parts, or for whom parts were created, so the director could have them around; and finally, the stars from Germany's commercial cinema, whom Fassbinder consciously courted, in some cases re-launching their careers: Karin Baal, Karlheinz Böhm, Ivan Desny, Cornelia Froboess, Adrian Hoven, Brigitte Mira, Luise Ullrich, Barbara Valentin. To these reassuring landmarks in

Fassbinder's world can be added the more exotic appearances by international celebrities: Eddie Constantine and Jeanne Moreau, Dirk Bogarde and Andrea Ferréol, Macha Méril, Bulle Ogier and Anna Karina, Gian Carlo Giannini and Mel Ferrer, Lou Castel, Brad Davis and Franco Nero.

These faces and voices, in their repetition and transformation gave a common feel to the films, a generic identity, like American studios in the 1930s who had invested much in building up supporting casts in order to furnish brand-identity. This Fassbinder achieved, and more successfully than any other director ever before in the German cinema, where finding 'extras' (i.e. reliable and capable bit-players) was reputedly very difficult.[5]

Not the least important element of cohesion in Fassbinder's films is the sound, mainly provided by Peer Raben, often his own compositions which uncannily blend with the recorded archive music taking in the Western repertoir from Vivaldi to Mahler, from Schubert to the Rolling Stones, from Verdi to the Walker Brothers. As instantly recognizable as the lighting, the decor and costumes, it is what gives the tactile presence and spatial intimacy its sensuous surface, but it also suggests a history for the characters' bodies and a utopia for their longings. The Fassbinder 'world' thus possesses a consistency, texture and verisimilitude entirely within its own terms, at once wholly artificial and wholly historical, the product of very distinct talents and unmistakeably the emanation of a singularity – that of the director.

A return to chronology and periodization helps bring to the fore certain thematic continuities, while also marking inner shifts and tensions in the narrative focus. For instance, the cycle about outsiders, petty criminals and pimps ostensibly shows the interaction of individuals in a group, yet the underlying dynamics is slanted towards exploring male friendships (LOVE IS COLDER THAN DEATH, GODS OF THE PLAGUE, THE AMERICAN SOLDIER). The melodramas centre on couples (quite often heterosexual: THE MERCHANT OF FOUR SEASONS, JAILBAIT, FEAR EATS THE SOUL, MARTHA), yet the ironic discrepancies of expectations and tragic incompatibilities between the partners suggest that something beyond the difficulties of domestic bonding is at issue. In the films about Germany – gravitating around the so-called BRD Trilogy (THE MARRIAGE OF MARIA BRAUN, LOLA, VERONIKA VOSS) and LILI MARLEEN – it is not only the historical canvas that matters: in each film the central magnetic pull is a strong woman character. Finally, as Fassbinder's cinematic testament, BERLIN ALEXANDERPLATZ combines the fascination about male friendships with an admiration for independent women, in a narrative replete with impossible heterosexual couples.

It seems, then, that the shift in genres, from gangster film to melodrama, from domestic drama to historic spectacle is less the result of a formal decision, or a cinephile move from one favourite Hollywood director (say, Raoul Walsh or Michael Curtiz) to another (Douglas Sirk), than the consequence of Fassbinder looking to genres for patterns of established meanings whose recognized truth he could either push further (as in the Sirk melodramas, giving them a very local habitat in Germany and Munich) or brush against the grain (as in the stylized gangster films, and the re-writing of the 1940s woman's picture in THE MARRIAGE OF MARIA BRAUN and LILI MARLEEN).

By concentrating on the narrative line, but also the structural features, the commentary tries to isolate typical plot configurations, but not necessarily in order to identify a Fassbinder *Ur-film*. Nor is there a desire to affirm, across the many echoes from film to film, from cycle to cycle, the author tautologically identical with himself.[6] Rather, the moves which follow, from film to film, describe a kind of spiral, digging deeper but also becoming more shallow. A cliché used by Fassbinder himself – that of the vicious circles – has served in a previous chapter as an orientation topos, to describe one of the inner movements of the films, alternatively giving rise to cognitive double-binds or three-dimensional picture puzzles. Here, the descending/ascending movement of the spiral also alludes to the different levels of interpretation identified throughout, from the documentary to the allegorical, from classically realist to the mimetic impulse of mirroring the spectator-screen relationship within the film. In this respect, the study of an author cannot but pick its way as best it can across the minefield of what interpretation is today, torn between modernism's rage for reading, realism's celebration of narratorial self-effacement, and postmodernism's diffracted and decentred textual allegories.

If Fassbinder's films can be understood as a corpus consisting of so many 'themes and variations', they are also 'rewritings': of basic human situations, of films and film-forms, of 'work-in-progress'. Incomplete and always already retrospective/reflective, Fassbinder's work has sustained a remarkable degree of openness, accommodating often eclectic sources, as well as contingencies, accidents, resistances. His impatience not to be fixed, for instance in literary adaptations, or the determination to subject even his fiercest admirers to tests of loyalty gave his films a dialogical dimension and their sequence a very peculiar scansion, as if one were in the presence of a body manifesting itself mostly by its irregular breathing. Perhaps Fassbinder the author did not so much express himself and inhabit his world as exhale himself and divest himself of his life.

Against this might be held that Fassbinder's films are not only autobiographical to a hitherto unparalleled degree, perpetually dramatizing quarrels and rivalries among the clique he surrounded himself with, but that he dwelt over and over on a rather cramped site of human behaviour: the vicious circles of emotional, sexual and economic exploitation he so often invoked in the interviews. A psychoanalytical interpretation of his films – the ambivalent dependence on mothers, the absence of credible father figures, the need for close friends to become the hero's double – can easily show the almost claustrophobic consistency of recurring motifs, from the aptly titled, but heavily disguised LOVE IS COLDER THAN DEATH through more than forty film and television productions, to the intensely personal celebration of love and death in QUERELLE and the apotheosis of Franz's crucifixion in the epilogue of BERLIN ALEXANDERPLATZ. Only in his contribution to GERMANY IN AUTUMN, an omnibus film on the repercussions of the 1977 hostage crisis and the triple suicide of the core of the Baader-Meinhof group, did Fassbinder seem to show himself (literally in the opening episode) naked and vulnerable, locked up with his lover and mother in a Munich apartment painted black, while police sirens and screeching car tires can be heard outside. Yet these highly conventionalized cinematic clichés of *angst* should warn the unwary: they indicate how much even this 'baring of the soul' was part of Fassbinder's fictionalized persona. He was and remained above all a storyteller, and probably the only German filmmaker this century to possess such a broad sympathetic vision of human beings, encompassing enough to engender (and 'gender') a world which is unmistakeably his and at the same time offers itself to be if not entered then, in any event, recognized by others.

The Gangster Films

Fassbinder's first creative period as filmmaker begins with four more or less self-conscious and stylized reworkings of gangster films, the Hollywood example having been filtered through such pastiche versions of the genre as A BOUT DE SOUFFLE, BANDE À PART, VIVRE SA VIE, directed by Jean Luc Godard between 1959 and 1963. It is a matter of speculation whether these models came to Fassbinder directly from the *nouvelle vague*, or via the debut films of Rudolf Thome, Klaus Lemke and Roland Klick, three 'tough-guy' directors also based in Munich in the late 1960s. What is more to the point is that Fassbinder's efforts have a quite distinct personal urgency absent from other bravura exercises, whether intended as homages, pastiches or parodies.[7]

LIEBE IST KÄLTER ALS DER TOD (Love Is Colder than Death)
d: Rainer Werner Fassbinder; sc: Rainer Werner Fassbinder; c: Dietrich Lohmann; ed: Franz Walsch (= Rainer Werner Fassbinder); m: Peer Raben, Holger Münzer; lp: Hanna Schygulla, Rainer Werner Fassbinder, Hans Hirschmüller, Katrin Schaake, Ingrid Caven, Ursula Strätz, Irm Hermann, Wil Rabenbauer (= Peer Raben), Kurt Raab, Rudolf Waldemar Brem, Yaak Karsunke; r: 88 min, b/w; p: antiteater-X-Film (Peer Raben, Thomas Schamoni), 1969.

In LOVE IS COLDER THAN DEATH, the occasional bank-robber Franz (played by Fassbinder) refuses to join The Syndicate, preferring to work for his own account. While Joanna (Hanna Schygulla), whose pimp is Franz, sulkily waits for him to marry her, Franz invites his friend, the smooth and handsome Bruno (Ulli Lommel), to move in. Bruno, who is working for The Syndicate, has orders to befriend Franz and accepts Franz's offer. By way of putting pressure on Franz, Bruno commits murders for which the police suspect Franz. Jealous of Bruno, Joanna betrays both of them to the police. But instead of her being killed by the hired gunman from The Syndicate, it is Bruno who dies in the ensuing melée with the police, while Franz and Joanna make their getaway.

GÖTTER DER PEST (Gods of the Plague)
d: Rainer Werner Fassbinder, Michael Fengler; sc: Rainer Werner Fassbinder; c: Dietrich Lohmann; ed: Franz Walsch (= Rainer Werner Fassbinder); m: Peer Raben; lp: Harry Baer, Hanna Schygulla, Margarethe von Trotta, Günther Kaufmann, Carla Aulaulu, Ingrid Caven, Yaak Karsunke; r: 91 min, b/w; p: Antiteater Munich, 1970.

GODS OF THE PLAGUE is both a variation on and a sequel to LOVE IS COLDER THAN DEATH. Straight from prison, Franz (now played by Harry Baer) looks up his old girlfriend Joanna (Hanna Schygulla) and discovers that his brother has been shot. Leaving the possessive Joanna for the more languid Margarethe (Margarethe von Trotta), Franz prefers the company of the 'Gorilla' (Günther Kaufmann) who freely admits that he killed Franz's brother. Franz, together with the 'Gorilla' and an ageing gangster, plans to rob a supermarket, not knowing that each of his jilted girlfriends has decided to betray him to the police. Shot dead in the botched robbery, Franz is avenged by the 'Gorilla', who kills the woman in the pornographer's shop (Carla Aulaulu), rightly suspecting her to have told Joanna about the intended raid, before succumbing to his injuries. The surviving women make up the mourners at Franz's funeral.

RIO DAS MORTES

d: Rainer Werner Fassbinder; sc: Rainer Werner Fassbinder, based on an idea of Volker Schlöndorff; c: Dietrich Lohmann; ed: Thea Eymèsz; m: Peer Raben; lp: Hanna Schygulla, Michael König, Günther Kaufmann, Katrin Schaake, Joachim von Mengershausen, Lilo Pempeit, Franz Maron, Rainer Werner Fassbinder; r: 84 min, col; p: Janus Film und Fernsehen / antiteater-X-Film, 1970.

In RIO DAS MORTES, Michael (Michael König) and Günther (Günther Kaufmann) discover an old map of Peru, supposedly showing the location of a buried treasure, near the Rio das Mortes. Against the pleas of Hanna (Hanna Schygulla) who not only dismisses their ideas about getting rich with sheep farming and cotton planting as fantastic, but also wants to marry and start a family with Michael, the two friends decide to emigrate. After finally persuading a rich widow to put up the money, they depart for the airport, followed by Hanna intent on shooting them as they step on the plane. She is foiled when a car suddenly blocks her view, and the two men depart, unaware of her presence.

DER AMERIKANISCHE SOLDAT (The American Soldier)

d: Rainer Werner Fassbinder; sc: Rainer Werner Fassbinder; c: Dietrich Lohmann; ed: Thea Eymèsz; m: Peer Raben; lp: Karl Scheydt, Elga Sorbas, Margarethe von Trotta, Hark Bohm, Ingrid Caven, Rainer Werner Fassbinder, Ulli Lommel, Irm Hermann; r: 80 min, b/w; p: antiteater Munich, 1970.

In THE AMERICAN SOLDIER Ricky (Karl Scheydt), a German-American Vietnam veteran visiting his mother in Munich is hired by three policemen to eliminate a number of suspects about whom the police have insufficient evidence for a legal arrest. Ricky agrees, and after meeting his old friend Franz Walsch (Fassbinder), he proceeds with his contracts. One of them turns out to be the woman who has fallen in love with him, but he kills her nonetheless. On his way home with Franz, the two friends are shot down at the train station by the police, who now have no further use for Ricky.

The underlying pattern in each film plays up the misogyny and homoeroticism implicit in many a classic *film noir*: a male friendship, thwarted by a jealous woman, ends in deception and violent death. Yet Fassbinder shifts the accent of his plots, underscoring paradoxical or tragic ironies: for his women, betrayal is the most authentic because most desperate proof of love, and the men show their manliness, and thus their worthiness as objects of love, by responding to a symbolic mandate: 'orders are orders', the Gorilla explains, after killing Franz's brother, an admission which only firms up Franz's intention to 'do a bank job' with him. Of Franz's other friends, Bruno (in LOVE IS COLDER THAN DEATH) works for The Syndicate and Ricky (in THE AMERICAN SOLDIER) for the police, after having been a volunteer in Vietnam. Similarly, Günther (in RIO DAS MORTES) does his German military service as a volunteer in order to prove his patriotism, being the son of a black GI stationed in Bavaria after the war. Such apparent gaps in the characters' motivation as well as their depravity and casual evil are dignified in these films by the stark schematism which love seems to impose on all the protagonists, male and female. One might object that this overlooks the basic bias, according to which the men's open duplicity (they are contract killers, they set up their best friend, or grass on him) only intensifies Franz's desire, whereas the women's covert duplicity (betrayal of the men to the authorities) is depicted as the natural state of their love and therefore leaves Franz indifferent. But this asymmetry is finally placed within another symmetry, the interchangeability of love and death, where men as much as women live under the same iron law: that of moral paradox and emotional perversity as the true logic of love. Fassbinder's formalism of structure thus not only gives his films a didactic rigour, it is the very condition for their moments of passion and intensity.

In other respects than narrative structure, the four films are quite different: in mood for instance, where GODS OF THE PLAGUE is relentlessly somber, while LOVE IS COLDER THAN DEATH tries at times a playful tone, as in the shop-lifting scene in a supermarket, with hand-held camerawork suggesting the carefree 'swinging sixties' and young people out for a lark. Also, the films often move from extreme stylization to moments of documentary realism, notably in RIO DAS MORTES. While Munich does not really become the movie capital of mythic presence[8] that the films of Truffaut, Melville and Godard fashion for Paris, a vivid portrait nonetheless emerges of the Munich suburbs and the *Hinterland*, especially in the scenes where Franz and the Gorilla look up the ageing 'heavy' Joe in GODS OF THE PLAGUE or the rain-sodden countryside following the raid on the supermarket. As political statements, the gangster films are about social outsiders and failures by the standards of the real world, who are the more human for their capacity in love, hurt, ambition (however second-hand their dreams might be).[9] Revolving around oddly assorted and badly matched couples, the narrative centre of the films is mostly 'Franz Walsh' who, as his name advertises, is modelled as much on Franz Biberkopf, the protagonist of BERLIN ALEXANDERPLATZ, as he is in the line of James Cagney's Hollywood gangsters, especially that monster of a mother-complex, Pat Cody from Raoul Walsh's WHITE HEAT.

Violence, Self-Aggression and In-Groups

The gangster films represent only part of Fassbinder's output during 1969 and 1970. A film version of his first stage play, *Katzelmacher*, is the most experimental of his early works, eliciting as much praise for its formal purity (the flat, frontal scenes, alternating with repeated forward tracking shots) as it appalled critics like Wim Wenders by its calculated coldness.[10] Brecht's influence is visible in the tableau-like scenes depicting the boredom and frustration of four suburban Munich couples who take out their spite, greed and sexual rivalry on a hapless immigrant worker. Generally concerned with the dynamics of in-groups, and the cycles of aggression they inflict on each other, as desperate tests and tentatively seeking reassurance, the films from this period are at once an extension of Fassbinder's theatre work with the *anti-teater* group, as a reflection on it, and thus entailing also a distancing and a detachment.

KATZELMACHER

d: Rainer Werner Fassbinder; sc: Rainer Werner Fassbinder, based on his play; c: Dietrich Lohmann; ed: Franz Walsch (= Rainer Werner Fassbinder); m: Franz Schubert; lp: Hanna Schygulla, Rudolf Waldemar Brem, Lilith Ungerer, Elga Sorbas, Irm Hermann, Harry Baer, Hans Hirschmüller, Rainer Werner Fassbinder; r: 88 min, b/w; p: antiteater-X-Film (Peer Raben), 1969.

The plot of KATZELMACHER is once more an elaborate conjugation of interdependent couples: 'Marie belongs to Erich, Paul sleeps with Helga, Peter lets himself be kept by Elisabeth, and Rosy does it with Franz, for money'.[11] This mutually sustaining network of exploitation and aggression is exacerbated by the arrival of Jorgos the Greek (played by Fassbinder), who rents a room from Elizabeth. While the men immediately gang up against him and use physical violence to scare him away, the women's responses are more ambivalent, be it because they know they can play off his reputed sexual potency against their own lovers (Helga, Rosy), because they want to use him economically (Elisabeth needs him as a lodger in order to keep Peter), or because they are genuinely attracted by his otherness (Maria).

The static takes and slow tracking shots draw constant attention to the presence of the camera, and Peer Raben's Schubertian music ironically counterpoints the action. The deadpan, deliberately wooden dialogue is intended to point to the characters' stark emotional isolation from each other, and it conveys well what a critic has called Fassbinder's 'poetry of the inarticulate'.[12] Shot in an overexposed, grainy black-and-white, its centre of attention is Maria (Hanna Schygulla) as the only one to side with Jorgos. KATZELMACHER can be seen as a particularly prescient film, in the light of the resurgence of xenophobia and racism after German unification, but at the time, it was more in line with the neo-Marxist analysis of the authoritarian personality, registering the fascist potential of people without jobs, education or social prospects ('I'm going to sign up in the Army, it's better than work' one of the men says at the end). What mitigates KATZELMACHER's didacticism and makes the film quite disturbing is that the laconic-poetic speech patterns in the verbal exchanges renders these bigots funny as well as outrageous, in ways familar whenever 'language speaks the subject'.

WARUM LÄUFT HERR R. AMOK (Why Does Herr R Run Amok?)

d: Rainer Werner Fassbinder; sc: Rainer Werner Fassbinder, Michael Fengler; c: Dietrich Lohmann; ed: Franz Walsch (= Rainer Werner Fassbinder), Michael Fengler; m: Christian Anders; lp: Kurt Raab, Lilith Ungerer, Amadeus Fengler, Harry Baer, Hanna Schygulla, Peer Raben, Irm Hermann, Ingrid Caven; r: 88 min, col; p: Antiteater/Maran Munich, 1970.

WHY DOES HERR R RUN AMOK? focuses even more strongly on what separates conscious behaviour and unconscious drives, expressed in dead speech as evidence of a society gone numb. In several other respects, it marks a break from earlier films. Co-directed by Michael Fengler, it was Fassbinder's first film in colour, and stars Kurt Raab in one of his most memorable roles. No longer set in the suburbs or among the social rejects, the film features model office worker Herr R in whose steady life monotony has taken over: television in the evenings with his wife and son, banalities at the dinner table, dull Sunday walks in the park. There are of course the worries about promotion at work, and his son does so badly at school that migraines send Herr R. to the doctor. Growing ever more morose and listless, he is briefly cheered by the visit of an old school friend (Peer Raben) with whom he sings the church hymns that used to be the torment of their boyhood. One evening, irritated by the chatter of his wife (Lilith Ungerer) with their neighbour (Irm Hermann) at the apartment door, he batters both women to death with an ornate candlestick and then kills his son. The next morning he hangs himself in the lavatory at the office.

Relentless in its insistence on banality of speech and gesture, the film hovers skilfully between appealing to the audiences' sadism and their masochism, exploiting the extremes of spectatorial identification and making its structures apparent, not least by playing out scenes with a pedantry reminiscent of Warhol. Unlike the previous films, whose narratives were driven by the balancing acts of group dynamics, WHY DOES HERR R RUN AMOK? follows a single line, accelerating suddenly in its downward plunge towards the inevitable, bloody end. Aggression, simmering beneath the surface, and emerging only once or twice as musical and humorous relief (e.g. in the scene in the record shop where Herr R makes the shop-assistants giggle by singing out of tune, or with his schoolfriend intoning church music), finally turns outward before it becomes self-aggression. With Kurt Raab at the centre, WHY DOES HERR R RUN AMOK? points forward to Raab's other starring roles for Fassbinder, as the mad and madly lucid poet Kranz in SATAN'S BREW, and the less demonic, though no less emotionally supercharged hapless hero in BOLWIESER. Structurally, WHY DOES HERR R RUN AMOK? anticipates THE MERCHANT OF FOUR SEASONS where the winding down of a life is even more subterranean, more grindingly painful and slow, and all the aggression is turned inward, first by a heart attack, and then in a methodically performed suicide.

DIE NIKLASHAUSER FART (The Niklashausen Journey)

d: Rainer Werner Fassbinder, Michael Fengler; sc: Rainer Werner Fassbinder, Michael Fengler; c: Dietrich Lohmann; ed: Thea Eymèsz, Franz Walsch (= Rainer Werner Fassbinder); m: Peer Raben, Amon Düül II; lp: Michael König, Michael Gordon, Rainer Werner Fassbinder, Hanna Schygulla, Walter Sedlmayr, Margit Carstensen, Franz Maron, Kurt Raab, Michael Fengler, Peer Raben, Magdalena Montezuma; r: 86 min, col; p: Janus Film und Fernsehen, 1970.

One of Fassbinder's least known films is THE NIKLASHAUSEN JOURNEY, made under the impact of the failure of the student movement of 1968, when the growing awareness of the problems of neo-colonialism in the wake of the Vietnam war and the liberation struggles in Latin America led to the formation of a radical, 'terrorist' wing from within the extra-parliamentary left. While political terrorism is a subject Fassbinder was to return to in several other films (GERMANY IN AUTUMN, MOTHER KÜSTER'S TRIP TO HEAVEN, THE THIRD GENERATION), the specific issues, and above all, the cinematic form chosen for them, remain unique to NIKLASHAUSEN. Its filmic forebears are Godard's WEEKEND (1968) and Glauber Rocha's ANTONIO DAS MORTES (1969), both films that mix declamatory rhetoric and readings from tracts with staged scenes, moving freely between past and present, and putting characters in historical costume and present day uniforms. Fassbinder based himself loosely on the story of a 15th century folk hero, Hans Böhm, who following a vision of the Virgin Mary proclaimed, in the company of an anabaptist priest, the gospel of social equality until he was arrested by the soldiers of the Bishop of Würzburg and burnt at the stake.

In the film, Böhm (Michael König) is a lay-preacher who finds support among a band of poor peasants and students, but who is 'masterminded' by the black monk (Fassbinder, in black leather jacket). Rejected by the Church authorities, Böhm radicalizes his social demands, but his supporters want a saint and miracleworker, while his benefactress, a rich society lady (Margit Carstensen), supports him mainly because she is sexually infatuated with him. Eventually, two German policemen, assisted by American Military Police, track the group down at a camping site, where they arrest the leaders and kill most of the followers. Crucified in the midst of wrecked cars piled sky-high, the socialist saint inspires a popular uprising, and under the leadership of the black monk, the surviving followers regroup, take to the hills, in order to lead, Che Guevara style, a revolutionary army to – one presumes – certain defeat.

Although there are a number of motifs which link NIKLASHAUSEN to other Fassbinder films (not least the role he gave himself as mediator, go-between and master-minder), it is best seen as his contribution not so much to Godard's or Rocha's political counter-cinema (for which it is too cynical and pessimistic), but to the debate of the New German Cinema about the failure of the radical left, and the filmmakers' resolve not to make 'political' films: THE NIKLASHAUSEN JOURNEY could, for instance, be usefully compared to Werner Herzog's SIGNS OF LIFE and EVEN DWARFS STARTED SMALL, Hans Jürgen Syberberg's SAN DOMINGO and SCARABEA: HOW MUCH EARTH DOES A MAN NEED, Alexander Kluge's ARTISTES AT THE TOP OF THE BIG TOP: DISORIENTED, and Edgar Reitz' CARDILLAC. All are cautionary, often highly abstruse and allegorical films about the filmmaker as false prophet and the audience/public as unreliable revolutionary agents of history.

WHITY

d: Rainer Werner Fassbinder; sc: Rainer Werner Fassbinder; c: Michael Ballhaus; ed: Franz Walsch (= Rainer Werner Fassbinder), Thea Eymèsz; m: Peer Raben; lp: Günther Kaufmann, Hanna Schygulla, Ulli Lommel, Harry Baer; r: 95 min, col, Cinemascope; p: Atlantis Film/Antiteater-X-Film, 1970.

Nothing at first sight could be further from an allegory of the political events of the day than WHITY, made the month before NIKLASHAUSEN. Set in 1878, in the prebellum American South (and shot in Almeria, Spain), it depicts life on a plantation, where the owner (Ron Randell), his wife (Katrin Schaake) and two sons, one a homosexual (Ulli Lommel), the other a half-wit (Harry Baer), have their eyes on Whity (Günther Kaufmann), a mulatto and bastard son, who serves as butler but also everyone's whipping-boy and confidant. When several family members want him to dispose of the others, Whity decides to kill them all and escapes with the saloon singer (Hanna Schygulla), the one person not to have exploited him. As they make for the desert it is clear that with no water or provisions, they are destined to perish, a fate they seem to accept with joyous abandon.

WHITY may seem a mere collection of remembered movie cliches and citations, from Walsh's BAND OF ANGELS and Vincente Minnelli's HOME FROM THE HILL to John Huston's TREASURE OF THE SIERRA MADRE, assembled into a brooding but also ghoulish soap opera. The film was uniformly disliked when shown at the Berlin Festival in 1971, though with hindsight it is much clearer where it fits into the work as a whole: in its emphasis on the group knit tightly by mutual hatred, jealousy and envy it picks up from KATZELMACHER (but also, perhaps, from William Faulkner's SANCTUARY); like WHY DOES HERR R RUN AMOK?, it shows an atmosphere of sullen tedium suddenly flaring into murderous violence; its dissection of family life foreshadows many of the films to follow, among them THE MERCHANT OF FOUR SEASONS and CHINESE ROULETTE; and while critics at the time were alienated by the artificiality of the setting and the technicolour-and-cinemascope exoticism, WHITY has surprising parallels with Pasolini's TEOREMA, made the year before, featuring a mysterious visitor whose presence shakes a bourgeois family to its foundations. With TEOREMA in mind, WHITY may not be that far from THE NIKLAUSHAUSEN JOURNEY after all, especially with the alien male at the centre, both sanctifed and vilified, who causes cathartic violence and abandons modern (city) life for the desert or the mountains. Even if such a vantage point 'from outside' remains ultimately a vain hope, both films suggest what might be meant by the 'utopian' perspective the director so often mentioned in interviews.[13]

WHITY has also been seen as Fassbinder's bid to aspire to the sultry, but also camp romanticism of a legionnaire's movie like Sternberg's MOROCCO,[14] though more striking is the fact that there can be no happy ending for this heterosexual couple, however promisingly mismatched a white singer from the local hotel might be with a black servant who has just killed his masters.

WARNUNG VOR EINER HEILIGEN NUTTE (Beware of the Holy Whore)

d: Rainer Werner Fassbinder; sc: Rainer Werner Fassbinder; c: Michael Ballhaus; ed: Franz Walsch (= Rainer Werner Fassbinder) Thea Eymèsz; m: Peer Raben, Gaetano Donizetti, Elvis Presley, Ray Charles, Leonard Cohen, Spooky Tooth; lp: Lou Castell, Eddie Constantine, Hanna Schygulla, Marquard Bohm, Rainer Werner Fassbinder, Ulli Lommel, Margarethe von Trotta, Herb Andress, Werner Schroeter; r: 103 min, col; p: antiteater-X-Film Munich/Nova International (Peer Raben) Rome, 1971.

The difficulties during the shooting of WHITY are sometimes cited as the ostensible reason for one of the key films of the early period, the openly self-reflexive and self-critical BEWARE OF THE HOLY WHORE, the whore of the title being the cinema in general and filmmaking in particular. Comparable (*mutatis mutandis*) to Fellini's 8 1/2, and the opposite of Truffaut's DAY FOR NIGHT,[15] Fassbinder's meta-film was probably very much in Wim Wenders' mind when he made THE STATE OF THINGS.

BEWARE OF THE HOLY WHORE features the actors and the crew of a production on location in a Spanish coastal hotel first waiting for the arrival of the director Jeff (Lou Castel), the international star (Eddie Constantine, as himself), and then for film stock and production money from Germany. Amidst the boredom, backbiting, sexual intrigues and power-games, Jeff is obliged to throw violent tantrums in order to impose himself, with partial success, since at one point he is beaten up by the camera crew, with no-one coming forward to help him. As tempers fray, only Eddie Constantine keeps his cool, which earns him the admiration of Hanna (Hanna Schygulla) who also stays above the melée. Eventually, shooting gets under way, Jeff having successfully split himself between acting the oriental despot of the team's psychodrama and remaining the craftsman-engineer, who works according to a blueprint-masterplan, ready in his head.

While Wolfgang Limmer claims that BEWARE OF THE HOLY WHORE is indeed more or less a documentary of what happened in Almeria during the shooting of WHITY,[16] the autobiographical and anecdotal interpretation tends to obscure some crucial features: first of all, the fact that with this film Fassbinder was able to analyse very clearly the dynamics of leader and led, and the emotional intimacy between victim and victimizer in any situation involving power, sexuality and creativity.[17]

Equally lucid is the analysis of the mutual dependencies existing between Fassbinder and his team, ever since the days of the action-theatre, an experience here depicted from a great distance, the distance, however, reflecting also moral closeness and emotional empathy. This paradoxical stance allows Fassbinder to make out of the many kinds of 'whoring' necessary to the creative endeavour in a collective art such as theatre or film, a most elegantly interwoven, cogently developed, deceptively spontaneous narrative. In short, stepping back from what he suffered and made others suffer, while stepping towards what he knew best and cared about most, Fassbinder seems to have experienced neither personal catharsis nor moral enlightenement, but a technical breakthrough in respect of his story-telling skills and his control of the mise-en-scène of a large cast of characters, each of whom has a point of view to embody and a position to defend.

The Sirkean Melodramas

Prompted by his discovery in 1971 of the middle-class, middle-America melodramas of German emigré Hollywood director Douglas Sirk,[18] Fassbinder conceived of a cycle of films focussing on the impossibility of love and happiness in the bourgeois family. Adapted to a German environment, the Sirkean formula seemed to succeed remarkably well, resulting in some of his best-known films. The second phase of Fassbinder's work thus begins in 1971 with THE MERCHANT OF FOUR SEASONS, set like the Sirk movies in the 1950s.[19]

DER HÄNDLER DER VIER JAHRESZEITEN (The Merchant of Four Seasons)
d: Rainer Werner Fassbinder; sc: Rainer Werner Fassbinder; c: Dietrich Lohmann; ed: Thea Eymèsz; m: "Buona Notte" (Rocco Granata); lp: Hans Hirschmüller, Irm Hermann, Hanna Schygulla, Andrea Schober, Kurt Raab, Klaus Löwitsch, Karl Scheydt, Ingrid Caven; r: 89 min, col; p: Tango (Rainer Werner Fassbinder, Michael Fengler), 1972.

Hans (Hans Hirschmüller) returns home after a spell in the French Foreign Legion: to a frosty mother (Gusti Kreissl) and a bickering wife Irmgard (Irm Hermann). He starts a new life selling fruit from a pushcart in the backyards of Munich tenement houses. His weakness is alcohol, which helps him forget domestic misery and the memory of the love of his life (Ingrid Caven).

After a particularly ugly scene with his wife, Hans collapses with a heart attack at a family dinner. He recovers and takes an assistant, who becomes his friend. What Hans does not know is that this man had had a casual affair with his wife. Anxious to keep her secret and jealous of the men's friendship, Irmgard maneuvers his dimissal. This leaves Hans in a depression, only briefly relieved by the appearance of a former friend from the Legion, who moves in as a lodger and assistant. Less and less interested in either his home life or the fruit stand, Hans visits his favorite sister (Hanna Schygulla), but, busy finishing a translation, she has no time for him. He returns to beer and schnapps, and in a slow, painful session, punctuated by memories of abandonment and betrayal, Hans drinks himself to death in a bar, in full view of his friends. His wife and child having long ago accepted the lodger as Hans' substitute, it is business as usual at the fruit stand. At the funeral, only Hans' love of his life seems to mourn for him.

THE MERCHANT OF FOUR SEASONS broke new ground not least in offering a scrupulously observed milieu that lost none of its atmospheric realism by being at the service of a story whose schematic simplicity has the strength of a parable and the stark economy of a tragedy. Fassbinder, building on the fluid style of BEWARE OF THE HOLY WHORE, shows himself completely in control of the medium, able to switch tone and mood, from self-pity to violence to sentimentality, as Hans, for instance, after a night of drunken self-incrimination, returns home and beats his wife. A mise-en-scène both poignant and supremely confident in its timing of dramatic effects evokes complex states of feeling as in the scene where Hans listens to a Rocco Granata ballad, his body language suggesting sunshine and south, while the chair he is slumped in denotes the cramped functionalism of hire-purchase affluence.[20]

Shot either in simple, pastel colours, or in sumptuous reds and gray, depending on the emotional tenor of each scene, the film has the power to move, enlisting compassion for its hero but avoiding bathos. Even though most of the story is told from Hans' point of view (uncannily, this includes the funeral, thus delving deeply into the narcissistic and masochistic fantasy underlying the story), Fassbinder is able to extend sympathy and understanding to the other characters as well: the flinty scorn of Hans' mother (who had to raise a family without a husband) and the wife's nagging and scheming hysteria are seen as no more than the result of daily worries wearing the women down, choking their own capacity for love. Sirk taught Fassbinder not only how to extend his emotional range, to encompass the lives of middle-class people, but also the filmic means that carry the audience with him. A significant advance on WHY DOES HERR R RUN AMOK? (whose narrative line it repeats, but also inverts), where the middle-class family is shown 'from outside' and appears as a gross caricature, THE MERCHANT OF FOUR SEASONS brought Fassbinder his first popular success, while taking him closer to his avowed aim of being a German Hollywood director. It also advertised his predilection for the 1950s, the decade that featured in several of his subsequent melodramas.

WILDWECHSEL (Jailbait)
d: Rainer Werner Fassbinder; sc: Rainer Werner Fassbinder, based on the play by Franz Xaver Kroetz; c: Dietrich Lohmann; ed: Thea Eymèsz; m: Beethoven; lp: Jörg von Liebenfels, Ruth Drexel, Eva Mattes, Harry Baer, Hanna Schygulla, Kurt Raab, Karl Scheydt, Klaus Löwitsch; r: 102 min, col; p: Intertel, 1972.

JAILBAIT is a return to the world of KATZELMACHER or the gangster films, insofar as it deals with people who, unable even to begin to articulate their feelings, bury them in inane phrases and violent acts. Based on a play by Franz Xaver Kroetz, a Brechtian specializing in rural Bavarian social drama, JAILBAIT tells the love story of Hanni, a fourteen-year-old schoolgirl (Eva Mattes) and a nineteen-year-old working class boy (Harry Baer). Betrayed by a friend to the girl's parents, Franz goes to prison for seducing a minor. After his release, he gets Hanni pregnant, and to prove his love, murders her feared and hated father. Back in prison, Franz is told by Hanni that their child died at birth and that their love was 'merely physical'. Uncomprehending, he nods in agreement, while stretching out his hand to touch her.

Kroetz took objection to Fassbinder's adaptation, calling it pornographic, and then taking court action.[21] Out of a sociological and somewhat sentimental play about the narrowness of a class and the bigotry of a community, Fassbinder built a study of corrupt innocence, making the girl in all her sweetness a femme fatale as deadly to the male as Barbara Stanwyck in DOUBLY INDEMNITY. Eva Mattes as Hanni is the centre of the film, in a part which was to lead to key roles of the New German Cinema in films by Werner Herzog, Helma Sanders-Brahms, Percy Adlon.[22] Her round face conveying the peasant faith of the simple soul, as well as peasant cunning, she also played Fassbinder himself in a biopic made after his death (Radu Gabrea's A MAN CALLED EVA, 1982).

ACHT STUNDEN SIND KEIN TAG (Eight Hours Do Not Make a Day)
d: Rainer Werner Fassbinder; sc: Rainer Werner Fassbinder; c: Dietrich Lohmann; ed: Marie Anne Gerhardt; m: Jean Geponint (= Jens Wilhelm Petersen); lp: Gottfied John, Hanna Schygulla, Louise Ullrich, Werner Finck, Kurt Raab, Renate Roland, Irm Hermann, Herb Andress; r: 5 part TV series, 101 min (part 1), 100 min (part 2), 92 min (part 3), 88 min (part 4), 89 min (part 5), col; p: Westdeutsche Rundfunk (WDR, Peter Märthesheimer) Cologne, 1972.

Fassbinder's melodramas are generally set more in a working class and petit-bourgeois milieu than Sirk's, with a greater emphasis on the workplace and economic problems. This approach succeeded particularly well in the television series EIGHT HOURS DO NOT MAKE A DAY, managing to deal seriously with wage disputes, union meetings and strikes, while unfolding in absorbing detail and with much suspense the complications of family life and domestic entanglements that belong to a proper television soap opera. The core characters are an extended family of three generations, in which the eldest and youngest are unattached, but in search of partners. This allows not only for the typical collusions and parallelisms between old and young, making common cause against the conformist and conservative nuclear couple, but the format also gives Fassbinder scope to introduce the sexual needs and erotic desires of the over-60 generation, a motif that is later taken up in FEAR EATS THE SOUL. Since the series is set in a working class family, Fassbinder dramatizes both class-conflict (especially middle-class parental prejudice against working-class boyfriends) and introduces the subject of foreign workers, also taken up in FEAR EATS THE SOUL. The real achievement, however, of the series must be the bold integration of family life and the workplace. While EIGHT HOURS DO NOT MAKE A DAY firmly belongs to the genre of the *Arbeiterfilm* (initiated by the Westdeutsche Rundfunk television network a few years earlier with films by Christian Ziewer, Theo Gallehr, Rolf Schübel, Ingo Kratisch and Marianne Lüdcke),[23] it remains an outstanding example of this brief, but brave attempt to open up state-controlled German television to portraits of West German social reality (the series was shot in the industrial Ruhr town of Mönchen-Gladbach). Fassbinder's five films are critical as well as entertaining, touching on topical issues and yet giving space to fantasies of a better and more empowering life to those who bore the brunt of the German economic miracle. As the intellectual fruit of the anti-authoritarian movement and the extra-parliamentary opposition, EIGHT HOURS DO NOT MAKE A DAY has a very clear eye for social contradictions, but avoids overt didacticism and indoctrination, showing Fassbinder's preference for clichés and stereotypes, in order to convey an emotional truth rather than documentary authenticity.

Fassbinder was able to extend the genre also in another direction, to include his own version of the 'women's picture',[24] by giving the women (the former star of the German commercial cinema of the 1950s, Luise Ullrich, and his own star Hanna Schygulla) strong roles, showing them fighting for the right to personal happiness, but also for social solidarity, somewhat in the spirit of Brecht's play *The Mother*.

PIONIERE IN INGOLSTADT (Pioneers in Ingolstadt)
d: Rainer Werner Fassbinder; sc: Rainer Werner Fassbinder, based on the play by Marieluise Fleißer; c: Dietrich Lohmann; ed: Thea Eymèsz; m: Peer Raben; lp: Hanna Schygulla, Harry Baer, Irm Hermann, Rudolf Waldemar Brem, Walter Sedlmayr, Klaus Löwitsch; r: 83 min, col; p: Janus-Antiteater, 1971.

Although he never adapted Brecht either in the theatre or for his films, Fassbinder did put on the play of one of Brecht's early disciples, Marie Luise Fleißer's *Pioneers in Ingolstadt*, about the tragic mismatch of a romantically selfless servant-maid (Hanna Schygulla) in love with her cynical soldier-boy (Harry Baer), just passing through town and looking for a sexual conquest.

In the film of the play one senses an odd tension, as if his admiration for Fleißer had prevented him from making the adaptation his own. The basic character constellation of the play did not seem to appeal to Fassbinder, since he effectively reversed it in JAILBAIT, and on the whole, Schygulla, while capable of self-sacrifice, is rarely tragically naive in his films. Instead, inspiration for the strong female characters in his work seems to have partly come from the same sources as Ingmar Bergman's: the Nordic dramatists. In Fassbinder's case Henryk Ibsen, whose *Hedda Gabler* and *A Doll's House* he produced, the first for the theatre (Bremen, 1973), the second for television (NORA HELMER, 1973). The ideal incarnation for the Ibsen woman was Margit Carstensen, for whom he wrote two plays during his stay in Bremen, *The Bitter Tears of Petra von Kant* and *Bremer Freiheit* (both 1971).

DIE BITTEREN TRÄNEN DER PETRA VON KANT (The Bitter Tears of Petra von Kant)
d: Rainer Werner Fassbinder; sc: Rainer Werner Fassbinder, based on his play; c: Michael Ballhaus; ed: Thea Eymèsz; m: The Platters, The Walker Brothers, Guiseppe Verdi; lp: Margit Carstensen, Hanna Schygulla, Irm Hermann, Eva Mattes, Katrin Schaake, Gisela Fackeldey; r: 124 min, col; p: Tango (Rainer Werner Fassbinder, Michael Fengler) Munich, 1972.

THE BITTER TEARS OF PETRA VON KANT became one of Fassbinder's great international triumphs when made into a film in 1972 and set the scene for several other essentially upper-middle-class melodramas, combining motifs from the Hollywood 'female paranoia' cycle of the 1940s, such as Hitchcock's SUSPICION and Fritz Lang's SECRET BEYOND THE DOOR with a more documentary approach to the clinical breakdown of a personality (FEAR OF FEAR, 1975). THE BITTER TEARS OF PETRA VON KANT deliberately avoids disguising its theatrical origins. Divided into five acts set in the same room, against the backdrop of a painted mural after Poussain, the performances powerfully underline the emotional claustrophobia of the film, never letting the spectator forget the high artifice of the dramatic situation. A successful fashion designer, Petra von Kant (Margit Carstensen) lives with her secretary and maid, the slavishly subservient Marlene (Irm Hermann). But Petra's control over her life is only apparent: it takes no more than the self-confident insolence of one of her models, Karin Thimm (Hanna Schygulla), to make Petra fall hopelessly and tragically in love. Karin is a working-class beauty, attracted by Petra's life style and sophistication, but too sure in her own values and (bi)sexuality to surrender to the love-hungry and possessive Petra. On her birthday, waiting for a sign from Karin, Petra has a nervous breakdown during the visit of her mother (Gisela Fackeldey) and daughter (Eva Mattes). Her recovery begins when she realizes that love means more than possession and dependence. She offers a partnership to Marlene, who had been a silent witness throughout, but the secretary packs a suitcase and leaves. Although not a single male appears in the film, Petra's bedroom-salon-studio is dominated by the Poussin painting, usually framed to give a view of a male nude's groin. Revolving around the phallus, a drama of loss (of love-object and of personal identity) is played out with Fassbinder's customary sense of dramatic symmetry and devastating irony.

MARTHA

d: Rainer Werner Fassbinder; sc: Rainer Werner Fassbinder, inspired by the short story *For the Rest of Their Lives* by Cornell Woolrich; c: Michael Ballhaus; ed: Liesgret Schmitt-Klink; m: G. Donizetti; lp: Margit Carstensen, Karlheinz Böhm, Barbara Valentin, Ingrid Caven, Günter Lamprecht, Peter Chatel, Gisela Fackeldey; r: 112 min, col; p: Westdeutscher Rundfunk (WDR) Cologne, 1973.

It is in MARTHA that Margit Carstensen gives her strongest performance as the highly strung Martha Hyer who, after a whirlwind romance in Rome, marries the suave and handsome engineer Helmut Salomon (Karlheinz Böhm). They rent a palatial house near Lake Constance, but with Helmut away on business, Martha finds herself mostly alone, listening to Donizetti's *Lucia di Lammermoor* and occasionally lunching with Kaiser (Peter Chatel), a former colleague from the library where she used to work. Helmut, who professes to adore his wife, always seems to steal up on Martha, with strangling solicitude. His mild-mannered but persistent attempts to improve her mind make Martha a prisoner in her own home, and his passion has the rapaciousness of a vampire, or so it feels to her. Gradually convinced that Helmut is terrorizing her into madness in order to keep her locked up, she persuades the young librarian to drive her to the country, but a car that follows them is for Martha proof of Helmut's murderous presence. Trying to shake him off, she takes hold of the steering wheel, and their car overturns. Martha wakes up in hospital to learn that she alone survived the crash. Permanently paralyzed, she is taken home in a wheelchair by Helmut, forever his.

The film is such a classic Hollywood subject that it comes as no surprise to learn that it is based on a Cornell Woolrich story and that Martha Hyer was a chilly Hollywood star of the 1950s and 1960s (starring in Sirk's BATTLE HYMN, and playing the frigid fiancé of Frank Sinatra in Minnelli's classic SOME CAME RUNNING). As in the most perfect examples of the genre, the spectator never knows what part of Martha's torment is due to a persecution mania and what is actually inflicted on her by her husband, whether Martha's total dependency at the end is tragic or a wish-fulfilling fantasy.[25] Thanks to Karlheinz Böhm and Margit Carstensen, the film transposes this material effortlessly and authentically into its German setting. Fassbinder's great achievement, however, is to have made a horror film in broad daylight and on sun-drenched terraces. Although masochism in Fassbinder's cinema is more often a male perversion (as in Sternberg's Dietrich films), as a study of a sado-masochistic couple MARTHA remains unrivalled. Not easily forgettable is the scene where Helmut, on their honeymoon and after a day at the beach, makes love to his wife, red as a lobster and almost fainting with pain from sunburn.

ANGST VOR DER ANGST (Fear of Fear)
d: Rainer Werner Fassbinder; sc: Rainer Werner Fassbinder, based on an idea by Asta Scheib; c: Jürgen Jürges, Ulrich Prinz; ed: Liesgret Schmitt-Klink, Beate Fischer-Weiskirch; m: Peer Raben; lp: Margit Carstensen, Ulrich Faulhaber, Brigitte Mira, Irm Hermann, Kurt Raab, Ingrid Caven, Lilo Pempeit; r: 88 min, col; p: Westdeutsche Rundfunk (WDR, Peter Märthesheimer) Cologne, 1975.

More clinical in its observation than MARTHA is FEAR OF FEAR, in which Carstensen plays a Cologne housewife, tormented by apparently groundless anxieties that lead to an attempted suicide, endless visits to doctors, drug stores and psychotherapists. One of the truly unsettling scenes (because balanced between horror and farce) is the mute encounter with a mad neighbour, who is later found hanged in his apartment. The fact that the neighbour is played by Kurt Raab indicates a close proximity to WHY DOES HERR R RUN AMOK? But unlike the earlier work, essentially a denunciation of a milieu, FEAR OF FEAR is the study of psychological borderline states. Here again, and typical of the melodramas, sympathy is extended to all the protagonists. Rare among Fassbinder's actresses, however, Margit Carstensen was able to give a convincing portrait of a psychology at once complex and extreme. For despite the hints at a sociological explanation, about the terrors of tidy pedestrian precincts and groomed front lawns, Carstensen's acting suggests that there need be no explanation for a nameless fear such as the one gripping her, other than the silence of the universe stifling a sensitive and questing soul.

ANGST ESSEN SEELE AUF (Ali – Fear Eats the Soul)
d: Rainer Werner Fassbinder; sc: Rainer Werner Fassbinder; c: Jürgen Jürges; ed: Thea Eymèsz; m: archive; lp: Brigitte Mira, El Hedi Ben Salem, Barbara Valentin, Irm Hermann, Rainer Werner Fassbinder, Marquard Bohm, Walter Sedlmayr; r: 93 min, col; p: Tango (Rainer Werner Fassbinder, Michael Fengler) Munich, 1974.

The theme of 'fear' also unites two other films made during the period 1973-1975, FEAR EATS THE SOUL and FONTANE EFFI BRIEST. In FEAR EATS THE SOUL, Emmi (Brigitte Mira), a sixty-year-old charwoman on her way home from work meets Ali (El Hedi ben

Salem), a North African in his thirties working as an auto mechanic. They move in together and marry, outraging Emmi's children, neighbours and her colleagues at work, until even the corner shop refuses to serve them. After a vacation together, social ostracism changes to accommodating exploitation, but now the relationship is beginning to show strains. Ali goes back to his old lover, the owner of the local bar, and one evening he collapses in Emmi's arms with a burst stomach ulcer. The doctor holds out little hope for a permanent cure: stress and an unaccustomed diet means foreign workers are always at risk.

Once again, Fassbinder constructs his storyline with the purity of a fable and the emotional impact of tragedy. The plot is similar to Sirk's ALL THAT HEAVEN ALLOWS, in which Jane Wyman and Rock Hudson play the lovers crossing the age and class barriers, but it is obvious that Fassbinder, choosing a much older actress and making his male lead a Moroccan, sharpened the conflict and with it, the unease initially provoked in the spectator when the couple break so many taboos. FEAR EATS THE SOUL was to become one of the key films of the New German Cinema and the one that first brought Fassbinder a wider international audience. The story, in fact, is first told by Franz's girlfriend in THE AMERICAN SOLDIER, but with an ending pointing to a quite different irony. One day, Emmi is found strangled, with the marks of crested ring on her neck bearing the initial A. Her Turkish boyfriend Ali is arrested, but protests his innocence: why should it be him, when Germans call every Turkish worker Ali ('Every Turk Is Called Ali' was Fassbinder's original film title).

FONTANE EFFI BRIEST (Effi Briest)
d: Rainer Werner Fassbinder; sc: Rainer Werner Fassbinder, based on the novel by Theodor Fontane; c: Dietrich Lohmann, Jürgen Jürges; ed: Thea Eymèsz; m: Camille Saint-Saëns and others; lp: Hanna Schygulla, Wolfgang Schenck, Karlheinz Böhm, Ulli Lommel, Ursula Strätz, Hark Bohm, Irm Hermann; r: 141 min, b/w; p: Tango, 1974.

FONTANE EFFI BRIEST, in many respects again a classic Hollywood 'women's picture,' is actually based almost verbatim on the eponymous novel by Theodor Fontane, itself indebted to Flaubert's *Madame Bovary* and Tolstoi's *Anna Karenina*. The seventeen-year-old Effi (Hanna Schygulla), daughter of a Prussian merchant, marries a man twenty years her senior, the sternly principled Baron von Instetten (Wolfgang Schenck), only to find that his love for her is above all pedagogic: Instetten even invents a haunted house in order to frighten Effi into submission; as she says, he had 'constructed a kind of calculated anxiety apparatus'. Unhappy, but fearful of her husband's gentle terror, Effi has an affair with Major Crampas (Ulli Lommel), a dashing young officer billeted in the small town. Years later her husband learns about the brief 'trespass'.[26] Being a 'man of honour' he challenges his former rival to a duel and kills him, divorcing Effi while keeping their child. After once more meeting with her daughter, whom Instetten has turned against her, Effi retires to her parental home where she dies.

Clearly, FONTANE EFFI BRIEST has many parallels with MARTHA, providing a telling contrast between the febrile Carstensen and the more languid Schygulla, both cast as the victims of men turned sadists out of an overweening sense of righteous duty. Yet the very similarity of the storylines only serves to underscore the differences in the emotional tone and impact of the films. Against MARTHA's vivid and burning colours, FONTANE EFFI BRIEST is shot in a particularly richly graded black-and-white, with every scene transition fading to the pure white of the printed page, as if the images rose from the words of Fontane (spoken in voice-over by Fassbinder himself). In MARTHA, all the ambivalence is concentrated on the heroine: are her fears real or imaginary? The intense pathos of FONTANE EFFI BRIEST stems from another source: the scrupulous fairness to all the characters, especially the self-tormented Instetten. This is in the spirit of the original, set in the 1890s, and very conscious of a momentous historical change, the passing away of the feudal Prussian aristocracy and the rise of an urban middle class. That these changes should be charted in their effects on the family and especially in the relations between the sexes is as typical of Fontane as it is central to Fassbinder's view of history.

FAUSTRECHT DER FREIHEIT (Fox and His Friends)
d: Rainer Werner Fassbinder; sc: Rainer Werner Fassbinder; c: Michael Ballhaus; ed: Thea Eymèsz; m: Peer Raben; lp: Rainer Werner Fassbinder, Peter Chatel, Karlheinz Böhm, Rudolf Lenz, Karl Scheydt, Kurt Raab, Harry Baer; r: 123 min, col; p: Tango/City Munich, 1975.

Given the importance male friendships have in his early films, it is perhaps surprising that not until FOX AND HIS FRIENDS did Fassbinder directly portray a homosexual love story; less surprisingly, it followed the pattern of economic and emotional exploitation established in his social melodramas. Franz Biberkopf (Fassbinder), a good-natured working-class homosexual, known as 'Fox, der tönende Kopf' among his fairground colleagues, wins half a million in a lottery and finds himself among the rich and glamorous gay community. Dazzled by the cool sophistication of his new friends, he falls in love with the shrewd and handsome Eugen (Peter Chatel), son of a middle-class printshop owner (Adrian Hoven), in dire need of capital. Father and son do their utmost to relieve Fox of his money, alternately flattering him with their attention and humiliating him by showing up his ignorance. Once the money is gone, so is love. Franz, homeless, swallows a bottle of sleeping pills; as he lies dying in a subway station, he is mugged by two small boys.

The film has been criticized mainly on two counts; for being excessively overt in the way it brings home its message, relentlessly humiliating its hero and punishing the audience with the dreadful inevitability of the story; and, secondly, for giving a crassly clichéd account of the homosexual milieu. Fassbinder said he wanted the spectator to forget it was a story between men, and indeed, the satirical crudity is no different from that found in his earlier pictures of bourgeois and petit-bourgeois households, such as WHY DOES HERR R RUN AMOK? and THE MERCHANT OF FOUR SEASONS. In these, however, male friendships are romanticized, since they formed the foil against which to measure the misery men and women inflicted on each other. If sexuality disappears as a barrier, those of class and education remain. In FOX AND HIS FRIENDS there is no exit, save the fleeting moments of compassion Fox receives from his sister (for once not Hanna Schygulla, but Barbara Valentin, Ali's under-standing ex-girlfriend in FEAR EATS THE SOUL). Fassbinder plays on a remarkable rupture of tone: the first half has such a sure touch of comedy that the self-pitying melodrama of Franz's stupidly uncomprehending degradation comes as a disagreeable shock.

It is tempting to see FOX AND HIS FRIENDS as both a sequel and a mirror-image of THE BITTER TEARS OF PETRA VON KANT. The perspective is twice inverted. In PETRA VON KANT the heroine's middle-class neuroses are exposed, rather than working-class insecurities; Karin is the sexually self-confident female who can negotiate social mobility and class differences through her looks, in a way apparently impossible for Franz in FOX, where it is the suave middle-class homosexuals who negotiate class differences.[27] PETRA is dedicated 'to him who here becomes Marlene'. Given that the dedication in FOX is 'for Armin and all the others,' it would seem that Fassbinder in the role of Fox plays his friend and lover Armin Meier, though he was said to have more in common with the manipulative Eugen.[28]

MUTTER KÜSTERS FAHRT ZUM HIMMEL (Mother Küster's Trip to Heaven)
d: Rainer Werner Fassbinder; sc: Rainer Werner Fassbinder, Kurt Raab; c: Michael Ballhaus; ed: Thea Eymèsz; m: Peer Raben; lp: Brigitte Mira, Ingrid Caven, Karlheinz Böhm, Margit Carstensen, Irm Hermann, Gottfried John, Armin Meier, Kurt Raab; r: 120 min, col; p: Tango, 1975.

The title of MOTHER KÜSTER'S TRIP TO HEAVEN alludes to a well-known working-class 'social problem' film of 1929, Piel Jutzi's MOTHER KRAUSE'S TRIP TO HAPPINESS, and the film begins where some of Fassbinder's others end. An assembly line worker kills his boss and commits suicide when rumors reach him that he is about to be made redundant. His widow (Brigitte Mira) and the two adult children have to cope not only with losing husband and father, but with the publicity the case receives in the scandal sheets. While the son (Armin Meier) and his wife (Irm Hermann) fear social disgrace, the daughter (Ingrid Caven), a nightclub singer, uses the notoriety of the Küster family name to advance her career. A journalist friend of hers (Gottfried John) ingratiates himself with Mother Küster and writes a particularly sensationalist story. In despair, she turns to a middle-class couple who are members of the Communist Party. They explain to her that her husband had had the right motives but resorted to the wrong means. Intent on rehabilitating his name, she joins the Party, but her straightforward decency is used by the couple for Party propaganda, and she begins to listen more to a young anarchist (Matthias Fuchs) who promises action. Together they occupy the office of the magazine that printed the offensive story, and to Mother Küster's horror, the activist takes hostages, demanding the release of all political prisoners. Both of them are shot by the police as they try to negotiate.

Made as a homage to Brigitte Mira (Emmi in FEAR EATS THE SOUL), the film is interesting in several respects. As a storyteller, Fassbinder felt so self-assured that, in the manner of classical tragedy, the dramatic framing events (the husband's initial suicide and the final showdown) happen off-stage. In fact, for the shoot-out with the police, the film simply reproduces pages from the script, which may explain why the American version used a quite different ending: the anarchist gives himself up, and Mother Küster moves in with a night-watchman, who instead of fabricating homemade bombs is an expert in home cooking. The happy ending (reminiscent of another famous film from the 1920s, Murnau's THE LAST LAUGH) is finally as absurd as the tragic one, and the film caused a heated debate, mainly because of its caustic and pessimistic look at the political left, with orthodox Communists and terrorist fringe alike being dismissed with sarcastic disdain.

In some ways the Communist couple are the most fascinating characters, since it is one of the very few times that the German cinema acknowledges the existence of a West German CP, and thus the subterranean links existing between West and East Germany during the 1970s. Nonetheless, they, too, remain caricatures as far as their politics are concerned and are interesting mainly because of the actors Fassbinder chose for the parts. Played by Karlheinz Böhm and Margit Carstensen, the sado-masochistic husband and wife in MARTHA, the couple are a good example of how Fassbinder, through his stock company and casting, weaves a kind of daisy-chain between his films. A leading actor in one genre may appear in a cameo role in another, but he or she will bring with them the memory of those parts, and so create subtle echo-effects and even uncanny reverberations that give the most direct storylines an undertow of both mystery and familiarity. Even if Fassbinder's actors do not quite elicit the recognition effects of the great international stars, they are richer in the meanings they add to a film than the stereotyped stock players of Hollywood genre films. Böhm, whom Fassbinder also used in FOX AND HIS FRIENDS as a smooth elderly homosexual, made his name as the effete crown prince opposite Romy Schneider in the SISSI series, three hugely popular films about the Habsburg Monarchy, before playing the psychopath film-maker in Michael Powell's PEEPING TOM. Margit Carstensen, on the other hand, dominated the women's roles in Fassbinder's middle period, as the upper-class intellectual alternative to Hanna Schygulla's more openhearted sensuality.

ICH WILL DOCH NUR, DASS IHR MICH LIEBT (I Only Want You to Love Me)
d: Rainer Werner Fassbinder; sc: Rainer Werner Fassbinder, after a book by Klaus Antes and Christiane Ehrhardt; c: Michael Ballhaus; ed: Liesgret Schmitt-Klink; m: Peer Raben; lp: Vitus Zeplichal, Elke Aberle, Alexander Allerson, Ernie Mangold, Johanna Hofer, Katharina Buchhammer, Wolgang Hess, Armin Meier; r: TV film, 103 min, col; p: Bavaria Atelier, 1975-1976.

Fassbinder's last working class-melodrama has one of the most programmatic titles of all his films: I ONLY WANT YOU TO LOVE ME. A television production, it tells a story reminiscent of both JAILBAIT and FOX. A young man (Vitus Zeplichal), growing up in a narrow-minded petit-bourgeois household, marries in order to escape, but finds that his wife (Elke Aberle) has no more genuine love for him than did his parents. Showering them all with presents, even building a house for his father in his spare time, he gets into ever deeper debts, finally losing his job with a construction firm. In a moment of panic, he kills the owner of the neighbourhood bar, a man who reminds him of his father. Sentenced to prison, he finds a sympathetic social worker.

While the title 'says it all', the story of someone compulsively buying love has often been applied all too directly to Fassbinder himself.[29] The narrative pattern, however, is close to those films where the central character turns aggression inward up to the moment where a sudden outburst makes him a murderer: in this case of a father-substitute, not unlike the parricide in JAILBAIT, with which it shares a certain misogyny (both mother and wife appear demanding and unloving: a constellation repeated stereotypically in Fassbinder from THE MERCHANT OF FOUR SEASONS onwards). In its sober, analytical but rather textbook-like demonstration of a social worker's case study, it recalls FEAR OF FEAR, although Margit Carstensen is able to suggest unplumbed depths in the disturbed housewife absent from the portrayal of deprived adolescence in the suburbs played by Vitus Zeplichal.

SATANSBRATEN (Satan's Brew)
d: Rainer Werner Fassbinder; sc: Rainer Werner Fassbinder; c: Jürgen Jürges; ed: Thea Eymèsz, Gabi Eichel; m: Peer Raben; lp: Kurt Raab, Margit Carstensen, Helen Vita, Volker Spengler, Ingrid Caven, Marquard Bohm, Ulli Lommel, Y Sa Lo; r: 112 min, col; p: Albatros/Trio, 1976.

Margit Carstensen's strangest, but strangely powerful performance for Fassbinder is in SATAN'S BREW, as a provincial spinster, her face covered in warts, masochistically sitting at the feet of the failed and frustrated writer Kranz (Kurt Raab). Kranz, a hen-pecked husband supporting an idiot brother (Volker Spengler), was briefly admired during the student movement as 'the poet of the Revolution'. When, after a prolonged writer's block, his latest poem turns out to be a plagiarism of 'The Albatross', a poem by the symbolist Stefan George, Kranz is persuaded he is George's reincarnation and surrounds himself with homosexual prostitutes, in imitation of George's circle of disciples. To support his lifestyle, Kranz has to borrow and steal. When mugged by one of his creditors, he discovers the pleasure of pain. This inspires his best-selling novel *Fascism Victorious, or No Funeral for the Führer's Dog*.

A cruel, 'over-the-top' satire of opportunism in the culture industry as well as the narcissism of the artist, SATAN'S BREW shocked critics by its graffiti-like directness, its shrill vulgarity and unsublimated violence: features ascribed to a self-flagellating impulse in Fassbinder himself. With hindsight, it fares better, and not only because it drew from Kurt Raab a bravura performance. As the rare attempt at a comedy from a filmmaker who is, as most commentators have noted, entirely devoid of humour, SATAN'S BREW shows Fassbinder giggling to himself rather than sharing a joke with either the audience or the actors. Yet there are moments of surreal logic reminiscent of late Buñuel, as in the scene where a policeman, come to investigate Kranz's role in a kinky sex-murder of a rich society-lady, ends up sharing a hot foot-bath with the suspect. At another level, SATAN'S BREW can be seen as a first study for DESPAIR, for it inaugurates the theme of the double as a historical figure, perhaps in recognition of Marx's dictum that those who do not learn from history are fated to repeat it, first as tragedy then as farce. But it is also reminiscent of WHITY (in its portrayal of a family 'gone mad') and BEWARE OF THE HOLY WHORE, where Fassbinder (playing the production manager) says 'the only feeling I can recognize as honest is despair.'

CHINESISCHES ROULETTE (Chinese Roulette)
d: Rainer Werner Fassbinder; sc: Rainer Werner Fassbinder; c: Michael Ballhaus; ed: Ila von Hasperg, Juliane Lorenz; m: Peer Raben; lp: Anna Karina, Macha Méril, Ulli Lommel, Brigitte Mira, Alex Allerson, Margit Carstensen, Andrea Schober, Armin Meier; r: 86 min, col; p: Albatros Film Munich (Michael Fengler)/ Les Films du Losange Paris, 1976.

Similarly bleak is CHINESE ROULETTE, a very unsmiling and un-Bergmanesque SMILES OF A SUMMER NIGHT in which the polio-stricken daughter (Andrea Schober) of a wealthy Munich couple engineers an embarrassing confrontation at the family's country house between her father (Alexander Allerson) and her mother (Margit Carstensen), each accompanied by a lover (Anna Karina and Ulli Lommel). Also present is the daughter's dumb governess (Macha Meril), the housekeeper (Brigitte Mira), and her son (Volker Spengler). The tense atmosphere of repressed hatred, jealousy and mutual recrimination finds its appropriate expression in the party game of the title. Each character has to think of him/herself as having played a prominent part in the Nazi regime, which the others have to guess. In the confusion that ensues, the mother shoots the governess. Shortly after, a second shot is heard, but the identities of victim and perpetrator are left to the spectator to imagine. A more glacial but no less camp variation on the theme of WHITY, the film is best described by the English title of a Fassbinder essay, 'Insects in a Glass Case,' devoted to the work of Claude Chabrol.[30] Not as sardonic as Chabrol, nor as supercilious, CHINESE ROULETTE is, despite its bright colours and precise, gliding camera-work, an unrelievedly gloomy film, which might be thought of as a distant relative of Buñuel's THE EXTERMINATING ANGEL and Pasolini's SALO. It marks Fassbinder's bid for a place as a European auteur and with two Godard actresses (Anna Karina and Macha Méril) signals his entry into international co-productions.

Art Cinema Auteur or Chronicler of German History?
By 1976/77 Fassbinder had himself become an international star. He began to receive Federal Film Prizes in Germany, but it was above all the retrospectives of his films in Paris (1976) and New York (1977) that made him a familiar name among cinephiles.[31] A first critical study of his work in English appeared in London in 1976, and it helped establish a following among university campus audiences making him a 'teachable' director.[32] He owned property in Paris and could be seen in gay bars in New York. Art house circuits avidly took up his films, and since by the time he was 'discovered' with FEAR EATS THE SOUL, FONTANE EFFI BRIEST and FOX AND HIS FRIENDS he had already fifteen films to his credit, the re-release of his earlier work, together with the steady stream of new films, made his productivity seem even more extraordinary. A potent cocktail was being mixed and served up as a media phenomenon: the Fassbinder myth was born.

His flamboyant and at the same time seedy lifestyle, his openly displayed and well advertised homosexuality, his boasts, scandals and bouts of self-pity ensured that in Germany, too, Fassbinder remained permanently in the news, making calculatedly outrageous headlines with statements such as 'I'd rather be a street-sweeper in Mexico than a filmmaker in Germany'.[33] The films received rather mixed notices from the national critics, many of whom only began to take Fassbinder seriously after the foreign press had hailed him as a genius. Commercially he was, like his fellow directors in the New German Cinema, successful only by the very special standards of the German film funding system, where a film need not recover its production costs to be classed a success. If seen by at least 300,000 paying spectators, it automatically qualified for a bonus, paid out of a levy on exhibitors' profits made on American and French box office successes, and available for future production.[34] This way, for most of the decade, Fassbinder was at least assured of development money for new projects.

Nevertheless, by the end of the year 1976 Fassbinder found himself at the crossroads. Having completed his first genuinely international film DESPAIR, an adaptation of a novel by Nabokov, with a script by Tom Stoppard, and Dirk Bogarde in the leading role, he seemed poised to follow the example of Bernardo Bertolucci, Louis Malle, Milos Forman or Roman Polanski, and make international films in Paris and Hollywood. After difficulties in Germany over two of his projects, such a move appeared almost inevitable, and Fassbinder publicly announced that he intended to emigrate. DESPAIR, however, was not quite the critical success he had expected, receiving neither a prize at Cannes nor returning its capital investment (it was largely financed by a company specializing in tax shelters for dentists), and no plans for making films abroad were actively envisaged.

BOLWIESER (The Station Master's Wife)
d: Rainer Werner Fassbinder; sc: Rainer Werner Fassbinder, based on the novel by Oskar Maria Graf; c: Michael Ballhaus; ed: Ila von Hasperg, Juliane Lorenz; m: Peer Raben; lp: Kurt Raab, Elisabeth Trissenaar, Bernhard Helfrich, Udo Kier, Volker Spengler, Armin Meier; r: TV version in 2 parts, 201 min, col; p: Bavaria Atelier GmbH Munich for Zweites Deutsches Fernsehen (ZDF) Mainz, 1976/1977.

The 1976/1977 season also saw Fassbinder completing one of his most ambitious works for television, the two-part, three-hour BOLWIESER, an adaptation of a novel first published in the 1931 by Oskar Maria Graf. Popular with television audiences and a critical success, it pointed to the dearth of fictional television drama about Germany, its history and people. By choosing a regional author such as Graf (whose work had been all but forgotten) rather than the usual literary adaptation of highbrow classics such as Kleist, Goethe or Thomas Mann, Fassbinder continued to mine a seam already opened with FONTANE EFFI BRIEST: reinterpreting the realist tradition of German literature as an entry-point to German social history. A film version of BOLWIESER was prepared by Fassbinder, who cut the original TV version down to 112 minutes, but for copyright reasons, it was not released until 1983, when it enjoyed posthumous fame of sorts on the first anniversary of Fassbinder's death.[35]

BOLWIESER might in fact be said to have opened the third major group of Fassbinder films, dealing with German history, although, as indicated, in retrospect it already began with FONTANE EFFI BRIEST, which was to have been followed by an adaptation of Gustav Freytag's *Soll und Haben*. When the project was turned down, in the wake of his play about Frankfurt, *Der Müll, die Stadt und der Tod*, meeting resistance because of the charge of anti-Semitism, Fassbinder's projects after 1977 took on a more self-consciously German tenor, partly capitalizing on his international reputation which meant that he had become identified with his native country, and partly out of a genuinely felt need to investigate more closely the origins of the Germany in which he lived and had grown up in. Furthermore, after the screening of the US television series HOLOCAUST, which caused a major soul-searching among German critics as well as filmmakers about West Germany 'mastering its past', German history (narrowed down to Hitler and National Socialism) became topical. Peter Märthesheimer, a successful television producer at WDR with whom Fassbinder had worked several times previously, also encouraged Fassbinder to devote himself to German subjects if he wanted to gain an international reputation.

BOLWIESER tells the story of a sexual infatuation against the background of a society morally in decay and facing an economic crisis. Bolwieser, a railway clerk and aspiring station master marries Hanni, the daughter of the wealthy local brewer, who has nothing but sadistic contempt for his new son-in-law. Blackmailed by one of his wife's lovers, Bolwieser ends up being sent to prison and, after serving his sentence, becomes a vagrant who finally takes the place of the ferry-master, rowing passengers across the river in a remote part of the country.

The film concentrates on the gradual self-destruction of a typically German petit-bourgeois, taunted by his colleagues, exploited by his in-laws and cuckolded by his wife. It may seem that Bolwieser is yet another of Fassbinder's flamboyant masochists who wants to be exploited, wants to be dependent on his wife's whims, and whose subaltern spirit marks him out as a typical subject of totalitarianism and charismatic dictatorship.[36] In this sense, BOLWIESER is MADAME BOVARY, but told from Charles Bovary's point of view: a masochistic male who enjoys suffering, humiliation and who feeds off the bigotry and envy which his small-town surroundings project on him. But the hero is also a petit-bourgeois 'Professor Unrat' (the literary source of THE BLUE ANGEL, said to have been the inspiration for Fassbinder's LOLA) with the emphasis – as in Heinrich Mann's novel – on the cuckold, a frequent icon of Wilhelmine and Weimar Germany whose power to evoke male anxieties Fassbinder expertly probes.

While the combination of sex and business (via the father's dynastic greed) harks back to Fassbinder's early 'prostitute and gangster' cycle, BOLWIESER, thanks also to Kurt Raab's performance, is a much more subtle portrait of a man on the brink of mental disintegration, holding on to an *ideé fixe* which he gradually transforms into a positive credo.

For the film, at least in the television version, takes the side of Bolwieser, and his cry of a tormented creature becomes a poignantly human testament to the possibility of selfless suffering. Bolwieser therefore, despite his misogynist rages, has someting in common with Erwin/Elvira (in IN A YEAR OF THIRTEEN MOONS), willing to divest himself of all conventional marks of identity for the sake of love.

As notable, perhaps, is the fact that BOLWIESER is, so to speak, the left-hand panel of a diptych, whose right-hand panel is DESPAIR. In both cases a man is tormented by an unfaithful, sexually voracious wife (Elizabeth Trissenaar plays Hanni in much the same way that Andréa Ferréol interprets Lydia), only too aware how the society around him turns to a radically sado-masochistic political solution, in order to escape the crisis of values and social stagnation. The difference is that in BOLWIESER, a petit-bourgeois functionary has to confront the dilemma, whereas in DESPAIR a duped aristocrat and cuckolded dandy tries to save himself into paranoia and insanity. The parallel suggests that although the crossroads Fassbinder found himself at in the mid-1970s opened up two different genres and media (television drama adapted from a realist author of the national literary canon, and international art-cinema adapted from a modernist author by a postmodernist playwright), thematically both films continue to explore the issue of German history and its crisis points.

EINE REISE INS LICHT (Despair)
d: Rainer Werner Fassbinder; sc: Tom Stoppard, after the novel by Vladimir Nabokov; c: Michael Ballhaus; ed: Reginald Beck, Juliane Lorenz; m: Peer Raben; lp: Dirk Bogarde, Andréa Ferréol, Bernhard Wicki, Volker Spengler, Klaus Löwitsch, Peter Kern, Roger Fritz; r: 114 min, col; p: NF Geria II/Bavaria Munich/SFP Paris (Peter Märthesheimer, Dieter Minx), 1978.

With DESPAIR, the director's most expensive film up to then, Fassbinder took extreme care over pre-production and the preparation of the script. Not unlike FONTANE EFFI BRIEST, Nabokov's story of Hermann Hermann, emigré heir to a chocolate factory in Berlin in the late 1920s, is a swan song for a passing civilization. But what drew Fassbinder to the subject, apart from the fact that Ingmar Bergman's elaborate set for THE SERPENT'S EGG was still available at cost price in Munich's Bavaria studios, was the hero's (Dirk Bogarde) dilemma: how to plan his own disappearance and escape his flighty, adulterous wife (Andréa Ferréol), his business responsibilities, and the rising tide of mob radicalism. At a fun fair Hermann spots among the many unemployed a man (Klaus Löwitsch) who, in his opinion, looks exactly like him. He bribes the stranger into swapping clothes, then shoots him, making the death look like suicide. Dressed as a vagrant, he escapes to Switzerland, where the police arrest him for murder: the plan had one fatal flaw, namely that between Hermann Hermann and his double, there was in fact no physical resemblance at all.

This denouement, a carefully timed surprise in the novel, must of necessity in the film be obvious from the start. Fassbinder (and Stoppard) concentrate on the disintegration of a hypersensitive personality, an aesthete who takes refuge in murder, self-delusion and madness. Most striking and original, however, is that Fassbinder depicts in Hermann Hermann's obsession with a double a link to the rise of fascism in Germany. Without drawing facile parallels between escaping from the political and economic chaos of the Weimar Republic into the 'madness' of fascism, Fassbinder sees in the German *Führer*-cult the search of an idealized ego, and suggests that in the drama of a schizophenic personality needing to suppress and yet exchange places with his double, there is a dilemma of wider significance. In fact, the trope of the double, highlighted by critics like Siegfried Kracauer as typical of the Weimar Cinema's troubled collective soul (THE STUDENT OF PRAGUE, WARNING SHADOWS, M), finds in Fassbinder a complement in DESPAIR's re-reading of Kracauer in the light of subsequent socio-psychological interpretations, such as Alexander Mitscherlich's *Society without the Father*.

Apart from being financed with tax-shelter money, DESPAIR had, unusually for a film by a New German director, a distribution guarantee from a US major company and was therefore shot simultaneously in English and German, an experiment Fassbinder was not keen to repeat. The film received a lukewarm reception at the Cannes film festival of 1977 and was subsequently disowned by its star, Dirk Bogarde, who claimed it had been re-cut by Fassbinder in a fit of depression.[37]

IN EINEM JAHR MIT DREIZEHN MONDEN (In a Year of Thirteen Moons)
d: Rainer Werner Fassbinder; sc: Rainer Werner Fassbinder; c: Rainer Werner Fassbinder; m: Peer Raben; lp: Volker Spengler, Ingrid Caven, Elisabeth Trissenaar, Gottfried John, Eva Mattes; r: 124 min, col; p: Tango Film/ Pro-Ject Film Munich, 1978.

DESPAIR's more private meaning may well lie in its parallel with IN A YEAR OF THIRTEEN MOONS, dedicated, like FOX AND HIS FRIENDS, to Armin Meier, who appears in several films (as Mother Küster's son, married to Irm Hermann, and as himself in the episode that Fassbinder shot for GERMANY IN AUTUMN). In May 1978 Armin was found dead in Fassbinder's apartment, having committed suicide when he learnt that his lover intended to terminate the relationship. Fassbinder immediately set about making a film that commemorates Armin, even as it places his life in a context where its sudden end is given meaning: that of belonging to Fassbinder's world. The film covers the last five days in the life of Elvira (Volker Spengler), a burly working-class transsexual originally named Erwin. She wanders the streets of Frankfurt with a friendly prostitute (Ingrid Caven) while looking up former friends and live-in lovers, including the man, now a powerful property speculator, for whose sake Erwin had undergone a sex change. Exhausted from the endless humiliations, Elvira cuts her wrists.

Here, the search for another identity, undertaken out of love, produces the fantasy of the double not merely in the mind, as for Kranz or Hermann Hermann, but inscribes itself on the body. The opening scene is also the film's strongest statement when Elvira is mistaken for a homosexual transvestite, stripped, and brutally beaten when it becomes evident that she is not a man. In another appallingly memorable sequence Elvira, visiting the slaughterhouse where he/she once worked, recounts her life story while cattle are slaughtered and prepared as meat.

IN A YEAR OF THIRTEEN MOONS is as much about Fassbinder's experience of the city of Frankfurt as about Armin Meier's experience of sexual loss and social isolation. After working as artistic director of Frankfurt's 'Theater am Turm' for a brief period and hating the cultural bureaucracy attached to a subsidized theatre, Fassbinder came to see the city as the epitome of the moral and political double standards pervading West Germany. A boom town during the 1970s, when it became the banking and insurance centre not only of Germany but for much of continental Europe, Frankfurt showed all the strains of a city not altogether able to mediate between its cultural prestige (the city of Goethe and of a long tradition in independent publishing and a liberal press) and its crassly commercial, international 'melting pot' image. In Fassbinder, this clash inspired a play, hastily written on a round trip flight to New York and entitled *The City, Garbage and Death* (1975). It featured a wealthy Jewish property-speculator, whose extreme ruthlessness in business matters and sexual lasciviousness is an open provocation, especially for his non-Jewish associates whose anti-Semitism and resentment against being made to feel guilty about the Holocaust hides behind philosemitic rhetoric. Surrounding himself by unsavoury underworld types, The Rich Jew focusses on himself all the fury of prejudice and self-repression. In its pattern of reverse identification, projection and with a scapegoat who acts the sadist at its centre, the play is a kind of blueprint of the structure underlying much of Fassbinder's work. Its 'model' character was taken to be literary crudity and lack of polish, while the depiction of a Jew as rich and exploitative was deemed to be unacceptable. *The City, Garbage and Death* thus gave enough arguments for censorship, and the production was cancelled. Suhrkamp, Fassbinder's publisher, also withdrew all copies of the play that had been printed. When it was made into a film (SCHATTEN DER ENGEL) in 1976 directed by Daniel Schmid and for Fassbinder's production company, Fassbinder acted the part of Raoul, while Karl Löwitsch, who plays Felix in DESPAIR, is The Rich Jew, and Ingrid Caven is the prostitute he (mercy-)kills.

The controversy led to two further film projects being cancelled, one an adaptation of Gustav Freytag's *Soll und Haben* (intended as a historical investigation into the roots of the German bourgeoisie), and the second an adaptation of Gerhard Zwerenz' novel *The Earth Is as Uninhabitable as the Moon*, again a Frankfurt novel, taking up the theme of the modern city.

DIE EHE DER MARIA BRAUN (The Marriage of Maria Braun)
d: Rainer Werner Fassbinder; sc: Peter Märthesheimer, Pea Fröhlich, Rainer Werner Fassbinder, based on an idea by Rainer Werner Fassbinder; c: Michael Ballhaus; ed: Juliane Lorenz, Franz Walsch (= Rainer Werner Fassbinder); m: Peer Raben; lp: Hanna Schygulla, Klaus Löwitsch, Ivan Desny, Gottfried John, Günter Lamprecht, Gisela Uhlen, Elisabeth Trissenaar; r: 120 min, col; p: Albatros (Michael Fengler)/Trio (Hanns Eckelkamp)/ Westdeutscher Rundfunk (WDR), Cologne, 1979.

By the time the storm broke over *The City, Garbage and Death*, Fassbinder had already directed THE MARRIAGE OF MARIA BRAUN, written and produced by Peter Märtesheimer and his wife Pia Fröhlich. It was to prove his most internationally and nationally profitable film and the best-known of his BRD [i.e. Bundesrepublik Deutschland] trilogy (completed with LOLA and VERONIKA VOSS). Viewed in isolation, THE MARRIAGE OF MARIA BRAUN is first of all the story of a self-made woman (Hanna Schygulla), whose rise to prosperity parallels that of West Germany between 1945 and 1954. At one level, the secret of her success is that she exploits men the way men usually exploit women. Beyond that, two principles keep Maria going: the skills as 'double agents' that women have to acquire in the world of sexual politics are useful in the economic battle as well; and, secondly, however much she loves her husband (Klaus Löwitsch), this love gives her strength only as long as it remains unconsummated. The perversity of these two precepts is not immediately apparent as the story of Maria unfolds: a war-bride, she waits in vain for the return of her husband from the front, and while she likes Bill (George Byrd), the GI lover who supplies her with cigarettes and nylons, she does not hesitate to kill him when it is a matter of proving whom she truly loves.

Similarly, her employer and benefactor Oswald (Ivan Desny) is allowed to sleep with her, but not to fall in love with her: it is the self-discipline of a ruthlessly double existence in body and soul rather than a split between body and soul that is the guarantee of Maria's success. When love and sex finally come together with the return of her husband, the wires get crossed and Maria accidentally blows up both of them, just at the moment when West Germany wins the football world championship, symbolically – and for Fassbinder highly ironically – finding itself once more as a 'nation'.

THE MARRIAGE OF MARIA BRAUN confirmed Hanna Schygulla as Fassbinder's ideal actress and set the style and tone for a number of historical films centered on strong female characters by German directors, some well-known abroad, like Helma Sanders-Brahms' GERMANY PALE MOTHER and Edgar Reitz' HEIMAT, others familar only to German audiences, like Jeanine Meerapfel's MALOU (which stars Ingrid Caven, a Fassbinder regular and his ex-wife, together with Ivan Desny, the industrialist from THE MARRIAGE OF MARIA BRAUN).

DIE DRITTE GENERATION (The Third Generation)
d: Rainer Werner Fassbinder; sc: Rainer Werner Fassbinder; c: Rainer Werner Fassbinder; ed: Juiliane Lorenz; m: Peer Raben; lp: Harry Baer, Hark Bohm, Margit Carstensen, Eddie Constantine, Günther Kaufmann, Udo Kier, Bulle Ogier, Lilo Pempeit, Hanna Schygulla, Volker Spengler, Y Sa Lo, Vitus Zeplichal; r: 111 min, col; p: Tango Film/Pro-ject (Harry Baer), 1979.

As a contemporary counter-example, THE THIRD GENERATION studies the disintegration of this same divided nation into a police state, in a story that explores the make-believe world and paranoid universe of urban terrorists, now in their third generation. The plot premise is that the activists' hunger for risk, adventure and playing with guns has not only eroded any political motive or strategic objective (hence the title, after the first generation of idealists and the second of pragmatists comes the third generation of opportunists). They are also cynically manipulated by multinational companies specializing in computer hardware and surveillance equipment. Financed by an electronics firm, the terrorists are tricked into kidnapping the firm's chief executive, whom they endlessly rehearse for his ransom note video appearance. The charade culminates at the annual masked carnival, where the terrorists not already betrayed by the infiltrated informer are shot by the police. The pattern, now much more politicized, is similar to that of the early gangster films, especially GODS OF THE PLAGUE and THE AMERICAN SOLDIER. What is different is the emphasis on politics as a branch of show business in which the powers that be are as implicated as their opponents.

LILI MARLEEN

d: Rainer Werner Fassbinder; sc: Manfred Purzer, Rainer Werner Fassbinder; c: Xaver Schwarzenberger; ed: Juliane Lorenz, Franz Walsch (= Rainer Werner Fassbinder); m: Peer Raben; lp: Hanna Schygulla, Giancarlo Giannini, Mel Ferrer, Christine Kaufmann, Hark Bohm, Karin Baal, Udo Kier, Gottfried John; r: 121 min, col; p: Roxy-Film Munich (Luggi Waldleitner)/Rialto-Film Berlin (Horst Wendlandt)/BR Munich/CIP, 1980.

Show business and politics is also the basic motif in Fassbinder's most explicitly 'commercial' film, LILI MARLEEN. Financed by a producer well-known for having made much of his money from porn and exploitation films, it seemed to be an attempt to follow up on the Maria Braun formula and its success. With Hanna Schygulla again in the lead, LILI MARLEEN looks more closely at Germany's fascination with fascist spectacle: even the Jews in the underground (improbably to some, offensively to others) smuggle sensational film and pull spectacular stunts. Ostensibly a fictionalized biography of Lale Anderson, performer of the famous wartime song of the title, it concentrates on Willie's (Hanna Schygulla) meteoric rise thanks to the protection of the Nazi hierarchy, while she is also conducting a secret love affair with Robert Mendelsson (Giancarlo Giannini), son of wealthy Swiss Jews masterminding the resistance within Germany and using their son's infatuation as a decoy. Willie's political naiveté is, like Maria Braun's, a function of her love, strengthened by absence and separation. Once the war is over, she discovers that Robert, following expediency rather than his feelings, has married someone else.

Too sophisticated in its play with clichés and too twisted in its storyline for the general public, the film's sardonic treatment of the Nazi war as only another face of show-business made many critics, especially abroad, nervous and suspicious. In the United States, for instance, it was felt to be in very poor taste, since it depicted the Zionists as either terrorists or multinational businessmen. Coming at the tail end of a Nazi film wave among European directors, it seemed to many critics to have missed its moment.[38]

LOLA

d: Rainer Werner Fassbinder; sc: Peter Märthesheimer, Pea Fröhlich, dialogues by Rainer Werner Fassbinder; c: Xaver Schwarzenberger; ed: Juliane Lorenz, Franz Walsch (= Rainer Werner Fassbinder); m: Peer Raben; lp: Barbara Sukowa, Armin Mueller-Stahl, Mario Adorf, Matthias Fuchs, Helga Feddersen, Karin Baal, Ivan Desny, Hark Bohm; r: 113 min, col; p: Rialto-Film Berlin (Horst Wendlandt)/Trio-Film Duisburg/Westdeutscher Rundfunk (WDR) Cologne, 1981.

LOLA presents another Maria Braun maneuvering between show business and big business. Loosely conceived as a reworking of THE BLUE ANGEL, its heroine (Barbara Sukowa) is the chief attraction in the brothel of Coburg, a small German town during the last years of the Adenauer era. Enjoying the protection of the all-powerful building contractor Schuckert (Mario Adorf), she profits from her exclusivity, while keeping an idealistic clerk in the local planning office pining and pliant. The cosy arrangement is upset when the new broom at the head of the building inspectorate, von Bohm (Armin Müller-Stahl) decides to clean up and crack down on Schuckert's cavalier ways with building regulations. But the self-righteous von Bohm is soon smitten by Lola, though persuaded that it is her soul he is after. By dividing body and soul, Lola (like Maria) is able to keep everyone happy, while reserving herself (and the financial lion's share) for herself. Particularly striking in its period decor, its garish lighting, and a deft way of introducing topical political issues as if they were no different from the cars and furniture supplied by the props department, LOLA has strong central performances. In particular, the harsh sultriness of Barbara Sukowa and the vulgar vigour of Mario Adorf give the film the astringency it needs to make its cynicism seem more than sentimentality in reverse.

DIE SEHNSUCHT DER VERONIKA VOSS (Veronika Voss)

d: Rainer Werner Fassbinder; sc: Peter Märthesheimer, Pea Fröhlich; c: Xaver Schwarzenberger; ed: Juliane Lorenz; m: Peer Raben; lp: Rosel Zech, Hilmar Thate, Cornelia Froboess, Armin Mueller Stahl, Elisabeth Volkmann, Rudolf Platte, Doris Schade; r: 105 min, col; p: Laura Film GmbH/Tango Film in Cooperation with Rialto- Film/Trio-Film and Maran-Film, 1982.

In a sense, both LILI MARLEEN and LOLA are more optimistic accounts of the schizophrenia of the (inescapable) double life than VERONIKA VOSS, which takes the disintegration of personality, under the pressure of living incompatible existences, to its ultimate conclusion. Veronika Voss (Rosel Zech), a film star from the 1940s once much admired by Goebbels, tries to make a comeback in a Munich studio. A sports reporter, after a chance encounter in a midnight tram, where she borrows money from him, follows her home and discovers that she is virtually kept a prisoner by a woman doctor who supplies her with heroin, expecting to inherit her remaining possessions. Fassbinder takes motifs both from the detective thriller and from the sensationalist German problem film of the 1950s to authenticate the feel and texture of the fable (again a particularly impressive use of black-and-white photography). But the most striking scenes are those where Veronika is confronted by the memory and image of her former self, as it has survived on film or as she tries to recreate it, on the occasion of her (final) birthday. While the gallant reporter, equally obsessed with his own image of her, tries to rescue her into and for the real world, it becomes clear that there is a deeper understanding between the diabolical doctor (all in white) and her patient: that Veronika is ultimately a willing victim because she is herself so fascinated by the mirror of corruption the doctor can hold up to her. This corruption is both historical and psychological, but only the cinema and show business seem in Fassbinder's later work to provide acceptable metaphors for the fatal fascination with one's double.

Return to the Beginnings?

For a final reckoning with German history – and with the figure of Franz – Fassbinder returned to the more intimate format of a television series, made between THE THIRD GENERATION and LILI MARLEEN. Expanding Alfred Döblin's 1929 novel *Berlin Alexanderplatz* into a fourteen part panorama of Germany from the end of the First World War to the rise of Hitler meant recreating an entire era. The production consumed 13 million DM (which was cheap for some fifteen hours' of film) and was shot between June 1979 and April 1980. Premiered at the Venice Film Festival, it was broadcast, starting around Christmas 1980 and taking three months, to the shrill notes of a campaign against the director and his work on the part of the right-wing press. Defended in the quality weeklies like *Die Zeit* and celebrated by critics abroad (where it was also shown in movie theatres) as one of the major achievements of world cinema, its domestic viewing figures were, after a promising start, disappointing. In subsequent years, it was shown on television in most European countries, though usually in late-night slots.

BERLIN ALEXANDERPLATZ

d: Rainer Werner Fassbinder; sc: Rainer Werner Fassbinder, based on the novel by Alfred Döblin; c: Xaver Schwarzenberger; ed: Juliane Lorenz; m: Peer Raben; lp: Gerhard Lamprecht, Barbara Sukowa, Hanna Schygulla, Ivan Desny, Gottfried John, Ingrid Caven, Brigitte Mira; r: TV film, 81 min (part 1), 59 min (each part from part 2 to part 13), 111 min (epilogue), col; p: Bavaria/RAI for WDR (Peter Märthesheimer), 1979/1980.

BERLIN ALEXANDERPLATZ is the story of Franz Biberkopf (Günther Lamprecht), a petty criminal and pimp, who in a fit of jealousy, killed his lover Ida and went to prison for manslaughter. The film begins with his release and his 'rescue' by two Jewish Talmud scholars. After regaining his manhood by virtually raping the sister of Ida and taking up with Lina, a Polish prostitute, Franz vows from now on to 'go straight' and remain decent. Given the economic slump and long lines of unemployed, lengthened further by war veterans and the disabled, this is a hard promise to keep, and Franz, after a handful of odd jobs, including street vendor of the Nazi newspaper and door-to-door salesman of shoelaces, soon finds himself back among the semi-criminal underworld, as a scout and 'fence' for Pums, a local gangster with respectable ambitions whose 'mob' includes Reinhold (Gottfried John), someone Biberkopf will fatally fall in love with, though never quite knowing what it is that draws him to the man with the stammer. The latter is, if anything, obsessively heterosexual, as is Franz, who proves his friendship to Reinhold by 'taking over' his women, as soon as Reinhold tires of them or finds their further presence in his life a burden. But Reinhold is also responsible for making Franz a 'cripple', by throwing him off the getaway truck after a botched warehouse robbery. Thus thrown back into the urban jungle of joblessness and worthlessness, Franz is once more rescued, this time by Mieze (Barbara Sukowa), a young prostitute 'given' to him not by Reinhold, but by his ex-lover Eva (Hanna Schygulla). Mieze supports him, takes care of him, and falls as much in love with him as he with her. One day, some time after a bloody argument and a tearful reconciliation, Mieze fails come back home, and Franz thinks she has left him, but in fact she has been murdered by Reinhold. When learning of her death, Franz has a nervous breakdown, is interned in a psychiatric clinic, and, upon release, is asked to testify against Reinhold at the trial. Not wishing to denounce his friend, he equivocates, and Reinhold receives a sentence for manslaughter rather than murder. Franz, unable to comprehend what all these setbacks and disasters in his life might mean, is happy to land a small job as a nightwatchman.

Döblin's book, which Fassbinder first read when he was fourteen, is, according to the director, the only true bracket between his life and his work. The adaptation puts the spotlight on the ominous, undeclared and lethal love between Franz and Reinhold, whereas the novel keeps this relationship submerged in the multifarious tragic and grotesque adventures of its Joe Average hero. Helped by the towering presence of Günther Lamprecht and Fassbinder's usual cast, the series draws from the material a truly spell-binding and terrifying picture of a world where, indeed, the 'little people are allowed to have big feelings'. These feelings, though, give them not much insight into the ways of the world, make them no class-conscious fighters for the just cause, but make them torment each other without knowing why. When it comes to deciding for or against democracy, Franz 'will probably vote for the National Socialists' (Fassbinder).

By appending an epilogue entitled 'My dream of the dream of Franz Biberkopf', a two-hour phantasmagoria stylistically located somewhere between Wagner, Syberberg and Pasolini, Fassbinder seems to be taking back into his own mind the huge external canvas of people and places, of personal and political disasters which the film spent so many hours making palpable. This epilogue leaves the viewer in turn numbed and exhausted by the bleakness of its vision, squirming because of its Bavarian kitsch version of the 'hell' which is our century, or astonished by Fassbinder's candour, exposing his own inner world, unprotected by genre conventions and melodrama, unless one realizes that, here too, the words are almost too painstakingly faithful to Döblin's text.

QUERELLE

d: Rainer Werner Fassbinder; sc: Burkhard Driest, Rainer Werner Fassbinder, based on the novel *Querelle de Brest* by Jean Genet; c: Xaver Schwarzenberger; ed: Juliane Lorenz; m: Peer Raben; lp: Brad Davis, Franco Nero, Jeanne Moreau, Laurent Malet, Hanno Pöschl, Günther Kaufmann; r: 107 min, col, Cinemascope; p: Planet-Film Munich (Dieter Schidor), 1982.

      At first glance, QUERELLE, after Jean Genet and Fassbinder's last film (shot but not edited at the time of his death), completes the cycle of characters fatally in love with their doubles. In the hermetically sealed artificial paradise of Brest harbour, luxuriating in an obsessively phallic world of sailors and leather boys, it becomes almost impossible to tell brother from brother, or to keep track of who over-identifies with whom and sees himself inversely doubled in whom. In this world of frosted glass and peep-show cubicles, not even cold-blooded murder or violent anal rape can shatter the mirrors that keep these anxious sleepwalkers of the lost reflection in thrall to their self-images. What emerges from the story of Querelle, the beautiful sailor, desired and exploited and in turn desiring and exploiting is once again a complex charade of disguises and doubles, brothers and lovers, betrayals and denials. While its overheated cloying atmosphere, its closed sets and artificial light, its choking, steaming, sweating, bleeding, oozing bodies are anything but conventional images of beauty, one can admire Fassbinder's honesty in creating such a democratic vision of perversion, and the discipline with which he gives the multifarious relationships between the protagonists the same unmistakable stamp of the authentically inauthentic that already determined the constellation of characters in his very first films. In another sense, QUERELLE could be seen as beginning something quite different, going well beyond the re-interpretation of the all-male relationships of the early gangster-films or the female melodramas, now no longer in drag.

Epilogue

Confronted with the magnum opus which is BERLIN ALEXANDERPLATZ, one is struck how this most egocentric and self-obsessed director, who is said to have fed off his associates, friends, lovers and collaborators, and who poured out film after film, without scarcely pausing to draw breath, possessed a very clear sense of wanting to give his furious productivity an almost morphological congruity. If for most critics BERLIN ALEXANDERPLATZ stands as his testament, gratifying one's sense of closure, mise-en-abyme and circularity, it is possible to see QUERELLE, and even more so two of the projects he was working on at the time of his death – an adaptation of a novel entitled *Cocaine*, and a life of *Rosa Luxemburg*, the socialist, feminist and revolutionary, murdered in 1919 – as vigorously continuing the twin tracks of his entire work. With *Cocaine*, the study of yet another vicious circle he was himself locked into, namely the mephistophelian wager his body had entered with mind-enhancing but also self-destructive stimulants, while in Rosa Luxemburg he had discovered another heroine faced with an impossible love, an impossible nationality, an impossible ethnic identity and impossible politics: all of these impossibilities at once energizing her life and using it up in and for German history.

These two projects also confirm that a reading of his work that stresses the psycho-biographical links and makes them the basis of the films' thematic coherence is as inviting as it is finally deeply unsatisfactory. Whatever one may think of this Fassbinder film or that on the scale of cinematic 'masterpieces', it will not do to treat any of them as the 'waste product'[39] of more or less unsavory episodes and anecdotes from a chaotic private and sexual life. What needed to be probed is why this singular and finally so strange body of work should be capable of elicting such strong emotional resonances, and yet, in some important respects, remain so remote. It once led me to speculate that the logic of independent filmmaking in Germany not only determined the director's working methods, but shaped his lifestyle as well.[40] In the films, however, this twofold historicity became the condition of possibility for a unique, and uniquely double (in its compassionate embracing of both elements of a contradiction) view of post-war West Germany. The argument I have tried to make in this book is that Fassbinder's films follow several distinct chronologies and enact quite distinct temporalities: pressing the case of him representing Germany, by embodying one 'approach' to being German in the latter half of the 20th century. His whole work can be seen as the effort to (once more) *become German*, and thus to help 'house' his country without immuring it in defensive guilt or aggressive self-identity. In this, he is not representative, but exceptional, and can claim to have done his share in (re)building the 'House' called Germany, even before Michail Gorbachov's appeal to the house called Europe. Like his Biblical culture hero, Moses, these very conditions of possibility seem to have banned Fassbinder from making this house his own habitation.

Appendix Two

Fassbinder's Germany 1945-1982: A Chronology

Rainer Werner Fassbinder (May 31, 1945—June 10, 1982) was born into a cultured bourgeois family in the small Bavarian spa town Bad Wörishofen. Raised by his mother as an only child, Fassbinder had only sporadic contact with his father, a doctor, after the divorce of his parents when he was five. Educated at a Rudolf Steiner elementary school and subsequently in Munich and Augsburg, the city of Brecht, he left school before passing any final examinations. A cinema addict ('five times a week, often three films a day') from a very early age, not least because his mother needed peace and quiet for her work as a translator, 'the cinema was the family life I never had at home.'

Fassbinder made his first short films at the age of twenty, persuading a male lover to finance them in exchange for leading roles. He also applied for a place at the Berlin Film School (DFFA), but was refused. He acted in both his early films: DER STADTSTREICHER *(The City Tramp)*, which also featured Irm Hermann (later often used in character roles); and DAS KLEINE CHAOS *(The Little Chaos)*. In the latter, his mother – under the name of Lilo Pempeit – played the first of many parts in her son's films. Only after these amateur directing-scripting-acting efforts did Fassbinder take lessons with a professional acting studio, where he met Hanna Schygulla, his most important actress, who thanks to him became an international star. It was through Schygulla that Fassbinder turned his interest to the theatre.

In 1967 Fassbinder joined the Munich action-theater. He directed, acted in, and adapted anti-establishment plays for a tightly knit group of young professionals, among them Peer Raben and Kurt Raab, who along with Schygulla and Hermann, became the most important members of his cinematic stock company. Jean-Marie Straub directed the action-theater in an eight-minute version of Bruckner's *Krankheit der Jugend*, using part of this stage production in his short film DER BRÄUTIGAM, DIE KOMÖDIANTIN UND DER ZUHÄLTER, 1968), with Fassbinder as the pimp. In 1968 Fassbinder directed the first play written by himself, *Katzelmacher*, a twenty-minute highly choreographed encounter between Bavarian villagers and a foreign worker from Greece, who with scarcely a word of German, becomes the object of intense racial, sexual, and political hatred among the men, while exerting a strangely troubling fascination on the women. A few weeks later, in May 1968, the Action theater was disbanded after its theatre was wrecked by one of its founders, jealous of Fassbinder's growing power within the group. It promptly reformed under Fassbinder's command as the *anti-teater,* which pursued an equally radical and frequently provocative production policy.

The years from 1969 to 1976 were Fassbinder's most prodigous and prolific period. An outstanding career in the theatre (productions in Munich, Bremen, Bochum, Nuremberg, Berlin, Hamburg and Frankfurt, where for two years he ran the 'Theater am Turm' with Kurt Raab and Roland Petri) was a mere backdrop for a seemingly unstoppable outpouring of films, TV film, adaptations, and even a TV variety show (in honour of Brigitte Mira). During the same period, he also did radio plays and took on roles in other director's films, among them the title part in Volker Schlöndorff's Brecht adaptation *Baal*. By 1976 Fassbinder had become an international star. Prizes at major film festivals, premieres and retrospectives in Paris, New York, Los Angeles, and a first critical study on his work appearing in London had made him a familiar name among cinephiles and campus audiences the world over. He owned a house in Paris and could be seen in gay bars in New York, earning him cult hero status but also a controversial reputation in and out of his films. Art house circuits avidly took up his films: because he had so many to his credit by the time he was 'discovered' with FEAR EATS THE SOUL, the re-release of his earlier films, together with the steady stream of new work, made his extraordinary productivity seem even more phenomenal.

This productivity has given rise to much speculation. He himself averred once that 'it must be some kind of sickness.' Others saw it as an escape from his personal life, a need to surround himself with people and commotion day and night. Kurt Raab has claimed that Fassbinder needed such a large 'surrogate family' in order to rehearse the situations of his films, and that – when not on the set, eating or asleep – he was mostly engaged in playing cruel private theatre and psychological power-games, in order to observe the reactions and the interpersonal dynamics. For Raab, who by his own admission loved him deeply and for years kept house for him, Fassbinder was only tolerable when one was alone with him. Peter Chatel, who tried to keep his distance, has also spoken of the pressure Fassbinder exerted on the members of his clan in order to have their assent and loyalty by a selective cruelty to others, making them the butt of his jokes, seeing this psycho-terror a necessary ingredient of his productivity. To Irm Hermann, who also knew him well, the source of his productivity was the anxiety of being abandoned, unloved, lonely – a fear she traced to an emotional coldness in his mother. The films were necessary to keep the 'family' which in turn provided the admiration that substituted for the missing love, of which he always had to reassure himself, by reenacting the originary lack, the mother's failure to be nurturing. In this sense, everything in Fassbinder's life becomes the displaced cause of everything else: the loveless mother the cause for his fear of solitude, the forced gregariousness the cause of the power-play and emotional manipulations, the manipulativeness the basis for his success as 'director', while being director provided the occasions for others to become involved with him. In this account – variations of which can also be found in Gerhard Zwerenz and Peter Berling – the films and their subjects are merely the consequence or by-products of having set up and then needing to service the apparatus of this particular kind of obsessive sociability, where glamour, attention, fame and financial rewards allowed Fassbinder to bind his collaborators to him, without himself having to be either loveable or loving.

Against such a psycho-portrait, however, one has to recall a number of other factors. Fassbinder was able to stimulate productivity in people who before coming into contact with him showed little promise or talent, inspiring them to give their best, which was very often better than anything they could do or had done on their own. From early on in his career, Fassbinder had also acquired the ability not only to recognize the basic principles of successful filmmaking, but to put them into practice: a regular team to ensure smooth working conditions and economic shooting schedules, a continuous flow of product to guarantee financial liquidity, and a turnaround of production capital. Working in a country without a viable film industry, where broadcast television was organized at the regional level and therefore highly decentralized, Fassbinder had opted for what he himself referred to as his 'mini-studio' system, a team of actors and technicians whom he could trust, if only to the extent that he knew how to exploit their dependence.

The high rate of output allowed most of his team to acquire technical skills. It speaks for his organizational ability and discipline that he could integrate and make his own the work of so many diverse individuals. In order to keep his team together Fassbinder had to give them regular work, and as a result, his films were shot fast and made cheaply, but with pretensions to production values to rival Hollywood, even if the budget rarely allowed crashing a single car in a chase or a shoot-out. The result was a shabby glamor that became the hallmark of his early style. As he grew more famous and his budgets larger, Fassbinder gradually replaced his original team with outside professionals, often from the German film and television industries.

To remain in business, German commercial producers had had to resort to making films in series – Karl May Westerns, Edgar Wallace thrillers, porn-films, classroom-comedies. Fassbinder's output by contrast, while also formula-bound in some respects, remained highly personal and distinctive, and testified to an unmistakable love and knowledge of the cinema. The films also reflected an innate and passionate professionalism, an admiration for the American cinema, the Hollywood studio system, its proven genres, and the box office power of its stars: 'I want to make Hollywood films – in Germany' Fassbinder was fond of saying.

In 1972 Fassbinder began his collaboration with a highly experienced and successful producer at West Germany's most prestigious television network, Peter Märthesheimer of WDR. Under Märthesheimer's influence, Fassbinder turned with even more determination to recognizably German subject matter. Together they made, among others, the tv series EIGHT HOURS DO NOT MAKE A DAY, and in 1978 co-wrote THE MARRIAGE OF MARIA BRAUN, Fassbinder's commercially most profitable film and the first in his 'post-war German trilogy'. For many foreign critics, his crowning achievement was the 13-part television adaptation of Alfred Döblin's *Berlin Alexanderplatz*, much maligned by the domestic press. Altough for VERONIKA VOSS Fassbinder received the Golden Bear at the 1982 Berlin Film Festival, a much-coveted Oscar nomination eluded him. As had often been noted, Fassbinder was the engine and motor (the 'heart' in Wolfram Schütte's words) of the New German Cinema. His sudden death from a drug overdose in June 1982 symbolically marked the end of the most exciting and experimental period the German cinema had known since the 1920s.

Chronology

Fassbinder 1945-1950

May 31st, 1945: Rainer Werner Fassbinder is born in Bad Wörishofen. His father is Dr. Helmuth Fassbinder, general practitioner, and his mother is Liselotte, born Pempeit, translator. RWF spent his first year in the Black Forest with the family of his father's twin brother (a country doctor), and returns to his parents, now in Munich in the Spring of 1946. The family rent a large apartment, combining surgery and living quarters, and are joined by a number of maternal relatives, including RWF's grandmother.

Germany 1945-1950

Major political events in 1945:

May 8th: unconditional surrender of German Armed Forces. Collapse of Hitler Germany.
June: The Four Allied Powers jointly assume governmental control.

Major media events in 1945:

August – December: Radio Hamburg goes on air, Radio Munich, Berlin, Frankfurt, Stuttgart, Cologne and Bremen follow suit.
British and American military governments jointly produce weekly newsreel *Welt im Film*.
First licensed newspaper *Frankfurter Rundschau* is produced in the U.S. military zone.
Allies set down first guidelines for new re-education policies.
Composer Anton v. Webern is shot dead in Mittersill/Salzburg by an American soldier.
TODESMÜHLEN, a documentary about the concentration camps is first shown.
News agencies in the British Zone are reconstituted as the *Deutscher Pressedienst* (later DPA)

Major publishing events in 1945:

Der Totenwald (report from the concentration camp Buchenwald) by Ernst Wiechert.
Magazines *Der Aufbau, Die Wandlung, Die Gegenwart* founded

Major political events in 1946:

January: first municipal elections in the U.S. zone
October 1st: 12 of the 24 accused at the Nuremberg war criminal trial are condemned to death.

Major film events in 1946:

Founding of DEFA in East Berlin; first feature film productions: DIE MÖRDER SIND UNTER UNS (The Murderers are Among Us), IRGENDWO IN BERLIN (Somewhere in Berlin), SAG DIE WAHRHEIT (Tell the Truth).

Major publishing events in 1946:

Das Glasperlenspiel by Hermann Hesse
Magazines *Der Ruf, Frankfurter Hefte* founded

Major cultural events in 1946:
Heinz Hilpert produces Carl Zuckmayer's *Des Teufels General* (about Hitler's army chiefs) at the Zurich Playhouse, which became the most frequently staged play between 1947 and 1950
Magda Hein's 'Möwe, Du fliegst in die Heimat' tops the charts and introduces the *Heimat*schlager in popular music.

Major political events in 1947:
January – April: the worst hunger months since the end of the war

Major publishing events in 1947:
First edition of the news magazine *Der Spiegel* (January)
Founding of the 'Gruppe 47', Germany's literary avantgarde (September)
Dr Faustus by Thomas Mann

Other events in 1947:
Soccer leagues begin training
First drawing of the 'Süddeutsche Klassenlotterie'
Architect Walter Gropius begins a lecture tour in Germany (invited by the American military government)

Major cultural events in 1947:
Wolfgang Borchert's play *Draußen vor der Tür* is aired on radio and performed in the *Hamburger Kammerspiele*.
Cultural magazine *Merkur* is founded
Popular hit songs with topical titles: 'Wer soll das bezahlen?' (who'll pay for all this?) and 'Wir sind die Eingeborenen von Trizonesien' (we're the natives of tri-zonasia)

Major film events of 1947:
IN JENEN TAGEN by Helmut Käutner, UND ÜBER UNS DER HIMMEL by Josef von Baky, ZWISCHEN GESTERN UND MORGEN by Harald Braun

Major political events in 1948:
June: Currency Reform in West Germany, Soviet blockade of Berlin, US/UK airlift
October: The Soviet zone becomes the German Democratic Republic

Major media events 1948:
First edition of illustrated weekly *Bunte Illustrierte*, followed by *Quick* and *Stern*.
Nordwestdeutsche Rundfunk (NWDR) is handed over to German management (January 1949)

Major literary and theatre events in 1948:
Herr Puntila und sein Knecht Matti by Bertolt Brecht premiers at the Zurich Playhouse

Major film events in 1948:
AFFAIRE BLUM by Erich Engel, FILM OHNE TITEL by Rudolf Jugert, BERLINER BALLADE by Robert A.Stemmle

Major political events in 1949:
April: NATO is founded
May: the 'Basic Law' of the Federal Republic is officially signed

September: Konrad Adenauer is narrowly elected first Federal Chancellor
October: the division of Germany into two states is internationally recognized

Major literary and theatre events in 1949:
Bertolt Brecht, together with wife Helene Weigel, founds the Berliner Ensemble in East Berlin and premiers *Mutter Courage und ihre Kinder.*
Thomas Mann gives lectures in East and West Germany (Frankfurt and Weimar)
Ernst Jünger's *Strahlungen* and Gottfried Benn's *Trunkene Flut* published

Major film event in 1949:
NACHTWACHE by Harald Braun

Major political event in 1950:
November: the German national soccer team defeats Switzerland 1:0

Fassbinder 1951-1955
1950: RWF's mother hospitalized with TB
1951: Parents separate, father moves to Cologne, RWF stays with his mother in Munich
1951-1955: RWF enters public school system, but in 1952 is moved to a Rudolf Steiner School, while his mother is frequently hospitalized or in sanatoria and RWF looked after by relatives and neighbours, first regular visits to the cinema.

Germany 1951-1955
Major political events in 1951:
March: production starts on the 'elastoplast bomber', a cheap and popular mass-market automobile
April: in Paris, Adenauer signs the 'Montan-Union' treaty, nucleus of the new Europe

Major film event in 1951:
DIE SÜNDERIN by Willy Forst (protest and boycott organized by the Churches)

Major political events in 1952:
September: Adenauer signs reparation treaty with Israel
December: first television broadcast in North and West Germany

Major political events in 1953:
17 June: East Berlin workers' uprising, crushed by Soviet tanks
October: Adenauer is re-elected Chancellor, with a right-of-centre coalition

Major political event in 1954:
4 July: German National Soccer Team wins the world championship against Hungary 3:2

Major film event in 1954:
DIE LETZTE BRÜCKE by Helmut Käutner

Major cultural event in 1954:
Bill Haley gives first rock'n'roll concerts in Hamburg and Frankfurt

Major political events in 1955:
June: West Germany becomes sovereign state, with its own army

July: Federal Republic is admitted into NATO

December: as 'economic miracle' takes off, the first 'Gastarbeiter' arrive from Italy and Greece

Major cultural event in 1955:
First *documenta* held in Kassel

Major film events in 1955:
HIMMEL OHNE STERNE by Helmut Käutner, SISSY by Ernst Marischka, starring Romy Schneider, DES TEUFEL'S GENERAL by Helmut Käutner

Fassbinder 1956-1960

1955/56: RWF attends Theresia Gymnasium in Munich

1956-1958: RWF attends St Anna Gymnasium in Augsburg, then move to Realgymnasium Augsburg and becomes boarder while his mother has operation, requiring a two-year recovery stay in a sanatorium. Frequent visits to the cinema

1959: After his mother marries journalist Wolff Eder, RWF once more changes school, and returns to Munich (Realgymnasium), but lives at a boarding school.

1960: RWF starts writing short stories and playlets

Germany 1956-1960

Major political events in 1956:
80th birthday of Chancellor Konrad Adenauer
Lower House of Parliament ratifies law decreeing compulsory military service
Franz Josef Strauß becomes minister of Defense
KPD (German Communist Party) is outlawed

Major cultural events in 1956:
Diary of Anne Frank is performed on numerous German stages
Bertolt Brecht dies

Major film events in 1956:
STRESEMANN by Alfred Braun, DIE TRAPP-FAMILIE by Wolfgang Liebeneiner, NIGHT AND FOG by Alain Resnais,
DIE HALBSTARKEN by Georg Tressler, DER HAUPTMANN VON KÖPENICK by Helmut Käutner, starring Heinz Rühmann

Major political events in 1957:
France cedes Saar region to Germany (January)
Germany signs Rome Treaty, founding the EEC (March)
Adenauer pleads for German nuclear armament, Otto Hahn and 18 other nuclear physicists sign an appeal for the German government to renounce atomic weapons
In Frankurt, a call-girl is found murdered; her clients are prominent politicians and industrialists

Major film event in 1957:
DAS WIRTSHAUS IM SPESSART by Kurt Hoffmann

Major media event in 1957:
Brecht's *Dreigroschenoper* on TV reaches 81,2% of viewers

Major political events in 1958:
First meetings between Adenauer and de Gaulle
Heinrich Lübke succeeds Theodor Heuss as President of the Federal Republic

Major film event in 1958:
German government attempts to ban the screening at the Venice Biennale of DAS MÄDCHEN ROSEMARIE by Rolf Thiele which deals with the death of the Frankfurt call-girl.

Major political events in 1959:
The Social-Democrat Party (SPD) ratifies the 'Godesberg Programme'
Ministry of Defense orders (ill-fated) 'Starfighters' from the US

Major film event in 1959:
DIE BRÜCKE by Bernhard Wicki

Major cultural events of 1959:
Hula-Hoop craze sweeps Germany
documenta 2 takes place in Kassel

Major political events in 1960:
The VW-Works are partially privatized, with 60% being sold as 'people's shares'
Adolf Eichmann is brought to Israel (sentenced in 1961 and executed in 1962)
The Social-Democrat Student Union (SDS) is expelled from the Party, eventually forming the Extra-parliamentary Opposition (APO)

Major media event:
Long-running (111 episodes since 1954), popular (70-90% audience share) television series *Die Familie Schölermann* is replaced by *Die Firma Hesselbach*

Fassbinder 1961-1964
1961-1963: RWF leaves school and joins his father to Cologne, for whom he works as rent collector, mainly tenement blocks let to 'Gastarbeiter' (foreign workers); attends evening classes, spends time in homosexual bars and writes stories
1963: RWF returns to Munich and continues to write: short plays, poems, stories, script-exercises, many of which have survived.
1963-1965: RWF works briefly in the research department of the *Süddeutsche Zeitung*
September 1963 to early 1964: RWF takes private acting lessons, before joining the Schauspielschule Fridl Leonhard

Germany 1961-1964
Major political events in 1961:
The Berlin Wall goes up
Adenauer is reelected as Federal Chancellor

Major media events in 1961:

Bayerischer Rundfunk stops transmission during a performance of *Lysistrata* (by Aristophanes, adapted by Fritz Kortner) because of offensive language.

Call to boycott Brecht's plays rejected by most West German theatres.

Cast of Bayreuth production of Wagner's *Tannhäuser* includes black singer Grace Bumbry which causes protest

Major political events in 1962:

On orders of Defense Minister Strauß, editorial offices of *Der Spiegel* are searched, publisher Rudolf Augstein and several other editors are arrested. The ensuing governmental crisis leads to FDP resignations and Strauß gives up his Cabinet post, allowing Adendauer to continue ruling with a CDU/CSU/FDP coalition.

US president John F Kennedy visits Berlin

Major media events in 1962:

The Beatles commence their career by performing in Hamburg

The 'Oberhausen Manifesto' of the 'Young German cinema' is published at the annual documentary festival

Major political events in 1963:

Adenauer (now 87) resigns after 14 years in office. His Finance Minister, Ludwig Erhard becomes his successor.

The Auschwitz trial begins in Frankfurt (until 1965)

Franco-German friendship treaty is signed

Major media event of 1963:

ZDF (Zweites Deutsches Fernsehen) goes on air

Major film event of 1963:

MACHORKA MUFF by Jean Marie Straub, after a story by Heinrich Böll

Fassbinder 1965-1966

1964-1966: RWF takes acting classes, where he meets Hanna Schygulla

1965: RWF meets Irm Hermann; first 8-mm films, small acting parts, and sound assistant on student productions

Fails entrance examination to federal acting academy, writes play about Auschwitz (*Nur eine Scheibe Brot*), which is awarded third prize in a youth drama competition

1966: applies to the Deutsche Film- und Fernsehakademie Berlin; fails entrance examinations, meets Daniel Schmid and decides to break off acting classes on his 21st birthday (31 May 1966)

Summer 1966: shoots first film (THIS NIGHT, 8mm-short film which has been lost)

November 1966: shoots DER STADTSTREICHER (with Christoph Roser, Irm Hermann, Michael Fengler and RWF)

Germany 1964-1966

Major political events in 1964:

SPD elects Willy Brandt as party chairman

Major cultural events in 1964:
documenta 3 in Kassel
Herbert Marcuse publishes *One-Dimensional Man*, the bible of the student protest movement
Mini skirt, invented by Mary Quant, becomes popular in Germany

Major political events in 1965:
Diplomatic relations established between West Germany and Israel
Ludwig Erhard re-elected as Chancellor. CDU/CSU/FDP coalition
Star-fighter planes continue to crash on training flights

Major media events in 1965:
high suicide rate at the 'New University' of Bochum
New York's Living Theatre (Julian Beck and Judith Malina) tour in Berlin and Munich.
Hans Magnus Enzensberger founds the periodical *Kursbuch*, rallying point of politicised intellectuals

Major film event of 1965:
NICHT VERSÖHNT by Jean Marie Straub, after a novel by Heinrich Böll

Major political events in 1966:
FDP ministers resign from Erhard's cabinet. No-confidence motion leads to Erhard's resignation. Kurt Georg Kiesinger (CDU) is elected Chancellor and enters into grand coalition with SPD. Willy Brandt takes over foreign affairs ministry and starts diplomatic opening to Eastern Europe ('Ostpolitik')

Major film events in 1966:
Karl-May series and Edgar Wallace thrillers are commercial hits
several 'Young German film' successful with the critics: ES by Ulrich Schamoni, YOUNG TÖRLESS by Volker Schlöndorff, ABSCHIED VON GESTERN by Alexander Kluge and SCHONZEIT FÜR FÜCHSE by Peter Schamoni

Fassbinder 1967

January: RWF shoots DAS KLEINE CHAOS on 35mm, meets Ulli Lommel, a promising young actor commuting between Bremen and Munich
First contacts with the Munich Action-Theater (Ursula Straetz, Peer Raben, Kurt Raab); tries once more, unsuccessfully, to enter Berlin film academy
At the Action-Theater, RWF first acts, then directs and co-directs with Peer Raben

Germany 1967

Major political events in 1967:
Konrad Adenauer dies
Founding of the 'Kommune I' in Berlin
State visit of the Shah of Iran. Violence erupts during protest demonstrations, where the student Benno Ohnesorg is shot dead by police.

Major cultural events in 1967:
Bremen becomes centre of German Theatre: Kurt Hübner, Peter Zadek, Wilfried Minks.

Martin Sperr's play *Landshuter Erzählungen* is performed in Munich
Peter Stein directs Edward Bond's *Saved* in Munich as a Bavarian dialect version

Major film event of 1967:
A new film subsidy law is passed, encouraging commercial producers to invest in cheap pornographic series
ZUR SACHE, SCHÄTZCHEN by May Spils

Fassbinder 1968

RWF adapts play by Marieluise Fleißer and writes his first play *Katzelmacher* which has its premiere in April at the Action-Theater
May: abrupt end of Action-Theater, when Horst Söhnlein destroys equipment and fittings
RWF founds 'antiteater' with ten members of the Action-Theater, among them Peer Raben, Hanna Schygulla, Rudolf Waldemar Brem, Kurt Raab. They play at the Büchner-Theater, then at the Akademie der Künste and finally, from the end of 1968 till the end of 1969, in the backroom of the pub 'Witwe Bolte' in Schwabing.
RWF adapts, writes and co-directs some eight plays, including *Der amerikanische Soldat*.

Germany 1968

Major political events in 1968:
Student revolts in Berlin and Frankfurt from April onwards
Student leader Rudi Dutschke is shot by right-wing fanatic and seriously wounded
Federal parliament passes 'emergency laws' which allow the government to curtail civil liberties

Major media events in 1968:
Peter Handke's play *Kaspar Hauser* opens in Frankfurt and Oberhausen.
The musical *Hair* draws huge audiences in Munich

Major film events in 1968:
CHRONICLE OF ANNA MAGDALENA BACH by Jean Marie Straub and Danièle Huillet and ARTISTS AT THE TOP OF THE BIG TOP: DISORIENTED by Alexander Kluge

Fassbinder 1969

April: shooting of the first film by the antiteater: LIEBE IST KÄLTER ALS DER TOD, which has its premiere at the Berlin Film Festival in June to mixed reviews (e.g. by Peter Handke); RWF writes *Pre-paradise sorry now* and *Anarchie in Bayern*, as well as scripts for several films
August: shooting of the second film by the antiteater: KATZELMACHER
October: premiere of KATZELMACHER at the Mannheim Film Festival, where it receives seven prizes
RWF meets Harry Baer, directs GODS OF THE PLAGUE and co-directs WHY DOES HERR R RUN AMOK; forced closure of 'Witwe Bolte'
Kurt Hübner at the Bremen Theater am Goetheplatz organizes the 'Fassbinder showdown' where the anti-theater team puts on all of Fassbinder's plays

RWF meets Margarethe von Trotta and acts in several films, including Volker Schlöndorff's
BAAL. Liaison RWF commences with Günther Kaufmann

Germany 1969
Major political events in 1969:
Gustav Heinemann (SPD) is elected Federal President
General election, after which SPD and FDP form coalition. Willy Brandt becomes Chancellor, with Walter Scheel as Minister of Foreign Affairs.

Major cultural events in 1969:
Georg Tabori writes and produces *Mein Kampf*, a fictional meeting between Hitler and Theodor Herzl in a night asylum
pop singer Heintje has several number one hits

Major film event in 1969:
OTHON by Jean Maire Straub and Danièle Huillet

Fassbinder 1970
RWF directs six films, among them BEWARE OF A HOLY WHORE. He makes one television
feature (DAS KAFFEEHAUS), writes and directs two radio plays
RWF has first contact with producers Günther Rohrbach and Peter Märthesheimer
RWF marries actress and chansonniere Ingrid Caven

Germany 1970
Major political events of 1970:
Chancellor Brandt and Willi Stoph (GDR) meet in Erfurt and Kassel: thaw in German-German relations
Signing of the German-Soviet peace treaty and the German-Polish peace treaty, Brandt makes genuflection at the Warsaw ghetto memorial

Major media events of 1970:
City of Hannover begins 'Aktion der Straßenkunst' (until 1973), a series of municipally funded art happenings in public spaces.
Hermann Nitsch slaughters lambs on stage and tears them into pieces, chanting and screaming

Major film event of 1970:
NICHT DER HOMOSEXUELLE IST PERVERS, SONDERN DIE SITUATION, IN DER ER SICH BEFINDET
by Rosa von Praunheim

Fassbinder 1971
RWF participates in the founding of Filmverlag der Autoren
End of antiteater and antiteater-X-Film
Founding of production company 'Tango Film-Rainer Werner Fassbinder', whose first film
is THE MERCHANT OF FOUR SEASONS
RWF writes two plays, among them his most successful *The Bitter Tears of Petra von Kant*

Through Peer Raben is alerted to the films of Douglas Sirk whose style and treatment of genre formulas have a profound effect on his filmmaking

RWF writes a play for Margit Carstensen, starts his relation with El Hedi ben Salem

RWF's mother, after the death of her husband Wolff Eder, takes over as RWF's business manager and accountant, warding off insolvency proceedings in the face of large liabilities in back taxes and outstanding debts

Germany 1971

Major political events in 1971:
Willy Brandt receives the Nobel Peace Prize
Bundesausbildungsgesetz (Bafög: student grants) is ratified: higher education expands dramatically

Major media events in 1971:
At the initiative of Hilmar Hoffmann, the first 'Kommunales Kino' (municipally subsidized programme cinema) is established in Frankfurt; in subsequent years some 150 such cinemas open all over West Germany
Joachim Fest publishes an attack on subsidized theatre ('Wozu das Theater'?) in *Der Spiegel*

Major film events in 1971:
LAND OF SILENCE AND DARKNESS by Werner Herzog; THE DEATH OF MARIA MALIBRAN by Werner Schroeter

Fassbinder 1972

RWF publishes major essay on six films by Douglas Sirk

Besides shooting two films starring Margit Carstensen, RWF begins FONTANE EFFI BRIEST with Hanna Schygulla and completes his workers' film television series EIGHT HOURS ARE NOT A DAY. Does a theatrical production of *Liliom* in Bochum and writes and directs another radio play

RWF separates from Ingrid Caven who moves to Paris

Germany 1972

Major political events in 1972:
Extremistenbeschluß: Heads of the Länder governments decide to ratify law which forbids civil servants to be members of 'radical political organizations'
The Axel Springer publishing house in Hamburg is fire-bombed by demonstrators
The Red Army Fraction's leaders (Andreas Baader, Jan-Carl Raspe, Gudrun Ensslin, Ulrike Meinhof) are arrested
The Palestinian terror group 'Black September' attacks the Israeli Team at the Munich Olympic Games

Major cultural event in 1972:
Franz Xaver Kroetz's play *Stallerhof* has the young actress Eva Mattes in the lead
The plays by Marie-Luise Fleißer and Ödön von Horvath have successful theatre revivals

Major film event in 1972:
AGUIRRE-WRATH OF GOD by Werner Herzog

Fassbinder 1973

More films starring Margit Carstensen (especially the extraordinary MARTHA), while also working at theartres in Bochum and Berlin. Splits up with El Hedi ben Salem, with whom (and for whom) he makes FEAR EATS THE SOUL, his international breakthrough film.

Germany 1973

Major political event in 1973:
West Germany becomes member of the United Nations

Major cultural event in 1973:
The end of the theatre crisis, according to *Theater heute*. The 'Theatre of the director' (Theater der Regisseure) is proclaimed.

Major film event in 1973:
ALICE IN THE CITIES by Wim Wenders

Fassbinder 1974

First Fassbinder-retrospective at the Cinémathèque in Paris
RWF becomes co-director at the TAT (Theater am Turm) in Frankfurt am Main, which practices a complicated co-determination model of decision making; RWF soon comes into conflict with members of the ensemble not belonging to his own inner circle, but puts on *Germinal* (adapted by Yaak Karsunke) and Chekhov's *Uncle Vanya*.
RWF writes a TV show in honour of Brigitte Mira, and directs a play by Peter Handke
Meets Armin Meier, who starts living with RWF

Germany 1974

Major political event in 1974:
Chancellor Brandt resigns when staff member Günter Guillaume is uncovered as a GDR spy. Helmut Schmidt takes over as Chancellor. Walter Scheel is elected Federal President

Major cultural event in 1974:
Heinrich Böll's novel *The Lost Honour of Katharina Blum* is published, castigating right wing tabloid journalism

Major film event of 1974:
KASPAR HAUSER by Werner Herzog

Fassbinder 1975

June: resigns from the TAT engagement before his contract runs out, and reputedly angered by the Frankfurt municipal bureaucracy, writes *The City, Garbage and Death*, as well as adapting the play for a film version
A Fassbinder-retrospective is organized by Richard Roud during the New York Film Festival; his films are now distributed by New Yorker (Dan Tabot) across the United States
Three films are completed, including MOTHER KUSTER which has a different ending for its US release

Germany 1975

Major political events in 1975:

Protest demonstrations against nuclear energy. Nuclear energy plant Wyhl is occupied.

Terrorist group 'Bewegung 2.Juni' takes CDU chairman hostage

In Stuttgart-Stammheim, the Baader-Meinhof trial opens

Major cultural event in 1975:

The 'Hitler Wave' sweeps the media, including a remarkable documentary, WINIFRED WAGNER UND DIE GESCHICHTE DES HAUSES WAHNFRIED by Hans-Jürgen Syberberg

Major film events in 1975:

FALSCHE BEWEGUNG' by Wim Wenders, scripted by Peter Handke

THE LOST HONOUR OF KATHARINA BLUM by Volker Schlöndorff and Margaretha von Trotta, after novel by Heinrich Böll

Fassbinder 1976

Spring: Fassbinder's play *Der Müll, die Stadt und der Tod* is called 'left-wing-fascist' by Joachim Fest, because of supposed anti-Semitism, and copies of the play are withdrawn by Suhrkamp-Verlag. Danièle Schmid's film SCHATTEN DER ENGEL, based on the play, is also withdrawn from distribution in Germany and leads to controversy and protests in Paris. Other plans for films after novels of Gerhard Zwerenz and Gustav Freytag are also cancelled, the subjects being judged potentially anti-Semitic. Fassbinder defends his position in several articles and essays.

RWF completes the black comedy SATAN'S BREW and BOLWIESER. Both films star Kurt Raab – a kind of farewell present before RWF breaks with Raab for good

End of the year: RWF becomes a partner of Filmverlag der Autoren.

Germany 1976

Major political events in 1976

Ulrike Meinhof commits suicide in Stuttgart-Stammheim

Helmut Schmidt is confirmed as Federal Chancellor at the head of SPD/FDP coalition

Major cultural event in 1976:

Polit-singer Wolf Biermann is expelled from the GDR and stripped of his citizenship while on tour in the Federal Republic.

Major film event in 1976:

KINGS OF THE ROAD by Wim Wenders

Fassbinder 1977

RWF sells his shares of the Filmverlag der Autoren.

RWF puts together his second international co-production, DESPAIR, and in three months dictates the bulk of his screenplays for BERLIN ALEXANDERPLATZ

End of the year: RWF contributes to the collective omnibus film DEUTSCHLAND IM HERBST and invites Douglas Sirk to make a film together. They collaborate on the student production BURBON STREET BLUES, in which RWF plays an alcoholic writer

Germany 1977

Major political events in 1977:

Chief Federal Prosecutor Siegfried Buback and his chauffeur are murdered by terrorists in Karlsruhe

Chief Executive of Dresdner Bank Jürgen Ponto is murdered in Oberursel

Hanns Martin Schleyer is abducted and found murdered in France (Schleyer was 'Präsident der Bundesvereinigung der Deutschen Arbeitgeberverbände und des Bundesverbandes der Deutschen Industrie')

After botched hijack by Palestine and German terrorists of Lufthansa plane to Mogadishu, the RAF prisoners – Baader, Ensslin, Raspe – commit suicide in Stuttgart-Stammheim

For several months in the autumn, West Germany is gripped by a state of siege and high-security alert, with house searches, arrests and near civil war conditions

Major cultural event in 1977:

HITLER – A FILM FROM GERMANY by Hans Jürgen Syberberg

Major film event of 1977:

THE AMERICAN FRIEND by Wim Wenders

Fassbinder 1978

Beginning of the year: RWF directs THE MARRIAGE OF MARIA BRAUN, with Hanna Schygulla playing the leading role, under tense personal and professional circumstances. After a trip to New York, Armin Meier commits suicide in their apartment in Munich, and RWF spends the summer writing (and then directing) IN A YEAR OF THIRTEEN MOONS.

RWF moves house and now lives with Juliane Lorenz, his regular editor since DESPAIR.

Germany 1978

Major political events in 1978:

Printers go on strike because of new electronic data printing methods.

Herbert Gruhl leaves the CDU/CSU, founds the ecological party 'Grüne Aktion Zukunft'.

Baden-Württemberg's President Hans Filbinger (CDU) has to resign when his activities as military judge during the Third Reich become public

Johannes Rau (SPD) becomes President of North Rhine Westphalia

Franz Josef Strauß (CSU) becomes President of Bavaria

Major media event in 1978:

Günther Rühle, in the (conservative) *Frankfurter Allgemeine Zeitung* accuses West German literature of shunning contemporary topics: 'Only the cinema is still dealing with current issues'. His articles signal the ascendancy of the right over the left in cultural policy (*Tendenzwende*)

Major film events in 1978:

GERMANY IN AUTUMN by Alexander Kluge et al, THE SECOND AWAKENING OF CHRISTA KLAGES by Margarethe von Trotta, welcoming the emergence of the women's movement

Fassbinder 1979

RWF shoots THE THIRD GENERATION in Berlin, with his own money, as subsidy is withdrawn in view of the politically sensitive subject matter. While still in Berlin, he begins shooting BERLIN ALEXANDERPLATZ in June, but moves production to Munich later in the year

Germany 1979

Major political events of 1979:

Renewed mass protest of opponents to nuclear energy (main target: Gorleben in Lower Saxony)

Karl Carstens is elected Federal President.

The Lower House decides that crimes against humanity and genocide cannot fall under the statute of limitations.

Major media event of 1979:

American television series HOLOCAUST is broadcast and has a great impact on younger and older generation

Major film event in 1979:

GERMANY PALE MOTHER by Helma Sanders-Brahms

Fassbinder 1980

April: end of shooting of BERLIN ALEXANDERPLATZ; RWF directs LILI MARLEEN for Luggi Waldleitner, a seasoned producer with international contacts; when BERLIN ALEXANDER-PLATZ airs later in the autumn, a press campaign puts him in the firing line, and RWF publishes several essays and interviews, clarifying his position, vigorously defending his ethical and aesthetic concepts

Germany 1980

Major political event of 1980:

Founding conference of the 'Green Party' in Karlsruhe

Ratification of a Law defining 'crime against the environment'

Major media event of 1980:

BERLIN ALEXANDERPLATZ by RWF

Major film event of 1980:

THE SUBJECTIVE FACTOR by Helke Sander

Fassbinder 1981

RWF plays the lead in KAMIKAZE by Wolf Gremm; he writes a screenplay of the novel *Cocaine* and directs three films, including a record of the Cologne theatre festival, the rarely seen THEATER IN TRANCE. With LOLA and VERONIKA VOSS he completes his 'BRD Trilogy'

Germany 1981

Major political events in 1981:

Squatters and police clash in West Berlin

Chancellor Schmidt visits the GDR

Introduction of Legal Aid System to facilitate access to courts of law

Leonid Brezhnev visits the Federal Republic

Major media event in 1981:
On the initiative of Bernt Engelmann, East and West German writers organize first joint meeting

Major film events in 1981:
THE GERMAN SISTERS by Margarethe von Trotta, ETWAS WIRD SICHTBAR by Harun Farocki, DAS LETZTE LOCH by Herbert Achternbusch

Fassbinder 1982

February: Golden Bear in Berlin for VERONIKA VOSS

March: shooting of QUERELLE

May: RWF at Cannes Festival, takes part in Wim Wenders' self-interview film CHAMBRE 666

June 10th: RWF dies in Munich of a drug overdose

Germany 1982

Major political event in 1982:
Violent protest actions against planned new runway at Frankfurt airport (Startbahn West)
Building Society scandal 'Neue Heimat'
Managers of Flick industrial conglomerate are subpoenaed on suspicion of having bribed CDU politicians
Chancellor Schmidt does not survive a vote-of-no-confidence, the FDP leaves the coalition, allowing Helmut Kohl to form a new FDP-supported coalition government. Fourteen years later, Kohl will have become Germany's longest-serving Federal Chancellor

Major media event of 1982:
The death of Rainer Werner Fassbinder

Fassbinder 1990-1992

Rainer Werner Fassbinder Foundation takes over the RWF estate, and in May 1992 organizes *Werkschau* (retrospective, exhibition, events) in Berlin, on the occasion of the 10th Anniversary of RWF's Death. Several book publications, television retrospectives and extensive reviews and reappraisals in the German press.

Germany 1990-1992

November 1990: Formal Unification of East and West Germany
December 1991: European Union integration treaty signed in Maastricht
October 1992: Willy Brandt dies

Appendix Three

A Fassbinder Bibliography

1. Collected Works, Screenplays and Writings by R.W. Fassbinder

a. Plays in German

Rainer Werner Fassbinder, *Anarchie in Bayern und andere Stücke* (Tropfen auf heiße Steine, Der amerikanische Soldat, Anarchie in Bayern, Werwolf). Frankfurt: Verlag der Autoren, 1985.

Rainer Werner Fassbinder, *Antiteater: Fünf Stücke nach Stücken* (nach Goethe: Iphigenie auf Tauris; nach Sophokles: Ajax; nach Gay: Die Bettleroper; nach Goldoni: das Kaffeehaus; nach Lope de Vega: Das brennende Haus), Frankfurt: Verlag der Autoren, 1986.

Rainer Werner Fassbinder, *Antiteater I* (Katzelmacher, Preparadise sorry now, Die Betteloper), Frankfurt: Suhrkamp, 1970.

Rainer Werner Fassbinder, *Antiteater II* (Das Kaffeehaus, Bremer Freiheit, Blut am Halsband der Katze), Frankfurt: Suhrkamp, 1972.

Rainer Werner Fassbinder, *Nur eine Scheibe Brot*, Frankfurt: Verlag der Autoren, 1992.

Rainer Werner Fassbinder, *Stücke 3* (Das brennende Dorf, Die bitteren Tränen der Petra von Kant, Der Müll, die Stadt und der Tod), Frankfurt: Verlag der Autoren, 1976.

Rainer Werner Fassbinder, *Sämtliche Stücke*, Frankfurt: Verlag der Autoren, 1991.

b. Screenplays in German

Rainer Werner Fassbinder, *Die Kinofilme 1* (Der Stadtstreicher, Das kleine Chaos, Liebe ist kälter als der Tod, Katzelmacher, Götter der Pest). Michael Töteberg (ed.), Munich: Schirmer Mosel, 1987.

Rainer Werner Fassbinder, *Fassbinders Filme 2* (Warum Läuft Herr R. Amok, Rio das Mortes, Whity, Die Niklaushauser Fart, Der amerikanische Soldat, Warnung vor einer heiligen Nutte). Michael Töteberg (ed.), Frankfurt: Verlag der Autoren, 1990.

Rainer Werner Fassbinder, *Fassbinders Filme 3* (Händler der vier Jahreszeiten, Angst essen Seele auf, Fontane Effi Briest). Michael Töteberg (ed.), Frankfurt: Verlag der Autoren, 1990.

Rainer Werner Fassbinder, *Fassbinders Filme 4/5* (Acht Stunden sind kein Tag, with additional – unproduced – scripts, interviews and documentation). Michael Töteberg (ed.), Frankfurt: Verlag der Autoren, 1991.

Rainer Werner Fassbinder, *Der Film Berlin Alexanderplatz: Ein Arbeitsjournal*, Harry Baer (ed.), Frankfurt: Zweitausendeins, 1980.

Rainer Werner Fassbinder, *Lili Marleen*. Lars Badram (ed.), Copenhagen: Gad, 1983.

Daniel Schmid, *Schatten der Engel: ein Film nach dem Theaterstück 'Der Müll, die Stadt und der Tod" von Rainer Werner Fassbinder*, Frankfurt/M.: Zweitausendeins, 1976 [contains

33 articles from various newspapers, as well as the dialogue of the motion picture, identical with the text of Fassbinder's play].

c. Collected Essays and Interviews

Rainer Werner Fassbinder, *Filme Befreien den Kopf*, Michael Töteberg (ed.), Frankfurt: Fischer, 1984.

Rainer Werner Fassbinder, *Die Anarchie der Phantasie*, Michael Töteberg (ed.), Frankfurt: Fischer, 1986.

d. Plays, Screenplays and Essays in English

Rainer Werner Fassbinder, *The Anarchy of the Imagination: Interviews, Essays, Notes*, Michael Töteberg and Leo A. Lensing (eds.), Baltimore: Johns Hopkins University Press, 1992.

Rainer Werner Fassbinder, 'Bremen Coffee', translated by Anthony Vivis, *Shakespeare the Sadist and Other Plays*, London: Eyre Methuen, 1977.

Rainer Werner Fassbinder, 'In a Year of Thirteen Moons', *October* 23, 1982.

Rainer Werner Fassbinder, 'Pre-Paradise Sorry Now', transl. by Peter Zander, *Gambit*, vol 6, no 21.

Rainer Werner Fassbinder, 'Cock-Artist (Katzelmacher)', transl. by Steve Gooch, *Gambit*, vol 10, no 39-40.

Rainer Werner Fassbinder, *The Marriage of Maria Braun*, Joyce Rheuban (ed.), New Brunswick: Rutgers University Press, 1986.

Rainer Werner Fassbinder, *Plays*, edited and translated by Denis Calandra, New York: PAJ Publications, 1985, 1992.

Rainer Werner Fassbinder, *Querelle: The Film Book*, Dieter Schidor and Michael McLernon (eds.), Munich: Schirmer/Mosel/Grove, 1982.

2. Books on Fassbinder

Harry Baer, *Schlafen kann ich wenn ich tot bin: Das atemlose Leben des Rainer Werner Fassbinder*, Cologne: Kiepenheuer & Witsch, 1982.

Peter Berling, *Die 13 Jahre des Rainer Werner Fassbinder: Seine Filme, seine Freunde, seine Feinde*, Bergisch-Gladbach: Gustav Lübbe, 1992.

Bernd Eckhardt, *Rainer Werner Fassbinder: in 17 Jahre 42 Filme. Stationen eines Lebens für den deutschen Film*, Munich: Heyne, 1982.

Paul Foss (ed.), *Fassbinder in Review*, Syndey, Melbourne: The Australian Filminsitute, 1983.

Annette Förster (ed.), *Rainer Werner Fassbinder: Science and Fiction*, Utrecht, Filmtheater 't Hoogt, 1993.

Achim Haag, *"Deine Sehnsucht kann keiner stillen": Rainer Werner Fassbinders Berlin Alexanderplatz*, Munich: Trickster Verlag, 1992.

Ronald Hayman, *Fassbinder Film maker*, London: Weidenfeld and Nicholson, 1984.

Peter W. Jansen and Wolfram Schütte (eds.), *Rainer Werner Fassbinder*, Munich: Hanser, 1975, 1987; Frankfurt: Fischer, 1992.

Robert Katz, *Love is Colder than Death: The Life and Times of Rainer Werner Fassbinder*, New York: Random House, 1987.

Yann Lardeau, *Rainer Werner Fassbinder*, Paris: Cahiers du Cinema, 1990.

Wolfgang Limmer, *Fassbinder*, Munich: Goethe Institute, 1973.

Wolfgang Limmer, *Rainer Werner Fassbinder: Filmemacher*, Reinbek: Spiegel/Rowohlt, 1981.

Juliane Lorenz (ed.), *Das ganz normale Chaos: Gespräche über Rainer Werner Fassbinder* Berlin: Henschel, 1995.

Ruth McCormick (ed.), *Fassbinder*, New York: Tanam, 1981.

Hans Günther Pflaum/Rainer Werner Fassbinder, *Rainer Werner Fassbinder: Das bißchen Realität das ich brauche*, Munich: Hanser, 1976.

Hans Günther Pflaum, *Rainer Werner Fassbinder: Bilder und Dokumente*, Munich: Edition Spangenberg, 1992.

Kurt Raab and Karsten Peters, *Die Sehnsucht des Rainer Werner Fassbinder*, Munich: Bertelsmann Verlag, 1982.

Tony Rayns (ed.), *Fassbinder*, London: British Film Institute, 1976, revised and enlarged 1979, 1980.

Dieter Schidor, *Rainer Werner Fassbinder dreht Querelle*, Munich: Schirmer/Mosel, 1982.

Marion Schmidt and Herbert Gehr (eds.), *Rainer Werner Fassbinder Werkschau: Dichter, Schauspieler, Filmemacher*, Berlin: Argon, 1992.

Hanna Schygulla, *Bilder aus Filmen von Rainer Werner Fassbinder*, Munich: Schirmer/Mosel, 1981.

Jane Shattuc, *Tabloids and Tears: Fassbinder and Popular Culture*, Minneapolis: University of Minnesota Press, 1995.

Giovanni Spagnoletti (ed.), *Fassbinder*, Milan: Carta Segreta, 1992

Herbert Spaich, *Rainer Werner Fassbinder: Leben und Werk*, Weinheim: Beltz Quadriga, 1992.

Wallace Steadman Watson, *Rainer Werner Fassbinder: Film as Private and Public Art*, University of South Carolina Press, 1996.

Christian Braad Thomsen, *Rainer Werner Fassbinder: Leben und Werk eines masslosen Genies*, Hamburg: Rogner und Bernhard, 1993.

Michael Töteberg (ed.), *Rainer Werner Fassbinder*, Munich: edition text + kritik, 1989.

Gerhard Zwerenz, *Der langsame Tod des Rainer Werner Fassbinder*, Munich: Schneekluth, 1982.

3. Books (in English) with chapters on Fassbinder

Richard Collins and Vincent Porter, *WDR and the Arbeiterfilm*, London: British Film Institute, 1981 [chapter on EIGHT HOURS DO NOT MAKE A DAY].

Paul Coates, *The Gorgon's Head*, Cambridge: Cambridge University Press, 1991 [chapter on LILI MARLEEN].

Timothy Corrigan, *New German Film: The Displaced Image*, Austin: University of Texas, 1983; 1994 [chapter on THE BITTER TEARS OF PETRA VON KANT]

Timothy Corrigan, *Cinema without Walls*, New York: Routledge, 1991 [chapters on IN A YEAR OF THIRTEEN MOONS and THE THIRD GENERATION].

Thomas Elsaesser, *New German Cinema: A History*, London: Macmillan 1989.

James Franklin, *New German Cinema: From Oberhausen to Hamburg*, Boston: Twayne, 1983.

Anton Kaes, *From Hitler to Heimat: The Return of History as Film*, Boston: Harvard University Press, 1989 [chapter on THE MARRIAGE OF MARIA BRAUN].

Klaus Phillips (ed.), *New German Filmmakers: From Oberhausen Through the 1970s*, New York: Frederick Ungar, 1984.

Hans Günther Pflaum and Hans Helmut Prinzler, *Cinema in the Federal Republic of Germany*, Bonn: Inter Nationes, 1983.

Eric Rentschler, *West German Film in the Course of Time*, Bedford Hills, New York: Redgrave, 1984.

Eric Rentschler (ed.), *German Film and Literature: Adaptations and Transformations*, London and New York: Methuen, 1986 [chapters on THE MARRIAGE OF MARIA BRAUN and BERLIN ALEXANDERPLATZ].

Eric Rentschler (ed.), *West German Filmmakers on Film*, New York: Holmes & Meier, 1988.

John Sandford, *The New German Cinema*, London: Oswald Wolff, 1980.

Steven Shaviro, *The Cinematic Body*, Minneapolis: Minnesota University Press, 1994 [chapter on QUERELLE].

Kaja Silverman, *Male Subjectivity at the Margins*, New York: Routledge, 1992 [chapters on FEAR EATS THE SOUL and BERLIN ALEXANDERPLATZ].

Hans Jürgen Syberberg, *Der Wald steht schwarz und schweiget*, Zurich: Diogenes, 1984 [chapter on Fassbinder and his reception in Germany]

4. General Articles on Fassbinder

Gilbert Adair, 'Fassbinder's Wristwatch', *Films and Filming*, 1983, no.347, 13-16.

Hans-Michael Bock (ed.), 'Fassbinder', *Cinegraph: Lexikon zum deutschsprachigen Film*, Munich: edition text + kritik, 1984).

Klaus Bohnen, '"Raum-Höllen" der bürgerlichen Welt: "Gefühlsrealismus" in der Theater- und Filmproduktion Rainer Werner Fassbinders', in: Gerhard Kluge (ed.), *Studien zur Dramatik in der Bundesrepublik Deutschland*, Amsterdam: Rodopi, 1983, 141-162.

Christian Braad Thomsen, 'Fassbinder's Holy Whores', *Take One*, 1973/74, no.6, 12-16.

Christian Braad Thomsen, 'Fassbinder und der Terrorismus', *Text und Kontext*, 1980, no.1, 145-164.

Barbara Bronnen and Corinna Brocher, *Die Filmemacher: Zur neue deutschen Produktion nach Oberhausen*, Munich: C. Bertelsmann, 1973.

Robert Burgoyne, 'Narrative and Sexual Excess', *October* 21, 1982, 51-61.

Vincent Canby, 'Rainer Werner Fassbinder – The Most Original Talent Since Godard. *The New York Times*, 6 March 1977.

Vincent Canby, 'A Beginner's Baedecker to the Genius of Fassbinder', *The New York Times*, 3 October 1982, 15, 22.

Richard Combs, '"Chinese Roulette" and "Despair"', *Sight and Sound*, Autumn 1978, 258-259

Douglas Crimp, 'Fassbinder, Franz, Fox, Elvira, Erwin, Armin and All the Others', *October* 21, 1982, 63-81.

Jan Dawson and Joe Medjuck, 'Fassbinder: A Year (or so) in the Life', *Take One*, Vol.4, no.12, July/August 1973.

David Denby, 'The Brilliant, Brooding Films of Rainer Werner Fassbinder', *The New York Times*, 1 February 1976.

Wolf Donner, 'Der Boß und sein Team', *Die Zeit*, 31 July 1970.

Richard Dyer, 'Reading Fassbinder's Sexual Politics', in: Tony Rayns (ed.), *Fassbinder*, London: British Film Institute, 1980, 54-64.

Peter W. Engelmeier, 'Der Anfasser', *Playboy* [German edition], October 1972.

Thomas Elsaesser, 'A Cinema of Vicious Circles', in: Tony Rayns (ed.), *Fassbinder*, London: British Film Institute, 1976/1979/1980, 24-36.

Thomas Elsaesser, 'Primary Identification and the Historical Subject: Fassbinder's Germany,' in Phil Rosen (ed.), *Narrative, Ideology, Apparatus*, New York: Columbia University Press, 1986, 544-48.

Thomas Elsaesser, 'Fassbinder', in: John Wakeman (ed.), *Dictionary of Film Directors*, New York: Wilson & Co, 1988, 318-330.

Thomas Elsaesser, 'Historicising the Subject: A Body of Work', *New German Critique* 63, Spring 1994, 11-33.

Manny Farber and Patricia Patterson, 'Fassbinder', *Film Comment*, 1975, vol 11, no 6, 5-7.

Howard Feinstein, 'BRD 1-2-3: Fassbinder's Postwar Trilogy and the Spectacle', *Cinema Journal*, vol.23, no.1, Fall 1983, 44-56.

Richard C. Figge, 'The Modus Operandi of Rainer Werner Fassbinder', *Die Unterrichtspraxis*, vol.12, no.2, Fall 1979.

Kurt Joachim Fischer, 'Zum Beispiel: Rainer Werner Fassbinder', *Kirche und Film*, August 1969, Nr.8.

Marie Luise Fleißer, 'Alle meine Söhne. über Martin Sperr, Rainer Werner Fassbinder und Franz Xaver Kroetz', *Theater heute*, Jahressonderheft 1972 (September).

James Franklin, 'The Films of Fassbinder: Form and Formula', *Quarterly Review of Film Studies*, 1979/80, vol.5, no.2.

Gordon Gow, 'Obsession', *Films and Filming*, vol 22, no 6, March 1976, 12-17.

Jacques Grant, 'Rainer Werner Fassbinder: étude, entretien et filmographie', *Cinéma* (Paris), 193, Dec 1974, 42-81.

Jürgen Harder, 'Filme des Rainer Werner Fassbinders', *Prisma* 3, 1972, 252-264.

Jim Hoberman, 'The Legacy of Rainer Werner Fassbinder', *American Film*, vol 7, no 10, September 1982.

Bernward Hoffmann, 'Leben als Film – Film als Leben', *medien praktisch* no.1, March 1983.

John Hughes and Brooks Riley, 'A New Realism: Fassbinder Interviewed', *Film Comment*, vol 11 no 6, Nov-Dec 1975, 14-17.

John Hughes and Ruth McCormick, 'RAiner Werner Fassbinder and the Death of Family Life', *Thousand Eyes Magazine*, April 1977, 5, 21.

Peter Iden, 'Rituale und Spiele aus anderen Spielen', *Frankfurter Rundschau*, 6 November 1969.

Sheila Johnston, 'A Star Is Born: Fassbinder and the New German Cinema', *New German Critique*, Fall/Winter 1981-82, no.24-25, 57-72.

Sheila Johnston, 'All That Television Allows', *Monthly Film Bulletin*, no.588, January 1983, 4-6.

John O'Kane, 'Rainer Werner Fassbinder: Art Cinema and the Politics of Culture', *Bennington Review*, 1983, no 15, 56-64.

Harlan Kennedy, 'Fassbinder's Four Daughters', *Film Comment*, 1982, vol.18, no.5, p.20-23.

Marsha Kinder, 'Ideological Parody in the New German Cinema', *Quarterly Review of Film and Video*, vol 12 no 1-2, 1990, 73-103.

Vincent Kling, 'The Dynamics of Defeat: Aspects of Rainer Werner Fassbinder's Art', *Film Studies Annual*, West Lafayette, Purdue Research Foundation, 1976, 157-166.

Gertrud Koch (ed.), 'Frauen bei Fassbinder. Eine Diskussion (with Ingrid Caven et al)', *Frauen und Film*, 1983, no.35, 92-96.

Gertrud Koch, 'Torments of the Flesh, Coldness of the Spirit: Jewish Figures in the Films of Rainer Werner Fassbinder', *New German Critique*, 38, Spring/Summer 1986, 28-38.

Horst Königstein, 'Fassbinders Showdown', *Film*, Dezember 1969, no.12.

Anna K. Kuhn, 'Rainer Werner Fassbinder: The Alienated Vision', in: Klaus Phillips (ed.), *New German Filmmakers*, New York: Ungar, 1984, 76-123.

Elisabeth Läufer, 'Fassbinder und Sirk', *Skeptiker des Lichts*, Frankfurt: Fischer, 1987, 186-221.

Yann Lardeau, 'Saint Fassbinder Comedien et Martyr', *Cahiers du Cinema*, 1988, vol.413, 30-32.

James Roy MacBean, 'The Success and Failure of Rainer Werner Fassbinder', *Sight and Sound*, vol.52, no.1, Winter 1982-83.

James Roy MacBean, 'The Cinema as Self-Portrait: The Final Films of R.W.Fassbinder', *Cinéaste*, vol 12, no 4, 1983.

James Roy MacBean, 'Between Kitsch and Fascism: Notes on Fassbinder, Pasolini & other Consuming Passions', *Cinéaste*, vol 13, no 4, 1984, 12-19.

Derek Malcolm, 'The Director Vanishes', *The Guardian*, 8 December 1979, 11.

Peter Märthesheimer, 'Das forschende Kind: Einige Steine des Hauses, das Rainer Werner Fassbinder zu bauen begonnen hatte', in: Hans Günther Pflaum (ed.), *Jahrbuch Film 82/83*, Munich: Hanser, 1982, 7-25.

Judith Mayne, 'Fassbinder and Spectatorship', *New German Critique*, Fall 1977, no.12, 61-74.

Ruth McCormick, 'Fassbinder and the Politics of Everyday Life', *Cineaste*, 1977, vol.8, no.2, 22-30.

Andy Medhurst, 'The Long Take: Fassbinder and Sexuality', *Sight and Sound* vol 6 no 2, February 1996, 20-23.

George Morris, 'Fassbinder x 5', *Film Comment*, vol. 17, no.5, September-October 1971.

George Morris, 'A Look at Fassbinder', *Thousand Eyes Magazine*, March 1975, 6.

Fritz Müller-Scherz, 'Fassbinders Erben', *Trans Atlantik*, February 1983, 12-21.

Camille Nevers, 'Le Secret de Rainer Werner Fassbinder', *Cahiers du cinema* 469, June 1993, 51-64.

Marcel Oms, 'A propos de R.W.F.', *Cahiers de la Cinématèque* 32, Spring 1981, 161-171.

Johannes G. Pankau, 'Figurationen des Bayerischen: Sperr, Fassbinder, Achternbusch', in: Helfried W. Seliger (ed.), *Der Begriff "Heimat" in der deutschen Gegenwartsliteratur*, Munich: Iudicium, 1987, 133-147.

Paul Pawlikowski, 'The Fassbinder Interview', *Stills*, vol 1 no 5, Nov-Dec 1982.

Tony Pipolo, 'Bewitched by the Holy Whore', *October*, 21, 1982, 83-114.

Hans Günther Pflaum, 'Fassbinder' *epd Film* no 6, 1992.

Ekkehard Pluta, 'Die Sachen sind so wie sie sind', *Fernsehen und Film*, 1970, vol.12, 15-20.

Ekkehard Pluta, 'Rapider Aufstieg jenseits der Routine', *Der Tagesspiegel*, 27 September 1970.

Carrie Rickey, 'Fassbinder and Altman: Approaches to Filmmaking', *Performing Arts Journal*, 1977, vol.2, no.2, 33-48.

Brooks Riley, 'Rainer Werner Fassbinder 1946-1982', *Film Comment*, vol 18 no 5, Sept/Oct 1982.

Wilhelm Roth, 'Versuchsanordnung: ein Mann, eine Frau...', *Süddeutsche Zeitung*, 19 April 1975.

Wilhelm Roth, 'Neues (?) über Fassbinder?', *epd Film*, January 1993, 12-13.

Richard Roud, 'Biter Bit', *Sight and Sound* vol 51, no 4, Autumn 1982, 288-289.

Hans Günther Rühle, 'Gruppe Fassbinder', *Frankfurter Allgemeine Zeitung*, 5 November 1969.

Fritz Rumler, 'Spaß fördert das Bewußtsein, *Der Spiegel,* 29 December 1969, Nr.53.

Peter Ruppert, 'Fassbinder, Spectatorship and Utopian Desire', *Cinema Journal*, Winter 1989, vol.28, no.2, 28-47.

Andrew Sarris, 'Can Fassbinder Break the Box-Office Barrier?', *The Village Voice*, 22 November 1976.

Andrew Sarris, 'Further Thoughts on Fassbinder', *The Village Voice*, 11 July 1977.

Andrew Sarris, 'Fassbinder and Sirk: The Ties That Unbind', *The Village Voice*, 3 September 1980.

Daniel Sauvaget, 'Rapports de Domination, Melodrame et Distanciation dans quelques Films de Fassbinder', *La Revue du Cinema/Image et Son*, 1978, vol.333, 43-46.

Dieter Schidor, *Rainer Werner Fassbinder dreht "Querelle"*, Munich: Heyne, 1982.

Wolfram Schütte, 'Das Herz', *Frankfurter Rundschau* 19 June 1982.

Wolfram Schütte, 'Sein Name: Eine Ära – Rückblick auf den späten Fassbinder', in: Peter W Jansen and Wolfram Schütte (ed.), *Rainer Werner Fassbinder*, Frankfurt: Fischer 1992, 63-74.

Jay Scott, 'The Sadomasochism Factory: Rainer Werner Fassbinder's Germany', in: *Midnight Matinees: Movies and Their Makers 1975-1985*, New York: Ungar, 1985, 45-59.

Jacques Segond, 'Le Baiser du Vampire', *Positif*, 1976, vol.183/184, 54-59.

Hans-Dieter Seidel, 'Genie aus Zufall', *Stuttgarter Zeitung*, 27 October 1972.

Daniel Selznick, 'Fassbinder: The Brain Won't Stop', *International Herald Tribune*, 19 October 1979.

Jane Shattuc, 'R.W.Fassbinder's Confessional Melodrama: Towards Historicizing Melodrama within the Art Cinema', *Wide Angle*, vol 12, no 1, January 1990, 44-59.

Kaja Silverman, 'Fassbinder and Lacan: A Reconsideration of Gaze, Look and Image', *Camera Obscura* 19, January 1989, 55-84.

Norbert Sparrow, '"I let the Audience Feel and Think": An Interview with Rainer Werner Fassbinder', *Cinéaste* vol 8, no 2, Fall 1977, 20-21.

John Russel Taylor, 'Wunderkind Rainer Werner Fassbinder', *The Movie*, Chapter 80, 1981.

Norbert Thomas, 'Säufer und Genie', *Stern*, no 34, 16 August 1970.

Paul Thomas, 'Fassbinder: The Poetry of the Inarticulate', *Film Quarterly*, vol 30, no 2, Winter 1976/77, 2-17.

Michael Töteberg, 'Rainer Werner Fassbinder', *Kritisches Lexikon zur deutschsprachigen Gegenwartsliteratur* (ed. Heinz Ludwig Arnold), München: edition text + kritik, 1981[ff].

Michael Töteberg, 'Fassbinder. Eine Recherche im Nachlaß', *epd film*, 1987, no.5, 25-28.

Felix Tretter, 'Filmgenie Fassbinder: Kreativität durch Drogen?", *Deutsches Ärzteblatt* no. 22, 23, June 1983.

Ralph Tyler, 'The Savage World of Rainer Werner Fassbinder', *The New York Times*, 27 March 1977.

Walter Vian, 'Fassbinder und seine Filme', *Zoom-Filmberater*, no. 1, 11 January 1973.

Rolf Vollmann, 'Wo Fassbinder geht, ist er gut', *Stuttgarter Zeitung*, 27 February 1971.

Craig Whitney, 'Fassbinder: A New Director Movie Buffs Dote on', *New York Times*, 16 February 1977.

David Wilson, 'Anti-Cinema Rainer Werner Fassbinder', *Sight and Sound*, Vol.41, no.2, Spring 1972.

David Wilson, 'Rainer Werner Fassbinder', in: Peter Cowie (ed.), *International Film Guide 1976*, London: Tantivy Press, 61-73.

David Wilson, 'Rainer Werner Fassbinder', in: Richard Roud (ed.), *Cinema. A Critical Dictionary*, vol.1, London: Secker and Warburg 1980, 335-339.

Katherine Woodward, 'European Anti-Melodrama: Godard, Truffaut, and Fassbinder', *Post-Script*, Winter 1984, vol.3, no.2, 34-47.

5. Essays on Selected Films

LOVE IS COLDER THAN DEATH, 1969

Jan Dawson, 'Liebe ist kälter als der Tod', *Monthly Film Bulletin*, no 534, July 1978.

Peter Handke, 'Ah Gibraltar!', *Die Zeit*, July 1969

KATZELMACHER, 1969

Vincent Canby, '*Katzelmacher* Hypnotizes and Amuses', *The New York Times*, 4 June 1977.

John O'Kane, 'Framing the Sixties', *Enclitic* vol 7, no 2, Autumn 1983.

GODS OF THE PLAGUE, 1969

Vincent Canby, 'Gods of the Plague', *The New York Times*, 11 June 1977.

Jan Dawson, 'Götter der Pest', *Monthly Film Bulletin*, no 533, June 1978.

WHY DOES HERR R RUN AMOK?, 1969

Vincent Canby, 'Fassbinder Sneers at German Affluence', *The New York Times*, 18 November 1977.

John Hughes, 'Why Herr R. Ran Amok', *Film Comment*, vol 11, no 6, Nov-Dec 1975, 11-13.

THE AMERICAN SOLDIER, 1970

John Rignall, 'The American Soldier', *Monogram* no 2, Summer 1971.

Roger Greenspun, 'White Heat', *Soho Weekly News*, 29 January 1976.

BEWARE OF A HOLY WHORE, 1970

Nicole Brenez, 'L'acteur en citoyen affectif', *Cinématèque* 9, Spring 1996, 84-93.

Christian Braad Thomsen, 'Fassbinder's Holy Whore', *Take One* vol 4 no 6, 1974, 12-16.

Claudia Wefel, 'Warnung vor einer heiligen Nutte', *epd Film*, no 6, 1992, 21-22.

THE MERCHANT OF FOUR SEASONS, 1971

Barbara Leaming, 'Structures of Alienation', *Jump Cut* no 10-11, Summer 1976, 39-40.

George Lellis, 'The Retreat from Romanticism', *Film Quarterly*, vol 28, no 4, 1975, 16-20.

Tony Rayns, 'The Merchant of Four Seasons', *Monthly Film Bulletin*, no 499, August 1975, 175-176.

THE BITTER TEARS OF PETRA VON KANT, 1972

David Ansen, 'Mad Love. The Bitter Tears of Petra von Kant', *The Real Paper* (Boston), 21 July 1976.

Cathy Johnson, 'The Imaginary and "The Bitter Tears of Petra von Kant"', *wide angle* vol 3, no 4, 1980.

Penelope Gilliatt, 'The Current Cinema', *The New Yorker*, 14 June 1976, 93-96.

Molly Haskell,'Sisterhoodwinked: Panting for Power', *The Village Voice*, vol 18, 25 October 1973, 92-93.

Lynne Kirby, 'Fassbinder's Debt to Poussin', *Camera Obscura*, 13-14 (1985-86), 5-27.

Ruth Perlmutter, 'Real Feelings, Hollywood Melodrama', *Minnesota Review* no 33, Autumn 1989.

FEAR EATS THE SOUL, 1973

Rob Burns, 'Fassbinder's Angst Essen Seele Auf: a mellow Brechtian drama', *German life and letters*, 48(1), 1995, 56-74.

Jim Franklin, 'Forms of Communication in Fassbinder's Angst Essen Seele Auf', *Literature/Film Quarterly*, Summer 1979, no.7, 182-200.

Denise Hartsough, 'Cine-Feminism Renegotiated: "Ali" as interventionist cinema', *wide angle* vol 12, no. 1, 1990, 18-29.

Laura Mulvey, 'Fassbinder and Sirk', *Spare Rib*, September 1974.

Michael Stern, 'The Inspired Melodrama and the Melodrama it Inspired', *A Thousand Eyes Magazine*, no 6, January 1976, 3-4, 18.

FONTANE EFFI BRIEST, 1974

Edith Borchardt, 'Leitmotif and Structure in Fassbinder's Effi Briest', *Film/Literature Quarterly*, vol 7, no 3, Summer 1979.

Renny Harrigan, 'Women Oppressed', *Jump Cut* 15, 1977, 3-5.

Anna K. Kuhn, 'Modes of Alienation in Fassbinder's Effi Briest', in: Sandra Frieden et al (eds.), *Gender and German Cinema* vol 1, Providence: Berg, 1991.

Jon Lewis, 'Effi Briest', *On Film* no 11, Summer 1983.

William R. Magretta, 'Reading the Writerly Film: Fassbinder's Effi Briest', in Andrew Horton and Joan Magretta (eds.), *Modern European Filmmakers and the Art of Adaptation*, New York: Ungar, 1981, 248-262.

FOX AND HIS FRIENDS, 1974

Andrew Britton, 'Fox and his Friends: Foxed', *Jump Cut*, November 1977, no.16, 22-23.

Bob Cant, 'Fassbinder's Fox', *Jump Cut*, November 1977, no.16, 22-23.

Roger Greenspun, 'Phantom of Liberty. Thoughts on Fassbinder's Fist-Right of Freedom', *Film Comment*, vol 11, no 6, November-December 1975, 8-10.

Jonathan Rosenbaum, 'Faustrecht der Freiheit', *Monthly Film Bulletin*, no 504, January 1976, 6.

SATAN'S BREW, 1975

Gilbert Adair, 'Satansbraten', *Monthly Film Bulletin*, no 553, February 1980.

Janet Maslin, 'Satan's Brew is Cold and Bitter', *New York Times*, 10 August 1977.

Andrew Sarris, 'A Summer Spate of Sugar and Spite', *The Village Voice*, 29 August 1977.

BOLWIESER (THE STATION MASTER'S WIFE), 1977

Sheila K. Johnston, 'Kindred Spirits: Fassbinder and Graf', *Philological Papers* (Morgantown), 1985, 49-57.

Gery Marta et al, 'Bolwieser' , *Film Review Annual 1983*, Englewood, NJ: J Ozer, 1984, 1114-1119.

Karl Prümm, 'Extreme Nähe und radikale Entfernung. Rainer Werner Fassbinder's Fernsehfilm "Bolwieser" (1977) nach dem Roman von Oskar Maria Graf', in: Franz-Josef Albersmeier and Volker Roloff (eds.), *Literaturverfilmungen*, Frankfurt: Suhrkamp, 1989, 155-182.

DESPAIR, 1977

Will Aitken, 'Despair', *Take One*, January 1979, 6-8.

Dolores M. Burdick, 'The Line Down the Middle: Politics and Sexuality in Fassbinder's "Despair"', in: Eugen J. Crook (ed.), *Fearful Symmetry: Doubles and Doubling in Literature and Film*, Tallahassee: University Presses of Florida, 1981, 138-148.

Thomas Elsaesser, 'Murder, Merger, Suicide: The Politics of "Despair"', in: Tony Rayns (ed.), *Fassbinder*, London: British Film Institute, 1980, 49-53.

Derek Malcolm, 'Exile in the kingdom of the bourgeoisie', *The Guardian* 6 July 1978, 12.

Edward M.V. Plater, 'Fassbinder's Despair: A Political Allegory', *Literature/Film Quarterly*, 1985, vol.4, 222-233.

Peter Ruppert, 'Fassbinder's Despair: Hermann Hermann Through the Looking-Glass', *Post Script*, 1984, vol.2, 48-64.

John Russell Taylor, 'Fassbinder Duo', *The Times*, 7 July 1978.

Wallace S. Watson, 'The Bitter Tears of RWF', *Sight and Sound* July 1992, 24-29.

GERMANY IN AUTUMN, 1978

Jan Dawson, 'Germany in Autumn', *Take One*, vol 6, no 12, November 1978, 14-15, 44-45.

Eric Rentschler, 'Life with Fassbinder', *Discourse* no 6, Autumn 1983, 75-90.

Marc Silberman, 'Introduction to Germany in Autumn', *Discourse* no 6, Autumn 1983.

IN A YEAR OF THIRTEEN MOONS, 1978

Don Ranvaud, 'In einem Jahr mit 13 Monden', *Monthly Film Bulletin*, no 561, October 1980, 195-196.

Jan Dawson, 'In a Year with 13 Moons', *The Listener*, 30 August 1979.

Sandra Frieden, 'In the Margins of Identity', in: Sandra Frieden et al (eds.), *Gender and German Cinema* vol 1, Providence: Berg, 1991.

Tony Rayns, 'In a Year with 13 Moons', *Time Out*, September 1980.

David Robinson, 'Tour de force of human oddity', *The Times*, 5 September 1980.

Richard Roud, 'Erwin had been a man...', *The Guardian*, 30 May 1979, 14.

THE MARRIAGE OF MARIA BRAUN, 1978

Richard Combs, 'Die Ehe der Maria Braun', *Monthly Film Bulletin*, no 559, August 1980, 155.

Mary Beth Haralovich, 'The Sexual Politics of The Marriage of Maria Braun', *wide angle* vol 12, no 1, 1990, 6-17.

Hans-Bernd Moeller, 'Fassbinder's Use of Brechtian Aesthetics', *Jump Cut* 35, April 1990, 102-107.

Robert C. Reimer, 'Memories from the Past', *Journal of Popular Film and Television* vol 9, no 3, Autumn 1981.

THE THIRD GENERATION, 1979

Martin Auty, 'Die Dritte Generation', *Monthly Film Bulletin*, no 561, October 1980, 191.

Jan Dawson, 'The Sacred Terror: Shadows of terrorism in the New German Cinema', *Sight and Sound*, Autumn 1979, vol.48, no.4, 242-245.

Richard Combs, 'Dilettantism and *realpolitik*: The Third Generation', *The Times Literary Supplement*, 19 September 1980.

Jacques Grant, 'La Troisième génération: Rainer Werner Fassbinder', *Cinéma*, July-August, no.247-248, 118-120.

BERLIN ALEXANDERPLATZ, 1980:

Thomas Basgier, 'In Memoriam Rainer Werner Fassbinder', *Filmfaust*, 1986, vol 53, 8-15.

Vinzenz B. Burg, 'Berlin Alexanderplatz', *medien und erziehung*, 1981, vol 2, 97-104.

Hermann Burger, 'Kein Platz für den Alexanderplatz', in: *Als Autor auf der Stör*, Frankfurt: Fischer, 1987, 180-188.

Vincent Canby, 'Is Berlin Alexanderplatz a Vision of the Movies' Future?', *The New York Times*, 10 July 1983.

Michael Dittmar and Horst Wegener, 'Fassbinders Millionen-Werk', *Der Spiegel*, 13 April 1980.

Thomas Elsaesser, 'Berlin Alexanderplatz: Franz Biberkopf/s/exchanges, *Wide Angle*, vol 12, no 1, 1990, 30-43.

Louis Ferron, 'Berlin Alexanderplatz: Fassbinder contra Döblin', The Hague: Bzztoh, 1980.

Louis Ferron, 'De Straf begint', *VPRO Gids* (Hilversum), 12 January 1992

Ulrich Greiner, 'Die Schrecken der Liebe', *Die Zeit*, 10 October 1980.

Ulrich Greiner, 'Fassbinder zum letzten', *Die Zeit*, 29 November 1980.

Michaal Hofmann, 'A Futurist Babel', *The Times Literary Supplement*, 20 September 1985, 1032.

Sheila Johnston, 'Fascism in Fourteen Parts', *City Limits* (London), 13-19 November 1981, 51.

Stanley Kauffmann, 'Maximum Opus', *The New Republic*, 8 August 1983.

Karl Korn, 'Berlin – metaphysisch', *Frankfurter Allgemeine Zeitung*, 2 January 1981.

James M. Markham, 'A Great Novel's Journey to Film', *The New York Times*, 7 August 1983.

Joachim Paech, 'Fassbinders "Berlin Alexanderplatz"' *Literatur und Film*, Stuttgart: Metzler, 1988, 144-150.

Eric Rentschler, 'Terms of Dismemberment: The Body in/of Fassbinder', *New German Critique* 34, 1985, 194-208.

Philip Romon, 'N.Y. fait un culte à R.W.F', *libération* 4 July 1983, 27.

Wolfram Schütte, 'Franz Mieze, Reinhold, Tod & Teufel', *Frankfurter Rundschau*, 11.10.1980.

Michael Schwarze, 'Das Prinzip Hoffnung', *Frankfurter Allgemeine Zeitung*, 3 September 1980.

Michael Stone, 'Welch ein Jahrhundert!', *Tagesspiegel*, 31 December 1980.

Susan Sontag, 'Novel into Film', *Vanity Fair*, September 1983, 86-90.

Karsten Witte, 'Hölle & Söhne', *Frankfurter Rundschau*, 18 October 1983.

Wolfgang Würker, 'Franz Biberkopf sucht seinen Weg', *Frankfurter Allgemeine Zeitung*, 14 October 1980.

Kristina Zerges, 'Die TV Serie Berlin Alexanderplatz. Dokumentation und Analyse eines Rezeptionsprozesses', *Spiel: Siegener Periodicum zur Internationalen Empirischen Literaturwissenschaft*, no 1, 1983, 137-181.

LILI MARLEEN, 1980:

David Bathrick, 'Inscribing History: Prohibiting and Producing Desire', *New German Critique*, 63, Fall 1994, 35-54.

Hans C. Blumenberg, 'Wie lustig ist die Tyrannei?', *Schuß/Gegenschuß*. Frankfurt: Fischer, 1984, 72-75.

Peter Buchka, 'Der Autorenfilm ist tot! Es lebe der Autor!', *Süddeutsche Zeitung*, 15 January 1981.

Thomas Elsaesser, 'Fassbinder, Fascism and the Film Industry', *October* 21, 1982, 115-140.

Annie Goldmann, 'Un nouveau Juif Süss: Lili Marleen', *Le Monde*, 16 May 1981.

Karen Jaehne, 'Lili Marleen', *Film Quarterly*, Spring 1982, 42-46.

Norbert Jochum, 'Nur ein Lied...', *Filme*, Berlin: 1981, vol.7, 44-45.

Sheila Johnston, 'A Song for Europe', *Time Out*, 8-14 January 1982, 22-23.

Judith Mayne, 'The Feminist Analogy', *Discourse* no 7, Autumn 1985.

Tom Milne, 'Lili Marleen', *Monthly Film Bulletin*, no 574, November 1981, 219-220.

Fred Ritzel and Jens Thiele, 'Ansätze einer interdisziplinären Filmanalyse am Beispiel "Lili Marleen"', *Lili – Zeitschrift für Literaturwissenschaft und Linguistik*, 1988, Beiheft 15, 109-132.

Andrew Sarris, 'Is History Merely an Old Movie?', *Village Voice*, 8-14 July, 1981, 33.

Wolfram Schütte, 'Verstimmtes Klavier', *Frankfurter Rundschau*, 17 January 1981.

Michael Stone, 'Springtime for Hitler', *Guardian*, 6 February 1981, 11.

LOLA, 1981

Werner Barg, '"Correct" history - Falsely told. Intertextuality and the interpretation of history in Rainer Werner Fassbinder's Lola and Lili Marleen' *Kodikas/Code, Ars Semeiotica*, 17 (1-4), 1994, 91-110.

Pascal Bonitzer, 'Lola et le Pantin', *Cahiers du cinema* 329, November 1981, 57-58.

Thomas Elsaesser, 'Fassbinder's Lola und die Logik des Mehrwerts, oder: nicht nur wer zahlt, zählt' in: A. Rost (ed.), *Der zweite Atem des Kinos*, Frankfurt: Verlag der Autoren, 1996, 53-88.

E. Ann Kaplan, 'Fassbinder as Political Voyeur', *Social Policy*, vol 14, no 1, Summer 1983.

Georg Seeßlen, 'Fassbinder Revisited. Lola', *epd Film*, no 6, 1992.

VERONIKA VOSS, 1981:

Anon, 'An Ex-Star is Born Veronika Voss', *Berlinale Tip*, 7/82, 18 February, 1982.

Serge Daney, 'Auf Wiedersehen, Veronika', *Libération*, 1 July 1982, 23.

David Robinson, 'Worthy testament to Fassbinder's gift', *The Times*, 18 March 1983, 10.

Philip French, 'From the Grave', *The Observer*, 20 March 1982.

Thomas Honickel (ed.), 'Die Sehnsucht der Sybille Schmitz', *Berlinale-Tip*, 5/82, 16 February, 1982.

Peter Märthesheimer, 'Oder wie oder was?', *Berlinale-Tip*, 7/82, 18 February, 1982.

Steve Jenkins, 'Die Sehnsucht der Veronika Voss', *Monthly Film Bulletin*, January 1983.

O.S., 'Rosel Zech. Le dernier amour de Fassbinder', *Libération*, 1 July 1982.

QUERELLE, 1982:

Geoff Brown, 'Potency of Fassbinder's hot-house imagination', *The Times* 12 August 1983

Joseph Hurley et al, 'Querelle', *Film Review Annual 1984*, Englewood, NJ: J Ozer, 1985, 918-928.

Christopher Sharett, 'The Last Stranger: "Querelle" and Cultural Simulation', *Canadian Journal of Political and Social Theory*, vol 13, no 1-2, 1989.

Steve Jenkins, 'Querelle', *Monthly Film Bulletin* 597, October 1983, 276-277.

Monika Treut, 'Man to Man', *Sight and Sound* vol 4, no 5, May 1994, 69.

6. Special Issues of Journals on Fassbinder

epd Film, no 6, 1992, Hans Günther Pflaum (ed.).

Film und Fernsehen, vol 20, no 4, 1992, Wilhelm Roth (ed.).

New German Critique, 63, Fall 1994, David Bathrick and Gerd Gemünden (eds.).

October 21, Summer 1982, Douglas Crimp (ed.).

text + kritik 103, 1989, Michael Töteberg (ed.).

Wide Angle, vol.3, no.4, 1980, Peter Lehman (ed.).

Wide Angle, vol.12, no.1, 1990, Jane Shattuc (ed.).

7. Articles Commemorating the 10th Anniversary of Fassbinder's Death in 1992

Michael Althen, 'Ein Stadtstreicher im Reich der Träume', *Süddeutsche Zeitung*, no.132, 10 June 1992, 12.

Nigel Andrews, 'Blissful Send-up of Tinseltown', *Financial Times*, 25 June 1992, 17.

Helmut Böttiger, 'Die Dialektik der Pflastersteine', *Frankfurter Rundschau*, 5 June 1992.

Peter Buchka, 'Das Phänomen Fassbinder', *Süddeutsche Zeitung*, 10 June 92, 13.

Manfred Etten, 'Der lange Abschied: Fassbinder und die Mythen des Neuen Deutschen Films' *Film Dienst*, May 1992.

Thomas Elsaesser, 'Dimendicando Fassbinder?', in: Giovanni Spagnoletti (ed.), *Rainer Werner Fassbinder*, Milan: Carte Segrete, 1992.

Wolfgang Jacobsen, 'Spätes Happy End', *die tageszeitung*, 21 June 1992.

Peter W Jansen, Holger Siemann et al, 'RWF Heute', *tip* 12/92, 4-17 June 1992, 22-39

Urs Jenny, 'Heiligsprechung eines Ungeheuers', *Der Spiegel*, 8 June 1992, 224-231.

Yaak Karsunke, 'Der Herr Karsunke ist da', *die tageszeitung*, 18 June 1992.

Andreas Kilb, 'Die Hölle? Die Unsterblichkeit', *Die Zeit*, 12 June 1992, 67-68.

Josef Nagel, 'Rainer war wirklich wie Jesus', *Film Dienst*, May 1992.

Sven Michaelsen, 'Magier und Monster', *Stern*, 4 June 1992, 44-54.

Gerd Midding, 'Schachspielen: Gespräch mit Hanna Schygulla', *die tageszeitung*, 19 February 1992.

André Müller, 'Der tote Sohn [interview with Liselotte Eder]', *Die Zeit*, no 18, 24 April 1992, 55-56.

Katrin Beate Müller, 'The Endless Tale of Loneliness', *Kulturchronik Inter Nationes* 5/92, May 1992.

Miriam Niroumand, 'Deutsch als Fremdsprache', *die tageszeitung*, 10 June 1992, 15-16.

Christiane Peitz, 'Ich heiße Franz', *Wochenpost*, no.25, 11 June 1992, 15.

Günther Pflaum, 'Ich hatte nur diese bestimmte Zeit: Zum 10. Todestag Rainer Werner Fassbinders am 10. Juni', *epd film*, no.6, June 1992.

Wolfram Schütte, 'Made in Germany', *Frankfurter Rundschau*, 10 June 1992, 22.

Michael Töteberg, 'Baumaterialien zu einem Haus', *Neue Zürcher Zeitung*, 13 October 1992.

Der Tagesspiegel (Berlin), 'Interview with Günter Lamprecht', *Der Tagesspiegel*, 31 May 1992.

Der Tagesspiegel (Berlin), 'Zitate aus Fassbinder Interviews', *Der Tagesspiegel*, 31 May 1992.

Leonoor Wagenaar, 'Fassbinders moeder en de leugens over der Rainer', *Het Parool*, 13 June 1992.

8. Further Literature

Karl-Heinz Assenmacher, "Das engagierte Theater" in: Gerhard Charles Rump (ed.), *Sprachnetze: Studien zur literarischen Sprachverwendung* (Mit Beiträgen zu Rainer Werner Fassbinder, Agatha Christie, Andre Breton und James Joyce). Hildesheim; New York: Olms, 1976, 1-85.

Sigrid Bauschinger et. al. (eds.), *Film und Literatur: Literarische Texte und der neue deutsche Film*, Berne: Francke, 1984.

Hans C. Blumenberg, 'Von Caligari bis Coppola: Junge deutsche Filmemacher in Hollywood auf den Spuren von Lubitsch, Murnau und Lang', *Die Zeit*, 22 February 1980.

Hans C. Blumenberg, 'Schreie und Flüstern', *Kinozeit*, Frankfurt: Fischer, 1980, 27-34.

Janusz Bodek, *Die Fassbinder-Kontroversen*, Frankfurt: Peter Lang, 1991.

Dirk Bogarde, *An Orderly Man*, New York: Knopf, 1983.

Denis Calandra, *New German dramatists*: A study of Peter Handke, Franz Xaver Kroetz, Rainer Werner Fassbinder, Heiner Müller, Thomas Brasch, Thomas Bernhard, and Botho Strauss. London: Macmillan, 1983.

Vincent Canby, 'The German Renaissance - No Room for Laughter or Love', *New York Times*, 11.12.1977, Section D, p.15.

Ingrid Caven, 'Entretien', *Cahiers du Cinéma* 469, June 1993, 59-61.

Gerald Clarke, 'Seeking Planets That Do Not Exist- The German Cinema is the Liveliest in Europe', *Time Magazine*, 20 March 1978, 51-53.

Jan Dawson, 'The Industry-German Weasels (Filmverlag Follies)', *Film Comment*, May-June 1977, vol 13, no 3, 33-34.

Jan Dawson, 'A Labyrinth of Subsidies', *Sight and Sound*, Winter 1980/81, 14-20.

David Denby, 'The Germans are Coming! The Germans are Coming!', *Horizon*, 1977, vol 20, no 1, 89-90.

Helmuth H. Diederichs, 'Filmverlag der Autoren', *epd film*, September 1985, 22-26.

Alfred Döblin, *Berlin Alexanderplatz: die Geschichte des Franz Biberkopf*, Berlin: Ullstein, 1929 [in English: *Berlin Alexanderplatz*, transl. by Eugene Jolas, New York: Ungar, 1983].

Wolf Donner, 'Die Deutschen kommen', *Die Zeit*, 21 November 1975.

Charles Eidsvik, 'Behind the Crest of the Wave: An Overview of the New German Cinema', *Literature/Film Quarterly*, vol 7, no 3, 1979, 167-181.

Thomas Elsaesser, 'The Post-War German Cinema', in: Tony Rayns (ed.), *Fassbinder*, London: British Film Institute, 1976, 1-16.

Thomas Elsaesser, 'Filming Fascism: Is History Just an Old Movie?', *Sight and Sound*, vol 2, no 5, Sept 1992, 18-21.

Thomas Elsaesser, 'The New German Cinema's Historical Imaginary', in: C. Wickham, B. Murray, (eds.), *Framing the Past: The Historiography of German Cinema and Television*, Carbondale: Southern Illinois University Press, 1992, 280-307.

Thomas Elsaesser, 'Subject Positions, Speaking Positions: From Holocaust and Heimat to Shoah and Schindler's List' in V. Sobchack, ed., *The Persistence of History*, New York: Routledge, 1996, 235-287.

Thomas Elsaesser, 'Moderne und Modernisierung: Der deutsche Film der Dreißiger Jahre', *montage/av*, vol 3, no 2, 1994, 23-40.

Rainer Werner Fassbinder, 'Seven Films by Douglas Sirk', in: Jon Halliday and Laura Mulvey (eds.), *Douglas Sirk*: Edinburgh: Edinburgh Film Festival, 1971, 91-104.

Rainer Werner Fassbinder, 'Insects in a Glass Case: Random Thoughts on Claude Chabrol', *Sight and Sound*, Autumn 1976, vol 45, no 4, 205-206, 252.

Rainer Werner Fassbinder, 'Klimmzug, Handstand, Salto mortale - sicher gestanden', *Frankfurter Rundschau*, 24 February 1979.

Joachim Fest, 'Reicher Jude von links', *Frankfureter Allgemeine Zeitung*, 19 March 1976.

Robert Fischer and Joe Hembus (eds.), *Der Neue Deutsche Film1960-1980*, Munchen: Goldmann, 1981.

Michel Foucault, 'Friendship as a Way of Life,' in Sylvère Lotringer (ed.), *Foucault Live*, New York: Semiotexte, 1989, 203-204.

Anne Marie Freybourg, *Bilder lesen: Visionen von Liebe und Politik bei Jean Luc Godard und Rainer Werner Fassbinder*, Vienna: PVS, 1996.

Saul Friedlander, *Reflexions of Nazism - An Essay on Kitsch and Death*, New York: Harper and Row, 1984.

Saul Friedlander (ed.), *Probing the Limits of Representation*, Cambridge, Mass.: Harvard University Press, 1992

Daniel F. Galouye, *Welt am Draht*, Munich: Goldmann, 1964.

Gerd Gemünden, 'Re-Fusing Brecht: The Cultural Politics of Fassbinder's German Hollywood', *New German Critique* 63, 1994, 55-76.

Olga Grüber, 'Armer Deutscher Film', *Trans Atlantik*, January 1981.

Boze Hadleigh, *Conversations with my Elders* (with essays on Sal Mineo 1939-1976, Luchino Visconti 1906-1976, Cecil Walter Hardy Beaton 1904-1980, George Dewey Cukor 1899-1983, Rainer Werner Fassbinder 1946-1982, Rock Hudson 1925-1985). New York: St. Martin's Press, 1986, 100-131.

Ron Holloway, 'Who's Who in West German Film Industry: A Directory of Directors and Filmmakers over the Period 1957-1977', *Variety*, 22 June 1977, 51-53, 55.

J. Hermand, H. Peitsch and K.R. Scherpe (eds.), *Nachkriegsliteratur in Westdeutschland 1945-1949*, vol.I, Berlin: Das Argument, 1982.

R. Herlt, 'Old Nazis in New Films: The German Cinema Today', *Cinéaste*, 1978, vol 9, no 1, 32-35.

Peter Katzenstein, *State and Terrorism in West Germany in the 1970s and 1980s*, Ithaca: Cornell University Press, 1991.

Anton Kaes, 'Distanced Observers: Perspectives on the New German Cinema', *Quarterly Review of Film Studies*, Summer 1985, 238-245.

Elisabeth Kiderlen (ed.), *Fassbinders Sprengsätze: deutsch-jüdische Normalität*. Frankfurt/M: Pflasterstrand, 1985.

Jörg Friedrich Krabbe, 'Die neuen Caligaris', Neues Forum (Vienna), July/August 1976.

Gunder Krasnova, 'Rainer Werner Fassbinder – Anstoß und Anregung für den Westdeutschen Film', *Kunst und Literatur 5*, 1984, 679-685.

Stan Lapinski, 'Het Fassbinder-universum in 22 minuten - het meisje en de wildeknokenman', *Skrien* 193, 1993, 18-21.

Al LaValley, 'The Gay Liberation of Rainer Werner Fassbinder: Male Subjectivity, Male Bodies, Male Lovers', *New German Critique* 63, 1994, 109-138.

Heiner Lichtenstein (ed.), *Die Fassbinder-Kontroverse oder Das Ende der Schonzeit*. Königstein/Ts: Athenaeum, 1986.

Juliane Lorenz, 'Entretien', *Cahiers du Cinéma* 469, June 1993, 65-67.

Arthur Lubow, 'Cinema's New Wunderkinder', *New Times*, 14 November 1975, 55.

Andrei Markovits, Seyla Benhabib, Moishe Postone, 'Rainer Werner Fassbinder's *Garbage, City and Death*: Renewed Antagonisms, *New German Critique* 38, Spring/Simmer 1986, 3-27.

Ruth McCormick, 'Metropolis Now: The New German Cinema', *In These Times*, 30 November 1979.

Peter Märthesheimer and Ivo Frenzel (eds.), *Der Fernsehfilm Holocaust*, Frankfurt: Fischer, 1979

Matthias Morgenstern, Antworten auf Fassbinder und andere Provokationen: Wie israelische Dramatiker mit der deutsch-jüdischen Vergangenheit umgehen, *Forum modernes Theater*, 10(1), 1995, p. 53-63.

Robert and Carol Reimer, 'Nazi-retro Film', New York: Twaine, 1992.

Eric Rentschler, 'Remembering not to Forget: Alexander Kluge's "Brutalität in Stein"' *New German Critique* 49 (Winter 1990) 23-41.

Eric Rentschler, 'The Use and Abuse of Memory: New German Film and the Discourse of Bitburg', *New German Critique*, Fall 1985, no.36, 67-90.

John Sandford, 'The New German Cinema', *German Life and Letters*, April 1979, vol.32, no.3, 206-228.

Eric Santner, *Stranded Objects: Mourning, Memory and Film in Postwar Germany* (Ithaca: Cornell University Press, 1990).

Andrew Sarris, 'The Germans are Coming, The Germans are Coming', *Village Voice*, 27 October 1975, 137-138.

Gerhard Zwerenz, *Die Erde ist unbewohnbar wie der Mond*; nebst notwendigen Vorbemerkungen von Jörg Schroeder, 'Knast und Kunst', Gerhard Zwerenz, 'Reicher Jude, links, rechts, zwo, drei, vier...' ; sowie einem Anhang: Die Erde ist unbewohnbar wie der Mond, Drehbuch nach dem Roman von Gerhard Zwerenz von Rainer Werner Fassbinder, Herbstein: April, April! Verlag (Schroeder), 1986.

Notes

Notes to Introduction

1 Two additions are Peter Berling, *Die 13 Jahre des Rainer Werner Fassbinder. Seine Filme, seine Freunde, seine Feinde* (Bergisch Gladbach: Gustav Lübbe Verlag, 1992) and Wallace Steadman Watson, *Rainer Werner Fassbinder: Film as Private and Public Art* (Columbia, S.C.: University of South Carolina Press, 1996). The latter reached me too late for full consideration or consultation of its substantial primary research.

2 Limmer 1981, 43-55.

3 For instance, Fassbinder's fantasy about re-writing the myth of *Phaedra*, with father and son ending up together, or his project of a film about (Freud's) Moses, "choosing" his people. Limmer 1981, 60-61.

4 See Appendix 2 for a brief biographical sketch.

5 Hayman 1984, 11.

6 Wilhelm Roth 'Neues (?) über Fassbinder', *epd Film* 1/1993, 12.

7 The subtitle of Bernd Eckhardt, *Rainer Werner Fassbinder* (Munich: Heyne, 1982).

8 Peter Chatel, one of Fassbinder's long-time collaborators who kept himself outside the 'inner circle' is fairly categorical, and thus fairly typical: 'I don't think he ever made a film one could call a masterpiece. The masterpiece are all the 41 films, the life, and everything together. The films are the waste products of this life.' Interviewed in Raab/Peters 1982, 292.

9 This is what Roth himself has attempted in his 'Kommentierte Filmographie', which together with Hans Helmut Prinzler's filmography and bibliography makes up the central part of the standard reference work on Fassbinder, Peter W. Jansen and Wolfram Schütte (eds), *Rainer Werner Fassbinder* (Frankfurt: Fischer, 1992).

10 'The fact that I made LILI MARLEEN is more of an accident'. Fassbinder in an (uncredited) interview from 1980, quoted in Ernst-Christian Neisel (ed.), *Werkschau: Programm* (Berlin: Argon, 1992), 78.

11 David Bordwell has some pertinent remarks on KATZELMACHER in his *Narration and the Fiction Film* (Madison: University of Wisconsin Press, 1985), 286-289.

12 See my 'Primary Identification and the Historical Subject', in Phil Rosen (ed.), *Narrative, Apparatus, Ideology* (New York: Columbia University Press, 1986), 548.

13 The filmography appendix lists the full references to these sources.

Notes to Chapter 1

1 Interview with Colette Godard, 'L'Allemagne, oeuvre complète', *Le Monde*, 14 April 1981.

2   For a collection of quotations, see 'Auskunft über Deutschland. Ausländische Reaktionen auf den Tod von Rainer Werner Fassbinder', *Frankfurter Allgemeine Zeitung*, 12 June, 1982 (with contributions by Karlheinz Bohrer, Ivan Nagel, Winfried Wiegand).

3   Hans Kohn, *The Mind of Germany* (New York: Charles Scribner's, 1960). See also Ernest Gellner, *Nations and Nationalism* (Oxford: Blackwell, 1983) and Eric Hobsbawm, *Nations and Nationalism since 1780: Programme, Myth, Reality* (Cambridge: Cambridge University Press, 1990).

4   The correspondence of Karl Jaspers and Hannah Arendt gives eloquent testimony in this respect.

5   Edgar Reitz, commenting on one of the episodes from his film HEIMAT. Edgar Reitz, *Drehort Heimat* (Frankfurt: Verlag der Autoren, 1993), 258.

6   See Ernst Bloch's essays from the late 1920s and early 1930s, warning the left to take mass-literature, movies and popular culture more seriously in the political struggle against the nascent right, collected in Ernst Bloch, *Heritage of Our Times* (California University Press, 1989).

7   Wim Wenders and Reinard Hauff were, for instance, attacked by Herbert Achternbusch, in *Semiotexte: the German Issue* no 11, 1982, 8-15.

8   Gabriele Förg (ed.), *Unsere Wagner* (Frankfurt/M: Fischer, 1984).

9   The tendency towards a certain monumentalism in the New German Cinema is undeniable: Herzog's Herculean feats as filmmaker, the length of Syberberg's OUR HITLER, Fassbinder's 13-part BERLIN ALEXANDERPLATZ, Reitz's HEIMAT (15 hours, 22 minutes) and DIE ZWEITE HEIMAT (nearly 26 hours).

10 See my 'Herbert Achternbusch and the German Avantgarde', *Discourse* no 6, 1983, 92-112.

11 'Interview: Lieber Straßenkehrer in Mexiko sein als Filmemacher in Deutschland', *Der Spiegel*, no 29, 11 July 1977.

12 'WHY DOES HERR R RUN AMOK is full of sneers for the same German affluence that has made Mr Fassbinder's extraordinary film career possible, but that's the way with many artists these days. They must bite the hands as long as they feed them'. Vincent Canby, 'Fassbinder Sneers at German Affluence' *The New York Times*, 18 November, 1977.

13 Wolfram Schütte, 'Unser Balzac ist tot', *Frankfurter Rundschau*, 11 June 1982.

14 Jansen/Schütte 1992, 64-65.

15 See Appendix for details of the 'hot autumn' of 1977.

16 Interview from 1980, quoted in *Werkschau: Programm*, 77-78.

17 Karsten Witte, 'Hölle & Söhne', *Im Kino* (Frankfurt: Fischer, 1985), 159.

18 In BEWARE OF THE HOLY WHORE, for instance, the motto is from *Tonio Kröger* and reads: 'Sometimes, I am tired to death, representing what is human without partaking in what is human'.

19 'What one looks for in vain, however, is evidence of Döblin's futurist techniques, of aural and visual impressionableness, of the intense, almost unhinging bombardment of walking

down a street in his Berlin.' Michael Hofmann, 'A Futurist's Babel', *Times Literary Supplement*, 20 September, 1985, 1032.

20 Pflaum/Fassbinder 1976, 60.

21 See also my 'A Cinema of Vicious Circles' in Rayns 1980, 24-36, reprinted and revised in *Rainer Werner Fassbinder* (New York: Museum of Modern Art, 1997).

22 A compilation film by this title was made by Robert von Ackeren in 1980.

23 Harry Baer, on the other hand, thought the series politically tame and opportunist: 'It wasn't radical enough for me, I found it trivial. That's when I took my leave, at any rate until FOX AND HIS FRIENDS. ... Many people found EIGHT HOURS DO NOT MAKE A DAY really great, but these grandma characters were too calculating and ingratiating for me.' Juliane Lorenz (ed.), *Das ganz normale Chaos* (Berlin: Henschel, 1995), 98.

24 Ingrid Caven 'Entretien' in *Cahiers du cinéma* 469, June 1993, 59-61.

25 For an overview of the political situation of West and East Germany in the 1970s, see Hartwig Bögeholz, *Die Deutschen nach dem Krieg: Eine Chronik* (Reinbek: Rowohlt, 1995).

26 See, for instance, Dan Diner (ed.), *Ist der Nationalsozialismus Geschichte?* (Frankfurt: Fischer, 1987) and Reinhard Kühnl (ed.), *Streit ums Geschichtsbild* (Cologne: Pahl-Rugenstein, 1987).

27 Fassbinder quoted in *Berlin tip*, 12/1992, 26.

28 With MARIA BRAUN's international success, Fassbinder was widely regarded as one of the most acute commentators on the Federal Republic at a crucial moment, according to Peter Märthesheimer, Ulrich Gregor and Karlheinz Böhm, interviewed in Hans Günther Pflaum ICH WILL NICHT NUR, DASS IHR MICH LIEBT, ZDF June 1992.

29 Interview in *Cahiers du cinéma* 469, June 1993, 60.

30 The witch-hunt against 'sympathizers' reached its climax on 11 October 1977, when the Christian Democrat Press Office published a list of citations from prominent SPD politicians, intellectuals and writers (including Böll), implying that they sided with terrorists. As a response, Böll wrote the script for the 'Antigone' episode of GERMANY IN AUTUMN.

31 For a synopsis of MOTHER KÜSTER, see *Appendix 1: Commented Filmography*.

32 Interview with Wilfried Wiegand, in Jansen/Schütte 1992, 86.

33 In the press handout to MARTHA, Fassbinder had made remarks which were taken up in a discussion with Margit Carstensen, 'Ein Unterdrückungsgespräch: Männer können nicht so perfekt unterdrücken, wie Frauen es gern hätten' (in English in Rentschler 1988, 168-171. But see also discussion in *Frauen und Film* 35, 1987, 92-96.

34 'I call this obscene, the way the film denounces its characters.[...] This film is no more than pornography with a fashionable touch of social critique'. *Filme befreien den Kopf*, 135.

35 Originally, in *Die Abendzeitung* (Munich), 12 March 1973. Reprinted in *Filme befreien den Kopf*, 123/4. Michael Töteberg points out a curious reversal. In 1981 Fassbinder cited

WILDWECHSEL as one of the New German cinema's 'most odious' films, while Kroetz, by 1984, conceded that the film had 'definite qualities'. (*Filme befreien den Kopf*, 136).

36 See Chapter 7 *Frankfurt, Germans and Jews*.

37 Limmer 1981, 82-3. 'The fact is: if you make films about women, Jews, homosexuals, you have to show them the way they are, how society made them, their faults as well.' 'I let the Audience Feel and Think', Interview with Norbert Sparrow, *Cineaste* VIII/2, Fall 1977, 20-22.

38 According to Robert Katz, Andreas Baader, the leader of the Baader-Meinhof group, was a frequent presence at the Munich *anti-teater* performances (Katz, 1986, 34).

39 Vincent Canby, 'Fassbinder Sneers at German Affluence' *New York Times*, 18 November, 1977.

40 'My films are about the exploitability of feelings, irrespective of who does the exploiting. It never ends, and that's my perennial subject.' *Die Anarchie der Phantasie*, 179.

41 Limmer 1981, 78.

42 Among the more critical obituaries were Mechthild Küpper, 'Faßbinder Superstar ist tot', *Die tageszeitung*, 11 June 1982; Ruprecht Skasa-Weiß, 'Ende eines Unaufhaltsamen', *Stuttgarter Zeitung*, 11 June 1982; Derek Malcolm, 'Radical without chic', *The Guardian* 11 June 1982; Vincent Canby, 'A Disturbing Talent' *New York Times*, 11 June 1982.

43 Among the critical essays by gay writers, one could mention Richard Dyer, 'Reading Fassbinder's Sexual Politics' (in Rayns 1980, 54-64) and Andrew Britton, 'Foxed', *Jump Cut* 16, November 1977.

44 'The more fatalistic a film is the more hopeful it is...' Interview with Norbert Sparrow, *Cineaste* VIII/2 (Fall 1977), 20.

45 Among the many examples from the 1970s, see Michael Schneider, *Marxismus und Psychoanalyse* (Frankfurt: Suhrkamp, 1972) and Bruno Reimann, *Psychoanalyse und Gesellschaftstheorie* (Darmstadt und Neuwied: Luchterhand, 1973).

46 The debate around the workers' films in Germany is documented in R. Collins, V. Porter, *WDR and the Arbeiterfilm: Fassbinder and others* (London: British Film Institute, 1976).

47 For instance, the debate between Colin McArthur and Colin McCabe about the progressive realist text in Christopher Williams (ed.,) *Realism and the Cinema*, (London: British Film Institute, 1980).

48 The phrase spoken by Fassbinder (in character) in BEWARE OF THE HOLY WHORE: 'the only feeling I can accept is despair', is commented in Chapter 3 *Murder, Merger Suicide: The Politics of despair*.

49 Interview with Wilfried Wiegand, Jansen/Schütte 1992, 89.

50 Jansen/Schütte 1992, 92.

51 Limmer 1981, 78.

52 Slavoj Zizek, 'Das Opfer als Liebling', *lettre international* 26, 1994, 22-24.

53 Gustav Freytag, *Soll und Haben*, Leipzig, 1855. It was made into a film in 1924 (directed by Carl Wilhelm).

54 First published in *Die Zeit*, 11 March 1977. Reprinted in *Filme befreien den Kopf*, 36.

55 *Filme befreien den Kopf*, 37.

56 '*Soll und Haben* is [...] a well constructed, exciting story, full of suspense, almost as if written for the cinema. This is entertainment [...] and it is fun, it gives pleasure to those who like to discover the breaks and badly joined patches in their own reality, and it encourages one to recognize a few contradictions which make up our reality.' *Filme befreien den Kopf*, 39.

57 'When I was prevented from making *Soll und Haben* for WDR, I could have said: fuck you, I'm never again going to work for television. But that would have been pretty stupid, because by turning one's back on television one loses a medium which I consider very important and even necessary.' *Die Anarchie der Phantasie*, 170.

58 'Warum denn Ärger mit Franz Biberkopf', *Frankfurter Allgemeinen Zeitung*, 29 December 1980.

59 A Fassbinder phrase used in the publicity material distributed by the Filmverlag der Autoren at the Cannes Film Festival, May 1979.

60 Yann Lardeau, 'Saint Fassbinder, comédien et martyr', *Cahiers du cinéma* no 413, 1988, 30-32.

61 Katz 1987, 55-59 and 210-221 (written by Peter Berling).

62 Not least by Fassbinder himself: 'With BEWARE OF A HOLY WHORE there began for me a decisively new phase.' (Interview with Wilfried Wiegand, Jansen/Schütte 1992, 88). See also interview with Peter W. Jansen: 'I have to say it once more, if despair there was, it was prior to [making the film]. The learning process took place during the filmmaking, and this is always a deeply pleasurable experience.' (Janse/Schütte 1992, 114).

63 'I went to him and said: "I've just read your script of MOTHER KÜSTER. I like it, but there's one thing I don't understand: I know you're against the right, I know you're against the left, you're against the extremists, the ones from below, the ones from above, you're against political parties, against established religion - so what exactly are you *for?*" He looked at me for a while, and then he said: "I think I just notice when it doesn't smell right, whether it's on the right or the left, above or below, I couldn't care less. It's just, when I notice it stinks, I fire in all directions".' Karlheinz Böhm 'Fließbandarbeit ist schwerer' in Lorenz 1995, 319.

64 *Die Anarchie der Phantasie*, 106.

65 Theo Hinz interview in Lorenz 1995, 245-246, but also Katz 1987, 145-154.

66 Jan Dawson 'The Sacred Terror', *Sight and Sound*, Autumn 1979, 242-245, and *Die Anarchie der Phantasie*, 106.

67 The terrorists' code word is (Arthur Schopenhauer's) 'the world as will and idea', which Fassbinder comments in an interview, saying that 'the main problem, [the reason I made the film], is that people who have no reason, no motive, no despair, no utopia can be used by others. [In the end] it makes no difference whether there ever was a chief executive officer who masterminded a terrorist cell in order to market more of his computers. [...]

One could even say, if he did not exist, he would have to be invented.' *Die Anarchie der Fantasie*, 137.

68 Fassbinder himself speaks of West Germans as living in a 'democracy handed to them as a present' (a common phrase at the time: 'Modell Deutschland: die geschenkte Demokratie', *Die Anarchie der Phantasie*, 138). This implies a question about the 'agency' the political subject can assume or put on (if only by mimicry) in reply to repression: 'we're not in control, and therefore not responsible,' thus hinting at one kernel of (inverted) truth in the emergent 'victim' cultures of the 1980s and 1990s.

69 A similar dilemma of how to respond to the symbolic mandate coming from a cult following has faced pop-stars. The black rapper of the 1990s, for instance, 'represents' a constituency which demands that his street-credibility of violence is not merely verbal and in the music. Tupac Shakur, the 'gangsta rapper' whose mother was a Black Panther militant, exposed himself to 'getting real' with fatal results. But as he is supposed to have said, 'all good niggers, all niggers who change the world, die in violence'.

70 Wilhelm Roth is reminded of the hero's suicide disguised as assassination in Robert Bresson's *Le Diable probablement*, a clip of which is in fact included in the film (Jansen/Schütte 1992, 225).

71 In an interview, Fassbinder called the media saturation of the film a form of 'aural terrorism' ('Schallterror'), *Die Anarchie der Phantasie*, 106.

72 When the writer Thomas Brasch asked Fassbinder to put on a theatre piece of his, Fassbinder wanted him to cut Hitler and Stalin out of a speech, saying 'leave out the politicians' names, your characters are fighting over power, but this struggle for power is not about political power, it's about something else'. Lorenz 1995, 355.

73 When an interviewer quoted Brecht's sentence that 'only the dumbest calves choose their own butchers' ('nur die allergrößten Kälber wählen ihren Metzger selber'), Fassbinder replied: 'ah, but there are so many kinds of calves'. Limmer 1981, 83.

74 Schlöndorff has since returned to Germany, to make big budget Euro-cinema (e.g. THE OGRE, 1996), while Petersen, along with the Dutch director Paul Verhoeven and fellow Germans Uli Edel and Roland Emmerich, has become a successful Hollywood director. Ironically, this is what Fassbinder often professed to be aiming for, and one can only speculate what road he might have taken.

75 Kohl coined the phrase about those 'blessed with the grace of the later born' ('die Gnade der späten Geburt'), among whom he included himself.

76 Willy Brandt is conspicuously the only chancellor not in 'negative' in the line of portraits from Hitler to Helmut Schmidt at the end of THE MARRIAGE OF MARIA BRAUN.

Notes to Chapter 2

1 'What I would like is a Hollywood cinema, that is to say, a cinema as wonderful and as generally accessible as Hollywood, but at the same time not so hypocritical'. Interview with Wilfried Wiegand, Jansen/Schütte 1992, 93-94.

2   See my 'Fassbinder and the Death of the New German Cinema', in Brian Wallis and Cynthia Schneider (eds.), *Global Television* (Cambridge, Mass: MIT Press, 1989), 119-136.

3   Laurens Straub talks about Fassbinder's bankability in Pflaum/Fassbinder 1976, 162.

4   Craig Whitney, 'A New Director Movie Buffs Dote on', *New York Times*, 16 February 1977.

5   'The basic problem with German cinema is that there is no middle ground between the mandarins and the masses, between the festival places and the grind houses... Fassbinder, I think, can provide pleasure even for the ordinary movie goer dwelling within the older boundaries of life. Fassbinder deftly balances style (Straub) with humanity (Herzog) in such a way that THE MERCHANT OF FOUR SEASONS manages to break the heart without betraying the mind.' Andrew Sarris, 'Lost Love, Found Despair', *The Village Voice*, 22 November 1973, 77.

6   KATZELMACHER received five of the federal film prizes of 1969, and thus made a handsome profit, even without any box-office returns: costing about 80,000 DM to make, it collected a total of 650,000 DM in prizes, with another 300,000 DM coming from the Film Subsidies Board two years later.

7   One of the scenes it incorporates was shot by Jean Marie Straub for his film THE BRIDEGROOM, THE COMEDIENNE AND THE PIMP (in which Fassbinder played the pimp).

8   Fassbinder has explained that the static camera set ups were due to the weight and bulk of the camera he was able to rent, which allowed for very little mobility in the indoor scenes. For a picture of the camera on the set, see Schmid/Gehr 1992, 194.

9   Critics certainly reacted to what they perceived as a provocation, the more so since the ensemble of the action theatre, as well as its successor, the anti-teater, were not averse to 'épater le public'. About Fassbinder's theatre work, see Yaak Karsunke, 'anti-teatergeschichte' and Peter Iden, 'Der Eindruck-Macher', both in Jansen/Schütte (eds), *Rainer Werner Fassbinder* (Munich: Hanser, 1974, 1985), and also in Ruth McCormack (ed.), *Fassbinder* (Tanam Press, 1985). Wiegand argues that there is a lot of aggression in the poverty of the decor and set, shown off with panache (Jansen/Schütte 1992, 30).

10 See Wim Wenders' review of KATZELMACHER, *Filmkritik*, December 1969, 751-2.

11 'Herr R is bored, but because he has no safety valve of impatience, he explodes. The camera has the habit of more or less settling down, as if it were someone vastly overweight filling up a chair. It watches what goes on with no special interest, but it hasn't the strength to move....and... often can't be bothered to turn to focus'. Vincent Canby, *New York Times*, 16 November 77.

12 There is another possible reading of KATZELMACHER, and especially of the central figure: the desire that keeps substitution going among the different members of the group is ultimately for a figure of authority. This quest is unsuccessful, and in the absence of such paternal authority, the power-struggles between men and women take on such an edge of

frustration. With Jorgos/Katzelmacher, a potent father figure does appear, but since he barely utters a word, his power is ambiguous, both present and merely imagined. When he does speak, the spell is broken, and the interminable sequence of pointless exchanges can finally end. This suggests a more allegorical than sociological meaning, also referring to Fassbinder's position within the group, which even suggests that BEWARE OF A HOLY WHORE is a sort of remake of KATZELMACHER.

13 'In giving as little grace to the victim as to the aggressors, Fassbinder at least plays fair; cynically fair.' Charles Lewsen, *The Guardian*, 14 November, 1974.

14 As far as his own love of the cinema is concerned, Fassbinder was an inveterate film-goer from a very early age onwards. He himself claimed to have gone 'three or four times a week', and to see in it a surrogate family. It seems his mother gave him money to go to the pictures so that she could work at home in peace. What Fassbinder saw in the mostly second-run cinemas near the Sendlinger Tor were American films dubbed into German. He also saw pornographic films, and the aesthetics of his early films are not so much derived from Brecht or Straub, as from cheaply made porn-films as they began to surface in the early 1960s. About Fassbinder's cinema going habits, see Kurt Raab, Karsten Peters, *Die Sehnsucht des Rainer Werner Fassbinder* (Munich: Goldmann, 1982), 56-57.

15 For a discussion of the New German Cinema 'in search of an audience', see my *New German Cinema A History* (London: Macmillan, 1989), chapters 4,5 and 6.

16 'I Let the Audience Feel and Think', Interview with Rainer Werner Fassbinder by Norbert Sparrow, *Cineaste* VIII/2, Fall 1977, 20-22.

17 Interview from 1974, quoted in Schmid/Gehr 1992, 194.

18 Interview with Wilfried Wiegand, Jansen/Schütte 1992, 92.

19 Exasperated by the frequent references to Godard as the key influence on his early films, Fassbinder once distanced himself from A BOUT DE SOUFFLE in a very characteristic way, saying 'I felt as if [Godard] had touched my cock, but not because he wanted to do something for me; he did it so that I would like his film.' Interview with Norbert Sparrow, *Cineaste* VIII/2, Fall 1977, 21.

20 Klaus Lemke and Roland Klick are now almost forgotten names, but at the time they were important influences on Fassbinder. See 'Hitliste des deutschen Films' in *Filme befreien den Kopf*, 127.

21 '"ganz sicher auch ein schwuler Film" ist Fassbinders knurriger Kommentar dazu', Wolf Donner, *Die Zeit*, 23 October, 1970.

22 John Hughes and Brooks Riley, 'A New Realism', *Film Comment* 11/6, November-December 1975. Already in KATZELMACHER, the women are shown to be addicted to romance fiction.

23 This is how Wim Wenders once described Rudolf Thome's RED SUN (1969), *Filmkritik*, January 1970, 9.

24 'Recognizing that I was gay and then acknowledging it was no problem for me. I was lucky. Maybe because I could not care less about anything. When I realized I was gay [at the age of 14], I went round telling everybody'. Limmer 1981, 74-75.

25 'There is a faction among the German public that says: "Fassbinder, we made you rich and famous, now give us art, make another Effi Briest, and we will love you" ... the other faction of the public says: "we accept Fassbinder as someone whose productivity derives from the fact that he will always be at odds with society".' Laurens Straub quoted in Pflaum/Fassbinder 1976, 162.

26 Interview with Norbert Sparrow, *Cineaste* VIII/2, Fall 1977, 20.

27 'Chronik und Bilanz des Internationalen Films', *Film* no 12, 1969, 62.

28 *Frankfurter Allgemeine Zeitung*, 30 June 1969.

29 'Sirk taught Fassbinder how to handle genre, which became an important facet of his audience-getting strategies.' Tony Rayns (ed.), *Fassbinder* (London: British Film Institute, 1980), 4.

30 'Fassbinder [...] created a cinema that used seeming naivety of gesture and image to refresh our perception of truth, jaded from long decades of looking at the true naivety of Hollywood or the overwrought sophistications of Europe', Nigel Andrews, *The Financial Times*, 25 June, 1992, 17.

31 See Tony Rayns, 'Merchant of Four Seasons', *Monthly Film Bulletin* 499, August 1975 and Barbara Leaming, 'Structures of Alienation', *Jump Cut* 11-12, Summer 1976.

32 See the scene of mother and daughter waiting, discussed in the previous chapter.

33 'The very love and friendship man seeks in order to cope with alienation is manipulated in structures of love and friendship'. Fassbinder, quoted in Ralph Tyler, 'The Savage World of Rainer Werner Fassbinder', *New York Times*, 22 March, 1977.

34 Pathos and irony may be seen as two ways of regulating the relationship of the spectator to the characters on screen, the first placing the spectator in a role of knowing no more than the character, the second giving the spectator a superior position of knowledge. In the various critical discussions around melodrama, these two stances were also 'gendered'. See Christine Gledhill, ed., *Home is where the Heart is* (London: British Film Iinstitute, 1986), and Steve Neale, 'Melodrama and Tears', *Screen* 27/6, 1986.

35 See my 'Tales of Sound and Fury', in Gledhill, 1986. Also Noel Carroll, 'Towards a Theory of Film Suspense', *Persistence of Vision*, 1, Summer 1984.

36 'The filmmakers were forced to shoot happy endings but a critical cineaste finds a way of getting around that, making one that is ultimately unsatisfactory. And that's what Sirk did ... and Jerry Lewis.' Interview with Norbert Sparrow, *Cineaste* VIII/2, Fall 1977, 20. Fassbinder also comments on the Hollywood happy ending in his Sirk essay, reprinted in *Filme befreien den Kopf*, 14.

37 For a fuller discussion of 'the subjectivity of the desiring subject', see Mary Ann Doane, *The Desire to Desire* (Bloomington, Indiana UP, 1987) and my review essay 'Desire Denied, Deferred, or Squared', in *Screen* 23/3, 1988, 106-115.

38 Judith Mayne discusses FEAR EATS THE SOUL in terms of a double structure of identification: the genre conventions yield a framework of recognition, which the stylization then draws attention to, by excessively formal, too perfect and stylized compositions. 'Fassbinder and Spectatorship', *New German Critique* 12, Fall 1977, 61-75.

39 So much so that in 1976 a critic could write in an excellent essay comparing ALL THAT HEAVEN ALLOWS with FEAR EATS THE SOUL: 'As much as I dislike invoking Brecht in discussions of movie aesthetics, it is worth noting here that his concept of *Verfremdungseffekte,* usually translated as 'alienation effect', can also be interpreted as 'strange making effect'.' Michael Stern, 'The Inspired Melodrama and the Melodrama it inspired' [a comparison of FEAR EATS THE SOUL and Sirk's ALL THAT HEAVEN ALLOWS], *Thousand Eye Magazine*, January 1976, 3-4.

40 See Robert Ray, *A Certain Tendency of the Hollywood Cinema* (Princeton: Princeton University Press, 1985) and Tim Corrigan, *A Cinema without Walls* (London: Routledge, 1991).

41 For an analysis of coincidence in LILI MARLEEN, see Chapter 6, below.

42 'A Cinema of Vicious Circles', in Tony Rayns (ed.), *Fassbinder* (London: British Film Institute, 1980), 24-36.

43 Interview with Hans Günther Pflaum, reproduced in ICH WILL NICHT NUR, DASS IHR MICH LIEBT, ZDF 1992.

44 See my discussion of the 'authenticity complex' in 'The New German Cinema's Historical Imaginary' in B. Murray and C. Wickham (eds.), *Framing the Past* (Carbondale: Southern Illinois University Press, 1992), 280-306. In a different context, Gertrud Koch once asked 'Can one become naive?' (reprinted in 'Dossier on HEIMAT', *New German Critique* 36, Fall 1985, 4-8).

45 Quoted in John Hughes and Ruth McCormick, 'Rainer Werner Fassbinder and the Death of Family Life', *Thousand Eyes Magazine*, April 1977, 4-5.

46 Michael Rutschky, *Erfahrungshunger* (Frankfurt: Fischer, 1982).

47 Klaus Kreimeier, *Die Ideologie der Traumfabrik: die Filme der Bundesrepublik*, Berlin: Freunde der deutschen Kinemathek, 1969.

48 Such a stance can go hand in hand with the ambition of making Hollywood films, themselves arguably 'perverse' in their spectator-positioning. See Raymond Bellour, 'Psychosis, Neurosis, Perversion', *Camera Obscura*, 3/4, Summer 1979, 104-134.

49 John Hughes and Ruth McCormick, 'Rainer Werner Fassbinder and the Death of Family Life', *Thousand Eyes Magazine*, April 1977, 4-5.

50 Gilles Deleuze and Felix Guattari, *Anti-Oedipus* (New York: Viking, 1977).

51 Rainer Werner Fassbinder, 'Imitation of Life. On Douglas Sirk' in L.Mulvey and J. Halliday, eds., *Douglas Sirk*, Edinburgh Film Festival, 1971, 95-107.

52 R.D. Laing, *Knots* (London: Penguin Books, 1970), 24.

53 See Dan Greenburg, *How to be a Jewish Mother* (Los Angeles, 1964).

54 Classic examples are questions such as 'Have you stopped beating your wife?', to which both 'yes' and 'no' are inappropriate answers, if the addressee is male and married, but has never laid a hand on his spouse.

55 Anthony Wilden, *System and Structure* (London: Tavistock, 1980) 110-124.

56 Michael Töteberg (ed.), *Fassbinders Filme 3* (Frankfurt: Verlag der Autoren, 1990), 9.

57 *ibid.*, 13.

58 Fassbinder's very first film DER STADTSTREICHER revolves around a double-bind: a tramp finds a gun in the park and doesn't know whether to keep it or throw it away. The dilemma is seen as both funny and tragic, since the means of defence are also the means of perdition: the man cannot get rid of the gun, he dare not hold on to the gun.

59 This is the situation also at the basis of GDR playwright Heiner Müller's theatre piece *Der Lohndrücker* and Andrzej Wajda's film *Man of Marble*.

60 Quoted by Wolfgang Roth, Jansen/Schütte 1992, 160.

61 See Rainer Werner Fassbinder, 'Talking about Oppression with Margit Carstensen' in R. Rentschler (ed.), *West German Filmmakers on Film* (New York: Holmes & Meier, 1988), 168-171.

62 Judith Mayne analyses the Fassbinder frame in terms of Brecht. 'Fassbinder and Spectatorship', *New German Critique* 12, Fall 1977, 70.

63 'Fassbinder's highly visible cinematic signifier points to a fetishisation of cinematic technique. [... He is] a director who approaches the Imaginary by means of a powerful attachment to and manipulation of cinematic technique as technique, while simultaneously barring entry to those of his audience who seek the imaginary in the invisible cinematic signifier.' Cathy Johnson, in *Wide Angle*, 3/4, 1980, 25.

64 Fassbinder himself apparently had a horror of shooting outdoors, and only felt comfortable within the artificiality and controllable conditions of the studio. Even when using interiors on location, he seemed to take little interest in them, leaving the details of the lay-out to his set designer, and only involving himself with the arrival of the camera. Pflaum/Fassbinder 1976, 134.

65 '[Using mirror-shots] is a way to create distance, for instance, vis-à-vis a character, with whom the audience is beginning to identify. With the mirror, identification all of a sudden disappears.' Limmer 1981, 87.

66 This mise-en-abyme of the frame is most reminiscent of the hallucinatory effect of Ingrid Bergman's dream about opening doors upon doors in Alfred Hitchcock's SPELLBOUND.

67 'A system protects itself against symmetry (the imaginary) by switching to complementarity.' See Anthony Wilden, *System and Structure*, 261.

68 Rainer Werner Fassbinder, 'Insects in a Glass Case', *Sight and Sound* 45/4, Autumn 1976.

69 In the vast literature on the topic, Laura Mulvey's article is the best known, reprinted, among other key essays, in Phil Rosen (ed.), *Narrative, Apparatus, Ideology* (New York: Columbia University Press, 1986). For a critique of Mulvey's position, see Kaja Silverman, *Male Subjectivity on the Margins* (London: Routledge, 1992), 152-153.

70 A feminist analysis of FEAR EATS THE SOUL can be found in Judith Mayne, 'The Feminist Analogy', *Discourse* 7, 1985, 34-40.

71 'Can one say that your films are a kind of camouflage, in the sense that homosexual relations are portrayed as heterosexual ones?' – 'No, that's what good old Marcel Proust did with his thing – the boys and girls – but not me.' Limmer 1981, 74.

72 Jacques Lacan, 'The mirror-stage as formative of the function of the I as revealed in psychoanalytic experience', *Ecrits: A Selection* (transl. Alan Sheridan, London: Tavistock, 1977). While paraphrases of Lacan's concept of the mirror-phase in film studies literature are legion, the most concise applications can perhaps be found in J.L. Baudry's 'Le dispositif' (reprinted in Phil Rosen, ed., *Narrative, Apparatus, Ideology*) and in Christian Metz, *The Imaginary Signifier* (London: Macmillan, 1984).

73 Limmer 1981, 87.

74 A quotation from the Rolling Stones that Fassbinder was fond of repeating himself. Watson (1996), 90.

75 In Bishop Berkeley's famous phrase.

76 Fassbinder, in John Hughes and Ruth McCormick, 'Rainer Werner Fassbinder and the Death of Family Life', *Thousand Eyes Magazine*, April 1977, 4-5.

77 'Although our look can never function as the gaze for ourselves, it can have that function for others, even at the moment that we assume the status of object for them. Exhibitionism unsettles because it threatens to explode the duplicity inherent in every subject, and every object.' Kaja Silverman, 'Fassbinder and Lacan: A Reconsideration of Gaze, Look and Image', *Camera Obscura* 19, 1989, 77.

78 The last words, spoken by the doctor. *Fassbinder's Filme 3*, 96.

79 'Fassbinder and Lacan: A Reconsideration of Gaze, Look and Image', *Camera Obscura* 19, 1989, 76.

80 'Every decent director has only one subject, and finally only makes the same film over and over again. My subject is the exploitability of feelings, whoever might be the one exploiting them. It never ends. It's a permanent theme. Whether the State exploits patriotism, or whether in a couple relationship, one partner destroys the other.' *Die Anarchie der Phantasie*, 179.

81 Slavoj Zizek, '*The Metastases of Enjoyment*' (London: Verso, 1994), 211.

82 In *The Imaginary Signifier*, Christian Metz discusses it as 'Primary Identification'. It is also analyzed by Jean Louis Baudry as at once a simulacrum and a meta-psychic machine. See also section on 'Narrative' in Phil Rosen (ed.), *Narrative, Apparatus, Ideology*.

83 Kaja Silverman defines the screen in the extended sense as the place where the two kinds of looks meet by intersecting but where they also always risk falling apart: the screen is 'something like a mask, a double, an envelope, a thrown off skin, thrown off in order to cover the frame of a shield.... although the subject has no identity without an alienating image, that image may be put in place either by the subject or by the other.' Kaja

Silverman, 'Fassbinder and Lacan: A Reconsideration of Gaze, Look and Image', *Camera Obscura* 19, 1989, 77.

84 A classic formulation of the double-bind as interpellation, injunction and demand comes from another Bavarian filmmaker, Herbert Achternbusch: 'Du hast keine Chance, aber nütze sie!'('You haven't got a chance, but be sure to use it!').

85 Michael Töteberg (ed.), *Die Kinofilme 1* (Munich: Schirmer/Mosel, 1987), 289.

86 In a brief note from 1971, Fassbinder wrote 'Someone, who has love in his belly doesn't need to play flipper, because love is enough of an achievement, not requiring a machine, against which one can, in any case, only lose.' After describing how difficult it is to love, the text ends as follows: 'I've decided to play flipper again, and let the machine win; after all, the one who finally wins is me.' *Fassbinder Filme befreien den Kopf*, 25.

87 How Fassbinder thought about GERMANY IN AUTUMN becomes clear in an article published in *Frankfurter Rundschau* in 1978, announcing his project THE THIRD GENERATION: 'GERMANY IN AUTUMN, a film by the way, which [...] in parts seems to me more terrible than terrible, is nonetheless a film that thanks to my great, Parzifal-like naivety I made my own. Incidentally, it was not the obscene moments that made this film an important one (and for the benefit of those who do not know it already, I do not consider obscene the way I play with my cock in front of the camera; I find obscene the way some people seemed to masturbate who would prefer to keep the existence of their cocks a secret from themselves).' *Fassbinder Filme befreien den Kopf*, 71-72.

88 Fassbinder has always tied to the body and to bodily existence the desire for self-less-ness, as the first step and necessary preparation for facing the condition of not-being. 'The sooner the certainty that we must die becomes a physical fact, the sooner we lose our existential pain – hatred, envy, jealousy. Our relations with each other are such cruel games because we cannot accept our end as something positive. It is positive, because it is real. The body must come to understand death.' *Die Anarchie der Fantasie*, 100.

Notes to Chapter 3

1 The line spoken by Fassbinder in character in BEWARE OF A HOLY WHORE, and in 'Despair: A Synopsis to a film that permits no summing up', *Die Anarchie der Phatnasie*, 103.

2 'Fassbinder's enterprise seems to be very much that of the old time music hall comedian: "You like that one? Oh, well, never mind, I've got a million of 'em". And so the films keep coming – hit or miss, highly wrought or thrown together on the spur of the moment, good, bad or indifferent.' John Russell Taylor, *The Times*, July 7th, 1978. The comparison with other great European auteurs became the stereotypical motif in the reviews: 'one of Fassbinder's best so far, moving him into the ranks of Bergman or Visconti.' Dieter E Zimmer, *Die Zeit*, 19 May 1975.

3 Rolf Zehetbauer had received an Oscar for his sets of *Cabaret* (1970).

4　'[DESPAIR] even has some curious echoes of a recent work from a director of totally opposed tendencies, Resnais' silly old PROVIDENCE, with which it has in common Dirk Bogarde as a leading performer'. John Russell Taylor, *The Times*, July 7th, 1978.

5　The preference for longer sequence and 'flatter' screen space has been typical of European filmmaking at least since the 1910s, when compared with the faster cutting and greater depth of field of the 'American' style. See the essays by Ben Brewster and Barry Salt in T. Elsaesser, ed., *Early Cinema: Space Frame Narrative* (London: British Film Institute, 1990).

6　Reviewers were either baffled by this lack of depth or saw it as technical virtuosity: 'There is something curiously artificial about the film, which blocks any spontaneous identification on the part of the viewer.[...] One is literally repulsed by the many mirrors and reflecting panes of glass [...] which stand in the way of one's comprehension.' H.G. Pflaum, *Süddeutsche Zeitung*, 19 May 1978. 'The way Fassbinder composes even the reflexes of his characters as shadows of their own selves into his images, the way his shots seem like ingeniously arranged mirrored superimpositions, shows a technical brilliance no-one today could hope to rival.' H.D. Seidel, *Stuttgarter Zeitung*, 19 May, 1978.

7　Nabokov wrote the novel in Russian, but translated it into English for its first publication in 1936. Fassbinder came across it when it was published in German in 1972.

8　In the novel, this realization only gradually dawns on the reader, while in the film it is evident from the start.

9　Contrary to remarks, according to which Fassbinder later in the film 'forgot' about the Nazi, their function is, as we shall see, central to the narrative.

10　In this it is reminiscent, again, of the work of European art directors, e.g. Resnais' JE T'AIME, JE T'AIME, Bergmann's THE SERPENT'S EGG, and Bernardo Bertolucci's THE CONFORMIST.

11　See Wallace Watson, 'The Bitter Tears of RWF', *Sight and Sound*, 4/5, July 1992, 24-29.

12　As one critic complained: 'We occasionally hear the ring of Stoppard's brightly polished brass, but it comes to us through a fog of higher intent'. Will Aitken, 'Despair', *Take One*, 7/2, January 1979, 6.

13　'Bogarde and Ferréol's performances are similarly mannered; at first they seem to be doing a spirited turn on the incessant archness of English drawing room comedy'. Will Aitken 'Despair', *Take One* 7/2, January 1979, 6.

14　'... there is clearly something missing. The film is never quite funny enough (how many German films ever are?). It is also a little too intricate and elliptical for its own good, especially since it does, after all, set out to be of wider appeal. Everything, I'm told, comes clear on a second viewing. But then, how many filmgoers can afford that?' Derek Malcolm, *The Guardian*, July 6th, 1978, 12. 'Tom Stoppard is said to be very unhappy about his collaboration with Fassbinder'. John Russell Taylor, *The Times*, July 7th, 1978.

15　For instance in Limmer 1981, 67/68.

16　Vladimir Nabokov, *Despair* (London: Weidenfeld & Nicolson, 1965), 163.

17 The parallels were noted by Will Aitken: 'Felix points a gun at Hermann through the transparent tunnels of a funhouse labyrinth; Felix fires at him, but the wound appears in Felix's stomach and he collapses on the funhouse floor. This is an obvious reference to LADY FROM SHANGHAI, but it adds no resonance to DESPAIR even though entirely appropriate'. Will Aitken, 'Despair', *Take One*, 7/2, January 1979, 7.

18 See the debate regarding FOX AND HIS FRIENDS, of who precisely, in 'real life' was Fox and who Eugen, the suggestion being that Fassbinder who plays Fox was more like Eugen than Fox. Katz 1987, 86-87, and Hayman 1984, 68-73, Raab/Peters 1982, 291-292.

19 See notes 5, 6 and 24, for instance.

20 As discussed in the previous chapter, with examples from THE BITTER TEARS OF PETRA VON KANT and MARTHA.

21 Fassbinder's preferred cogito (*esse est percipi*) was discussed in the previous chapter.

22 A Brechtian reading might call this spectator role that of a witness ('of a traffic accident', Brecht called it in *Der Dreigroschenprozess*, where he details his theory of cinematic spectatorship), but as we shall see, this abstracts perhaps too much from the more context-dependent function this role has in Fassbinder.

23 In actual fact, DESPAIR is 'dedicated to Antonin Artaud, Vincent van Gogh and Unica Zürn' – all artists who might be said to have escaped into insanity to keep their vision intact.

24 'There is so much distancing in DESPAIR we end up wishing we were out in the lobby', Will Aitken, *Take One*, 7/2, January 1979, 6.

25 Vladimir Nabokov, *Despair*, 222.

26 Nabokov apparently revised the novel prior to its English re-issue in 1965, so this surmise may not be strictly accurate. See Watson 1996, 198 and 201.

27 One major difference between novel and film is that the novel's perspective is that of Hermann Hermann as first person narrator, with whom the 'author' plays his own cat-and-mouse game.

28 I am here subsuming the critique of this notion of the cinematic apparatus by feminist film theory, and the subsequent critique of this critique. See, among the ample literature, Stephen Heath, Teresa de Lauretis (eds.), *The Cinematic Apparatus* (London: Macmillan, 1984), Mary Ann Doane and Patricia Mellencamp (eds.), *Re-Vision: Feminism and Film Theory* (Frederick, MA: American Film Institute, 1984), Constance Penley (ed.), *Feminism and Film Theory* (New York: Routledge, 1988) and Joan Copjec, *Read My Desire* (Cambridge, Mass: MIT Press, 1994).

29 Alexander Mitscherlich, *Society without the Father* (London: Tavistock, 1969), 283.

30 *ibid.*, 284.

31 Alexander Mitscherlich and Margarethe Mitscherlich, *The Inability to Mourn* (London: Tavistock, 1975), 65.

32 *ibid.*, 64.

33 Hermann, on the other hand, has a knowledge – his pact with Oswald – that she does not share. See the following chapter for a fuller discussion.

Notes to Chapter 4

1 As noted in Jansen/Schütte 1992, 294.

2 Katz 1987, 10-12.

3 As quoted in Katz 1987, 133.

4 See Peter Märthesheimer and Michael Ballhaus interviews in Lorenz 1995, 139-142 and 203-206. Ballhaus maintains that Michael Fengler had to blackmail Fassbinder into shooting the film at all. In Peter Berling's version, as told by Katz, Fassbinder took on MARIA BRAUN as a quickie, in order to fill a gap of six months before shooting on BERLIN ALEXANDERPLATZ could commence, much to the alarm of Berling who wanted Fassbinder to give this mega-project his total concentration. Katz 1987, 132-134.

5 Both at Cannes and at a promotional tour in New York, arranged by United Artists, Fassbinder is reputed to have been extremely upset by the amount of media attention his star seemed to be diverting from himself. Katz 1987, 166.

6 The seeming continuity disguises some not insignificant breaks between Fassbinder and Schygulla, who once again fell from grace after she gave an interview to *Variety* at the 1981 Cannes festival, suggesting she would be starring in LOLA.

7 These continued after Fassbinder's death. See Fritz Müller-Scherz, Fassbinders Erben, *Transatlantik* February 1983, 12-21.

8 Raab/Peters 1982, 363. Katz 1987, quoting Berling, 132-34. For another account of the relationship, sympathetic to Michael Fengler, see Raab/Peters, 83-84.

9 Lorenz 1996, 204.

10 *Westfälisches Volksblatt* 10 October 1979, quoted in Rheuban 1986, 3.

11 Raab/Peters 1982, 337. Raab also claims that the story is substantially his, and that he authored the original treatment of 300 pages during a holiday on the Greek island of Skopelos, following talks with Fassbinder. Raab/Peters 1982, 302.

12 Zwerenz is the author of *Die Erde ist unbewohnbar wie der Mond* which Fassbinder wanted to make into a film and from which he took certain motifs for his play *Der Müll, die Stadt und der Tod*. Zwerenz also acted in a number of Fassbinder films, BOLWIESER, IN A YEAR OF THIRTEEN MOONS and BERLIN ALEXANDERPLATZ. Apart from MARIA BRAUN, Zwerenz also turned Fassbinder's life into a 'novelization': Gerhard Zwerenz, *Der langsame Tod des Rainer Werner Fassbinder* (Munich: Schneekluth, 1982).

13 In July 1977 Fassbinder gave an interview to *Der Spiegel*, provocatively entitled 'Rather streetsweeper in Mexico than filmmaker in Germany', which was widely quoted. Kurt Raab comments 'sometimes he threatened to move to Paris, sometimes that he'd emigrate to the USA. But he was too intelligent and too aware of his own limits to think seriously of making films there. He was only too conscious of the fact that his films were German,

and had to be made in Germany, that they could have their impact abroad only if they transported the immediacy of what he lived and felt.' Raab/Peters 1982, 226.

14 That Fassbinder's financial 'clout' in Germany was nonetheless precarious is evident when one recalls that the two films made immediately after THE MARRIAGE OF MARIA BRAUN (but, it must be added, before the film was released) were largely produced with Fassbinder's own money, and while in the case of the first, IN A YEAR OF THIRTEEN MOONS, Fassbinder may have wished it this way, for the other, THE THIRD GENERATION, for the reasons mentioned earlier, he was refused both federal film subsidy and Berlin funding, with the result that television co-finance was also withdrawn.

15 This is how they are read by Howard Feinstein, 'BRD 1-2-3 Fassbinder's Postwar Trilogy and the Spectacle', *Cinema Journal* 23/1, Fall 1983, 50.

16 Wilhelm Roth, 'Kommentierte Filmographie' in Jansen/Schütte 1992, 216.

17 But Anton Kaes compares Maria Braun also with Moll Flanders, the heroine of Daniel Defoe's novel, giving the figure a rather longer pedigree than the fashionable female role models of the 1970s. *From Hitler to Heimat* (Cambridge, Mass: Harvard University Press, 1989), 84.

18 Christopher Sharp, in *Women's Wear Daily*, 12 October 1979, quoted in Rheuban 1986, 215.

19 Ruth McCormack, quoted in Rheuban 1986, 222.

20 *ibid.*, 227.

21 Peter W Jansen, quoted in Rheuban 1986, 221. This interpretation would seem to apply more to Helma Sanders-Brahms' GERMANY PALE MOTHER (1980), a film made under the impact of MARIA BRAUN, but with a different historical and gender agenda.

22 There were several films on this topic, from the independent documentary ROSIE THE RIVETER using archive material to the Hollywood production SWING SHIFT, with Goldie Hawn as the lead.

23 Jansen, quoted in Rheuban 1986, 221.

24 Frank Rich, *Time Magazine*, 22 October, 1979.

25 Another intertext is German post-war literature, notably the novels of Heinrich Böll and Günther Grass, where the singular point of view is used to voice the authors' misgivings about the kind of society Germany had become. In addition, popular novelists like Walter Kempowski, whose nostalgic tales of family life in the Weimar Republic and the Third Reich were very successful also on television, whetted the public's appetite for more fictional glimpses of how 'our parents' lived and loved.

26 See Marsha Kinder, 'Ideological Parody in the New German Cinema', *Quarterly Review of Film and Video* 12/1-2, 1990, 73-104.

27 Anton Kaes 1989, 86.

28 Hayman 1984, 114.

29 Barabara Baum, 'Jeder Film eine Herausforderung', in Lorenz 1995, 289.

30 'A brief description how he saw the film, a few of the dramatic climaxes that were important to him, a few of his favourite films that were important for his work and which he wanted to watch with us, that's how he inspired the team. For LOLA, for instance, he just told me it had to look like an early Hollywood colour film'. *ibid.*, 289.

31 In LOLA another chancellor, Ludwig Erhard, makes an important speech the day von Bohm has his first television installed. We hear the speech while von Bohm watches – the test card. The bulky set echoes the television given to Emmi by her children in FEAR EATS THE SOUL, itself, of course, a scene lifted, in respectful homage, from Douglas Sirk's ALL THAT HEAVEN ALLOWS.

32 The quotation continues: '(They hear nothing of the women's humming or the fist-fight at the train station.) ... Fassbinder's breakthrough soundtrack gives the tearjerking melodramatic dramaturgy the coolness of marble sculpture he requires.' Peter W Jansen, in Rheuban 1986, 219-220.

33 Hans Dieter Seidel, quoted in Rheuban 1986, 218.

34 For the importance of Kleist in general and this novella in particular for the 1970s, see my 'The New German Cinema's Historical Imaginary' in Bruce Murray and Christopher Wickham (eds.), *Framing the Past* (Carbondale: University of Southern Illinois, 1992), 281-282 and my *New German Cinema: A History* (London: Macmillan, 1989), 87-92.

35 Norbert Jürgen Schneider, *Musikdramaturgie im Neuen Deutschen Film* (Munich: Ölschläger, 1986), 187.

36 Schneider 1986, 186-187.

37 Schneider 1986, 88.

38 Schneider also comments on the aural frames that reverse the meaning of the music: '[...] in LOLA, there are authentic hits from the 50s, sung by the characters in the film, but there is also typical film music which narrates and illustrates the emotions present at a given point in the action. This music, however, is 'phoney', in keeping with the corrupt dishonesty of the characters. But then there is a third layer, a sort of depth-psychological one, where the music once more provides something like an honest commentary.' Schneider 1986, 189.

39 For a different reading, see Howard Feinstein, 'BRD 1-2-3 Fassbinder's Postwar Trilogy and the Spectacle', *Cinema Journal* 23/1, Fall 1983, 44-56. There, Feinstein defines the framing devices as 'the vicious circle over which characters have no control' (45).

40 This point is well made by Kaes 1989, 89.

41 Kurt Raab claims that Fassbinder knew in fact very little of German history, but that he used very judiciously the information about particular figures and events which he got from talking to other people, notably Raab and Märthesheimer. Raab: 'the sloppy mistakes he made in LILI MARLEEN while not excusable are understandable.' Wallace Watson has argued that a not inconsiderable source of political and historical education might have been Wolff Eder, his stepfather, a left-liberal journalist. Watson 1996, 15.

42 Feinstein, *Cinema Journal*, 23/1, Fall 1983, 45-49.

43 Interview with Walter Reisch, Los Angeles, 1982.

44 'Sybille Schmitz: Geschichte für einen Spielfilm', in Michael Töteberg (ed.), *Rainer Werner Fassbinder* (Munich, text + kritik, 1989), 11-19.

45 Yann Lardeau, *Rainer Werner Fassbinder* (Paris: Edition de l'Etoile, 1990), 268.

46 See entry on 'Trümmerfilme' in G.Vincendeau (ed.), *Encyclopedia of European Cinema* (London: BFI/Cassell, 1995).

47 Lardeau 1990, 268.

48 Lardeau 1990, 269.

49 Jacques Aumont has discussed the 'migration' of certain medical and depth-psychological associations in VERONIKA VOSS, pointing out, for instance, the motif of milk in the film (it is how the maid gets Krohn to meet Dr Katz, by inviting him to breakfast), and how it takes up similarly sinister associations in Hitchcock, notably in SUSPICION when Ingrid Bergman is given by Cary Grant, her solicitous husband, a glass of milk she has reason to suspect is poisoned, or in SPELLBOUND, when Ingrid Bergman hands a glass of soothing milk to Gregory Peck, after a particularly difficult psychoanalytic session. Aumont speaks of the quality of whiteness, of its invading impersonality, which fits well with the connotations that Fassbinder gives to the whiteness that invades Krohn's life, once he has come into contact with Veronika. Jacques Aumont, 'Migrations', *Cinématèque* 7, (Spring 1995), 45.

50 Fassbinder uses similar fades to white, and for a comparable purpose in EFFI BRIEST.

51 Serge Daney suggests both, when in an obituary for Fassbinder, called 'Auf Wiedersehen, Veronika', Daney speaks of the drug-taking Veronika as a metaphor for Germany: 'the soft sleep of forgetting', and then goes on to say, 'pity the country that has no cinema, because it has not dreams.' *Libération*, 1 July 1982, 23.

52 The combination of the central female character and German history makes MARIA BRAUN a genuinely new start for Fassbinder, even if, from another vantage point, he had already made other women's films (notably MARTHA and THE BITTER TEARS OF PETRA VON KANT) and had touched on the impact of fascism on subjectivity and class relations in both DESPAIR and BOLWIESER (neither of which had been the popular success Fassbinder had envisaged).

53 Actually, rather than being spoken by Nana/Anna Karina, it is one of the early intertitles in the film, where Godard quotes Blaise Pascal.

54 The full context of the famous quotation is: 'A capitalist tool by day, and by night an agent of the proletarian masses,' which is of course the language of the politicised 1970s rather than the original voice of the 1950s, and thus another deliberately ironic anachronism.

55 See Raymond Bellour about the centrality of family as institution and the bourgeoisie as class forming the twin supports of cinema. 'Alternation, Segmentation, Hypnosis: An Interview', *Camera Obscura* 3/4, Summer 1979, 70-103.

56 See my 'The New German Cinema's Historical Imaginary' in Murray/ Wickham 1992, 285-291.

57 Michael Schneider, 'Fathers and Sons, Retrospectively', *New German Critique* 31, Winter 1984, 3-51.

58 For a fuller discussion, see my 'Spectators of Life: Time, Place and Self in the Films of Wim Wenders' in D. Cook and G. Gemünden (eds.), *Wim Wenders* (Wayne State University Press, 1996).

59 The male hero's fatal attraction for Veronika effectively commences also with an economic barter: she asks him to lend her 300 Marks, with the invitation to collect it back from her the next day.

60 See the comments by Margarethe von Trotta in H.G. Pflaum, ICH WILL NICHT NUR DASS IHR MICH LIEBT, ZDF, 1992.

61 See Marcel Mauss, *Essay sur le don*, and more recently, Jacques Derrida's commentary on symbolic exchange in *Specters of Marx* (London: Routledge, 1994), 155-163.

Notes to Chapter 5

1 Walter Benjamin, 'Theses on the Philosophy of History', *Illuminations* (New York: Schocken, 1969) 255.

2 The German word 'Vergangenheitsbewältigung' is more telling, with its suggestion of 'Gewalt' (violence) and struggle where one might either defeat or be defeated by the past.

3 See Ian Buruma, *The Wages of Guilt: Memories of War in Germany and Japan* (London: Jonathan Cape, 1994), about these two countries' different ways of 'mastering the past'.

4 One of the most significant landmarks on the way to answering this question was the May 8th speech of the then President of the Federal Republic, Richard von Weizsäcker, in 1985.

5 See Norbert Seitz, *Die Unfähigkeit zu feiern* (Frankfurt: Neue Kritik, 1985), 10-14.

6 Anton Kaes, *From Hitler to Heimat* (Cambridge, Mass: Harvard University Press, 1989), 89.

7 The fact that 'two nations' emerged from the defeat of Hitler saddled West Germany with a task that only came on the agenda 45 years later, again mainly thanks to outside developments, namely how to master the unification of 1990.

8 See, for instance, Jürgen Habermas, *The New Conservatism: Cultural Criticism and the Historians' Debate* (Cambridge, Mass.: MIT Press, 1989); Dan Diner (ed.), *Ist der Nationalsozialismus Geschichte* (Frankfurt: Fischer, 1987); and Reinhard Kühnl (ed.), *Streit ums Geschichtsbild* (Cologne: Pahl-Rugenstein, 1987).

9 Among an extensive literature, one can usefully consult Charles S. Maier, *The Unmasterable Past* (Cambridge, Mass.: Harvard University Press, 1988) and Saul Friedlander (ed.), *Probing the Limits of Representation* (Cambridge, Mass.: Harvard University Press, 1992).

10 Jürgen Habermas, *The New Conservatism*, 230.

11 Berel Lang, 'The Representation of Limits' in Friedlander 1992, 317.

12 For a comprehensive list of titles, see Robert C. Reimer and Carol J. Reimer, *Nazi-Retro Film: How German Narrative Film Remembers the Past* (New York: Twayne, 1992), and also Ilan Avisar, *Screening the Holocaust: Cinema's Images of the Unimaginable* (Bloomington: Indiana University Press, 1988).

13 For arguments about the 'melodramatic' as an autonomous representational mode, see Peter Brooks, *The Melodramatic Imagination* (New York: Columbia University Press, 1985) and Christine Gledhill (ed.), *Home is where the Heart is* (London: BFI Publishing, 1988).

14 This is the line taken, for instance, in parts of Joachim C. Fest's HITLER-EINE KARRIERE (1977).

15 Hans Dieter Schäfer, *Das gespaltene Bewußtsein: Deutsche Kultur und Lebenswirklichkeit 1933-1945* (Munich: Carl Hanser, 1981).

16 Saul Friedländer, *Reflections of Fascism* (New York: Harper & Row, 1983).

17 Quoted in *Werkschau:Programm* 1992, 77-78.

18 Quoted in Jan Dawson, *Wim Wenders* (New York: Zoetrope, 1976), 7.

19 The 'revisionist' tendency culminated in Andreas Hillgruber, *Zweierlei Untergang: Die Zerschlagung des Deutschen Reiches und das Ende des europäischen Judentums* (Berlin: Siedler, 1986) which provoked the historians' debate mentioned earlier.

20 'The operative ideological border zone known as *Stunde Null*, that vastly mythologized marker of 1945 which was to serve politically, psychologically, and apologetically as an immediate and synthetic cleansing to the reborn.' David Bathrick, 'Inscribing History' in *New German Critique* 63 (Fall 1994), 36.

21 See my *New German Cinema: A History* (Brunswick, NJ: Rutgers University Press, 1989), 87-92.

22 'The historical obsession of contemporary cinema is not concerned so much with the representation of "real" events in the form of a story, but rather with the representation of cinematic events in the form of other stories.' Guiliana Bruno, 'Towards a Theorization of Film History', *Iris*, 2/2, 1984, 53-54.

23 Wim Wenders, 'That's Entertainment: Hitler', originally in *Die Zeit*, 5 August, 1977. Translated in Rick Rentschler (ed.), *West German Filmmakers, Visions and Voices* (New York: Holmes & Meier, 1988), 126-131. Wenders is reviewing the Joachim Fest film, which he criticised for presenting as documentary record the visual material shot by the Nazis for their own self-promotion and propaganda.

24 See, for instance, Syberberg's contribution at the Aschaffenburg Streitgespräch, quoted in Karl-Heinz Janßen, 'Wir – zwischen Jesus und Hitler' *Die Zeit*, July 14, 1978.

25 Edgar Reitz, 'Statt "Holocaust": Erinnerungen aufarbeiten', *Medium*, May 1979, 21.

26 See the many book titles in German on this topic: e.g. H.M.Enzensberger, *Die Furie des Verschwindens* (1980); Hans von Hentig, *Das allmähliche Verschwinden der Wirklichkeit* (1984); P.Hamm, *Die verschwindende Welt* (1985).

27 Wim Wenders, in Rentschler 1988, 128.

28 The reference point being, inevitably, Leni Riefenstahl's TRIUMPH OF THE WILL (1935).

29 Walter Benjamin, 'The Work of Art in the Age of Mechanical Reproduction' in *Illuminations* (New York: Schocken Books, 1969), and Susan Sontag, 'Fascinating Fascism' reprinted in Bill Nichols, *Movies and Methods I* (Berkeley and Los Angeles, University of California Press, 1980), 31-43.

30 See, for instance, Robert Burgoyne, 'The Imaginary and the Neo-Real', *Enclitic,* Spring 1979, 16-34.

31 There were, in Italian cinema, illustrious precedents, both in the popular cinema (the long tradition of the 'peplum') and in auteur cinema, notably Visconti's SENSO (1954) and THE LEOPARD (1963): films that Fassbinder held in high esteem.

32 See my 'Chronicle of a Death Retold: The European Art Cinema', *Monthly Film Bulletin,* June 1987.

33 'The Third Reich itself was often reduced [...] to a semiotic phenomenon: SS uniforms, swastikas, shaved napes, black leather belts and boots, intimidating corridors and marble stairs have become mere signs unmistakeably signalling "fascism"'. Kaes 1989, 22.

34 The so-called 'Hitler-wave' broke with Albrecht Speer's memoirs in 1968, Joachim Fest's Hitler biography (1973) and subsequent film HITLER-A CAREER in 1977. It washed into high-culture with novels by Michel Tournier and George Steiner, and ebbed away with the farcical fraud around Hitler's diaries in 1986. Its symptomatic importance lies also in the fact that it encompassed the whole spectrum of culture, from garish comics and pornographic magazines, accessories in sex shops and s/m boutiques, or glossy reproductions of period photographs in coffee-table books, to the growing shelves of novels, biographies, autobiographies and scholarly publications devoted to the Third Reich, Hitler, and every conceivable aspect of Nazism.

35 'Film and Popular Memory', originally in *Cahiers du cinéma* 251/2, July/August 1974, in English in Sylvère Lotringer (ed.), *Foucault Live* (New York: Semiotexte, 1989), 89-106.

36 Jean Baudrillard, 'Holocaust', *Cahiers du cinéma* 302, July-August 1979.

37 Max Horkheimer, 'Die Juden und Europa', *Zeitschrift für Sozialforschung,* VIII 1/2 (1939), 115.

38 Ernst Nolte, *Three Faces of Fascism*, transl. Leila Vennewitz (New York: Holt, Rinehart and Winston, 1969).

39 Alexander and Margarethe Mitscherlich, *The Inability to Mourn: Principles of Collective Behavior*, trans. Beverley A. Plaszek (New York: Grove Press, 1975).

40 For a discussion of 'mourning work' and cinema, see Elsaesser 1989, 239-248 and Eric L. Santner, *Stranded Objects* (Cornell: Cornell University Press, 1990).

41 See Rick Rentschler, 'Remembering not to Forget: Alexander Kluge's BRUTALITY IN STONE' in *New German Critique* 44, 1990, 23-41.

42 The autumn in question was the highpoint of the RAF terrorist acts, the politically motivated assassinations, the cutbacks in civil liberties, the crisis of the social democratic government under Helmut Schmidt. For a more detailed discussion of GERMANY IN AUTUMN, see Kaes 1989, 25-28 and above, Chapter 2.

43 Produced for NBC in 1976, it was directed by Marvin J. Chomsky, based on a script by Gerald Green. The impact of HOLOCAUST in West Germany has given rise to a sizeable literature (see F. Knilli, S. Zielinski, *Holocaust zur Unterhaltung* (Berlin: Elephanten Press, 1982)). For a comprehensive assessment in English, see Michael E Geisler, 'The Disposal of Memory: Fascism and the Holocaust' in B. Murray, C. Wickham (eds.), *Framing the Past* (Carbondale, Ill: Southern Illinois University Press, 1992), 220-260.

44 Heinz Höhne, in *Der Spiegel*, quoted (and translated) in Kaes 1989, 30-31.

45 The exhibitionist side was in some sense highlighted by the fact, as every German commentator pointed out, that the world's eyes were on Germany, to see how it reacted to the series. Kaes 1989, 31-35 comments on the international dimension of the HOLOCAUST reception.

46 quoted in Kaes 1989, 31.

47 There were, however, a vast number of documentaries dealing with both the Third Reich and the 'Final Solution'. See Volker Lilienthal, 'Das gepriesene Schreckbild', in Joachim Schmitt-Sasse (ed.), *Widergänger: Faschismus und Anti-Faschismus im Film* (Münster: Maks, 1992), 173-201.

48 Christian Meier, quoted in Kühnl 1987, 258.

49 For a more detailed discussion of films made from a feminist and family perspective, see Elsaesser 1989, 232-238 and 264-267; Julia Knight, *Women in New German Cinema* (London: Verso, 1992).

50 J. Hoberman, 'Once Upon a Reich Time', *Village Voice*, 16 April, 1985, 52.

51 In the case of HEIMAT, the much-despised but perennially popular *Heimatfilm* was one of the genres Reitz set out to rewrite, for he shows no rural, pre-industrial idyll, and instead, his characters' lives and histories are transformed by modern communication technologies: the women go to the movies (to see a film called HEIMAT), and the men spend all their time with ham radio sets, are chronically obsessed photographers, or on active duty as cinematographers on the Eastern front.

52 See my 'Myth as the Fantasmagoria of History: Syberberg, Cinema and Representation', *New German Critique* 24-25, Fall/Winter 1981-82, 108-154.

53 See also Eric L. Santner, *Strangled Objects* (Ithaca: Cornell University Press, 1990), 104-105.

54 Gertrud Koch, 'How Much Naivety Can We Afford'? *New German Critique* 36 (Fall 1985), 4-6.

55 Eric L. Santner, 'On the Difficulty of Saying "We"': The Historians' Debate and Edgar Reitz's "Heimat"', in Murray/Wickham 1992, 273-274.

56 Edgar Reitz, 'Statt "Holocaust": Erinnerungen aufarbeiten', *Medium* 5/79, 21.

57 For instance, Hans Jürgen Syberberg 'Wie man den neuen Haß züchtet', *Frankfurter Allgemeine Zeitung*, 12 September, 1990.

58 Enno Patalas, director of the Munich Filmmuseum, once contrasted the public's reaction on showing Veit Harlan's KOLBERG (1945), where no-one protested, with that of showing Harlan's OPFERGANG (1944), after which he received threats. (Quoted in Bernadette Klasen, 'Eine Frau wird erst schön durch die Liebe', in Joachim Schmidt-Sasse 1992,38). It seems that audiences have a secure subject position in a film they 'know' to be propaganda (KOLBERG), but feel threatened when a strong emotional reaction to a melodrama (OPFERGANG) conflicts with their awareness that this is a 'fascist' film.

59 See the writings by Alexander and Margarethe Mitcherlich mentioned above, and discussed in Chapter 3.

60 For a discussion of the temporal structures in Fassbinder, see Chapter 3 and Chapter 8.

61 As already noted, flashbacks are exceedingly rare in his work.

Notes to Chapter 6

1 Peter Sloterdijk, *Die Kritik der zynischen Vernunft* (Frankfurt: Suhrkamp, 1983) vol 2, 586.

2 Friedrich Luft, 'Opa's Kino in Aspik', *Die Welt*, 16 January 1981; Wilhelm Roth, 'Verschwimmende Positionen im perfekten "Hit" [muddled perspectives and the perfect hit]', *Spandauer Volksblatt*, 16 January 1981; Ruprecht Skasa-Weiß, 'Grob, genial und gefährlich [blunt, inspired, dangerous]', *Stuttgarter Zeitung* 16 January 1981. In France, critics drew ominous parallels: Annie Goldmann, 'Un nouveau Juif Süss: Lili Marleen', *Le Monde*, 16 May 1981.

3 This is the argument Schäfer makes about the Nazis' policy towards 'deviant' popular culture. Hans Dieter Schäfer, *Das gespaltene Bewußtsein* (Munich: Hanser, 1981), 160-177.

4 The full title of Andersen's autobiography is *Der Himmel hat viele Farben. Das Leben mit einem Lied* (Stuttgart: Deutsche Verlagsanstalt, 1972) and the best-known biography is by her daughter, Litta Magnus Andersen, called *Lale Andersen – die Lili Marleen* (Munich: Universitas, 1981).

5 As David Bathrick notes: 'Fassbinder's Germany [in LILI MARLEEN] is always already the Germany of mass culture, of consumption and leisure industries, of Hollywood spectacle'. David Bathrick, 'Inscribing History, Prohibiting and Producing Desire', *New German Critique* 63 (Fall 1994), 37. See also my 'Moderne und Modernisierung', *Montage a/v* 3/2, 1994, 23-40.

6 See my 'Myth and the Fantasmagoria of History: Syberberg, Cinema and Representation', *New German Critique*, 24/25 (Fall-Winter 1981/82), 108-154.

7 Syberberg's politics are discussed in Eric Santner, 'The Trouble with Hitler', *New German Cinema* 57, 1992, 15-18.

8 Walter Benjamin, 'The Work of Art in the Age of Mechanical Reproduction' *Illuminations* (New York: Schocken, 1969) 243.

9 Tom Milne and Jean Narboni (eds.), *Godard on Godard* (London: Thames & Hudson, 1972), 243.

10 For recent studies of popular culture in Nazi Germany, besides Hans Dieter Schaefer, *Das gespaltene Bewusstsein* (Munich: Hanser, 1981), see Michael H. Kater, *Different Drummers* (Oxford/New York: Oxford University Press, 1992) and Detlev Peukert, *Inside Nazi Germany* (New Haven, Yale University Press, 1987).

11 Asked whether critics would not accuse him of succumbing to the spell of fascist glamour, Fassbinder replied: 'I know that is what they will say. I knew this already before I started. But I always said that the subject Nazism is only of interest to me if I do something that noone else has done before: to make the 'Third Reich' reveal itself via the fascinating details of its self-representation.' Limmer 1981, 91.

12 See Fassbinder on A TIME TO LOVE AND A TIME TO DIE, 'Imitation of Life: Six Films by Douglas Sirk' in Jon Halliday, Laura Mulvey (eds.), *Douglas Sirk* (Edinburgh: Edinburgh Festival, 1972), 104.

13 *ibid.,* 98.

14 'Love is colder than death', it will be remembered, is the title of Fassbinder's first full-length film.

15 See also below, Chapter 9.

16 For feminist readings of film noir, see Annette Kuhn, ed., *Women in film noir* (London: British Film Institute, 1979), and Mary Anne Doane 'Gilda', *Femmes Fatales* (New York: Routledge, 1992).

17 As in a Hollywood film, where the ending would either be the formation of the couple, or an explicit act of sacrifice by the female character, as in Max Ophuls' LETTER FROM AN UNKNOWN WOMAN.

18 'It is a costly business digging up Germany's recent past [...]. LILI MARLEEN will have to gross over 11 million DM at the box office just to recover its production cost [...]. With Fassbinder's favourite actress, Hanna Schygulla in the title role, the film is a slap in the face of anybody who ever thought Fassbinder is an important director.' Derek Malcolm, *The Guardian*, 6 February, 1981.

19 As Fassbinder had done in SATAN'S BREW and was to do again for IN A YEAR OF THIRTEEN MOONS (see Chapter 8).

20 The narrative of *Holocaust* is based on the 'classical' principle of parallel and counterpoint, via the contrasting fates of two familes, the (Aryan) Dorf and the (Jewish) Weiss family, their fortunes and fate criss-crossing at certain crucial points.

21 Andrew Sarris, who disliked LILI MARLEEN, read it as moving towards just such a narrative of closure, asking in his review, rhetorically: 'Is History Merely an Old Movie?', *The Village Voice*, 8 July 1981.

22 As Willie receives the information about the number of fans who comprise her audience, her face is lit by a lamp, placed conspicuously in the foreground. Her Nazi friend, standing diagonally opposite in the background, idly spins a globe. The glamour lighting of the star image is here conspicuously associated with the global strategies of war, trade and dominion.

23 Although Fassbinder was not particularly fond of Fritz Lang ('in his later films... incapacity is everywhere in evidence'), there are in fact echoes of Lang in the way Fassbinder conceives of the double agent, counter-intelligence plotlines in several of his films (e.g. GODS OF THE PLAGUE and THE THIRD GENERATION). One might even say that LILI MARLEEN's thriller element reworks M (in which police and organised crime are both in pursuit of the same suspect) and the MABUSE films (which are constructed entirely on the exchange and substitution of objects whose values are redefined). Hitchcock's 'Wrong Man' motif also comes to mind. In Lang's work, one could name CLOAK AND DAGGER and HANGMEN ALSO DIE as examples of films that examine symmetries that are non-equivalences. That Fassbinder should have 'invented' a Hagana-type Jewish underground in order to create such a set of non-equivalent symmetries has outraged many commentators. See Annie Goldmann, 'Un nouveau Juif Süss', Le Monde 16 May, 1981.

24 In the way the Jewish resistance is portrayed one senses the quotations from other films: Claude Chabrol's LA LIGNE DE DEMARCATION, for instance, and Pierre Melville's L'ARMEE DES OMBRES. For some of warfare footage and scenes of detonations, Fassbinder utilized out-takes from Sam Peckinpah's STEINER – CROSS OF IRON, made at Bavaria studios the year before.

25 The question of why so much popular or 'pulp' culture is concerned with the death drive, nostalgia and the compulsion to repeat has been examined in Slavoj Zizek, Looking Awry (Cambridge, Mass.: MIT Press, 1991), 107-114.

26 Generically speaking, LILI MARLEEN is a pastiche of the Ufa/Nazi musical (e.g. a Lilian Harvey Revuefilm) which has been 'deconstructed' via the pastiche of a Veit Harlan female melodrama (e.g. OPFERGANG, 1943). By counterpointing these two crucial Ufa genres, Fassbinder locates the 'split consciousness' of Nazi popular culture. See also his remarks on Gustav Freitag's Soll und Haben, discussed in Chapter 1.

27 For a discussion of the function of emblems, logos, brand-names in Nazi Germany, see B. Hinz (ed.), Die Dekoration der Gewalt (Gießen, 1979).

28 The song here serves the same 'mirror-effect' as the face/eyes of the film star, whose function it is to present to the camera a wholly expressionless face. See Fassbinder in Werkschau Programm, 1992, 45.

29 On Straub/Huillet, see Barton Byg, Landscapes of Resistance (Berkeley and Los Angeles: University of California Press, 1995), 233-248.

30 The motif of the excessive light is introduced earlier, when she is led to an audience with the Führer, whom we never see, except for the portals at the top of the stairs, whose

brightness swallows her. See also the discussion in Chapter 4 of whiteness and light in VERONIKA VOSS.

31 Despite roles in films directed by Schlöndorff, von Trotta, Jean Luc Godard, Andrzej Wajda and many other European directors of note, Hanna Schygulla did not find a role or persona as potent and definitive as the one she embodied for Fassbinder, across two dozen parts. Already in 1980, Fassbinder was brutally candid: 'Hanna has a simple problem. She has made films with me, and each time she was visibly good. Then she made films with other directors, and there she was visibly not so good. And because she did not want to believe it, she walked away.' *Die Anarchie der Phantasie*, 177.

32 Fassbinder called them 'a sort of mosaic'. Interview with Klaus Eder, *Frankfurter Allgemeine Zeitung*, 29 December 1980.

Notes to Chapter 7

1 'Le drame d'un homme, c'est d'oublier jusqu'à ses rêves d'enfant. Le drame d'un cineaste, c'est d'avoir grandi dans un pays sans rêves, donc sans cinema.' Serge Daney, 'Auf Wiedersehen, Veronika', *Liberation* 1 July 1982, 23.

2 Joachim Fest's documentary compilation film, HITLER – EINE KARRIERE (1977), gives less than three out of 96 minutes to Nazi policy towards the Jews and the concentration camps.

3 Even today, pre-Auschwitz German anti-Semitism is a contested topic. See the impact of Daniel Goldhagen's *Hitler's Willing Executioners* (New York: Knopf, 1995) and the controversies it provoked, both in the United States (e.g. *New York Review of Books* 43/7, and 9, 18 April and 23 May 1996) and in Germany (e.g. *Die Zeit*, 16-18/1996, 20-25/1996, 32/1996).

4 The memorial to the Holocaust by the Austrian artist Hrdlika at the Dammtor station in Hamburg, for instance, continued for years to give rise to protest and defacement until it was eventually removed.

5 Primo Levi, *Ist das ein Mensch? Die Atempause* (Munich: dtv, 1988), 359.

6 Hermann Glaser, *Die Kulturgeschichte der Bundesrepublik Deutschland: Zwischen Protest und Anpassung* (Fischer: Frankfurt, 1990) 342.

7 'The emphasis on anti-Semitism has served to underline the supposed total character of the break between the Third Reich and the Federal Republic, and to avoid a confrontation with the social and structural reality of National Socialism, a reality which did not completely vanish in 1945.' Moishe Postone, 'Anti-Semitism and National Socialism', *New German Critique* 19 (Winter 1980), 98.

8 *Die Anarchie der Phantasie*, 82.

9 Jörg Friedrich, *Die kalte Amnestie*, quoted in Glaser 1990, 343.

10 Ralph Giordano, *Die zweite Schuld oder Von der Last Deutscher zu sein* (Hamburg: Claasen, 1987), 11.

11 See reference below, note 79, and also Neil Ascherson, 'The Cost of Bitburg', *Games with Shadows* (London: Century Hutchinson, 1988), 168-171.

12 'In other words, what happened to the Jews has been instrumentalized and transformed into an ideology of legitimation for the present system. This instrumentalization was only possible because anti-Semitism has been treated primarily as a form of prejudice, as a scapegoat ideology – a view which has obscured the intrinsic relationship between anti-Semitism and other aspects of National Socialism.' Postone 1980, 98.

13 For a brief analysis of the Springer press, see Neil Ascherson, 'Axel's Castles', *Games with Shadows* (London: Century Hutchinson, 1988), 164-167.

14 An excellent account of the debates and positions up to the late 1970s can be found in *New German Critique* 'Germans and Jews' 19, 20, 21 (Winter/Spring 1980-Fall 1980).

15 Among the books that looked once more at race and anti-Semitism, now with the emphasis on gender, the best-known is Klaus Theweleit, *Männerphantasien* I/II (Frankfurt: Roter Stern, 1977/78).

16 Michael Geisler, 'The Disposal of Memory: Fascism and the Holocaust on West German Television', Bruce A. Murray and Christopher J. Wickham (eds.), *Framing the Past* (Carbondale: Southern Illinois Press, 1992), 220-260.

17 Quoted by Henryk Broder, 'Antisemitismus – ja, bitte' *Süddeutsche Zeitung*, 18 January 1986, reprinted in Heiner Lichtenstein (ed.), *Die Fassbinder-Kontroverse, oder das Ende der Schonzeit* (Königstein/Ts: Athenäum, 1986), 213.

18 Broder referred to this as 'the anger of the perpetrators against the victims, whose existence is a provocation, difficult to support.' Lichtenstein 1986, 213.

19 Neil Asherson, Lecture at the Goethe Institut, London, 20 February 1990.

20 RW Fassbinder, *Filme befreien den Kopf* (Frankfurt: Fischer, 1984), 36-39.

21 This is the account given by Peter Chatel in Raab 1982, 292. According to Daniel Schmid, the play was written on a flight from Frankfurt to Dakar, and rather than the result of his anger about Frankfurt, it was more a dare, to show his Theater-am-Turm team how fast he could work (Katz 1987, 100). Another account argues that Fassbinder was only interested in adapting the Zwerenz novel, which was to have been his first big production ever. The play was simply fodder for the theatre, put together as a collage of loose scenes (Lichtenstein 1986, 72). Chatel, on the other hand, thinks the play was very important to Fassbinder (Raab 1982, 292).

22 Fest was alerted by a book review in the *Frankfurter Rundschau* discussing the play when it was published in a Suhrkamp volume (later withdrawn and pulped) of Fassbinders' theatre pieces. Joaching Fest 'Reicher Jude von links', *Frankfurter Allgemeine Zeitung*, 19.3.1976. See 'Special issue on the German-Jewish Controversy' *New German Critique* 38 (Spring/Summer 1986). While focussing on the attempt to stage the play in Frankfurt in the autumn of 1985, the volume usefully fills in the background also to the scandal of 1976. Both controversies are most fully documented in Lichtenstein 1986.

23 According to Fassbinder, once he and Daniel Schmid had made SHADOWS OF ANGELS, the play had served its purpose, and he saw no reason to have others produce it on stage (*Anarchie der Phantasie*, 68, 75). As to Zwerenz's novel, Fassbinder always maintained that he wanted to make the film, but only as a big budget production (*Anarchie*, 160). Zwerenz re-edited his novel, and published it together with the screenplay in 1986. See also his comments in *Der langsame Tod des Rainer Werner Fassbinder* (Munich: Schneekluth, 1982).

24 '[Fassbinder's] attempts to explore the most sensitive area of German memory, the memory of anti-Semitism and systematically planned and executed genocide, all failed.' Anton Kaes, *From Hitler to Heimat* (Cambridge, Mass: Harvard University Press, 1989), 90.

25 Katz 1987, 95.

26 Joachim Fest, 'Zensur für Fassbinder?', *Frankfurter Allgemeine Zeitung*, 30 July 1985, quoted in Lichtenstein 1986, 62.

27 For references, see Chapter 5, above.

28 The background to the Bitburg controversy is extensively discussed in Geoffrey Hartmann (ed.), *Bitburg in Moral and Political Perspective* (Bloomington: Indiana University Press, 1986).

29 The speech is reprinted in *Frankfurter Allgemeine Zeitung*, 18 October 1985 and also in Lichtenstein 1986, 77.

30 'Studies of latent and manifest anti-Semitism [in Germany], such as those by Alphons Silbermann, were nowhere so decisively rejected as 'questionable' as among the representatives of the Central Council of Jews. They conducted, in the words of Silbermann, a "head-in-the-sands-policy" and pretended that everything was fine as long as leading German politicians continued to make dignified speeches at the opening of one more Solidarity Week.' Henryk Broder, reprinted in Lichtenstein 1986, 212.

31 Valuable material can be found in the transcript of a symposium devoted to the topic, with statements by Andrei S. Markovits, Seyla Benhabib and Moishe Postone, *New German Critique* 38 (Spring/Summer 1986), 3-27.

32 Andrej S Markovits, *New German Critique* 38, 10.

33 Rainer Werner Fassbinder, *Sämtliche Stücke* (Frankfurt: Verlag der Autoren, 1991), 675.

34 *Sämtliche Stücke*, 1991, 675.

35 Jean Améry, 'Shylock, der Kitsch und die Gefahr', reprinted in Lichtenstein 1986, 40. Améry continues 'as author of this play [Fassbinder is] bare of all psychological insight, un-philosophical, and a-historical.' *ibid.*, 40.

36 Hellmuth Karasek, *Der Spiegel* 15, 1976, reprinted in Lichtenstein 1986, 35.

37 Gerhard Zwerenz, 'Politik mit Vorurteilen', reprinted in Lichtenstein 1986, 246.

38 'Even if Zwerenz and Fassbinder did not intend it, how can they know that someone might not use their 'Rich Jew' in order to stitch together an alibi for his undigested, murderous prejudices?' (Hellmuth Karasek, in Lichtenstein 1986, 36). Peter Zadek, on the other

hand, argues that 'of course, the play is anti-semitic, anyone who has read it can tell. This is exactly why it ought to be put on. I am sure that today in Germany, the theatre-going public is mature enough to realize that it is being presented with a play of *Stürmer*-ish anti-semitism.' Letter to the Editor, *Die Zeit*, 13 September, 1985.

39 *New German Critique* 38, 20, and Lichtenstein, 1986, 83.

40 'Whatever I do, it always ends up as a scandal.' *Die Anarchie der Phantasie*, 168.

41 *Die Anarchie der Phantasie*, 82, 84-85.

42 Reinhold Grimm, 'The Jew, the Playwright and Trash', *Monatshefte* 81/3, 1991, 26, also quoted in Gerd Gemünden, 'Remembering Fassbinder', *New German Critique* 63 (Fall 1994), 7.

43 Fassbinder, *Sämtliche Stücke*, p 702.

44 See the discussion about representativeness in the chapter 'Fassbinder representing Germany'.

45 Interview in *Der Spiegel*, 11 July 1977, reprinted in *Die Anarchie der Phantasie*, p 99.

46 See the previous chapter on LILI MARLEEN. On Fassbinder's disaffection with the theatre, see Juliane Lorenz quoted in Yann Lardeau, *Rainer Werner Fassbinder* (Paris: *Cahiers du cinéma,* 1990), 45.

47 Fassbinder was financially involved in Daniel Schmid's film of the play, SCHATTEN DER ENGEL (1975), which was produced by Albatros Production (Michael Fengler). Besides featuring familiar Fassbinder actors like Klaus Löwitsch (Abraham, the Rich Jew), Ingrid Caven (Lily/Roma B), Irm Hermann, Ulli Lommel, Peter Chatel and Harry Baer, Fassbinder himself played Franz B (named Raoul in the film version).

48 In the case of other stories that were first produced for the stage, such as *The Bitter Tears of Petra von Kant*, it is quite clear that the film version, despite keeping the act division, obeys the principles of a typical Fassbinder screenplay rather than becoming a filmed Fassbinder play.

49 As argued in a previous chapter, Fassbinder does not use the father-son paradigm of GERMANY IN AUTUMN, typical of the generational confrontation with fascism in much of West German cinema and literature from the 1970s.

50 *Sämtliche Stücke*, 681.

51 *Sämtliche Stücke*, 704.

52 As analyzed in Walter Benjamin, *Der Ursprung des deutschen Trauerspiels*, written as a doctoral dissertation in the late 1920s, and much discussed in the 1960s, in the course of the Benjamin revival.

53 *MST* might in this respect be usefully compared with *The Measures Taken*, one of Bertolt Brecht's 'Lehrstücke', or political morality plays.

54 *Sämtliche Stücke*, 693.

55 Lichtenstein 1986, 212.

56 *Franz B*: 'what sort of a guy was it then? The son of a millionaire? A tennis player? How can one love something like that. I spit on his money, I spit on it.' *Roma B*: 'It's a Jew.

A fat ugly Jew. None of those you hate, Franz, no tennis player. Just a Jew.' *Sämtliche Stücke*, 682-3.

57 In this, she is close to Willie in LILI MARLEEN who also refuses to submit to the patriarchal law even of the 'good' Jews, or of Fassbinder himself in GERMANY IN AUTUMN, rejecting the patriarchal succession of father and sons.

58 *Die Anarchie der Phantasie*, 83.

59 Herbert Riehl-Heyse, 'Lehrstück auf dünnem Eis', *Süddeutsche Zeitung*, 23 October 1985, reprinted in Lichtenstein 1989, 83.

60 quoted by Broder, Lichtenstein 1986, 214.

61 *Filme befreien den Kopf*, 38.

62 See the debate in Paris over SHADOWS OF ANGELS in *Le Nouvel Observateur* 28 February 1977 and *Le Monde* 5, 18, 22, 23 February 1977, as well as the protests in Rotterdam in November 1987.

63 *New German Critique* 38, 19.

64 See also the discussion of Fassbinder's *Soll und Haben* project in Chapter 1, above.

65 *Die Anarchie der Phantasie*, 88.

66 Already in 1969 Fassbinder advised Kurt Raab to play the King in Georg Büchner's *Leonce and Lena* not like he imagined an absolutist king, but rather like a petit-bourgeois audience would imagine him (Raab 1982, 44).

67 Gertrud Koch, 'Torments of the Flesh, Coldness of the Spirit', *New German Critique* 38, 35.

68 See Eric L. Santner, 'The Trouble with Hitler', *New German Critique* 57, (Summer 1992) 5-24.

69 See Saul Friedlander (ed.), *Probing the Limits of Representation* (Cambridge, Mass.: Harvard University Press, 1992)

70 Especially Henryk Broder 'Anti-Semitismus – ja, bitte', reprinted in Lichtenstein 1986, 212-215.

71 See Chapter 2, above.

72 Norbert Seitz (ed.), *Die Unfähigkeit zu feiern* (Frankfurt: Verlag Neue Kritik, 1985), quoted in my 'Between Bitburg and Bergen-Belsen', in *On Film* 14, 1985, 38-40.

73 Philipp Jenninger, 'Von der Verantwortung für das Vergangene' [On the Responsibility for the Past], reprinted in *Die Zeit*, 25 November 1988.

74 On November 9th, 1989, a year after Jenninger's speech, East Germans first crossed the Berlin wall. Eric Santner has spoken of a 'mnemonic readjustment' taking place, making November 9th 'newly available for libidinal investment'. Eric L. Santner, 'History beyond the Pleasure Principle', in Friedlander 1992, 144.

75 Andreas Hillgruber, *Zweierlei Untergang: Die Zerschlagung des Deutschen Reiches und das Ende des europäischen Judentums* (Berlin: Siedler, 1986).

76 Perry Anderson has a high regard for the historical merits of Hillgruber's analysis. See 'On Emplotment: Two Kinds of Ruin', in Friedlander 1992, 62-63.

77 *ibid.*, 58.

78 For references, see Chapter 2 above.

79 Eric Rentschler makes this point in 'Remembering not to Forget: Alexander Kluge's BRUTALITY IN STONE', *New German Critique* 49 (Winter 1990), 23-41.

Notes to Chapter 8

1 Kurt Raab: 'First you annihilate people, and then you erect for them a monument.' Raab/Peters 1982, 367.

2 '[After the death of Armin] I felt the necessity to do something. There were basically three possibilities. One was to go to Paraguay and become a farmer [...]. Another possibility was to stop being interested in what was happening around me. That would have been like a mental illness. The third possibility was to make a film – certainly the easiest for me.' Limmer 1981, 95, also quoted in *October* 21 (Summer 1982), 75.

3 'What is important for me is that I managed to make a film which does not simply translate my emotions about the suicide. That is my pain and mourning about the fact that I may have failed in some respects in this relationship, but that I made a film [...] which goes far beyond this; which tells a lot more than I could have told about Armin. And for me this was a decision for life.' Limmer 1981, 96.

4 But see Nigel Andrews' remarks in *The Financial Times*, 29 June 1992, 17.

5 Jansen/Schütte 1992, 217-218.

6 Hans Dieter Seidel, 'Monströse Frankfurter Passion, *Stuttgarter Zeitung*, 18 November 1978.

7 'The film is largely a solo by the actor Volker Spengler, and fails to make any specifically human or philosophical point to account for its two hours and more of discouraging glumness'. David Robinson , *The Times*, 5 September 1980.

8 Richard Roud, 'Armin/Erwin/Elvira: Rest in Peace.' *The Guardian*, 30 March 1979.

9 Jan Dawson, *The Listener*, 30 August 1979, and Tony Rayns, *Time Out London*, 4 September 1980. This view was encouraged by the press release which in part read: 'The film is set in Frankfurt, a city with a specific structure that virtually provokes biographies like this one. [...] Frankfurt is not a place of amiable mediocrity, reconciliation of opposites, it's neither peaceful nor kind.'

10 In taking this risk, the present chapter wants to offer more than a different reading of one of the director's most baffling films: it would be invidious to call it an 'unreadable' film, in order then to proceed to explain it.

11 Limmer 1981, 96.

12 As to a sociological reading of love as the very trope of impossibility, see Niklas Luhmann, who called love a semiotic system, which offers the paradox of 'a semantics of instability and of suffering – at once fact and symptom of impossibility'. Niklas Luhmann, *Liebe als Passion: zur Codierung von Intimität* (Frankfurt: Surkamp, 1982), 212.

13 'In a Year of Thirteen Moons' *October* 21 (Summer 1982), 35-36 (translation slightly amended from German transcript of soundtrack).

14 See also previous chapter. The so-called 'Battle of the Westend' is one of the key episodes in the modern history of Frankfurt, discussed in the novel by Gerhard Zwerenz (*Die Erde ist unbewohnbar wie der Mond*), featured in a film by Alexander Kluge (IN GEFAHR UND GRÖSSTER NOT BRINGT DER MITTELWEG DEN TOD), and the subject of several major sociological studies. See also Elisabeth Kiderlen (ed.), *Deutsch-jüdische Normalität... Fassbinders Sprengsätze* (Frankfurt: Pflasterstrand, 1985) and J. Roth, *Z.B. Frankfurt: Die Zerstörung einer Stadt* (Frankfurt: Fisher, 1975).

15 All of Erwin/Elvira's relations are sound in human/moral/emotional terms (nobody can be said to be exploiting the other), and they are sound also formal in terms, in the sense that they are not only 'normal', but portrayed in ways that refer us to conventional, even ritualized interpersonel situations.

16 From KATZELMACHER onwards, Fassbinder has shown that in the face of oppression, there is little solidarity between outsiders, however much they have 'objective' interests in common. See my 'A Cinema of Vicious Circles' in Rayns 1980, 31-33.

17 'In a Year of Thirteen Moons', *October* 21 (Summer 1982), 5.

18 'In a Year of Thirteen Moons', *October* 21 (Summer 1982), 42.

19 *Zora*: 'She just had everything down there cut off.' *Soul Frieda*: So? That's not the reason she's unhappy. She was probably always a woman in her soul'. *Zora*: 'No, that's just it. She just did it. [...] I don't think she was even gay.' In a Year of Thirteen Moons, *October* 21 (Summer 1982), 20-21.

20 See Al LeValley's description of Elvira in *New German Critique*, 63, Fall 1994, 130-131.

21 *Filme befreien den Kopf*, 43-68.

22 This novel Fassbinder adapted as a two-part television film in 1973, WELT AM DRAHT.

23 The film obliquely implies that Saitz and his gang are now making their living from petty street crime and robberies.

24 If the unrepresentable in IN A YEAR OF THIRTEEN MOONS becomes the problem of impossibility, it also dispels the notion that Fassbinder wanted to centre on the Jew as 'subject' (with the attendant charge of 'mythification') or on anti-Semitism (as the projection of a repressed part of the self onto an 'other', and thus a form of 'scapegoating').

25 Dan Diner, 'Negative Symbiose: Deutsche und Juden nach Auschwitz', *Babylon* 1, 1986, 9.

26 What has been called 'das deutsch-jüdische Gemeinschaftswerk' (Henryk Broder, in Lichtenstein 1986, 212) has to be compared with the statistics of persistent anti-Semitism in Germany, quoted in Kiderlen 1985, 58.

27 See the remark by the writer Robert Neumann, quoted by Fassbinder, to the effect that 'a philosemite is an anti-Semite who loves Jews.' *Anarchie der Phantasie*, 83.

28 Frank Stern, *The Whitewashing of the Yellow Badge. Antisemitism and Philosemitism in Postwar Germany* (Oxford: Pergamon Press, 1992).

29 In contrast to the GDR which never took responsibility for any of the Nazi crimes committed on its territory again Jews – until the very last weeks of the its existence in 1989, when the Modrow Government published an official apology which in crucial respects actually went further than any official statement pronounced by the Federal Republic.

30 See also Henryk Broder: 'The trouble is not that anti-Semitism exists in West Germany, the trouble is that there is nobody who admits to it' and Yaacov Ben Chanan: 'What we need to be afraid of is not overt anti-Semitism, but the repressed feelings of the Germans towards us'. Lichtenstein 1986, 211, 241.

31 Notably in the literature of young German-Jewish writers of the 1980s and 1990s. Sander L. Gilman, *Jews in Today's German Culture* (Bloomington: University of Indiana Press, 1995).

32 The German nouns 'Schuld' and 'Schulden' are almost identical, especially when used as the singular and the plural. Both mean debt, but in the singular, 'Schuld' also means guilt, while in the plural, it mostly refers to an outstanding financial obligation.

33 Especially during the *Historikerstreit* and the Bitburg visit discussed in the previous chapter, it was this – hopelessly naive, insultingly relativizing – equivalence of 'their' victims against 'our' victims that became one of the major issues. Geoffrey Hartman (ed.) *Bitburg in Moral and Philosophical Perspective* (Bloomington: Indiana University Press, 1986), 4-8.

34 Andrei S. Markovits, *New German Critique* 38 (Spring/Summer 1986), 5.

35 See Sander L. Gilman's discussion of masochism and guilt as thematized by Rafael Seligmann around the 'power' of the Jew in post-war Germany, *Jews in Today's German Culture*, 40-45.

36 In Helmuth Kohl's infamously famous phrase. The asymmetrical equivalent of the 'Auschwitz bonus' is, of course, the cartoon caption already quoted : 'Die Schuld lassen wir uns nicht nehmen (we won't let them take away our guilt).'

37 'Genug ist genug', 'Das Ende der Schonzeit', 'Man muß endlich einen Schlußstrich ziehen' were the cliché phrases that kept cropping up in the West German debate. See Kiderlen 1985 and Lichtenstein 1986.

38 Peter Gay, *Freud, Jews and other Germans* (Oxford: Oxford University Press, 1978), ix.

39 In her long monologue during the slaughterhouse scene, however, Elvira describes how Christoph used to take an interest in her clients, repeating almost verbatim the lines of Roma B wondering about Franz B's obsession with the men she slept with. 'In a Year of Thirteen Moons', *October* 21 (Summer 1982), 14.

40 See quotation in footnote 33, following chapter.

41 See also Zizek on the perversion of him who, in order to prove his love, maims the beloved, scars her, because now he can show her that he loves her not for her beauty alone. Slavoj Zizek, 'Das Subject Opfer', *Lettre international* 19, 1996, 63.

42 This is where Gerhard Zwerenz seemed to miss the point, during the 'Fassbinder Controversy', when he argued that Fassbinder should have used, as the Jewish hero of his play, the well-known and respected Hesse trial judge Franz Bauer ('Das Verschweigen des Sozialisten Fritz Bauer'). Lichtenstein 1986, 247.

43 In fact, Elvira's situation is not that different from that of Hans Epp, in THE MERCHANT OF FOUR SEASONS, who knows he is a good policeman by the fact that he recognizes that he had to be sacked from the force. See above, Chapter 2.

44 Klaus Theweleit, *Männerphantasien* II (Frankfurt: Roter Stern, 1978).

45 As socio-political, culture-critical ruminations, there is something both dangerously naive and historically absurd in this 'what-if' nostalgia for a better and purer Germany, but one can also recognize in this picture the populist and anti-modernist mirror image of the Frankfurt School's high-modernist equation of the American culture industry with German fascism.

46 Syberberg radicalizes his anti-American position, by suggesting that West Germany after 1945 lost its cultural identity twice over: the majority's embrace of American popular culture as an antidote to having been caught out by the mass-deception of fascist entertainment is only one side of the coin, whose other side is West Germany's intellectual establishment who also over-identified with the other's 'other': this time, with the Jewish émigrés and their view of German culture.

47 See also Eric L. Santner, 'The Trouble with Hitler: Postwar German Aesthetics and the Legacy of Fascism', *New German Critique* 57 (Summer 1992), 5-24.

48 This allegorical mode put him at odds also with those German filmmakers, whose own 'proper coping' (Eric Santner's phrase) so often approached the Nazi past as a purely German-German relation, confronted within the family, across the generations (in the films of Margarethe von Trotta and Helma Sanders-Brahms, for instance), or was grasped by trying to identify victims, and across victims, find a solidarity that might allow for recognition of the 'other', and thus make possible the mourning work, the supposed absence of which dominated the HOLOCAUST debate. Where such reconciliation takes place across an oedipal exchange between guilty fathers and angry sons, it became known as the 'Hamlet' phase of West German culture. As such, it was not confined to films, and could be found in literary autobiographies (see Michael Schneider, 'Fathers and Sons Retrospectively', *New German Critique* 31, Winter 1984, 3-51). Focusing on the bad father whom the children/sons cannot go on hating forever (which in the cinema appears in Thomas Harlan's WUNDKANAL, Helma Sanders Brahms' DEUTSCHLAND BLEICHE MUTTER, DEUTSCHLAND IM HERBST – the Kluge part – as well as DIE REISE and DIE BLEIERNE ZEIT), Henryk Broder derisively commented: 'it seems that the children of the executioners do not have an easy time of it [...]. Sometimes I'm grateful that my parents stood on the right side of the concentration camp fence'. Lichtenstein 1986, 214.

49 See my 'The German Postwar Cinema and Hollywood' in Rob Kroes/David Ellwood (eds.), *Hollywood Europe* (Amsterdam: Vrije Universiteit Press, 1994), 283-302.

50 See the discussion of this scene in Chapter 2, above.

51 'In a Year of Thirteen Moons', *October* 21 (Summer 1982), 7.

52 *ibid.*, 12.

53 Kaja Silverman, 'The Ruination of Masculinity', *Male Subjectivity on the Margins* (New York: Routledge, 1992), 266-270.

54 Gertrud Koch, 'Torments of the Flesh, Coldness of the Spirit', *New German Critique* 38 (Spring/Summer 1986), 28-38.

55 See Geoffrey Nowell-Smith, 'Minnelli and Melodrama', in Bill Nichols, ed., *Movies and Methods II* (Berkeley and Los Angeles: California University Press, 1985), 192.

56 As Gertrud Koch seems to imply. *New German Critique* 38, 34-35.

57 See Eric Santner, 'Visual Pleasure and the Primordially Repressed', Lynne Cooke and Peter Wollen (ed.), *Visual Display* (Seattle: Bay Press, 1995), 242-243.

Notes to Chapter 9

1 Fassbinder, 'Die Städte des Menschen und seine Seele', in Michael Töteberg (ed.), *Filme befreien den Kopf* (Frankfurt: Fischer Verlag, 1984), 82.

2 The essay was first published in *Die Zeit*, 14 March 1980.

3 This is the position taken, for instance, by Yann Lardeau, a key chapter of whose book is called 'The Ten Faces of Franz Walsch', where he puts 'BERLIN ALEXANDERPLATZ at the centre of the work', calling it 'la matrice thematique'. *Rainer Werner Fassbinder* (Paris: Editions de l'Etoile/Cahiers du Cinéma, 1990), 58. A similar premise can be found in Achim Haag, *'Deine Sehnsucht kann keiner stillen'* (Munich: Trickster, 1992), a full-length study of the autobiographical, intertextual and philosophical dimension of BERLIN ALEXANDERPLATZ.

4 Directed by Piel Jutzi and starring Heinrich George as Franz Biberkopf.

5 In the moment of existential crisis depicted in GERMANY IN AUTUMN, Fassbinder is at work on the adaptation. One sees the paperback copy of the book, and he is dictating dialogue and shot breakdowns into a tape recorder.

6 'A work of art was crucially decisive for the course of my life'. *Filme befreien den Kopf*, 85.

7 'On second reading, from page to page, it became ever clearer to me [...] that a huge part of myself, my behaviour, my reactions, in other words, much that I had considered to be my own, was in fact nothing other that what Döblin had described in *Berlin Alexanderplatz. Filme befreien den Kopf*, 84.

8 *Filme befreien den Kopf*, 84. For an illuminating perspective on Fassbinder's experience in this respect, see David Bergman's *Gaity Transfigured* (Madison: Wisconsin University Press, 1992). 'Gay people are specially receptive to cultural images presented by books and films because, in the years when they are settling their sense of their own identity, they are uniquely on their own. [...] As a result, there is a uniquely cultural transaction in

which the concept of homosexuality [...] becomes a literary construct'. Quoted by Richard Davenport-Hines, 'Making Gay', *Times Literary Supplement*, 25 December 1992, 9.

9   Eric Rentschler has drawn attention to Fassbinder's thoughts on adaptation in the preface to QUERELLE in 'Terms of Dis-Memberment: The Body in/and/of Fassbinder's BERLIN ALEXANDERPLATZ' *New German Critique* 34 (Winter 1985), 196-197.

10 Writing about Werner Schroeter: 'I don't know anyone else, apart from myself, who chases a probably infantile, foolishly naive utopia of love with the same desperate intransigence.' 'Klimmzug, Handstand, Salto mortale – sicher gestanden'. *Filme befreien den Kopf*, 77-78.

11 *Filme befreien den Kopf*, 83.

12 'Nicht angetörnt' is the phrase he uses. *Filme befreien den Kopf*, 81.

13 For a synopsis, see Appendix 1, Commented Filmography, and also Fassbinder's own in 'The Cities of Man and his Soul', *Filme befreien den Kopf*, 85-88.

14 See the two interviews on the reception of BERLIN ALEXANDERPLATZ, reprinted in Michael Töteberg (ed.), *Die Anarchie der Phantasie* (Frankfurt: Fischer, 1986) 167-185.

15 Fassbinder calls this 'a reverse process of catharsis' which by the end makes Biberkopf both a 'useful member of society' and 'probably a Nazi voter'. *Filme befreien den Kopf*, 88.

16 Kaja Silverman has made this ambivalence at the extremes central to her reading of BERLIN ALEXANDERPLATZ, theorizing it in the concept of 'masochistic ecstasy'. Kaja Silverman, *Male Subjectivity at the Margins* (London: Routledge, 1992), 214-296.

17 Rentschler 1985, 195-196.

18 *Filme befreien den Kopf*, 89.

19 See the scene where Franz tells Lina the story of the bald man persecuted because he liked a boy, called him "my sunshine" and took him to a hotel room. While Lina is disgusted because she suspects Franz of having homosexual leanings himself, Franz is outraged that the hotel propretor had drilled holes in the walls to spy on his guests.

20 Typical in this respect is Franz's refusal of the political divisions between 'Kommunist' vs 'Hakenkreuzler' (National Socialist). Unable to comprehend, in the crisis years of the Weimar Republic, the growing polarization among members of the same class or community, he finds himself isolated and at odds with the doctrines of the day. The working men that were once his friends taunt him by singing the 'International' after he pleads for class solidarity *and* national solidarity, to which he replies by intoning the (nationalist) 'Watch on the Rhine'.

21 When accused of being a Nazi and a traitor to his class, Franz sings defiantly 'ich hatt einen Kameraden... er fiel von meiner Seite, als wär's ein Stück von mir' (well-known song from the Napoleonic and Franco-Prussian wars, and also very popular among the veterans of World War I). The text alludes to male comradeship and bonding beyond death.

22 'Ich bin ein romantischer Anarchist' in *Die Anarchie der Phantasie*, 186-194.

23 *Filme befreien den Kopf*, 83.

24 As Franz says to Meck at one point: 'It's better if we don't discuss Reinhold. I don't think there is anyone with whom I can really talk about him, perhaps least of all myself.' R.W.Fassbinder and Harry Baer, *Berlin Alexanderplatz: Ein Arbeitsjournal* (Frankfurt: Zweitausendeins, 1980), 306.

25 In this respect similar to Hermann Hermann 'recognizing' Felix in DESPAIR.

26 Franz agrees to the trading of women with Reinhold because, as he says at one point, it reminds him of the days of inflation.

27 This constellation is also discussed in Lardeau 1990, 68, 170.

28 An important prefiguration of this economy occurs in episode four, where Franz's tenement neighbours, the Greiner couple, whom he spies on by listening through the wall, make common cause with the thieves who regularly break into the basement liquor store.

29 It occurs in one of those 'perverse' ways in which Reinhold periodically assures himself of his masculinity involving Franz. After Franz tells him that he does not blame Reinhold for the 'accident' which cost him his arm because he regards it as the 'punishment' he deserved, Reinhold wants to inspect the open wound ('die offene Stelle'). Reinhold's desire to see Franz' amputated stump, and even more, Franz' willingness to show it, make this complicit showing and looking among males almost the inverse of the 'fetishization' of the woman. Evidently linked to Reinhold's pathological castration anxiety, this display betwen the men involves the physical body as the site of a different symbolic transaction. If one recalls that it is in fact Reinhold who inflicted this wound on Franz, then the perversity of this exhibitionist act becomes quite vertiginous. However, it becomes comprehensible, from Franz' point of view, as 'material' proof of the gift he is making his beloved – comparable, again, to Erwin/Elvira in IN A YEAR OF THIRTEEN MOONS, whereas from Reinhold's point of view, Franz's forgiveness is terrifying. Threatened by so much self-abandoning generosity, he finds the sight of the site of Franz's incompleteness as visible on the body reassuring.

30 To 'cover' his wound, he dissembles it by playing the war veteran, pinning an Iron Cross to his jacket.

31 Regarding the symbolic economy of the gift, one might usefully consult the discussion of a symbolic exchange around which Jacques Derrida has argued one of his disagreements with Jacques Lacan. See Slavoj Zizek, *The Metastases of Enjoyment* (London: Verso, 1994), 194-195.

32 On the other hand, Franz seems less concerned with the fact that Mieze is dead, than with the fact that she didn't leave him, but was murdered: for in this sense she still belongs to him in death as she did in life, and can never leave him. One is reminded of Joanna in GODS OF THE PLAGUE, when she betrays Franz to the police, and cries at his grave. When Franz digs Mieze up from the grave in the epilogue, he makes the same movements with his arms as when he killed Ida. Perhaps at a deeper level, that is precisely why Reinhold

killed her, or that is the way that Franz can understand Reinhold killing her: to make sure she belongs to Franz forever.

33 'Christoph was as good as paralyzed. Oh this went on for years, this being paralyzed from depression, until Christoph finally decided for himself to go back to the way he was taught to be – that men are active, decisive, and should act independent. Until then, he lived off me. Believe me, Zora, that was important to me. It wasn't like he was my pimp, or anything, although our money came from other men who paid to have me.' *October* 21, (Summer 1982) 14. Since this narrative is itself a repetition of Roma B's story about her relation to Franz B in the play *Der Müll, die Stadt und der Tod*, the circle closes itself and the two Franz B's are indeed related.

34 One could construct a sort of allegory, according to which Reinhold is to Franz what Hollywood and its narratives of desire are to Fassbinder's own 'German Hollywood' cinema: the German cinema painfully recording the shattering of oedipal trajectories and of phallic identity, which Hollywood maintains, pathologically but powerfully, because assured of the loyalty of those thereby 'victimized'.

35 This, for instance, is the typical situation in the films of Robert Siodmak, for instance, such as THE KILLERS or CRISS CROSS.

36 To continue the analogy, one could argue that the 'phallic' version of this in *film noir* is the hero on the run having his wounds tended by a minstering angel, as in several Humphrey Bogart films, notably THE BIG SLEEP, DARK PASSAGE and HIGH SIERRA.

37 When Franz takes Mieze to meet the gang, the event is momentous because it inscribes into the systems of exchange one of 'devaluation' that could be called 'showing and looking'. By being 'shown' to his friends, she loses her phallic power for Franz and seems to become just one 'object of the look' among others.

38 The films most typical of this conjuncture are: FONTANE EFFI BRIEST (the decline of the Prussian monarchy), BOLWIESER (the collapse of the Austro-Hungarian empire), BERLIN ALEXANDERPLATZ (unemployment and the collapse of the Weimar Republic), DESPAIR (the rise of Fascism), LILI MARLEEN (the world war), THE MARRIAGE OF MARIA BRAUN (the post-war years, and the beginning of the economic miracle), LOLA (the reconstruction boom), GERMANY IN AUTUMN (the hostage crisis), IN A YEAR OF THIRTEEN MOONS (the gay movement), THE THIRD GENERATION (urban terrorism and the state apparatus).

39 'Interview mit Wolfram Schütte', reprinted in *Die Anarchie der Phantasie*, 136.

40 As mentioned above, every review at the time discussed the complaints about the murky lighting in the opening episode. Fassbinder replied that far from being the result of careless workmanship or haste, such lighting is one of the most difficult kinds of film lighting, and he and Xaver Schwarzenberger had worked hard to achieve it.

41 See the discussion of the role 'Marlene' plays in THE BITTER TEARS OF PETRA VON KANT, the examples from FEAR EATS THE SOUL and THE MERCHANT OF FOUR SEASONS, the analysis of GERMANY IN AUTUMN and DESPAIR in Chapters 2 and 3.

42 There is an intertext which (as so often in Fassbinder) refers to German film history: much of so-called 'Expressionist' cinema is condensed in these opening scenes, so completely fashioned around being looked at. Furthermore, cast and crew had to watch Junghans' SO IST DAS LEBEN before and during shooting. And Franz's sympathy for the bald man who calls his young friend "you are my sunshine" seems almost certainly a reference to Peter Lorre in M; debates around the difference between nationalism and class solidarity such as those between Franz and his former comrades figure prominently in HITLERJUNGE QUEX (itself the national-socialist 'reply' to KUHLE WAMPE and its plea for an internationalist proletarian consciousness). Finally, Franz's final job as a nightwatchman at a hotel recalls Murnau's THE LAST LAUGH. Döblin himself was a great cinema fan, publishing several key articles about the cinema of the first decades, and his novel *Berlin Alexanderplatz* has a number of references to Franz's cinema-going.

43 In actual fact, one quickly adjusts to the lower light levels and derives from it a very intense experience and a heightened involvement. Despite an extremely adverse and shrill tabloid campaign against Fassbinder and BERLIN ALEXANDERPLATZ, the series – badly placed in the schedule on a Monday evening – had an average of 16% of the viewing audience.

44 Rentschler 1985, 196.

45 This alignment of non-discursiveness in the mode of representation, and non-utilitarianism in matters of love and sexuality might serve as a reference point for discussing Fassbinder's specifically homosexual aesthetics, not only for BERLIN ALEXANDERPLATZ. An explicitly 'Deleuzian' reading of QUERELLE which also touches on some of these issues has been attempted by Steven Shaviro, *The Cinematic Body* (Minneapolis: Minnesota University Press, 1994), 159-198.

46 'We know what we know, the price has not been low' is the motto of the epilogue and a phrase Biberkopf keeps repeating.

47 Wallace Watson, for instance, complains about the 'freewheeling and heavy-handed cinematic symbolism'. Watson 1996, 242.

48 'He will probably become a Nazi'. See Limmer 1981, 39, *Anarchy* 65, Watson 1996, 247, but see also Heinz Brüggemann, 'Berlin Alexanderplatz', *Text + Kritik* 103, 1989, 59.

Notes to Chapter 10

1 'I let the Audience Feel and Think', Interview with RWF by Norbert Sparrow, *Cineaste* VIII/2 (Fall 1977), 21.

2 See the filmography for key articles from June 1992.

3 Rosa von Praunheim, 'From Beast to Beast', reprinted in Eric Rentschler, *West German Filmmakers on Film* (New York: Holmes & Meier, 1988), 201-203.

4 The Finnish director A.Kaurismäki has occasionally been called a 'second Fassbinder' (*VPRO Guide*, Hilversum, March 1994), and it might be argued that the Danish director

Lars von Trier (ZENTROPA, THE KINGDOM, BREAKING THE WAVES) has been majorly 'influenced' by Fassbinder.

5   For instance, Andreas Kilb, 'Die Hölle? Die Unsterblichkeit', *Die Zeit*, 12 June 1992, p 67.

6   This is the view, after Schütte's obituaries, of virtually all commentators, confirmed ten years later, for instance by Georg Seßlen, 'Fassbinder revisited: LOLA' *epd-Film* 6/1992, 23-24. For a counter argument see my *New German Cinema A History* (New Brunswick: Rutgers University Press, 1989), 310-11.

7   As discussed in Chapter 7 *Frankfurt, Germans and Jews*.

8   Ronald Hayman, *Fassbinder film maker* (London: Weidenfeld & Nicolson, 1984), 16.

9   Fritz Müller-Scherz, "Fassbinders Erben", *Transatlantik* (February 1983), 42-47.

10 The organizers of the 1992 *Werkschau*, the Rainer Werner Fassbinder Foundation, to which Fassbinder's mother made over her part of his estate, has as one of its aims the fund raising necessary to redeem the rights and settle outstanding suits. The second aim is to make sure the films, including the television work, is preserved. *Press Release*, Berlin 1993.

11 For a report from the mid-1980s on the extent and contents of Fassbinder's posthumous papers, see Michael Töteberg, 'Fassbinder -Eine Recherche im Nachlass', *epd Film* 5/87, 25-28. In May 1990, at the Stiftung Deutsche Kinemathek in Berlin, I spoke to Harry Baer, as he and Juliane Lorenz were working on these papers. At that point, access appeared to be restricted to Baer and Lorenz. Since the *Werkschau* of 1992, the Fassbinder Foundation, located in Berlin and directed by Juliane Lorenz, now controls access to the papers.

12 See, for instance, Gerd Gemünden and Roger F. Cook (eds.), *The Cinema of Wim Wenders* (Detroit: Wayne State University Press, 1996).

13 'One never has the impression in Fassbinder that the actors want to say or show something – they talk and move, in the midst of incredible dialogues and a camera heavy with sensuality, giving their everything of body, looks, gestures. They're not the support of ideas, but presences, facing us. They are 'there', which is to say, neither 'true' or 'false'. Jacques Grant on THE THIRD GENERATION, *Cinéma*, July-August 1979, no 247-248, 120.

14 Haag speaks of 'biographical parallels' and 'Fassbinder's alter ego'. Haag 1992, 24-26, 52.

15 Douglas Crimp, 'Fassbinder, Franz, Fox, Elvira, Erwin, Armin and All the Others', *October* 21 (Summer 1982), 68. Crimp gives a useful description of the *auteur* dilemma, when he writes: 'A filmmaker who is gay evidently has only two choices: either he makes films which are not about homosexuality, in which case a disguised homosexuality will be the inevitable result – or he makes films about homosexuality, in which case he necessarily presents his *version* of homosexuality. Homosexuality, it seems, cannot merely be there. No matter what the film's official pretext, the subject is "coming out."' *ibid.*, 69.

16 A view, for instance, argued in Paul Coates, *The Gorgon's Gaze* (Cambridge University Press, 1991), 135-141.

17 'Daniel Schmid always said: "[Fassbinder] is lying, whenever he opens his mouth, except when he eats." In the films, though, he told truths, not personal ones, about himself to you or me.' Peter Chatel, in Raab/Peters 1982, 298.

18 One could give a synoptic list of all the films to demonstrate how they are interconnected, charting them in terms of 'agents' or roles, e.g. pimp, prostitute, gangster, son, street vendor, black marketeer, businessman, but also showing certain recurring places/spaces: bar, home, the street, the woods, the stage, etc. Such a tabulation would not only index the motifs, but also represent a kind of Greimasian reading, where the narrative logic could reveal quite a lot about the textual economy of the oeuvre as a whole. It might be adduced to show how and why Fassbinder could be so prolific, in that the same constellations crop up, connected to a deep structure which can be recognized, and which corresponds to the vague sense of feeling onself in a familiar world when seeing a Fassbinder film, without one having to resort to regarding the work as a *roman à clef*.

19 These oscillations are vividly described because keenly suffered by Kurt Raab, in *Die Sehnsucht des Rainer Werner Fassbinder* (Munich: Goldmann, 1982).

20 See passages from uncredited interview, cited in *Werkschau: Programm* (1992), 77-78.

21 Katz 1987, throughout, but see also the chapters entitled 'The Group and the Team', 'Paying for Love', 'The Necessary Cruelty' in Ronald Hayman, *Fassbinder film maker* (London: Weidenfels & Nichols, 1984).

22 In one of the earliest (1974) analyses of Fassbinder's work, Wilfried Wiegand referred to the 'Russian doll' principle in Fassbinder's work. Jensen/Schütte 1992, 29.

23 'The films I made in the beginning were always films about films. That doesn't interest me anymore. Film has become something for me that is there, and which I do not want to problematize anymore.' John Hughes and Ruth McCormick, 'Rainer Werner Fassbinder and the Death of Family Life'. *Thousand Eyes Magazine* (April 1977), 4-5.

24 This is well captured in two films of Hartmut Bitomsky, REICHSAUTOBAHN and VW-KOMPLEX. See my 'Moderne und Modernisierung: Der deutsche Film der dreißiger Jahre', *montage/av* 3/2 (1994), 23-40.

25 For references to Fassbinder in Saul Friedlander, *Reflections of Fascism*, see chapter five and six. For an argument trying to establish a more directly historical dimension, see David Bathrick, 'Inscribing History, Prohibiting and Producing Desire in Lili Marleen', *New German Critique* 63, Fall 1994, 35-53.

26 A full-scale comparison might well be in order. While no-one, to my knowledge, has given a comparative account of the three directors' work, the closing remarks in Yann Lardeau, *Rainer Werner Fassbinder* (Paris: Cahiers du Cinema, 1990), 271-272, are directed at some of the parallels between them.

27 Volker Spengler, 'Diese polarisierende Beobachtung der Gesellschaft', in Lorenz 1995, 300.

28 The Bargan-Croze relationship, echoing that of Baal and Ekart (in *Baal*), and of Garga and Shlink (from *In the Jungle of the Cities*) may well have served both Döblin and Fassbinder for the feelings of Franz towards Reinhold in *Berlin Alexanderplatz*. 'He let everything go for him, and probably was glad that the man he loved was not a good person, but a malevolent, greedy child, who sucked him dry like a raw egg, in one go.' (Bert Brecht, 'Bargan läßt es sein' *Der neue Merkur*, 1921, no 6, 23.)

29 Raab/Peters 1982, 292.

30 In an article written shortly after Fassbinder 'banished' him, in the men's magazine *lui* (German edition) no 11, 1979..

31 Gilles Deleuze and Felix Guattari, *Kafka: For a Minor Literature* (Minneapolis: University of Minnesota Press, 1983).

32 Deleuze/Guattari 1983, 23-50.

33 'The roles played by women are much more varied and interesting. Women are more imaginative in shading them. Moreover, women are the social underdogs. It is sometimes easier to understand the oppressor by showing the behaviour of the oppressed and his – her – way of coping with it', Paul Pawlikowski, "The Fassbinder Interview", *Stills*, vol 1 no 5, Nov-Dec 1982.

34 Ingrid Caven, 'Frauen in Fassbinder', *Frauen und Film*, 35 (Summer 1987), 92-96.

35 Rosel Zech, interviewed in *Libération*, 1 July, 1982, 5.

36 Kurt Raab, as the one closest to the flame, seems to have stayed capable of hurt thanks to his love and remained lucid thanks to his jealousy. However unreliable he may be in certain factual details, his speaking position is never in doubt. See Raab/Peters 1982.

37 Ronald Hayman: 'Like Strindberg [Fassbinder] had no difficulty in finding lovers eager to help him, but like Strindberg he savaged those who loved him most. [...] Each of them was good at writing about women because in doing so he could write about himself while taking sides against himself.' Hayman 1984, 11.

38 'Fassbinder's characteristic obsession [is] with relationships as theatrical exchanges, emotional goods being bought and sold. [...] The suggestion that Germany, in begging, borrowing or stealing its way back to nationhood since the war, has lost its sense of reality [...] nags away at some abstract, unrealised level. Richard Combs, 'The Marriage of Maria Braun', *Monthly Film Bulletin* no 559, August 1980, 155.

39 Some examples: Judith Mayne, 'Fassbinder and Spectatorship', *New German Critique* 12 (Fall 1977) 61-74; Bob Cant, 'Fassbinder's Fox', and Andrew Britton, 'Foxed', both reprinted in *Jump Cut* 16 (November 1977) 22-23.

40 Richard Dyer, 'Reading Fassbinder's Sexual Politics', in Tony Rayns (ed.), *Fassbinder* (London: British Film Institute, 1980), 54-64.

41 As Robert Burgoyne has argued in 'Narrative and Sexual Excess', *October* 21 (Summer 1982), 51-61.

42 Michel Foucault, 'Friendship as a Way of Life', in Sylvère Lotringer (ed.), *Foucault Live* (New York: Semiotexte, 1989), 203-204.

43 Kaja Silverman, *Male Subjectivity at the Margins* (New York: Routledge, 1992), 296.

44 *ibid.*, 255-270.

45 Steven Shaviro, *The Cinematic Body* (Minneapolis: Minnesota University Press, 1994), 159-198.

46 Leo Bersani, 'Is the Rectum a Grave?', *October* 43 (1987), 205-222.

47 [In PETRA VON KANT we see] two women, and that is what they are supposed to be.' Wolfgang Limmer, *Rainer Werner Fassbinder Filmemacher* (Hamburg: Spiegel Verlag, 1981), 74.

48 See Chapter 2 and 3 above.

49 Eric Rentschler makes this telling point in 'Remembering not to Forget: Alexander Kluge's BRUTALITY IN STONE' in *New German Critique* 49 (Winter 1990), 23-41. Helke Sander's POWERS OF OCCUPATION (1993) – a film about German women raped by American and Soviet soldiers after 1945 – raises similar questions about the gender and status of victimhood.

50 About *Cocaine*, Fassbinder wrote in 1980: 'Apart from the fact that no really comparable film yet exists, which comes up to my idea of *Cocaine*, there is nonetheless AMARCORD by Fellini, SALO by Pasolini, EMPIRE OF THE SENSES by Oshima, and my own 14th part [the epilogue] of BERLIN ALEXANDERPLATZ.' Quoted in Marion Schmid, Herbert Gehr, eds., *Werkschau Katalog* (Berlin: Argon, 1992), 248.

51 Fassbinder was often exasperated about the German Left's model of explaining history: 'When I meet people who talk as if it was still 1968 I get very aggressive.' Rainer Werner Fassbinder, *Die Anarchie der Phantasie*, ed. Michael Töteberg (Frankfurt: Fischer Verlag, 1986), 75.

52 Gertrud Koch has written perceptively about Fassbinder's villains in 'Torment of the Flesh, Coldness of the Spirit', *New German Critique* 38 (Spring/Summer 1986), 28-38.

53 What comes to mind are some of Welles' overreachers, notably Quinlan in TOUCH OF EVIL, a film Fassbinder greatly admired. See *Werkschau-Programm* 1992, 124, 135.

54 One is reminded of Woody Allen, remarking to his female companion in BROADWAY DANNY ROSE: 'how can you live without guilt? Without guilt, you're not human!'

55 Hanna Schygulla: 'out of his ugliness, he reclaimed another kind of beauty ('der Kampf gegen diese Häßlichkeit ist daß man sich die Schönheit anders zurückerobert'), *Frauen und Film* 35 (1987), 93.

Notes to Appendix one

1 A famous quotation from Rainer Maria Rilke ('those without a house, shall not build one now'). They are almost the first lines spoken in LOLA, sarcastically introducing the film's central theme: housing contracts, building regulations, corruption in local government.

2 Quoted from an uncredited interview in *Fassbinder Werkschau*, 254. Peter Märthesheimer entitled his obituary 'The investigating child. Some bricks of the house

that Rainer Werner Fassbinder had begun to build', in Hans Günther Pflaum (ed.), *Jahrbuch Film* (Munich: Hanser 1982/83).

3   Pascal Bonitzer, reviewing LOLA, wondered whether Fassbinder had not mixed too much straw with his bricks. 'Lola et le pantin', *Cahiers du cinéma* 329 (November 1981), 57.

4   The metaphor also compares interestingly with similar projects that other German artists were working on during the 1970s and 1980s, for instance, the painter Jörg Immendorf's *Cafe Deutschland* cycle, or Anselm Kiefer's *Besetzung*.

5   H.G. Pflaum and R.W. Fassbinder, *Das bißchen Realität* (Munich: Hanser, 1976), 150.

6   'The *auteur* hypothesis [is] the phenomenological positing of some central subject or consciousness embodying itself in a distinctive 'world' and 'style'. [T]his kind of rewriting (which constructs a new textual object) leads on to the false problem of subjectivity, unless it raises the (historical) question of its own condition of possibility'. Fredric Jameson, 'Spatial Systems in NORTH BY NORTHWEST', in S. Zizek, ed., *Everything you always wanted to know about Lacan but were afraid to ask Hitchcock* (London: Verso, 1992), 47.

7   'From all these inserts and quotations emerged a very personal film, which can also be distinguished from comparable films of other contemporary directors, such as Lemke's FORTY-EIGHT HOURS TO ACAPULCO and Thome's DETECTIVES: Fassbinder's film is shabbier, more desolate and even further away from Hollywood than these other two thrillers set in Munich.' Wilhelm Roth, 'Kommentierte Filmographie', in Schütte/Jansen 1992, 122.

8   'Maybe it is typical that the longest scene set in Munich in any of Fassbinder's films is not by him at all. In LOVE IS COLDER THAN DEATH the camera tracks for several minutes along the Landsbergerstrasse, past the lone prostitutes, and taking in the nocturnal desolation on the other side of the railway lines. This travelling is an out-take from a film by his colleague Jean Marie Straub. Munich in Fassbinder always remained in quotation marks, cobbled together from the movie cities of Godard and Melville. Munich has to play Paris, or Chicago: the show-down at the main railway station in THE AMERICAN SOLDIER, a bar at the Stachus in I ONLY WANT YOU TO LOVE ME, the Post office bank building in SATAN'S BREW. Always a kind of gentle melancholy that Munich is the way it is, regret almost, mingled with pity.' Michael Alten, 'Ein Stadtstreicher im Reich der Träume', *Süddeutsche Zeitung* (10 June, 1992), 12.

9   'What remains, when one has seen this film is not that someone killed six people [...] but that here, a few poor sods had to make a life, who didn't know how, who simply found themselves in this place, who weren't given a chance, in fact who didn't have a chance.' Fassbinder, introducing LOVE IS COLDER THAN DEATH, in *Film* 8/1969, 20.

10 'The most horrible thing about this film is how bored it is with itself, down to the smallest detail. The cuts are like the listless switching of tv channels on a Saturday night, each change of programme only increasing one's anger and depression. And the fact that all the characters look so grim is not because they're supposed to represent the provinces

and prejudice, but because of the grim schema into which they are pressed... – Only Hanna Schygulla is so alive in this dead film that one has the impression of seeing her in colour.' Wim Wenders, 'Katzelmacher', *Filmkritik* 12/69, 751-2.

11 Fassbinder, in 'Spielfilme im Deutschen Fernsehen', *ARD Broschüre* 1973, 55 and quoted by Wilhelm Roth in Jansen/Schütte 1992, 123-4.

12 Paul Thomas, 'Fassbinder: The Poetry of the Inarticulate', *Film Quarterly*, 30/2 (Winter 1976/77). Wilhelm Roth, by contrast, notes that he suspects the film enjoys cult status north of the Bavarian border mainly because of its stilted dialogue masquerading as authentic Munich dialect. Wilhelm Roth, in Jansen/Schütte 1992, 127.

13 'As far as I can think, I see no hope. Only beyond where my thoughts can take me, there I see some.' Fassbinder, quoted by Wilfried Wiegand in Jansen/Schütte, 49.

14 'In MOROCCO the singer Marlene Dietrich prefers the simple soldier Gary Cooper, just as Hanna prefers Whity, the black. Marlene gives Cooper an apple, Hanna gives Whity a rose. Both couples finally trek off to the desert...'. Wolfgang Roth in Jansen/Schütte 1992, 136.

15 Miriam Niroumand, 'Deutsch als Fremdsprache' *die Tageszeitung*, 10 June 92. Her argument is that in Fassbinder there is a sado-masochistic daisy chain linking the characters to each other, whereas in Truffaut, the film crew is indeed a kind of surrogate family. But perhaps the more appropriate comparison would be to the pornographic daisy-chain demanded by the boss from his office staff in Jean-Luc Godard's SAUVE QUI PEUT...LA VIE (1980).

16 Limmer 1981, 184, but see also Hayman 1984, 46-48 and Katz 1987, 210-221.

17 The fact that the making of WHITY is the ostensible pretext and material for BEWARE OF THE HOLY WHORE can also lead to the realization that 'the Fassbinder clan was not his substitute family, but a social laboratory in which he conducted experiments', Peter Buchka, 'Das Phänomen Fassbinder', *Süddeutsche Zeitung*, 10 June 92.

18 'Imitation of Life. Über Douglas Sirk', *Fernsehen und Film* 2 (February 1971), translated as 'Six Films by Douglas Sirk', in Laura Mulvey, Jon Halliday (eds.), *Douglas Sirk* (Edinburgh: Edinburgh Festival, 1972), 95-108.

19 The six films were ALL THAT HEAVEN ALLOWS (1956), WRITTEN ON THE WIND (1957), INTERLUDE (1957), THE TARNISHED ANGELS (1958), A TIME TO LOVE AND A TIME TO DIE (1958), and IMITATION OF LIFE (1959).

20 Barbara Leaming has noted that Hans' apartment is 'a series of boxlike rooms without connecting passages between them'. 'Structures of Alienation: The Merchant of Four Seasons', *Jump Cut* 10/11 (Summer 1976).

21 The Kroetz-Fassbinder controversy is documented by Michael Töteberg, in Rainer Werner Fassbinder, *Filme befreien den Kopf* (Frankfurt: Fischer 1984), 135-6.

22 STROSZEK (Werner Herzog, 1977); GERMANY PALE MOTHER (Helma Sanders-Brahms, 1979); CELESTE (Percy Adlon, 1981).

23 For a full accont, see Richard Collins, Vincent Porter (eds.), *WDR and the Arbeiterfilm: Fassbinder, Ziewer and others* (London: British Film Institute, 1981).

24 Christine Gledhill (ed.), *Home is where the Heart is* (London: BFI, 1986) for discussions of the maternal melodrama and the woman's picture. Also for the paranoia cycle, see Mary Ann Doane, *The Desire to Desire* (Bloomington: Indiana University Press, 1991), chapter 4.

25 In a discussion with Margit Carstensen about her role in MARTHA, Fassbinder came up with a number of aphorisms which became notorious among feminist critics: 'Women who let themselves be oppressed often are more beautiful than women who fight back' and 'Most men simply cannot oppress women as perfectly as women would like them to'. R. W. Fassbinder, 'Talking about Oppression with Margit Carstensen' in E. Rentschler (ed.), *West German Filmmakers on Film* (New York: Holmes and Meier, 1988), 169-171. See also 'Frauen bei Fassbinder', *Frauen und Film* 35 (October 1983), 92-96.

26 Fontane's novel was adapted as DER SCHRITT VOM WEGE (The Trespass, 1936) and directed by Gustav Gründgens.

27 Fassbinder described the film as 'the story of a young entrepreneur whose firm is about to go bust, and who manages with a few private tricks to steal money from someone else in order to save his business. It's the private battle between an entrepreneur and a non-entrepreneur, who wants to be one'. Interview with Kraft Wetzel, *Kino* 18/19, 1974.

28 'Once at the Lincoln Centre in New York I found Rainer in one of the projection theatres. Tears ran down his face as he was watching himself in FOX AND HIS FRIENDS. The odd thing is that he is actually [Eugen] the character played by me, the one who exploits. The character that he plays [Fox] is how he would have liked to have been, the tender, sensitive proletarian he never was.' Peter Chatel, in K. Raab, K. Peters, *Die Sehnsucht des Rainer Werner Fassbinder* (Munich: Bertelsmann, 1982), 291-92.

29 Ronald Hayman, 'Paying for Love', *Fassbinder film maker* (London: Weidenfeld and Nicolson, 1984), 62.

30 This was written for a volume on Chabrol edited by W. Schütte and P. Jansen in the Hanser film book series. 'Insects in a Glass Case' was first published in English in *Sight and Sound*, 45/4 (Autumn 1976).

31 Craig Whitney, 'A New Director Movie Buffs Dote on', *New York Times*, 16 February 1977.

32 The first time I was invited to lecture on Fassbinder in the United States was in October 1977.

33 *Der Spiegel*, 11 July 1977; reprinted in *Die Anarchie der Fantasie* (1986), 94-99.

34 On the functioning of the subsidy system, and Fassbinder's response, see my *New German Cinema A History* (London: Macmillan, 1989), 8-35.

35 Hans Christoph Blumenberg, 'Hervorragend', *Die Zeit*, 10 June 1983 and Peter Buchka, 'Eine gute Liebe lieben', *Süddeutsche Zeitung*, 10 June 1983.

36 Wilhelm Roth notes that running the railways is a good metaphor for the 'Untertanengeist' (spirit of subordination), and as in DESPAIR, Fassbinder introduced men in SA uniforms to point to things to come. Jansen/Schütte 1992, 200.

37 Dirk Bogarde, interviewed in an *Arena Special* (BBC 2, 1992). No independent evidence of such a re-edit exists. There is a correspondence between Fassbinder and Bogarde, which Bogarde transposed into a dialogue in his autobiography. See Wallance Watson, 'The Bitter Tears of RWF', *Sight and Sound* 2/3 (July 1992), 24-29.

38 See Andrew Sarris, 'Is History Merely an Old Movie?' *Village Voice*, 8-14 July 1981. For a different view, see Chapter 6, above.

39 Peter Chatel's phrase, in Raab/Peters 1982, 292.

40 'A Cinema of Vicious Circles', in Rayns (ed.), *Fassbinder* 1980, 35-36.

Index

Page numbers in *italics* refer to the chapters dedicated to the films in question.
Page numbers in **bold** refer to the Commented Filmography, with credits and synopsis.
RWF's films are listed under their original titles in the Commented Filmography.
Footnotes are not indexed.